PUBLIC LAW

Third edition

PUBLIC LAW

Third Edition

By

Paul Reid
Advocate, Ampersand

First Edition 2003 by Jane Munro
Second Edition 2007 by Jane Munro

Published in 2015 by W. Green, 21 Alva Street,
Edinburgh EH2 4PS
Part of Thomson Reuters (Professional) UK Limited (Company No.1679046).
Registered in England and Wales.
Registered office: 2nd Floor, 1 Mark Square,
Leonard Street, London EC2A 4EG.

Typeset by Wright and Round Ltd, Gloucester
Printed and bound in Great Britain by
CPI Group (UK) Ltd, Croydon, CR0 4YY

No natural forests were destroyed to make this product;
only farmed timber was used and re-planted.

A CIP catalogue record for this book is available from the British Library.

ISBN 978-0-414-01908-9

Thomson Reuters and the Thomson Reuters logo are
trademarks of Thomson Reuters.

2015 Thomson Reuters (Professional) UK Limited

PREFACE

The first edition of *Public Law* in Greens' Concise Scots Law series was published in 2003, about 10 years after I properly acquainted myself with constitutional and administrative law for the first time. During those 10 years, the subject had changed very much. My early education was mostly a matter of legal and constitutional history. The great post war decisions in administrative law were hardly new; and many lawyers and legal scholars of that vintage regarded the 1980s, in particular, as a retrograde period in the development of the law on civil liberties and human rights. This was the perspective that informed the commitment of the Labour government elected in 1997 to devolution, freedom of information and the enactment of the Human Rights Act. It is fair to say that, at the time, I thoroughly applauded these developments.

They meant, however, that constitutional law and administrative law were no longer only of historic interest. That being so, the writing of the first edition of *Public Law* was a considerable undertaking, one I was only able to assume because I had time to devote to it after completing the Diploma in Legal Practice at Edinburgh University in 2003 with a view to being called to the Scots Bar (as I was in July 2005). The second edition of *Public Law* was published in the autumn of 2007. Even by that time, it was felt that enough had happened to warrant an updating of the first edition. I realised in the course of preparing the second edition, during the summer vacation of 2007, that I would not care to prepare the third. In the event, eight years have passed since the publication of the second edition and the developments in that time have called less for an updating of the book than its rewriting. Paul Reid, Advocate, has undertaken that task and the purpose of this preface is to express my gratitude to him, and my profound admiration. He modestly claims to have built on my original text, but this book is Paul's. I have learned a great deal from it. To my mind, it achieves what a textbook in this series ought to achieve: the right combination of thoroughness and rigour, conveyed in an accessible and intelligible way. I wish the book, and its author, every success.

Jane Smith
June 2015

ACKNOWLEDGEMENTS

Since the last edition was published the constitutional landscape of both Scotland and the United Kingdom has changed significantly. That has resulted in the structure of this book evolving: chapters on the more specialist areas of freedom of information and immigration have been replaced with chapters on the process of constitutional change and the use of referendums. Some of the material that would otherwise be lost has been harvested for a rebranded chapter on the citizen and the state. Public law has an endless but increasing capacity to generate case law. This work has never been a casebook so this edition seeks to reflect any significant changes in the case law but not necessarily every case that simply illustrates the application of an existing principle. I have sought to update the text that formed the second edition so that it reflects the law, the best that I can, as at 1 May 2015 (although account has been taken of the outcome of the 2015 General Election and some other developments where possible).

A number of thanks are necessary. First, to Jane Smith for letting me update her existing text. Most of the hard work was done by Jane in the earlier editions which allowed me to build on the structure and content that was already in place. A number of colleagues at the Faculty of Advocates have offered much support throughout the writing process. Kenneth Campbell, QC, Andrew Devlin and Ross McClelland each deserve special thanks for the time they have given to discussing various aspects of the book, as do my clerks at the Ampersand Stable who have shown almost boundless patience as I have tried to find the time to work on this project. Emma Broddesson, Henrik Norinder and the staff at the law library of Lund University accommodated me as I escaped for a final push to get the manuscript completed. Josie Hayes and Dr Daniel Carr between them read most of the book in draft and offered valuable input, although the usual disclaimers apply. And of course, the team at W. Greens who have been very supportive and, in particular, indulging so far as the regular requests for more time were concerned.

Finally, my family, in particular my parents, Yvonne and George, who have supported me at every turn and in all that I have done, and Kimberley, who has had to live with this book for years, has shown endless patience and has always been there to console me when it looked like the book would never be finished. We made it in the end!

Lastly, for my part, this book is dedicated to grandfathers, Tom and George.

Paul Reid
Advocates' Library
20 June 2015

CONTENTS

Table of Cases

xiv *Table of Cases*

Table of Statutes

Acts of the Parliament of Scotland

Table of Statutory Instruments

Chapter 1

SCOTLAND'S CHANGED CONSTITUTION

Introduction

Any discussion of contemporary public law in Scotland will, sooner or later, **1–01** arrive at events of September 2014. So it is there that we shall begin. On 18 September 2014, 84.6 per cent of Scotland's registered electorate (which included, for the first time, 16 and 17 year olds) voted by a margin of 55.3–44.7 per cent for Scotland to remain part of the UK. The vote was unprecedented. As we shall see in Ch.5, below the UK has only limited experience of using a referendum. The issue at stake was also unprecedented: the future of the "forever" Union was being decided.[1] That Union endures but in the aftermath of the referendum, there was a sense that things would never be the same again, a feeling perhaps reinforced by the 2015 General Election result. The legal issues presented by Scotland's referendum were many: the legal basis on which the Scottish Parliament could legislate for a referendum on independence; the extension of the franchise to 16 and 17 year olds and the blanket disenfranchisement of serving prisoners; the rules for the campaign, both its conduct and its funding; securing confidence in the result; and if there was a "yes" vote, when would independence be declared and what would it look like on "day one"? These issues are considered in this chapter.

The issues thrown up by the result are just as varied: the rights of Scottish MPs at Westminster in relation to subjects that have been devolved to Scotland (an issues that has been thrown into even sharper focus by the SNP's increased representation following the 2015 general election); the extension of the franchise to 16 and 17 year olds for future Scottish elections; further devolution of powers to the Scottish Parliament; and securing the Scottish Parliament within the UK's constitutional structures. These issues are briefly discussed at the end of this chapter but more fully considered where they arise in the course of the subsequent chapters.

Public law, especially that which would traditionally be regarded as "constitutional" law, often finds itself operating on the border where law meets politics. Never has that been truer than Scotland's referendum. To understand the lead up to the September 2014 vote, we need to start with politics because the Scotland Act 1998 was clear: the Union of the Kingdoms of Scotland and England was a matter that was expressly reserved to the UK Parliament.[2] So how was it that the Scottish Parliament came to legislate for a referendum on Scottish independence

---

[1] Act of Union 1707, s.1 provided that, "That the Two Kingdoms of Scotland and England shall upon the first day of May next ensuing date hereof and forever after be United into one Kingdom by the name of Great Britain . . . ".

[2] Scotland Act 1998 Sch.6 para.1(b).

and why did it become accepted that the Scottish Parliament was entitled so to legislate?

CALLING THE REFERENDUM—THE POLITICAL BASIS

1–02 Irrespective of the terms of the Scotland Act 1998, for reasons of practical politics the Scottish Parliament would never legislate for a referendum on independence unless it had a majority of nationalist MSPs.[3] So it was a necessary political prerequisite that the SNP hold an overall majority in the Scottish Parliament. As we will see in Ch.4, below the electoral system used for the Parliament was one that should ordinarily produce coalition or minority government.[4] Given the absence of a second chamber that was not a surprising choice. But the practical consequence was that the SNP required to have an exceptional degree of electoral success before the possibility of calling a referendum on independence could even begin to be envisaged and the question of the Scotland Act discussed. In 2007, the SNP were returned as the largest party with 47 MSPs (one less than the Scottish Labour Party). That was significantly short of the 65 required to have a majority in the Parliament. In 2010, the SNP Government consulted on a draft Referendum (Scotland) Bill.[5] Without a parliamentary majority[6] the Bill was withdrawn before it was put to a vote. The political landscape changed significantly as a result of the 2011 Scottish general election. That election saw the SNP again returned as the largest party in the Parliament. But this time they had 69 MSPs and thus an overall majority. If a similar Bill were to be introduced in this parliamentary session, the Scottish Government could expect to have the votes to secure its passage. And with a clear manifesto commitment to hold such a referendum, the newly returned SNP Government claimed the democratic mandate and legitimacy to hold a referendum. The politics now being in place, the introduction of the necessary enabling legislation appeared inevitable. That required the legal basis on which such a referendum could be held to be addressed.

CALLING THE REFERENDUM—THE LEGAL BASIS

1–03 As we have already noted, the terms of the Scotland Act appeared to be clear and appeared to prohibit the Scottish Parliament legislating to hold an independence referendum. In the 2010 consultation the Scottish Government had maintained that if the question was worded appropriately, the Scottish Parliament would have the power to legislate for a referendum.[7] That view was disputed by the UK

---

[3] The majority of nationalist MSP belong to the Scottish National Party ("SNP") but the Scottish Green Party also supported independence. For ease of reference, the discussion that follows talks of the SNP holding a majority but that is shorthand for a nationalist majority in the Scottish Parliament.
[4] See para.4–08, below.
[5] Scottish Government, *Scotland's Future: Draft Referendum (Scotland) Bill Consultation Paper* (Scottish Government, 2010) *http://www.gov.scot/resource/doc/303348/0095138.pdf* [Accessed 27 May 2015].
[6] Support from the Scottish Green Party (two votes) and an independent MSP (Margo McDonald) gave the SNP Government only 50 votes.
[7] Scottish Executive, *Choosing Scotland's Future: A National Conversation* (The Stationery Office, 2007) p.35.

Government. They insisted that any Bill that sought to authorise the holding of an independence referendum, whatever the precise wording of the question might be, would "relate to" the Union and thus fall outside the competence of the Scottish Parliament.[8] The Scottish and the UK Governments did agree that the SNP Government had won a mandate to hold an independence referendum and that it was better for the legal basis to be put beyond doubt rather than be subject to challenge in the courts. That common accord gave rise to what became known as the Edinburgh Agreement.[9] On 15 October 2012, the Scottish and UK Governments signed an agreement that was to allow the Scottish Parliament to legislate for an independence referendum. The Scottish Parliament was to be given the competence to legislate for the referendum by means of a "section 30 Order": that is an Order in Council made in terms of s.30(2) of the Scotland Act 1998 to modify the list of reserved matters. It was a condition of that transfer of power that the referendum be held by the end of 2014 and that a single question be put to the voters with only two possible answers.[10] The date of the referendum, the precise wording of the question and the franchise for the vote were all matters to be determined by the Scottish Parliament. On 12 February 2013 the Privy Council made the Scotland Act 1998 (Modification of Schedule 5) Order 2013[11] giving effect to the terms of the Edinburgh Agreement. The Scottish Parliament now had the legislative competence to pass a Bill authorising the holding of an independence referendum.

THE FRANCHISE

The first step taken by the Scottish Parliament on the road to authorising the **1–04** referendum was to determine the franchise. This was fixed by the Scottish Independence Referendum (Franchise) Act 2013 ("the Franchise Act"). Here the most noticeable provision was the extension of the franchise to 16 and 17 year olds, which reflected the Scottish Government's policy that the franchise be extended to that group for all elections. The Franchise Act therefore had to make provision for the registration of those individuals for the purposes of the referendum.[12] Other than that (significant) change, the franchise reflected that for Scottish parliamentary and local government elections. That was consistent with the approach taken for the devolution referendum in 1997.[13] The consequence was eligibility to vote in the referendum was basically tied to residency in Scotland on the date of the referendum: Scots who worked and lived outside Scotland were generally not entitled to vote. The other provision of significance

---

[8] Scotland Office, *Scotland's Constitutional Future: A consultation on facilitating a legal, fair and decisive referendum on whether Scotland should leave the United Kingdom* (The Stationery Office, 2012), Cm.8203, p.11. That view was based on the wording, and interpretation, of s.29(3) of the Scotland Act 1998.

[9] The Edinburgh Agreement is available at *http://www.gov.scot/About/Government/concordats/Referendum-on-independence* [Accessed 27 May 2015].

[10] The 2010 consultation by the Scottish Government had proposed that there be two questions: one about independence and one about so-called "devo-max" (a substantial further transfer of powers to the Scottish Parliament). In 2012, the UK Government was opposed to a second question, insisting that a single, clear, question be put so as to ensure a clear and decisive result.

[11] Scotland Act 1998 (Modification of Schedule 5) Order 2013 (SSI 2013/242).

[12] That provision is made in the Scottish Independence Referendum (Franchise) Act 2013 ss.4–9, which required the creation of a "register of young voters" for each electoral area.

[13] Referendums (Scotland and Wales) Act 1997.

was the blanket disenfranchisement of serving prisoners. That ban, which was found in s.3 of the Franchise Act, was to be subject to judicial challenge.

1–05   As we will see in Ch.4, below the provision of the Representation of the People Act 1983 that provides for the disenfranchisement of serving prisoners (s.3) has been held to be incompatible with art.3 of Protocol 1 to the European Convention on Human Rights.[14] Despite the Grand Chamber refusing to revisit their interpretation of art.3 of Protocol 1, and insisting that a blanket ban on serving prisoners voting in parliamentary elections is unlawful, the UK Parliament has not legislated to amend the offending provision. The Franchise Act repeated the prohibition contained in s.3 of the 1983 Act.[15] A number of serving prisoners judicially reviewed the competence of that provision.[16] They were unsuccessful in both the Outer House[17] and the Inner House.[18] There was a superficial attraction to the petitioners' argument: if participating in a parliamentary election every four or five years was a fundamental human right surely participating in a referendum of such constitutional significance as the independence referendum was also protected? That argument, however, ran into difficulties when it confronted the wording of art.3 of Protocol 1. Article 3 of Protocol 1 requires the UK to "hold free elections at reasonable intervals" to ensure the free expression of the electorate "in the choice of the legislature". The Strasbourg court had held that art.3 of Protocol 1 did not cover referendums.[19] The "reasonable intervals" requirement caused an obvious tension: the independence referendum was said to be a "once in a generation" event. If art.3 of Protocol 1 applied so as to afford serving prisoners a vote, it raised at least the possibility of a challenge in the years to come that the "reasonable intervals" requirement had been infringed. It was an issue that divided the Supreme Court: the ban survived by five votes to two.

Influential to the minority (Lord Kerr and Lord Wilson) was the fact that the Convention is a "living instrument" whose interpretation evolves with the times. Accordingly, the fact that referendums were not in the contemplation of the framers of the Convention was not fatal to the prisoners' argument.[20] Article 3 of Protocol 1, said Lord Kerr, had to be interpreted in light of its object and purpose.[21] When that was borne in mind:

> "it is difficult to see how that purpose would be other than frustrated by preventing the safeguard applicable to ordinary legislative elections from applying to the most fundamental of votes."[22]

---

[14] *Smith v Scott* [2007] CSIH 9; 2007 S.C. 345; see para.4–13, below and the cases cited therein.

[15] Franchise Act s.3; see para.10 of the explanatory notes that accompanied the Bill which made the intention to repeat the ban contained in the 1983 Act clear.

[16] *Moohan, Petitioner* [2014] UKSC 67; 2015 S.L.T. 2. As explained in Ch.6 below, any provision of an Act of the Scottish Parliament that is incompatible with a Convention right is outwith the legislative competence of the Scottish Parliament with the effect that it is "not law" (Scotland Act 1998 s.29).

[17] *Moohan, Petitioner* [2013] CSOH 199; 2014 S.L.T. 213.

[18] *Moohan, Petitioner* [2014] CSIH 56; 2015 S.C. 1.

[19] *X v United Kingdom* (Application No.7096/75) Unreported 3 October 1975 European Court of Human Rights (concerning the UK referendum on continued membership of the then EEC) and *Bader v Austria* (1996) 22 E.H.R.R. CD213 (concerning the Austrian referendum on accession to the then EC).

[20] *Moohan, Petitioner* [2014] UKSC 67; 2015 S.L.T. 2 per Lord Kerr at [67].

[21] *Moohan, Petitioner* [2014] UKSC 67; 2015 S.L.T. 2 per Lord Kerr at [67].

[22] *Moohan, Petitioner* [2014] UKSC 67; 2015 S.L.T. 2 per Lord Kerr at [68].

The "regular intervals" requirement was, in the minority's view, secondary to the primary aim of art.3 of Protocol 1 that citizens should have a full role in the selection of who shall govern them.[23] So far as the Strasbourg case law was concerned, according to Lord Wilson, it was not, as the majority described it, "unequivocal" on the point and the Supreme Court could, and should, go further and extend the application of art.3 of Protocol 1 to the independence referendum.[24] The majority took a much narrower view. Lord Hodge, who gave the leading judgment for the majority, found that there was a clear and constant line of decisions from the Strasbourg court that excluded referendums from the scope of art.3 of Protocol 1 and that line ought to be followed by the Supreme Court.[25] The "regular intervals" requirement was also influential to the majority: that requirement suggests the framers of the Convention did not have referendums in mind.[26] Indeed, it would be, said Lord Neuberger, "little short of absurd" to suggest that a referendum on a "classic 'one off' issue" such as independence should be held at "regular intervals".[27] Furthermore, Lady Hale held that art.3 of Protocol 1 does not, and cannot, require a referendum on Scottish independence to be held thus it follows that the protections that have been implied into art.3 of Protocol 1 cannot be applicable to such a vote.[28]

Perhaps the most surprising reason cited by the majority (and expressed in the judgment of Lord Neuberger, with whom the rest of the majority agreed) was what was said to be the consequence of the referendum:

" . . . while the main political parties had committed themselves to accept the result of the Referendum, a 'yes' vote would not of itself have triggered independence for Scotland. If there had been a 'yes' vote[29], Scotland would not have achieved independence unless and until the UK Parliament had voted in favour, and, whatever the main parties had promised, Members of Parliament would have been free, indeed constitutionally bound, to vote as they saw fit."[30]

Whilst no doubt correct as a strict proposition of law, it serves to highlight how many of the issues surrounding the referendum operated at the very boundary of the law and politics. Had there been a "yes" vote, the idea that the UK Parliament would then refuse to pass legislation giving effect to that vote is almost unthinkable. But if the unthinkable happened, a unilateral declaration of independence by Scotland would almost certainly have followed. And as the experience of the break up of the Empire shows, whatever the strict constitutional

---

[23] *Moohan, Petitioner* [2014] UKSC 67; 2015 S.L.T. 2, per Lord Kerr at [69], per Lord Wilson at [93]–[96].
[24] *Moohan, Petitioner* [2014] UKSC 67; 2015 S.L.T. 2 at [103]–[105]. For discussion of the regard that should be had to Strasbourg authorities, see paras 11–05—11–06.
[25] *Moohan, Petitioner* [2014] UKSC 67; 2015 S.L.T. 2 at [9]–[13].
[26] *Moohan, Petitioner* [2014] UKSC 67; 2015 S.L.T. 2, per Lord Hodge at [8].
[27] *Moohan, Petitioner* [2014] UKSC 67; 2015 S.L.T. 2 at [45].
[28] *Moohan, Petitioner* [2014] UKSC 67; 2015 S.L.T. 2 at [54]–[55].
[29] Although the outcome of the appeal was advised later the same afternoon (24 July 2014) after the oral arguments had concluded, it was not until 17 December 2014 that the written reasons were provided which allowed Lord Neuberger to reflect the outcome in his judgment.
[30] *Moohan, Petitioner* [2014] UKSC 67; 2015 S.L.T. 2 at [47]. See also the decision of the Supreme Court of Canada in *Reference re Secession of Quebec* [1998] 2 S.C.R. 217 where the limits of the law were expressly recognised by that court.

theory may be, when that happens, the law simply has to recalibrate to the new reality.[31]

That was to prove the only time any aspect of the independence referendum was tested in the courts. But it demonstrated that the issues were both legally complex and impossible to divorce entirely from the prevailing political climate. However, the short point to note is the disenfranchisement of serving prisoners stood and the vires of the Franchise Act was vindicated.

THE SCOTTISH INDEPENDENCE REFERENDUM ACT 2013

1–06   The substantive legislation that regulated the referendum, the Scottish Independence Referendum Act 2013 ("the Referendum Act"), was passed on 14 November 2013 and received Royal Assent a month later. Section 1 provided for a referendum to be held on 18 September 2014[32] on the question: "Should Scotland be an independent country?"[33] The original wording proposed by the Scottish Government was: "Do you agree that Scotland should be an independent country?" The Electoral Commission was asked for their advice on the wording and intelligibility of that question. "Do you agree . . . " was found by the Electoral Commission's research to have the possibility of leading people towards voting yes hence they recommended the wording that actually appeared in the Referendum Act.[34] It was necessary for the Referendum Act to make provision for the conduct of the campaign. Detailed provision on the conduct of a referendum campaign had been made in the Political Parties, Elections and Referendums Act 2000.[35] The independence referendum, however, having been legislated for by the Scottish Parliament and not Westminster, was not a referendum for the purposes of the 2000 Act.[36] Detailed provision therefore had to be made by the Referendum Act. The principal provisions of note were: the Electoral Commission were to be responsible for monitoring and securing compliance with the campaign rules (s.12); the Electoral Commission were required to take steps to promote public awareness and understanding of the referendum, the question and how to vote (s.23)[37]; and no challenge to the result was permitted other than by judicial review and any such petition had to be lodged within six weeks of the declaration of the result (s.34). The "referendum period" (the time during which the campaigning and funding rules applied) was fixed at 16 weeks (Sch.8) and thus began on 30 May 2014. Schedule 4 to the

---

[31] *Madzimbamuto v Lardner-Burke* [1969] 1 A.C. 645 PC (Rhodesia); *Manuel v Attorney General* [1983] Ch. 77 CA (Civ Div) at 89; see para.3–07, below.

[32] Scottish Independence Referendum Act 2013 s.1(4). The Scottish Ministers had the power to vary this date if it became "impossible or impracticable" to hold the referendum on that date (s.1(5)) so long as the alternative date was no later than 31 December 2014 (s.1(6)).

[33] The question was prescribed by s.1(2).

[34] Electoral Commission, *Referendum on independence for Scotland: advice of the Electoral Commission on the proposed referendum question* (Electoral Commission, 2013), *http://www.e-lectoralcommission.org.uk/__data/assets/pdf_file/0007/153691/Referendum-on-independence-for-Scotland-our-advice-on-referendum-question.pdf* [Accessed 27 May 2015].

[35] Political Parties, Elections and Referendums Act 2000 Pt VII. See para.5–10 et seq.

[36] Political Parties, Elections and Referendums Act 2000 s.101.

[37] Given the remarkable turnout (just under 85%) there was clearly no issue as to a lack of awareness or understanding!

Referendum Act made provision for detailed "campaign rules".[38] These cover the registration of "permitted participants" (Sch.4 para.3), the selection of "designated organisation" (in other words, the official "yes" and "no" campaigns) (Sch.4 para.6), the regulation of expenses (Sch.4 paras 10–25) and the control of donations to the permitted participants (Sch.4 paras 29–44). These rules largely mirror the provision made in the Political Parties, Elections and Referendums Act 2000 for a referendum that falls within its scope and which are discussed in Ch.5, below.

THE CAMPAIGN

The "referendum period" may have only begun on 30 May 2014 but the **1–07** campaign was long underway by that stage. In May and June 2013 the "Yes" and "Better Together" campaigns were launched, and in November 2013 the (SNP) Scottish Government launched its White Paper *Scotland's Future: Your Guide to an Independent Scotland*.[39] It might have been called a White Paper, but in substance it was a campaigning document and one that the Scottish Government would deliver for free (on request) to any house in the UK. In this document 26 March 2016 was identified as "independence day". From the UK Government came a series of documents (19 in all) called *Scotland Analysis*.[40] These covered a range of topics such as banking, currency, energy, the EU and defence. On 19 June 2014 a concluding document (*United Kingdom, united future: Conclusions of the Scotland analysis programme*)[41] was published setting out the benefits Scotland had gained, and would continue to gain, from the Union. Just like the Scottish Government's White Paper, these documents are best viewed as campaign documents. The Scottish and UK Governments were not the only contributors to the debate. People and organisations from almost all sections of society participated and nothing close to a comprehensive review of the campaign can be attempted in this work.[42] Almost every major campaign issue had a constitutional law implications: currency choice (and possible currency "union"); continued membership of the EU (which was an important political issue not just in Scotland but in Spain and other EU countries with separatist parties operating in various regions); and the relative merits of "devo-plus" as opposed to "devo-max" as opposed to independence. By the time polling day arrived, normal politics had been suspended for quite some time and Scotland had a very well informed electorate, who were daily debating and wrestling with

---

[38] Schedule 5 made provision for the Electoral Commission to investigate alleged breaches of the campaign rules; Sch.6 made provision for civil sanctions that attached to certain breaches; and Sch.7 made provision for various offences that were created by the Scottish Independence Referendum Act 2013.

[39] Scottish Government, *Scotland's Future: Your Guide to an Independent Scotland* (Scottish Government, 2013) *http://www.scotland.gov.uk/Publications/2013/11/9348/downloads* [Accessed 27 May 2015].

[40] See *https://www.gov.uk/government/collections/scotland-analysis* [Accessed 27 May 2015].

[41] HM Government, *United Kingdom, united future: Conclusions of the Scotland analysis programme* (The Stationery Office, 2014), Cm.8869, *https://www.gov.uk/government/uploads/system/uploads/attachment_data/file/321369/2902216_ScotlandAnalysis_Conclusion_acc2.pdf* [Accessed 27 May 2015].

[42] For another account of the Independence Referendum, see: Christopher M.G. Himsworth and Christine M. O'Neill, *Scotland's Constitution: Law and Practice*, 3rd edn (Haywards Heath: Bloomsbury Professional, 2015) Ch.4.

fundamental constitutional problems. Most of these issues were rendered especially difficult because they were "what if . . . " issues. Many pages could be devoted to considering these, and the many other, issues that were debated during the campaign. For present purposes, there is one in particular that is worth dwelling on. What would the constitution for a newly independent Scotland look like?

WHAT IF. . . ?

1–08   "What if there is a 'yes' vote?" was a question that occurred throughout the referendum campaign, on a variety of issues, and the answer to which rarely achieved a cross-party consensus. The *Scotland's Future* White Paper was designed to answer some of those questions. For constitutional lawyers (but admittedly not the rest of the electorate), one of the most interesting subsets of the "what if . . . " question was: "What will the constitution for an independent Scotland look like in the event of a 'yes' vote?" The timescale between the referendum (18 September 2014) and what would have been "independence day" (26 March 2016) was relatively short in which to negotiate secession and adopt a new constitution. It was widely accepted that an independent Scotland would have a written constitution and that had been made plain in the Scottish Government's White Paper, *Scotland's Future*.[43] That White Paper told us a number of things about what would be expected of the constitution of an independent Scotland: it would set out and protect the rights of the people of Scotland; it would define the role of government; it should set out the aspirations of the country; it should reflect "the fundamental constitutional truth—that the people, rather than politicians or state institutions, are the sovereign authority in Scotland".[44] As we shall see in the next chapter, the UK constitution may well embody a number of those ideas, but it has never been felt necessary to capture them in a single document that we call "the Constitution". So the question became: who decides what should form part of the constitution of an independent Scotland, what rights should be protected, how should they be protected and how should that decision be made? In June 2014, the Scottish Government published its proposed answers to those questions and put them out to consultation.

   Those proposals came in the form of a draft Scottish Independence Bill. Like the *Scotland's Future* White Paper, it was at least in part a campaigning document. That draft Bill had three main purposes: to make provision for Scotland to become independent; to provide an interim constitution; and to make provision for holding a Constitutional Convention to draft a permanent constitution. Constitution drafting is a new art in the UK so it is worth spending a moment to consider the terms of what would have been the interim constitution of an independent Scotland. There is a preliminary point to note. It was proposed that the Bill be enacted in the period following the referendum but before "independence day". Unsurprisingly, the draft Bill relates to a number of reserved matters (indeed, some of the most fundamental reserved matters). For the Scottish Parliament to pass the Bill before "independence day" the UK Parliament would have had to devolve the power to do so (presumably by means

---

[43] Scottish Government, *Scotland's Future: Your Guide to an Independent Scotland*, p.351.
[44] Scottish Government, *Scotland's Future: Your Guide to an Independent Scotland*, p.351. That latter idea is one that can be traced back to the Declaration of Arbroath in 1320.

of a s.30 order).[45] On "independence day", "all laws" that were in effect before independence would continue in effect unless and until amended or repealed by the Scottish Parliament.[46]

As for the draft constitution itself, this was set out in Pt II of the draft Bill. It contained the provisions one would expect of a constitution: establishing the institutions of the state; setting out the rights of the people; and containing several statements of an aspirational nature about the sort of country Scotland wanted to be. The Scottish Parliament and the Scottish Government would continue but the powers of both were subject to the constitution.[47] Her Majesty the Queen was to remain as Head of State.[48] Local government and the civil service were also provided for in the draft interim constitution.[49] The Court of Session and the High Court of Justiciary would be the Supreme Courts of Scotland (they already are the Supreme Courts of Scotland) but they would also be the final courts of appeal and no appeal would lie against their decision. That, however, was subject to the continuing jurisdiction of the Court of Justice of the European Union and the European Court of Human Rights and the jurisdiction of any other international court under an international agreement to which Scotland was a party.[50] It appears implicit in the draft constitution that the Supreme Courts would have had jurisdiction to strike down Acts of the (independent) Scottish Parliament as contrary to the constitution.[51]

The Scottish Parliament would not be "sovereign" in the Westminster sense. **1–09** That view was reinforced by cll.2 and 3:

> **"2 Sovereignty of the People**
> In Scotland, the people are sovereign.
> **3 The nature of the people's sovereignty**
>   (1) In Scotland, the people have the sovereign right to self-determination and to choose freely the form in which their State is to be constituted and how they are to be governed.
>   (2) All State power and authority accordingly derives from, and is subject to, the sovereign will of the people, and those exercising State power and authority are accountable for it to the people."

The idea of the people of Scotland as the source of power (as opposed to the Crown) is one that can trace its roots back to at least the Declaration of Independence that was signed in Arbroath Abbey in 1320. It also reflected the

---

[45] This is a point made clear by cl.35 of the draft interim constitution which purports to repeal the Union with England Act 1707 which, in terms of the Scotland Act 1998, the Scottish Parliament currently has no power to authorise.
[46] Scottish Independence Bill cl.34.
[47] Scottish Independence Bill cll.10 and 11, respectively. On the latter point, see also cl.1(3).
[48] Scottish Independence Bill cl.9.
[49] Scottish Independence Bill cll.17 and 16, respectively.
[50] Scottish Independence Bill cl.14.
[51] Scottish Independence Bill c.24(2) provided that "Scots law is of no effect so far as it is inconsistent with EU law" and cl.26(2) provided that "Scots law is of no effect so far as it is incompatible with [the European Convention on Human Rights]". Enforcing those provisions would require the courts to provide "strike down" powers. That is not a radical development on the powers over the current Scottish Parliament but is a significant difference to the powers of the UK Parliament.

prominent role of "the people" under the draft constitution. Clause 12, for example, specifically provides that both the Scottish Parliament and the Scottish Government would be "accountable to the people". On the international stage, the draft interim constitution provided for Scotland to be a "dualist" state[52] and was premised on Scotland remaining a member of the European Union and the Council of Europe.[53] The draft interim constitution then made provision for what might best be described as the "aspirational" clauses. In reality, they were campaigning clauses, setting out the Scottish Government's vision for what an independent Scotland would look like. For example "every person is entitled to live in a healthy environment",[54] that Scotland's national resources were to be used in a manner which is "best calculated to be sustainable",[55] that the Scottish Government enter negotiations to procure the removal of nuclear weapons based in Scotland[56] as well as requirements of equality[57] and the promotion of the wellbeing of children.[58] Not all of those provisions could be judicially enforceable[59] but that does not prevent them finding a home in a constitution.[60]

1–10   Of particular interest were the provisions of cl.33 which made provision for establishing a permanent constitution for Scotland. That required the Scottish Parliament to establish, "as soon as possible" after independence day, an independent Constitutional Convention to draw up a written constitution to be agreed by or on behalf of the people of Scotland. A number of questions flow from that and how it was to go about its business. Who was to be a member of this Constitutional Convention? How was any proposed constitution to be adopted? To what extent, if any, were the provisions of the interim constitution binding? Was it open to the Constitutional Convention to reject, for example, nuclear disarmament? That last point hints at another question: what was the process for constitutional amendment? The draft interim constitution was silent on that matter. Perhaps that would not have been a problem given it was only ever designed to be an interim constitution. But what if consensus over a "permanent" constitution proved elusive? In the event this, along with the rest of the draft interim constitution, was rendered academic. The consultation period ended on 20 October 2014. By that time the referendum had been held and the result was known. But the publishing of the draft interim constitution was an interesting insight into constitution formation in the 21st century and an indication as to what an independent Scotland may have looked like.

---

[52] Scottish Independence Bill cl.22; see para.2–12, below.
[53] Scottish Independence Bill cl.26. From cl.27, however, it is only what are currently defined as "Convention rights" under the Human Rights Act 1998 that would have effect under the draft interim constitution.
[54] Scottish Independence Bill cl.31.
[55] Scottish Independence Bill cl.30.
[56] Scottish Independence Bill cl.23.
[57] Scottish Independence Bill cl.28.
[58] Scottish Independence Bill cl.29.
[59] For example, what is a "healthy environment" and what sanction is there, and on whom, for breach?
[60] For example, art.21 of the Indian Constitution ("Protection Of Life And Personal Liberty: No person shall be deprived of his life or personal liberty except according to procedure established by law") has been interpreted to include, inter alia, a right to sufficient food to avoid starvation, a right to a healthy environment including fresh air and clean water and a right to health (see S.P. Sathe, "India: From Positivism to Structuralism" in J. Goldsworthy (ed), *Interpreting Constitutions: a comparative study* (Oxford: Oxford University Press, 2006) Ch.5).

THE VOTE

On 18 September 2014, Scotland went to the ballot box. With the eyes of the **1–11** world focused upon her, Scotland determined the future of the 307 year old Union. The vote, in terms of its organisation and the logistics, passed off without incident and coped with an unprecedented turnout (turnout was no lower than 75 per cent, with an average turnout of just under 85 per cent). Then, shortly after 6am on the morning of 19 September the result from Fife was declared and a "no" vote became inevitable. The official declaration of the result would not come for a number of hours yet (bad weather delayed some of the ballot papers for the Western Isles getting to the counting centre) but the Union would continue. The question now was in what form would it continue?

WHAT NEXT . . . ?

Shortly after that declaration, the Prime Minister announced a number of **1–12** measures, accompanied by a seemingly demanding timetable. Those measures included promises for "English votes on English law" and further devolved powers for Scotland. It was apparent that things would never be the same again. "English votes on English law" was to feature prominently in the 2015 general election campaign, especially when opinion polls started to suggest that the SNP would increase their representation at Westminster (to the point, it was suggested in one poll, of winning *all* of the Scottish constituencies). Superficially attractive, the idea of "English votes on English laws" is this: when the House of Commons debates and is then asked to pass legislation that would only apply to, and impact upon, England only MPs representing English constituencies should be permitted to vote on the matter. What could be wrong with that? Nothing, in principle; it is, after all, just another way of describing devolution. But "English votes on English laws" is not a call for a devolved English legislature. It is a call for changes in House of Commons procedure for particular Bills. When that becomes clear, we do not need to pause and reflect on the proposal for long before a whole host of difficulties occur. For example, what are "English laws"? In a system of asymmetric devolution, identifying matters that are exclusively English would not be easy. It is a problem that would only intensify if further power were transferred to Scotland but not to Wales and Northern Ireland. Taken to its logical conclusion, there would be at least four types of Bill: those that all MPs could vote on; those that only English MPs could vote on; those that only English and Welsh MPs could vote on; those that English and Northern Irish MPs could vote on. Remembering that the UK Parliament retains the power to legislate on devolved matters, if a Bill was presented that only concerned Scotland and which covered reserved matters, ought only Scottish MPs to vote on the matter? That all suggests that some sort of harmonisation of devolved competences would be necessary for there to be a stable and long term solution. Several other issues arise from the proposal. How would "English only" Bills be determined? As we will see when we look at the competences of the Scottish Parliament, where to draw the line can be controversial and in some instances it has divided the Supreme Court.[61] Proceedings in Parliament are not reviewable

---

[61] For example, *Martin v Most* [2010] UKSC 10; 2010 S.C. (U.K.S.C.) 40; see para.6–32.

by the courts.[62] But would a Speaker's certificate[63] certifying that the Bill was "English" be sufficient? When Acts of the Scottish Parliament have been reviewed by the court, the Presiding Officer and the Law Officer's views about competence has been held to be irrelevant.[64] So some system for determining who can vote will be necessary but any system that allows recourse to the court threatens to undermine one of the central provisions of the Claim (and Bill) of Rights. Assuming a workable solution could be found that allowed the House of Commons to pass a Bill that had been voted on by only a part of its membership, what would the status of the resulting Act be? Would it be an Act of Parliament in the traditional sense, that is, the Act of the sovereign legislature the validity of which could not be questioned in any court?[65] There are two main reasons to doubt that could be. First, what if, as a matter of fact, the provisions of the Act did impact on Scottish (or Welsh, or Northern Irish) law? It would be almost unthinkable that this would be done deliberately but it is possible as a result of an oversight or a failure to appreciate the impact of the provision. Would that provision remain law? Would there be no mechanism (outside Parliament) to review that matter? The second reason concerns the protection of fundamental human rights. Each of the devolved legislatures has their competence defined by reference to Convention Rights.[66] To the extent that any provision they adopt is incompatible with a Convention right it is "not law". Acts passed by Westminster, on the other hand, remain law (and remain enforceable) despite an incompatibility with a Convention right having been found.[67] Would a measure passed by the House of Commons by only English MPs benefit from that protection? If it did, it would produce the curious result that the fundamental human rights of those living in England would have a lower standard of protection than the other parts of the UK.[68]

What of the formation of a government in a House of Commons that operated under an "English votes on English law" rule? By convention (there being no detailed law that regulates the selection of Prime Minster and the formation of a government) the Prime Minster is the person best able to command the support of a majority in the House of Commons. What if that person changes when

---

[62] That is based on the terms of art.9 of the Claim (and Bill) of Rights. For a recent discussion of the principle by the Supreme Court, see *R. v Chaytor (David)* [2010] UKSC 52; [2011] 1 A.C. 684.

[63] That is what is required under the Parliament Act 1911 to determine what is a "money Bill" and thereby falling within the terms of that Act.

[64] *Imperial Tobacco Ltd v Lord Advocate* [2012] UKSC 61; 2013 S.C. (U.K.S.C.) 153, per Lord Hope of Craighead at [7]; *A v Scottish Ministers* [2001] UKPC D5; 2002 S.C. (P.C.) 63, per Lord Hope of Craighead at [7].

[65] The extent to which the conventional view of parliamentary sovereignty still holds true is discussed in Ch.3, below.

[66] Scotland Act 1998 s.29(2); Government of Wales Act 2006 s.103(6); Northern Ireland Act 1998 s.6(2).

[67] Human Rights Act 1998 s.4. The best illustration is the continuing disenfranchisement of serving prisoners that we have just discussed and which is considered further in para.11–13.

[68] As Lord Rodger of Earlsferry explained in *Somerville v Scottish Ministers* [2007] UKHL 44; 2008 S.C. (H.L.) 45 at [94]: "The Scotland Act confers wide, but nevertheless limited, powers on the Scottish Parliament and the Scottish Executive. Essentially, the limitations on the powers of both institutions are similar. In particular, it is beyond the competence of either to do anything that is incompatible with Convention rights . . . The limitation also affords protection to the Conventions rights of all those who are affected by the acts of the institutions. This is important since the changes brought about by the Scotland Act are actually intended to benefit people by improving the government of Scotland." The same must surely be true of any change introduced to give effect to "English votes for English laws".

Scottish MPs are left out of account? That raises the prospect of different party leaders being in a position to command a majority on different issues. It being the UK Parliament, and the UK Government, it may be assumed that the Prime Minister should be the person best able to command the support of a majority of MPs when all are included. But if that is correct, and the non-English MPs are excluded from voting on devolved issues (for example, most aspects of health) the Prime Minister may be lacking a majority on those issues. Indeed, if the Prime Minister represents a non-English constituency, they may themselves be unable to vote on what may be flagship policies of their own government. Could that give rise to a convention that the Prime Minister represents an English constituency? An equivalent convention probably exists in relation to portfolios that have been devolved.[69] But it would likely be objectionable to the other parts of the UK if there was now an expectation that the Prime Minister represent an English constituency. So despite the superficial attractiveness of "English votes on English laws", accommodating it within the existing constitutional framework appears to be fraught with difficulties.

On 19 September 2014, the Prime Minister also announced the establishment **1–13** of a commission to report on what further powers should be devolved to Scotland. This fulfilled "the vow" made by the leaders of the three main Westminster parties in the final days of the referendum campaign.[70] A commission, chaired by Lord Smith of Kelvin, recommended a range of further powers for the Scottish Parliament, including control over the voting system and franchise for the Scottish Parliament and establishing the Scottish Parliament and the Scottish Government as permanent institutions. The UK Government undertook to implement the recommendations of the Smith Commission and in January 2015 published a White Paper *Scotland in the United Kingdom: An enduring settlement* which contained a series of "draft clauses" to give effect to the Smith Commission recommendations.[71] Before turning to look at a few of the most significant clauses a word on process is appropriate. The Smith Commission had been formed, met, consulted, deliberated and reported by the end of November 2014, barely two months after the referendum. By January 2015 the draft clauses had been produced to "make it possible to quickly translate the [Smith Commission Agreement] into law at the beginning of the next Parliament and transfer power to Scotland".[72] The House of Lords Constitution Committee in particular has been critical of this approach to such significant and potentially wide reaching constitutional reform:

> "We do not believe that the referendum and subsequent events constitute a 'clearly justifiable' reason for adopting such an unusual process for

---

[69] The appointment of Dr (now Lord) John Reid as Health Secretary in June 2003 was controversial as Dr Reid represented a Scottish constituency and health had been more or less fully devolved to the Scottish Government. There has been no subsequent appointment of this nature.

[70] "The Vow" was a signed pledge by David Cameron, Ed Miliband and Nick Clegg that was published on the front page of the *Daily Record* on 16 September 2014 which promised "extensive new powers" for the Scottish Parliament.

[71] HM Government, *Scotland in the United Kingdom: An enduring settlement* (The Stationery Office, 2015) Cm.8990, *https://www.gov.uk/government/uploads/system/uploads/attachment_data/file/397079/Scotland_EnduringSettlement_acc.pdf* [Accessed 27 May 2015].

[72] HM Government, *Scotland in the United Kingdom: An enduring settlement*, p.7.

initiating significant constitutional change. The undue haste with which the process was conducted . . . undermines confidence in the outcome."[73]

The point is well made: by the time voters in Scotland went to the poll, the options on the ballot paper were independence and further significant devolution. To underscore the point, it is helpful to consider a few of the draft clauses.

First, ss.1 and 44 of the Scotland Act 1998 would be amended as follows: "(1A) A Scottish Parliament is recognised as a permanent part of the UK's constitutional arrangements" (s.1); and "(1A) A Scottish Government is recognised as a permanent part of the UK's constitutional arrangements" (s.44). These clauses can only, on a conventional view, be declaratory and not a binding statement of the law.[74] As explained in Ch.3, below on a traditional understanding of the UK constitution, the Westminster Parliament has the power to make or unmake any law and the only limit on its competence is that it cannot bind its successors.[75] So the language of permanence can only be a statement of desire and not a legally binding commitment. The next draft clause falls into the same category. The Smith Commission recommended that the Sewel convention (that the UK Parliament will not normally legislate on devolved matters in Scotland without the consent of the Scottish Parliament) be put on a statutory footing. That is achieved with a proposed amendment to s.28 of the Scotland Act 1998:

> "But it is recognised that the Parliament of the United Kingdom will not normally legislate with regard to devolved matters without the consent of the Scottish Parliament."

Following, as it does, immediately after a statutory assertion of the UK Parliament's continuing authority to legislate for Scotland on any matter (s.28(7)) this clause can be no more than a statement of desire, which cannot bind future parliaments (nor even the parliament that enacts it) and cannot be judicially enforceable.[76] There are other draft clauses that appear to have more substance to them. Draft cl.4 proposes the introduction of the concept of "protected subject-matter" which could only be modified by an Act of the Scottish Parliament if that Act was passed by two-thirds of the total number of MSPs. It is proposed that the "protected subject-matter" be the proposed new competences over the electoral system for the Parliament, the franchise for such elections and the number of constituencies. A qualified majority is a sensible provision to guard against the risk of these new competences being exercised for party political advantage by any party that obtained a simple majority in the Parliament. But two questions arise.

---

[73] House of Lords Select Committee on the Constitution, *Proposals for the devolution of further powers to Scotland, 10th Report of Session 2014–15* (The Stationery Office, 2015) HL Paper 145, para.47.

[74] For the contrary argument, see K. Campbell, "The 'Scotland Clauses' and 'Parliamentary Supremacy' ", 2015 Jur. Rev. forthcoming.

[75] See para.3–02—3–08, below for a discussion of this orthodox statement of constitutional principle and the current challenges to it.

[76] Even assuming the UK Parliament were to be held to be no longer sovereign, the wording of the clause is so vague ("will not normally legislate") that even if the courts could review the legality of an Act of Parliament, it is hard to see how they could ever review it on the grounds it infringed the proposed s.28(8) of the Scotland Act 1998.

First, are there any other issues that should fall within the "protected subject-matter"? For example, the rules on the appointment and removal of the judiciary. These are issues that are fundamental to securing the rule of law. Do they deserve the protection that a qualified majority brings? If not, why not? A by-product of the manner in which the draft clauses were produced is that there has been little opportunity to consider how they sit in the wider constitutional framework. That brings us to the second point. Is it appropriate to have devolved these powers to the Scottish Parliament? Voting system and number of members are not too controversial but the ability to modify the voting age is. If the voting age for Holyrood elections is lowered to 16 (and draft legislation to that effect is already before the Parliament, a s.30 order having been made to transfer the necessary power)[77] it throws up yet another anomaly in the UK constitutional arrangements. In 2020 the UK and Scottish general elections are due to clash. Another of the draft clauses (cl.5, which would insert s.2(2A) into the Scotland Act 1998) provides that the Scottish general election must be held on a date other than that of the UK general election and that that date must be no less than two and no more than six months after the date of the UK general election. Is it sustainable that on 7 May 2020, 16 and 17 year olds in Scotland will not get to vote in one parliamentary election but two months or so later get to vote in a different parliamentary election (bearing in mind that 16 and 17 year olds in Wales and Northern Ireland will, as things stand, not be permitted to vote in elections for their devolved legislatures)? The speed with which the draft clauses arrived has allowed no proper debate on whether lowering the voting age is appropriate, let alone whether setting different voting ages in different parts of the country is desirable. Of course, all of this is said without discussion of the further competences that it is proposed be devolved to Scotland. But three years after the Scotland Act 2012, which followed the Calman Commission and lengthy consultation, was enacted, it is surprising that extensive further powers are being transferred without, at the very least, a similar sort of consultation process. The process of constitutional change is something we will discuss in a moment. Before that, however, a few words about the 2015 election result are necessary.

2015 GENERAL ELECTION

Until well into the count after the polls had closed, it appeared that again the **1–14** electorate would have failed to return a majority government. In the end, the Conservative party passed the 326 seats needed to form a majority government. In Scotland, the SNP increased their representation: from six seats in 2010 to 56 in 2015. That left only three constituencies that did not return an SNP MP. The political consequences of the result, in particular what it means for Edinburgh--London relations, cannot be known at the time of writing. But there is one point that deserves mention now. In Ch.4, below we discuss the different electoral systems employed in the UK. In particular, we discuss the case for reforming the first past the post system used for the House of Commons and the referendum that was held in 2011 on the proposed change to that system. The 2015 result again highlights the case for reform.

---

[77] Scottish Elections (Reduction of Voting Age) Bill 2015; Scotland Act 1998 (Modification of Schedules 4 and 5 and Transfer of Functions to the Scottish Ministers etc.) Order 2015 (SI 2015/692).

Table 1: 2015 general election result in UK

Party	Votes	%	Seats	%
Conservative	11,334,920	36.9	331	50.9
Labour	9,347,326	30.4	232	35.7
Liberal Democrat	2,415,888	7.9	8	1.2
SNP	1,454,436	4.7	56	8.6
UKIP	3,881,129	12.6	1	0.2
Greens	1,157,613	3.8	1	0.2

Total votes cast: 30,698,210   Turnout: 66.1 per cent   Seats available: 650

On a purely proportionate allocation of seats (recognising that even systems of proportionate representation rarely produce an exact representation of the votes cast), the allocation of seats in the House of Commons would have been: Conservative 240; Labour 198; Liberal Democrat 51; SNP 31; UKIP 82 and Greens 25. No party would be close to a majority and the third largest party in the House of Commons would be UKIP. The most startling comparison is between the fortunes of UKIP and the Greens (whether individually or taken together) as compared to the SNP. In return for just under 1.5 million votes the SNP have secured 56 seats in the House of Commons. For just under 5 million and 1.2 million votes respectively, UKIP and Greens have secured a single seat each. On a proportionate allocation of seats, UKIP would have secured almost three times more seats than the SNP. In a representative democracy, an electoral system that can produce such a result must be a matter of concern. Of course, the SNP only fielded candidates in 59 of the 650 constituencies so necessarily have a more concentrated vote. It is a known feature of the first past the post system that it rewards parties that have such a support. As we will see in Ch.4, below the Liberal Party (in its various incarnations throughout the years) has regularly suffered from this feature of the system. But the SNP anomaly cannot be justified, or explained, by pointing to the results in Scotland alone. They simply make the problem more acute.

Table 2: 2015 general election result in Scotland

Party	Votes	%	Seats	%
SNP	1,454,436	50.0	56	94.9
Labour	707,147	24.3	1	1.7
Conservative	434,097	14.9	1	1.7
Liberal Democrat	219,675	7.5	1	1.7

Total votes case: 2,910,465   Turnout: 71.1 per cent   Seats available: 59

The SNP have secured 95 per cent of the seats in Scotland on 50 per cent of the votes cast (which in turn represents 35.5 per cent of the registered electorate). They can be seen to be large benefactors from the first past the post system. A purely proportionate result would have given the SNP 30 seats (still five times more than they won at the 2010 election and thus, on any measure, a significant electoral success), Labour 15 seats, the Conservative Party 8 or 9 seats and the Liberal Democrats 4 or 5 seats. This result raises a real question about the democratic deficit in Scotland and about an electoral system that allows a landslide in terms of seats in Parliament on only half of the vote.

Those results make a strong case for reform of the first past the post electoral system. Such calls are not new. But that system becomes increasingly unacceptable as the two party system moves further into the annuls of history. That begs the question: what should replace it? The alternative vote (which is, in reality, little better) was rejected by the electorate in 2011. The other systems employed in the UK are discussed in Ch.4, below. Most of them would require at least some departure from the constituency based system that is currently used and which has such a strong place in UK democracy. So any change would be significant and any change would likely require the sanction of the electorate in a referendum: certainly that was the view of the House of Lords Constitution Committee and arguably the 2011 referendum creates a "convention" to that effect.[78] That raises the question as to whether any change to the electoral system ought not to go hand in hand with other constitutional change (a revised settlement for Scotland and reform of the House of Lords, to take two examples)? This all leads to questions about the process of constitutional change, an issue that has often been neglected and one that we have touched upon in relation to the "draft clauses". It is appropriate that we finish with a few words about it.

THE PROCESS OF CHANGE

We have begun by talking about Scotland's changed constitution which, in large **1–15** part, can be attributed to the independence referendum. But throughout the remainder of this book, examples of constitutional change are noted: the introduction of fixed terms for Parliament[79]; the growth of the referendum, in particular as a result of the European Union Act 2011[80] and the unsuccessful attempt to change the voting system for elections to the House of Commons.[81] The structure of this book means that these changes are discussed at various different points. As a consequence, it is easy to lose sight of an important point that arises: the process by which these changes have been made. As we will see in Ch.3, below it remains trite to say that the UK Parliament can effect wide ranging constitutional reform in an ordinary Act of Parliament. But the process that gives rise to that Act merits consideration (particularly in light of the 2015 general election result which renders further constitutional change very likely). And when that is done, the patchwork and disjoined approach to constitutional reform in the UK become clear. The House of Lords Constitution Committee has expressed its concern about the ad hoc approach to constitutional reform that is regularly adopted and has called for a clear and consistent approach to be adopted for all significant constitutional changes.[82] That of course raised the question of

---

[78] House of Lords Select Committee on the Constitution, *Referendums in the United Kingdom, 12th Report of Session 2009–10* (The Stationery Office, 2010) HL Paper 99, para.94.

[79] See para.6–02.

[80] See para.10–43.

[81] See para.4–05.

[82] House of Lords Select Committee on the Constitution, *The Process of Constitutional Change, 15th report of Session 2010–12* (The Stationery Office, 2011) HL Paper 177, para.15.

what is "constitutional" in a country without a single written document it calls "the constitution". The working definition adopted by the committee was:

> "the set of laws, rules and practices that create the basic institutions of the state, and its component and related parts, and stipulate the powers of those institutions and the relationship between the different institutions and between those institutions and the individual."[83]

Recognising that the current system for constitutional change was flexible, and this was regard by some as a virtue, the committee explained that it did not overcome the weaknesses inherent in the ad hoc approach to constitutional reform adopted in the UK.[84] Those criticisms included: lack of constrains on government; failure to have regard to wider constitutional arrangements; lack of coherence within government; lack of consistency in the use of particular processes; possibility of changes being rushed; and lack of consultation.[85] What the committee proposed was the introduction of a requirement that a written statement be made to each House of Parliament, by the Minister responsible for the Bill in that House, setting out the Minister's view on whether the Bill provides for significant constitutional change.[86] Where the Minister is of the view that it does provide for such change, they should then be required to explain the processes that the Bill has been subject to and their outcomes.[87]

The report was published over three years before the independence referendum. In response to that vote, significant constitutional change was promised, change that had not been included in the most recent manifesto of any of the leading parties, and on which no prior consultation had taken place. Proposals were formulated in an exceptionally short period of time and there was no meaningful debate on whether the status quo was (or should be) an option. In short, the process adopted presents the most compelling case yet for the adoption of a fixed and defined process for constitutional reform in the UK. As the Constitution Committee had warned when reporting on the Fixed Term Parliaments Bill (itself a constitutional measure enacted swiftly after the 2010 General Election without proper consultation or regard for its impact on other parts of the constitution),[88] process matters:

> "Process is critical in terms of upholding, and being seen to uphold, constitutional values: particularly those of democratic involvement and transparency in the policy-making process. Moreover, we believe that a

---

[83] House of Lords Select Committee on the Constitution, *The Process of Constitutional Change, 15th report of Session 2010–12*, para.10. That definition was first proposed by the same committee in its very first report: House of Lords Select Committee on the Constitution, *Reviewing the Constitution: Terms of Reference and Method of Working, 1st report of Session 2001–2002* (The Stationery Office, 2001) HL Paper 11, para.20.
[84] House of Lords Select Committee on the Constitution, *The Process of Constitutional Change, 15th report of Session 2010–12*, paras 20–22.
[85] The concerns are discussed in turn in House of Lords Select Committee on the Constitution, *The Process of Constitutional Change, 15th report of Session 2010–12*, paras 20–46.
[86] House of Lords Select Committee on the Constitution, *The Process of Constitutional Change, 15th report of Session 2010–12*, para.71.
[87] House of Lords Select Committee on the Constitution, *The Process of Constitutional Change, 15th report of Session 2010–12*, para.72.
[88] See further, para.6–02.

proper process is the foundation upon which successful policy is built: the lack of a proper process makes an ineffective outcome more likely."[89]

As we face what is likely to be a further period of significant constitutional change, the process by which that change is made will be all the more important.

---

[89] House of Lords Select Committee on the Constitution, *Fixed-term Parliaments Bill, 8th Report of Session 2010–2011* (The Stationery Office, 2010) HL Paper 69, para.160.

CHAPTER 2

SOURCES

2–01 "A constitution is a thing antecedent to government, and a government is only the creature of a constitution."[1] Clearly, this will not do to describe the British constitution.[2] We do not have a single authoritative document identifying the principal institutions of the state and the powers held by each[3]; and even where a system has a constitution in this sense; it never offers a complete description of that system's constitutional law. The House of Lords Constitution Committee proposed the following definition of the constitution:

> " . . . the set of laws, rules and practices that create the basic institutions of the state, and its component and related parts, and stipulate the powers of those institutions and the relationship between the different institutions and between those institutions and the individual."[4]

The committee also recognised five basic tenants of the UK constitution: sovereignty of the Crown in Parliament; the rule of law; the union state; representative democracy; and membership of the Commonwealth, the European Union and other international organisations.[5] Whilst admittedly not definitive, it has proved to be a helpful working definition.

It is not correct to say that the British constitution is "unwritten".[6] Our constitution is the aggregate of several sources, some written, some not; some legal in character, others non-legal in the sense of not being judicially enforceable or of deriving rather from the realms of legal and political theory. The process of constitutional reform that began in the late 1990s with devolution, in, as we shall see, different forms, to Scotland, Wales and Northern Ireland, and the enactment of the Human Rights Act 1998 saw the constitution become

---

[1] Thomes Paine, *The Rights of Man*.
[2] There is, however, something of Paine's idea in the arguments of those who suggest that the UK does possess an "antecedent" constitution in the form of the Acts and Treaty of Union of 1707: see, e.g. T.B. Smith, "The union of 1707 as fundamental law" [1957] P.L. 99; D.N. MacCormick, "Does the United Kingdom have a constitution?" (1978) 29 N.I.L.Q. 1; M. Upton, "Marriage vows of the elephant" (1989) 105(Jan) L.Q.R. 79.
[3] Although, up to a point, the Scotland Act 1998 may be said to serve as such for Scotland.
[4] House of Lords Select Committee on the Constitution, *The Process of Constitutional Change, 15th report of Session 2010–12* (The Stationery Office, 2011) HL Paper 177, para.10. That definition was first proposed by the same committee in its very first report: House of Lords Select Committee on the Constitution, *Reviewing the Constitution: Terms of Reference and Method of Working, 1st report of Session 2001–2002* (The Stationery Office, 2001) HL Paper 11, para.20.
[5] House of Lords Select Committee on the Constitution, *The Process of Constitutional Change, 15th report of Session 2010–12*, para.10.
[6] The distinction between "written" and "unwritten" constitutions, and the consequences thought to flow from that distinction, has rightly been described as misleading and inexact: C.R. Munro, "What is a constitution?" [1983] P.L. 563.

increasingly "written". That process has continued: the Constitutional Reform Act 2005 (which created the UK Supreme Court), the Government of Wales Act 2006 (which as ultimately led to the transfer of limited legislative competence to the Welsh Assembly), the European Union Act 2011 and the Scotland Act 2012 have all resulted in an expansion of the written aspects of the constitution. But the unwritten (or at least, non-statutory) remains as significant as the written: both the Scotland Act and the Human Rights Act are, on the face of it, ordinary statutes enacted in the ordinary way and bearing no imprint of "constitutional" status, but, as we shall see, the courts ascribe to these and other statutes a superior status by virtue of their subject matter, and as a matter of the common law.

Already, then, we have identified two sources of those norms which go to make up our constitutional law: the law of Parliament as enacted in legislation, and the common law as expounded and applied by the courts. These take up much of, but do not exhaust, the field. Inter- and intra-institutional relations are very much the province of any system of constitutional law, and here we must look less at legal rules and more to what are known as constitutional conventions, to the law and custom of Parliament and indeed to broader concepts of legal and political theory, such as the separation of powers and the rule of law, from which certain conclusions about the appropriate balance of power between the institutions of the state may be drawn. It would also be inappropriate to ignore claims to "popular sovereignty" or "the will of the people" which, if they have not made much impact on constitutional law and practice hitherto, have in recent years, especially in Scotland, been asserted with greater vigour and may in the future illuminate not only political choices (e.g. as to the appropriateness of this or that piece of legislation) but also judicial decisions (e.g. as to the relationship between national law and EU law, or as to the legality of Westminster legislation trenching upon the legislative competence devolved to the Scottish Parliament). Finally, one should never be insular in looking for the sources of constitutional law. True it is that the term "the United Kingdom constitution" implies a strong connection between a constitution, or constitutional law, and the state. But just as the monolithic conception of the state has been weakened from within, by the asymmetric devolution of power from the central legislative and/or executive authorities of the UK to Scotland, Wales and Northern Ireland, so too has it been weakened from without. Most obviously, this has been a consequence of the UK's membership of the European Union. But it has also been the consequence of the UK's wider engagement in the global community, wherein the state is increasingly in competition with other authoritative sites of power.[7] These developments have posed significant challenges to British constitutional traditions, and the process of accommodating those challenges within our constitutional law is continuing.

LEGISLATION

Let us begin, at any rate, with legislation—Acts of Parliament—as a source of **2–02** constitutional law, and let us begin, as it were, at the beginning.[8] Parliament,

---

[7] N. Walker, "Beyond the unitary conception of the United Kingdom constitution" [2000] P.L. 384; N. MacCormick, *Questioning Sovereignty: Law, State and Nation in the European Commonwealth* (Oxford: Oxford University Press, 1999).

[8] Even this is not going back far enough. Pre-Union enactments of the English and Scottish Parliaments which remain in force include, most importantly, the Bill of Rights 1689 and Claim

meaning the UK Parliament at Westminster, is in its present form the creation of legislation, which legislation might in that sense be described as "constitutive". Before 1707 there were separate Scottish and English Parliaments. After 1707 there was a Parliament of Great Britain: by the Acts and Treaty of Union, the separate legislatures provided for their own extinction and the creation of a new entity.[9] That entity was enlarged again by the Union with Ireland Act 1800, the effects of which were reversed in large part by the legislation providing for the establishment of the Irish Free State.[10] Over the years, the Parliament thus established progressively redefined its internal composition by means of the Reform Acts,[11] the legislation to modify the power of the House of Lords to block legislation approved by the Commons[12] and, latterly, the legislation to remove altogether the right of hereditary peers to sit and vote in the Lords.[13] By the European Communities Act 1972, Parliament incorporated into national law the whole body of what is now called EU law, including future accretions thereto, and, whether intentionally or not, made possible recognition by the courts of the primacy of EU law over inconsistent national law.[14] In the Human Rights Act 1998, Parliament ordained all courts to read and give effect to its enactments, existing and future, in a manner compatible with the "Convention rights",[15] so far as possible; and, where such interpretation was not possible, conferred on the higher courts jurisdiction to make "declarations of incompatibility" in respect of

---

of Right 1688, whereby the Parliaments finally refuted the claims of the Stuart monarchs to govern by prerogative right; and the Act of Settlement 1700 (extended to Scotland by the Treaty of Union in 1707), which regulated succession to the Crown. As to the status of pre-Union legislation, while many Acts of the Scottish Parliament were repealed pursuant to the Treaty of Union, many were not, and unless subsequently repealed (see, e.g. the Statute Law Revision (Scotland) Acts of 1906 and 1964) or in desuetude, continue in force.

[9] Upton, "Marriage vows of the elephant" (1989) 105 L.Q.R. 79, suggests that the Union involved a delegation of authority by the Scottish and English Parliaments, and that even if, after the Union, there was no need for the old Parliaments, this did not mean that they were "abolished" or that it would be legally impossible to recall them. Suffice to say that, despite the rhetoric attending the first meeting of the new Scottish Parliament on 12 May 1999, that body was indeed new, the creation of an Act of the Westminster Parliament on the terms therein contained, and not the revival of the body dormant since 1707.

[10] Government of Ireland Act 1920, Irish Free State (Constitution) Act 1922 and Irish Free State (Agreement) Act 1922. These provided for the establishment of the Irish Free State as a dominion within the Commonwealth subject to a mechanism—promptly utilised—allowing the six counties of Ulster to opt out. The Irish Free State (or Eire) declared itself a sovereign independent state in the Irish Constitution of 1937; the UK recognised this independence in the Ireland Act 1949.

[11] Notably the Representation of the People Acts 1832, 1867 and 1918. The law relating to the franchise is now contained in the Representation of the People Act 1983, as amended.

[12] Parliament Acts 1911 and 1949.

[13] House of Lords Act 1999. Section 1 of the Act is qualified, however, by s.2, which "saves" the right of the Earl Marshal, Lord Great Chamberlain and 90 other hereditary peers elected by their fellows to sit and vote pending further reform of the House of Lords. The exact nature of that reform remains unresolved. As we shall see below, completing the process of reform that began in 1911 has not proved easy.

[14] For discussion of the meaning of the "primacy" of EU law, see further below at para.3–09—3–12, below and the discussion of the European Union Act 2011 at para.12–45, below. As to whether Parliament knew what it was about in 1972, see D. Nicol, *EC Membership and the Judicialisation of British Politics* (Oxford: Oxford University Press, 2001). The author contends that, despite the explicit assertions by the European Court of Justice of the autonomy and primacy of EU law, MPs did not appreciate the legal and constitutional consequences of accession.

[15] "Convention rights" are those articles of the European Convention on Human Rights listed in Sch.1 to the Human Rights Act 1998.

the offending statutory provision(s).[16] In the same session, Parliament made provision for the devolution of legislative competence in relation to Scotland to the Scottish Parliament, subject to various reservations and conditions, and for different forms of devolution to the National Assembly for Wales and Northern Ireland Assembly.

In their different ways—because they are constitutive or definitional, or concern the fundamental rights and freedoms of the individual, or confer authority on new constitutional actors—all of these statutes may be described as "constitutional" in a general sense. The question is whether this carries with it any higher legal status. Traditional constitutional doctrine has it that it does not:

> "[No] Act of the sovereign legislature (composed of the Queen, Lords and Commons) [can] be invalid in the eyes of the courts; . . . it [is] always open to the legislature, so constituted, to repeal any legislation whatever; . . . therefore no Parliament [can] bind its successors; and . . . the legislature [has] only one process for enacting legislation, whereby it is declared to be the joint Act of the Crown, Lords and Commons in Parliament assembled. . . . [It] is an invariable rule that in case of conflict between two Acts of Parliament, the latter repeals the earlier."[17]

In other words, there is no difference in status between (for instance) the Acts of Union on the one hand and the Dentists Act on the other. This is because, on the above reasoning, the only thing that the Westminster Parliament cannot do is detract from its own continuing sovereignty—its ability to make or unmake any law whatever. That being so, any attempt to "entrench" legislation regarded as "constitutional" or otherwise significant would be an exercise in futility: the statute would remain as vulnerable as any other to repeal (express or implied) by a subsequent statute passed in the ordinary way.

We consider that theory in more detail in the next chapter. For now, it suffices **2–03** to note that it no longer occupies the position of impregnability it once enjoyed. In particular, there has been judicial recognition that the status of Acts of Parliament does differ and that some Acts ought to be regarded as "constitutional". In *Thoburn v Sunderland City Council*, it was argued that provisions of the European Communities Act 1972 had been impliedly repealed by a subsequent, inconsistent Act of Parliament. Laws LJ held that this was not possible:

> "Ordinary statutes may be impliedly repealed. Constitutional statutes may not. For the repeal of a constitutional Act or the abrogation of a fundamental right to be effected by statute, the court would apply this test: is it shown that the legislature's *actual*—not imputed, constructive or presumed—intention was to effect the repeal or abrogation? I think the test could only be met by express words in the later statute, or by words so specific that the inference of an actual determination to effect the result contended for was

---

[16] The operation of the Human Rights Act 1998 (which the current Government has promised to repeal) is discussed in Ch.11, below.
[17] H.W.R. Wade, "The basis of legal sovereignty" [1955] C.L.J. 172.

irresistible. The ordinary rule of implied repeal does not satisfy this test. Accordingly it has no application to constitutional statutes."[18]

If this is so—if "constitutional" statutes are entrenched against implied override—the question is, what qualifies as a constitutional statute? Laws LJ gave some examples: Magna Carta, the Bill of Rights 1689, the Act of Union, the Reform Acts, the European Communities Act 1972, the Human Rights Act 1998 and the devolution statutes. The Supreme Court has more recently included the Claim of Right 1689 and the Constitutional Reform Act 2005 on a similar list.[19] More broadly, Laws LJ described a constitutional statute as:

> "one which (a) conditions the legal relationship between citizen and state in some general, overarching manner, or (b) enlarges or diminishes the scope of what we would now regard as fundamental constitutional rights."[20]

This definition is not without difficulties.[21] Those difficulties have not prevented the Supreme Court endorsing the assertions of Laws LJ.[22] We may, therefore, safely speak of a category of constitutional statutes (albeit a somewhat open-ended one), which are, at least, resistant to repeal by anything other than express terms or the necessary intendment of a later Act of Parliament.

COMMON LAW

2-04 Professor Mitchell noted the importance of judicial decisions "either as an original source of principle or as a secondary source, when the courts are interpreting a statute".[23] To these categories (which overlap) might be added a third: determining the scope of prerogative power, which is recognised by but not founded as such on the common law, and supervising the manner of its exercise. Dicey was referring to the courts as the source of original principles when, in his account of the rule of law, he wrote that, "the general principles of the

[18] *Thoburn v Sunderland City Council* [2002] EWHC 195 (Admin); [2003] Q.B. 151 at [63] (emphasis in original). This deals with the situation where a "constitutional" statute clashes with an "ordinary" statute. How the courts would deal with a clash between competing "constitutional" statutes is not clear: see the discussion by Lord Neurberger PSC and Lord Mance JSC in *R. (on the application of Buckingham CC) v Secretary of State for Transport* [2014] UKSC 3; [2014] 1 W.L.R. 324 at [207]–[208].
[19] "The United Kingdom has no written constitution, but we have a number of constitutional instruments. They include Magna Carta, the Petition of Right 1628, the Bill of Rights and (in Scotland) the Claim of Rights 1689, the Act of Settlement 1701 and the Act of Union 1707. The European Communities Act 1972, the Human Rights Act 1998 and the Constitutional Reform Act 2005 may now be added to that list": *R. (on the application of Buckingham CC) v Secretary of State for Transport* [2014] UKSC 3; [2014] 1 W.L.R. 324, per Lord Neuberger PSC and Lord Mance JSC at [207].
[20] *Thoburn v Sunderland City Council* [2002] EWHC 195 (Admin); [2003] Q.B. 151 at [62].
[21] See the discussion by Lord Rodger of Earlsferry in *Watkins v Secretary of State for the Home Department* [2006] UKHL 17; [2006] 2 A.C. 395, especially at [62]; G. Marshall, "Metric measures and martyrdom by Henry VIII clause" (2002) 118 L.Q.R. 493.
[22] *R. (on the application of Buckingham CC) v Secretary of State for Transport* [2014] UKSC 3; [2014] 1 W.L.R. 324 at [207]–[208].
[23] J.D.B. Mitchell, *Constitutional Law*, 2nd edn (Edinburgh: SULI; W. Green, 1968) p.23.

constitution (as, for example, the right to public liberty, or the right of public meeting) are with us the result of judicial decisions".[24]

In fact, this was a highly questionable proposition. The courts would intervene to protect invasions of individual rights for which there was no lawful authority.[25] But the common law was subordinate to the law enacted by Parliament, at least after 1688–89,[26] and it was less accurate to speak of "rights" of speech, property, assembly and so on than of such residue of liberty as remained after subtracting all the statutory (and common law) restrictions placed upon it. To be sure, the courts had the task of interpreting statutes, and might be more or less protective of the liberty of the subject in doing so.[27] But it is only relatively recently that the courts have begun to speak in terms of "common law constitutional rights".[28] Even there, they draw as much, if not more, inspiration from the post-war human rights movement, in particular the European Convention on Human Rights, as from the ancient traditions of the common law itself.[29]

The subjection of the common law to the law of Parliament was a corollary of the asserted supremacy of Parliament, as explained (in differing terms) by writers such as Blackstone and Dicey.[30] It is important to note that at the time Blackstone and (to a lesser extent) Dicey were writing, the law of Parliament encroached upon fewer areas of life than it does today.[31] In that sense, the role of the courts was as much a creative as an interpretive one, for in all the areas untouched by legislation, the common law was the law of the land.[32] This state of affairs did not last. The powers of the state and its organs increased exponentially in the nineteenth and, particularly, twentieth centuries. This was not necessarily for sinister reasons: the establishment and development of the welfare state, for one thing, and the prosecution of two world wars for another, required it, and it came

---

[24] A.V. Dicey, *Introduction to the Law of the Constitution*, 10th edn (London: Macmillan, 1959) p.195.

[25] The classic exemplar being *Entick v Carrington* (1765) 19 State Trials 1029.

[26] cf. *Dr Bonhams Case* (1610) 8 Co. Rep. 121, where Coke CJ asserted that "when an Act of Parliament is against common right and reason, or repugnant, or impossible to be performed, the common law will control it, and adjudge such Act to be void".

[27] Probably the least tolerance was shown to statutory provisions purporting to authorise invasions of rights of property: see, e.g. *Cooper v Wandsworth Board of Works* (1863) 14 C.B. N.S. 180. It has been suggested that *Entick v Carrington* is less a ringing assertion of the subjection of government to law than part of this property-fixated tradition: see K.D. Ewing, "The politics of the British constitution" [2000] P.L. 405.

[28] For example, the comments by Lord Hope (at [48]–[52]) and Lord Reed (at [149]–[153]) of *AXA General Insurance Co Ltd v Lord Advocate* [2011] UKSC 46; 2012 S.C. (U.K.S.C.) 122.

[29] For an instructive blending of the two traditions, see Lord Browne-Wilkinson, "The infiltration of a Bill of Rights" [1992] P.L. 397, in which his Lordship suggested that the restrictive approach taken by the courts to the construction of penal and taxing statutes—which threaten, respectively, the liberty and property of the individual—be applied equally to statutes impinging upon other rights as enshrined in the European Convention on Human Rights.

[30] See P.P. Craig, "The sovereignty of the United Kingdom Parliament after *Factortame*" (1991) 11 Y.B.E.L. 221.

[31] Dicey's *Law of the Constitution* was first published in 1885. The same year, Sir Henry J.S. Maine published *Popular Government* (London: 1885), which deplored both the increasing reach of statute law and the increasing domination of Parliament by the executive.

[32] The reference to the common law must include, in Scotland, reference to the civil law, which was a major influence on the development of Scots private law, if not of its public law. Likewise, the institutional writers are regarded as a source of law in Scotland, in the absence of subsequent judicial decisions to the contrary; but as Mitchell noted, the great institutional writers tended not to discuss public law so fully as private law or criminal law. Most constitutional "books of authority" are the works of English writers, and may carry less authority north of the border in consequence: see, generally, Mitchell, *Constitutional Law* (1968) pp.19–26.

about at the behest of a legislature which was (at least after 1928) elected on the basis of universal adult suffrage. Its consequence, however, was that the role of the courts in developing the common law became less important than their role in interpreting and applying statutes and instruments made under them.

The interpretive role is not value neutral and we may identify two strands of criticism (not necessarily mutually exclusive) levelled at the courts for the way in which they have performed this task. One school depicts the courts as ever apt to thwart the intentions of the legislature when its enactments conflict with the values—or class prejudices—of the judiciary.[33] Others are more concerned with the apparent readiness of the courts (at least in the past) to allow the claims of administrative efficiency and convenience to prevail over the protection of individual freedoms.[34] Associated with the latter if not the former has been a growing perception that the protection of what might be termed "constitutional values" should no longer be left to Parliament alone, or even primarily, given the subordination of Parliament to the executive where the latter commands a majority in the House of Commons. As Lord Hope explained in *AXA General Insurance Co Ltd v Lord Advocate*:

> "While the judges, who are not elected, are best placed to protect the rights of the individual, including those who are ignored or despised by the majority, the elected members of a legislature of this land are best placed to judge what is in the country's best interests as a whole."[35]

The judicial response to this tension has fused, in a sense, the function of expounding original principle and the function of statutory interpretation. It has been repeatedly held that, in construing legislation, it is to be presumed, absent express words or necessary implication to the contrary, that Parliament intended no infringement of certain "fundamental" rights.[36] In this way, the courts reasserted the authority of the common law as a source of constitutional norms, to such an extent that one commentator discerned a "new and still emerging constitutional paradigm, no longer of Dicey's supreme Parliament to whose will the rule of law must finally bend, but of a bi-polar sovereignty of the Crown in Parliament and the Crown in its courts".[37]

2-05   There is another, discrete sense in which the common law is important as a source of constitutional doctrine, and that is in its treatment of the Crown and prerogative powers. The nature of the Crown and of the prerogative is considered in greater detail in Ch.7; suffice to say for now that the courts have successively

---

[33] See, in particular, J.A.G. Griffith, *The Politics of the Judiciary*, 5th edn (London: Fontana, 1997); also, Ewing, "The politics of the British constitution" [2000] P.L. 405.

[34] See, in particular, the surveys by Sir Stephen Sedley, "The sound of silence: constitutional law without a constitution" (1994) 110 L.Q.R. 270 and "Human rights: a twenty-first century agenda" [1995] P.L. 386.

[35] *AXA General Insurance Co Ltd v Lord Advocate* [2011] UKSC 46; 2012 S.C. (U.K.S.C.) 122 at [49].

[36] See, for example, *R. v Lord Chancellor Ex p. Witham* [1998] Q.B. 575 QBD; *R. v Secretary of State for the Home Department Ex p. Pierson* [1998] A.C. 539 HL; *R. v Secretary of State for the Home Department Ex p. Simms* [2000] 2 A.C. 115 HL; *R. (on the application of Morgan Grenfell & Co Ltd) v Special Commissioners of Income Tax* [2002] UKHL 21; [2003] 1 A.C. 563, per Lord Hoffmann at [8].

[37] Sedley, "Human rights: a twenty-first century agenda" [1995] P.L. 386, 389.

denied the Crown any autonomous legislative authority,[38] affirmed the pre-eminence of statute over the prerogative,[39] and asserted the subjection of the prerogative to the supervisory jurisdiction of the courts provided its exercise raises justiciable questions.[40] As we shall see, despite all this, the subjection of the prerogative to law is often more a matter of principle than reality. That is not always, or necessarily, a matter of concern, for in certain circumstances political rather than legal control is apposite.

Like the prerogative, the privileges of Parliament are rooted in custom,[41] but may be said to exist within the common law in the sense that they are recognised by the courts and (so far as the courts are concerned) are subject to the common law, for while the courts concede Parliament's exclusive jurisdiction in matters of privilege where properly claimed, they assert for themselves the last word on where the outer limits of privilege lie.[42]

CONSTITUTIONAL CONVENTION

In his account of our constitutional rules, Dicey distinguished the legal **2–06** rules—statutory and common law—from another set of rules consisting of the,

> "conventions, understandings, habits or practices which, though they may regulate the conduct of the several members of the sovereign power, of the ministry, or of their officials, are not in reality laws at all since they are not enforced by the courts. This portion of constitutional law may, for the sake of distinction, be termed the 'conventions of the constitution' or 'constitutional morality'."[43]

For Dicey, the central significance of constitutional conventions was that they prescribed the manner in which the prerogatives of the Crown (or of ministers or servants of the Crown) fell to be exercised. This far from exhausts the field, but it is certainly true that these are the most important, or most clearly established, conventions, and chief amongst them is the convention which requires that the Queen act only on the advice of her ministers.[44] As we shall see, even this rule may admit of exceptions in certain circumstances. One might therefore wonder how is it possible to speak of conventions as "rules" of the constitution at all, if it is neither necessary that they be always obeyed nor possible (through recourse to the courts) to enforce their observance.[45]

---

[38] *Case of Proclamations* (1611) 12 Co. Rep. 74 and, in Scotland, *Grieve v Edinburgh and District Water Trustees*, 1918 S.C. 700.

[39] *Attorney General v De Keysers Royal Hotel Ltd* [1920] A.C. 508.

[40] *Council of Civil Service Unions v Minister for the Civil Service* [1985] A.C. 374.

[41] Although the privilege of freedom of speech was given statutory force by the Bill of Rights 1689 art.9.

[42] *R. v Chaytor (David)* [2010] UKSC 52; [2011] 1 A.C. 684, per Lord Phillips of Worth Matraves PSC at [15]–[16].

[43] Dicey, *An Introduction to the Law of the Constitution* (1959) p.24. His insight was not a new one. Mitchell, *Constitutional Law* (1968) cites Gilbert Stuart, who wrote in his *Observations concerning the public law, and the constitutional history of Scotland: with occasional remarks concerning English antiquity* (Edinburgh: William Creech, 1779) that "habits tend to establish a rule, and custom is often as effectual as law".

[44] R. Brazier "Royal Assent to legislation" (2013) 129 L.Q.R. 184.

[45] As to the judicial non-enforceability of convention, see *Attorney General v Jonathan Cape Ltd* [1976] Q.B. 752 QBD.

In asking that question, one risks falling into the error of equating conventions with legal rules. They are not legal rules, by definition. Legal rules are the product of sources we recognise as law constitutive: the Queen in Parliament, the Scottish Parliament acting within the sphere of its competence, and the courts. Conventions, by contrast, are founded on practice and precedent. Breach of a legal rule—stealing, speeding, committing murder—does not invalidate the rule. Breach of a convention, on the other hand, may have a destructive effect, depending on the "degree of stringency and definiteness" the convention possesses.[46] Short of that, the breach may restrict the range of circumstances over which the convention is felt to hold sway, or diminish its binding force within its allotted sphere.[47] What is critical to the crystallisation and survival of a convention, however, is that it has this binding quality: "feeling obliged" is a necessary condition for the existence of a convention, but neither a necessary nor a sufficient condition for the existence of a legal rule.[48]

2–07   The necessity that the key constitutional actors are left "feeling obliged" to adhere to a convention can create some uncertainty as to whether a convention has in fact been established. What then is required to create a constitutional convention? Jennings explained it thus:

> "We have to ask ourselves three questions: first, what are the precedents, secondly, did the actors in the precedents believe that they were bound by a rule; and thirdly, is there a reason for the rule? A single precedent with a good reason may be enough to establish the rule. A whole string of precedents without such a reason will be of no avail, unless it is perfectly certain that the persons concerned regarded them as bound by it."[49]

Constitutional conventions are normally "the product of a slow process of evolution".[50] That is not always so. The more rapid creation of a convention can be illustrated by asking: does the government require the approval of the House of Commons before engaging the military in armed conflict overseas? As we will see in Ch.7, the deployment of the armed forces and the declaration of war are prerogative powers, exercisable by the executive without prior approval by the legislature. However, before deploying armed forces in Iraq in 2003 the then Prime Minister, Tony Blair, asked the House of Commons to vote on his motion requesting approval for the use of military force "to ensure the disarmament of Iraq's weapons of mass destruction".[51] That motion was carried. It was subsequently suggested that events of 2003 meant that similar approval would "almost certainly" have to be obtained in similar circumstances in the future.[52] The next Prime Minister, Gordon Brown, proposed in a Green Paper that a convention to the effect that the consent of the House of Commons should be

---

[46] See F.W. Maitland, *The Constitutional History of England* (Cambridge: The University Press, 1911) p.398.

[47] See J. Jaconelli, "The Nature of Constitutional Convention" (1999) 19 L.S. 24 at 33; J. Jaconelli, "Do Constitutional Conventions Bind?" [2005] C.L.J. 149.

[48] C.R. Munro, *Studies in Constitutional Law*, 2nd edn (London: Butterworths, 1999) pp.78–87.

[49] Sir Ivor Jennings, *The Law and the Constitution*, 5th edn (London: University of London Press, 1959) p.136.

[50] A. McHarg, "Reforming the United Kingdom constitution: law, convention and soft law" (2008) 71 M.L.R. 853.

[51] *Hansard*, HC Vol.401, col.760 (18 March 2003).

[52] Lord Wilson of Dinton, "The robustness of conventions in a time of modernisation and change" [2004] P.L. 407.

required before sending the military into armed conflict. That proposal was never taken forward. When the prospect of military intervention in Syria arose however, the Prime Minister of the day, by now David Cameron, felt obliged to seek approval of UK involvement in any such military intervention. When the House of Commons did not grant that approval, the Prime Minister undertook not to exercise the government's prerogative power to nevertheless deploy the military in Syria and the UK did not participate in the subsequent military campaign.[53] Events of 2003 proved to have been a sufficient single event to produce the rule: it was, to use Jenning's language, a single precedent underpinned by a very good reason.[54]

The requirement of "feeling obliged" may also help us to clarify what we mean when we speak of "breaches" of convention. The very language betrays a sense of being obliged to act in a particular way, and an expectation of criticism if one acts otherwise. It also suggests that a constitutional actor who acts in a manner other than that ordained by convention will have thought long and hard before doing so, and will probably feel (rightly or wrongly) that they have a good reason for acting in the way they have chosen.[55] For these reasons, the term "breach" may not always, or necessarily, be apposite. But while conventions are not "rules of law" they can be regarded as "rules of the constitution". The difference between a legal rule and a convention being simply the method of enforcement: the former is enforced by the courts and the latter by the political process.[56]

The key characteristics of the operation of constitutional conventions can be **2–08** illustrated by considering the cardinal convention that governs the exercise of so called "personal prerogatives" of the Queen (assenting to legislation, appointment of the Prime Minister and so on). This list previously included the dissolution of Parliament and the calling of a general election. That personal prerogative has, however, been removed by legislation.[57] By convention, the Queen is required to exercise these only in accordance with the advice of her ministers.[58] Constitutional practice is consistent (if not altogether without ambiguity) and the reasons for it can be located in the importance we attach to such values as responsible government and democratic accountability. Thus in

---

[53] *Hansard*, HC Vol.566, cols 1555–1556 (29 August 2013).

[54] See McHarg, "Reforming the United Kingdom constitution: law, convention and soft law" (2008) 71 M.L.R. 853, who discusses why the Green Paper should not be considered the source of the convention.

[55] Jaconelli, "The Nature of Constitutional Convention" (1999) 19(1) L.S. 24 discusses this point under reference to Ronald Dworkin's account of the nature of practices in *Law's Empire* (London: Fontana, 1986). Dworkin agrees that practices have an element of uncertainty which is open to interpretative dispute. On this view, it is not enough to act solely on the basis of the "raw empirical data" consisting in past precedents; rather, one must supplement the data with questions of the rationale for applying the convention in the present circumstances.

[56] C. Turpin and A. Tomkins, *British Government and the Constitution: text and materials*, 7th edn (Cambridge: Cambridge University Press, 2011) pp.182–183.

[57] Fixed-Term Parliaments Act 2011 s.3; s.6(1) of the 2011 Act preserves Her Majesty's power to prorogue Parliament. The 2011 Act, however, otherwise prescribes when, and in what circumstances, an election can now be called. Parliament is then dissolved on the seventeenth working day before the election (s.3(1)). For a critical analysis of the 2011 Act see M. Ryan, "The Fixed-Term Parliaments Act 2011" [2012] P.L. 213.

[58] R. Blackburn, "Monarchy and the personal prerogatives" [2007] P.L. 546 (who argues that the approach of "personal prerogatives" is "wrong, misconceived, and belongs to an earlier era"; despite the cogency of his argument, the phrase remains in common currency and is used here, subject to Professor Blackburn's warnings); see also R. Blackburn, "The prerogative power of dissolution of Parliament: law, practice and reform" [2009] P.L. 766.

normal circumstances, the Queen will appoint as Prime Minister the person best able to command the confidence of the House of Commons. In other words, the Queen will appoint either the leader of the largest party (especially where that party has an overall majority) or, where a coalition has been formed, the leader of the largest party within that coalition.

As we saw in 2010, the Queen exercised no personal choice in the aftermath of a general election that produced no clear winner. In 2010, there were three possibilities: a Conservative-Liberal Democrat coalition, a Labour-Liberal Democrat coalition or a minority Conservative government.[59] Coalition talks between the Conservatives and the Liberal Democrats took a number of days. During that period, the incumbent Prime Minister, Gordon Brown, remained in office. By failing to tender his resignation immediately after the election (as would ordinarily be expected of a defeated incumbent) he afforded space to the parties to negotiate a coalition agreement. As a result, the Queen was not placed in a position where she may have required to intervene in those discussions. Events of May 2010 underscore the flexibility of the constitution, and in particular the conventions surrounding the appointment of the Prime Minister. Just as King George V was not required to exercise any personal choice in the 1920s when twice a general election failed to produce a clear winner, nor was his granddaughter nearly a century later: political circumstances dictated the outcome. Any alternative, which saw an unelected and hereditary Head of State exercise a personal choice in the appointment of Prime Minister, in a representative democracy, could be described as, at best, unfortunate.[60]

What does this tell us about the conventions surrounding the choice of Prime Minister? It suggests that despite being labelled a "personal prerogative" of the Sovereign, the prevailing political atmosphere should ensure that no personal choice is required on the Sovereign's part. Any other situation would be dangerous for the monarchy as an institution. The 2011 Act removes the need to theorise about when, if at all, the Queen could act contrary to the advice of her Prime Minister in relation to the dissolution of Parliament. History, however, teaches us that it would only have been in the rarest of circumstances that such a course would have been appropriate. In 1926, the minority Liberal Prime Minister in Canada requested a dissolution from the Sovereign's representative, the Governor General. The Governor General believed that the Conservative leader could form a government having majority support in the existing Parliament, and refused. The Prime Minister resigned and the Governor General appointed the Conservative leader in his place. Days later, the new government was defeated on a motion of confidence, leading to the dissolution which had been denied to its Liberal predecessor. In the general election that followed, the Liberals were returned with a convincing majority. Again, in 1975, the Governor General of Australia was moved to exercise the prerogative of dismissing a Prime Minister and his government.[61] The Australian Senate (in which the opposition had a majority) had refused to pass money bills authorising government expenditure. This had led to a rapid depletion in the funds available to maintain public services. Prime Minister Whitlam requested the Governor General to

---

[59] For a general and insightful discussion of the issues arising from the 2010 election result, see V. Bogdanor, *The Coalition and the Constitution* (Oxford: Hart, 2011).

[60] Blackburn, "Monarchy and the personal prerogatives" [2004] P.L. 546.

[61] This despite the fact that the exercise of the prerogative of dismissal had been described not so very long before as "not being within the scope of practical politics": *Adegbenro v Akintola* [1963] A.C. 614 PC (Nigeria), per Lord Radcliffe at 631.

dissolve the Senate. The Governor General insisted on a full dissolution so that a general election could be held. When Whitlam refused to change his advice, the Governor General dismissed him and his government and appointed the Leader of the Opposition in his place on condition that he would guarantee supply and advise a dissolution and general election.

It is not obvious that the circumstances of either case were so extreme as to justify departure from the normal convention. In the Australian case, for instance, the more astute course would have been to follow the advice given and let the electorate decide, in the fullness of time, whether Whitlam's advice had been sound. Resolution of the crisis would then have rested where it properly belonged, firmly in the arena of democratic politics. On this view, the Sovereign should only exercise her prerogatives personally and without advice where the advice tendered is clearly an abuse of the system or where necessary to safeguard the parliamentary and democratic bases of the constitution. The point remains that even this convention is less than absolute in its terms, and does not altogether exclude the possibility of the Sovereign exercising effective political power. This may not commend itself to those of a republican bent. On the other hand, it generally works; and it is not as though the alternative solutions to such occasional crises are themselves free of problems.[62]

Other conventions are less prescriptive still, perhaps not least the convention **2–09** of ministerial responsibility. This has a collective and an individual dimension. Collective ministerial responsibility,

> "requires that Ministers should be able to express their views frankly in the expectation that they can argue freely in private while maintaining a united front when decisions have been reached. This in turn requires that the privacy of opinions expressed in Cabinet and Ministerial Committees, including in correspondence, should be maintained."[63]

A Minister that cannot adhere to this principle ought to resign from the government.[64] Individual ministerial responsibility in its classic form involves the minister in charge of a government department assuming responsibility for all that is done by his officials in his name, such that an official's mistake is deemed to be the Minister's mistake and, if sufficiently serious, warrant for his resignation. The sanction attaching to a lapse from collective ministerial responsibility is clear enough: if the Minister neglects to resign, they may simply be sacked. The sanction attaching to a departure from the strictures of individual ministerial responsibility, however, is less clear. In the days when Parliament was less apt to operate on rigid party lines, MPs might have forced an incompetent Minister's resignation by withdrawing their confidence from him. Now, this is

---

[62] See A. Tomkins, "In Defence of the Political Constitution" (2002) 22 O.J.L.S. 157. The author contrasts the British constitutional handling of a hung Parliament with the debacle that followed the American Presidential election in 2000, suggesting that the latter demonstrates the futility and undesirability of seeking to find the answer to all political disputes in law (see *Bush v Gore* (2000) S31 US 98).

[63] Cabinet Office, *Ministerial Code* (The Stationery Office, 2010) para.2.1, *https://www.gov.uk/government/uploads/system/uploads/attachment_data/file/61402/ministerial-code-may-2010.pdf* [Accessed 2 June 2015].

[64] In this context, "Minister" includes all members of the Government, including parliamentary private secretaries (para.3.9 of the Ministerial Code).

virtually inconceivable provided the government has majority support: government backbenchers are unlikely, to put it mildly, to force the resignation of one
of their own. Is there, then, evidence that Ministers resign in circumstances of
departmental failure through a sense of obligation to do so? Professor Finer
doubted it.[65] Having studied the instances of ministerial resignation over the
course of the preceding century, he concluded that:

> "All [the convention] says (on examination) is that if the minister is
> yielding, his Prime Minister unbending and his party out for his blood—no
> matter how serious or trivial the reason—the minister will find himself
> without parliamentary support. [But] that is a statement of fact, not a
> code."

It is of note that the Ministerial Code now talks about a Minister's duty to
account as opposed to their responsibility.[66] As we will see in Ch.7, the
distinction between "accountability" and "responsibility" has become of
increasing importance in recent years. It is true that Ministers do not routinely
fall on their swords in the manner the convention seems to prescribe. Famous
examples do not denote consistent compliance.[67] But some Ministers at least
have felt an obligation to resign, and "in everyday political discourse, too, the
rule continues to be treated as if it had practical content".[68] Thus we need not
accept Finer's conclusion that there is no convention of resignation at all, even
if we concede that it is not a convention of great "stringency and definiteness".
Further, as we shall see in Ch.7, it does not necessarily do to focus exclusively
on the "blame and sanction" aspect of the convention of ministerial responsibility. It has been forcefully argued that the convention has had a strong influence
on the internal structuring of government.[69] Moreover, in point of fact, Ministers
do answer to Parliament for the actions and decisions of their departments, and
do not routinely or systematically mislead Parliament in doing so. Viewed thus,
whether or not a Minister resigns may be less important than the adequacy (or
otherwise) of the convention as a vehicle for securing the accountability of the
executive to Parliament.

2–10   So far we have been talking about the operation of constitutional conventions
at the UK level. To what extent may it be said that conventions have developed
in the context of the devolved Scottish institutions? It may still be too soon to
speak of "indigenous" conventions, the products of consistent and uniform
practice. In the last decade, we have seen coalition government, minority
government and the supposedly impossible majority government. What should

---

[65] S.E. Finer, "The Individual Responsibility of Ministers" (1956) 34(4) *Public Administration*
377.
[66] For example, para.4.6 of the Ministerial Code: "The Minister in charge of a department is solely
accountable to Parliament for the exercise of the powers on which the administration of that
department depends."
[67] Among the classic cases are those of Sir Thomas Dugdale, who resigned as Minister of
Agriculture in 1954 after an inquiry found maladministration by officials in his department; the
Foreign Secretary, Lord Carrington, and two Foreign Office ministers, who resigned in 1982
amidst claims that the Foreign Office had culpably misinterpreted signals of Argentinian intention
in the period preceding the Falklands conflict; and the Home Secretary, Leon Brittan MP, who
resigned in 1986 after one of his officials leaked confidential legal advice to the press.
[68] Munro, *Studies in Constitutional Law* (1999) p.86.
[69] T. Daintith and A. Page, *The Executive in the Constitution: Structure, Autonomy and Internal
Control* (Oxford: Oxford University Press, 1999).

be considered "the norm" is yet to be established. But two aspects of the devolution settlement are interesting in this regard. First, the Scotland Act clothes in the language of legislation the conventions that, at Westminster, govern the choice of Prime Minister.[70] The appointment of the First Minster is made by the Queen from among the members of the Scottish Parliament. Section 46(4) of the Scotland Act 1998 provides that the Presiding Officer shall recommend to the Queen the appointment of that MSP who is nominated by the Parliament in accordance with the section. Nowhere does the Act state in terms that the nomination must be accepted, but the intention of the section is clear; whatever arguments might be made about the strict legal position, here at least we can probably speak of a convention, even at this stage, that the Queen will act in this matter on the advice of the Presiding Officer alone.

Secondly, there is said to be a convention—the "Sewel convention"—whereby Westminster is obliged to seek the consent of the Scottish Parliament before proceeding to enact legislation touching on devolved matters.[71] This is at variance with s.28(7) of the Scotland Act, which provides that the devolution of legislative competence to the Scottish Parliament "does not affect the power of the Parliament of the United Kingdom to make laws for Scotland". The Sewel convention is named for the Scottish Office Minister who, during the parliamentary debates on the Scotland Bill, sought to assuage concern that, after devolution, Westminster would exploit its unimpaired legislative competence to frustrate the work of the Scottish Parliament:

> "The government would expect a convention to be established that Westminster would not normally legislate with regard to devolved matters in Scotland without the consent of the Scottish Parliament."[72]

This principle was endorsed by the House of Commons Select Committee on Procedure in 1999, and further reinforced by guidance concerning its operation in the Memorandum of Understanding between the UK Government and Scottish Executive and documents issued by the Privy Council Office in 1999 and by the Constitution and Parliamentary Secretariat in 2001. Where consent is required, it is sought by way of a "legislative consent motion" (formerly known as "Sewel motion") laid before the Scottish Parliament[73] by the appropriate Scottish Minister following consultation between the UK Government and the Scottish Government.

It was not anticipated that legislative consent motions would be used routinely. **2–11** In fact, they are commonplace.[74] So far, Westminster has sought, and obtained, the Scottish Parliament's consent each time it has wished to enact legislation

---

[70] The Scottish Parliament has always been a fixed term parliament. The Scotland Act 1998 was effectively a codification of the conventions that, at that time, regulated Westminster. Those conventions have now been codified for Westminster as well in the form of the Fixed-Term Parliaments Act 2011.

[71] See B.K. Winetrobe, "Counter-devolution? The Sewel convention on devolved legislation at Westminster" (2001) 6(4) S.L.P.Q. 286; N. Burrows, "It's Scotland's Parliament: Let Scotland's Parliament Legislate", 2002 Jur. Rev. 213; A. Page and A. Batey, "Scotland's Other Parliament: Westminster Legislation about Devolved Matters in Scotland since Devolution" [2002] P.L. 501; J. Munro, "Thoughts on the 'Sewel Convention'", 2003 S.L.T. (News) 194.

[72] *Hansard*, HL Vol.592, col.791 (21 July 1998).

[73] Standing Orders of the Scottish Parliament Pt 9B.

[74] As at May 2015 167 legislative consent motions had been passed by the Scottish Parliament, *http://www.scotland.gov.uk/About/Government/Sewel/SewelMemosPdf* [Accessed 2 June 2015].

touching on devolved matters. The practice is therefore consistent, and there are good reasons for it. But the Sewel convention raises interesting doctrinal points. First, does it merit the name? Is it possible for a convention in the true sense of the term to "spring fully armed from the head of a particular procedure"?[75] Jaconelli suggests that, even if ultimately we may trace the emergence of a convention back to a particular event, such as a statement made in the legislature, the statement "attains that status in truth only when [it has] set in motion a chain of actions and expectations based on [its] observance". Secondly, the terms in which Sewel tends to be discussed suggest not only that we take its force as a constitutional convention for granted but also that we place it at the "stringent and definite" end of the spectrum. Does either conclusion follow? If "feeling obliged" is a necessary component of a constitutional convention, we might wish to pause before ascribing that status to Lord Sewel's dictum. What if the Scottish Parliament under the control of a majority government were to refuse all legislative consent motions on principle, even where the arguments for UK-wide legislation were compelling? Would Westminster "feel obliged" to refrain from legislating within the sphere of devolved competence? It is hard to conceive of the UK Government and Parliament refusing to legislate in the face of such an arbitrary policy. Would the decisive factor prove to be the popular support the Scottish Government's stance attracted? If so, the resolution would lie in the realm of politics and not law. The real test of a convention comes when it constrains constitutional actors to behave in a way other than that which they would, left to themselves, have chosen. The proposal to repeal the Human Rights Act may provide such a test. The Human Rights Act is, itself, reserved to Westminster. To that end, there is no need for a legislative consent motion to repeal it. However, the concept of Convention rights to woven deep into the fabric of the Scotland Act. Repeal of the Human Rights Act, it appears, would necessitate some amendment to the Scotland Act. If that is so, the Sewel convention would dictate that the consent of the Scottish Parliament be obtained. At the time of writing, the Scottish Government (which holds a majority in the Parliament) is opposed to repeal of the Human Rights Act and has vowed to refuse to give such consent. Given the increasing strain the very existence of the Union has had placed on it, it would be unfortunate if now was the first time that Westminster asserted its continuing sovereignty and proceeded to amend the devolution settlement against the wishes of the Scottish Parliament.

INTERNATIONAL LAW

2–12 As a Member State of the European Union, the UK is obliged to give effect to and apply directly effective norms of EU law, and that obligation is discharged through the medium of the European Communities Act 1972. The incorporation of EU law has had momentous consequences for our constitutional law, as we shall see the next chapter. But to what extent might other international legal norms serve as a source of domestic constitutional law? Rules of customary international law, the product of consistent and uniform state practice which comes to reflect an *opinio juris* that particular conduct is proscribed or, as the case may be, required by international law, constitute rules of Scots law, whether

---

[75] Jaconelli, "The Nature of Constitutional Convention" (1999) 19(1) L.S. 24 at 33.

or not codified in international treaties.[76] Thus, established principles of international humanitarian law on the prohibition of torture and other crimes against humanity would form part of Scots law independently of their incorporation (or otherwise) into national law by statutes. Rules of international law derived from treaties (unless they have customary law status) differ. Some constitutional systems, which are described as "monist", hold that, when a state signs and ratifies an international treaty, the contents of that treaty automatically become part of its domestic law, directly enforceable as such before its courts. The UK, however, subscribes to the "dualist" position, which holds that a treaty does not form part of national law unless and until incorporated into the law by legislation. The process for ratification of treaties by the UK has now been put on a statutory footing.[77] Unless incorporated, however, the treaty cannot create rights or duties enforceable before the national courts. The rationale for this is that the signing of a treaty is an executive, not a legislative, act, and the government should not be permitted to burden citizens with obligations unsanctioned by Parliament.[78] Lord Steyn has noted that this reasoning is quite beside the point in relation to human rights treaties, which by definition do not impose burdens on individuals.[79] Lord Kerr (in the course of dissenting) has adopted this argument and strongly advocated that human rights enshrined in international treaties to which the UK is party should be directly enforceable in domestic law.[80] Nonetheless, the weight of authority remains firmly in favour of dualist orthodoxy.[81]

This is not to say that unincorporated international treaties have no domestic legal effect. As Diplock LJ held in *Salomon v Commissioners of Customs and Excise*:

"There is a *prima facie* presumption that Parliament does not intend to act in breach of international law, including therein specified treaty obligations; and if one of the meanings that can reasonably be attributed to the

---

[76] See *R. (on the application of European Roma Rights Centre) v Prague Immigration Officer* [2004] UKHL 55; [2005] 2 A.C. 1; *Lord Advocates Reference (No.1 of 2000)*, 2001 J.C. 143. It follows that, whereas questions of foreign law (including English law) constitute questions of fact on which evidence may be led, questions of customary international law constitute questions of law for the judge to determine.

[77] Constitutional Reform and Governance Act 2010 Pt 2.

[78] See *JH Rayner (Mincing Lane) Ltd v Department of Trade and Industry* [1990] 2 A.C. 418 HL, per Lord Oliver at 500.

[79] *Re McKerr* [2004] UKHL 12; [2004] 1 W.L.R. 807, per Lord Steyn at [49]–[50]. These comments built on his extrajudicial comments: Lord Steyn, "Democracy Through Law" [2002] E.H.R.L.R. 723. Under reference to *Thomas v Baptiste* [2000] 2 A.C. 1 PC (Trinidad and Tobago) and *Lewis v Attorney General of Jamaica* [2001] 2 A.C. 50 PC (Jamaica), in which the Judicial Committee of the Privy Council held that condemned men in Caribbean countries could not be executed until the determination of their appeals to the Inter-American Human Rights Committee, a body whose jurisdiction depends upon an unincorporated treaty, Lord Steyn suggests that there is "scope for the evolution of a more realistic notion", which would place human rights treaties in a special category. See also Lord Collins, "Foreign Relations and the Judiciary" (2002) 51(3) I.C.L.Q. 485. For a robust response to this argument see, P. Sales and J. Clement, "International Law in Domestic Courts: The Developing Framework" (2008) 124 L.Q.R. 388.

[80] *R. (on the application of JS) v Secretary of State for Work and Pensions* [2015] UKSC 16; [2015] 1 W.L.R. 1449 at [254]–[256].

[81] See, in addition to *JH Rayner (Mincing Lane) Ltd v Department of Trade and Industry* [1990] 2 A.C. 418, *R. v Lyons (Isidore Jack)* [2002] UKHL 44; [2002] 3 W.L.R. 1562, per Lord Hoffmann at [27], [28]; and *Whaley v Lord Advocate*, 2004 S.C. 78, per Lord Brodie at [41]–[44].

legislation is consonant with the treaty obligations and another or others are not, the meaning which is so consonant is to be preferred." [82]

Thus where a statutory provision was ambiguous, international treaties to which the UK was party could be relied on as an aid to construction and there is a strong presumption in favour of interpreting a statute so as to avoid placing the UK in breach of its international law obligations.[83] An equivalent presumption applies when developing the common law[84] and unincorporated treaties can be used to resolve ambiguities in the common law.[85] As we shall see, prior to the incorporation of the "Convention rights" by the Human Rights Act 1998, the European Convention on Human Rights was particularly influential in this respect.[86] But there is no reason in principle why exactly the same approach should not apply in relation to other, as yet unincorporated, treaty provisions,[87] in particular in the field of human rights. The European Court of Human Rights is already prepared to have regard to unincorporated international treaties to which the UK is a party when determining whether there has been an infringement of the Convention rights.[88]

---

[82] *Salomon v Commissioners of Customs and Excise* [1967] 2 Q.B. 116 CA at 143. See also Lord Hughes' summary of the circumstances where an unincorporated international treaty may be relevant in domestic law in *R (on the application of JS) v Secretary of State for Work and Pensions* [2015] UKSC 16; [2015] 1 W.L.R. 1449 at [137] and Lord Kerr's fuller discussion on the status of international law in the same case at [234]–[257].

[83] *Assange v Swedish Prosecution Authority* [2012] UKSC 22; [2012] 2 A.C. 471, per Lord Dyson at [122].

[84] *A v Secretary of State for the Home Department (No.2)* [2005] UKHL 71; [2006] 2 A.C. 221, per Lord Bingham of Cornhill at [27].

[85] *Derbyshire CC v Times Newspapers Ltd* [1993] A.C. 534 HL.

[86] If only latterly in Scotland. It was held in *Kaur v Lord Advocate*, 1980 S.C. 319 that, "as the Convention was not part of the municipal law of the United Kingdom, the court was not, so far as Scotland was concerned, entitled to have regard to the Convention either as an aid to construction or otherwise" (per Lord Ross at 330). This remained the position in Scots law until the First Division held in *T, Petitioner*, 1997 S.L.T. 724, that it could no longer be justified and should be departed from. Section 3 of the Human Rights Act 1998 now requires the courts to read and give effect to all legislation, whenever enacted, consistently with the Convention rights so far as possible to do so; s.4 authorises certain higher courts to make declarations of incompatibility in respect of provisions of primary legislation which cannot be so construed (and it should be noted that provisions of Acts of the Scottish Parliament which are incompatible with the Convention rights are invalid and may be struck down accordingly).

[87] Indeed reference is regularly made to such treaties as the Universal Declaration of Human Rights, the International Covenant on Civil and Political Rights and the UN Convention on the Rights of the Child: see R. Clayton and H. Tomlinson, *The Law of Human Rights* (Oxford: Oxford University Press, 2000) paras 2.09–2.60. So far as the latter Convention is concerned, it was precisely what status it had in domestic law that divided the Supreme Court on the question of whether the "benefits cap" was lawful: *R. (on the application of JS) v Secretary of State for Work and Pensions* [2015] UKSC 16; [2015] 1 W.L.R. 1449.

[88] See, for example *Wilson v United Kingdom* (2002) 35 E.H.R.R. 20, where regard was had to the European Social Charter 1961 and International Labour Organisation Conventions Nos 87 and 98.

Chapter 3

FOUNDATIONS

Introduction

Less than half a century ago, the central tenet of the law of the constitution, that **3–01** of the supremacy of Parliament, was so firmly established that the Senior Law Lord felt able to say:

> "The idea that a court is entitled to disregard a provision in an Act of Parliament on any ground must seem strange and startling to anyone with any knowledge of the history and law of our constitution."[1]

It may, therefore, be thought surprising that the First Division of the Court of Session, in 2011, felt able to say:

> "There can accordingly be seen to be an as yet unresolved issue at the highest judicial level as to whether an Act of the United Kingdom Parliament could, in any circumstances, be open to challenge in the courts."[2]

Those comments were echoed in the Supreme Court.[3] In this chapter, we begin by considering the supremacy of Parliament and we will look at the recent developments that led the highest courts in the land to openly speculate about its future. Any fall in support for the supremacy of Parliament appears to have been offset by a rise in support for the rule of law, "[t]he rule of law enforced by the courts is the ultimate controlling factor on which our constitution is based."[4] It has also been declared by Parliament to be "an existing constitutional principle".[5] The rule of law is an idea that can be traced back as far as Aristotle[6] and

---

[1] *British Railways Board v Pickin* [1974] A.C. 765 HL, per Lord Reid at 782; he went on to say, "In earlier times many learned lawyers seem to have believed that an Act of Parliament could be disregarded in so far as it was contrary to the law of God or the law of nature or natural justice, but since the supremacy of Parliament was finally demonstrated by the Revolution of 1688 any such idea has become obsolete." That comment is worth bearing in mind as we discuss the contemporary debate around parliamentary supremacy.

[2] *AXA General Insurance Co Ltd v Lord Advocate* [2011] CSIH 31; 2011 S.C. 662 at [67].

[3] *AXA General Insurance Co Ltd v Lord Advocate* [2011] UKSC 46; 2012 S.C. (U.K.S.C.) 122, per Lord Hope of Craighead DPSC at [50], "The question whether the principle of the sovereignty of the UK Parliament is absolute or may be subject to limitation in exceptional circumstances is still under discussion."

[4] *R. (on the application of Jackson) v Attorney General* [2005] UKHL 56; [2006] 1 A.C. 262, per Lord Hope of Craighead at [107].

[5] Constitutional Reform Act 2005 s.1(a).

[6] B.Z. Tamanaha, *On the Rule of Law: History, Politics, Theory* (Cambridge: Cambridge University Press, 2004) pp.8–9; *Aristotle's Politics and Athenian Constitution*, edited and translated by J. Warrington (London: J.M. Dent, 1959) book III, s.1287, p.97.

it was a concept that Dicey too wrote about.[7] Despite that pedigree it has proved a notoriously difficult concept to define. In the second part of this chapter we will look at the various tenets of the rule of law and consider how they relate to the continuing supremacy of Parliament. Finally, we look at the separation of powers, a concept that for many years the United Kingdom did not appear, formally at least, to adhere to. In recent years, however, steps have been taken to ensure an institutional separation of powers which compliments the pre-existing functional separation. But it is with what was traditionally seen as the "bedrock"[8] of the constitution that we begin: the supremacy of Parliament.

PARLIAMENTARY SUPREMACY

The traditional approach

3–02   "The principle of parliamentary sovereignty means neither more nor less than this, namely, that Parliament . . . has, under the English constitution, the right to make or unmake any law whatever; and further, that no person or body is recognised by the law as having a right to override or set aside the legislation of Parliament."[9]

That statement of principle has the support of a long and impressive line of authority. We have already seen what Lord Reid had to say about the matter in *British Railways Board v Pickin*. He was not the first senior judge to make such remarks nor was he the last. As to the first proposition (that Parliament can "make or unmake any law whatever") it is of course true that "one does not establish that Parliament can do anything merely by pointing to a number of things that it has done, however impressive".[10] But some support for Dicey's thesis can be drawn from the many statutes that Parliament has passed, both before and after Dicey's time, whereby important constitutional change, or retrospective or extraterritorial legislation, has been enacted.[11] The second proposition (that no person or body can set aside the legislation of Parliament) has, as we shall see, an even stronger pedigree.

The Diceyian doctrine of parliamentary supremacy has three consequences. First, it has a positive effect and ensures that the courts obey any new Act of Parliament. As Lord Morris explained in *Pickin*, "In the courts there may be argument as to the correct interpretation of the enactment: there must be none as to whether it should be on the statute book at all."[12]

---

[7] A.V. Dicey, *The Law of Constitution*, 10th edn (London: Macmillan, 1959) pp.99–119.

[8] *R. (on the application of Jackson) v Attorney General* [2005] UKHL 56; [2006] 1 A.C. 262, per Lord Bingham of Cornhill at [9].

[9] Dicey, *The Law of the Constitution* (1959) pp.39–40.

[10] C.R. Munro, *Studies in Constitutional Law*, 2nd edn (London: Butterworths, 1999) p.13.

[11] That is not to say that important constitutional change does not require special consideration. See the consideration of the process of constitutional change by the House of Lords Select Committee on the Constitution, *The Process of Constitutional Change, 15th report of Session 2010–12* (The Stationery Office, 2011) HL Paper 177, para.1: "The constitution is the foundation upon which law and government are built. The fundamental nature of the constitution means that it should be changed only with due care and consideration."

[12] *British Railways Board v Pickin* [1974] A.C. 765 at 789. Ungoed-Thomas J made the same point in *Cheney v Conn* [1968] 1 W.L.R. 242 (ChD) at 247: " . . . what the statute itself enacts cannot be unlawful . . . and it is not for the court to say that a parliamentary enactment, the highest law in the country, is illegal." As we will see below, these comments must now be read as subject to what happened in *R. (on the application of Jackson) v Attorney General* where a challenge to the

That bars any argument that Parliament lacked the legal power to enact any particular law. It is important to distinguish between *political* limitations on Parliament's ability to legislate and *legal* limitations. Dicey himself recognised the former: Parliament may have the legal power to pass any legislation it wished but that was not the same as saying there were no limits whatsoever on the legislative competence of Parliament.[13] Moral or political considerations may prevent Parliament legislating as it wishes. But once it has legislated, the court cannot entertain an argument that an Act of Parliament is beyond its competence or somehow "unconstitutional". As Lord Reid explained in *Madzimbamuto v Lardner-Burke*:

> "It is often said that it would be unconstitutional for the United Kingdom Parliament to do certain things, meaning that the moral, political and other reasons against doing them are so strong that most people would regard it as highly improper if Parliament did these things. But that does not mean that it is beyond the power of Parliament to do such things. If Parliament chose to do any of them, the courts could not hold the Act of Parliament invalid."[14]

The question that flows from this is: what is an Act of Parliament? Dicey described the Queen in Parliament as the sovereign power. It is not the House of Commons alone that is supreme but it is the will of the House of Commons, the House of Lords (subject to the provisions of the Parliament Acts 1911–1949) and the Queen that is accorded this special status. This reflected a number of decisions at the time Dicey was writing (and which have gone unquestioned since).[15] Once an Act of Parliament reaches the statute book, there can be no inquiry by the court as to how it got there. To do otherwise would be to review the internal proceedings of Parliament. Such a review is precluded by the terms of art.9 of the Claim (and in England and Wales, the Bill) of Rights. This gives rise to what is known and the "enrolled bill rule". Lord Campbell LC explained the rule in (the Scottish case) *Edinburgh & Dalkeith Railway v Wauchope*:

> "All that a Court of Justice can do is look to the Parliamentary Roll; if from that it should appear that a Bill has passed both Houses and received Royal Assent, no Court of Justice can inquire into the mode in which it was introduced into Parliament, nor into what was done previous to its

---

validity of the Hunting Act 2004 was heard by the court, a situation that the Court of Appeal recognised as novel ([2005] EWCA Civ 126; [2005] Q.B. 579 at [11]–[13]) as did the House of Lords ([2005] UKHL 56; [2006] 1 A.C. 262, per Lord Bingham of Cornhill at [8] and Lord Nicholls of Birkenhead at [49]). Of particular note is the concession by the Attorney General that "there was no absolute rule that the courts could not consider the validity of a statute".

[13] Dicey, *The Law of the Constitution* (1959) pp.76–84.

[14] *Madzimbamuto v Lardner-Burke* [1969] 1 A.C. 645 PC (Rhodesia) at 723.

[15] "If an Act be penned that the King with the assent of the Lords, or with the assent of the Commons, it is no Act of Parliament, for three ought to assent to it scilicet the King, the Lords and the Commons, or otherwise it is not an Act of Parliament": *The Prince's Case* (1606) 8 Co. Rep. 481; *Stockdale v Hansard* (1839) 9 Ad. & El. 1, per Lord Denman at 108. *The Prince's Case* ought be treated with caution, referring as it does to the pre-Union Parliament of England and not the post-Union Parliament.

introduction, or what passed in Parliament during its progress through Parliament."[16]

If there is a suggestion that an Act, whether private or public, has been obtained improperly or through fraud that is a matter for Parliament to investigate and, if necessary, repeal the offending Act. Whilst it remains on the statute book however, the courts must give effect to it.[17]

What, however, of an Act of Parliament that is passed in accordance with the provisions of the Parliament Acts 1911–1949: do such Acts benefit from the enrolled Bill rule as explained by Lord Campbell LC? That question arose in *R (on the application of Jackson) v Attorney General*.[18] The Parliament Acts allow for a Bill to pass without the consent of the House of Lords. Where a Bill is passed using that procedure, it becomes an Act of Parliament and primary legislation. It is not of an inferior quality because the House of Lords did not assent it to.[19] But it is not an Act of a sovereign parliament, one with the power to make or unmake any law, because the Parliament Acts prohibit the passing of certain legislation (for example, extending the life of Parliament) without the assent of the House of Lords.[20] The workings of the Parliaments Acts are considered in more detail in Ch.6. For present purposes, however, it is important to note the challenge that was mounted to the Hunting Act 2004. This controversial piece of legislation, which sought to make it an offence to hunt wild animals with a dog, was passed under the Parliament Acts after the House of Lords refused to pass it. After Royal Assent was given, a number of individuals with an interest in fox-hunting challenged the Act arguing that it was not a valid Act of Parliament. On a simple application of the dicta from *Edinburgh & Dalkeith Railways* and *Pickin* the challenge ought to have fallen to be rejected. But the claim was entertained by the courts, and was ultimately determined by an unprecedented panel of nine Law Lords. Why? Lord Bingham explained that he was persuaded that the case should be heard for two reasons. First, unlike *Pickin* the court was not being asked to enquire into the internal workings of Parliament to ascertain whether it had been misled when enacting the legislation and, unlike *Edinburgh & Dalkeith Railways*, the court looks to the parliamentary roll and does not see a Bill that has passed both Houses of Parliament. That gave rise not to a question of parliamentary procedure but to a question of law. Lord Bingham's second reason was "more practical":

> "The appellants have raised a question of law which cannot, as such, be resolved by Parliament. *But it would not be satisfactory, or consistent with the rule of law, if it could not be resolved at all.* So it seems to me necessary

---

[16] *Edinburgh & Dalkeith Railway v Wauchope* (1842) 8 Cl. & F. 710.

[17] *Lee v Bude and Torrington Junction Railway* (1871) L.R. 6 C.P. 576; *British Railways Board v Pickin* [1974] A.C. 765.

[18] *R. (on the application of Jackson) v Attorney General* [2005] UKHL 56; [2006] 1 A.C. 262. For a general discussion of this important case, see Lord Cooke of Thorndon, "A Constitutional Retreat" (2006) 122 L.Q.R. 224; M. Plaxton, "The Concept of Legislation: *Jackson v Her Majesty's Attorney General*" (2006) 69 M.L.R. 249.

[19] *R. (on the application of Jackson) v Attorney General* [2005] UKHL 56; [2006] 1 A.C. 262, per Lord Bingham of Cornhill at [24]–[25].

[20] Although commenting obiter, the majority of the House of Lords held that such limitations could not be removed by a two-step process: amending the Parliament Acts, using their own procedure, to remove the limit and then passing legislation to extend the life of Parliament. It is noteworthy that this was not a view shared by Lord Bingham.

that the courts should resolve it, and that to do so involves no breach of constitutional propriety."[21]

From *Jackson* we learn that the rule that appears from *Pickin* and *Edinburgh & Dalkeith Railways* is not absolute: it does not apply to Acts passed under the Parliament Acts. Furthermore, we learn that the court has jurisdiction to entertain a challenge to the validity of an Act of Parliament where the rule of law demands it. That is an idea we shall return to shortly.

The second consequence of the Diceyian doctrine of parliamentary supremacy is a negative effect. Nobody else can override the wishes of Parliament, be it the courts or another, competing, legislature. For example, in relation to matters where legislative competence has been devolved to the Scottish Parliament, the UK Parliament retains the power to legislate (with or without the blessing of the Scottish Parliament).[22] In relation to the courts, Dicey recognised that:

"Parliament is the supreme legislator, but from the moment Parliament has uttered its will as law giver, that will becomes subject to the interpretation put upon it by the judges."[23]

But to ensure that the courts do not override the wishes of Parliament, the process of statutory interpretation is an attempt to discover the intention of Parliament in using the words it has chosen, thereby giving effect to that intention.[24] As we shall see below, the Human Rights Act 1998, and the interpretative obligation imposed on the courts by virtue of s.3 of that Act, have required the courts to be careful not to overstep the bounds of their legitimate constitutional role.

Finally, the supremacy of Parliament has the effect that Parliament cannot bind **3–03** her successors.[25] This, for Dicey, was the only limit on the powers of a sovereign legislature. Sovereignty was continuing and, on Dicey's logic, inescapable short of revolution. It followed that there could be no difference in the "ranking" of Acts of Parliament: all Acts were of equal standing and authority. That produced what is known as the doctrine of implied repeal:

"The Legislature cannot, according to our constitution, bind itself as to the form of subsequent legislation, and it is impossible for Parliament to enact that in a subsequent statute dealing with the same subject matter there can

---

[21] *R. (on the application of Jackson) v Attorney General* [2005] UKHL 56; [2006] 1 A.C. 262 at [27] (emphasis added); Lord Nicholls (at [51]) reached the same conclusion for similar reasons: "This question of statutory interpretation is properly cognisable by a court of law even though it relates to the legislative process. Statutes create law. The proper interpretation of a statute is a matter for the courts, not Parliament. This principle is as fundamental in this country's constitution as the principle that Parliament has exclusive cognizance (jurisdiction) over its own affairs"; and Lord Hope of Craighead at [107] and [110]–[116].

[22] Scotland Act 1998 s.28(7) makes the point specifically but it was unnecessary to secure the result. With regard to how the UK Parliament exercises its legislative powers in devolved areas, see the discussion in relation to legislative consent motions at para.2–10.

[23] Dicey, *The Law of the Constitution* (1959) p.413.

[24] On interpretation of legislation, see *Craies on Legislation: A Practitioners' Guide to the Nature, Process, Effect and Interpretation of Legislation*, edited by D. Greenberg, 10th edn (London: Sweet and Maxwell, 2012) Ch.16; F.A.R. Bennion, *Statutory Interpretation*, 6th edn (London: LexisNexis, 2013) Pt XI; *Edwards v Chesterfield Royal Hospital NHS Foundation Trust* [2011] UKSC 58; [2012] 2 A.C. 22, per Lord Phillips of Worth Matravers PSC at [79].

[25] See Lord Hope's comments in *R. (on the application of Jackson) v Attorney General* [2005] UKHL 56; [2006] 1 A.C. 262 at [113].

be no implied repeal. If a subsequent Act of Parliament chooses to make it plain that the earlier statute is being to some extent repealed, effect must be given to that intention just because it is the will of the Legislature."[26]

The result of the doctrine of implied repeal is that the court gives effect to the most recent expression of Parliament's intention: if the terms of an Act from 2005 and 2015 are irreconcilable, the court will give effect to the terms of the 2015 Act on the basis it has impliedly repealed the 2005 Act. The doctrine of implied repeal has, however, undergone modification in recent years.[27] In *Thoburn v Sunderland City Council* Laws LJ recognised that not all Acts of Parliament are equal: there are some statutes which should be regarded as "constitutional" and thus protected from implied repeal as it is traditionally understood.[28] This distinction between "ordinary" Acts and "constitutional" Acts, although difficult to draw,[29] has subsequently been endorsed by the Supreme Court.[30] And although Laws LJ made reference to "Acts" and "statutes" it is probably better to think of constitutional "provisions", recognising the fact that one section of an Act may be "constitutional" whereas the rest of its provisions may be very "ordinary".[31] The distinction that Laws LJ drew is traced back to the court's core function when interpreting an Act of Parliament, namely to ascertain the intention of Parliament when passing the legislation.[32] As Laws LJ explained:

> "Ordinary statutes may be impliedly repealed. Constitutional statutes may not. For the repeal of a constitutional Act or the abrogation of a fundamental right to be effected by statute, the court would apply this test: is it shown that the legislature's actual—not imputed, constructive or presumed—intention was to effect the repeal or abrogation? I think the test could only be met by express words in the latter statute, or by words so specific that the inference of an actual determination to effect the result contended for was

---

[26] *Ellen Street Estates Ltd v Minister of Health* [1934] 1 K.B. 590 CA, per Maugham LJ at 597. See also: *Vauxhall Estates Ltd v Liverpool Corp* [1932] 1 K.B. 733 (KBD) and, for a more modern statement of the same rule, *Thoburn v Sunderland City Council* [2002] EWHC 195 (Admin); [2003] Q.B. 151 at [37]: "The rule is that if Parliament has enacted successive statutes which on the true construction of each of them makes irreducibly inconsistent provisions, the earlier statute is impliedly repealed by the latter."

[27] For a discussion of the uncertainty surrounding the scope of implied repeal, see A.L. Young, *Parliamentary Sovereignty and the Human Rights Act* (Oxford: Hart, 2009) Ch.2.

[28] *Thoburn v Sunderland City Council* [2002] EWHC 195 (Admin); [2003] Q.B. 151 at [59]–[64].

[29] D. Feldman, "The nature and significance of 'constitutional' legislation" (2013) 129 L.Q.R. 343.

[30] *R. (on the application of Buckingham CC) v Secretary of State for Transport* [2014] UKSC 3; [2014] 1 W.L.R. 324, per Lord Neuberger PSC and Lord Mance at [207]–[208].

[31] Feldman, "The nature and significance of 'constitutional' legislation" (2013) 129 L.Q.R. 343, 352–353.

[32] For the moment, we are considering how the idea of constitutional statues impacts on the doctrine of implied repeal. It is worth noting at this stage, however, that the courts have held that the same approach should be taken to the interpretation of "constitutional" legislation as any other legislation (*Imperial Tobacco Ltd v Lord Advocate* [2012] UKSC 61; 2013 S.C. (U.K.S.C.) 153; *Attorney General v National Assembly for Wales Commission* [2012] UKSC 53; [2013] 1 A.C. 792; D. Feldman, "Statutory interpretation and constitutional legislation" (2014) 130 L.Q.R. 473). This point is developed further in Ch.6, when considering the operation of the Scotland Act.

irresistible. The ordinary rule of implied repeal does not satisfy this test. Accordingly, it has no application to constitutional statues."[33]

This idea that Parliament requires to use clear language to obtain particular results was not new nor does it necessarily undermine parliamentary supremacy. Lord Hoffmann had explained a few years earlier that, in relation to fundamental principles of human rights, Parliament, because it was supreme, had the power to legislate contrary to those rights but the courts would only accept Parliament intended to do so where express and clear words had been used.[34] Laws LJ did little more than apply the same rule of statutory interpretation to "constitutional" statutes more generally. So far as parliamentary supremacy is concerned, the modification to the doctrine of implied repeal set out by Laws LJ preserves Parliament's right to "make or unmake any law". All it does is require Parliament to do so using words which make that intention clear (expressly or giving rise to an "irresistible" inference) when it comes to statutes which condition the relationship between the citizen and the state or alter the scope of fundamental constitutional rights.[35] In *H v Lord Advocate*[36] the Supreme Court, in the context of explaining how the Scotland Act could be repealed or modified, said this:

> "But in my opinion only an express provision [*modifying s.57(2) of the Scotland Act*] could be held to lead to such a result. This is because of the fundamental constitutional nature of the settlement that was achieved by the Scotland Act. This in itself must be held to *render it incapable of being altered otherwise than by an express enactment*. Its provisions cannot be regarded as vulnerable to alteration by implication from some other enactment in which an intention to alter the Scotland Act *is not set forth expressly on the face of the statute*."[37]

It has been suggested that these remarks qualified what Laws LJ had said in *Thoburn* with the result that an "irresistible" inference was no longer sufficient to amend the Scotland Act (and, by implication, any other "constitutional" statute).[38] That argument, however, appears to overstate what the Supreme Court said in *H v Lord Advocate*. The Supreme Court heard limited oral argument on the point (it arose in the context of whether the Supreme Court had jurisdiction to hear an extradition appeal from the High Court of Justiciary which in turn required that apparently conflicting provisions of the Extradition Act 2003 and the Scotland Act 1998 be reconciled). Had there been an intention to review, with a view to modifying, what Laws LJ had said in *Thoburn* the court can be

---

[33] *Thoburn v Sunderland City Council* [2002] EWHC 195 (Admin); [2003] Q.B. 151 at [63]

[34] *R. v Secretary of State for the Home Department, Ex p. Simms* [2000] 2 A.C. 115 HL, per Lord Hoffmann at 131. In *R. (on the application of Jackson) v Attorney General* [2005] UKHL 56; [2006] 1 A.C. 262 at [159] Baroness Hale made the same point: " . . . courts will, of course, decline to hold that Parliament has interfered with fundamental rights unless it has made its intentions crystal clear."

[35] *Thoburn v Sunderland City Council* [2002] EWHC 195 (Admin); [2003] Q.B. 151 at [60] and [64]

[36] *H v Lord Advocate* [2012] UKSC 24; 2012 S.C. (U.K.S.C.) 308; [2013] 1 A.C. 413.

[37] *H v Lord Advocate* [2012] UKSC 24; 2012 S.C. (U.K.S.C.) 308; [2013] 1 A.C. 413, per Lord Hope of Craighead DPSC at [30] (emphasis added).

[38] A. Perry and F. Ahmed, "The Quasi-Entrenchment of Constitutional Statues" (2014) 73 C.L.J. 514.

expected to have insisted upon the point being fully argued.[39] Furthermore, when Law LJ's decision in *Thoburn* was discussed a little over a year later in *R. (on the application of Buckingham CC) v Secretary of State for Transport* there was no suggestion that his remarks had been qualified by what Lord Hope said in *H v Lord Advocate*. For the moment, the better view is that for Parliament to amend or repeal the provisions of a "constitutional" statute, it must use words that make that intention clear, whether expressly or by way of an irresistible inference.

3–04   Challenges to the doctrine of parliamentary supremacy are not new. We consider three contemporary challenges below: the European Union, common law constitutionalism and the Human Rights Act 1998. But first it is necessary to examine some older arguments against the idea of parliamentary supremacy. The first challenge we need to consider relates to the Acts of Union and the argument that the UK Parliament was "born unfree".[40] Is Parliament limited by the terms of the Acts of Union, for example that the Court of Session continues for all time coming?[41] Dicey's view was clear, " . . . neither the Act of Union with Scotland nor the Dentists Act 1878 has more claim than the other to be considered a supreme law."[42]

There is an obvious difference between the Act of Union and the Dentists Act 1878 (and, indeed, any other Act passed by Parliament): the Dentists Act was passed by Parliament whereas the Act of Union *founded* Parliament. Dicey did recognise that the drafters of the Union legislation intended it to be binding on the legislature it created.[43] The argument that the Acts of Union represent "fundamental law" and thus impose some limits on the legislative competence of the UK Parliament has found some judicial support. In *MacCormick v Lord Advocate* Lord President Cooper famously observed:

> "The principle of the unlimited sovereignty of Parliament is a distinctively English principle which has no counterpart in Scottish constitutional law . . . I have difficulty in seeing why it should have been supposed that the new Parliament of Great Britain must inherit all of the peculiar characteristics of the English Parliament but none of the Scottish Parliament, as if all that happened in 1707 was that Scottish representatives were admitted to the Parliament of England. That is not what was done."[44]

In that case, the Lord Advocate conceded that certain articles of the Union were unalterable, for example those protecting the Church and the independent legal

---

[39] *H v Lord Advocate* [2012] UKSC 24; 2012 S.C. (U.K.S.C.) 308; [2013] 1 A.C. 413, per Lord Mance at [73].

[40] T.B. Smith, "The Union of 1707 as fundamental law" [1957] P.L. 99. See also J.D.B. Mitchell, *Constitutional Law*, 2nd edn, (Edinburgh: SULI; W. Green, 1968) pp.93–98; N. MacCormick, "Does the United Kingdom have a constitution?" (1978) 29 N.I.L.Q. 1; M. Upton, "Marriage vows of the elephant: the Constitution of 1707" (1989) 105 L.Q.R. 79; J.D. Goldsworthy, *The Sovereignty of Parliament: History and Philosophy* (Oxford: Clarendon Press, 1999), pp.165–173; Munro, *Studies in Constitutional Law* (1999) pp.137–142; E. Wicks, "A new constitution for a new state? The 1707 Union of England and Scotland" (2001) 117 L.Q.R. 109; *R. (on the application of Jackson) v Attorney General* [2005] UKHL 56; [2006] 1 A.C. 262, per Lord Hope of Craighead at [106].

[41] Act of Union 1707 art.XIX.

[42] Dicey, *The Law of the Constitution* (1959) p.145.

[43] Dicey, *The Law of the Constitution* (1959) p.69.

[44] *MacCormick v Lord Advocate*, 1953 S.C. 396 at 411. There is some suggestion in the institutional writers that the pre-Union Parliament of Scotland was in fact sovereign. See, for example, Stair, IV, 1, 61.

system. The Lord President, however, went on to doubt whether a breach of the Acts of Union would be a justiciable issue in the courts of either Scotland or England and Wales. It is also worth noting that although the Lord President questions whether Scots and English law took the same view of parliamentary supremacy before the Union, Scottish courts have supported the Diceyian orthodox since.[45] In *Gibson v Lord Advocate* Lord Keith reserved his opinion as to the effect of a hypothetical Act of Parliament purporting to abolish the Church of Scotland or the Court of Session but held that arguments about whether changes to Scots private law were "for the evident utility" of the subjects of Scotland (as required by art.XVIII of the Union legislation) would not be justiciable. There is a logical attraction to the fundamental law argument but sustaining it faces significant difficulties.[46] As Munro explains, nearly every article of the legislation has been altered or repealed to a greater or lesser extent.[47] Even T.B. Smith, a great proponent of the fundamental law theory, accepted that "many changes have been made, even of the most fundamental clauses".[48] That leaves one asking what exactly is beyond the reach of Parliament? The requirement (in art.XXII) that a prescribed number of Scots sit in the House of Lords was competently altered by the House of Lords Act 1999,[49] the Acts of Union now take effect subject to the provisions of the Scotland Act 1998[50] and the appellate jurisdiction of the House of Lords has been abolished and transferred to the new Supreme Court,[51] a matter which was previously thought to have been inhibited by the terms of the Acts of Union.[52]

In reality, we will only learn if certain provisions of the Union legislation are beyond the reach of Parliament if an attempt is made to legislate contrary to them. That the Acts of Union confer no power on the courts to review Acts of Parliament on the grounds of non-conformity with the terms of the Union cannot be decisive: the constitution of the United States did not confer such a power on the Supreme Court but it was claimed as necessary to uphold the constitution.[53] Whether the Scottish (or England and Welsh) court would claim a similar power if faced with an Act of Parliament that, say, purported to abolish the Court of Session is unknown. They have, however, never thought it necessary to qualify their clear statement on the supremacy of Parliament that we considered above to guard against the possibility.

The next challenge we need to consider is the "manner and form" argument: **3–05** if Parliament cannot bind its successors as to the content of future legislation can

---

[45] *Mortensen v Peters* (1906) 8 F. (J.) 93, per Lord Justice General Dunedin at 100 (sitting with a full bench), the continuing force of which was affirmed by the Lord Ordinary (Brodie) in *Whaley v Lord Advocate*, 2004 S.C. 78.

[46] As Lord Hope of Craighead put it in *Lord Gray's Motion*, 2000 S.C. (H.L.) 46 at 59D–E, " . . . the argument that the legislative powers of the new Parliament of Great Britain were subject to the restrictions expressed in the Union Agreement by which it was constituted cannot be dismissed as entirely fanciful." Lord Slynn of Hadley, in the same case, doubted whether even a provision regarded as fundamental to the constitution could not be altered by Parliament (at p.49I).

[47] Munro, *Studies in Constitutional Law* (1999) p.138–139.

[48] T.B. Smith, "Two Scots Cases" (1953) 69 L.Q.R. 512, 515.

[49] *Lord Gray's Motion*, 2000 S.C. (H.L.) 46.

[50] Scotland Act 1998 s.37.

[51] Constitutional Reform Act 2005 Pt 3.

[52] Mitchell, *Constitutional Law* (1968) p.11; Wicks, "A new constitution for a new state? The 1707 Union of England and Scotland" (2001) 117 L.Q.R. 109, 118–119.

[53] *Marbury v Madison* (1803) 1 Cranch 137.

it bind them as to the process by which they legislate?[54] On this argument, should Parliament wish to entrench a particular statute, it could provide that none of the provisions of the Act might be repealed or amended without, for example, a two-thirds majority in both Houses of Parliament.[55] The evidence to support this view is derived primarily from Commonwealth cases, notably *Attorney General of New South Wales v Trethowan*[56] and *Bribery Commissioner v Ranasinghe*,[57] both decisions of the Privy Council, as well as the South African case of *Harris v Minister of the Interior*.[58] In *Trethowan* the legislature of New South Wales passed an Act, in 1929, providing that no Bill that would abolish the upper house of the legislature be presented for Royal Assent unless it had been approved by the electorate in a referendum. The opposition Labour party in 1929 were committed to the abolition of the upper house. When they won the general election of 1930 two Bills were passed by both houses: the first repealing the referendum requirement and the second abolishing the upper house. Neither were approved by a referendum. An injunction was granted by the Supreme Court of New South Wales and an appeal to the Privy Council was unsuccessful. On one level, that decision supports the "manner and form" argument. But it is not very helpful in understanding the extent to which the Westminster Parliament is subject to such an argument. Dicey had little difficulty classifying the New South Wales legislature as a non-sovereign body.[59] It was subordinate to the Colonial Laws Validity Act 1865 and in particular s.5.[60] The decision therefore turned on the correct interpretation of s.5 of the 1865 Act, which was held to require the offending legislation to be approved in a referendum. So to compare the legislature of New South Wales with the Westminster Parliament is to compare apples and oranges.

Harris perhaps presents a closer analogy. *Harris* concerned the Separate Representation of Voters Act 1951, passed pursuant to the new apartheid policy of the Union Parliament of South Africa, acting by simply majority, both Houses sitting separately. Voters who were deprived of their rights by the 1951 Act argued that it was invalid because it was contrary to s.35 of the South Africa Act 1909 (an Act of the UK Parliament). Section 35 required certain legislation of the South African Parliament, including the 1951 Act, to be passed by both Houses sitting together and agreed to by not less than two-thirds of the total number of members of both Houses. The South African Government argued that the Union Parliament had, since 1909, full legislative sovereignty and so was free to disregard the provisions of s.35 of the 1909 Act. The court disagreed, with Centlivres CJ holding:

---

[54] On this, see generally J.D. Goldsworthy, *Parliamentary Sovereignty: Contemporary Debates* (Cambridge: Cambridge University Press, 2010) Ch.7.

[55] See, for example, Sir Ivor Jennings, *The Law and the Constitution*, 5th edn (London: University of London Press, 1959) pp.152–159; R.F.V. Heuston, *Essays in Constitutional Law*, 2nd edn (London: Stevens, 1964) Ch.1.

[56] *Attorney General of New South Wales v Trethowan* [1932] A.C. 526 PC (Australia).

[57] *Bribery Commissioner v Ranasinghe* [1965] A.C. 172 PC (Ceylon).

[58] *Harris v Minister of the Interior* [1952] 1 T.L.R. 1245.

[59] Dicey, *The Law of the Constitution* (1959) Ch.2.

[60] Section 5 of the 1865 Act provided: " . . . every Representative Legislature shall, in respect to the Colony under its jurisdiction, have, and be deemed at all times to have had, full power to make laws respecting the Constitution, Power and Procedure of such legislature; provided that such laws shall have been passed in such manner and form as may from time to time be required by any Act of Parliament, Letters Patent, Order in Council, or Colonial law for the time being in force in the said colony."

"A State can unquestionably be sovereign although it has no legislature which is completely sovereign ... In the case of the Union, legal sovereignty is or may be divided between Parliament as ordinarily constituted and Parliament as constituted under [s.35]. Such a division of legislative power is no derogation from the sovereignty of the Union and the mere fact that that division was enacted in a British statute which is still in force in the Union cannot affect the question in issue. ... The South Africa Act created the Parliament of the Union. It is that Act ... which prescribes the manner in which the constituent elements of Parliament must function for the purpose of passing legislation. ... [I]t follows that ... courts of law have the power to declare the Act of 1951 invalid on the ground that it was not passed in conformity with the provisions of section 35."[61]

While this passage crisply articulates the nub of the manner and form argument it again does not tell us much about the UK Parliament. The decision in *Harris* turned on the application of s.35 of the 1909 Act. But as Lord Pearce explained in *Ranasinghe* "in the United Kingdom there is no governing instrument which prescribes the law-making powers and the forms which are essential to those powers".[62] There being no such instrument in the United Kingdom, it is hard to see how the "manner and form" argument could gain much traction as against our Parliament.

We have seen that the courts accept whatever the Queen in Parliament enacts **3–06** (both Houses acting by simple majority) as law. That being a rule of the common law, on one view it should be open to modification by Parliament. Does this allow a change to the "manner and form" of legislation? No. For Parliament to modify the rule would be to limit (or potentially abandon) its sovereignty and that, as we have seen, is the one thing Parliament cannot do. The point was explained by Professor Wade in his seminal article in 1955:

"[T]he rule that the courts obey Acts of Parliament is above and beyond the reach of statute ... because it is itself the source of authority of statute. This puts it into a class by itself among rules of the common law ... The rule of judicial obedience is in one sense a rule of common law, but in another sense—which applies to no other rule of common law—it is the ultimate political fact upon which the whole system of legislation hangs. Legislation owes its authority to the rule: the rule does not owe its authority to legislation. To say that Parliament can change the rule ... is to put the cart before the horse. The rule is unique in being unchangeable by Parliament—it is changed by revolution, not by legislation; it lies in the keeping of the courts and no Act of Parliament can take it from them."[63]

---

[61] *Harris v Minister of the Interior* [1952] 1 T.L.R. 1245.

[62] *Bribery Commissioner v Ranasinghe* [1965] A.C. 172 at 195.

[63] H.W.R. Wade, "The basis of legal sovereignty" [1955] C.L.J. 172, 187; this analysis that was approved by Lord Denning MR in *Blackburn v Attorney General* [1971] 2 All E.R. 1380 at 1387; it is not an approach that found favour with Lord Bingham: "To my mind, it has been convincingly shown that the principle of parliamentary sovereignty has been recognized as fundamental in this country not because the judges invented it but because it has for centuries been accepted as such by judges and others officially concerned in the operation of our constitutional system. The judges did not by themselves establish the principle and they cannot, by themselves, change it" (T.H. Bingham, *The Rule of Law* (London: Allen Lane, 2010) p.167).

Such a revolution occurred in Rhodesia when the Rhodesian courts ceased to recognise UK statutes as supreme and instead relocated their rules of recognition to the revolutionary constitution of 1965.[64] But there has been no such change in the United Kingdom and what the courts recognise as law remains the will of the Queen in Parliament.

3–07   Finally, did Parliament bind its successors when legislating for the independence of former British colonies? Take, for example, s.4 of the Statute of Westminster 1931 that provided that no subsequent Act of Parliament would extend, or be deemed to extend, to a dominion unless it was expressly declared in the Act that the dominion had requested and consented to its enactment. Did Parliament thereby deprive itself of the competence to legislate for a dominion without the request and consent of the dominion? Lord Sankey LC described the notion that Parliament could repeal or disregard s.4 as "theory [having] no relation to realities"[65] and in *Ndlwana v Hofmeyr*, Stratford ACJ insisted that "freedom once conferred cannot be revoked".[66] But here we see again the difference between the legal limits on the legislative competence of Parliament and the political or other limits. As a matter of legal theory, Parliament could have repealed or disregarded the terms of s.4 of the 1931 Act. That is not the same thing as the courts of the dominion paying heed to it. As Sir Robert Megarry VC explained in *Manuel v Attorney General*:

> "I have grave doubts about the theory of the transfer of sovereignty as affecting the competence of Parliament. . . . As a matter of law the courts recognise Parliament as being omnipotent in all save the power to destroy its own omnipotence. Under the authority of Parliament the courts of a territory may be released from their legal duty to obey Parliament, but that does not trench on the acceptance by the . . . courts of all that Parliament does. Nor must validity in law be confused with practical enforceability."[67]

So independence to the colonies did not undermine the legislative supremacy of Parliament; it simply released certain courts from the obligation to give effect to the will of Parliament.

3–08   Having examined some of the traditional challenges to the supremacy of Parliament, it is time to turn and consider three more contemporary challenges. The first comes in the form of the European Union and the consequences of UK membership. Then we will consider the rise of what is known as common law constitutionalism before finally assessing the impact of the Human Rights Act. Bogdanor has said: "In practice . . . if not in law, Parliamentary sovereignty is no longer the governing principle of the British constitution."[68] Have these three

---

[64] *R. v Ndhlovu* (1968) 4 S.A. 515; see also *Madzimbamuto v Lardner-Burke* [1969] 1 A.C. 645 which held that the regulations made by the rebel regime were void.

[65] *British Coal Corp v The King* [1935] A.C. 500 PC (Canada).

[66] *Ndlwana v Hofmeyr* [1937] A.D. 229.

[67] *Manuel v Attorney General* [1983] Ch. 77 CA (Civ Div) at 89.

[68] V. Bogdanor, *The New British Constitution* (Oxford: Hart, 2009) pp.13–14; for a discussion of Bogdanor's views on sovereignty, see R. Gordon QC, "Constitutional Change and Parliamentary Sovereignty—the Impossible Dialetic" in M. Qvortrup (ed), *The British Constitution: Continuity and Change, A Festschrift for Vernon Bogdanor* (Oxford: Hart, 2013) Ch.9. See also A. Bradley, "The Sovereignty of Parliament—form or substance?" in J. Jowell and D. Oliver (eds), *The Changing Constitution*, 7th edn (Oxford: Oxford University Press, 2011) Ch.2.

contemporary challenges to the supremacy of Parliament really taken us to that stage?

Parliamentary supremacy and the European Union

To understand the significance of UK membership of the European Union, it is **3–09** necessary to first understand a bit about the state of EU law when the UK joined in 1973.[69] In 1963, in the case of *Van Gend en Loos v Nederlandse Administratie der Belastingen*, the European Court of Justice explained: " . . . the Community constitutes a new legal order of international law for the benefit of which states have limited their sovereign rights."[70] The court returned to this theme a year later, in the Italian case of *Costa v ENEL*. The language could hardly have been clearer:

> "By creating [the] Community . . . the Member States have limited their sovereign rights, albeit within limited fields, and have thus created a body of law which binds both their nationals and themselves. . . . The transfer by the states from their domestic legal systems to the Community legal system of the rights and obligations arising under the Treaty carries with it a permanent limitation of their sovereign rights, against which a subsequent unilateral act incompatible with the concept of the Community cannot prevail."[71]

The primacy of EU law over conflicting national law was not explicit in the founding treaties. However, within little more than a decade, the ECJ had made it clear that national law must come second where there was a conflict. In *International Handelsgesellschaft* the European Court of Justice confirmed that EU law in all its forms prevails over national law, including the provisions of national constitutions, where there is a conflict.[72] All of this was clear, or at least ought to have been, when the UK sought membership in the early 1970s. For completeness, it is worth noting that the European Court of Justice took these various statements to their logical conclusion in their judgment in *Simmenthal* where they said that a national court must "apply Community law in its entirety and protect rights which the latter confers on individuals, and must accordingly set aside any provision of national law which may conflict with it, whether prior or subsequent to the Community rule".[73] Those statements from the European Court of Justice are obviously irreconcilable with a conventional understanding of the Diceyian doctrine of parliamentary supremacy.

In passing the European Communities Act 1972 Parliament had to, as best it could, allow the UK to fulfil its obligations under the treaties and join what is now the EU. The key provision is s.2 of the 1972 Act. Subsection (1) provides:

[69] Throughout this section reference is made to the "European Union" and the "EU". This is done for simplicity. As is explained in Ch.10, below the EU as we know it today has gone through various iterations and it was, in fact, the EEC that the UK joined in 1973.
[70] *Van Gend en Loos v Nederlandse Administratie der Belastingen* (C–26/62) [1963] E.C.R. 1 at 12.
[71] *Costa v Ente Nazionale per l'Energia Elettrica (ENEL)* (C–6/64) [1964] E.C.R. 585 at 593.
[72] *International Handelsgesellschaft MbH v Einfuhr und Vorratsstelle fur Getreide und Futtermittel* (C–11/70) [1970] E.C.R. 1125.
[73] *Amministrazione delle Finanze dello Stato v Simmenthal SpA* (C–106/77) [1978] E.C.R. 629.

"All such rights, powers, liabilities, obligations and restrictions from time to time created or arising by or under the Treaties, and all such remedies and procedures from time to time provided for by or under the Treaties, as in accordance with the Treaties are without further enactment to be given legal effect or used in the United Kingdom shall be recognised and available in law, and be enforced, allowed and followed accordingly."

At a stroke, Parliament had commanded that directly effective provisions of EU law should prevail over inconsistent national law and, as we have seen, EU law would require that rule to apply to Acts of Parliament as well.[74] We have already seen that the 1972 Act is now regarded as part of the group of "constitutional statutes" identified by Laws LJ in *Thoburn* and so is immune from implied repeal. But could Parliament do what it sought to achieve in s.2? Is s.2 not a clear attempt to bind its successors? And despite what the European Court of Justice may have said, would the domestic courts really set aside an Act of Parliament if it conflicted with the terms of EU law? An early indication of the attitude of the courts was given by Lord Denning MR in *Macarthys Ltd v Smith*, where he held:

"Under section 2(1) and (4) of the European Communities Act 1972, the principles laid down in the Treaty are 'without further enactment' to be given legal effect in the United Kingdom; and have priority over any enactment 'passed or to be passed' by our Parliament . . . In construing our statute, we are entitled to look to the Treaty as an aid to its construction; but not only as an aid but as an overriding force. If . . . it should appear that our legislation is deficient or is inconsistent with Community law by some oversight of our draftsmen then it is our bounden duty to give priority to Community law. Such is the result of section 2(1) and (4) of the European Communities Act 1972."[75]

This answer avoids the main issue however. The Act in question in *Macarthys* was the Equal Pay Act 1970, in other words an Act that pre-dates the 1972 Act. Any conflict could be resolved by an application of the doctrine of implied repeal in its classic sense. The more important question was how would the court treat an Act that post-dates the 1972 Act and which conflicts with EU law? That was the issue that arose in the *Factortame* litigation.

3–10   In *Factortame* a number of English-registered companies whose managers and shareholders were primarily Spanish nationals lost their right to exploit the UK's fishing quota when the Merchant Shipping Act 1988 made the right conditional on nationality requirements they were unable to meet. The companies argued that the 1988 Act was unlawful as being in breach of the EU treaties. The House of Lords referred the case to the European Court of Justice for a preliminary ruling; that court duly held that the 1988 Act was incompatible with EU law. The case then returned to the House of Lords where the question of remedy arose. What was the House of Lords to do with an Act that post-dated the 1972 Act but which was inconsistent with EU law? The European Court of Justice authorities were,

---

[74] For a contemporary discussion of the issues, see S.A. de Smith, "The Constitution and the Common Market: A Tentative Appraisal" (1971) 34 M.L.R. 597; H.W.R. Wade, "Sovereignty and the European Communities" (1972) 88 L.Q.R. 1.
[75] *Macarthys Ltd v Smith* [1979] 3 All E.R. 325 at 329.

as we have seen, clear on the point: the Act must be disapplied. In the House of Lords, Lord Bridge held:

> "Some public comments on the decision of the Court of Justice . . . have suggested that this was a novel and dangerous invasion by a Community institution of the sovereignty of the United Kingdom Parliament. But such comments are based on a misconception. If the supremacy within the European Community of Community law over the national law of Member States was not always inherent in the EEC Treaty it was certainly well established in the jurisprudence of the Court of Justice long before the United Kingdom joined the Community. Thus whatever limitation of its sovereignty Parliament accepted when it enacted the European Communities Act 1972 was entirely voluntary. Under the terms of the 1972 Act it has always been clear that it was the duty of a United Kingdom court, when delivering final judgment, to override any rule of national law found to be in conflict with any directly enforceable rule of Community law."[76]

Two points of significance arise from this passage. First, Lord Bridge speaks of a "limitation of sovereignty". This is something that is inconsistent with the very essence of the Diceyian theory of parliamentary supremacy. The House of Lords had, argued Wade, effected a revolution.[77] Secondly, Lord Bridge is at pains to emphasise that any limitation of Parliament's sovereignty was its own choice.[78] This again conflicts with the Diceyian view of parliamentary supremacy: being sovereign it was said Parliament could not abandon its own sovereignty. A similar approach was taken by the House of Lords a few years later when, in *R. v Secretary of State for Employment Ex p. Equal Opportunities Commission* which confirmed that the UK courts had jurisdiction to review primary legislation said to be in breach of EU law.[79]

It has been argued that the decision in *Factortame* does not necessarily **3–11** undermine the doctrine of parliamentary supremacy. As Goldsworthy has explained, the conflict between the Merchant Shipping Act 1988 and the 1972 Act was inadvertent and Parliament had been assured during the passage of the 1988 Act that it was compatible with EU law. What the court did in *Factortame* was to correct an oversight by Parliament and give effect to its intention: that the 1988 Act not breach EU law.[80] That is to overlook what the House of Lords in fact did: it questioned and then set aside an Act of Parliament on the grounds it was not consistent with EU law. That cannot be reconciled with Dicey's statement that "that no person or body is recognised by the law as having a right to override or set aside the legislation of Parliament".[81] The Diceyian doctrine of parliamentary supremacy now had to be read as subject to the requirements of EU law. It was that factor which led Wade to describe the decision as a "revolution".

---

[76] *R. v Secretary of State for Transport Ex p. Factortame Ltd* [1991] 1 A.C. 603 HL at 658–659.
[77] H.W.R. Wade, "Sovereignty—Revolution or Evolution? (1996) 112 L.Q.R. 568.
[78] Which is contrary to Wade's view that parliamentary sovereignty lies in the keeping of the courts: Wade, "The basis of legal sovereignty" (1955) 13 C.L.J. 172, 187, discussed at para.3–03, above.
[79] *R. v Secretary of State for Employment Ex p. Equal Opportunities Commission* [1995] 1 A.C. 1 HL.
[80] Goldsworthy, *Parliamentary Sovereignty: Contemporary Debates* (2010) pp.288–290.
[81] Dicey, *The Law of the Constitution* (1959) pp.39–40.

3–12   *Factortame* did leave one question open: what if Parliament expressly stated its intention to derogate from EU law but without withdrawing from the EU? This produces an acute tension: on the one hand, there is the power to make or unmake any law, while on the other hand a clear rule of EU law that conflicting national rules, whatever their domestic standing, must be set aside if in conflict with EU law. Could the UK pick and chose the EU law obligations it complied with?

Lord Denning MR addressed this issue in *Macarthys*:

> "If the time should come when our Parliament deliberately passes an Act with the intention of repudiating the Treaty or any provision of it or intentionally of acting inconsistently with it and says so in express terms then I should have thought that it would be the duty of our courts to follow the statute of our Parliament."[82]

That view is supported by Goldsworthy: "It is the business of the government and Parliament, not the courts, to decide whether or not Britain should abide by its treaty commitments."[83] But that is to ignore the content of EU law. As the European Court of Justice emphasised in *Costa*:

> "The executive force of Community law cannot vary from one State to another in deference to subsequent domestic laws, without jeopardising the attainment of the objectives of the Treaty."[84]

As long as s.2 of the 1972 Act remains in force effect has to be given to the treaties and, in particular, the rule that EU law takes precedence. By virtue of s.2 the entire corpus of EU law is a part of domestic law. That has led other commentators to suggest that it would not be open to Parliament to pick and choose the EU obligations it complied with: it is all or nothing.[85] That would appear to be the preferable view. The functioning of the EU is contingent upon Member States not selecting the obligations they are willing to comply with while seeking to draw all the benefits of membership. As we saw, this aspect of EU law was clear when the UK joined and it is one they ought to be held to whilst remaining a member. Not dissimilar arguments were advanced in *Thoburn*. As we have seen, Laws LJ held that the 1972 Act was exempt from the doctrine of implied repeal. But he rejected the argument that was because of requirements of EU law. Rather, it was the result of national law:

> "The British Parliament has not the authority to authorise [a limit on its sovereignty]. Being sovereign, it cannot abandon its sovereignty. Accordingly there are no circumstances in which the jurisprudence of the Court of Justice can elevate Community law to a status within the corpus of English

---

[82] *Macarthys Ltd v Smith* [1979] 3 All E.R. 325 at 329. That is consistent with what Lord Diplock had said in *Gartland v British Rail Engineering Ltd* [1983] 2 A.C. 751 HL at 771 where he said that legislation passed after a treaty was entered into "are to be construed, if they are reasonably capable of bearing such a meaning, as intended to carry out the obligation".
[83] Goldsworthy, *Parliamentary Sovereignty: Contemporary Debates* (2010) p.287.
[84] *Costa v ENEL* (C–6/64) [1964] E.C.R. 585 at 594.
[85] P. Craig, "Report on the United Kingdom" in A.M. Slaughter, A.S. Sweet and J.H.H. Weiler (eds), *The European Court and National Courts: Doctrine and Jurisprudence* (Oxford: Hart, 1998).

domestic law to which it could not aspire by any route of English law itself. This is, of course, the traditional doctrine of sovereignty. If is to be modified, it certainly cannot be done by the incorporation of external texts. The conditions of Parliament's legislative supremacy in the United Kingdom necessarily remain in the United Kingdom's hands."[86]

While this does not answer directly the question of whether Parliament can pick and choose its EU law obligations it makes one thing clear: should the need arise, the answer will be found in domestic, and not EU, law.[87] Parliament has also made a similar statement, in the form of s.18 of the European Union Act 2011.[88]

Thoburn also belongs to a group of cases that form the second contemporary attack on the classic Diceyian view of parliamentary sovereignty and which found the basis for our discussion of common law constitutionalism.

Parliamentary supremacy and common law constitutionalism

From the discussion above the common law's view of parliamentary supremacy ought to have appeared fairly clear: the idea that the provisions of an Act of Parliament could be set aside should appear "strange and startling". Starting with a number of extrajudicial writings in the 1990s,[89] however, the suggestion that there were some, albeit extreme, circumstances where the common law would reject legislation passed by Parliament began to take hold. As we have just seen, reflecting his extrajudicial writings, the idea of common law constitutionalism is woven through Law LJ's judgment in *Thoburn*. The debate reached a new level, however, following some obiter dicta comments by Lord Steyn, Lord Hope of Craighead and Barnoess Hale of Richmond in their speeches in the case of *R. (on the application of Jackson) v Attorney General*.[90] The relevant passages merit repetition. First, Lord Steyn: 3–13

> "The classic account given by Dicey of the doctrine of the supremacy of Parliament, pure and absolute as it was, can now be seen to be out of place in the modern United Kingdom. Nevertheless, the supremacy of Parliament is still the *general* principle of our constitution. It is a construct of the

---

[86] *Thoburn v Sunderland City Council* [2002] EWHC 195 (Admin); [2003] Q.B. 151 at [59]. The approach was approved by Lord Reed in *R. (on the application of Buckingham CC) v Secretary of State for Transport* [2014] UKSC 3; [2014] 1 W.L.R. 324 at [79]. On that case the various constitutional issues that were discussed see P. Craig, "Constitutionalising constitutional law: HS2" [2014] P.L. 373.

[87] The same approach has been taken by the constitutional courts of a number of other Member States, for example Germany, Czech Republic and Poland. See D.A.O. Edward and R.C. Lane, *Edward and Lane on European Union Law* (Cheltenham: Edward Elgar, 2013) para.6.19 and cases cited therein.

[88] See the discussion at para.10–45, below on the need for, and effect of, this particular statutory provision.

[89] Lord Woolf, "Droit public—English style" [1995] P.L. 57; Sir John Laws, "Law and democracy" [1995] P.L. 72; Sir Stephen Sedley, "Human rights: a twenty-first century agenda" [1995] P.L. 386. For a response, see J.A.G. Griffith, "The brave new world of Sir John Laws" (2000) 63 M.L.R. 159. A similar argument had opened up in New Zealand, in the 1980s, a country also thought to possess a legislature with unlimited sovereign power (and, of course, a country with an uncodified constitution): *Taylor v New Zealand Poultry Board* [1984] 1 N.Z.L.R. 394, per Cooke J at 398: "Some common law rights presumably lie so deep that even Parliament could not override them."

[90] *R. (on the application of Jackson) v Attorney General* [2005] UKHL 56; [2006] 1 A.C. 262.

common law. The judges created this principle. If that is so, it is not unthinkable that circumstances could arise where the courts may have to qualify a principle established on a different hypothesis of constitution-alism."[91]

Lord Hope went on to say:

"Our constitution is dominated by the sovereignty of Parliament. But parliamentary sovereignty is not longer, if it ever was, absolute. . . . It is no longer right to say that its freedom to legislate admits of no qualification whatever. Step by step, gradually but surely, the English principle of the absolute legislative sovereignty of Parliament which Dicey derived from Coke and Blackstone is being qualified."[92]

Lord Hope continued:

"The rule of law enforced by the courts is the ultimate controlling factor on which our constitution is based. The fact that your Lordships have been willing to hear this appeal and to give judgment upon it is another indication that the courts have a part to play in defining the limits of Parliament's legislative sovereignty."[93]

Finally, Baroness Hale:

"The courts will treat with particular suspicion (and may even reject) any attempt to subvert the rule of law by removing governmental action affecting the rights of the individual from all judicial scrutiny."[94]

In the same passage, Lady Hale went on to say: "In general, however, the constraints upon what Parliament can do are political and diplomatic rather than constitutional."

These passages are remarkable for the fact they contain dicta openly questioning the continuing validity of the central tenet of the constitution that is, as we have seen, supported by an almost unwavering line of judicial authority. It was in large part these remarks that led the First Division in *AXA General Insurance Co Ltd v Lord Advocate* to describe the question of parliamentary supremacy as an "as yet unresolved issue".[95] Are there other principles of the constitution that could trump that of parliamentary supremacy? Lord Hoffmann spoke of "principles of fundamental human rights which exist at common law" in *R. v Secretary of State for the Home Department, Ex p. Simms*[96] and Lord

---

[91] *R. (on the application of Jackson) v Attorney General* [2005] UKHL 56; [2006] 1 A.C. 262 at [102] (emphasis in original).

[92] *R. (on the application of Jackson) v Attorney General* [2005] UKHL 56; [2006] 1 A.C. 262 at [104]; Lord Hope has also discussed his comments in *Jackson* extrajudicially: Lord Hope, "Sovereignty in Question" (W.G. Hart Legal Workshop, 28 June 2011) *http://www.supreme-court.uk/docs/speech_110628.pdf* [Accessed 10 August 2015].

[93] *R. (on the application of Jackson) v Attorney General* [2005] UKHL 56; [2006] 1 A.C. 262 at [107].

[94] *R. (on the application of Jackson) v Attorney General* [2005] UKHL 56; [2006] 1 A.C. 262 at [159].

[95] *AXA General Insurance Co Ltd v Lord Advocate* [2011] CSIH 31; 2011 S.C. 662 at [67].

[96] *R. v Secretary of State for the Home Department, Ex p. Simms* [2000] 2 A.C. 115 at 131G.

Reed, in *AXA*, spoke of Parliament, when enacting the Scotland Act 1998, not having legislated in a vacuum but having legislated for "a liberal democracy founded on particular constitutional principles and traditions".[97] In *Walton* Lord Reed also explained that the "constitutional function" of the court when exercising its supervisory jurisdiction was "maintaining the rule of law".[98] That statement was unqualified. Could it include maintaining the rule of law in the face of an Act of Parliament that would otherwise undermine it? There is no reason, in principle, why that should not be so. As we have seen, the constitution of the United States does not expressly authorise the court to strike down legislation that conflicts with the constitution. It was a power claimed by the Supreme Court as necessary to protect the constitution.[99] In Canada, the Supreme Court has read in principles that underlie the constitution and which will be protected by the courts.[100] And in India, the Supreme Court has gone as far as to strike down a constitutional amendment (which was otherwise passed in accordance with the written constitution) because it offended principles that underpin the constitution.[101] The more difficult question, perhaps, is whether such a change should be made by the courts acting on their own initiative.[102] As Professor Wade explained:

"Even without a [break in legal continuity] there might be a shift in judicial loyalty if we take into account the dimension of time . . . [N]ew generations of judges might come to accept that there had been a new constitutional settlement based on common consent and long usage, and that the old doctrine of sovereignty was ancient history . . . The judges would then be adjusting their doctrine to the facts of constitutional life, as they have done throughout history."[103]

A change to such a fundamental rule of the constitution ought to be made, if possible, with the consent of the various constitutional actors. If the courts cease to recognise Acts of Parliament as beyond challenge it would be preferable if this was the result of a consensus having emerged as to what the new fundamental

[97] *AXA General Insurance Co Ltd v Lord Advocate* [2011] UKSC 46; 2012 S.C. (U.K.S.C.) 122 at [153]. The First Division has recently spoken of established principles of the Scottish constitution: *Taylor Clark Leisure Plc v Commissioners for Her Majesty's Revenue and Customs* [2015] CSIH 32; 2015 S.L.T. 281, per Lord President (Gill) at [16]. The "established principle of the Scottish constitution" discussed in that case was rights of audience before the Court of Session. But the Lord President's remarks do raise the intriguing question of what other principles of the Scottish constitution exist and to what extent, if any, they may differ from the "English" or the "UK" constitution.
[98] *Walton v Scottish Ministers* [2012] UKSC 44; 2013 S.C. (U.K.S.C.) 67 at [90].
[99] *Marbury v Madison* (1803) 1 Cranch 137.
[100] *Reference re the Secession of Quebec* [1998] 2 S.C.R. 217.
[101] *Golaknath v Punjab*, 1967 A.I.R. 1643; see the discussion of the "Basic Structure Doctrine" in S.P. Sathe, "India: From Positivism to Structuralism" in J.D. Goldsworthy (ed), *Interpreting Constitutions: A Comparative Study* (Oxford: Oxford University Press, 2006) pp.242–248. The idea of a constitution that has a basic structure, or architecture, has also been discussed in Canada: *Reference re Senate Reform*, 2014 S.C.C. 32 at [25]–[27].
[102] On the process of constitutional change, see House of Lords Select Committee on the Constitution, *The Process of Constitutional Change, 15th report of Session 2010–12*. The sovereignty of Parliament had earlier been recognised by the same committee as one of the central tenets of the constitution: House of Lords Select Committee on the Constitution, *Reviewing the Constitution: Terms of Reference and Method of Working, 1st report of Session 2001–2002* (The Stationery Office, 2001) HL Paper 11, para.20.
[103] H.W.R. Wade, *Constitutional Fundamentals* (London: Stevens, 1989).

rule of the constitution ought to be, as opposed to one branch of the state unilaterally declaring it.[104]

3–14　　But the United Kingdom is not there yet. Common law constitutionalism is only to be found in academic journals and obiter dicta comments. There is no "common consent" that there has been a shift away from parliamentary supremacy. Quite the reverse. A staunch defence of the Diceyian view of parliamentary supremacy was given by Lord Bingham, writing after his retirement. Lord Bingham argued:

> "We live in a society dedicated to the rule of law; in which Parliament has power, subject to limited, self-imposed restraints, to legislate as it wishes; in which Parliament may therefore legislate in a way which infringes the rule of law; and in which the judges, consistently with their constitutional duty to administer justice according to the laws and usages of the realm, cannot fail to give effect to such legislation if it is clearly and unambiguously expressed."[105]

The same argument was advanced by Goldsworthy[106] along with several eminent judges.[107] If, however, it is accepted that there are some limits to the legislative competence of Parliament (for example, as a result of EU law) then it is hard to understand why, as a matter of principle, there should be no other limits.[108] Why should an Act of Parliament yield to the requirements of the free movement of goods within the EU but not to fundamental principles of human rights? It may be dangerous for Parliament to assume it could, in a modern democracy, legislate in flagrant breach of the rule of law or fundamental human rights.[109] If it did, it may find it had not the power to do so. In the Human Rights Act 1998 the UK now has a stronger protection of such rights. And that Act represents the third contemporary challenge to the Diceyian orthodox.

Parliamentary supremacy and the Human Rights Act[110]

3–15　The working of the Human Rights Act 1998 is considered in more detail in Ch.11. For present purposes, we are interested in how the Act impacts on parliamentary supremacy. The Human Rights Act has been said to have been carefully crafted to ensure that parliamentary supremacy was preserved whilst allowing certain rights within the European Convention on Human Rights to be

---

[104] Bogdanor, *The New British Constitution* (2009) pp.280–282; Bingham, *The Rule of Law* (2010) p.170. See generally C. Turpin and A. Tomkins, *British Government and the Constitution: Text and Materials*, 7th edn (Cambridge: Cambridge University Press, 2011) pp.71–75; Young, *Parliamentary Sovereignty and the Human Rights Act* (2009) pp.82–93.

[105] Bingham, *The Rule of Law* (2010) p.168.

[106] Goldsworthy, *Parliamentary Sovereignty: Contemporary Debates* (2010) pp.304–318.

[107] Lord Neuberger MR (as he then was), "Who are the Masters Now?" (Lord Alexander of Weedon Lecture, 7 April 2011); and Jonathan Sumption, QC (as he then was), "Judicial and Political Decision-Making: the uncertain boundary" (F.A. Mann Lecture, 2011) *http://www.legalweek. com/digital_assets/3704/MANNLECTURE_final.pdf* [Accessed 3 June 2015].

[108] A. Kavanagh, *Constitutional Review under the Human Rights Act* (Cambridge: Cambridge University Press, 2009) pp.413–415

[109] J. Jowell, "The Rule of Law and its Underlying Values" in *The Changing Constitution* (2011) p.32.

[110] See generally, Young, *Parliamentary Sovereignty and the Human Rights Act* (2009) and Kavanagh, *Constitutional Review under the Human Rights Act* (2009) Chs 10 and 11.

available in domestic courts.[111] Similar statements were made repeatedly in the Bill's passage through both Houses of Parliament. The key provisions for this present discussion are ss.3 and 4 of the Act. Section 3 provides:

> "So far as it is possible to do so, primary legislation and subordinate legislation must be read and given effect in a way which is compatible with the Convention rights."

Section 4 provides that where the courts are satisfied that a legislative provision is incompatible with Convention rights, and that incompatibility cannot be cured by using s.3, then a "declaration of incompatibility" shall be made. Such a declaration does not affect the continuing validity, operation or enforcement of the offending provision.[112] The courts, therefore, are given no power to strike down or disapply an Act of Parliament. Where a declaration of incompatibility is made, the offending legislation can be cured by means of subordinate legislation.[113] So far, so good for the traditional view of parliamentary supremacy.

However, the key question is when should the courts interpret a provision **3–16** using their power under s.3 and when should they make a declaration under s.4? The more readily the courts are prepared to resort to s.4, the greater the control that Parliament retains over the content and meaning of its legislation. However, if greater use is made of s.3 to interpret, gloss, stretch, or potentially change, the meaning of the words used by Parliament, the less control Parliament retains over the effect of its legislation. In other words, over use of s.3 threatens to restrict or impinge upon parliamentary supremacy by giving the words used by Parliament a meaning or effect that was never intended by it.[114] There were early tensions within the House of Lords over to what extent s.3 should be used to interpret legislation in a manner consistent with Convention rights.[115] In *Ghaidan v Godin-Mendoza* Lord Rodger of Earlsferry explained the correct approach to s.3 of the Act:

> "[The] key to what it is possible for the courts to imply into legislation without crossing the border from interpretation to amendment does not lie in the number of words that have to be read in. The key lies in a careful consideration of the essential principles and scope of the legislation being interpreted. If the insertion of one word contradicts those principles or goes beyond the scope of the legislation, it amounts to impermissible amendment. On the other hand, if the implication of a dozen words leaves the essential principles and scope of the legislation intact but allows it to be read in a way which is compatible with Convention rights, the implication is a legitimate exercise of the powers conferred by section 3(1)."[116]

---

[111] See, for example, Lord Steyn's comments in *R v DPP Ex p. Kebeline* [2000] 2 A.C. 326 at 367.

[112] Human Rights Act 1998 s.4(6)(a).

[113] Human Rights Act 1998 s.10.

[114] These issues are more fully discussed at paras 11–07—11–13, below.

[115] Compare Lord Steyn's approach in *R. v A* [2001] UKHL 25; [2002] 1 A.C. 45 which advocated an extensive use of s.3 and Lord Nicholls more moderate approach in *Re S (Children) (Care Order: Implementation of Care Plan)* [2002] UKHL 10; [2002] 2 A.C. 291.

[116] *Ghaidan v Godin-Mendoza* [2004] UKHL 30; [2004] 2 A.C. 557 at [122].

Where s.3 cannot be used in that manner, it falls to the court to make a declaration of incompatibility under s.4. This approach to ss.3 and 4 proceeds on the understanding that Parliament had not intended to legislate in breach of Convention rights and thus the court corrects, where it can, any inadvertent or unintended incompatibility with Convention rights. In that respect, the Minister responsible for the Bill must state to Parliament whether, in his or her view, the Bill is compatible with Convention rights or, alternatively, that he or she unable to make such a statement but the government nevertheless wish the House to proceed with the Bill.[117] Thus if Parliament intends to legislate contrary to Convention rights, it ought to be clear that that was the intention. Furthermore, where the courts issue a declaration of incompatibility it is open to Parliament to take no remedial action, as has happened in respect of the blanket ban on prisoners voting.[118] Seven years after the declaration of incompatibility was originally made, the Supreme Court refused to make a further declaration: the matter was one for Parliament.[119]

3–17   It can be seen, therefore, that the Human Rights Act ultimately leaves the last word with Parliament. A consequence of that approach is that the protection of some Convention rights is incomplete (for example, those of disenfranchised prisoners) but parliamentary supremacy remains intact. But the Human Rights Act does not compromise Parliament's ability to legislate contrary to Convention rights if it so desires but to do so effectively it will need to use clear and express language. As Lord Bingham explained (when speaking about the presumption expressed by Lord Hoffmann in *Simms* and which has parallels to s.3) this is no bad thing:

> " . . . if, as sometimes happens, the executive as the proponent of legislation wants to introduce a provision that would strike ordinary people as unfair or disproportionate or immoral, the need to spell out that intention explicitly on the face of the bill must operate as a discouragement, not least because of the increased risk of media criticism and parliamentary and popular resistance."[120]

If that is the combined effect of ss.3, 4 and 19 of the Human Rights Act then far from undermining Parliament, it ought to strengthen it.

Conclusions on parliamentary supremacy

3–18 Despite the contemporary debate about whether the Diceyian model of parliamentary supremacy *ought* to endure, there can be little doubt that it does in fact endure. It is vouched by authority of the highest order that has never been overruled. But there is undoubtedly a shift in attitudes. Openly speculating on the continence of the doctrine in the highest courts would have been unthinkable two or three decades ago yet, as we have seen, judges in both the Inner House of the Court of Session and the Supreme Court/House of Lords have engaged in just such speculation. Perhaps the more important question is if there is to be a shift away from parliamentary supremacy as the touchstone of our constitution, who

[117] Human Rights Act 1998 s.19.
[118] See the discussion below at para.4–13; the relevant provision of the Representation of the People Act 1983 was declared to be incompatible by the Registration Appeal Court (Scotland) in *Smith v Scott* [2007] CSIH 9; 2007 S.C. 345.
[119] *McGeoch v Lord President of the Council* [2013] UKSC 63; 2014 S.C. (UKSC) 25.
[120] Lord Bingham, "Dicey Revisited" [2002] P.L. 39, 48.

should initiate the move. Lord Millett, in *Ghaidan v Godin-Mendoza*, accepted that the doctrine of parliamentary supremacy was not "sacrosanct" but if it were to be changed, it should be done by the legislature and not "judicial activism".[121] That view is supported by a number of other judges.[122] However, Laws LJ, Lord Steyn and Lord Hope would say that parliamentary supremacy is a creature of the common law and what the common law giveth, the common can taketh away. Professor Wade would support this stance. At present, the rule of parliamentary supremacy represents the "rule of recognition"[123] or "*grundnorm*"[124] in our legal system. It has attained that status, and derived its authority, from its acceptance by the judges and other constitutional actors. Any change in that rule of recognition ought not to lie exclusively in the hands of the courts or the legislature but in both, acting together, to form a new consensus, a consensus shared by the people.

A point that has not arisen in our discussion so far is the increasing use of referendums in the United Kingdom.[125] What, if any, impact does that have for parliamentary supremacy? Dicey himself came to advocate the introduction of the referendum in the UK.[126] He proposed a Referendum Act that would require popular approval of any legislative measure that alters provisions of the highest constitutional importance. Any measure not so approved should be "held invalid by every court of law".[127] Such a proposal would flatly contradict the classic, Diceyian, view of parliamentary supremacy. We discuss the rise of the referendum in Ch.5. If the referendum does become a common feature of our constitution, a fourth flank is likely to be opened in the battle over continuing parliamentary supremacy. And this line of attack appears to have been endorsed by Dicey himself.

At present, however, the law remains clear: assuming Parliament uses sufficient clear language, it retains the power to make or unmake any law, subject to the courts ability to disapply any provision that conflicts with EU law. If that is to change, it is likely to be justified, at least in part, by a need to secure the rule of law. And it is to the rule of law that we now turn.

THE RULE OF LAW

Introduction

The idea of the rule of law began to develop as a principle of the British **3–19** constitution in the nineteenth century but it has more ancient roots.[128] Its

---

[121] *Ghaidan v Godin-Mendoza* [2004] UKHL 30; [2004] 2 A.C. 557 at [57].
[122] Bingham, *The Rule of Law* (2010) Ch.12; Lord Neuberger MR, "Who are the Masters Now?" (Lord Alexander of Weedon Lecture, 7 April 2011); and Jonathan Sumption QC, "Judicial and Political Decision-Making: the uncertain boundary" (F.A. Mann Lecture, 2011) *http://www. legalweek.com/digital_assets/3704/MANNLECTURE_final.pdf* [Accessed 3 June 2015].
[123] H.L.A. Hart, *The Concept of Law*, 2nd edn (Oxford: Clarendon Press, 1994) pp.149–150.
[124] H. Kelsen, *Pure Theory of Law* (translation from the revised 2nd edn, German edn by M. Knight); H. Kelsen, *General Theory of Law and State* (translated by A. Wedbery) (Cambridge Mass.: Harvard University Press, 1949).
[125] On which see Bogdanor, *The New British Constitution* (2009) Ch.7.
[126] A.V. Dicey, "The Referendum and its Critics" (1910) 212 *Quarterly Review* 538; see also: R. Weill, "Dicey was not Diceyan" (2003) 62 C.L.J. 474; Young, *Parliamentary Sovereignty and the Human Rights Act* (2009) pp.98–101.
[127] Dicey, "The Referendum and its Critics" (1910) 212 *Quarterly Review* 538, 554.
[128] Tamanaha, *On the Rule of Law: History, Politics, Theory* (2004) pp.8–9; *Aristotle's Politics and Athenian Constitution* (1959) book III, s.1287, p.97.

importance as a constitutional principle is now taken as read and has found itself embodied in statute.[129] Section 1 of the Constitutional Reform Act 2005 provides:

> "This Act does not adversely affect—(a) the existing constitutional principle of the rule of law; or (b) the Lord Chancellor's existing constitutional role in relation to that principle."

Section 17 of the Act goes on to amend the terms of the Promissory Oaths Act 1868 so as to require the Lord Chancellor to take an oath that he will "respect the rule of law, defend the independence of the judiciary and discharge my duty to ensure the provision of resources for the efficient and effective support of the courts for which I am responsible".

No attempt is made to define "the rule of law" in the 2005 Act. That reflects the fact that there is no general consensus about what it includes. Some argue that the rule of law should be content free.[130] In other words, the rule of law should be about the form that law takes and the procedures for making law. It should not, the argument goes, trouble itself with the content of the law. The rule of law, on this understanding, should not be confused with, or be seen to require, other attributes (such as democracy, social justice, equality or the protection of human rights) to which a "good" constitution ought to aspire. The attributes that this narrow view of the rule of law would require include a requirement that laws be prospective in operation, open and clear. The law should be relatively stable. The making of particular laws or rules, whether legislative or administrative in nature, should be guided by open, stable, clear and general norms. This all requires that the courts play a role in securing even this narrow vision of the rule of law. An independent judiciary, who observe the principles of natural justice, and ready access to open courts are important features of this construction of the rule of law.[131] Rather than trying to capture all of the virtues of the state under the banner "the rule of law", this vision of the rule of law makes the more modest claim that respect for the rule of law is a necessary, if not a sufficient, condition for respecting individual freedom and human dignity.

The narrow view of the rule of law has the problem that it could maintain a state that supported arbitrary discrimination or other human rights abuses so long as the law was made in the appropriate manner and administered by independent courts. That has led others to argue for a fuller vision of the rule of law, one which includes specific rights for individuals.[132] Such a model is not without its difficulties. Which rights are protected by the rule of law? Are they unalienable

---

[129] As Lord Steyn put it, an "overarching principle of constitutional law": Lord Steyn, "Democracy through law" [2002] E.H.R.L.R. 723. But the usefulness of the doctrine was not always so readily accepted: "The ground is then shifted slightly and what becomes sacred and untouchable is something called the Rule of Law. The Rule of Law is an invaluable concept for those who wish not to change the present set-up" (J.A.G. Griffith, "The Political Constitution" (1979) 42 M.L.R. 1, 15).

[130] Perhaps the strongest advocate of this vision of the rule of law was Joseph Raz, see, in particular: J. Raz, "The Rule of Law and its Virtue" (1977) 93 L.Q.R. 195.

[131] See, for example, *Guardian News and Media Ltd v AB and CD* [2014] EWCA Crim B1, per Gross LJ at [2].

[132] See, for example, Woolf et al, *De Smith's Judicial Review*, 7th edn (London: Sweet & Maxwell, 2013) para.1–021. For a comparison between the two models, see R. Dworkin, "Political Judges and the Rule of Law" in R. Dworkin, *A Matter of Principle* (Oxford: Oxford University Press, 1985) Ch.1.

and thus beyond the reach of future generations who may wish to order society differently? A further problem arises in the British constitutional context. The logical conclusion of any substantive vision of the rule of law requires the imposition of legal limitations on the legislature.[133] On this view, the rule of law sets its face against arbitrary power; arbitrary power is power unconstrained by law; the legislative supremacy of Parliament is unconstrained by law and therefore arbitrary; being arbitrary, it must be subject to judicial control (even if only on limited grounds). But since there "cannot be an infinite regress of lawmakers able to impose limits on the authority of each one in turn",[134] this argument necessarily involves the substitution of judicial for legislative supremacy. Only one institution can have the last word on whether or not law is valid.

The suggestion that, as a matter of the rule of law, that institution must be the courts can be resisted on a number of grounds. The first argument deployed is usually that such "judicial supremacy" is undemocratic.[135] The substantive rights said to be captured by the rule of law are rarely absolute. Once it is accepted these rights require to be qualified or balance against each other, difficult choices are not made any easier by leaving the decision to the judiciary as opposed to the elected legislature.[136] The argument runs deeper than the democratic accountability of judges. Judicial decisions arise out of adversarial litigation. That process is ill suited to the balancing of various competing interests and rights: that is a quintessentially legislative function.[137] Finally, given judicial decision making is inherently retrospective, there is a necessary tension with the rule of law's emphasis on the prospectivity of the law.[138]

In *A v Secretary of State for the Home Department*, however, Lord Bingham defended judicial decision making and its democratic values:

> "I do not in particular accept the distinction which [the Attorney General] drew between democratic institutions and the courts. It is of course true that the judges in this country are not elected and are not answerable to Parliament. It is also of course true . . . that Parliament, the executive and the courts have different functions. But the function of independent judges charged to interpret and apply the law is universally recognised as a cardinal feature of the modern democratic state, a cornerstone of the rule of law itself. The Attorney General is fully entitled to insist on the proper limits of judicial authority, but he is wrong to stigmatise judicial decision-making as in some way undemocratic."[139]

---

[133] We have seen the seeds of this argument above, at para.3–13, where the idea of common law constitutionalism was discussed.

[134] J.D. Goldsworthy, "Legislative sovereignty and the rule of law" in T. Campbell, K.D. Ewing and A. Tomkins (eds), *Sceptical Essays on Human Rights* (Oxford: Oxford University Press, 2001) Ch.4.

[135] See, for example, Griffith, "The brave new world of Sir John Laws" (2000) 63 M.L.R. 159; K.D. Ewing, "The Human Rights Act and Parliamentary Democracy" (1999) 62 M.L.R. 79.

[136] Griffith, "The political constitution" (1979) 42 M.L.R. 1.

[137] L.L. Fuller, "The Forms and Limits of Adjudication" (1978) 92 Harvard L.R. 353.

[138] R. Ekins, "Judicial Supremacy and the Rule of Law" (2003) 119 L.Q.R. 127.

[139] *A v Secretary of State for the Home Department* [2004] UKHL 56; [2005] 2 A.C. 68 at [42]; see also Lord Hope at [108]. For support for Lord Bingham's stance, see J. Jowell, "Judicial Deference: Servility, Civility or Institutional Capacity?" [2003] P.L. 592 and R. Clayton, "Judicial deference and 'democratic dialogue': the legitimacy of judicial intervention under the Human Rights Act 1998" [2004] P.L. 33.

That does not allow the courts to second guess the judgment of the executive or the legislature without restraint. As Lord Bingham also explained, it is necessary to have regard to the concept of "relative institutional competence":

> "The more purely political . . . a question is, the more appropriate it will be for political resolution and the less likely it is to be an appropriate matter for judicial decision. The smaller, therefore, will be the potential role for the court. It is the function of political and not judicial bodies to resolve political questions. Conversely, the greater the legal content of any issue, the greater the potential role of the courts, because under our constitution and subject to the sovereign power of Parliament it is the function of courts and not of political bodies to resolve legal questions."[140]

That suggests that a middle way can be found. Lord Bingham acknowledges the role of the court, even where the legal content is high, is subject to the supremacy of Parliament. That is a clear rejection of the logical end point of a fuller ideal of the rule of law. But it is also a rejection of the narrow formulation favoured by Raz and others. To understand how such a middle way can be navigated, it is necessary now to turn and consider what the rule of law actually means. Can we find an acceptable definition of this important term (one which has been described as the "ultimate controlling factor" upon which our constitution is based)?[141] To do that, we will consider two theories. First, Dicey and his views on the rule of law, which despite coming under heavy criticism, remain influential. The second is the vision of the rule of law set out by Lord Bingham after his retirement as the Senior Law Lord. Once we have done that, we then turn to consider the different means by which the rule of law is protected in the United Kingdom.

Dicey on the rule of law

3–20 Dicey's approach to the rule of law perhaps exemplifies the debate that has been outlined above and the difficulty in drawing any hard and fast lines. Dicey has been described as offering both a formal[142] and a substantive[143] concept of the rule of law. Dicey's views on the rule of law have been the subject of substantial, and sustained, criticism but they were the first clear articulation of the concept in terms of British constitutional law. For Dicey the rule of law sat with parliamentary sovereignty as the two fundamental doctrines of the constitution.[144] While parliamentary supremacy concerned itself with Parliament's relationship with the law, the rule of law concerned the executive's relationship with the law.

Dicey understood the rule of law to have three facets.[145] First, he took the rule of law to mean "the absolute supremacy or predominance of regular law as opposed to the influence of arbitrary power".[146] Arbitrariness, prerogative, even

---

[140] *A v Secretary of State for the Home Department* [2004] UKHL 56; [2005] 2 A.C. 68 at [29].
[141] *R. (on the application of Jackson) v Attorney General* [2005] UKHL 56; [2006] 1 A.C. 262, per Lord Hope of Craighead at [107].
[142] For example, P. Craig, "Formal and substantive conceptions of the rule of law: an analytical framework" [1997] P.L. 467.
[143] Perhaps most trenchantly by Jennings, *The Law and the Constitution* (1959).
[144] Dicey, *The Law of the Constitution* (1959) pp.183–184.
[145] Dicey, *The Law of the Constitution* (1959) pp.188–203.
[146] Dicey, *The Law of the Constitution* (1959) p.202.

"wide discretionary authority on the part of government" were, for Dicey, incompatible with the rule of law. But this equation of discretion and arbitrariness is misconceived. No workable scheme of social welfare or regulation can be cast in terms of rules alone. Those charged with implementing and administering the scheme must be entrusted with a discretion in order to adapt and apply its general principles to the circumstances of specific cases. Consequently, Parliament regularly confers wide discretionary powers on public authorities and officials. That is plainly compatible with a narrow view of the rule of law: having the imprimatur of the legislature, its legal pedigree is beyond question. However, discretionary power and the rule of law can coexist. This does not dismiss Dicey's first branch of the rule of law entirely. Dicey's attack was on arbitrary power, which is not readily reconcilable with the idea of government under law. The issue thus becomes whether we have appropriate legal (and political) controls with which to regulate the exercise of discretionary power so as to ensure that it is not exercised in an arbitrary manner. Those controls are considered below.

Secondly, Dicey saw the rule of law as requiring "the equal subjection of all classes to the ordinary law of the land administered by the ordinary Law courts".[147] Dicey drew a distinction between the arrangements in Britain and those in continental systems, such as France, which had a distinct system of public law administered by separate courts. "With us", Dicey explained, "every official, from the Prime Minister down to a constable or collector of taxes, is under the same responsibility for every act done without legal justification as any other citizen." This proposition too is hard to sustain. It is simply wrong to say that there is equality before the law in the United Kingdom today. Leaving aside issues of access to the courts (which are touched on below) the state has a whole host of special rights, privileges and immunities before the law.[148] Furthermore, the distinction between ordinary courts in Britain and the administrative courts in France has become less marked during the twentieth century as Parliament moved an increasing number of disputes away from the courts and into specialist tribunals.[149]

Finally, the rule of law, according to Dicey, means that:

> "with us the law of the constitution, the rules which in foreign countries naturally form part of a constitutional code, are not the source but the consequence of the rights of individuals, as defined and enforced by the Courts".[150]

The British constitution, on this account, was the product of the ordinary law, developed by the courts on a case by case basis, as distinct from (and, implicitly, superior to) a constitutional order superimposed in the manner of a written

---

[147] Dicey, *The Law of the Constitution* (1959) p.202.

[148] To take but a few examples: in the absence of express terms (or necessary implication) to the contrary, the Crown is not bound by the burden of a statute (*Lord Advocate v Dumbarton DC*, 1990 S.C. (H.L.) 1); the Crown has immunity from coercive remedies (interdict and implement in Scotland; injunction and specific performance in England and Wales) in civil proceedings (Crown Proceedings Act 1947), although "civil proceedings" has now been held not to include proceedings for judicial review (*M v Home Office* [1994] 1 A.C. 377 HL; *Davidson v Scottish Ministers* [2005] UKHL 74; 2006 S.C. (H.L.) 41).

[149] These have now been brought together under the unified tribunal structure: Tribunals, Courts and Enforcement Act 2007 and Tribunals (Scotland) Act 2014.

[150] Dicey, *The Law of the Constitution* (1959) p.203.

constitution. This third meaning of the rule of law is perhaps the most curious. Dicey clearly regarded individual rights and liberties as secured by the rule of law: the right to personal freedom, right to freedom of discussion and the right of public meeting were all discussed by Dicey in the section concerned with the rule of law.[151] In that sense Dicey gave a fuller, or substantive, account of the rule of law. But he did not (obviously) take that to the logical conclusion discussed above. Parliament retained the right to make or unmake any law. That being so, if the government of the day, commanding a majority in the House of Commons, forces through illiberal legislation (perhaps using the Parliament Acts) there is nothing the courts can do about it. For Dicey, however, parliamentary supremacy and the rule of law were not to be viewed as counterbalancing forces but in fact being mandated by each other. They are complementary.[152] This appears to be based on Dicey's belief that Parliament would not enact laws harmful to the interests of its electors: Dicey only ever advocated the absence of *legal* limits on the competence of Parliament. As he explained:

"Parliament, though sovereign, unlike a sovereign monarch who is not only a legislator but a ruler, that is head of the executive government, has never been able to use the powers of the government as a means of interfering with the regular course of law; and what is even more important, Parliament has looked with disfavour and jealously on all exemptions of officials from the ordinary liabilities of citizens or from the jurisdiction of the ordinary Courts; Parliamentary sovereignty has been fatal to the growth of 'administrative law'."[153]

The last sentence, at least, is clearly out of place in the modern United Kingdom. But the rest of this passage also highlights how times have changed since Dicey was writing. Parliament has been, in modern times, dominated by the executive. It is a necessary condition (by convention at least) that the executive commands the support of the majority of the House of Commons. That fact, coupled with the provisions of the Parliament Acts, do allow a confusion between executive and legislative functions.[154] Thus a tension can be seen between the Diceyian model of parliamentary supremacy and the rule of law. Maintaining the former necessarily leads to at least the risk of an incomplete protection of the latter.

Bingham on the rule of law[155]

3–21 A more contemporary definition of the rule of law was given by Lord Bingham:

[151] Dicey, *The Law of the Constitution* (1959) pp.206–283.
[152] Dicey, *The Law of the Constitution* (1959) p.406. See also T.R.S. Allan, *Law, Liberty and Justice: the Legal Foundations of British Constitutionalism* (Oxford: Clarendon Press, 1994) p.282 and Laws, "Law and Democracy" [1995] P.L. 72.
[153] Dicey, *The Law of the Constitution* (1959) p.409.
[154] This increasingly troubled Dicey and was at the root of his proposed Referendums Act, discussed in Ch.5, below.
[155] What follows is a necessarily brief synopsis of Lord Bingham's discussion of the rule of law that is set out in his lecture on the topic, "The Rule of Law", which is published at [2007] C.L.J. 67 the themes of which are more fully discussed in his book, Bingham, *The Rule of Law* (2010). The book in its entirety is commended to anyone who has an interest in the issue of the rule of law.

"The core of the existing principle is, I suggest, that all persons and authorities within the state, whether public or private, should be bound by and entitled to the benefit of laws publically made, taking effect (generally) in the future and publically administered in the courts."[156]

Lord Bingham acknowledged that this formulation of the rule of law has been heavily influenced by Dicey. Lord Bingham went on to explain that his formulation of the rule of law brings with it eight sub-rules[157]:

(i)   "the law must be accessible and so far as possible intelligible, clear and predictable";
(ii) "questions of legal right and liability should ordinarily be resolved by application of the law and not the exercise of discretion";
(iii) "the laws of the land should apply equally to all, save to the extent that objective differences justify differentiation";
(iv) "ministers and public officers at all levels must exercise the powers conferred on them in good faith, fairly for the purpose for which the powers were conferred, without exceeding the limits of such powers and not unreasonably";
(v)   "the law must afford adequate protection of fundamental human rights";
(vi) "means must be provided for resolving, without prohibitive cost or inordinate delay, bona fide civil disputes which the parties themselves are unable to resolve";
(vii) "adjudicative procedures provided by the state should be fair"; and
(viii) "the rule of law requires compliance by the state with its obligations in international law as in national law".

Lord Bingham's formulation and his sub-rules can been seen to share characteristics of both the narrow view of the rule of law (for example, sub-rules (i)–(iv)) but also a more substantive vision of the rule of law (for example, sub-rules (v) and (vi)). Access to justice is a topical example to choose.[158] As Lord Bingham explained an "unenforceable right or claim is a thing of little value to anyone" and it is important the courts are not open to everyone in the same way that anyone (who has the money) can stay at the Ritz Hotel.[159] The jurisdictions of the United Kingdom have long subsidised access to the courts for those that did not have the means to pay for professional representation. But legal aid, especially for civil litigation, is a contentious issue. As successive cuts are made to legal aid budgets, and access to the courts becomes more difficult for more and more families, strain in placed on the rule of law.[160] But would there come a point when legal aid was cut so far that it would infringe the rule of law? And if so,

---

[156] Bingham, *The Rule of Law* (2010) p.8.
[157] Bingham, *The Rule of Law* (2010) Chs 3–10 (respectively).
[158] See, generally, Lord Neuberger, "Justice in the Age of Austerity" (Tom Sargant Memorial Lecture, 15 October 2013) *http://www.supremecourt.uk/docs/speech-131015.pdf* [Accessed 3 June 2015].
[159] Bingham, *The Rule of Law* (2010) pp.85–86.
[160] See, for example, the controversy surrounding whether a complex fraud trial could continue where barristers involved refused to appear at the reduced legal aid rates that had been imposed: *R. v Crawley (Scott)* [2014] EWCA Crim 1028; [2014] 2 Cr. App. R. 16.

could such legislation (assuming the cut to have been made by Act of Parliament) be reviewable on the grounds it does not comply with the rule of law?

3–22   Despite supporting a more substantive content to the rule of law, Lord Bingham denies that his formulation necessarily leads to the rule of law supplanting parliamentary supremacy as the ultimate rule of our constitution. As we have already seen, Lord Bingham argues that Parliament retains the right to legislate contrary to the rule of law if sufficiently clear words are used.[161] That potentially gives rise to an incomplete protection of the rule of law. As Lord Bingham noted earlier in his work:

> "It is a good start for public authorities to observe the letter of the law, but not enough if the law in a particular country does not protect what are regarded as the basic entitlements of a human being."[162]

The protection of the rule of law, as Lord Bingham recognised, rests on trusting Parliament not to abuse its legislative supremacy. An obvious assault on the rule of law (for example, the fabled legislation requiring the slaughter of all blue-eyed babies) can safely be ruled out. But as we saw with legal aid, more subtle infringements of the rule of law cannot be excluded. Lord Bingham recognises that the constitution has become "unbalanced" in this regard and may, in time, require reconsideration.[163]

As we have seen, both Dicey and Bingham's visions of the rule of law result in incomplete protection so long as parliamentary supremacy remains. But to what extent is that only an academic concern? To answer that, we need to consider how the rule of law is currently safeguarded in the United Kingdom.

Protecting the rule of law

3–23 All three branches of the state (judiciary, legislature and executive) have an important role to play in protecting the rule of law. We have already seen the statutory obligation placed on the Lord Chancellor in that regard. He, with the other Law Officers, play an important role in ensuring the executive respect the rule of law. The legislature (be it Westminster or Holyrood) have a role to play as well. For example, s.1 of the Judiciary and Courts (Scotland) Act 2008 places an obligation on the First Minister, the Lord Advocate, the Scottish Ministers and MSPs to "uphold the continued independence of the judiciary": as we have seen, an essential component of the rule of law. But it is the judiciary that play the most important role in securing the rule of law, through applying the common law and interpreting the legislation passed by Parliament.

3–24   Dicey (through his second characteristic of the rule of law) and Bingham (through his third sub-rule) saw the courts playing an important role in the protection of the rule of law. This is most commonly done through the common law. In our discussion of common law constitutionalism we have seen the courts asserting the common law's role in giving content to, and protection for, the rule of law. The common law has long protected some basic rights, which have been said to include: access to a judicial remedy, right to life, liberty of the person, right to a fair hearing, prohibition on the retrospective imposition of criminal

---

[161] Bingham, *The Rule of Law* (2010) p.168; see para.3–14, above.
[162] Bingham, *The Rule of Law* (2010) p.84.
[163] Bingham, *The Rule of Law* (2010) p.169.

penalty, freedom of expression and many others.[164] At its core, is the principle of legality. This requires the courts to apply the rule of law and other constitutional principles unless Parliament has clearly and expressly excluded them.[165] It also requires the executive to act in accordance with the law, including the law of delict. Thus in *Entrick v Carrington*, the court rejected the assertion that "state necessity" was sufficient warrant for authorising the King's Messengers to break in to Entrick's house and seize his books and papers:

> "Every invasion of private property is a trespass. No man can set his foot upon my ground without my licence, but he is liable to an action . . . If he admits the fact, he is bound to show by way of justification that some positive law has empowered or excused him. The justification is submitted to the judges, who are to look into the books, and see if such a justification can be maintained by the text of the statute law, or principles of the common law . . . It is said that it is necessary for the ends of government to lodge such a power [*of search and seizure*] with a state officer . . . but with respect to the argument of state necessity, or to a distinction that has been aimed at between state offences and others, the common law does not understand that kind of reasoning, nor do our books take notice of any such distinction."[166]

A more recent example is *R. v Davis*, where the House of Lords held that the common law conferred a right on an accused to confront his accusers.[167] An order by a trial judge that allowed witnesses to use pseudonyms, to be hidden behind a screen, have their voice mechanically distorted and prohibited the accused's counsel from asking any questions which may have allowed the witnesses to be identified was unlawful.[168]

But the protection offered by the principle of legality is limited. It does not require the state to found on a positive legal authority for all that it does. Rather, such authority is only required where necessary to validate what would otherwise constitute a legal wrong. *Malone v Metropolitan Police Commissioner* illustrates the significance of that distinction.[169] Mr Malone was prosecuted for handling stolen goods. It came to light during his trial that evidence had been recovered in the form covert recordings of his telephone conversations (in other words, a phone tap). The Secretary of State, on the request of the police, had authorised the Post Office (who then ran the telephone network) to record Mr Malone's telephone calls. Mr Malone sought a declaration that such phone tapping was unlawful. He was unsuccessful. There had been no trespass on to his property and the common law, at that point, did not protect a person's privacy. Accordingly,

[164] Woolf et al., *De Smith's Judicial Review* (2013) para.5–042.
[165] *R. v Secretary of State for the Home Department Ex p. Simms* [2000] 2 A.C. 115, per Lord Hoffmann at 131; subject to the caveat that the courts *may* reject a blatant attempt to subvert the rule of law: *R. (on the application of Jackson) v Attorney General* [2005] UKHL 56; [2006] 1 A.C. 262, per Baroness Hale of Richmond at [159].
[166] *Entrick v Carrington* (1765) State Trials 1030.
[167] *R. v Davis (Iain)* [2008] UKHL 36; [2008] 1 A.C. 1128.
[168] That result was swiftly reversed by legislation in the form of the Criminal Evidence (Witness Anonymity) Act 2008 although the effect was ameliorated by requiring the trial judge to ensure that the requirements of art.6 of the European Convention on Human Rights were still fulfilled.
[169] *Malone v Metropolitan Police Commissioner* [1979] Ch. 344 (ChD).

Mr Malone could point to no unlawful act by those that had recorded his telephone conversations. That was fatal to his claim:

> "If the tapping of telephones by the Post Office at the request of the police can be carried out without any breach of the law, it does not require any statutory or common law power to justify it: it can lawfully be done simply because there is nothing to make it unlawful."[170]

When Mr Malone's case reached the European Court of Human Rights in Strasbourg, however, the absence of a legal basis for the actions of the police was fatal to its compatibility with art.8 of the European Convention on Human Rights.[171] *Malone* is simply one example of the haphazard protection of the rule of law by the common law. An equally stark example is that of *Liversidge v Anderson* which saw the House of Lords uphold the detention of Mr Liversidge without charge, without trial and without limit of time.[172] The case is most memorable for Lord Atkin's stinging dissent:

> "In this country, amid the clash of arms, the laws are not silent. They may be changed, but they speak the same language in war as in peace."[173]

But his comments were just that, a dissent. The laws must have sounded very quiet indeed to Mr Liversidge as he languished in his prison cell at the behest of the Secretary of State. It took the best part of four decades before the common law recognised that Lord Atkin had been correct all along.[174] Whatever the reasons for decisions such as *Malone* or *Liversidge*, they serve to underscore the uncertain protection that the common law can afford to the rule of law.

It is not just through the common law that the judiciary seek to protect the rule of law. The approach of the courts to statutory interpretation also plays an important role. Once Parliament has spoken (in the form of legislation) the meaning to be given to those words is a matter for the courts. As we have seen, the court will not uphold a construction of an Act that infringes fundamental rights unless Parliament has clearly and expressly authorised such an infringement. This rule can obviously be overcome by the legislature but to do so, Parliament must confront squarely what it is doing.

Conclusions on the rule of law

3–25 Despite its increasingly important place in our constitution, a definition of the rule of law that is acceptable to all remains elusive. The truth appears to lie somewhere between the narrow and the substantive visions of the rule of law that have been advocated. What we have seen, however, is that while parliamentary

---

[170] *Malone v Metropolitan Police Commissioner* [1979] Ch. 344, per Sir Robert Megarry VC at 367A.

[171] *Malone v United Kingdom* (1984) 7 E.H.R.R. 14.

[172] *Liversidge v Anderson* [1942] A.C. 206 HL; see also Lord Bingham, "Mr Perlzweig, Mr Liversidge, and Lord Atkin", 16 October 1997, republished in Lord Bingham, *The Business of Judging* (Oxford: Oxford University Press, 2000) pp.211–221. Further discussion at para. 13–02.

[173] *Liversidge v Anderson* [1942] A.C. 206 at 244.

[174] *Inland Revenue Commissioners v Rossminster Ltd* [1980] A.C. 952 HL, per Lord Diplock at 1011.

supremacy remains in its orthodox form, the protection of the rule of law can never be complete.

SEPARATION OF POWERS

For supposedly fundamental doctrines of the constitution, the meaning and force **3–26** of both parliamentary supremacy and the rule of law turn out to be surprisingly contested questions. So too the doctrine of the separation of powers, which Britain was once taken to exemplify, which was subsequently written off as irrelevant, but which seems withal to have clung on to its claim to be a central feature of the constitution.[175]

The classic statements of the separation of powers doctrine were made in the period prior to the Glorious Revolution although the idea underpinning the doctrine can be found in the experiments with mixed government in Ancient Greece and Rome. The classic formulation of the doctrine was give by Montesquieu in *The Spirit of the Laws*:

> "In every government there are three sorts of power . . . that of making laws, that of executing public affairs and that of adjudicating on crimes and individual cases . . . When the legislative and executive powers are united in the same person or in the same body of magistrats, there can be no liberty . . . Again, there is no liberty if the power of judging is not separated from the legislature and executive. There would be an end to everything if the same man or the same body . . . were to exercise those powers."[176]

Thus the crucial evil which the separation of powers seeks to avoid is the concentration of power in too few hands, with all that that implies in terms of loss of liberty. This may be achieved by a rigid separation of the legislative, executive and judicial functions, and their allocation to three distinct agencies; more probably, it will be achieved by structuring the institutions of the state in such a way that no one institution has complete autonomy in the exercise of its functions, but is subject to a degree of control by one or both of the others.[177] On this account, it is less important correctly to identify and distribute particular functions of the state than to ensure that at no one time does one branch of the state have too much power by comparison with the others: the "health" of a constitution is a function of the efficacy of the "checks and balances" whereby the different institutions may encroach upon one another's territory.

On the face of it, our constitutional arrangements appear to conform to this doctrine: we have legislatures, executive authorities and judicial organs, each performing its respective role. Why then did it become so fashionable to dismiss

---

[175] In defence of the separation of powers, see M.J.C. Vile, *Constitutionalism and the Separation of Powers* (1967); Munro, *Studies in Constitutional Law* (1999) Ch.8; E. Barendt, "Separation of powers and constitutional government" [1999] P.L. 599; N.W. Barber, "Prelude to the separation of powers" [2001] C.L.J. 59.

[176] Montesquieu, *The Spirit of the Laws* (1749). Although influenced by British constitutional arrangements, the theories of Montesquieu were to have their greatest impact in the exercise in constitutional design which took place in the United States of America following the Declaration of Independence.

[177] Montesquieu insisted, however, that the judicial power be wholly independent of the other two branches of government.

the separation of powers as a "tiresome talking point"?[178] There are obvious institutional overlaps.[179] When not simply ignoring it, critics of the separation of powers would enumerate in exhaustive detail the instances of Parliament performing non-legislative functions, of the government making laws and adjudicating upon them,[180] of the judiciary acting non-judicially. There is some truth in these observations, but they tend to give an incomplete and distorted impression. Thus it is true that Parliament has a penal jurisdiction in the protection and enforcement of its privileges but it has not been used for more than a century.[181] A great deal of legislative power is delegated by Parliament to ministers, local authorities and others; but primary legislation prescribes the scope and limits of these powers, subordinate legislation is subject to parliamentary approval, and the courts can invalidate subordinate legislation which is found to be ultra vires. Certain judicial functions are performed by administrative tribunals or officials; but since the Franks Report on administrative tribunals and inquiries, and the legislation to which it led, such tribunals have been absorbed into the machinery of justice, and their determinations are subject either to appeal or review by the ordinary courts.[182] So the various functions of the state do stray across institutional boundaries to some extent. But Montesquieu himself did not insist on an absolute division of the functions of the state between separate institutions. It may be that the critics of the doctrine have perpetuated the pure theory which, in its lack of correspondence to actual constitutional arrangements, is easier to knock down.

3–27   There are numerous references in the case law to the separation of powers. For example, in *Duport Steels Ltd v Sirs*, Lord Diplock remarked:

> "At a time when more and more cases involve the application of legislation which gives effect to policies that are the subject of bitter public and parliamentary controversy, it cannot be too strongly emphasised that the British constitution, though largely unwritten, is firmly based on the separation of powers: Parliament makes the laws, the judiciary interprets them."[183]

---

[178] S.A. de Smith, "The Separation of Powers in New Dress" (1966) 12 McGill L.J. 491.

[179] The Sovereign, for example, is part of the legislature, the executive and the judiciary, if only in a formal sense; the government is drawn from Parliament; and, until October 2009, the most senior judges sat in the House of Lords.

[180] Something which the recent Government got a taste for: consider, for example, the general anti-avoidance rule contained in s.207 of the Finance Act 2013 which make financial arrangements "abusive" if they "exploit" "shortcomings" in the Act. So the Finance Act 2013 means not only what Parliament said, but what the Government would wish it had said when and if a loophole is found. As Greenberg explains, this is a very serious blurring of the separation of powers as between the three institutions of the state and one which was introduced without any constitutional complaints: D. Greenberg, "Dangerous Trends in Modern Legislation" [2015] P.L. 96, 100–103 (the article rewards consideration in full).

[181] It is almost inconceivable that it will ever be used again, certainly since the decision of the European Court of Human Rights in *Demicoli v Malta* (1991) 14 E.H.R.R. 47. There, a journalist had been convicted of a breach of parliamentary privilege for criticising MPs by a tribunal numbering amongst its membership two of the MPs named in his article. The court held that his rights to a fair trial under art.6 had been violated. See also *R. v Chaytor (David)* [2010] UKSC 52; [2011] 1 A.C. 684 for a discussion of the House of Commons penal jurisdiction.

[182] Although review by the courts of tribunal decisions is increasingly restricted: *Eba v Advocate General for Scotland* [2011] UKSC 29; 2012 S.C. (U.K.S.C.) 1; *R. (on the application of Cart) v Upper Tribunal* [2011] UKSC 28; [2012] 1 A.C. 663.

[183] *Duport Steels Ltd v Sirs* [1980] 1 W.L.R. 142 at 157.

Again in *Secretary of State for the Home Department v Rehman*, where the question was whether and to what extent the Special Immigration Appeals Committee could question the Home Secretary's decision that a person's deportation was "in the interests of national security", Lord Hoffmann held:

> "However broad the jurisdiction of a court or tribunal, whether at first instance or on appeal, it is exercising a judicial function and the exercise of that function must recognise the constitutional boundaries between judicial, executive and legislative power. Secondly ... limitations on the appellate process ... arise from the need, in matters of judgment and evaluation of evidence, to show proper deference to the primary decision-maker."[184]

Similarly in Belmarsh, on the question whether there existed "a public emergency threatening the life of the nation" so as to entitle the government to derogate from the United Kingdom's obligations under the European Convention on Human Rights, the majority of the House of Lords accepted that this was an issue calling for the exercise of "pre-eminently political judgment", in consequence of which great (if not overriding) weight was to be attached to the views of executive and legislature.[185]

Invocation of the separation of powers does not always involve judicial **3–28** restraint. The Privy Council has on a number of occasions struck down retrospective criminal legislation or legislation transferring sentencing powers to the executive as unconstitutional usurpations of the judicial function,[186] and separation of powers thinking may be said to inform decisions such as *Commissioners of Customs and Excise v Cure & Deeley Ltd*,[187] where the Court of Appeal declined to interpret a statute so as to permit an administrative authority to make the final decision on a person's liability to tax. More broadly, it is notable how often the separation of powers crops up as a tool of criticism of aspects of constitutional practice. The Franks Report in 1957, and the concerns that prompted the establishment of the Committee on Administrative Tribunals and Inquiries, may be seen as a powerful vindication of the continuing relevance of the reasoning underpinning the separation of powers doctrine.[188] To speak of one institution of the state "usurping" the functions of another is pejorative, and reflects a sense of offence to the proper order of things. As with the rule of law, then, it is possible to load too much weight on to the doctrine of the separation of powers. But the ideas are interconnected in our modern constitution. As Lord Phillips explained *R. (on the application of Cart) v Upper Tribunal*:

> "The administration of justice and upholding of the rule of law involves a partnership between Parliament and the judges. Parliament has to provide the resources needed for the administration of justice. ... Parliament has not

---

[184] *Secretary of State for the Home Department v Rehman* [2001] UKHL 47; [2003] 1 A.C. 153 at [49].

[185] *A v Secretary of State for the Home Department* [2004] UKHL 56; [2005] 2 A.C. 68, per Lord Bingham of Cornhill at [29]; Lord Hoffmann dissented on that point at [95]–[97].

[186] See, e.g. *Liyanage v The Queen* [1967] 1 A.C. 259 PC (Ceylon) and *Hinds v The Queen* [1977] A.C. 195 PC (Jamaica).

[187] *Commissioners of Customs and Excise v Cure & Deeley Ltd* [1962] 1 Q.B. 340.

[188] As may the earlier report of the Donoughmore Committee on Ministers' powers, which reported in 1929 and which was set up to consider whether the increasing use of delegated legislative power required to be checked. The committee concluded that it did not, subject to appropriate safeguards to prevent abuse.

sought to oust or fetter the common law powers of judicial review of the judges of the High Court and I hope that Parliament will never do so. It should be for the judges to decide whether the statutory provisions for the administration of justice adequately protect the rule of law and, by judicial review, to supplement these should it be necessary. But, in exercising the power of judicial review, the judges must pay due regard to the fact that, even where the due administration of justice is at stake, resources are limited."[189]

In that passage, Lord Phillips captures the need for institutional respect between the organs of the state and a need that each respects the competences of the other. Whilst the United Kingdom may not have the formal, and strict, separation of powers that can be found in countries such as the United States, the idea remains an important element of our constitution.

As ever, the tide ebbs and flows. Recently, the courts have been more willing to review areas which may previously have been thought to be "off limits". For example, in *Belhaj v Straw* the claimants sought to challenge the alleged "rendition" and subsequent mistreatment in which the UK Government was said to have been complicit.[190] Pleas that the action be dismissed on account of state immunity and the "act of state" doctrine were rejected by the Court of Appeal:

" ... the stark reality is that unless the English courts are able to exercise jurisdiction in this case, these very grave allegations against the executive will never be subjected to judicial investigations ... there is ... no alternative international forum with jurisdiction over these issues. As a result, these very grave allegations would go uninvestigated and the appellants would be left without any legal recourse or remedy."[191]

Here we see the Court of Appeal, although not expressly, balancing the rule of law (the need for the executive to be held to account) and the separation of powers (the court respecting its proper constitutional function). As we shall see in Ch.13, below, it is often cases involving terrorism, and the response to its threat, that tests each of the fundamental principles of the constitution.[192]

3–29 Going forward, it may be argued that the tripartite division of powers, and indeed the whole focus of the doctrine on the state, no longer provides an accurate or adequate picture of a constitution. This is not to abandon the doctrine, but to seek to strengthen it: the separation of powers in the modern age is as much concerned with the proper allocation of competence between national and supranational institutions, or between separate legislatures, as it is with the balance between legislature and executive, or legislature and the courts.[193] On this view, the separation of powers, properly understood, aims not only to

[189] *R. (on the application of Cart) v Upper Tribunal* [2011] UKSC 28; [2012] 1 A.C. 663 at [89].
[190] *Belhaj v Straw* [2014] EWCA Civ 1394; [2015] 2 W.L.R. 1105.
[191] *Belhaj v Straw* [2014] EWCA Civ 1394; [2015] 2 W.L.R. 1105 at [119].
[192] For a general discussion of the issues surrounding the courts approach to respecting its proper constitutional function, see A. Paterson, *Final Judgment* (Oxford: Hart, 2013) Ch.7.
[193] Barber, "Prelude to the separation of powers" (2001) 60(1) C.L.J. 59.

safeguard individual liberty, but also to secure efficiency in government, in the sense that a given function should be allocated to the institution best fitted to discharge it.[194] In that regard, the separation of powers doctrine may acquire added significance as the devolution settlement beds down and questions are raised about the balance of competences it presently enshrines.

---

[194] Barber, "Prelude to the separation of powers" (2001) 60(1) C.L.J. 59, under reference to John Locke, James Madison (The Federalist Papers, No.47) and the decision of the Supreme Court in *Myers v United States* (1926) 272 U.S. 52.

Chapter 4

ELECTIONS

Introduction

4–01 In a democratic society, a number of basic decisions have to be made about how the holders of elected office are to be chosen: by what system will a candidate be elected; who will be entitled to vote in any election; who will be entitled to stand as a candidate; how frequently shall an election be held; how is any election campaign to be funded and conducted. The United Kingdom is under an obligation, in terms of art.3 of the First Protocol to the European Convention on Human Rights:

> "to hold free elections at reasonable intervals by secret ballot, under conditions which will ensure the free expression of the opinion of the people in the choice of the legislature".

The substantive content of that right is a matter that has proved controversial and we shall return to it later. But there is a universal consensus that elections be by secret ballot and regular meetings of Parliament pre-date (by centuries) the modern concept of democracy but the principle endures.[1] There is a general consensus that all those above a certain age (and who are not subject to a legal disability) be entitled to vote although there is disagreement around the edges: what should the age at which an individual becomes eligible to vote be (16 or 18?) and should criminals serving a prison sentence be automatically disenfranchised? The former arose from the Scottish independence referendum, where the voting age was 16 and there will soon be different voting ages for Scottish and UK parliamentary elections.[2] The latter arises from a series of court

---

[1] Meeting of Parliament Act 1694 s.2 required that Parliament be summoned afresh every three years. The Septennial Act 1715 extended that period (as the name suggests) to seven years only for it to be shorted to five years by the Parliament Act 1911 s.7. These were minimum requirements. The Fixed-term Parliaments Act 2011 now specifies the precise date on which the general election will be held and, as a consequence, prescribes the length of Parliament (now fixed at five years). On the 2011 Act, see para.6–02, below. On some of the technical legalities surrounding summoning a new Parliament, see O. Gay and B.K. Winetrobe, "Putting out the Writs" [1997] P.L. 385.

[2] See the Smith Commission proposals, adopted by the UK Government, that the Scottish Parliament be empowered to determine the franchise, including the voting age, for Scottish Parliamentary elections; HM Government, *Scotland in the United Kingdom: An enduring settlement* (The Stationery Office, 2015) Cm.8990. A s.30 order (Scotland Act 1998 (Modification of Schedules 4 and 5 and Transfer of Functions to the Scottish Ministers etc.) Order 2015 (SI 2015/692)) has already been made to transfer competence to determine the voting age. The Scottish Elections (Reduction of Voting Age) Bill 2015 has been passed by the Scottish Parliament and awaits Royal Assent.

decisions to the effect that art.3 of the First Protocol prohibits the automatic disenfranchisement of serving prisoners.[3] Both are discussed more fully below. The idea of free, fair and regular elections is easy to state but the devil, as all too often is the case, lurks in the detail. Political interest in reforming electoral law is normally inversely proportionate to the ability to do anything about it.[4] That is perhaps unsurprising, given the prevailing system will have produced the election of those holding power. But the result is a rather patchwork electoral law, based largely on Victorian laws, which is often confusing for both the electorate and those seeking election.[5] Until recently, one saving grace was that electoral law was largely reserved and thus while the electoral systems employed varied, the regulatory framework was broadly consistent throughout the United Kingdom. That may now change with the Scottish Parliament set to gain control of the rules governing elections to that body.[6]

In this chapter we will consider the following topics. First, we will look at electoral systems. Voters in Scotland currently use four different systems depending on which representatives they are being asked to elect. Next, we will consider the question of the franchise: who is entitled to vote? Thirdly, we will consider the rules on candidacy and who is entitled to seek election. Finally, we will review the regulations governing the funding and conduct of election campaigns. Each of those topics are concerned with "representative democracy": the selection by the electorate of individuals to take collective decisions on their behalf. Until recently, the United Kingdom could safely be described as a representative democracy. There has, however, been a recent growth in "direct democracy": the use of the referendum to canvass the opinion of the electorate on a particular question. The increasing resort to direct democracy in the United Kingdom, its interrelationship with representative democracy and its consequences for the constitution are considered in the next chapter. But before that, and before considering the detail of the UK's electoral arrangements, it is helpful to briefly consider what we mean by a "representative democracy".

The House of Commons, the Scottish Parliament and the various other elected **4–02** assemblies comprise of members who have been elected to represent a certain section of the population. The section they represent is invariable determined on a geographical basis. But what is the role of these representatives? There are two competing theories.[7] On the one hand these representatives can be seen as a

---

[3] *Hirst v United Kingdom* (2005) 42 E.H.R.R. 41; *Smith v Scott* [2007] CSIH 9; 2007 S.C. 345; *R. (on the application of Chester) v Secretary of State for Justice* [2013] UKSC 63; 2014 S.C. (U.K.S.C.) 25; [2014] A.C. 271; *McHugh v United Kingdom* (51987/08), *The Times*, 12 February 2015. This line of authority is more fully discussed below at paras 4–11—4–13, above.

[4] Independent Commission on the Voting System, *Report of the Independent Commission on the Voting System* (The Stationery Office, 1998) Cm.4090–I, para.23.

[5] A joint consultation was launched by the Law Commission, the Scottish Law Commission and the Northern Ireland Law Commission in December 2014 having reviewed electoral law with a view to bringing forward proposals for reform to rationalise the law and ensure it was fit for modern times. The Commissions are due to report in the summer of 2015. The consultation paper is available at *http://lawcommission.justice.gov.uk/docs/cp218_electoral_law.pdf* [Accessed 4 June 2015].

[6] HM Government, *Scotland in the United Kingdom: An enduring settlement*, paras 1.4.1 to 1.4.13. See para.1–12.

[7] What follows is a brief overview. This issue is more fully discussed in C. Morris, *Parliamentary Elections, Representation and the Law* (Oxford: Hart, 2012) Ch.2.

delegate sent by their constituents to represent the views of those constituents. This requires the representative to ascertain or understand their constituents' views on a particular matter and to vote in accordance with those views. In short, they should reflect the wishes of their constituents. On the other hand, there is the "trustee" theory. A representative is not elected to simply advocate the local interests of the area they represent and to do as their constituents would wish. Once elected they are to act in the national interest. They cannot be bound by the views of their constituents because they have not participated in the debates and do not have regard to the "bigger picture". What is represented is not the people of the constituency but their interests. Which theory prevails? In the UK, the answer is neither. Members of Parliament are expected to advocate local causes where appropriate but equally are not expected to be bound by local views when they come to cast their vote. The party system, and the whipping of the vote, does not allow for that. The answer probably depends on the circumstance. Ordinarily representatives act as "trustee" and their constituents are quite content that they exercise their own judgment and vote as they see fit.[8] But some matters are of greater concern to constituents. Issues which would have a direct (and normally negative) impact on the constituency are issues on which constituents will expect their representative to have regard to their views and, in some circumstances, vote in accordance with their wishes. Bearing in mind that any representative requires his mandate to be renewed by his constituents, ignoring their wishes on such issues can prove (politically) fatal.

ELECTORAL SYSTEMS

Introduction

4–03 Different systems are used to elected representatives for different bodies. In Scotland, four different systems are used: first past the post for elections to the UK Parliament; the additional member system for elections to the Scottish Parliament; the regional list system for elections to the European Parliament; and the single transferrable vote for local government elections in Scotland.

UK Parliament

4–04 Elections to the UK Parliament are conducted under the first past the post system (which is also referred to as the plurality system). It is a system that is also used in Canada and the United States but otherwise eschewed by the most of the democratic world. It requires the electoral area (in the case of elections to Westminster, the entire UK) to be divided into a number of constituencies.[9] There are currently 650 constituencies: this figure is to be reduced to 600 in time for the

---

[8] Their MP will, after all, have ordinarily been standing under the banner of a political party and that party's election manifesto will have given voters a fair idea as to how their MP would vote on a range of issues.

[9] Provision for which is made by the Parliamentary Constituencies Act 1986 (which was a consolidation of pre-existing legislation on the matter, namely the House of Commons (Redistribution of Seats) Acts 1949 to 1979).

2020 election.[10] Each of these constituencies should be broadly the same size.[11] A single Member of Parliament is then returned by the electorate of each constituency. The greatest virtue of the first past the post system is its simplicity: the winner is the person who gets the most votes. There is no need to receive a majority of the votes cast (never mind a majority of the voters in the constituency) but just one more vote than the nearest rival. In other words, the winner takes it all. Casting a vote under the first past the post system is also simple. All that a voter need do is place a cross against his or her preferred candidate. And counting the votes is also simple for each ballot paper should only have one cross on it, against one candidate. Any ballot paper that has more than a single cross will be discarded as spoilt and not counted. The simplicity of the count also makes the system relatively cheap to operate. Furthermore, the first past the post system is said to provide a strong link between the constituency and the MP: whether they voted for him or her or not, each voter knows who their designated representative in Parliament is. Finally, it is said that the first past the post system should produce a clear result and with it a "strong" government. That argument lost a degree of credibility following the outcome of the 2010 UK general election, which produced the Conservative-Liberal Democrat coalition government with no one party having achieved an overall majority in the House of Commons. 2010 was the first time since February 1974 that the result of the general election had not produced a government with an overall majority in the House of Commons. "Normality" (somewhat unexpectedly) resumed in 2015 with a majority government being returned.[12] But as we saw in Ch.1, above the 2015 election result raised other questions about the first past the post system.

If the first past the post system is so simply and relatively cheap to operate then why do so few countries employ it? Because the first past the post system comes at a price and that price is the translation of the electorates' votes into seats allocated to the various parties in the House of Commons. As Munro put it, "[the first past the post system] provides only a rough and ready translation of electors' wishes".[13] That might seem like a fairly fundamental flaw in the electoral system

---

[10] Parliamentary Constituencies Act 1986 Sch.2 para.1 requires that there be 600 constituencies. The number (600) was fixed by the Parliamentary Voting and Constituencies Act 2011 s.11(1). Prior to that amendment, the 1986 Act required the number of constituencies to "not be substantially greater than" 613, no fewer than 35 of which should be Welsh and between 16 and 18 (and ordinarily 17) of which should be in Northern Ireland. The requirement that there be not fewer than 71 Scottish constituencies was removed by the Scotland Act 1998 (Sch.9 para.1). Prior to the establishment of the Scottish Parliament Scotland had been proportionately over-represented and the advent of devolution was regarded as the right time to equalise representation throughout Great Britain. The reduction to 600 MPs was due to come into effect in time for the 2015 general election. However, in January 2013 Parliament voted to defer the necessary boundary review until October 2018 with the effect that there will remain 650 MPs until the 2020 general election (Electoral Registration and Administration Act 2013 s.6).

[11] Parliamentary Constituencies Act 1986 Sch.2 para.2 requires that the electorate in any constituency shall be no less than 95%, and no more than 105%, of the United Kingdom electoral quota. The "United Kingdom electoral quota" is the total electorate of the United Kingdom (excluding the Isle of Wright (which shall have two constituencies), Orkney and Shetland (which shall be one constituency) and Comhairle nan Eliean Siar (which shall also be a single constituency) on account of their particular geographical locations: Sch.2 para.6) divided by 596.

[12] V. Bogdanor, *The Coalition and the Constitution* (Oxford: Hart, 2011) pp.123–127.

[13] C.R. Munro, *Studies in Constitutional Law*, 2nd edn (London: Butterworths, 1999) p.107.

of a representative democracy. What does Munro mean? That is best explained by considering a number of recent election results and the number of seats won by each of the three main parties.

Table 1: Share of the vote and seats in House of Commons (1983–2015)

	2001		2005		2010		2015	
	% vote	Seats (%)	% vote	Seats (%)	% vote	Seats (%)	% vote	Seats (%)
Con	31.7	166 (25.2)	32.3	197 (30.5)	36.1	306 (47.7)	36.9	331 (50.9)
Lab	40.7	412 (62.5)	35.2	356 (55.1)	29.0	258 (40.2)	30.4	232 (35.7)
Lib Dem	18.3	52 (7.9)	22.1	62 (9.6)	23.0	57 (8.9)	7.9	8 (1.2)
Other	9.3	29 (4.4)	10.4	31 (4.8)	5.9	20 (3.1)	24.8	78 (12)

	1983[14]		1987		1992		1997	
	% vote	Seats (%)	% vote	Seats (%)	% vote	Seats (%)	% vote	Seats (%)
Con	42.4	397 (61.1)	42.2	375 (57.5)	41.9	336 (51.6)	30.7	165 (25.0)
Lab	27.6	209 (32.2)	30.8	229 (35.1)	34.4	271 (41.6)	43.2	418 (63.4)
Lib Dem	25.4	23 (3.5)	22.6	22 (3.4)	17.8	20 (3.1)	16.8	46 (7.0)
Others	4.6	21 (3.2)	4.4	26 (4.0)	5.8	24 (3.7)	9.3	30 (4.6)

The first past the post system favours a two party system. As a consequence, the third party (and other smaller parties) is significantly disadvantaged.[15] To succeed under the first past the post system a political party requires to have concentrated support in a number of constituencies rather than a moderate, across the board, support. For it does not matter that a party comes second, or a close third, by a narrow margin in dozens of seats as that will not translate into seats. To win a seat, a candidate need only poll one more vote than any of the others. With that comes absolutely victory in that constituency. The problems caused by the potentially unrepresentative outcomes produced by the first past the post system were easily overlooked when the two main parties (Conservatives and

---

[14] The Liberal Democrats were then in the form of the Liberal/SDP Alliance (as they were again in 1987).

[15] The 2015 result altered that traditional narrative slightly. The SNP are now the "third party" in the House of Commons and far from being disadvantaged by the first past the post system, it benefitted them significantly. But that was a result of the fact the SNP only contested seats in Scotland. Again, see the discussion of the 2015 election in Ch.1, above.

Labour) dominated: between 1931 and 1970, on average they received over 90
per cent of the vote between them. That is no longer the case. In 2015, more than
a third of the votes were for parties other than the two main parties. As can be
seen from Table 1, this was not a new issue. The Liberal Democrats (or their
previous incarnations) have regularly received a much smaller allocation of the
seats in the House of Commons than their share of the vote would suggest was
fair. The result of the 1983 election remains, over 30 years on, one of the best
examples of the deficiencies in the first past the post system: Labour and the
Liberals received 27.6 per cent and 25.4 per cent of the vote respectively but the
first past the post system translated that into 209 seats for Labour and 23 seat for
the Liberals. The 1983 election is not an isolated example. In 1992, despite
polling just under 18 per cent of the vote, the Liberals won only 3 per cent of the
seats. Five years later, their share of the vote fell by 1 per cent but their share of
the seats in the House of Commons more than doubled. Little had changed by
2010 when the Liberal Democrats received 23 per cent of the vote, only 6 per
cent less than Labour but that translated into to 8.9 per cent of the seats for the
Liberal Democrats but 40.2 per cent of the seats for Labour (not too dissimilar
from 1983!). Lest it be thought that the first past the post system only
disadvantages the smaller parties, Labour and the Conservatives could have
cause to grumble. For example, compare the Conservative result in the 2010
election (36.1 per cent of the vote yielding 306 seats) with the Labour result in
2005 (35.2 per cent of the vote yielding 356 seats). Nonetheless, it is little
wonder that the Liberal movement have advocated reform of the electoral system
for more than a century.[16]

It was a condition of the coalition agreement that was forged by the **4–05**
Conservatives and the Liberal Democrats in May 2010 that a referendum be held
on changing the voting system for elections to the House of Commons.[17]
Securing electoral change was a long held ambition of the Liberal Democrats.
Alternatives to the first past the post system were studied in exhaustive detail by
the independent commission appointed after the 1997 general election under the
chairmanship of the late Lord Jenkins. The commission recommended that the
first past the post system be replaced by a two vote mixed system, described in
the Jenkins Report as "limited AMS" or "AV top-up". "AMS" stands for the
additional member system of voting.[18] As the name implies, it is not a system
which operates alone; its object, rather, is to mitigate the unfairness involved in
a strictly majoritarian system. In effect, at any election involving the additional
member system, there are two types of candidate: the constituency candidates,
elected by the first past the post system or some similar method, and the
additional or top up candidates, elected in accordance with proportional
representation. "AV" stands for the alternative vote system. It works on the basis
of single member constituencies in the same way as the first past the post system.
It differs from the first past the post system in that the voter does not simply cast
his vote for his preferred candidate, but ranks the candidates listed on his ballot

---

[16] The first past the post system survived a challenge that is was incompatible with art.3 of the First
Protocol to the European Convention on Human Rights (read with art.14): *Liberal Party v United
Kingdom* (1980) 4 E.H.R.R. 106.
[17] See Bogdanor, *The Coalition and the Constitution* (2011) Ch.5.
[18] As we shall see, this forms part of the system adopted for elections to the Scottish Parliament.

paper in order of preference. If one candidate wins 50 per cent or more of the first preference votes, that candidate is elected to represent the constituency. Failing that, the candidate receiving the lowest number of first preferences is eliminated and his supporters' second preferences are redistributed. The process of elimination and redistribution continues until one candidate secures an overall majority of votes by comparison to the others.[19] But this is to use the word "majority" in the loosest sense: the alternative vote system may produce results even less representative of voter preferences than the first past the post system. The Jenkins Commission itself recognised that the alternative vote system unmitigated by a second, more proportionate method of voting, would not constitute an acceptable alternative to first past the post. Hence its recommendation for a combination of the alternative vote and additional member systems, whereby some four-fifths of MPs would be elected on the basis of single member constituencies, but using the alternative vote system rather than the first past the post system, with the remaining top up members being elected on a second vote based on regional lists. The alternative vote top up was not, however, the alternative to the first past the post system that the electorate were offered in the 2011 referendum.[20] What was offered was the alternative vote system: the system rejected by the Jenkins Commission and derided by the Liberal Democrats themselves. The alternative vote system did not offer proportionate representation thus it did not address the fundamental concern of many of those that advocated electoral reform. The electorate were presented with a choice between the first past the post system and the alternative vote system. The choice did not engender much enthusiasm amongst voters with a turnout of only 42.2 per cent (dropping as low as 27.2 per cent in one area). Those that did vote were fairly emphatic with 67.9 per cent voting "no". Thus the first past the post survived, warts and all, and the prospect of electoral reform in relation to the House of Commons appeared to have retreated to the very distant horizon.

That was until 2015 general election result, which threatens to return it to the fore much earlier than anyone could have expected. As we have seen, the disparities thrown up by the first past the post system were again highlighted, not so much as between the main two parties but as between the fortunes of the other parties. In Scotland, the Scottish National Party ("SNP") secured 95 per cent of the seats on 50 per cent of the votes cast. Whereas the United Kingdom Independence Party ("UKIP") won a single seat, in return for securing just under 3.9 million votes—more than double the votes cast for the SNP and nearly 1.5 million votes more than the Liberal Democrats (who won eight seats). Similarly,

---

[19] The alternative vote system was recommended for use in county constituencies by an all-party Speaker's Conference in 1917; and in 1931, a Bill providing for the adoption of the system was actually passed by the House of Commons. The Bill was rejected by the House of Lords and nothing more was heard of it after the fall of the second Labour Government later that year.
[20] The referendum was enabled by the Parliamentary Voting System and Constituencies Act 2011. That Act provided that the Minister "must" make an order bringing into force the provisions that would have introduced the alternative vote system in the event that more votes were cast for "yes" than "no" in the referendum (s.8(1)). Any by-election during the term of the 2010–2015 would have been conducted under the first past the post system with the alternative vote system being introduced for the 2015 general election (s.8(3)). In the event, there were more "no" votes than "yes" and accordingly the relevant provisions of the 2011 Act have now been repealed (s.8(2); Parliamentary Voting System and Constituencies Act 2011 (Repeal of Alternative Vote Provisions) Order 2011 (SI 2011/1702)).

the Green Party polled 1.1 million votes and won a single seat. Unsurprisingly, there were complaints about the first past the post system in the aftermath of the election. If there is to be another attempt at change for the electoral system for the House of Commons, that is likely to require a further referendum.[21] It is noteworthy, however, that when the House of Commons has had to choose an electoral system for other bodies, it has invariably chosen some form of proportionate representation.

Scottish Parliament

Voters in the Scottish Parliamentary elections require to cast two votes: one for **4–06** a constituency MSP and one for a "regional" MSP. Constituency MSP's are elected using the first past the post system (styled the "simple majority system" in the Scotland Act 1998) while "regional" MSP's are elected using the additional member system of proportionate representation.[22] There are 73 single member constituencies for the Scottish Parliament.[23] There are eight "regions", each returning seven MSPs.[24] Accordingly, there are 129 MSPs in total. Candidates may stand as both a constituency candidate and a regional candidate in the same election.[25] But a candidate may only stand for election in one constituency[26] and in one region.[27] So far as the regions are concerned, a registered political party[28] may list up to 12 candidates in each region but the list may include only one person.[29] The purpose of the regional members, and allocating those seats under a system of proportionate representation, is to ameliorate the effects of the first past the post system. The consequence should be a parliament that is more representative of the votes actually cast. As Table 2 shows, the electoral system has been fairly successful in this respect.

---

[21] See para.5–06, below.
[22] Scotland Act 1998 s.1(2) and (3).
[23] Scotland Act 1998 Sch.1 para.1. The Scotland Act originally provided that the constituencies for the Scottish Parliament would be the same as those for the UK Parliament (save for Orkney and Shetland being split into separate constituencies for the purposes of the Scottish Parliament). However, when Scottish representation was reduced at Westminster it was not thought appropriate to reduce the number of MSPs. Accordingly, the Scotland Act was amended by the Scottish Parliament (Constituencies) Act 2004 and the number of constituencies is now a matter regulated by Order in Council (Sch.1 para.6). The matter is currently regulated by the Scottish Parliament (Constituencies and Regions) Order 2014 (SI 2014/501) Sch.1). The size of each constituency should be as near the "electoral quota" as is "practicable" (Scotland Act 1998 Sch.1 para.12 r.2(1)). The "electoral quota" is the total electorate divided by 71 (Scotland Act 1998 Sch.1 para.12 r.2(3)). It should be noted that determination of constituencies of the Scottish Parliament is presently a reserved matter (Scotland Act 1998 Sch.4 para.4) but the Smith Commission recently proposed that this matter be devolved.
[24] The current regions are: Central Scotland, Glasgow, Highlands and Islands, Lothian, Mid Scotland and Fife, North East Scotland, South Scotland and West Scotland (Scottish Parliament (Constituencies and Regions) Order 2014 (SI 2014/501) Sch.2). Each region consists of specific constituencies, which are listed in the 2014 Order. The electorate in each region should, as far as is "practicable", be the same (Scotland Act 1998 Sch.1 para.13 r.2).
[25] Scotland Act 1998 s.5(1).
[26] Scotland Act 1998 s.5(2).
[27] Scotland Act 1998 s.5(8).
[28] As defined as Pt II of the Political Parties, Elections and Referendums Act 2000 ("PPERA") (Scotland Act 1998 s.5(9)). The (legal) concept of a political party was first introduced by the Registration of Political Parties Act 1998.
[29] Scotland Act 1998 s.5(6).

Table 2: Results of General Elections to the Scottish Parliament (2003-2011)[30]

Party/Year	Constituency		Regional		
2003	% vote	Seats (%)	% vote	Seats (%)	Total Seats (%)
Lab	34.6	46 (63.0)	29.3	4	50 (38.8)
SNP	23.8	9	20.9	18	27 (20.9)
Lib Dem	15.4	13	11.8	4	17 (13.2)
Con	16.6	3	15.5	15	18 (14.0)
Other	7.7	2	16.5	15	17 (13.2)
2007	% vote	Seats (%)	% vote	Seats (%)	Total Seats (%)
Lab	32.1	37 (50.1)	29.1	9 (16.1)	46 (35.7)
SNP	32.9	21 (28.9)	31.0	26 (46.4)	47 (36.4)
Lib Dem	16.2	11 (15.1)	11.3	5 (8.9)	16 (12.4)
Con	16.6	4 (5.5)	13.9	13 (23.2)	17 (13.2)
Other	0.2%	0 (0%)	8.9%	3 (5.4%)	3 (2.4%)
2011	% vote	Seats (%)	% vote	Seats (%)	Total Seats (%)
Lab	31.7	15 (20.5)	26.3	22 (39.3)	37 (28.7)
SNP	45.4	53 (72.6)	44.0	16 (28.6)	69 (53.5)
Lib Dem	7.9	2 (2.7)	5.2	3 (5.4)	5 (3.9)
Con	13.9	3 (4.1)	12.4	12 (21.4)	15 (11.6)
Other	1.1	0 (0)	12.1	3 (5.4)	3 (2.3)

In 2007, as a result of the additional member system, the result of the election was altered: on the first past the post votes alone, Labour would have had a

---

[30] Source, Scottish Parliament, "Election Results", *http://www.scottish.parliament.uk/msps/election-results.aspx* [Accessed 4 June 2015].

majority in the Scottish Parliament of a single seat, having won 37 of the 73 constituencies on offer. However, once the regional members were added, the SNP became the largest party, albeit without an overall majority, and proceeded to govern as a minority administration. The 2011 election also provides a good example of the effects of the additional member system. On first past the post votes the SNP won a landslide, securing almost three-quarters of the seats but on only 45 per cent of the vote. The final result, however, still handed the SNP more seats than a strictly proportionate allocation would have afforded them (69 or 53.5 per cent) and allowed them to govern this time as a majority government. But they governed not with the overwhelming majority they would have achieved under the first past the post system. The 2003 election saw a similar correction of a first past the post landslide: this time reducing Labour's 63 per cent of the constituency seats to only 39 per cent of the total number of seats and thus compelling them to govern in coalition with the Liberal Democrats. So in securing a more representative result, and in avoiding one party governing as a result of the grossly exaggerated allocation of seats, the combination of the first past the post system with the additional member system has served the Scottish Parliament reasonably well.

As is common with systems of proportionate representation, a common consequence is coalition or minority government. This was true of the Scottish Parliament until the 2011 election in which the SNP achieved the supposedly impossible: an absolute majority. There are good reasons why that was meant to be impossible and we will touch on those in a moment. But before that, it is necessary to explain how the regional seats are allocated under the additional member system.

The method of allocating the seven available regional seats in each region is **4–07** complex and will only be outlined here. Once the regional votes have been counted, each party and each individual candidate is allotted a "regional figure" calculated in accordance with a formula prescribed by s.7(2) of the Scotland Act 1998. The first regional seat is awarded to the party or individual candidate having the highest regional figure. Where a seat is awarded to a party in this way, it is then necessary, in order to maintain proportionality in the distribution of seats, to recalculate that party's regional figure. Again the arithmetic is prescribed by the Act. Each successive seat is awarded to the party or candidate having, on that particular round, the highest regional figure, until all seven seats are filled. If at any stage of the process, that figure is shared between two parties or between a party and an individual candidate, the Act provides that a regional seat shall be allocated to each. The use of party lists in the election of regional members obviates the need for by-elections should a regional seat fall vacant during the life of the Parliament: the regional returning officer will simply notify the Presiding Officer of the next named nominee in the appropriate party's regional list (no doubt having first ascertained that he or she is willing to serve). On purely practical grounds, the Scotland Act makes no provision for regional by-elections in other situations, as where a party's regional list is exhausted, or where a regional seat held by an individual candidate falls vacant. This has happened only once so far (following the death of Margo MacDonald MSP in April 2014). Having been elected as a regional MSP from a list that contained only her name, the seat remains vacant until the 2016 election. Constituency MSPs, however, are replaced during the life of the Parliament by means of a by-election. Where the seat of a constituency MSP falls vacant by reason of the death, disqualification or resignation of the incumbent, the Presiding Officer will appoint a date for a by-election to fill the vacancy unless such date would fall within three months of the date of the next ordinary general election. In that event, the seat will remain vacant until filled in the usual way.

4–08   It is worth pausing to reflect on why it was thought necessary to devise a system that produced a more proportionate result. Democratic claims cannot be enough. If they were, the continuing use of the first past the post system for the House of Commons would be indefensible. But an electoral system must also serve the institution it selects members for. The obvious difference between Holyrood and Westminster is the absence of a second chamber in Edinburgh. As discussed in more detail in Ch.6, the House of Lords acts as a form of handbrake on the House of Commons (dominated as it necessarily is by the executive): the executive can almost always prevail (using the Parliament Acts if necessary) but like driving a car with the handbrake on, forcing legislation through against the wishes of the House of Lords takes longer, makes more noise and risks causing significant damage. Had the Scottish Parliament been elected using only the first past the post system there was no equivalent "handbrake". Instead, the handbrake function is built in to the electoral system: by ensuring a more proportionate representation the chances of a single party having an overall majority are significantly reduced. That required the executive (where it lacked an overall majority) to either compromise when forming a coalition with one or more of the other parties or to govern as a minority administration and thus compromise on its legislative agenda. It was not expected that the electoral system adopted for the Scottish Parliament would produce a single party majority government. That made the 2011 election result all the more remarkable. For when there is a single party majority government at Holyrood, there is no effective "handbrake" function on the executive. That gives rise to obvious concerns (as discussed in Ch.3) in relation to the separation powers.

4–09   At the time of writing, most of the electoral law governing the Scottish Parliament is a reserved matter. The Smith Commission, set up shortly after the referendum, recommended that many of those powers be devolved. In January 2015 the UK Government published draft clauses to give effect to that (and other) recommendations.[31] Each of the three main political parties at Westminster are committed to enacting such legislation early in the life of the 2015–2020 Parliament. It is therefore helpful to discuss the changes these clauses would make. Under the proposals, the power to determine the franchise for elections to the Scottish Parliament, the electoral system that is used at those elections, the number of constituencies, the number of regions and the number of members each region shall return will be devolved to the Scottish Parliament. The proposals introduce the concept of a "super-majority" for the passage of certain legislation.[32] A "super-majority" requires a Bill to be passed either without division or with the number of members voting in favour being not less than two-thirds of the total number of seats in the Parliament. Any of the changes to the electoral system under the newly devolved powers must be passed under this procedure. In practice, the power is most likely to be used to reduce the voting age to 16 following the

[31] HM Government, *Scotland in the United Kingdom: An enduring settlement.*
[32] Clause 4 of the Draft Scotland Clauses 2015, annexed to the Command Paper, HM Government, *Scotland in the United Kingdom: An enduring settlement.* Clause 4 would insert at new s.30A into the Scotland Act 1998. That provision is discussed at para.6–17.

perceived success of enfranchising 16 and 17 year olds for the referendum. A
s.30 order to allow the Scottish Parliament to lower the voting age was made
by the Privy Council in March 2015.[33] A Bill to that effect has been passed
by the Scottish Parliament and is awaiting Royal Assent.[34]

European Parliament

Elections to the European Parliament are, in Great Britain, conducted under the **4–10**
regional list system.[35] This operates in much the same way as the second vote for
the Scottish Parliament. There are currently 73 MEPs elected in the United
Kingdom.[36] The United Kingdom is divided into a number of electoral regions:
Scotland, Wales and Northern Ireland each constitute a region and England and
Gibraltar is divided into nine regions.[37] The 73 seats in the European Parliament
are then divided between the regions. In the year before a European Parliamentary election, the Electoral Commission[38] must review the distribution of MEPs
between the regions and report to the Secretary of State. In carrying out that
review, the Commission must consider whether the ratio of electors to MEPs is
as nearly as possible the same for each region. If it is not, the Commission's
report to the Secretary of State must include a recommendation of a distribution
of seats that would achieve that result.[39] Under the current allocation, Scotland
returns six MEPs.[40]

On polling day, voters are presented with a ballot paper that lists each of the
political parties that are fielding candidates along with any independent candidates. It is a "closed list" system: the voter does not rank a party's candidates in
order of preference; they simply vote for their preferred party (or independent
candidate) and any seats are allocated in accordance with the order in which
candidates have been ranked by their party.[41] Once the votes have been tallied for
the region, seats are allocated using a quota system.[42] A party's "quota" is the
number of votes they have received divided by the number of seats they have
already received plus one. This is probably best illustrated with an example
rather than more words:

[33] The Scotland Act 1998 (Modification of Schedules 4 and 5 and Transfer of Functions to the Scottish Ministers etc.) Order 2015 (SI 2015/692).
[34] Scottish Elections (Reduction of Voting Age) Bill 2015.
[35] European Parliamentary Elections Act 2002 s.2. In Northern Ireland, the single transferrable vote system is employed: s.3 of the 2002 Act. That is the system employed in Scottish local government elections and is explained at para.3–10, below.
[36] That number has fluctuated as the size of the European Union has changed. When the 2002 Act was first enacted, the number was 87 but was most recently fixed by the European Union Act 2011 s.16(2).
[37] The regions are prescribed in Sch.1 to the 2002 Act. They currently are: East Midlands, Eastern, London, North East, North West, South East, South West (which includes Gibraltar), West Midlands and Yorkshire and the Humber.
[38] On which, see para.4–16.
[39] European Parliamentary Elections Act 2002 Sch.1A.
[40] European Parliamentary Elections Act 2002 s.1(3).
[41] European Parliamentary Elections Act 2002 s.2(8).
[42] European Parliamentary Elections Act 2002 s.2(5)–(7).

Table 3: allocation of seats under regional list system

	Region x; six seats to be allocated					
Party	**Seat 1**	**Seat 2**	**Seat 3**	**Seat 4**	**Seat 5**	**Seat 6**
A	250,000/1	250,000/1	250,000/2 125,000	250,000/2 125,000	250,000/2 125,000	250,000/2 125,000
B	450,000/1	450,000/2 225,000	450,000/2 225,000	450,000/3 150,000	450,000/3 150,000	450,000/4 112,500
C	100,000/1	100,000/1	100,000/1	100,000/1	100,000/1	100,000/1
D	175,000/1	175,000/1	175,000/1	175,000/1	175,000/2 87,500	175,000/2 87,500
	Party B	**Party A**	**Party B**	**Party D**	**Party B**	**Party A**

In that example, the final seat allocation is three for party B, two for party A and one for party D. In percentage terms, party B won 50 per cent of the seats, party A won 33.3 per cent of the seats and party D won 16.7 per cent of the seats. Their respective share of the vote was: party A 25.6 per cent, party B 46.2 per cent, party C 10.2 per cent and party D 17.9 per cent. So we can see that the regional list system also produces a broadly proportionate allocation of seats.

Local government

4–11 Finally, Scottish voters use another form of proportional representation when electing their local government representatives: the single transferrable vote. These were the only Scottish elections that were initially devolved to the Scottish Parliament and it was the Scottish Parliament that adopted the single transferrable vote under the Local Governance (Scotland) Act 2004. The single transferrable vote was first used at the local government elections in 2007. The single transferrable vote requires each local government area[43] to be divided into a number of wards. There is a separate election for each ward and each ward returns three or four councillors.[44] With the single transferrable vote the voter does not merely vote for one party or candidate, but expresses his preferences for the candidates in numerical order. The first candidate whose "first preference votes" meet a predetermined quota is awarded the first seat in the constituency.[45] His second (and subsequent) preference votes are then redistributed to the appropriate candidates until someone else achieves the quota figure. If no candidate meets the quota on the first round of counting, the candidate receiving the lowest number of first preferences is eliminated, with second and subsequent preferences being redistributed to other candidates as appropriate. The process continues until enough candidates have met the quota to fill the seats available in the constituency. Complex it may be, but it was adopted in Northern Ireland with the acknowledged aim of reducing the risk of the electorate splitting along sectarian lines and in practice has worked well there. It also appears to have

---

[43] A "local government area" is defined by the Local Government etc. (Scotland) Act 1994, which in its present form provides for Scotland to be subdivided into 32 local government areas.
[44] Local Governance (Scotland) Act 2004 s.1(2).
[45] That quota, and the allocation of seats, is prescribed by the Scottish Local Government Election Rules (Scottish Local Government Elections Order 2011 (SSI 2011/399) Sch.1 rr.47–53).

worked well in the two Scottish local government elections that have been held under it.[46]

THE FRANCHISE

The franchise (that is, who is entitled to vote) is determined by the Representa- **4–12** tion of the People Act 1983. That Act was itself a consolidation of the pre-existing law that dated back to Victorian times[47] but has been heavily amended, most recently (and most significantly) by the Political Parties, Elections and Referendums Act 2000. Critical to being entitled to vote is being registered to vote.[48] Entitlement to be registered depends (together with criteria relating to age, capacity and citizenship) on being resident in the constituency or electoral area on the "relevant date". Previously, the 1983 Act prescribed a single annual qualifying date[49] on which a person's residence fell to be tested. The 2000 Act amended s.4 of the 1983 Act so as to define the "relevant date" as the date on which an application for registration is made or, in the case of a person applying for registration pursuant to a declaration of local connection or a service declaration, the date on which the declaration was made. This "rolling system" allows a person to be entered on and removed from the electoral register at any time of year.

Sections 5 and 7 of the 1983 Act make provision as to the meaning of "residence" for the purposes of registration.[50] Patients resident in a mental hospital, whether on a voluntary or detained basis, are able either to register in respect of the hospital, if they are likely to be there some time; or to register at some other address (such as the address the patient would regard as their home address were they not in hospital). Alternatively, such patients may make a "declaration of local connection". Remand prisoners[51] may register at the

---

[46] The single transferable vote was recommended for adoption in the UK's urban constituencies by the 1917 Speaker's Conference, and was actually used in a number of the old multi-member university seats until their abolition in 1948. The principal objection to its adoption for Westminster elections, at least, was identified by the Independent Commission on the Voting System, *Report of the Independent Commission on the Voting System* in the following terms (para.94): "In Britain, with a population of 58.5 million as against Ireland's 3.5 million, the multi-member STV constituencies (unless there were to be a massive increase in the number of MPs, which the Commission regards as unacceptable) would need to be approximately four or five times as large as the Irish constituencies. This would make them geographically far-flung in rural or semi-rural areas, and, even in concentrated urban areas, constituencies of about 350,000 electors would entail a very long ballot paper and a degree of choice which might be deemed oppressive rather than liberating."

[47] The Representation of the People Act 1983 (1983 Act) is, according to its long title, a consolidation of the Representation of the People Acts of 1949, 1969, 1977, 1978 and 1980. The 1949 Act was again a consolidation of "certain enactments relating to parliamentary... elections" (according to its long title), the main such enactment being the Representation of the People Act 1867.

[48] Being registered to vote is also a precondition to being entitled to make a donation to a political party: see para.4–19, below.

[49] 10 October.

[50] Without prejudice to the case law which has accumulated on whether a person is resident in a constituency such as to be entitled to be registered to vote there, see, e.g. *Scott v Phillips*, 1974 S.L.T. 32; *Hipperson v Newbury District Electoral Registration Officer* [1985] Q.B. 1060 CA (Civ Div).

[51] For whom provision is made in the new s.7A of the 1983 Act, inserted by the Political Parties, Elections and Referendums Act 2000.

establishment where they are being held, at some other address or by means of a declaration of local connection. The position of convicted prisoners is controversial and is considered in a moment. Homeless persons who would not otherwise be able to satisfy a residence-based test may also make a declaration of local connection. Declarations of local connection must state the declarant's name, an address to which correspondence may be sent (or an undertaking to collect correspondence from the electoral registration office), the date of the declaration and a statement that the declarant falls into one of the categories permitted to make a declaration of local connection. They must also state that the declarant conforms to the nationality requirements and is 18 years of age or over (or, if not, his date of birth). Section 7 of the 2000 Act repeals and replaces s.12 of the 1983 Act, enabling service personnel to vote in the same way as other voters or as overseas electors as well as by way of a service declaration. Lastly, s.12 of and Sch.4 to the 2000 Act make significant changes to the rules relating to absent voting (voting by post or by proxy) at parliamentary or local government elections, including local elections in Scotland.

4–13   The scope of the franchise is largely uncontroversial, save for the blanket exclusion of convicted prisoners. That matter has attracted significant judicial attention in recent years. The 1983 Act deprives any person who has been convicted of a criminal offence and who is serving a prison sentence (irrespective of length) of the right to vote.[52] To that extent, the 1983 Act is incompatible with art.3 of the First Protocol to the European Convention on Human Rights and a declaration to that effect was first made by the (Scottish) Electoral Registration Court in 2007.[53] The Grand Chamber of the European Court of Human Rights has declined to change its stance on the correct interpretation of art.3 of the First Protocol.[54] The Supreme Court has accepted the Grand Chamber's interpretation.[55] That has not been an end of the matter. Parliament had not remedied the incompatibility. Indeed, it has specifically refused to do so.[56] The saga of the right of prisoners to vote is considered in more detail in Ch.11 in the context of the Human Rights Act 1998 and the limits of a declaration of incompatibility.[57] For present purposes, it is sufficient to note that it is acceptable, in terms of art.3 of the First Protocol for some convicted prisoners to be disenfranchised as a result of their imprisonment; but such disenfranchisement must be proportionate; a blanket ban on serving prisoners voting in an election is not proportionate and is incompatible with art.3 of the First Protocol; there is a clear and consistent line of authority from the Grand Chamber to that effect; that line of authority has been accepted (although to some extent reluctantly) by the Supreme Court; s.3 of the

---

[52] See s.3 of the 1983 Act.
[53] *Smith v Scott* [2007] CSIH 9; 2007 S.C. 345. The matter was most recently considered by the Supreme Court in *R. (on the application of Chester) v Secretary of State for Justice* [2013] UKSC 63; 2014 S.C. (U.K.S.C.) 25; [2014] A.C. 271. Interestingly, as is discussed in the following chapter, art.3 of the First Protocol to the European Convention was not infringed by the blanket disenfranchisement of serving prisoners for the Scottish independence referendum: *Moohan, Petitioner* [2014] UKSC 67; 2015 S.L.T. 2 (a point on which the Supreme Court split 5:2).
[54] *Hirst v United Kingdom* (2005) 42 E.H.R.R. 41; *Scoppola v Italy* (2012) 56 E.H.R.R. 19.
[55] *R. (on the application of Chester) v Secretary of State for Justice* [2013] UKSC 63; 2014 S.C. (U.K.S.C.) 25; [2014] A.C. 271, where it was made clear (albeit with some reluctance on the part of several justices) that the European Court's jurisprudence on art.3 of the First Protocol stands.
[56] There are arguments both ways, as Laws LJ explained in *R. (on the application of Chester) v Secretary of State for Justice* [2010] EWCA Civ 1439; [2011] 1 W.L.R. 1436 at [32]–[34].
[57] See para.11–13.

1983 Act is therefore incompatible with art.3 of the First Protocol; but it is for Parliament to address the issue as it is not possible to read the offending section in such a way as to remedy the incompatibility. Despite the UK being required, as a matter of international law, to amend the 1983 Act so as to address the incompatibility, there is (perhaps understandably) little political enthusiasm for enfranchising even a proportion of the prison population. Those prisoners that were disenfranchised at the 2010 UK general election, and who complained to the Strasbourg Court, had their complaint that their right under art.3 of the First Protocol had been infringed upheld but were refused any financial compensation.[58] At the time of writing, eight years after the declaration of incompatibility in *Smith v Scott*, the blanket disenfranchisement of serving prisoners remains in place.

CANDIDATES FOR ELECTION

There are relatively few rules on who may stand as a candidate for election to the **4–14** House of Commons. Statute does not positively define who may be a candidate.[59] Instead, a person may stand as a candidate for election provided they do not fall within any of the prescribed exclusions. "Aliens" (persons who are neither Commonwealth citizens nor British protected person nor a citizen of the Republic of Ireland)[60] are not eligible to be members of Parliament.[61] A candidate must have attained the age of 18 on the day they are nominated.[62] Mental illness is no longer a bar to membership of the House of Commons.[63] Peers that have a seat in the House of Lords cannot be a member of the House of Commons but those hereditary peers who are excluded in terms of the House of Lords Act 1999 may now be a member of the House of Commons.[64] The House of Lords Reform Act 2014 makes provision for members of the House of Lords to resign their membership of that House. A peer that resigns in terms of that Act becomes eligible for membership of the House of Commons.[65] Other persons that are excluded from membership of the House of Commons include: clergy that sit in the House of Lords as Lords Spiritual[66]; certain bankrupts[67]; holders of any office prescribed by the House of Commons Disqualification Act 1975[68]; persons convicted of an offence and sentenced to a period of imprisonment of one year or more, while detained (or unlawfully at large) in pursuance

---

[58] *McHugh v United Kingdom* (51987/08), *The Times*, 12 February 2015.
[59] "Candidate" is defined by statute (1983 Act s.118A, inserted by s.135(2) of PPERA) but it is restricted to the time after the election has been called.
[60] British Nationality Act 1981 s.50(1); Ireland Act 1949 s.3; Electoral Administration Act 2006 s.18.
[61] Act of Settlement 1700 s.3; *Tipperary* case (1875) 3 O'M. & H. 19.
[62] Electoral Administration Act 2006 s.17.
[63] Mental Health (Discrimination) Act 2013 s.1(2).
[64] House of Lords Act 1999 ss.1–3.
[65] House of Lords Reform Act 2014 s.4(5).
[66] House of Commons (Removal of Clergy Disqualification) Act 2001.
[67] Insolvency Act 1986 ss.426A–427 (as amended by the Enterprise Act 2002 s.266).
[68] The list is constantly changing but includes: most judicial office holders (House of Commons Disqualification Act 1975 Sch.1) members of a wide range of bodies (from the Forestry Commission to the UK Sports Council including civil servants and police officers) (Sch.2) and an even wider range of specific offices (Sch.3).

of that sentence[69]; a person convicted of being personally guilty of corrupt practices[70]; a person convicted of being personally guilty of illegal practices.[71] Where a person wishes to stand as a candidate on behalf of a party, that party must be a registered party in accordance with the Political Parties, Elections and Referendums Act 2000.[72] A candidate must pay a deposit, which is lost in the event they receive few than one-twentieth of the votes cast.[73] Qualification to stand for election to, and to be a member of, the Scottish Parliament is prescribed by s.15 of the Scotland Act 1998 and the Scottish Parliament (Disqualification) Order 2010.[74] Those provisions largely apply the disqualifications that apply to the House of Commons to the Scottish Parliament. Specific rules are made in relation to the European Parliament. They are not set out in full here. In short, any person who has reached the age of 18 and is not disqualified from being a member of the European Parliament may stand as a candidate. A citizen of the EU has the right to stand as a candidate in their Member State of residence: the consequence is that any citizen of an EU state that is resident in the United Kingdom may stand for election in a UK electoral region.[75]

CONDUCT OF ELECTIONS

Introduction

4–15   Article 3 of the First Protocol to the European Convention on Human Rights requires that the state provide for "free elections . . . which will ensure the free expression of the opinion of the people". Accordingly, the conduct of election campaigns is a heavily regulated matter. Prior to 2000, the controls on the conduct of elections focused on the constituency level of an election campaign: there were virtually no controls on the conduct of the national campaign or on the expenditure incurred by parties at that level, or indeed on the financing of political parties. The Political Parties, Elections and Referendums Act 2000 ("PPERA") changed all of that. The PPERA made fresh provision for the registration and regulation of political parties[76]; for the financing and expenses of registered political parties; for the conduct of election and referendum campaigns; and for proceedings in connection with elections.[77] The older controls on

---

[69] Representation of the People Act 1981 s.1. That produces the frankly absurd result that a prisoner serving a sentence of less than 12 months can stand for election but is prohibited from voting in that election. The Recall of MPs Act 2015 now provides that an MP that is sentenced to a term of imprisonment or suspended from the House of Commons for at least 21 days may face a "recall petition" which would trigger a by-election in his constituency should a sufficient number of his constituents support such a move. At the time of writing the 2015 Act had not yet been brought into force.

[70] 1983 Act s.160. The disqualification lasts for five years from conviction.

[71] 1983 Act s.159. The disqualification lasts for three years from conviction.

[72] PPERA s.22(1). This does not prevent a person standing as an "independent" candidate. On registration of political parties, see para.4–17, below.

[73] 1983 Act Sch.1 rr.9 and 53(3). The deposit is currently £500.

[74] Scottish Parliament (Disqualification) Order 2010 (SI 2010/2476).

[75] Treaty on the Functioning of the European Union art.22. For further details see: *Schofield's Election Law* (London: Sweet & Maxwell) Vol.1, paras.2–016—2–020.

[76] Re-enacting, with modifications, the provisions of the Registration of Political Parties Act 1998.

[77] It should however be noted that many of the amendments made to earlier legislation by the Political Parties, Elections and Referendums Act 2000 do not apply to Scottish local government elections (which are, with the exception of the franchise, a devolved matter).

the conduct of campaigns at a constituency level, provided for by the Representation of the People Act 1983, continue in force. Before turning to consider the various provisions introduced by PPERA, it is helpful to start with the body that was created to oversee this new system of regulation of elections, the Electoral Commission.

The Electoral Commission

The Electoral Commission was established by Pt 1 of PPERA. Its statutory remit **4–16** is considerable. It is charged, first, with reporting on the administration of, inter alia, parliamentary general elections, European parliamentary general elections, Scottish parliamentary general elections and certain referendums. Its other functions include reviewing, and reporting to the Secretary of State on, matters relating to elections and referendums, including the distribution of seats at parliamentary elections; the conduct of local government elections; the registration and regulation of political parties; and political party funding.[78] It must be consulted on changes to electoral law.[79] It may express views on party political broadcasting, to which independent broadcasters are required to have regard. It may provide advice and assistance on electoral matters to bodies including registered political parties, the Scottish Parliament, Scottish Government and councils constituted under the Local Government etc. (Scotland) Act 1994. More broadly, it has a general duty to promote public awareness of electoral systems, systems of local and national government in the United Kingdom (including the devolved administrations, but excluding Scottish local government unless the Scottish Ministers by order provide otherwise) and the institutions of the EU.

In January 2007, the Committee on Standards in Public Life published *A Review of the Electoral Commission*.[80] It was withering in its assessment of the Commission's performance since its establishment. During that time, as the *Review* points out, there has been a marked fall in confidence in the integrity of the system of electoral administration and in the framework for the regulation of political party funding—both matters falling within the statutory remit of the Commission.[81] The width of that remit, in the view of the Committee on Standards in Public Life, is at the root of the problem.[82] It recommended a

---

[78] The Commission does not, however, have power to review or report on (among other things) the funding of political parties under s.97 of the Scotland Act 1998; the conduct of referendums held pursuant to an Act of the Scottish Parliament (although it was given a role in the independence referendum by the Scottish Independence Referendum Act 2013 s.12); or (subject to s.19 of PPERA) on the conduct of local elections in Scotland.

[79] Including changes to provision made by the Secretary of State pursuant to the Scotland Act 1998 s.12 for the conduct of elections in Scotland.

[80] Committee on Standards in Public Life, *A Review of the Electoral Commission, 11th Report* (The Stationery Office, 2007) Cm.7006.

[81] This fall in confidence the Committee attributes, on the one hand, to the perceived increase in voter fraud (driven in part by the introduction of such initiatives as on-demand postal voting); and, on the other, to the controversy surrounding undeclared loans taken out by the major political parties prior to the 2005 general election. The latter prompted the Prime Minister to appoint Sir Hayden Phillips to conduct a review of party funding. Sir Hayden's report, *Strengthening Democracy: Fair and Sustainable Funding of Political Parties* (The Stationery Office, 2007) was published in March 2007. In relation to the proper role of the Electoral Commission, it endorses the views of the Committee on Standards in Public Life in every material respect.

[82] As the *Review* observes, the various functions with which the Commission is charged are not mutually compatible and, in choosing to concentrate on issues such as the promotion of public engagement in the electoral process, the Commission has neglected its more contentious regulatory roles.

comprehensive reconfiguration of the Electoral Commission, so as to focus its role as the regulator of party funding and campaign expenditure on the one hand, and electoral administration on the other. The result was the Political Parties and Elections Act 2009, which strengthened the Electoral Commission's investigatory powers[83] and provides the Commission with a range of civil sanctions that it can now impose.[84] The introduction of these civil sanctions was important: previously the Commission faced a choice of doing nothing or instigating a criminal prosecution. That had led to the Commission, on occasion, to take no action in response to acknowledged breaches of PPERA.[85] A more proportionate response is now available to the Commission and is to be welcomed.

Registration of political parties

4–17 Until the introduction of a voluntary register by the Registration of Political Parties Act 1998, there was no system for the registration of political parties in the UK. The PPERA changed that and the whole regulatory regime contained in that Act now revolves around the registration of political parties. Unless registered a party cannot field candidates at any election in the UK other than elections to community councils (or their English equivalents, parish councils).[86] This is without prejudice to the right of any person who does not purport to represent any party[87] to stand for election. The register of political parties previously maintained by the Registrar of Companies under the Registration of Political Parties Act 1998 was replaced with two new registers maintained by the Electoral Commission.[88] The Great Britain Register contains details of parties intending to contest elections in one or more of England, Scotland or Wales; the Northern Ireland Register contains details of parties intending to contest elections in Northern Ireland. An entry in the Great Britain Register must be marked to indicate the part or parts of Great Britain in respect of which the party in question is registered. A party can apply to be registered in both registers, but the party as registered in the Great Britain Register and the party as registered in the Northern Ireland Register are required to be constituted as two separate parties with separate financial affairs.

Each registered party must register a person as the party's leader, the party's nominating officer and the party's treasurer (although the same person may hold all three offices).[89] The nominating officer has responsibility for the submission by representatives of the party of lists of candidates for elections; the issuing of certificates attesting that a candidate in an election is a representative of the party; and the approval of descriptions and emblems used on nomination and ballot

---

[83] See now PPERA s.146 and Sch.19B.
[84] See now PPERA s.150 and Sch.19C.
[85] See, for example, the much criticised decision the Commission took in relation to Wendy Alexander and her failure to timeously return an impermissible donation, Electoral Commission, "Statement by the Electoral Commission" (3 June 2008), *http://www.electoralcommission.org.uk/i-am-a/journalist/electoral-commission-media-centre/news-releases-donations/statement-by-the-electoral-commission* [Accessed 4 June 2015]. The Alexander affair (and its wider implications) are discussed in: N.S. Ghaleigh, B. Kemp and P. Reid, "Politics as a profession: electoral law, Parliamentary standards and regulating politicians" [2012] P.L. 658.
[86] Nor, in terms of PPERA s.37 can broadcasters transmit party political broadcasts on behalf of a party which is not registered.
[87] That is, a person whose nomination paper describes him as "independent" or as "the Speaker seeking re-election", or which gives no description at all.
[88] PPERA s.23.
[89] PPERA s.24.

papers at elections. The treasurer has responsibility for compliance on the part of the party with the provisions of Pts III and IV of PPERA (concerning accounting requirements[90] and the control of donations) and, unless a different person is registered as the party's campaigns officer, with the provisions of Pts V–VII (concerning campaign expenditure, third party expenditure and referendums).

A party may not be registered unless it has adopted a scheme which sets out the arrangements for regulating the financial affairs of the party for the purposes of PPERA and which has been approved in writing by the Electoral Commission.[91] In particular, the scheme must specify whether the party is to be regarded as a single organisation with no division of responsibility for the financial affairs and transactions of the party for the purposes of PPERA's accounting requirements, or as consisting of a central organisation and one or more separate accounting units (that is, constituent or affiliated organisations each of which is responsible for its own financial affairs). In the latter case, the scheme must identify the various accounting units within the party by name; and in every case, must include such other information as may be required by regulations made by the Electoral Commission. The Commission may either approve a scheme as submitted, or give notice to a party requesting it to submit a revised scheme. The same process applies where a registered party wishes to replace an approved scheme with a revised scheme.

Applications for registration must be in the form prescribed by PPERA,[92] **4–18** specifying a name to be the party's registered name[93]; the address of the party's headquarters, or an address to which communications to the party may be sent; the name and home address of each of the party's registered officers; a copy of the party's constitution and a draft of the accounting scheme submitted to the Electoral Commission; (where the party has accounting units) the name of each accounting unit, its address and the name of its treasurer; and such additional information as the Electoral Commission may prescribe in regulations. A party may also apply to register up to three emblems to be used by the party on ballot papers. The Electoral Commission is obliged to grant applications unless the application falls foul of the conditions prescribed in s.28(4).[94] Applications must be signed by the proposed registered leader or nominations officer, the treasurer and (where a party has one) by the campaigns officer, each of whom must declare that they are authorised to sign the application on the party's behalf. Thereafter, subject to applying to change registered particulars, the registered treasurer of a party must at the time of sending its annual statement of accounts to the Electoral Commission also give notification to the commission confirming that its registered particulars remain accurate.

---

[90] Unless the party has accounting units, in which case the treasurer is only responsible for compliance with the accounting requirements by the party's central organisation. Compliance with the requirements of PPERA Pts III and IV by each accounting unit is the responsibility of the person registered as treasurer of the unit.

[91] PPERA s.26.

[92] PPERA s.28 and Sch.4 Pt 1.

[93] As to registered names and descriptions, see now also Pt 7 of the Electoral Administration Act 2006.

[94] For example, the party proposes to register a name which has already been registered by another party, which is likely to result in voters confusing the party with another registered party, which comprises more than six words, or which is obscene, offensive or includes words the publication of which might amount to the commission of an offence.

Donations to political parties[95]

4–19   One of the main objectives in requiring political parties to be registered was to
allow greater control of, and transparency in respect of, their funding. Following
PPERA, donations to political parties is now a heavily regulated matter.[96] It was
not always so. Funding of political parties has long been a controversial topic.[97]
Political parties have access to very limited public funds. Once a party has
managed to secure a foothold in Parliament it is eligible for a contribution from
public funds towards its parliamentary work (but not its election expenses).[98] At
election time, candidates are entitled to such benefits as free postage (for one
constituency mail shot) and free use of public buildings for election meetings. If
a party is sufficiently sizeable to register on the national scale, it is also entitled
to at least one party election broadcast.[99] Beyond that, the amount a party has to
spend at election time on advertising and other forms of promotion depends on
its membership income (which, for almost all parties, is in radical decline)[100]
and, crucially, support from companies, trades unions, private individuals and
others. It is the latter, and the terms on which it is provided, which has
perennially caused controversy. Having investigated the matter in the context of
its Fifth Report, the Committee on Standards in Public Life was unpersuaded of
the case for state funding of political parties. Its recommended solution involved
limits on campaign expenditure coupled with new requirements of disclosure and
registration. Those recommendations provided the foundation for Pt IV of
PPERA concerning donations to political parties.

4–20   "Donation" is defined by s.50 of PPERA to include any gift to a party of
money or other property[101]; any sponsorship provided in relation to the party[102];
any subscription or other fee paid for affiliation to, or membership of, the party;
any money spent (otherwise than by or on behalf of the party) in paying any
expenses incurred by the party; any money lent to the party otherwise than on
commercial terms; and the provision otherwise than on commercial terms of any

---

[95] What follows is necessarily an overview of what is becoming an increasingly complex and
technical subject; M. Smyth, P. Barratt and F. Campbell, *The Law of Political Donations* (London:
Wildy, Simmonds & Hill, 2012) is commended to anyone in search of further detail.

[96] Donations to members of registered parties, members associations and certain elected offices are
also controlled by a near identical scheme: see PPERA s.71 and Sch.7.

[97] See K.D. Ewing, *The Funding of Political Parties* (Cambridge: Cambridge University Press,
1987); more recently, Committee on Standards in Public Life, *The Funding of Political Parties
in the United Kingdom, Fifth Report* (The Stationery Office, 2008) Cm.4057–I and, now, the
House of Commons Constitutional Affairs Committee, *Party Funding, First Special Report of
Session 2006–2007* (The Stationery Office, 2007) HC 222 and Phillips, *Strengthening Democracy: Fair and Sustainable Funding of Political Parties*.

[98] Known as "Short money" in the House of Commons and "Cranborne money" in the House of
Lords, this system of funding has a statutory foundation in relation to the Scottish Parliament in
the Scotland Act 1998 s.97.

[99] On party election broadcasts, see para.4–26, below.

[100] The SNP buck that trend having seen a huge growth in their membership following the 2014
referendum.

[101] This includes the provision of property, services, facilities or other consideration of monetary
value for payment of a sum less than the market value of the property transferred; and also
includes bequests.

[102] Defined in s.51 as money or other property transferred to the party or to any person for the benefit
of the party for the purpose of helping the party to meet any defined expenses (i.e. expenses in
connection with a conference, meeting or other event organised by or on behalf of the party; the
preparation, production or dissemination of any publication by or on behalf of the party; or any
study or research organised by or on behalf of the party) or to secure that to any extent such
expenses are not incurred.

property, services or facilities for the use or benefit of the party, including the services of any person. Anything given or transferred to any officer, member, trustee or agent of a registered party in that capacity is also to be regarded as a donation to the party. Section 52 then lists items which are not to be regarded as donations, including: grants made to cover security costs at party conferences; payments made by or on behalf of the European Parliament for the purpose of assisting MEPs in the performance of their functions; the transmission by a broadcaster, free of charge, of a party political broadcast or referendum campaign broadcast; any other facilities provided in pursuance of any right conferred on candidates or a party at an election or a referendum by any enactment; the voluntary provision by any individual of his own services, in his own time and free of charge; payments made for the hire of a stand at a party conference (provided the payment does not exceed a maximum deemed by the Electoral Commission to be reasonable). Any donation worth less than £500 also falls outwith PPERA scheme entirely.[103]

Donations may only be accepted from "permissible donors".[104] The concept of a "permissible donor" was at the heart of PPERA reforms. In short, the objective was to prevent foreign donations to political parties. The rational is obvious: only those that have a sufficient connection to the UK should be allowed to contribute to funding politics in the UK. Where a political party receives a donation from an impermissible donor (or it is unable to satisfy itself that the donor is permissible), it must return the donation within 30 days.[105] Failure to do so is a criminal offence.[106] Who, then, is a "permissible donor"? A list is set out in s.54(2) and includes: an individual registered in an electoral register[107]; a registered company[108]; a registered party; a registered trade union; a building society; a registered limited liability partnership; a registered friendly society; and an unincorporated association which carries on its activities wholly or mainly in the UK. The objective of the list was to provide a clear and simple way of verifying a donor's entitlement to make a donation. It was with that in mind that a proposal that an individual who was not on the electoral register but was entitled to be on it should be a permissible donor was rejected.[109] Ascertaining the permissibility of a donation from an individual was therefore a clear and simple process. Changes introduced by the Political Parties and Elections Act 2009 will complicate this issue in some circumstances. The 2009 Act (although the relevant provision has not yet been bought into force) requires any person making a donation in excess of £7,500 (whether in a single donation or a series of donations in the same calendar year) to be domiciled and tax resident in the

---

[103] PPERA s.52(2)(b). The limit was originally £200 but it was increased to £500 by the Political Parties and Elections Act 2009 s.20(1).

[104] PPERA s.54.

[105] PPERA ss.56(1) and 57.

[106] PPERA s.56(3).

[107] An "electoral register" is defined by PPERA s.54(8).

[108] Registered under the Companies Act 2006, incorporated in the UK or another EU Member State and carrying on business in the United Kingdom.

[109] The recommendation was made by the Neill Committee in Committee on Standards in Public Life, *The Funding of Political Parties in the United Kingdom, Fifth Report*, para.5.20. The recommendation was specifically rejected in the Government's response to the Neill Committee's report: HM Government, *The Funding of Political Parties in the United Kingdom: the Government's proposals for legislation in response to the Fifth Report of the Committee on Standards in Public Life* (The Stationery Office, 1999) Cm.4413, para.4.6.

United Kingdom.[110] Thus, a political party receiving such a donation will need to check not only that the donor is on the electoral register but also his tax status. There is no register that can be checked to ascertain that and determining a person's residence for tax purposes and their domicile is often a complicated business.[111] Whilst the policy behind the amendment (to restrict donations from those that although on the electoral register do not pay tax in the United Kingdom) is understandable, it results in an unfortunate dilution of what was otherwise a clear system and renders compliance more difficult that the original scheme anticipated.

4–21   Retaining an impermissible donation has two consequences. First, the party and its treasurer commit a criminal offence.[112] It is a defence for a party or its treasurer to show that all reasonable steps were taken to verify (or ascertain) whether the donation was permissible and as a result the treasurer believed the donation to be permissible.[113] As an alternative to criminal prosecution, the Electoral Commission now has a range of civil sanctions that it may impose upon a person that commits an offence under PPERA.[114] Secondly, the Electoral Commission can seek an order for forfeiture of "an amount equal to the value of the donation".[115] Forfeiture allows the political party to be deprived of the benefit of an impermissible donation. Such an application is made to the sheriff (in Scotland) or to the magistrate (in England and Wales)[116] and can be made irrespective of whether proceedings have been brought for an offence connected with the donation.[117] An appeal lies, at the instance of the political party, to the Court of Session or the Crown Court.[118] The decision of the sheriff (or magistrate) is amenable to judicial review at the instance of the Electoral Commission.[119] Whether to order forfeiture, and how much of the impermissible donation should be forfeited, are matters of discretion for the sheriff (or magistrate). That was made clear by the Supreme Court in *R. (on the application of Electoral Commission) v Westminster Magistrates' Court*.[120] That case was the culmination of litigation arising out of UKIP's acceptance of 69 donations totalling over £350,000 from a party member who was not on the electoral register and was thus an impermissible donor. Sixty two of those donations were made when both UKIP and the donor were ignorant of the fact he was an impermissible donor. The remaining seven (amounting to just under £15,000)

---

[110] Political Parties and Elections Act 2009 s.10, inserting s.54(2ZA) and s.54B into PPERA.

[111] Smyth, Barratt and Campbell, *The Law of Political Donations* (2012) pp.43–46.

[112] PPERA s.56(3) and (4). Upon conviction on indictment the court may impose a fine or a period of imprisonment of up to one year; upon summary conviction the court may impose a fine up to the statutory maximum or a period of imprisonment of up to six months (PPERA s.150 and Sch.20).

[113] PPERA s.56(3A); this provision was inserted by the Political Parties and Elections Act 2009 s.12 and reflects the grounds on which the Electoral Commission did not initiate criminal proceedings against Wendy Alexander in 2008 when she failed to return an impermissible donation within the 30 day period.

[114] These were introduced by the Political Parties and Elections Act 2009 and are now to be found in PPERA s.147 and Sch.19C.

[115] PPERA s.58(2).

[116] PPERA s.58(5).

[117] PPERA s.58(4).

[118] PPERA s.59.

[119] *R. (on the application of Electoral Commission) v Westminster Magistrates' Court* [2009] EWHC 78 (Admin); [2009] A.C.D. 23.

[120] *R. (on the application of Electoral Commission) v Westminster Magistrates' Court* [2010] UKSC 40; [2011] 1 A.C. 496.

were made after UKIP became aware the donor was not a permissible donor. The Electoral Commission made an application for a forfeiture order covering all donations that were in excess of £200 (the then minimum threshold to fall within the 2000 Act scheme). At first instance, the magistrate ordered forfeiture in the sum of £14,481 (representing the seven donations received once the donor's status was known to UKIP). The Electoral Commission sought judicial review of that decision. By the time the case reached the Supreme Court the issue had become focused: was there a presumption in favour of forfeiture where a donation came from an impermissible donor? The Supreme Court split 4:3. The minority (Lords Rodger, Brown and Walker) were of the view that there was a strong presumption in favour of forfeiture, especially in a case such as the present where the donation had been retained by the party.[121] As Lord Brown put it:

> " . . . in any case where neither the benefit nor its value has ever been returned, it is difficult to see how the discretion could properly be exercised other than by an order for forfeiture. How, in those circumstances, could a court properly allow a party to retain the value of a donation which Parliament has plainly ordained that it should never have accepted?"[122]

That reasoning is fairly compelling and would have resulted in forfeiture of the entire amount that UKIP had received. But the majority (Lords Phillips, Mance, Kerr and Clarke) took a more nuanced view of the forfeiture rules: where a donation has been accepted from an impermissible source, there is an initial presumption in favour of forfeiting the donation; there is an onus on the party to show why such a donation should not be forfeited; a "first step" in discharging that onus will be show that it was not in fact a "foreign donation"; that can be done by showing an individual was entitled to be entered on the electoral register; if it can be shown that the individual was in a position to qualify as a permissible donor, the initial presumption in favour of forfeiture will have been rebutted.[123] In relation to the sum to be forfeited, the majority went on to hold that the power to order forfeiture of "an amount equal to the value of the donation" was not an all or nothing power: it implicitly contains the power to order forfeiture of a lower sum.[124] That was necessary, said Lord Phillips, to ensure the sum forfeited was proportionate to the culpability of the party.[125] Nothing in this decision

---

[121] *R. (on the application of Electoral Commission) v Westminster Magistrates' Court* [2010] UKSC 40; [2011] 1 A.C. 496, per Lord Rodger at [69] and Lord Brown at [95].

[122] *R. (on the application of Electoral Commission) v Westminster Magistrates' Court* [2010] UKSC 40; [2011] 1 A.C. 496 at [95]. Lord Rodger's interpretation of s.54(1) (at [58]) was equally compelling: "Nothing could be clearer than the language used by Parliament and nothing could be clearer than the intention behind the language: political parties were not to accept donations from any individual who was not registered in an electoral register. In particular, parties were not to accept donations from individuals who were entitled to be registered, but who were not on the register. That situation would be adequately catered for by the simple expedient of the individual concerned getting himself registered: the party could then accept a donation from him."

[123] *R. (on the application of Electoral Commission) v Westminster Magistrates' Court* [2010] UKSC 40; [2011] 1 A.C. 496, per Lord Phillips at [47]–[49].

[124] *R. (on the application of Electoral Commission) v Westminster Magistrates' Court* [2010] UKSC 40; [2011] 1 A.C. 496, per Lord Phillips at [50]–[51].

[125] Again, the minority's view on this point is compelling: *R. (on the application of Electoral Commission) v Westminster Magistrates' Court* [2010] UKSC 40; [2011] 1 A.C. 496, per Lord Rodger at [64]–[69] and Lord Brown at [90]–[92]. As Lord Rodger explains in that passage, the consequence of the majority's decision appears to be that large impermissible donations are harder to forfeit than smaller impermissible donations: that would be an odd result.

changes the fact that a party may not accept a donation from a person that is not on the electoral register and to do so remains a criminal offence. But it does mean that forfeiture of that donation is unlikely if the donor was eligible to be on the electoral register. To that extent, what appears on the face of PPERA to be a strong incentive to carefully check the electoral register on receipt of a donation has been significantly watered down.

Campaign expenditure

4–22 The idea that an election result can be "bought" should be repugnant in a democracy. As we have just seen, regulation of donations to political parties is a relatively new development.[126] Such expenditure is now controlled by a combination of the Representation of the People Act 1983 and Pts V and VI of PPERA. So far as the 1983 Act is concerned, the relevant provisions are to be found in Pt II of that Act, in particular ss.72–90D. A summary of the key provisions will suffice.[127] The 1983 Act concerns itself with "election expenses". An "election expense" is any expense incurred at any time after the date on which a person becomes a candidate in respect of matters specified in Pt 1 of Sch.4A and which is used for the purpose of the candidate's election.[128] The matters prescribed in Sch.4A include: advertising of any nature; unsolicited material addressed to electors; transport costs; public meetings; costs of engaging an election agent; and accommodation and administrative costs.

4–23	The Political Parties, Elections and Referendums Act 2000 now adds to those rules. Part V concerns the control of campaign expenditure. "Campaign expenditure" is defined as "expenses incurred by or on behalf of the party which are expenses falling within Part 1 of Schedule 8 and so incurred for election purposes"[129] but it excludes anything that falls to be included in a return as election expenses by a candidate.[130] The matters listed in Pt 1 of Sch.8 include: party political broadcasts; advertising of any nature; unsolicited material addressed to electors; any manifesto or equivalent document; costs associated with polling or market research; the provision of services or facilities in connection with press conferences or other media dealings; transport; and rallies or other party meetings (but excluding party conferences). Campaign expenditure does not include anything which falls to be included in a return as to election expenses in respect of a candidate or candidates at a particular election. Nor does it include such items as expenses in respect of newsletters issued by or on behalf of the party in order to inform the local electorate about a representative or candidate; the costs of employing party staff; or travelling expenses incurred by an individual from his own resources and not reimbursed.[131] Responsibility in relation to campaign expenditure is vested in the treasurer of a party and such

---

[126] The rules in the UK can be contrasted to the approach taken in the US, where there are few restrictions on campaign expenditure as the US Supreme Court has consistently taken the view that such regulations infringe the First Amendment of the US Constitution. Most recently, see *Citizens United v Federal Election Commission*, 558 U.S. 310 (2010).

[127] Fuller discussion of these provisions can be found in R. Clayton, *Parker's Law and Conduct of Elections* (Croydon: Charles Knight, 1996) Ch.8.

[128] 1983 Act s.90ZA(1); "for the purpose of the candidate's election" is widely defined as "with a view to, or otherwise in connection with, promoting or procuring the candidate's election at the election" (s.90ZA(3)).

[129] PPERA s.72(1).

[130] PPERA s.72(7).

[131] PPERA Sch.8 Pt 1 para.2.

deputy treasurers (not exceeding 12) as they may appoint.[132] No "campaign expenditure" may be incurred without authorisation of the treasurer, a deputy or somebody that is authorised on their behalf.[133] The obligations imposed by PPERA are onerous and time consuming, especially for smaller parties that have limited resources. Limits are imposed on the amount of "campaign expenditure" that may be incurred during specified periods. Those limits are set out in Sch.9 of the 2000 Act. For a UK general election, Scotland, Wales, Northern Ireland and England are treated separately. The amount of "campaign expenditure" a party may incur is (at least in the first instance) tied to the number of seats they are contesting in each part of the UK. Where a registered party contests one or more seats in a part of the UK the amount of campaign expenditure that may be incurred in that part of the UK is £30,000 per constituency in that part of the country.[134] There is, in relation to Great Britain, a minimum amount a party fielding a candidate may spend: in England that is £810,000, in Scotland £120,000 and in Wales £60,000.[135] For a Scottish general election, campaign expenditure is limited to £12,000 per constituency that is being contested and £80,000 for each region that is contested.[136] There is no minimum amount. Breaching those limits is a criminal offence, which is committed both by the treasurer (or deputy) that authorised the expenditure and by the party.[137]

It may be helpful to put those figures into context:

Table 4: Campaign expenditure during 2010 UK and 2011 Scottish general elections[138]

Party	2010 UK general election	2011 Scottish general election
Con	£16,682,874	£273,462
Lab	£8,009,483	£816,889
Lib Dem	£4,787,595	£176,300
SNP	£315,776	£1,141,662
Cap if contesting all[139] constituencies	£18,960,000	£1,516,000

From those figures alone, it is clear that there is a wide disparity in the amount the different parties spent during a general election campaign. The amount spent in 2010 and 2011 was substantially less than was spent in 2005 and 2007

---

[132] PPERA s.74.

[133] PPERA s.75.

[134] PPERA Sch.9 para.3(2) and (4).

[135] PPERA Sch.9 para.3(3).

[136] PPERA Sch.9 para.5(2). The power to vary this sum will be devolved if legislation is passed to give effect to the Smith Commission. At the time of writing, the current draft of the relevant clause is cl.7 of the Draft Scotland Clauses 2015 which are annexed to the Command Paper, HM Government, *Scotland in the United Kingdom: An enduring settlement*.

[137] PPERA s.79(2).

[138] Source, the Electoral Commission. At the time of writing figures were not available for the 2015 UK general election.

[139] In relation to the 2010 UK general election, that is all constituencies in Great Britain

respectively. Although no party has yet spent the limit of their entitlement, imposing a limit on expenditure does ensure that there is only so far that the gulf can open.

Part VI of PPERA is concerned with controls on third party participation in national election campaigns. These provisions are a response to the European Court of Human Rights decision in *Bowman v United Kingdom*.[140] As it then stood, s.75 of the 1983 Act made it an offence for a person other than a candidate or his agent to incur expenditure in excess of £5 during an election period "with a view to promoting or procuring the election of a candidate" at that election, which might be contravened as much by denigrating a candidate (since his opponents stood to benefit) as by actively promoting him. That rule was held to be a disproportionate restriction on freedom of expression contrary to art.10 of the Convention. Part VI now allows for greater third party participation in national election campaigns but still subject to strict limits.[141] For the 2010 general election just under £3,000,000 of "controlled expenditure" was incurred by third parties. In the 2011 Scottish general election approximately £10,000 of such expenditure was incurred. The Pt VI regime was further expanded by the Transparency of Lobbying, Non-Party Campaigning and Trade Union Administration Act 2014 which brought charities, certain Scottish partnerships and certain bodies established by Royal Charter within the scope of Pt VI of the 2000 Act.[142] The 2014 Act also introduces limits to the amount third parties can spend in a single parliamentary constituency.[143]

Television coverage, electoral broadcasts and debates

4-24 Television coverage of election campaigns has long been regulated. The power and reach of television means it could have a significant impact on the outcome of an election if favourable coverage was to be given one party or candidate as compared to the rest. There are no equivalent restrictions on the printed media: newspapers and the like are free to be as partisan as they please during an election campaign. Under s.320 of the Communications Act 2003, in relation to matters of political or industrial controversy or current public policy, broad-casters (both television and radio) must avoid all expressions of the views or opinions of the broadcaster, preserve due impartiality and prevent undue prominence being given to the views of any particular person or body. The preservation of impartiality can be satisfied by a series of programmes taken as a whole and the prevention of undue prominence can be secured by viewing the service in question's coverage as a whole. "Political" in this context is not restricted to party political but includes social advocacy bodies.

4-25 Adverts "directed towards a political end" are prohibited in the United Kingdom.[144] That phrase is given a wide meaning and includes, inter alia, a

---

[140] *Bowman v United Kingdom* (1998) 26 E.H.R.R. 1.
[141] In relation to a Scottish general election, the limit is £75,800 of "controlled expenditure" during the "relevant period": PPERA Sch.10 para.5. The limits for a UK general election vary as between Scotland, England, Wales and Northern Ireland and are determined in accordance with PPERA Sch.10 para.1.
[142] Transparency of Lobbying, Non-Party Campaigning and Trade Union Administration Act 2014 s.32 (which amends PPERA s.88).
[143] Transparency of Lobbying, Non-Party Campaigning and Trade Union Administration Act 2014 s.29 (which amends PPERA ss.94, 96 and Sch.10). A mechanism is introduced to calculate the limit, which is currently £9,750.
[144] Communications Act 2003 s.321(2).

broadcast with the purpose of influencing the outcome of an election or referendum, bringing about a change in the law, influencing the policies or decisions of a government, influencing public opinion on a matter of public controversy and promoting the interests of any group for political ends.[145] Having such a blanket ban on access to the broadcast media is an obvious restriction of the art.10 right to freedom of expression. It is, however, a proportionate interference with that right.[146] Lord Bingham, in *R. (on the application of Animal Defenders International) v Secretary of State for Culture, Media and Sport*, explained the rationale that underpins the duties imposed on broadcasters and the ban on political adverts:

"The fundamental rationale of the democratic process is that if competing views, opinions and policies are publicly debated and exposed to public scrutiny the good will over time drive out the bad and the true prevail over the false. It must be assumed that, given time, the public will make a sound choice when, in the course of the democratic process, it has the right to choose. But it is highly desirable that the playing field of debate should be so far as practicable level. This is achieved where, in public discussion, differing views are expressed, contradicted, answered and debated. It is the duty of broadcasters to achieve this object in an impartial way by presenting balanced programmes in which all lawful views may be ventilated. It is not achieved if political parties can, in proportion to their resources, buy unlimited opportunities to advertise in the most effective media, so that elections become little more than an auction. Nor is it achieved if well-endowed interests which are not political parties are able to use the power of the purse to give enhanced prominence to views which may be true or false, attractive to progressive minds or unattractive, beneficial or injurious. The risk is that objects which are essentially political may come to be accepted by the public not because they are shown in public debate to be right but because, by dint of constant repetition, the public has been conditioned to accept them. The rights of others which a restriction on the exercise of the right to free expression may properly be designed to protect must, in my judgment, include a right to be protected against the potential mischief of partial political advertising."[147]

Political parties (or at least some of them) are given some access to the airwaves. **4–26** Broadcasters and licenced radio stations are required to carry "party political broadcasts".[148] In the run up to an election, these are known as party election broadcasts. It is for the broadcasters, following, in the case of commercial broadcasters, the rules set down by Ofcom, to determine the number of broadcasts each political party should receive having regard to their duty to

---

[145] Communications Act 2003 s.321(3). These restrictions do not have a territorial limitation: they apply to *any* election, referendum, government, policy or body and not just those in the United Kingdom. See *R. (on the application of London Christian Radio Ltd) v Radio Advertising Clearance Centre* [2013] EWCA Civ 1495; [2014] 1 W.L.R. 307.

[146] *R. (on the application of Animal Defenders International) v Secretary of State for Culture, Media and Sport* [2008] UKHL 15; [2008] 1 A.C. 1312; *Animal Defenders International v United Kingdom* (2013) 57 E.H.R.R. 21.

[147] *R. (on the application of Animal Defenders International) v Secretary of State for Culture, Media and Sport* [2008] UKHL 15; [2008] 1 A.C. 1312 at [28].

[148] Communications Act 2003 s.333(1).

ensure a fair overall coverage. Under the current Ofcom rules,[149] the "major parties" (in Great Britain they were the Conservative Party, Labour and the Liberal Democrats)[150] should receive at least two broadcasts. In determining the allocation of broadcasts, regard is had to each party's past electoral support and/ or current levels of support. For these purposes, each nation of the UK is considered separately. For the UK general election, at least one broadcast should be allocated to any party that is contesting at least one-sixth of the seats that are up for election. Detailed rules are made by Ofcom about the length of broadcasts and the time of day that broadcasters must carry them. Unsurprisingly, the allocation of broadcasts is controversial.

A more recent development are debates between the party leaders in the run up to an election. Unlike party political broadcasts, there is little regulation about the number and content of any debates (as the run up to the 2015 election showed). They were first used in advance of the 2010 general election in which the leaders of the three main parties (Labour, the Conservatives and the Liberal Democrats) took part. Such debates are an import from the US, where televised debates between the presidential candidates have been a feature of elections since the mid-1970s.[151] Matters are simpler in the US where the two main parties (the Republicans and the Democrats) dominate and where the electorate are voting to choose the President rather than electing a legislature.[152] Presidential debates normally consist of the candidate from each party.[153] It is not as straightforward in the UK. A challenge was mounted to the 2010 debates by the SNP, who claimed their leader was entitled to participate, representing as he did the largest party in Scotland. Accordingly it was argued that broadcasting the debates in Scotland would breach the broadcasters' obligation of impartiality.[154] Their application for interim interdict to prevent the broadcasting of the debate in Scotland failed.[155] It did so for a number of reasons: placed in the context of the planned coverage of the election campaign, broadcasting the debate did not prevent impartial coverage of the overall campaign; it was too late to prevent broadcast of the third debate (it being likened to denying the audience act three of a three act play); and the terms of the order lacked sufficient precision. Although unsuccessful, the case highlights a problem with presidential-style

---

[149] Ofcom, *Ofcom Rules on Party Political and Referendum Broadcasts* (March 2013) *http:// stakeholders.ofcom.org.uk/binaries/broadcast/guidance/ppbrules.pdf* [Accessed 4 June 2015].

[150] The SNP are a "major party" in Scotland.

[151] The first debate was in the 1960 campaign between Kennedy and Nixon. It was not until 1976 that a presidential debate was held again and since then they have been an ever present feature of the US presidential election campaign. The number, timing and location of the debates is always a controversial matter and one which is determined by the Commission on Presidential Debates, *http://www.debates.org* [Accessed 4 June 2015].

[152] The United States adheres to a strict version of the separation of powers. With the exception of the Vice-President who chairs the Senate (the upper chamber of the US legislature) members of the executive do not sit in the legislature. Voters in the US cast a different ballot to elect their "Senator" (who sits in the upper chamber) and the "Representative" (who sits in the lower chamber).

[153] In 1992 the Republican (President G.H.W. Bush) and Democrat (then Governor Clinton) candidates were joined by independent candidate Ross Perot and in 1976 a third candidate (Congressman Anderson) sought to participate in the debates. Otherwise, the debates have been a two party affair.

[154] The challenge was made to the broadcast of the third debate, which was due to be screened by the BBC. At the point the case was heard the first two debates had already been broadcast by other broadcasters.

[155] *Scottish National Party v BBC* [2010] CSOH 56; 2010 S.C. 495.

debates in a parliamentary democracy in the UK: whilst voters in Scotland may have an interest in seeing a representative of the SNP (or Welsh voters seeing Plaid Cymru) the voters in Yorkshire or East Anglia or Devon will have little, if any, interest as they are unlikely to have the option of voting for a candidate from those regional parties. That issue arose in 2015 where the parties again disagreed on who should be entitled to participate in any televised debates. Eventually there was a single debate, with seven party leaders appearing.[156] That still led to complaints from the Democratic Unionist Party in Northern Ireland about their omission. Other debates followed between the opposition leaders, and in Scotland between the Scottish political leaders. But the agreement was forged against the background of broadcasters threatening to leave an empty chair in the place of any leader who did not participate and sharp divisions between the leaders on the appropriate number and form of debate. This all highlighted that televised leadership debates in the run up to a general election do not sit easily with the UK's parliamentary style democracy. But they are likely to be here to stay and thus ought to be properly regulated. Just as it took the US a number of electoral cycles to learn to work with such debates, the same seems likely to be true of the UK.

CHALLENGING AN ELECTION RESULT[157]

It was previously an aspect of parliamentary privilege that it was for the House **4–27** of Commons, and the House of Commons alone, to determine the outcome of any controverted election. That remained the position until the Parliamentary Elections Act 1868 by which the House delegated its jurisdiction to the civil courts.[158] The Representation of the People Act 1983 now governs challenges to an election result and primarily relies upon private challenge. The 1983 Act applies to elections to the UK Parliament and local government.[159] Almost identical provision is made in the Scottish Parliament (Elections etc.) Order 2010 in relation elections to the Scottish Parliament.[160] Legal proceedings questioning an election must be taken in accordance with Pt III of the Representation of the People Act 1983.[161] The procedure set out below relates to the challenge to an election to the UK Parliament. The same procedures have, however, been largely adopted in relation to the Scottish Parliament.[162]

---

[156] Conservative, Labour, Liberal Democrat, SNP, Plaid Cymru, UKIP and the Greens.

[157] Law Commission, Scottish Law Commission and Northern Ireland Law Commission, *Electoral Law: A Joint Consultation* (The Stationery Office, 2014) L.C.C.P. 218, S.L.C.D.P. 158, N.I.L.C. 20, Ch.13 contains a comprehensive survey of this particularly complex corner of electoral law with a number of proposals for reform.

[158] For a brief history, see *Erskine May Parliamentary Practice*, edited by M. Jack, 24th edn (London: LexisNexis Butterworths, 2011) p.217.

[159] So far as local government elections in Scotland are concerned, that is as a result of the Scottish Local Government Elections Order 2011 (SSI 2011/399).

[160] Scottish Parliament (Elections etc.) Order 2010 (SI 2010/2999). Specific provision is made for European Parliamentary elections and it will not be discussed further here as it too broadly follows the schemes that have been enacted for domestic elections The relevant legislation is: European Parliamentary Elections Act 2002 and the European Parliamentary Elections Regulations 2004 (SI 2004/293).

[161] In what follows, we consider the procedure for challenging a parliamentary election result. Broadly similar provision is made by the 1983 Act to challenge a local government election result.

[162] Scottish Parliament (Elections etc.) Order 2010 (SI 2010/2999) art.84 and Sch.6.

A challenge must come in the form of a parliamentary election petition. [163] These are essentially private proceedings, which is surprising given the obvious public interest in the legitimacy of an election result. Three categories of persons have title to raise such a petition: (a) a person who voted, or who had the right to vote, at the election; (b) a person claiming to have had the right to be elected or returned at the election; and (c) a person alleging himself to have been a candidate at the election.[164] The respondent to such a petition is either the person whose election or return is being complained of or, where the petition complains about the conduct of the returning officer, the returning officer.[165] The form of petition and the procedures to be adopted in determining the petition are prescribed by the Rules of Court.[166] The timescales for challenging an election result are, for understandable reasons, short. The default time limit for presenting a parliamentary election petition is within 21 days of the election that is complained about.[167] Where, however, the complaint is of corrupt practices and specifically alleges a payment of money or other reward in furtherance of the alleged corrupt practice, a petition may be presented within 28 days of the date of the payment.[168] Other time limits apply where the allegation is of an illegal practice.[169] The grounds of challenge are not easily distilled from the various statutes that apply. In their consultation paper, the Law Commissions identified three grounds on which an election result can be annulled:

"(a) a breach of electoral law during the conduct of the election which was either: (i) fundamental; or (ii) materially affected the result;
(b) corrupt or illegal practices committed either: (i) by the winning candidate personally or through that candidate's agent; or (ii) by anyone else, to the benefit of the winning candidate, where such practices were so widespread that they could reasonably be supposed to have affected the result; or
(c) the winning candidate was at the time of the election disqualified from office".[170]

A parliamentary election petition is tried by two judges, who constitute "the election court".[171] The election court has the same powers, jurisdiction and authority as a judge of the Court of Session but importantly it is not the Court of Session.[172] It is a separate court exercising a jurisdiction which was previously the exclusive preserve of Parliament itself.[173] Unlike civil cases, where the Court

---

[163] 1983 Act s.120.
[164] 1983 Act s.121(1).
[165] 1983 Act s.121(2).
[166] In Scotland, Ch.69 of the Rules of the Court of Session 1994, read with ss.136 to 157 of the 1983 Act.
[167] 1983 Act s.122(1).
[168] 1983 Act s.122(2).
[169] 1983 Act s.122(3) and (4). Generally, 31 days after delivering an election expenses return to the returning officer or, where it is alleged that payment of money or some other act has been done, within 28 days of that payment or act.
[170] Law Commission, Scottish Law Commission and Northern Ireland Law Commission, *Electoral Law: A Joint Consultation*, para.13.12.
[171] 1983 Act s.123(1). A rota is maintained of judges who may be selected to hear election petitions. At the time of writing, the Scottish judges who could hear such petitions were Lord Eassie and Lady Paton (Court of Session Practice Direction No.1 of 2014).
[172] 1983 Act s.123(2).
[173] Until the Parliamentary Elections Act 1868 transferred that jurisdiction to the courts.

of Session always sits in Parliament House in Edinburgh, the election court should ordinarily sit within the constituency for which the election was held.[174] Having heard the necessary evidence, the election court must then determine whether the member whose election is complained of has been duly returned or elected or whether that election was void.[175] That determination must be communicated to the Speaker of the House of Commons forthwith.[176] Where the court is divided on whether the member has been properly elected (being a court of two judges there will be no majority) the election shall stand.[177] Where an allegation of corrupt or illegal practices was made in the petition, the election court shall also report to the Speaker (or Clerk to the Scottish Parliament) whether any such allegation has been proved to have been committed by or with the knowledge and consent of any candidate at the election and the nature of the corrupt or illegal practice.[178] The report must also name all those who have been proved to have been guilty of any corrupt or illegal practice, but where they were not a party to the petition proceedings, the election court must first give that person the opportunity to be heard and, if appropriate, lead evidence to defend why they should not be so reported.[179] A candidate's election is void if they are reported by an election court as personally guilty, or guilty by their agents, of any corrupt or illegal practice.[180] Where the election court finds that corrupt or illegal practices or illegal payments, employments or hirings were made in the context of the election campaign and with the view to procuring the election of any person prevailed so extensively that they may be reasonably supposed to have affected the result the election result shall be void.[181] The 1983 Act makes no provision for an appeal from the findings of the election court. Any decision is, however, amenable to judicial review.[182] Having reported to the Speaker, the election court is functus; there is no standing election court.

Thankfully, such challenges are rare. But the rules concerning challenges to **4–28** election results are, in the Law Commissions' words, "complex and inaccessible".[183] At the time of writing, the outcome of the Commissions' consultation is awaited but their provisional proposals for reform included bringing the law regarding challenging elections together in a single piece of primary legislation, the grounds of challenge should be restated and positively set out, the election court should be abolished with challenges being heard by the ordinary courts, returning officers should be given standing to raise a petition and the possibility of introducing "public interest" challenges. Whatever the outcome of the consultation, some codification of the rules relating to challenging election results would be welcome.

---

[174] 1983 Act s.123(3).
[175] 1983 Act s.144(1).
[176] 1983 Act s.144(2); in the case of the Scottish Parliament, the determination is relayed to the Clerk of the Scottish Parliament.
[177] 1983 Act s.144(3)(a).
[178] 1893 Act ss.144(4) and 158.
[179] 1983 Act s.160.
[180] 1983 Act s.159(1).
[181] 1983 Act s.164.
[182] *R. (on the application of Woolas) v Parliamentary Election Court* [2010] EWHC 3169 (Admin); [2012] Q.B. 1.
[183] Law Commission, Scottish Law Commission and Northern Ireland Law Commission, *Electoral Law: A Joint Consultation*, para.13.13.

CHAPTER 5

REFERENDUMS

INTRODUCTION

5–01 In the previous chapter we considered the electoral systems by which democracy in the United Kingdom has been traditionally assured. Referendums, or at least the promise of referendums, are, however, becoming increasingly popular. There is now detailed regulation of how a referendum ought to be conducted but there is little regulation of when a referendum ought to be held. The effect of the referendums on devolution in 1978 and 1997 appear to have established a convention that the people should be asked to approve a scheme of devolution.[1] In 2011 the people of Wales were asked to approve the transfer of limited legislative competence to the Welsh Assembly. They did, with 63.5 per cent of those voting in favour. The people of Scotland, however, were not asked to approve the changes to their devolution settlement that were introduced by the Scotland Act 2012. So even in relation to devolution, it is unclear when a referendum ought to be called. The people of Scotland, of course, have just been asked for their view not on devolution but on independence. By a margin of 55:45 (on an unprecedented turnout of 85 per cent) they voted to remain part of the UK. It had always been accepted that Scotland could not leave the Union without a positive vote in such a referendum. Similarly, legislation provides that Northern Ireland shall not leave the Union without the people of that province voting to do so in a referendum. So devolution and independence appear to require (politically at least) a referendum. The European Union Act 2011 now requires a referendum before certain amendments to the treaties can be ratified by the United Kingdom. As we have seen, a proposal to change the electoral system for the House of Commons was submitted to a referendum, it having long been accepted that direct approval by the people was necessary before any such change could be made. A range of other issues have been submitted to the people for approval, ranging from continued membership of what was then the EEC (in 1975; a similar question will be posed before the end of 2017) to the people of Aberdeen being asked to approve plans to replace Union Terrace Gardens (in 2012). This ad hoc use of the referendum, often for political as opposed to constitutional reasons, has been lamented by the House of Lords Constitution Committee.[2] The first question we will consider in this chapter is when, in a

---

[1] This applies not only to sub-national devolution but also to regional devolution: a referendum preceded the establishment of the Greater London Assembly and the creation of a directly elected mayor. The people of the north east of England rejected regional devolution in a referendum and as a result none has been forthcoming. Similarly, 9 out of 10 cities that were asked whether they wanted a directly elected mayor in 2012 said no.

[2] House of Lords Select Committee on the Constitution, *Referendums in the United Kingdom, 12th Report of Session 2009–2010* (The Stationery Office, 2010) HL Paper 99, para.62.

representative democracy, should resort be had to the people in a referendum? Despite the fact the first nationwide referendum was not held until 1975, use of the referendum has been advocated for over a century. One such advocate was Dicey and we will begin by considering some of his thoughts on the use of referendums. We will then turn to consider the range of circumstances in which a referendum has been held, or where legislation now requires that one be held, in an attempt to understand what the contemporary requirements of the constitution are.

The second issue we will consider in this chapter is the regulation of referendums and referendum campaigns. Despite the infrequency with which they have been held, detailed provision was introduced for their regulation in 2000. That regulatory framework will be outlined. Perhaps the most notable omission from this chapter on referendums is the 2014 Scottish independence referendum: we have already considered that in Ch.1.

DICEY ON THE REFERENDUM[3]

Given what we have seen about Dicey's views on parliamentary supremacy, it is **5–02** perhaps surprising to learn that he was a strong advocate for the introduction of the referendum:

> " ... the final decision of the nation's destiny must be referred to a more august tribunal than the House of Commons, or even than Parliament"[4]

Dicey's comments have to be set in the context of the time he was writing. He was a staunch opponent of Irish Home Rule, a measure that the House of Commons seemed determine to pass but which Dicey thought the majority of the population were opposed to. He was also increasingly concerned by the role played by the party system in the House of Commons which was, by the end of the nineteenth century, becoming increasingly powerful. The consequence, feared Dicey, was that the House of Commons, freely chosen by the electorate, may nonetheless fail to represent the views of the nation.[5] Dicey proposed a Referendum Act that would require approval by the people of any Act of Parliament effecting constitutional reform. The requirement, Dicey believed, should be judicially enforceable. His proposed Act provided:

> "Any Bill, or so-called Act, passed by both Houses of Parliament and assented to by the Crown, which, whilst affecting any one of the scheduled Acts, had not been sanctioned by and on appeal under the Referendum Act, should be held invalid by every court of law throughout the British Empire."[6]

---

[3] See generally: A.V. Dicey, "The Referendum" (1894) 23 *National Review* 65; A.V. Dicey, "The Referendum and its Critics" (1910) 212 *Quarterly Review* 538; R. Weill, "Dicey was not Diceyan" (2003) 62(2) C.L.J. 474.

[4] Dicey, "The Referendum" (1894) 23 *National Review* 65, 71.

[5] Dicey, "The Referendum and its Critics" (1910) 212 *Quarterly Review* 538.

[6] Dicey, "The Referendum and its Critics" (1910) 212 *Quarterly Review* 538, 554.

Such a provision obviously causes a problem for what is regarded as the Diceyian view of parliamentary supremacy: it simultaneously purports to bind Parliament's successors (but perhaps only in terms of the "manner and form" of legislation),[7] it appears to recognise a hierarchy of Acts of Parliament[8] and it authorises the courts to invalidate an Act of Parliament. In other words, it appears to contradict the three cardinal features of Dicey's own vision of parliamentary supremacy. Dicey sought to reconcile his Referendum Act and parliamentary supremacy by explaining no party leader would wish to incur the resentment of the electorate by denying them their say in a referendum but that Parliament could override his proposed Referendum Act if it was necessary to protect the State "against imminent peril, e.g. foreign invasion".[9] Dicey's Referendum Act would ultimately have been binding only in a political sense and the supremacy of Parliament preserved.

Leaving that to one side for now, for present purposes it is helpful to consider the function that Dicey saw the referendum performing. The referendum, for Dicey "places the electorate in the position once occupied in England by the Crown; it is the nation's veto ... It establishes the only conservative check on legalisation which is clearly in harmony with those democratic principles which in the modern world form the moral bases of government."[10]

Dicey recognised that there were forceful arguments against his vision of the referendum: it was conservative in that it can only block change not iniate it; the referendum ought to be useless because a fairly elected House of Commons should represent the wishes of the nation; and the referendum threatened to diminish the importance of Parliament.[11] Those concerns were, for Dicey, outweighed by the benefits of the system: it allows the people to pronounce on whether a particular change *should* be made while leaving to Parliament the detail of *how* such a change was implemented; and it "cuts at the root of parliamentary intrigue" allowing the people to override the will of the politicians.[12]

Despite Dicey's best efforts, however, Home Rule for Ireland was passed, the absolute veto of the House of Lords restricted and the referendum never adopted. It would be nearly three-quarters of a century until the United Kingdom used the referendum. Dicey's discussion of the referendum, however, offers a helpful introduction to the more contemporary issues that now arise.

THE REFERENDUM IN THE UK

5–03 It was in 1975 that the United Kingdom had its first nationwide referendum. Two years previously, a border poll had been held in Northern Ireland to determine whether the province should remain within the United Kingdom. On a 58.7 per cent turnout, 98.9 per cent of the votes cast were in favour of remaining in the

[7] See para.3–05, above.
[8] A consequence Dicey had already recognised: "[The referendum] may undoubtedly be so used as to establish a clear distinction between laws which effect permanent changes to the Constitution and ordinary legislation" (Dicey, "The Referendum" (1894) 23 *National Review* 65, 69).
[9] Dicey, "The Referendum and its Critics" (1910) 212 *Quarterly Review* 538, 555.
[10] Dicey, "Parliamentarism", lecture of 30 August 1898, reproduced in J.W.F. Allison (ed), *Comparative Constitutionalism: AV Dicey* (Oxford: Oxford University Press, 2013) p.147.
[11] Dicey, "Parliamentarism" in *Comparative Constitutionalism: AV Dicey* (2013) pp.148–149.
[12] Dicey, "Parliamentarism" in *Comparative Constitutionalism: AV Dicey* (2013) p.148.

United Kingdom. The poll was, however, boycotted by the nationalist community. In 1975, however, the people of the United Kingdom were asked: "Do you think the UK should stay in the European Community (Common Market)?"[13] Whether to hold a referendum was a deeply controversial topic, primarily due to concerns about its effect on the doctrine of parliamentary supremacy.[14] Continued membership of the EEC was said to be so significant that it was the sole exception to the principle that decisions be taken by Parliament and not by the people directly in a referendum.[15] Once the referendum genie was out of the bottle, however, others feared that it would not be possible to get it back in. Despite those constitutional arguments on whether the poll should have been held in the first place, when it came to the vote, on a 65 per cent turnout, 67 per cent voted in favour of the UK remaining within the "Common Market".

Despite government assurances in advance of the 1975 referendum that no precedent was being set and the vote was in response to a unique situation, it was not the last referendum of the decade. The devolution legislation of the 1970s, as originally introduced, contained no requirement for approval by the people of Scotland and Wales, respectively, in a referendum. Backbench pressure saw the government amend the Scotland and Wales Bill so as to introduce a referendum requirement. When the Scotland and Wales Bill ran out of parliamentary time, devolution legislation was again introduced in the 1977–78 session of Parliament, this time in the form of separate Bills for Scotland and Wales. This time, however, the Scotland Bill was amended during its passage to introduce what would become s.85(2) of the Scotland Act 1978. Section 85(2) required the Secretary of State to lay before Parliament an Order in Council for the repeal of the Act if it appeared that less than 40 per cent of the persons *entitled to vote* in the referendum had voted "yes".[16] An abstention therefore became a "no" vote and thus the lower the turnout the larger the margin of victory would have to be before a "yes" on the ballots cast became an effective "yes". In the event, on a turnout of 63 per cent, 52 per cent voted "yes" which equated to approximately 33 per cent of the electorate. Devolution for Scotland had, at that stage, been rejected.[17] When Labour returned to power in 1997, however, devolution was resurrected. Again, it was accepted that the people of Scotland and Wales should express a desire for devolution in a referendum before any system was implemented. But this time, the poll was to be held before Parliament passed devolution legislation. The Referendums (Scotland and Wales) Act 1997 was passed requiring polls to be held in September 1997. This time, no turnout threshold was included. On 11 September 1997 Scotland voted in favour of the establishment of a Scottish Parliament (74 per cent "yes", 26 per cent "no", turnout 61 per cent) and to vest it with limited tax varying powers (64 per cent "yes", 36 per cent "no"). Matters were much closer in Wales a week later: on a 50 per cent turnout, 50.3 per cent voted in favour of the establishment of a Welsh

---

[13] Referendum Act 1975 Schedule.
[14] For example, see C. Dike, "The case against parliamentary sovereignty" [1976] P.L. 283.
[15] *Hansard*, HC Vol.881, cols 1742–1743 (22 November 1974) quoted by V. Bogdanor, *The New British Constitution* (Oxford: Hart Publishing, 2009) p.182.
[16] An equivalent amendment was made to the Wales Bill, resulting in what became s.80(2) of the Wales Act 1978. In the event, it was academic. On a 58% turnout, only 20% voted "yes" and thus Welsh devolution was comprehensively rejected.
[17] The appropriate Order in Council was laid before Parliament and approved but not before the government considered asking its MPs to vote against it and thus save the devolution project. See the discussion by Bogdanor, *The New British Constitution* (2009) pp.183–184.

Assembly with 49.7 per cent voting against. The following year, the Scotland Act and the Government of Wales Act were passed by Parliament and the inaugural elections for the two new bodies were held in May 1999. We will return to consider what lessons can be learned from the UK's experience of the referendum thus far. But at this point it worth noting that had the 40 per cent threshold applied to the 1997 devolution referendums Scotland would have a Parliament *without* tax varying powers and Wales would have no Assembly.

Two other referendums took place in 1998: in Northern Ireland the Belfast Agreement was approved by the people of that province (71 per cent "yes", 29 per cent "no", turnout 80 per cent)[18] and in London the establishment of the Greater London Authority with a directly elected mayor and council were approved, in a manner of speaking, by Londoners (72 per cent "yes", 28 per cent "no", but a turnout of only 34 per cent). Similar devolution to the north east of England proved significantly less popular with the electorate there in 2004: on a 48 per cent turnout, only 22 per cent voted in favour. There have been no further referendums on devolution to other regions of England and the relevant legislation (the Regional Assemblies (Preparations) Act 2003) has now been repealed in its entirety.[19]

5–04	Two further referendums were held in 2011. First, on 3 March 2011 the people of Wales were asked to decide whether limited legislative competence should be granted to the Welsh Assembly. Unlike 1997, when Parliament had not yet passed legislation on the matter, provision had been made in the Government of Wales Act 2006. Under the 2006 Act, it was for the Welsh Assembly to request that the Secretary of State hold a referendum on the subject.[20] As with 1997, what was required was a majority of *votes cast* in a referendum and not any specific percentage of the electorate. The transfer of limited legislative competence to the Welsh Assembly was approved with 63.5 per cent voting in favour (36.5 per cent voting "no", with a turnout of 35.6 per cent). Then, in May 2011, only the second ever UK wide referendum was held. The electorate were asked to approve a change to the voting system for the House of Commons. This was a central plank of the Liberal Democrats coalition negotiations following the 2010 general election. When it was put to the electorate, however, it was roundly defeated. Turnout was only 42.2 per cent (the highest it reached was 63 per cent in Eastwood but it sunk as low as 27.2 per cent in Newham, London)[21] and 67.9 per cent of those voting voted "no".

---

[18] A referendum was simultaneously held in the Republic of Ireland as the Good Friday Agreement required approval in both referendums. For a discussion of some of the particular issues arising from the Good Friday Agreement referendums, see G. Gilbert, "The Northern Ireland Peace Agreement, Minority Rights and Self-Determination" (1998) 47 I.C.L.Q. 943.

[19] Local Democracy, Economic Development and Construction Act 2009 Sch.7(4) para.1.

[20] Government of Wales Act 2006 s.104. Similar provision is now made under the Wales Act 2014 (s.12) in relation to the possible transfer of limited powers in relation to income tax. Curiously, it is for the Welsh Assembly, in requesting that the referendum be held, to state the voting age (16 or 18) (s.13(2)). Sixteen was of course the voting age in Scotland for the independence referendum but, as matters stand at the time of writing, 18 will be the voting age for the proposed EU referendum (European Union Referendum Bill cl.2).

[21] C. Rallings and M. Thrasher, *The 2011 Referendum on the Parliamentary Voting System: aspects of participation and administration* (Plymouth: Elections Centre, University of Plymouth, 2011), *http://www.electoralcommission.org.uk/__data/assets/pdf_file/0018/141336/Plymouth-referendum-report-WEB.pdf* [Accessed 5 June 2015], prepared on behalf of the Electoral Commission.

Finally, of course, the Scottish people went to the polls on 18 September 2014 to answer the question: "Should Scotland be an independent country?" On a turnout of 84.6 per cent, 44.7 per cent answered that question "yes" whereas 55.3 per cent answered the question "no".[22] The obvious consequence of that result is that Scotland shall, for the time being at least, remain a part of the UK. Some of the issues arising from that result have already been discussed in Ch.1, above.

Before turning to consider what we can learn from the UK's experience of the referendum, it is worth noting that referendums happen on a local level too. For example, residents of Edinburgh were asked to approve the introduction of a congestion charge in 2005. That was a postal referendum and the proposal was rejected: 74.4 per cent voted "no" on a turnout of 61.8 per cent. In 2012, the people of Aberdeen were asked to choose between two proposals for the redevelopment of Union Terrace Gardens. Again, this was a postal referendum (although online and telephone voting were available). Turnout was 52 per cent with the City Garden Design Project being favoured by 52.3 per cent of the voters. Despite the failure of regional government in England and Wales in 2004, in 2012 referendums were held in 10 different cities across England asking the local population whether they wished to have a directly elected mayor. Only Bristol voted in favour.[23] Various other local referendums have been held across the country. As we will consider below, referendums at this level present some of their own issues.

One final point before moving: there is no (enforceable) obligation to hold a referendum. In Ch.14 we consider when a substantive legitimate expectation that gives rise to an enforceable right in public law can arise. For present purposes, however, it is sufficient to note that a ministerial (even a Prime-ministerial) promise to hold a referendum on any particular issues cannot give rise to an enforceable obligation on the Government to arrange such a referendum.[24]

That brief review of the use of the referendum in the United Kingdom helps **5–05** us answer the question posed above: when, in a representative democracy, should resort be had to the people in a referendum? But it also shows that the question really has two parts to it: first, on what issues should a referendum be held and secondly, should the referendum be held before or after Parliament has legislated on the matter? A further question arises from the UK's experience of the referendum: what provision, if any, should be made in relation to minimum levels of turnout to legitimise a referendum result? We will now turn to consider each of those issues.

---

[22] The turnout was noteworthy: 3.62 million votes were cast out of an electorate of 4.28 million. That level of public participation in democracy was unprecedented in modern times. Turnout peaked in East Dumbartonshire (at 91 per cent) and dropped no lower than 75 per cent (in Glasgow).

[23] The cities that rejected a directly elected mayor were: Birmingham, Bradford, Coventry, Leeds, Manchester, Newcastle-upon-Tyne, Nottingham, Sheffield and Wakefield. Doncaster voted to retain their mayor. The referendums were held in terms of s.9N of the Local Government Act 2000 (that section having been inserted by Sch.2 para.1 of the Localism Act 2011). See Electoral Commission, *Local elections and referendums in England 2012: Report on the administration of the elections and referendums held on 3 May 2012* (Electoral Commission, 2012), http://www.electoralcommission.org.uk/__data/assets/pdf_file/0004/149422/2012-English-locals-election-report-web.pdf [Accessed 5 June 2015].

[24] *R. (on the application of Wheeler) v Office of the Prime Minister* [2008] EWHC 1409 (Admin) at [41]; *Wheeler v Office of the Prime Minister* [2014] EWHC 3815 (Admin); [2015] 1 C.M.L.R. 46 at [41]–[48].

Statute now requires that a referendum be held on a number of issues, including: (a) before Northern Ireland can cease to be part of the UK[25]; (b) before any new exclusive competence is conferred upon the EU, or an existing competence extended[26]; (c) before limited tax varying powers are conferred on the Welsh Assembly[27]; (d) the adoption of certain planning decisions in England and Wales[28]; and (e) increasing, in certain circumstances, council tax charges in England and Wales.[29] That apart, the calling of a referendum is a matter for the government of the day, constrained to a certain extent by convention. Generally referendums have been called where the decision was believed to be of significant constitutional importance (devolution, independence or continued membership of the EU). Referendums on each of these issues can be labelled "constitutional referendums". This is a phrase that Tierney defines as "any direct citizen vote on the specific issue of constitutional change or constitutional creation".[30] Tierney identifies four types of constitutional process where the referendum is now regularly used: founding of new states (e.g. Montenegro in 2006); amendment or adoption of a constitution; establishing devolution; and transfer of sovereign powers to international institutions.[31] A border poll under the Northern Ireland Act 1998, which is necessary before Northern Ireland could leave the UK, would also fall into this category. Convention must now require a referendum to approve the introduction of devolution to a region: the effect of the 1998 vote in London and, more particularly the 2004 vote in the north east would appear to provide a precedent. The extension of devolution, however, is not as clear cut. The Government of Wales Act 2006 required approval in a referendum before limited legislative competence was conferred on the Welsh Assembly. Similarly, the Wales Act 2014 now requires a referendum before income tax varying powers are conferred on the Assembly. On the other hand, the Scotland Act 2012 was introduced without being approved by the Scottish people in a referendum. Although the 2012 Act made limited changes to the legislative competences of the Scottish Parliament it did significantly alter the devolved competences in relation to taxation. Despite a specific question on that issue being posed in the 1997 referendum, there was no great call for a referendum on the 2012 Act. Similarly, there has been no suggestion that a referendum be held on whatever becomes of the Smith Commission. That may be explained by attention being focused on the 2014 independence referendum: it would have

---

[25] Northern Ireland Act 1998 s.1 and Sch.1.

[26] European Union Act 2011 s.4. Various other matters that require a referendum are enumerated in s.4 but do not need to be discussed here. The 2011 Act is considered in more detail at para.10–42, below.

[27] Wales Act 2014 s.12.

[28] Town and Country Planning Act 1990 Sch.4B (as inserted by Sch.10 of the Localism Act 2011).

[29] Local Government Finance Act 1992 Ch.4ZA (as inserted by the Localism Act 2011 s.72 and Sch.5).

[30] S. Tierney, *Constitutional Referendums: The Theory and Practice of Republican Deliberation* (Oxford: Oxford University Press, 2012) p.11.

[31] Tierney, *Constitutional Referendums: The Theory and Practice of Republican Deliberation* (2012) p.1. Tierney also explains (pp.11–14) that "constitutional referendums" can be further subdivided into "constitution-changing" and "constitution-framing". The former occur within the existing constitutional structure of the state whereas the latter usually transcend the existing constitutional order. In the United Kingdom, referendums (including the Scottish independence referendum and the provisions of the Northern Ireland Act 1998) are best understood as falling into the former category as they have all been accommodated within the existing constitutional structure of the state.

been odd if the Scottish people were asked to approve a revised devolution scheme at the same time as plans were being laid for a referendum on independence. Conversely, in Wales, the result in 1997 can explain the requirement for a referendum before the Welsh Assembly was granted legislative competence. The margin of victory for the "yes" vote was so slight that testing the people of Wales continuing enthusiasm for devolution before extending it further appears eminently reasonable. What the contrast between Scotland and Wales shows is the continuing flexibility of the United Kingdom's constitutional arrangements and its ability to tailor a solution for a particular set of circumstances. Referendums have, however, also been called for apparently political reasons. The 1975 referendum on continued membership of the EEC falls into that category, as would the promised, but never held, referendum on adopting the euro. Both issues were highly controversial and divisive within the government. By submitting (or, in the case of the euro, undertaking to submit) the matter to the people in a referendum the political sting was drawn from it. Legislation is now before Parliament which will require a referendum to be held on the UK's continued membership of the European Union before the end of 2017.[32] The local referendums in Edinburgh and Aberdeen on congestion charging and redeveloping Union Terrace Gardens perhaps fall into this category as well.

The House of Lords Constitution Committee expressed their concern at the ad **5–06** hoc manner in which referendums have been used and called for cross-party agreement on the circumstances in which they should be used.[33] The Committee recommended that if they are to be used, they should be restricted to "fundamental constitutional issues". Recognising that a comprehensive definition of "fundamental constitutional issues" would be impossible (and unwise) they considered that any of the following issues would fall to be determined by a referendum: proposal to abolish the Monarchy; proposal to leave the EU; secession of the nations of the UK from the Union; abolition of either House of Parliament; changes to the electoral system for the House of Commons; adoption of a written constitution; and a proposal to change the currency used in the UK.[34] In relation to local referendums (of the sort that took place in Edinburgh and Aberdeen), the Committee was left unconvinced that they were the most effective way to increase citizen engagement with the local democratic process.[35]

The other issue to consider in relation to the calling of a referendum is the **5–07** question of timing. As we saw, the 1978 devolution referendums were called after Parliament had legislated on the matter. The people were being asked to approve the legislation enacted by Parliament. This was the Diceyian vision of the referendum: "the nation's veto". But by asking the people to vote after Parliament has legislated a number of problems arise. First, Parliament may find itself enacting legislation that its members are not actually in favour of but they would prefer to take the chance of trying to persuade the people to reject it. This leads to a second problem. In that scenario, it is not in the interests of those opposed to the substance of the measure to seek to improve the legislation as it makes its way through Parliament. The more problems they can point to in the

---

[32] European Union Referendum Bill (introduced to Parliament on 28 May 2015).
[33] House of Lords Select Committee on the Constitution, *Referendums in the United Kingdom, 12th Report of Session 2009–2010*, para.62.
[34] House of Lords Select Committee on the Constitution, *Referendums in the United Kingdom, 12th Report of Session 2009–2010*, para.94.
[35] House of Lords Select Committee on the Constitution, *Referendums in the United Kingdom, 12th Report of Session 2009–2010*, para.140.

legislation, the greater the chance they can persuade the people to reject the measure. Thirdly, it is a considerable waste of parliamentary time for potentially complex and controversial issues to be debated by both Houses and then passed only for it to be vetoed by the electorate. Finally, having the approval of the people before the legislative process begins helps secure the passage of the legislation when it comes before Parliament. Dicey conceived of the referendum as a purely negative weapon, unable to instigate change. Yes, if it is held after the event. But where it was held in advance, the referendum can have a positive effect. This last reason in particular saw the 1997 devolution referendums be held before legislation was introduced to Parliament.[36] Holding the referendum before Parliament legislates is not without its difficulties either. The primary argument is that the people need to have a clear idea of what they are voting for. That line of argument led to some calls in the early stage of the Scottish independence referendum debate for a second vote after the terms of secession had been agreed. There has been no consistent practice in the UK. Reform of the electoral system for the House of Commons was put to the people before legislation had been passed whereas, as we have seen, the people of Wales were asked about conferring legislative competence on the Welsh Assembly only after Parliament had enacted the necessary measures. What can perhaps be drawn from the UK's experience is that the more politically controversial the issue, the better it is to get the people's view in principle before Parliament debates the issue.

5–08	The UK's experience of the referendum also raises an interesting question about the need for, and the appropriateness of, a turnout threshold to legitimise the referendum and the result.[37] A threshold can be a response to two questions: when is the turnout so low that the result should have no authority; and, especially in relation to constitutional issues, when is the result sufficiently clear to sanction the proposed change? As we have seen, a threshold has only once been used in the United Kingdom, in the 1978 devolution referendums where 40 per cent of those eligible to vote had to vote in favour of devolution for the proposals to be implemented. That was an example of a voter-registered threshold, linked as it was to the number of registered voters and not the number of votes cast. On an 80 per cent turnout a 40 per cent requirement needs 50 per cent of those voting to support the proposal. But if turnout falls to 60 per cent, two-thirds of those voting must vote in favour. The threshold of success therefore varies according to the turnout. Where the referendum concerns an issue of constitutional change or importance, a voter-registered threshold requirement can be justified so as to ensure the measure attracts sufficiently broad support within the population. Imagine the result of the Scottish independence referendum had been different and 55 per cent of those voting had voted in favour of independence but this time on a turnout of only 65 per cent. Would 35.8 per cent of Scots voting for independence have been regarded as a sufficient majority to end the Union? At the very least, it would have risked a bitter argument as to what the effect of the result actually was. Such a threshold requirement can, however, also serve to depress turnout: failing to vote is a tantamount to a "no" vote. Such a threshold requirement therefore risks artificially lowering the

[36] That this was the main reason for holding the referendum before, and not after, the legislation passed through Parliament was made clear by Tony Blair in his memoirs: Blair, *A Journey* (London: Hutchison, 2010) p.252.
[37] See Tierney, *Constitutional Referendums: The Theory and Practice of Republican Deliberation* (2012) pp.271–278; Bogdanor, *The New British Constitution* (2009) pp.192–194.

turnout. It can also lead to problems after the vote where an overwhelming number of those voting supported a measure only for it to fall by having narrowly missed the threshold requirement. Most states, therefore, eschew a voter-registered threshold requirement. As we have seen, so too has the United Kingdom for all subsequent referendums.

But turnout in those subsequent referendums (save only the Scottish independence referendum), in particular the 1998 referendum on the establishment of the Greater London Authority and the 2011 referendum on the transfer of limited legislative competence to the Welsh Assembly (34 per cent and 35.6 per cent, respectively), raise the question of whether a threshold related to a minimum percentage of the registered electorate voting is appropriate. The 1998 and 2011 results translate as 24.5 per cent and 22.6 per cent, respectively, of the electorate in each of those referendums actually voting in favour of the proposal. As Tierney explains, turnout threshold is common throughout European countries that use the referendum as part of their constitution. Only a handful of countries have no such threshold requirement and they are very much the exception.[38] Had a 50 per cent turnout threshold been set for each referendum that has been held in the UK, there would be no Mayor of London, Wales would have an Assembly (just) but without legislative competence and reform of the voting system for the House of Commons would have failed at the first hurdle. Yet in each case the validity of the result was not questioned because of the turnout.

Of course, there is nothing magic about achieving a 50 per cent turnout. All that demonstrates is half of the population care sufficiently about the question that is being asked of them to express their opinion. If a simple majority is sufficient to "win" a referendum with a 50 per cent turnout threshold, the victory is still achieved with little more than a quarter of the electorate positively supporting the measure. Again, the significance of the issue probably plays a major role. If the choice is the style of garden design for the city centre (as it was in Aberdeen in 2012) ought it really to be blocked because so few people engaged with the issue? Whether to leave the EU, or to change currency, on the other hand, has much longer term consequences. As a result, there is a stronger case for ensuring that the proposed change has sufficient support from the electorate before proceeding. After all, the very fact a referendum has been called indicates that the legislature consider is at least prudent to seek specific approval from the people direct. It should, of course, be hoped that in those circumstances a turnout threshold becomes academic. If a referendum is reserved for genuinely important constitutional issues, assuming the electorate have been properly informed of not only the arguments for and against but why the issue is important, the electorate ought to be willing to engage in direct democracy and express their view. Recognising that the Scottish independence referendum was of unique character, it did demonstrate the levels of public engagement that can be achieved when the people are aware of the importance and significance of the issue. But the issues that the European Union Act 2011 require be submitted to a referendum rather risk voter fatigue as opposed to widespread engagement.

The referendum and the sovereignty of Parliament

A referendum result cannot, legally, bind Parliament. As we have already seen, **5–09** on an orthodox understanding of the constitution, the UK Parliament retains the

---

[38] Tierney, *Constitutional Referendums: The Theory and Practice of Republican Deliberation* (2012) p.272.

power to make or unmake any law. The people having expressed their view on the matter in a referendum does not qualify that power. Of course, the result of a referendum may act as a *political* limitation on Parliament's ability to legislate on a particular matter. But Parliament has long had political or other non-legal limitations on its legislative options. None of them detract from its legal supremacy. However, the greater the recourse to the referendum, the greater the strain that parliamentary sovereignty is likely to come under. The UK remains a representative democracy. As we saw in Ch.4, above, the role of the elected representative is as much "trustee" as it is "representative" and they are not always (indeed may rarely be) required to vote in line with the views of the majority of their constituents. But where the people have been consulted directly, the case for their elected representative (having agreed, in the first place, to consult the people) declining to follow the expressed will of the people is, at best, thin. However, in *Moohan*, Lord Neuberger (with whom the other justices in the majority agreed), in the context of considering the consequence of a "yes" vote in the Scottish independence referendum, said that Members of Parliament would not be bound to vote so as to give effect to the result but instead would have been "free, indeed constitutionally bound, to vote as they saw fit".[39] If that would be true of a UK-wide referendum (and there is no reason to doubt that, on the current understanding of parliamentary sovereignty, it would be) then that may well preserve Parliament's ability to reject the result of a referendum. But should Parliament ever vote so as to deny effect to the views expressed in a referendum, in the absence of some compelling justification, inordinate strain would undoubtedly be placed on the continuing doctrine of parliamentary sovereignty.

REGULATION OF REFERENDUMS

Introduction

5-10 Despite the fact that only a handful of referendums have ever been held, detailed provision was made about them in 2000. Part VII of the Political Parties, Elections and Referendums Act 2000 introduced detailed rules on who may participate in a referendum campaign, the funding of such a campaign and the conduct of any vote. Part VII of the 2000 Act applies to any referendum "held, in pursuance of any provision made by or under an Act of Parliament, on one or more questions specified in or in accordance with any such provision".[40]

Consequently, the Scottish independence referendum did not fall within the scope of the Act (called, as it was, by the Scottish Parliament). A poll held under s.64 of the Government of Wales Act 2006 (which allows the Welsh Ministers to hold a poll to ascertain the views of the Welsh public on how any of its powers should be exercised) is also excluded from the scope of the Act.[41] Specific provisions are made for these referendums. What follows is a brief overview of the main provisions of PPERA that would apply to a referendum that is called by the UK Parliament.

---

[39] *Moohan, Petitioner* [2014] UKSC 67; 2015 S.L.T. 2 at [47].
[40] Political Parties, Elections and Referendums Act 2000 ("PPERA") s.101(2).
[41] PPERA s.101(3).

Preliminaries

The provisions of the Political Parties, Elections and Referendums Act 2000 **5–11**
begin to apply even before the legislation authorising a referendum has been
enacted. Where the Bill proposing the referendum specifies the wording of the
question that will be posed, the Electoral Commission is required to publish a
statement of any views that it has as to the proposed question's intelligibility.
That statement should be published, in such manner as the Commission may
determine, as soon as practicable after the Bill is introduced.[42] An equivalent
procedure is to be followed when the wording of the question is to be determined
by secondary legislation.[43] An Act that sanctions the holding of a referendum
should also prescribe a "referendum period".[44] During the "referendum period"
controls on the spending of "permitted participants" apply. It is important,
therefore, to understand who these controls apply to.

Permitted participants and campaign funding

Regulation of the campaign, and in particular its funding, is tied to the concept **5–12**
of the "permitted participant".[45] A "registered party" can make a declaration to
the Commission stating the referendum to which it relates and the outcome that
the party proposes to campaign for. An individual or certain legal entities listed
in s.54 of PPERA can also notify the Commission of their intention to campaign
in a referendum and the outcome they propose to campaign for.[46] A declaration
by a registered party or a legal entity must identify the person responsible for
compliance with the financial controls that are imposed. The Commission is
required to maintain a register of declarations and notifications.[47] The Commission has the power to designate certain permitted participants as "organisations
to whom assistance is available".[48] Where there are only two possible outcomes
to a referendum, the Commission may only designate one permitted participant
as representing those campaigning for the outcome in question.[49] Where there are
more than two possible outcomes, the Secretary of State may, having consulted
the Commission, specify the possible outcomes in relation to which permitted
participants may be designated by the Commission.[50] A permitted participant
may apply for designation by the Commission and such an application must be
made within 28 days of the start of the referendum period.[51] The Commission
must make its decision within 14 days of the end of that 28 day period. The
referendum can be held no earlier than 28 days after the period for the

---

[42] PPERA s.104(2).
[43] PPERA s.104(3)–(6).
[44] PPERA s.102. For the 2011 referendum on the proposed change to the voting system for the
House of Commons the "referendum period" began on the day the Parliamentary Voting System
and Constituencies Act 2011 was passed (16 February 2011") and ended on the day of the
referendum (5 May 2011): Sch.1 para.1.
[45] PPERA s.105.
[46] Those entities are: a company registered under the Companies Act 2006 or another Member State
and carrying out business in the UK; a trade union; a building society; a limited liability
partnership; a friendly society; or an unincorporated association (PPERA ss.54(2)(b) and (d)–(h)
and 106(4)(b)).
[47] PPERA s.107.
[48] PPERA s.108.
[49] PPERA s.108(2).
[50] PPERA s.108(3).
[51] PPERA s.109(1) and (2).

Commission to make its decision has expired.[52] Where there is only one application to represent a particular outcome, the Commission shall designate that applicant unless it appears that they do not adequately represent those campaigning for that outcome.[53] Where there is more than one applicant to represent a particular outcome, the Commission shall designate the applicant that appears to them to represent to the greatest extent those campaigning for that outcome.[54] The participants designated by the Commission shall each receive a grant, of the same amount, not exceeding £600,000.[55]

That narrative is the statutory basis on which a referendum campaign ends up with an "official" "yes" campaign and an "official" "no" campaign. The ordinary political parties will normally make a declaration to the Commission so that they can participate in the campaign. But they are unlikely to be the "official" campaign for any particular outcome. A particular, one off, organisation is likely to be formed for that purpose. Referendum questions do not normally divide neatly along party lines that make "official" campaigns on either side a better vehicle by which to ensure there is a coherent campaign for both sides of the argument. It also allows fund raising to be done in the name of the campaign and not the party which allows those that may have no political loyalty to the party (or parties) leading the campaign they support to participate without feeling they are supporting, financially or otherwise, a political party they do not.

5-13   Once participants have registered with the Commission, and the referendum period has begun, they become subject to PPERA's financial controls. These controls are set out in Ch.2 of Pt VII and come in three parts: incurring costs associated with the referendum; spending limits; and receiving donations. Starting with costs incurred, PPERA defines "referendum expenses" as expenses that fall within Pt 1 of Sch.13[56] and incurred for referendum purposes.[57] Various anti-avoidance provisions are made in s.112 to prevent circumvention of the spending limits.[58] The Act then imposes controls on permitted participants incurring referendum expenses. It is an offence for any referendum expenses to be incurred without the consent of the responsible person (who was identified to the Commission at the time of registration) or a person authorised, in writing, by the responsible person.[59] Similarly, it is an offence to make a payment (of whatever nature) in respect of any referendum expenses that has been, or will be, incurred unless it is made by the responsible person or a person authorised, in

[52] PPERA s.103.
[53] PPERA s.109(4).
[54] PPERA s.109(5).
[55] PPERA s.110.
[56] There are eight categories set out in Pt 1 of Sch.13: referendum campaign broadcasts, advertising of any nature; unsolicited material addressed to electors; certain promotional material; market research or canvassing for the purposes of ascertaining voting intentions; provision of services and facilities in relation to press conferences or other dealings with the media; transport by any means of persons to any place with a view to obtaining publicity in connection with a referendum campaign; and rallies and other events, including public meetings (but not party conferences) with a view to obtaining publicity in connection with the campaign.
[57] PPERA s.111(2). "For referendum purposes" means, read short, promoting or procuring a particular outcome (s.111(3)).
[58] PPERA s.112 which concerns "notional referendum expenses", for example, where employees are made available to a campaign or where property is transferred for a discount of more than 10% of its market value.
[59] PPERA s.113(1) and (2).

writing, by the responsible person.[60] Any payment of more than £200 must be supported by an invoice or receipt and where the payment is made by a person authorised by the responsible person, it is an offence if that persons fails to provide the responsible person with the invoice or receipt and notification that they have made the payment as soon as possible after it has been made.[61] Any claim for payment incurred in respect of referendum expenses by a permitted participant during the referendum period must be submitted to the responsible person (or a person authorised by them to incur the expenses) within 30 days of the end of the referendum period.[62] It must be paid within 60 days of the end of the referendum period.[63] It is an offence to contravene either of these periods, although leave can be sought from the court to extend them. Such leave may only be granted if for any special reason it is appropriate to do so.[64]

Financial limits apply during the referendum period to any individual or body who is not a permitted participant. If they did not, there would be no incentive to register with the Commission and incur the reporting obligations that follow. That limit is currently £10,000 and it is an offence to incur expenses in excess of it.[65] Where the expenses are incurred by a body the offence is committed by both the body and any person who knew, or ought reasonably to have known, that expenses would be incurred in excess of the limit.[66] So far as permitted participants are concerned, the bodies designated under s.108 (in other words, the "official" campaigns) may incur no more than £5,000,000 of referendum expenses during the referendum period.[67] The limit imposed on political parties is tied to their share of the vote at the previous UK general election. The relevant limits are these[68]:

Relevant % at last election	Limit
Greater than 30%	£5,000,000
More than 20% but not more than 30%	£4,000,000
More than 10% but not more than 20%	£3,000,000
More than 5% but not more than 10%	£2,000,000
Not more than 5% or no relevant %	£500,000

For any other person or body that notified the Commission the limit is £500,000. These limits apply to UK wide referendums. Where a referendum falls within the scope of PPERA but only relates to part of the UK, the Secretary of State shall prescribe the necessary limits by order.[69] It is again an offence to exceed these limits. For a political party, the offence is committed by the responsible person

---

[60] PPERA s.114(1) and (4).
[61] PPERA s.114(2)–(4).
[62] PPERA s.115(1).
[63] PPERA s.115(2).
[64] PPERA s.115(3)–(5). Where the entitlement to payment is disputed, nothing in s.115 prevents an action for payment of any sums that are claimed to be due: s.116.
[65] PPERA s.117(1)–(2).
[66] PPERA s.117(3)–(4).
[67] PPERA s.118 and Sch.14 para.1(2).
[68] PPERA s.118 and Sch.14 para.1(2)(b).
[69] PPERA s.118 and Sch.14 para.2(2).

and any deputy treasurer (assuming they knew, or ought reasonably to have known, that the limit would be exceeded) and the party itself.[70] For other permitted participants, the offence is committed by the responsible person (again assuming they had the necessary knowledge) and the body itself.[71]

Donations to political parties are regulated in the normal manner (which is set out in Pt IV of PPERA).[72] For those individuals and bodies that are permitted participants but not registered political parties, special provision is made.[73] These rules, which need not be rehearsed here, broadly replicate the scheme in place for political parties. For example, the definition of "permissible donor" is the same, the de minimis threshold of £500 is retained and the reporting requirements are almost identical. Irrespective of which set of rules govern the receipt of donations, for all permitted participants that incur any referendum expenses during the referendum period, detailed returns must be submitted to the Commission within six months of the end of the referendum period.[74] Where the referendum expenses incurred by a permitted participant exceeded £250,000, the return to the Commission must be accompanied by a report prepared by a qualified auditor.[75] Various offences are committed by failing to comply with the requirement to make a return to the Commission.

The campaign

5–14 The Political Parties, Elections and Referendums Act 2000 goes on to make a number of particular provisions in relation to the conduct of the campaign. First, it restricts the material that can be published by any Minister of the Crown, government department or local authority in the 28 days immediately before the referendum.[76] The restrictions do not prevent any of these bodies answering specific requests for information, the issuing of press notices or publishing information concerning the holding of the poll. It does prohibit, however, the publication of any material that puts arguments for or against the referendum question or is in any way designed to encourage voting at the referendum. The purpose of the restriction is clear. The government will invariably have a position on any referendum (and particular local governments may take a contrary view from that of the central government). Indeed, depending on the question posed, the very future of the government may depend on the result. The government is invariably in a much strong position, in terms of the resources available to it and its access to the media, than other bodies that may be campaigning. Restricting its activities in the four weeks before a vote is a sensible measure to level the playing field. Next, PPERA requires that no material wholly or mainly relating to the referendum may be published during the referendum period unless it complies with certain stipulated requirements.[77] In short, such material must include the name and address of the printer of the material, the promoter of the material, and any person on behalf of whom the material is being published. It is an offence to not comply with these requirements. Finally, broadcasters are

---

[70] PPERA s.118(2)(a).
[71] PPERA s.118(2)(b).
[72] Outlined at para.4–19, above.
[73] PPERA s.119 and Sch.15.
[74] PPERA ss.120–124.
[75] PPERA s.121.
[76] PPERA s.125.
[77] PPERA s.126.

prohibited from carrying any referendum campaign broadcast made by any person or body not designated by the Commission under s.108 (in other words, only the "official" campaigns may make a referendum campaign broadcast).[78] This duty, taken with the broadcasters' existing duty of impartiality, is designed to ensure that each side of the campaign has equal access to free airtime for referendum broadcasts.

In relation to the vote itself, it is conducted under the supervision of the Chief **5–15** Counting Officer. The Chief Counting Officer shall be the chairperson of the Commission. They shall appoint a counting officer for each relevant area in Great Britain.[79] The Secretary of State is empowered to make such orders as they consider expedient in relation to the conduct of the referendum. Before making such an order, however, they shall consult the Commission. They may not make any order in relation to matters for which specific provision has been made in another enactment.[80]

---

[78] PPERA s.127.
[79] PPERA s.128.
[80] PPERA s.129.

CHAPTER 6

PARLIAMENTS

6–01 Since 1 July 1999, the Scottish Parliament has exercised legislative competence in the increasing sphere of devolved competence. It is a competence that is shared with the Westminster Parliament. The Scotland Act 1998 is explicit on that point.[1] Outwith that sphere, the Westminster Parliament retains exclusive legislative competence. In particular, terms of devolution are reserved to Westminster thus the Scottish Parliament remains subordinate to it.[2]

There are significant differences between the Westminster Parliament and the Scottish Parliament, which go beyond the differences in their legislative competences. Westminster is a bicameral legislature, the Scottish Parliament unicameral. Westminster and Scottish parliamentary committees have different functions (perhaps most prominently, the committees of the Scottish Parliament have a power to initiate legislation, which the Westminster committees do not yet share). But there are also many similarities and parallels between the two institutions. Both perform the same general functions of a representative, law-making body in a "parliamentary system": the enactment of legislation, the provision of a government and the sustaining of that government in office, and the important function of holding the government and other public authorities to account on behalf of the public as a whole. The rules and procedures governing both bodies have much in common, in so far as those applicable in Scotland often represent a statutory rendering of the conventions that have grown up at Westminster. The same is true in matters of privilege and standards, in that both bodies have jurisdiction to regulate their own procedures and the conduct of their members. The two Parliaments are therefore considered side by side, high-lighting the distinctions between them where such exist, but noting also what they have in common where that is the case.

LIFE OF PARLIAMENT

Westminster

6–02 The life of a Parliament at Westminster begins when the Sovereign exercises her prerogative to summon it to meet. By convention, the Queen exercises this prerogative following a general election. Parliament must meet in the subsequent

---

[1] Scotland Act 1998 ("SA 1998") s.28(7). The extent to which Westminster may enact legislation for Scotland the subject matter of which falls within the definition of devolved competence is regulated for the present by the so called "Sewel convention", whereby Westminster will not normally enact such legislation without first obtaining the consent of the Scottish Parliament: see para.2–11, above.

[2] SA 1998 s.28(7); *AXA General Insurance Co Ltd v Lord Advocate* [2011] UKSC 46; 2012 S.C. (U.K.S.C.) 122, per Lord Reed at [146].

years of its life to approve the appropriation of monies for the provision of public services and perform its other constitutional functions. It was, until 2011, for the Queen to dissolve Parliament. This was done on the advice of the Prime Minster and had to be done no later than five years after the previous general election.[3] In practice, Parliament was dissolved before this time, usually during its fourth year. The Fixed-term Parliaments Act 2011 removes that prerogative power.[4] The last UK general election was held on 7 May 2015[5] and future elections will ordinarily be held on the first Thursday of May every five years.[6] The Prime Minister can, by statutory instrument, delay the election date by up to two months.[7] There are two mechanisms by which an earlier election can be called. Both lie in the hands of the House of Commons and not the Prime Minister or the Sovereign. First, the House of Commons can pass a motion that there shall be an early general election. Such a motion requires a two-thirds majority in the House of Commons.[8] Secondly, an early general election can be prompted by a vote of no confidence in the government. This only requires a simple majority and shall trigger an election only if a motion of confidence is not then passed within 14 days.[9] Where an election is held in such circumstances, and the poll takes place before the first Thursday in May, the next general election is on the first Thursday in May in the fourth calendar year following the election. Where such a poll takes place after the first Thursday in May, the next election takes place in the fifth calendar year following the election (again on the first Thursday in May).[10]

The case for Parliament to operate on a fixed-term basis had long been made. Both Labour and the Liberal Democrats went in to the 2010 election with a manifesto promise to legislate for a fixed-term Parliament. The advantage of a fixed-term Parliament is primarily in restricting the power of the executive to call an election at a time of their choice. Prior to the 2011 Act, the decision rested with the Prime Minister alone, which allowed the election to be held on a date that would maximise the political advantage to the government. Fixing the length of Parliament also allows for the better planning of the legislative programme and, especially in times of coalition, can offer stability and security to the government. How real these benefits are has been questioned.[11] In 2010, a fixed-term Parliament was important to the junior members of the coalition (the Liberal Democrats) so that the Prime Minister could not end the coalition at will (and at a time which gave him the greatest political advantage). Whether one is a supporter of fixed-term Parliaments or not there are a number of criticisms that

---

[3] Parliament Act 1911 s.7.

[4] Fixed-term Parliaments Act 2011 s.3(2); see generally M. Ryan, "The Fixed-term Parliaments Act 2011" [2012] P.L. 213; R. Brazier, "A small piece of constitutional history" (2012) 128 L.Q.R. 315.

[5] Fixed-term Parliaments Act 2011 s.1(2).

[6] Fixed-term Parliaments Act 2011 s.1(3).

[7] Fixed-term Parliaments Act 2011 s.1(5); the reason for this provision lies in ensuring sufficient flexibility to deal with a situation such as the foot and mouth outbreak that promoted Tony Blair to delay the 2001 election by a month so as to deal with the crisis.

[8] Fixed-term Parliaments Act 2011 s.2(1).

[9] Fixed-term Parliaments Act 2011 s.2(3).

[10] Fixed-term Parliaments Act 2011 s.1(4). Compare with the provisions of the Scotland Act 1998: where an "extra-ordinary general election" (e.g. one that follows a vote of no confidence in the Scottish Government) does not interrupt the normal four year parliamentary cycle.

[11] Brazier, "A small piece of constitutional history" (2012) 128 L.Q.R. 315, 316–317; V. Bogdanor, *The Coalition and the Constitution* (Oxford: Hart, 2011) Ch.6.

can be levelled at the 2011 Act. Why, for example, was a five-year period chosen? Under the Parliament Act 1911 that was the *maximum* length of a Parliament but in practice most lasted for less than four years. Four years was selected as the appropriate length of time between elections for devolved legislatures and is the most common period in other European countries. A five-year cycle also meant that the 2015 election would fall on the same day as elections to the Scottish Parliament. The 2011 Act addresses that problem by extending the current session of the Scottish Parliament by a year.[12] That, however, only delayed the problem until 2020 when the elections would have again clashed. As we shall see shortly, consideration is still being given to a permanent solution to this by-product of the 2011 Act.[13] Furthermore, the 2011 Act leaves no residual power for the sovereign to dissolve Parliaments. The Queen retains such a residual function, which could only be appropriately used in exceptional circumstances, in relation to Canada, Australia and New Zealand but not now in relation to the United Kingdom. Why that decision was taken is not at all clear. Fixed-term Parliaments are not in themselves objectionable. Yet the 2011 Act represents another bit of piecemeal reform of the constitution which is likely to need reconsidered in the years ahead.

The Queen's Speech takes place early on in a newly summoned Parliament, and at the commencement of subsequent parliamentary sessions of the Parliament. It marks the formal opening of each new session following the summoning or re-summoning of Parliament. Sessions[14] usually run for about 12 months from November to November, although there is no legal requirement that they should. A session is brought to an end either by the dissolution of Parliament or by its prorogation. The significance of prorogation is that it suspends all parliamentary business until the next session (which may begin the following day). In particular, public Bills which do not complete their parliamentary stages before the end of the session lapse and must start again in the session following (although there is now provision for the carrying over of government legislation from one session to the next with the agreement of the House of Commons).[15]

Holyrood

6–03 The life cycle of the Scottish Parliament is fixed by the Scotland Act 1998. It begins on a date falling within the period of seven days beginning with the day immediately after that on which the poll at a general election was held.[16] Ordinarily, it will end with its dissolution with a view to a general election being held on the first Thursday in May of the fourth calendar year following that in

---

[12] Fixed-term Parliaments Act 2011 s.4; similar provision is made for Wales and Northern Ireland so as to avoid elections to those legislatures being held on the same day as an election to the UK Parliament (s.5 of the 2011 Act).

[13] With respect to the Welsh Assembly, the problem has been solved by increasing that body's term from four to five years (Wales Act 2014 s.1).

[14] A "Session" of the UK Parliament is usually a year but a "Session" of the Scottish Parliament is the entire period (usually four, but currently five, years) between elections.

[15] In Scotland, Bills have the full remaining spread of the parliamentary cycle following their introduction in which to complete their parliamentary stages.

[16] SA 1998 s.2(3)(b). For the purposes of calculating the seven day period, Saturday and Sunday, Christmas Eve and Christmas Day, Good Friday, a Scottish bank holiday or a "day appointed for public thanksgiving or mourning" are to be disregarded: s.4.

which the previous ordinary general election was held.[17] Should the first Thursday in May be unsuitable for some reason unsuitable, the Presiding Officer of the Scottish Parliament may propose an alternative date, no earlier than one month before and no later than one month after the first Thursday in May, to the Queen; and the Queen may[18] then by proclamation dissolve the Parliament, require the poll to be held on the date proposed and require the new Parliament to meet within the period of seven days beginning with the date of the poll. Should the recommendations of the Smith Commission be enacted, the Scotland Act will be amended to prevent a clash with the scheduled election date for the UK Parliament.[19] The draft clauses prepared by the Smith Commission included a proposed s.2A to be inserted into the Scotland Act. If enacted, the four-yearly election cycle of the Scottish Parliament would be interrupted where the Scottish general election would clash with a UK, European or Scottish local government election. Where there would otherwise be a clash, s.2A (if enacted) would require the Scottish general election to be held no less than two months and no more than six months after the date on which the election should otherwise be held. Surprisingly, the draft s.2A makes no provision for (and by when) how the actual date of the election will be chosen. Given the power already vested in the Presiding Officer in relation to varying the election date, she would be the obvious choice. The consequence is that while the first Thursday in May of the fourth calendar year following an election remains the default, the lifespan of the Scottish Parliament will now vary between four and a half years and three and a half years, with a four-year Parliament becoming the exception. This all appears to be an unintended by-product of the hastily enacted Fixed-term Parliaments Act 2011.

Section 3 of the Scotland Act makes provision for extraordinary general elections. Where no fewer than two-thirds of the total number of MSPs (that is, at least, 86 MSPs) vote in favour of a resolution that the Parliament be dissolved, the Presiding Officer must propose a date for the holding of an election and the Queen may, by proclamation, dissolve the Parliament, require an extraordinary general election to be held on the date proposed and enjoin the new Parliament to meet within seven days of the date of the poll.[20] An extraordinary general election may also be required where the Parliament fails to nominate one of its members for appointment as First Minister within 28 days of a general election, or of the resignation or death of an incumbent First Minister, or of the incumbent First Minister ceasing to be an MSP otherwise than by virtue of a dissolution of the Scottish Parliament.[21] In any of these situations, if the extraordinary election is held within the six month period prior to the first Thursday in May, and an

---

[17] SA 1998 ss.2(3)(a). If the election is to be held on the first Thursday in May, the Parliament must be dissolved at the beginning of the "minimum period" ending with the date of the poll. The "minimum period" is specified in accordance with orders made under s.12, which confers power on the Secretary of State to make provision about Scottish elections.

[18] Here, "may" not "shall" (cf. SA 1998 s.2(3)(a)). Presumably this is to preserve an element of discretion on the Queen's part as the ultimate safeguard against abuse (although it is significant that it is the Presiding Officer, not the First Minister, who is charged with proposing an alternative date), but it presents another odd contrast with the Fixed-term Parliaments Act 2011 which divested the Queen of any discretion in the dissolution of Parliament.

[19] HM Government, *Scotland in the United Kingdom: An enduring settlement* (The Stationery Office, 2015) para.1.4, *https://www.gov.uk/government/uploads/system/uploads/attachment_data/file/397079/Scotland_EnduringSettlement_acc.pdf* [Accessed 7 June 2015].

[20] SA 1998 s.3(1)(a) and (2)(b).

[21] SA 1998 s.3(1)(b); and see also s.46.

ordinary election was due to take place on the latter date, the ordinary election will not be held.[22]

COMPOSITION

The Sovereign

6–04 As we have seen, the Sovereign has an important, if formal, role to play in the dissolution and summoning of the Westminster and Scottish Parliaments. But the Sovereign is also a component part of the Westminster Parliament—"the King, Lords and Commons assembled"—in that Acts of Parliament are Acts of the Queen in Parliament, and must receive Royal Assent in order to become law.[23] The Queen is not part of the Scottish Parliament even in this formal sense, but Royal Assent is nonetheless necessary in order that a Bill passed by the Parliament may become an Act of the Scottish Parliament.[24]

Westminster

House of Lords

> "No one shall be a member of the House of Lords by virtue of a hereditary peerage."

6–05 At a stroke (promptly qualified), s.1 of the House of Lords Act 1999 did away with what was widely accepted as an indefensibly undemocratic blemish on British constitutional arrangements. But it has to be put in its historical context: in 1911 the powers of the House of Lords to block legislation approved by the House of Commons were curtailed by the Parliament Act, the long title of which declared:

> "it is intended to substitute for the House of Lords as it at present exists a Second Chamber constituted on a popular instead of hereditary basis, but such substitution cannot be immediately brought into operation".

A century on, the wait continues.[25] Perhaps the most that could be said for the historic right of hereditary peers to sit and vote in the House of Lords was that they offered some form of counterweight to the "elective dictatorship" flowing from the command of a majority in the House of Commons. But it was not a particularly compelling argument for retention of the hereditary principle: if nothing else, there was a question about how even-handed a counterweight the hereditary peers actually were.

---

[22] SA 1998 s.3(3). This does not affect the year in which the subsequent ordinary general election will be held: s.3(4).

[23] By convention, of course, the Sovereign never refuses Royal Assent. The last time this happened was in the reign of Queen Anne, and even then seems to have been on the advice of her Ministers.

[24] SA 1998 s.28(2)–(4).

[25] See C. Ballinger, *The House of Lords 1911–2011: A Century of Non-Reform* (Oxford: Hart, 2012).

The House of Lords remains in a transitional state, pending final reform. There are about 790 peers in total, comprising about 650 life peers,[26] 26 Lords Spiritual (being bishops and archbishops of the Church of England) and 92 hereditary peers exempted from the effects of the 1999 Act. Members of the judiciary (be they former Lords of Appeal in Ordinary[27] or other members of the judiciary) are now disqualified from sitting and voting in the House of Lords.[28] Following the enactment of the 1999 Act, the government appointed a Royal Commission under the chairmanship of Lord Wakeham to consider and make recommendations on the changes needed to bring about a fully reformed and modernised second chamber.[29] The Wakeham Commission reported in January 2000.[30] It recommended no substantial changes to the functions of the House of Lords or to the balance of power between the two Houses of Parliament, but dealt in detail with the question of the composition of a reformed upper house. In essence, Wakeham favoured a mixed membership of about 550, consisting of elected "regional members" and members appointed on the nomination of an independent statutory appointments commission charged with securing a "broadly representative" chamber. Some one-fifth of the members of this reformed House of Lords would sit on the cross-benches; the remaining, politically affiliated members would be required to reflect the voting preferences expressed at the most recent general election. The government endorsed Wakeham's recommendations, but its attempts to take them forward have run repeatedly into the sand.[31] Having undertaken to allow a free vote in Parliament on the composition of a reformed House of Lords in its manifesto for the 2005 general election, the government published a further White Paper in February 2007 in order to provide a framework within which such a vote might take place.[32] On 7 March 2007 a series of votes were held in the House of Commons on various reform options.[33]

[26] The Life Peerages Act 1958 provided for the conferment of life peerages on men and (for the first time) women with the right to sit and vote in the Lords. Life peers have helped to mitigate, if not remove, the political imbalance in the upper house; and, to the extent that life peerages are conferred in recognition of outstanding public service and/or expertise in particular fields, have brought to the House of Lords a rather wider range of experience and specialism than tends to exist in the Commons. But as appointees, life peers have no obviously greater claim to democratic legitimacy than hereditary peers.

[27] The House of Lords judicial function (save as in so far as it retains jurisdiction to determine peerage claims: *Erskine May Parliamentary Practice*, edited by M. Jack, 24th edn (London: LexisNexis Butterworths, 2011) pp.182–183) was abolished on the creation of the Supreme Court on 1 October 2009.

[28] Constitutional Reform Act 2005 s.137.

[29] For the government's own thoughts on the matter, see HM Government, *Modernising Parliament: Reforming the House of Lords* (The Stationery Office, 1999) Cm.4183.

[30] Royal Commission on the Reform of the House of Lords, *A House for the Future* (The Stationery Office, 2000) Cm.4534.

[31] The government set out its proposals in a further White Paper, HM Government, *The House of Lords: Completing the Reform* (The Stationery Office, 2001) Cm.5291, which was then the subject of public consultation. The crucial outcome of that consultation process was the rejection, by almost 90% of respondents, of the government's proposal for a predominantly appointed second chamber. The government thereupon handed the matter over to Parliament; but the joint committee of both Houses of Parliament established in 2002 and charged with finding a way through to the next stage of reform met with no more success. A further, fruitless, public consultation took place in 2003–2004 on the proposals contained in yet another White Paper, Department for Constitutional Affairs, *Constitutional Reform: Next Steps for the House of Lords* (The Stationery Office, 2003) CP14/03.

[32] HM Government, *The House of Lords: Reform* (The Stationery Office, 2007) Cm.7207.

[33] They were: fully appointed House of Lords; fully elected; 20% elected; 40% elected; 50% elected; 60% elected; and 80% elected.

The House of Commons voted in favour of *both* a fully elected House of Lords and an 80 per cent elected House. A week later, the House of Lords voted against all of the proposals other than a wholly appointed House. The impasse continued. Despite this, a further Green Paper was published in July 2007, restating the government's commitment (now under Gordon Brown's leadership) to complete reform[34] and each of the three main parties went into the 2010 general election with manifestos containing commitments to complete the reform of the House of Lords. It was therefore unsurprising that the coalition agreement that followed the election contained a pledge to bring forward proposals for a wholly or mainly elected House of Lords. In 2012, the House of Lords Reform Bill was introduced by the Deputy Prime Minister, Nick Clegg.[35] The Bill proposed a mainly elected (80 per cent) chamber, with members elected for a 15 year term by means of proportionate representation.[36] There would eventually be 360 elected members, 90 appointed members, 12 Lords Spiritual and any "ministerial members".[37] The Bill only made it to the second reading in the House of Commons. In the face of increasing opposition in the House of Commons (primarily from Conservative backbench MPs), the government announced in August 2012 that it would not proceed with the Bill.[38] As a result, the only reforming legislation that was passed during the 2010–2015 Parliament was the House of Lords Reform Act 2014. But this did not contain substantive change to the structure and composition of the House. Rather, it made provision for members of the House of Lords to resign, for them to cease to be Members of the House if they failed to attend during a parliamentary session and their removal from the House upon conviction of a "serious offence" (an offence for which a period of imprisonment in excess of a year was imposed).

The task of reforming the House of Lords is not to be underestimated.[39] It is much easier to propose questions than identify solutions. How do you constitute the House of Lords on a popular basis without threatening the primacy of the House of Commons? Assuming some form of proportionate representation was employed for any elections to the House of Lords, and assuming the first past the

---

[34] HM Government, *The Governance of Britain* (The Stationery Office, 2007), Cm.7170.
[35] A draft Bill had been published a year earlier (HM Government, *House of Lords Reform Draft Bill* (The Stationery Office, 2011), Cm.8077, *https://www.gov.uk/government/uploads/system/uploads/attachment_data/file/229020/8077.pdf* [Accessed 7 June 2015]) which was then considered by a joint committee of the two Houses (Joint Committee on the Draft House of Lords Reform Bill, *Draft House of Lords Reform Bill, Report Session 2010–12* (The Stationery Office, 2012), HL Paper 284–I, HC 1313–I, *http://www.publications.parliament.uk/pa/jt201012/jtselect/jtdraftref/284/284i.pdf* [Accessed 7 June 2015]). There was no consensus from the joint committee with an alternative report being published by 12 of the committee's members. The government accepted the majority of the recommendations of the joint committee: HM Government, *Government Response to the Report of the Joint Committee on the Draft House of Lords Reform Bill* (The Stationery Office, 2012), Cm.8391, *https://www.gov.uk/government/uploads/system/uploads/attachment_data/file/228718/8391.pdf* [Accessed 7 June 2015].
[36] The system proposed was the closed list system of proportionate representation (which is currently used to elect "regional members" of the Scottish Parliament and for elections to the European Parliament). Under the proposal, the United Kingdom would be divided into 12 electoral regions (Scotland, Wales and Northern Ireland each representing a single region).
[37] Achieving a House in that form would take 15 years as 120 elected members would be returned at each general election (cl.4) and those elections would take place on the same day as elections to the House of Commons (cl.3).
[38] This led to allegations by the Deputy Prime Minster (that were denied by the Prime Minister) that the Conservative Party had broken the coalition agreement.
[39] For a further discussion, see V. Bogdanor, *The New British Constitution* (Oxford: Hart, 2009) Ch.6.

post system continued to be employed by the House of Commons, that would probably give rise to a second chamber that was more representative of the views of the electorate.[40] How, on democratic grounds, could the House of Commons then claim a mandate to exercise the powers of the Parliament Acts if its legislation was rejected? More fundamentally, would it continue to be appropriate that the executive be drawn principally from the House of Commons? If the House of Commons moves to a system of proportionate representation, what system should be employed to prevent the House of Lords mirroring the composition of the Commons? If the House of Lords is to be appointed (in whole or in part), who makes the appointments? On what basis? For what term? What, if any, element of the House of Lords should be democratically elected? All of these are difficult questions. And they all defy an answer unless reform of the House of Lords goes hand in hand with wider constitutional reform. But the continuing irony is that whilst the undemocratic nature of the House of Lords (in particular the remaining hereditary element) remains objectionable in a modern democracy, it actually performs the role expected of an upper chamber to a reasonably good standard.[41]

House of Commons

At present, 650 MPs sit in the House of Commons, of whom 59 represent **6–06** Scottish constituencies. Prior to the 2005 general election, there were 72 Scottish MPs. The reduction in their number constitutes the then government's response to what is dubbed the "West Lothian question"[42]—namely, whether it can be right that Scottish MPs should retain the ability to vote on legislation intended to apply only to England and Wales[43] when English and Welsh MPs have forfeited that ability in relation to matters devolved to a Scottish Parliament. Reducing Scottish representation at Westminster mitigates, but does not go to the root of, the problem. We have already discussed the problems associated with the current proposal of "English votes on English laws". Arguably, only a shift to a federal model of constitutional organisation could provide a long-term solution.[44] Plainly, so long as Westminster continues to enact legislation for the whole of the UK, an appropriate level of Scottish representation must be maintained. It is not obvious, however, that the West Lothian question can be dismissed as an incidental, and ultimately minor, untidiness occasioned by devolution.[45] As further powers are devolved to Scotland, the case for addressing it becomes

---

[40] We have seen the problems facing the first past the post system in Chs 1 and 4, above.

[41] The difficulties similar to those inherent in reforming the House of Lords have arisen in Canada, which has a Senate modeled on the House of Lords. The Supreme Court of Canada has recently considered the constitutionality of various options for reforming the Canadian Senate. It offers an interesting discussion of similar issues to those that have arisen in the United Kingdom: *Reference re Senate Reform* [2014] S.C.C. 32.

[42] So called because it was articulated in the debates on the earlier Scotland Bill in the 1970s by Tam Dalyell, then MP for West Lothian.

[43] Occasionally with decisive effect, as where the government's majority is secured by its Scottish MPs.

[44] A. Olowofoyeku, "Decentralising the United Kingdom: The federal argument" (1999) 3 Edin. L.R. 57.

[45] During the debates on the Scotland Bill in the late 1970s, an amendment was tabled which would have provided for the taking of a second vote in such circumstances (the idea being that, in the meantime, the Scottish MPs could be persuaded to abstain). The government of the day rejected the idea as a "constitutional imbecility", but it has resurfaced in the current debate and something like it may in the longer run require to be adopted.

stronger, and in recent months the calls to finally resolve the anomaly have grown even louder.

Holyrood

6–07 The Scotland Act 1998 provides that there shall be 129 Members of the Scottish Parliament.[46] Seventy three of these are elected by the familiar "first past the post" or simple majority method in each of the constituencies from which, until the 2005 general election, Scottish MPs were returned (with Orkney and Shetland split into two separate constituencies). The remaining 56 members are elected in accordance with the "additional member" system of proportional representation from each of the eight European parliamentary constituencies provided for by the European Parliamentary Constituencies (Scotland) Order 1996[47] (although for European elections these have now been supplanted by the electoral system provided for by the European Parliamentary Elections Act 2002, under which Scotland constitutes a single region for the purposes of electing its eight MEPs). Thus seven regional members are returned from each region.[48]

ELIGIBILITY AND DISQUALIFICATION

6–08 The conditions of eligibility to stand for election to the House of Commons and the Scottish Parliament were considered in Ch.4, above.[49] As we saw, those conditions were broadly the same. The provisions differ, however, as to the consequences of disqualification. At Westminster, a person claiming that an individual disqualified by virtue of the House of Commons Disqualification Act 1975 has been elected to the House of Commons may apply to the Judicial Committee of the Privy Council for a declaration to that effect under s.7. The Judicial Committee may direct that the issue be tried in the High Court of England and Wales, the Court of Session or the High Court of Northern Ireland, depending on the location of the constituency in question; if so, the decision of that court is final. In Scotland, if a disqualified person is elected to the Scottish Parliament either as a constituency or a regional member, his election is void and his seat vacant.[50] Where a person becomes disqualified during the currency of his membership, he ceases to be an MSP and his seat falls vacant accordingly.[51] Where an MSP becomes disqualified on grounds of bankruptcy, his seat is not automatically vacated but he does become ineligible to participate in the proceedings of the Parliament and may lose other rights and privileges incidental to membership. In any of these situations, the Parliament may by resolution elect to disregard the member's disqualification under s.16(4) of the Scotland Act, if it considers that the ground of disqualification has been removed or that it is proper to disregard any disqualification incurred by the member.[52] Anyone who

---

[46] SA 1998 s.1 and Sch.1.

[47] European Parliamentary Constituencies (Scotland) Order 1996 (SI 1996/1926).

[48] For an account of the process governing elections to the Scottish Parliament, see paras 4–06—4–09, above.

[49] See para.4–14, above.

[50] SA 1998 s.17(1).

[51] SA 1998 s.17(2).

[52] But no such resolution may be adopted where an election petition has been presented in respect of the member, or where the disqualification has been established in election petition proceedings or proceedings under SA 1998 s.18. Mental illness is no longer a ground to suspend a member's participation in the work of the Parliament: Mental Health (Discrimination) Act 2013.

believes that a person is or has become disqualified from membership of the Scottish Parliament may apply to the Court of Session for a declarator to that effect.[53] It should be noted that the jurisdiction of the Court of Session in this respect extends to all possible grounds of disqualification, not merely, as with the Judicial Committee of the Privy Council, those arising from the House of Commons Disqualification Act 1975.

FUNCTIONS OF PARLIAMENTS

The Westminster and Scottish Parliaments alike have three essential functions: to provide and sustain a government in office; to make law; and to hold the executive to account.[54] The first of these we touched on in Ch.2, above, in the context of the constitutional conventions (or, in Scotland, statutory rules) surrounding the appointment and resignation of governments; we revisit the matter in the next chapter. Suffice to say here that the democratic legitimacy of a government in a parliamentary system depends upon its ability to command the continuing confidence of the House of Commons or Scottish Parliament as the case may be; that confidence withdrawn, the government must fall. Under the Scotland Act 1998 the First Minister (s.45(2)) and her Ministers (s.47(2)(c)) must resign if a motion of no confidence is passed in relation to the Scottish Government.[55] An extraordinary general election will then follow only if the Parliament fails to nominate one of its number as First Minister within 28 days of that resignation (s.3(1)(b)). So far as Westminster is concerned, the matter is now, as we have seen, regulated by the Fixed-term Parliaments Act 2011. Where a motion of no confidence is passed in the government, a general election follows *if* a motion of confidence is *not* passed in a new government within 14 days. Both Parliaments, therefore, have provisions that delay the calling of an election in order that an attempt can be made to form an alternative government before resort is had to an unscheduled election. **6–09**

---

[53] SA 1998 s.18. The procedure provides an alternative mechanism for challenging a person's election to the election petition procedure laid down by the Representation of the People Act 1983, with the possible advantage that, whereas election petitions must be presented within 21 days of the contested election, there is no comparable time limit on proceedings under s.18. However, the jurisdiction of the court under s.18 is excluded if an election petition has already been presented; it is also excluded if the Scottish Parliament has adopted a resolution under s.16(4) to disregard a member's disqualification.

[54] Plainly that is not an exhaustive account. There are other parliamentary functions, such as the regulation of internal procedures and the supervision of parliamentary standards; and as elected representatives MPs and MSPs have a variety of functions in relation to their constituents and constituencies.

[55] The Scotland Act 1998 makes no provision for the possibility that, for 28 days and the period leading up to and immediately following an extraordinary general election, there would be no Scottish Government at all. It is open to the Parliament within that 28 day period to resolve that it should be dissolved, which would trigger the duty of the Presiding Officer under s.3(1)(a) to recommend to the Queen a date for an extraordinary election. But such a resolution requires the support of at least two-thirds of the total number of MSPs, and if the political complexion of the Parliament is such that it is unable within 28 days to nominate a replacement First Minister, it may be equally unfavourable to securing a resolution for dissolution. At Westminster, a government which loses a vote of confidence continues in office de facto on a caretaker basis during the currency of the election period, and arguably some such arrangement would require to be made in Scotland in the circumstances envisaged here; but there is no basis for it in the Scotland Act.

The primary legislative function of the Parliaments we examine later in this chapter. There is of course a salient difference between the UK and Scottish Parliaments in this respect, in that while the legislative competence of the former is traditionally understood to be subject to no legal limits, the legislative competence of the latter is restricted in terms of the Scotland Act 1998.[56] It should not necessarily be assumed, however, that the legislative sovereignty of the Westminster Parliament means that it is wholly unfettered. True it is that a government in command of a reliable majority in the House of Commons may secure the enactment of legislation that is in some sense disagreeable or offensive to popular (or elite) sentiments. Nonetheless, a process, more or less protracted, must be followed in order to obtain the seal of parliamentary approval, and if the process provides no guarantee as to the substance of the legislative outcomes, it offers a measure of procedural protection the importance of which, in structuring and confining the will of the executive, is often overlooked.[57]

6–10   The role of the Parliaments in holding the executive to account is frequently disparaged. As we shall see in Ch.7, below, there is certainly scope for doubting the adequacy of the convention of ministerial responsibility to Parliament as a mechanism for securing accountability for the exercise of political power. Much is made, for example, of the persistent failure of Ministers to resign in response to departmental wrongdoing or error, as if this were a vital component of the concept. The emphasis on resignation flows from the fact that, as a matter of nineteenth century practice, before the emergence of the modern party system and the consolidation of government control over the legislature, Parliament could and sometimes did force the resignation of a Minister or Ministry in whose fitness for office it had lost confidence. Nowadays, such events are vanishingly rare.[58] But however ephemeral the sanction attaching to ministerial responsibility, the expectation that Ministers should answer to Parliament, and account as fully and clearly as possible for their and their departments' actions and decisions, even to the extent of acknowledging errors where errors are made, remains very much alive. Not only that, but Ministers do appear before Parliament and parliamentary committees, do subject themselves to questioning, and do not routinely mislead Parliament in the process (even if their answers may be evasive or at least less comprehensive than parliamentarians would like). To be sure, difficulties remain in "investigating the facts, agreeing on the application of the convention [of ministerial responsibility] to the facts, and enforcement",[59] difficulties which are attributable, at least in part, to what has been justly described as "the intense inefficiency of our parliamentary system".[60] The tabling of parliamentary questions, for example, is not an especially efficient means of eliciting information; and parliamentary debates are frequently notable only for the absence of any meaningful debate. But the convention of ministerial responsibility is not the only mechanism, nor even the only parliamentary mechanism, of accountability. Parliamentary committees both at Westminster and Holyrood provide a more exacting forum for the scrutiny of the executive than the parliamentary floor. Their fact finding capacities may have been blunted

---

[56] As we shall see, there are also significant differences between the two Parliaments in relation to legislative procedures.

[57] See K.D. Ewing and C.A. Gearty, *The Struggle for Civil Liberties: Political Freedom and the Rule of Law in Britain, 1914–1945* (Oxford: Oxford University Press, 2000) pp.12 and 13.

[58] The last time the government lost a vote of confidence was in 1979.

[59] I. Leigh, "Secrets of the Political Constitution" (1999) 62 M.L.R. 298.

[60] D. Judge, "Parliament in the 1980s" (1989) 60 *Political Quarterly* 400.

in the past, and their effectiveness unduly dependent on ministerial co-operation, but the first of these at least may have been enhanced by the enactment of freedom of information legislation, the utility of which is in no sense confined to pressure groups and busybodies.

LEGISLATIVE PROCESSES

Westminster

At Westminster, proposals for legislation (known as "Bills") are either public, **6–11** private or hybrid.[61] Private bills provide for the conferment of special powers, benefits or exemptions on a person or body of persons in excess of or in conflict with the general law. There are two categories of public Bills. First, there are government Bills.[62] All government sponsored legislation is enacted by means of public Bills. Government Bills are introduced by the relevant Minister. Secondly, there are private members' Bills. Public bills introduced by any other Member fall into this category. Often thought of as referring to Bills introduced by backbench MPs, private members' Bills also include any Bill introduced by the opposition parties. In other words, they are "non-government" Bills. There is no procedural distinction between the different categories of public Bills. However, in the House of Commons, all Bills are not equal and very limited time is made available for private members' Bills. Accordingly, any private members' Bill that is at all controversial has very limited chance of passing into law.[63]

A government Bill first comes to the formal notice of Parliament at first reading, although it contents may have been more or less extensively trailed in advance of that.[64] First reading is a purely formal stage, after which the Bill is printed and published. Explanatory notes now ordinarily accompany a government Bill[65] and an "impact assessment" is now required.[66] A Bill can be

---

[61] *Erskine May Parliamentary Practice* (2011) describes hybrid Bills as "public bills which are considered to affect specific private or other local interests, in a manner different from the private or local interests of other persons or bodies of the same category". After second reading, a hybrid Bill is sent to a select committee. If petitions objecting to the Bill are received, the committee deals with it in much the same way as a private Bill; if not, the Bill is recommitted to a standing committee or Committee of the Whole House and dealt with as a public Bill. An example is the Channel Tunnel Rail Link Act 1996. The only hybrid Bill to be enacted by the Scottish Parliament is the Forth Crossing Act 2011.

[62] For a detailed account of the entire legislative process, see Cabinet Office, *Guide to Making Legislation* (The Stationery Office, 2014) *https://www.gov.uk/government/uploads/system/uploads/attachment_data/file/328408/Guide_to_Making_Legislation_July_2014.pdf* [Accessed 6 June 2015].

[63] *Erskine May Parliamentary Practice* (2011) pp.525–526.

[64] In addition to established forms of pre-legislative consultation, such as the publication of White Papers or Royal Commission reports, the government has since 1997 published draft Bills where possible in order to facilitate pre-legislative scrutiny by the appropriate select committee. The House of Commons Select Committee on Modernisation has recommended that where it is not possible to produce a draft Bill, the government should instead submit detailed policy proposals for pre-legislative scrutiny: House of Commons Select Committee on Modernisation, *Modernisation of the House of Commons: A Reform Programme, Second Report of Session 2001–02* (The Stationery Office, 2002) HC 1168–I.

[65] Following the recommendation in the House of Commons Select Committee on Modernisation, *Second Report of Session 1997–98* (The Stationery Office, 1997) HC 389.

[66] Cabinet Office, *Guide to Making Legislation*, pp.110–115.

introduced into either House, with the exception of "money Bills"[67] that must originate in the House of Commons.[68] We will illustrate the passage of a Bill based on it having been introduced in the Commons.[69] At second reading, the principles of the Bill are considered. If the Bill is passed (and it is rare for a government Bill to be denied a second reading), the Bill proceeds to committee. If, following line by line scrutiny, the Bill is amended in committee, it is reprinted as amended and "reported" to the Commons. At third reading, the Bill is debated in final form, and thereafter proceeds to the House of Lords. Procedure in the Lords is much the same as the Commons, except that Bills are normally considered by a Committee of the Whole House after second reading, amendments may be made at third reading as well, in committee and at report, and there is no provision in the Lords for curtailing debate. In the Commons, by contrast, the Minister responsible for a Bill may move an allocation of time, or guillotine, motion to fix the time available for its remaining stages; and increasing use is also being made of programme motions, whereby the whole progress of the Bill through the Commons is timetabled in advance.[70]

If the Lords make no amendments to the Bill, it may be sent forward at once for Royal Assent.[71] If amendments are made, the Bill returns to the Commons, which may agree to the amendments, substitute amendments of its own or reject the amendments outright. In the latter two cases, the Bill is sent back to the Lords with the Commons' reasons. As a rule, the Lords acquiesce in the wishes of the Commons; but from time to time, they stand their ground. The Bill will then be batted back and forth between the two Houses until some form of compromise is reached, as usually happens. If, exceptionally, the two Houses fail to reach agreement within the parliamentary session, the Bill will lapse. Where such failure is attributable to insoluble differences between the two Houses, the Parliament Acts 1911 and 1949 provide for the will of the Commons to prevail over that of the Lords. The House of Lords may delay a public Bill for one session (other than a Bill certified by the Speaker of the House of Commons as a money Bill, which may be sent forward for Royal Assent if at the end of one month the Lords have failed to pass it), but it is open to the Commons to revive the measure in the following session, bypass the Lords and proceed directly to Royal Assent.

Three Acts of Parliament were enacted under the procedure contained in the 1911 Act as originally enacted: the Government of Ireland Act 1914, the Welsh Church Act 1914 and the Parliament Act 1949 itself, which reduced the length of the Lords' delaying power from two years to one. The amended procedure was not then used until the enactment of the War Crimes Act 1991. The Labour Government of 1997–2001 had to resort twice to the procedure, to secure the

---

[67] As a result of the Parliament Act 1911 removing the House of Lords power to block or amend such Bills.

[68] As a general rule, more controversial Bills are likely to be introduced in the House of Commons. Bills that implement law reform or Law Commission proposals are ordinarily introduced in the House of Lords. Any Bill where the government may wish to resort to the Parliament Acts to ensure its passage must be introduced in the House of Commons.

[69] See *Erskine May Parliamentary Practice* (2011) Chs 27–29 for the detailed rules and procedure relating to the passage of a public Bill.

[70] While sensible in principle, in practice programme motions often have the effect of seriously constraining the time available for proper scrutiny of the detail of a Bill in committee. See Cabinet Office, *Guide to Making Legislation*, pp.184–188.

[71] Even major Bills—as witness, e.g. the Anti-Terrorism, Crime and Security Act 2001—may complete their parliamentary stages in a matter of days.

enactment of the European Parliamentary Elections Act 1999 and the Sexual Offences (Amendment) Act 2000. It was also required to secure the enactment of the Hunting Act 2004, which was then the subject of legal challenge in *R. (on the application of Jackson) v Attorney General.*[72] The claimant's argument was that the Parliament Act 1911 did not permit the enactment of a statute amending its own terms, as the Parliament Act 1949 did, without the consent of the Lords. Since the 1949 Act was enacted without the consent of the Lords, it was accordingly invalid; and the statutes enacted under the Parliament Acts procedure since, including the Hunting Act, were likewise invalid. The argument depended upon the proposition that legislation enacted under the 1911 Act was a species of delegated legislation in the sense that, by its terms, the King, Lords and Commons had delegated to the King and Commons the power, in specified circumstances, to enact Acts of Parliament without the Lords' consent. If that were correct, then it followed that the legislative power conferred upon the King and Commons by s.2(1) of the 1911 Act could not be enlarged by them in the absence of clear statutory words authorising them to do so. This was simply a consequence of ordinary principles of statutory interpretation.

The House of Lords, sitting as a panel of nine, rejected the argument.[73] Sections 1 and 2 of the 1911 Act identified legislation enacted in accordance with its terms as "Acts of Parliament", an expression

> "used, and used only, to denote primary legislation . . . The 1911 Act did, of course, effect an important constitutional change, but the change lay not in authorising a new form of sub-primary parliamentary legislation but in creating a new way of enacting primary legislation".[74]

In any event, it was not possible to characterise the 1911 Act as a "delegation" of legislative power: " . . . the overall object of the 1911 Act was . . . to restrict, subject to compliance with specified statutory conditions, the power of the Lords to defeat measures supported by a majority of the Commons"[75] in the context of an unprecedented constitutional crisis. Accordingly it was open to Parliament, constituted as King and Commons, to rely on the 1911 Act for the purposes of enacting the amending 1949 Act; and since the 1949 Act was a valid Act of Parliament, so too were the statutes subsequently enacted in accordance with its terms.

There are a number of procedures whereby an MP may introduce a private **6–12** members' Bill. Shortly after the start of each new parliamentary session, a ballot is held among backbench MPs to determine priority in the use of the time set aside for private members' business; in practice, only the first 20 names in the

---

[72] *R. (on the application of Jackson) v Attorney General* [2005] UKHL 56; [2006] 1 A.C. 262.
[73] It had previously been rejected by the Divisional Court (*R. (on the application of Jackson) v Attorney General* [2005] EWHC 94 (Admin)) and, albeit on different grounds, by the Court of Appeal (*R. (on the application of Jackson) v Attorney General* [2005] EWCA Civ 126; [2005] Q.B. 579).
[74] *R. (on the application of Jackson) v Attorney General* [2005] UKHL 56; [2006] 1 A.C. 262, per Lord Bingham at [24].
[75] *R. (on the application of Jackson) v Attorney General* [2005] UKHL 56; [2006] 1 A.C. 262, per Lord Bingham at [25].

ballot have a realistic chance of seeing their Bills through to the statute books.[76] Private members' Bills have precedence over government business on 13 Fridays in each session.[77] Ten minute rule Bills may be introduced on a motion under standing orders, seeking leave to present a Bill to the Commons; and "ordinary presentation" bills may be introduced by MPs under standing orders in the same way as a government Bill.[78] Similar procedures obtain in the House of Lords, although with this difference: a private members' Bill from the Lords cannot be proceeded with, or even printed, in the Commons until an MP has indicated a willingness to take it up, whereas, when a Commons private members' Bill is sent up to the Lords, it is deemed already to have had a first reading and is printed at once (although a peer must still be found to pilot it through its stages in the Lords).

Making it through to the statute books is not the only criterion of success for a private members' Bill.[79] Some are introduced to publicise a cause, or to prompt the government to take action. But many are introduced with the aim and intention of changing the law, and have proved an important means of achieving this, particularly in areas of social or moral controversy which cross party lines and where governments are unwilling to risk their own hard pressed legislative time. The abolition of the death penalty, and reform of the law on abortion and homosexuality, for example, were brought about by private members' Bills.

6–13   Private legislation, designed to obtain special rights or privileges over and above those provided by the general law, is introduced by parliamentary agents acting on behalf of the prospective beneficiary. Since the powers sought may interfere with the rights and interests of others, who might therefore wish to object, the promoters of a private Bill must comply with requirements concerning publicity and notification.[80] Subject to that, and provided the Bill is otherwise competent and in proper form, private Bills go through essentially the same stages as public Bills. After second reading,[81] the Bill will be sent either to an opposed Bill committee or unopposed Bill committee, depending on whether objections have been lodged. In either case, the committee sits in a quasi-judicial capacity to determine whether the case for having the provision sought by the Bill is established; if it finds that it is not, the Bill is effectively thrown out. If, however, the committee finds the Bill to be acceptable, it reports accordingly (together with any amendments it may have made). The Bill is then read for a third time, and if it is passed it proceeds to the other House where it undergoes much the same process once again.

---

[76] Assuming they have a Bill. A common practice is for MPs to wait to see where they are placed in the ballot and then choose between the draft Bills proffered them by interest groups or, indeed, the government, if it has been unable to find time for a measure in its own programme for the session.

[77] House of Commons Standing Orders r.14(9)

[78] But such Bills cannot be presented until the ballot Bills have been presented and set down for second reading, which is likely to exhaust the time available for private members' business.

[79] The success rate in that sense is variable. In some sessions, only a handful of private members' Bills are enacted into law; in others, upward of 20.

[80] *Erskine May Parliamentary Practice* (2011) Ch.42 ("Preliminary Proceedings in Both Houses on Private Bills").

[81] Whether a private Bill commences in the Commons or the Lords is determined by the Commons' Chairman of Ways and Means and the Lord Chairman of Committees; as a rule, private Bills promoted by local authorities or those raising complex issues commence in the Lords.

A special procedure applies to the enactment of private legislation intended **6–14** solely for application in Scotland which relates to matters reserved to West-minster by the Scotland Act 1998.[82] Under the Private Legislation Procedure (Scotland) Act 1936, the promoter lodges a petition for a provisional order with the Secretary of State, on or before 27 November or 27 March in any year. Petitions objecting to the order sought must be received by 23 January or 24 May, whichever follows the date of submission of the petition for the order. The Secretary of State may grant or refuse the petition, or may order that an inquiry be held. The Commissioners of Inquiry sit in Scotland and follow the procedure of an opposed Bill committee; if they recommend that the order be granted, the Secretary of State may so grant it, with or without modifications. A provisional order granted by the Secretary of State, whether or not following an inquiry, then requires to be confirmed by Parliament.[83]

Holyrood

The Scotland Act requires that the proceedings of the Parliament be regulated by **6–15** standing orders,[84] and in places specifies the content of standing orders,[85] but beyond this the Parliament is free to adopt such procedures as it chooses. The rules relating to the legislative procedure are presently contained in Chs 9 and 9A of the standing orders (relating respectively to public Bills and private Bills). In total, the standing orders provide for no fewer than 12 different species of Scottish legislation.[86] Rules 9.2–9.13A of the standing orders lay down general rules applicable to all public Bills introduced in the Parliament, except to the extent that the special rules set out in rr.9.14–9.16 and 9.17A–9.21 are inconsistent with the general rules in relation to particular types of Bill. In that event, the special rules prevail to the extent of the inconsistency.

Government Bills are the most important type of bill in numerical terms, being Bills introduced by a member of the Scottish Government in order to carry forward the Government's legislative agenda. The rules make provision for the form and manner of introduction of government Bills, and for the lodging of various accompanying documents. These are: a written statement by the Scottish Minister in charge of the Bill stating that in his view its provisions are within the competence of the Parliament[87]; a written statement signed by the Presiding Officer, indicating whether in her view the provisions of the Bill would be within the competence of the Parliament and, if in her view they would not be, his reasons[88]; a memorandum on delegated powers; a financial memorandum and

---

[82] *Erskine May Parliamentary Practice*, 22nd edn (1997), Ch.41. The procedure has not been invoked since 2000. Private legislation on devolved matters in Scotland naturally falls now to be enacted by the Scottish Parliament itself: see SA 1998 s.36(3)(c), Scottish Parliament Standing Orders Ch.9A, and see also para.6–16.

[83] By virtue of SA 1998 s.94, where any pre-devolution enactment requires an order to be confirmed by Act of Parliament or approved by way of special procedure (as to which see the Statutory Orders (Special Procedure) Act 1945), and the order-making power is one which passed to the Scottish Ministers under s.53 on 1 July 1999, the power to confirm falls to be exercised by the Scottish Parliament.

[84] SA 1998 s.22.

[85] See SA 1998 Sch.3.

[86] Namely, government Bills, members' Bills, committee Bills, budget Bills, Scottish Law Commission Bills, consolidation Bills, codification Bills, statute law repeals Bills, statute law revision Bills, emergency Bills, private Bills and hybrid Bills.

[87] SA 1998 s.31(1).

[88] SA 1998 s.31(2).

policy memorandum; explanatory notes summarising the purposes and effects of the Bill; and (if the Bill contains provisions charging expenditure on the Scottish consolidated fund) a report signed by the Auditor General for Scotland setting out his views on whether the charge is appropriate. Once the Bill and its accompanying documents have been lodged with the Clerk to the Parliament, it is the job of the clerk to arrange for their printing and publication. The substantive part of the legislative process then gets underway.

At stage one, the Parliamentary Bureau[89] refers the Bill to the committee within whose remit its subject matter falls.[90] The committee considers the general principles of the Bill, often taking evidence from experts and interested parties, and, in the case of a government Bill, the accompanying policy memorandum. Having done so, it reports to the Parliament on whether the general principles of the Bill should be agreed. The Parliament is not bound by the committee's recommendation. If the Parliament does approve the general principles, the Bill proceeds to stage two, where it undergoes detailed scrutiny by the committee or lead committee in charge of it.[91] Bills may be amended at stage two, and any MSP may lodge amendments for the committee's consideration following the completion of stage one. If at the end of stage two the Bill has been amended, it is reprinted in amended form. Further amendments may be lodged at stage three, at which point the Parliament decides whether to pass or reject the Bill.[92] If there is a division at stage three on whether the Bill is passed, the result will be valid only if at least one-quarter of the total number of MSPs vote, whether for or against or to abstain. If the result of the division is not valid, the Bill is deemed to be rejected.

6–16   Space precludes detailed consideration of all the other species of Scottish legislation, but it is worth noting the rules applicable to members' Bills, committee Bills, emergency Bills and private Bills.[93] Members' Bills are the equivalent in Scotland of private members' Bills at Westminster, although again the applicable procedural rules differ considerably. Any MSP who is not a Scottish Minister may introduce up to two members' Bills in any one session (bearing in mind that in the Scottish Parliament, the term "session" denotes the full (ordinarily) four year cycle of the Parliament, not each year within that cycle). The MSP proposing a member's Bill must notify his proposal by lodging it with the clerk, setting out his name, the short title of the Bill and a brief summary of its purposes. The notice is published in the Business Bulletin which signifies the start of a "consultation period" and the proposal is sent to the

---

[89] The bureau is comprised of the Presiding Officer, a representative of each political party having five or more MSPs in the Parliament, and the representative of any group formed by MSPs representing parties with fewer than five MSPs in the Parliament (provided that the group itself numbers at least five MSPs). It has responsibility for organising the business of the Parliament: see Scottish Parliament Standing Orders Ch.5.

[90] If the subject matter of the Bill falls within the remit of more than one committee, the Parliamentary Bureau will move that one be designated lead committee on the Bill. The other committee(s) report to the lead committee, which must take its (or their) views into account in preparing its report for the Parliament.

[91] Unless the Parliamentary Bureau successfully moves that stage two be taken by a different committee or by a Committee of the Whole Parliament.

[92] There is no need for the Minister responsible for the Bill or the Presiding Officer to restate his or her view on whether the amended Bill is within the Parliament's legislative competence. Such a requirement may have avoided the unfortunate case of *Salvesen v Riddell* [2013] UKSC 22; 2013 S.C. (U.K.S.C.) 236 (on which, see para.6–33, below).

[93] Note that the Scottish Parliament's tax varying power, as provided for by SA 1998 Pt IV, is exercisable by way of resolutions rather than primary legislation.

committee within whose remit the proposal falls. Once the consultation period has concluded, the final proposal must, within one month, attract the support of at least 18 other MSPs for the Bill to be introduced. Thereafter it is subject to the same procedure as a government Bill.

Committee Bills are an innovation: each of the Parliament's committees may make a proposal for a Bill relating to a competent matter falling within its remit. A proposal for a committee Bill consists of a report to the Parliament setting out the committee's recommendations for legislation together with an account of why the legislation is needed. The committee may, but need not, append to its report a draft Bill.[94] If the Parliament agrees to the proposal, the committee convenor may instruct that a Bill be drafted (if necessary) and may subsequently introduce the Bill in the Parliament. The subsequent stages of the Bill are the same as those applicable to government Bills, except that at stage one with the Bill being referred to the Finance Committee to consider and report on the financial memorandum. The need for report on the Bill's general principles is, understandably, dispensed with.

The very first Act of the Scottish Parliament[95] was an emergency Bill. These are a species of government Bill in relation to which a member of the Scottish Government or a junior Scottish Minister moves that it be treated as an emergency Bill. If agreed, the Bill is referred directly to the Parliament at stage one for consideration of its general principles and a decision on whether these are agreed; stage two is taken by a Committee of the Whole Parliament; and the final vote at stage three is taken immediately thereafter. Unless the Parliament decides otherwise, all of the stages of an emergency Bill must be taken on the day on which the Parliament agrees to treat it as such.

As to private legislation, and as at Westminster, the role of the Parliament is not merely to legislate but also to arbitrate between the competing private interests of the promoter of the legislation and any objectors. The Parliament has considered 16 private Bills so far in its lifetime.[96] The applicable procedures, which are contained in Ch.9A of the standing orders, must therefore be both parliamentary and quasi-judicial in nature. The promoter must submit a text of the Bill, together with a substantial amount of supporting documentation,[97] to the clerk at least three weeks before the proposed date of introduction.[98] The promoter must also comply with requirements for notification and advertisement of the Bill in order to draw it to the attention of potential objectors. The Bill is introduced when it is formally lodged with the clerk. Any person, body corporate or unincorporated association may lodge objections to the Bill, within 60 days of

---

[94] The Parliament has established a Non-Government Bills Unit to assist MSPs, committees and the promoters of private legislation in the drafting and formatting of Bills.

[95] Mental Health (Public Safety and Appeals) (Scotland) Act 1999. See also, more recently, the Senior Judiciary (Vacancies and Incapacity) (Scotland) Act 2006.

[96] Many have concerned railways or tram lines. Full details are available on the Parliament's website, Scottish Parliament, "Private Bills", *http://www.scottish.parliament.uk/parliamentarybusiness/Bills/29669.aspx* [Accessed 7 June 2015].

[97] This includes a statement by the Presiding Officer on legislative competence; explanatory notes; a promoter's statement and memorandum; and, where the Bill seeks to authorise the construction or alteration of certain classes of works or the compulsory acquisition of land or buildings, various maps and plans, a book of reference and an environmental statement.

[98] This in order to allow the clerk to arrange for the distribution of copies of the Bill and supporting documentation to "partner libraries" throughout Scotland.

its introduction, if it would adversely affect their private interests.[99] A Private
Bill Committee is convened following introduction of the Bill to consider its
provisions and report to Parliament. It will have up to five members, and
although the normal rules on party political balance do not apply to its
composition, it may not include among its number any MSP who resides in, or
represents, a constituency falling wholly or partly within the area which would
be affected by the Bill. The Bill is then subject to a three stage process. At the
preliminary stage, the committee considers the general principles of the Bill and
whether these should be agreed. It may take evidence from the promoter or his
legal representatives, and should certainly do so if it is minded to recommend
that the Bill be rejected. If following the committee's preliminary stage report the
Parliament agrees to the general principles of the Bill, it proceeds to the
consideration stage, which falls into two parts. In the first, quasi-judicial, part, the
committee hears evidence on the Bill and the objections to it. On completion of
this part, the committee prepares a report giving its decisions on the objections
considered, with reasons where appropriate. In the second part, the committee
sits in a legislative capacity to consider and dispose of amendments to the Bill.[100]
At the final stage, at which further amendments are competent, the Parliament
votes on whether or not to pass the Bill.[101] As with other enactments of the
Scottish Parliament, the Presiding Officer may not send the Bill as passed
forward for Royal Assent until after the expiry of the four week period during
which the Law Officers or Secretary of State may intervene in terms of ss.33 or
35 of the Scotland Act.

6–17   The amendments proposed to the Scotland Act by the Smith Commission
would introduce a special category of legislation that would require a "super-
majority" to enact.[102] The following matters would require members representing at least two-thirds of the seats in the Parliament to vote for the Bill to become
law: the franchise for Scottish parliamentary elections; the electoral system
employed at such elections; the number of constituencies; the number of regions;
and the number of members to be returned by those regions.[103] These issues are
referred to as "protected subject-matters" and the Presiding Officer will be
required to certify, on or before introduction, whether a Bill relates to such
subject matters.[104] The "super-majority" provisions relate to new powers
concerning composition and election that it is proposed be transferred to the
Scottish Parliament. Setting the two-thirds requirement is clearly designed to
minimise the potential for these rules to be changed by, and for the advantage of,
any one political party. As we saw in Ch.3, above, imposing such a requirement

---

[99] The Private Bill Committee charged with consideration of the Bill has a discretion to admit late
objections where reasonable cause is shown for the delay, but not beyond the expiry of the
preliminary stage.
[100] If substantial amendments are made, the promoter is expected to produce revised or supplementary explanatory notes.
[101] Only one private Act of the Scottish Parliament was enacted in the 1999–2003 Parliament. Seven
private Acts were enacted, out of a total of 60, in the 2003–2007 Parliament. A further six have
been enacted in the period 2008–2015 (including three in 2014).
[102] HM Government, *Scotland in the United Kingdom: An enduring settlement*, para.1.4.12. See now
the Scotland Bill that was introduced to Parliament on 28 May 2015.
[103] Clause 4 of the draft clauses, introducing what would become s.30A of the Scotland Act
1998.
[104] Clause 4 of the draft clauses and what would be s.31(2A) of the Scotland Act 1998. This
requirement replicates what is currently required of the Presiding Officer in relation to the
legislative competence of the Parliament in respect of a proposed Bill.

on the UK Parliament would, on a traditional understanding of parliamentary sovereignty, be ineffective.[105] It binds, however, the Scottish Parliament and unsurprisingly the proposed s.30A would be a reserved matter.[106]

At Westminster and Holyrood alike, there is concern about the capacity of **6–18** existing procedures to cope with the pressures placed on them. It is arguable, as is implicit in many of the recommendations made by the Modernisation Committee of the House of Commons, that the only way of alleviating the strain on legislative procedures is to move much of the debate over the policies and principles of legislative proposals back to the pre-legislative stage, so that at least the main outstanding areas of disagreement are focused for the legislative process proper. In this respect, the greater willingness of government north and south of the border to engage in greater pre-legislative consultation is an important advance, although it is fair to say that the Scottish Parliament has made better efforts to institutionalise public participation in the legislative process, via the practice of committees of taking evidence on the general principles of Bills at stage one.[107] The problems of overload may not yet have manifested themselves quite as seriously at Holyrood as at Westminster, but it is still noticeable that much the greater part of legislative time is spent on government bills, contrary to an expectation in the early days that more legislation would emanate from committees or members.[108] At Westminster, there is widespread disquiet that the advance programming of major Bills precludes proper scrutiny of their finer points; on more than one occasion in recent years, large numbers of amendments tabled for consideration in committee have had to be abandoned for simple lack of time. This matters, for to the extent that much of the parliamentary time devoted to legislation is (quite properly) spent on government Bills, the legislative process provides as much an opportunity for holding the government to account as questions and debates.

LEGISLATIVE COMPETENCE

Introduction

In relation to the legislative competence of the Westminster Parliament, there is **6–19** little one can usefully add to the earlier discussion of the supremacy, or sovereignty, of Parliament.[109] If there are things Westminster would not do on

---

[105] Despite that, a two-thirds majority is to be found in s.2 of the Fixed-term Parliaments Act 2011 in relation to the dissolution of Parliament. Of course, the UK Parliament could, by simple majority, repeal that provision.

[106] The introduction of super majorities for constitutional legislation in the UK Parliament was rejected by the House of Lords Select Committee on the Constitution, *The Process of Constitutional Change, 15th Report of Session 2010–2012* (The Stationery Office, 2011) para.99.

[107] This is not to say that external perspectives will not influence the legislative process at Westminster, for MPs and peers alike draw on the views expressed to them by interested groups and parties in their contributions to legislative debate; the difference, however, is that in Scotland that participation is direct rather than filtered through the medium of elected members.

[108] This expectation was founded on the recommendations of the Consultative Steering Group on the Scottish Parliament, established in advance of devolution to consider parliamentary procedures, geared towards the achievement of (among other things) "power-sharing" in the new Parliament. This was felt to imply if not equality as between executive and non-executive Bills, at least greater priority for the latter than they have in fact received.

[109] See paras 3–02—3–08, above.

moral or political grounds, there are nevertheless no legal limitations, as the law is traditionally understood, on its ability to enact whatever legislation it chooses.[110] The focus of this section is therefore on the legislative competence of the Scottish Parliament, which is limited in terms of s.29(2) of the Scotland Act. A number of mechanisms exist to ensure, so far as possible, that the Scottish Parliament does not stray outwith the bounds of its competence. Most of these operate at the pre-Assent stage, i.e. before a Bill becomes an Act of the Scottish Parliament on the signifying of Royal Assent. However, it follows from the fact that an Act, or provision of an Act, "is not law"[111] if it is outside the legislative competence of the Parliament that its validity may be questioned after it has been enacted and entered into force. A question of this sort may be raised as a "devolution issue" in terms of s.98 and Sch.6 of the Scotland Act 1998 or a "compatibility issue" in terms of s.288ZB of the Criminal Procedure (Scotland) Act 1995.

It is worth noting the terms of s.29(2) in full:

"(2) A provision is outside [the legislative competence of the Scottish Parliament] so far as any of the following paragraphs apply—

(a) it would form part of the law of a country or territory other than Scotland, Scotland,

(b) it relates to reserved matters,

(c) it is in breach of the restrictions in Schedule 4,

(d) it is incompatible with any of the Convention rights or with Community it is incompatible with any of the Convention rights or with Community

(e) it would remove the Lord Advocate from his position as head of the it would remove the Lord Advocate from his position as head of the systems of criminal prosecution and investigation of deaths in Scotland."

The reference to extraterritorial effect in subpara.(a) must be understood in light of s.126(1), whereby the term "Scotland" includes "so much of the internal waters and territorial sea of the United Kingdom as are adjacent to Scotland". The reservation in relation to the functions of the Lord Advocate in subpara.(e) reflects the perceived need to secure his or her independence as public prosecutor and head of the system of investigation of deaths in Scotland, even though the Lord Advocate ceased on devolution to be a member of the UK Government and became instead a member of the Scottish Government. The principal restrictions on the competence of the Scottish Parliament, however, are those contained in s.29(1)(b)–(d): reserved matters, the protection of certain enactments from modification by the Scottish Parliament, and compatibility with the Convention rights and EU law.

---

[110] The caveat reflects the comments of the First Division of the Inner House in *AXA General Insurance Co Ltd v Lord Advocate* [2011] CSIH 31; 2011 S.C. 662 at [67]: "There can accordingly be seen to be an as yet unresolved issue at the highest judicial level as to whether an Act of the UK Parliament could, in any circumstances, be open to challenge in the courts." We have discussed the current debate around this issue in Ch.3, above.

[111] SA 1998 s.29(1).

Reserved matters

The list of matters reserved to the exclusive competence of the Westminster **6–20**
Parliament is contained in Sch.5 to the Scotland Act, which is arranged in three
parts.[112] Part I sets out a number of "general reservations" under six headings.[113]
Part II sets out a number of "specific reservations" grouped under 11 headings.[114] Part III contains five paragraphs of general provisions relating primarily
to the reservation of certain public bodies.

A provision of an Act of the Scottish Parliament will fall foul of this restriction
if it "relates to" one of the reserved matters specified in Sch.5. Section 29(3)
provides that

> "the question whether a provision of an Act of the Scottish Parliament
> relates to a reserved matter is to be determined, subject to subs.(4), by
> reference to the purpose of the provision, having regard (among other
> things) to its effect in all the circumstances".[115]

In *Martin v Most* Lord Walker described the phrase "relates to" as

> "familiar in this sort of context, indicating more than a loose or con-
> sequential connection, and the language of section 29(3), referring to a
> provision's purpose and effect, reinforces that".[116]

---

[112] Under SA 1998 s.30, the list may be modified by Order in Council as necessary or expedient (as
was done, for example, to confer competence to hold the independence referendum). See para.
1–03.

[113] The constitution (including the Crown, but not Her Majesty's prerogative and other executive
functions, or functions exercisable by any person acting on behalf of the Crown; the Union of the
Kingdoms of Scotland and England; the UK Parliament; and the continued existence of the High
Court of Justiciary and the Court of Session); the registration and funding of political parties;
foreign affairs (with the important exception of "observing and implementing international
obligations, obligations under the Human Rights Convention and obligations under EU law"); the
civil service of the state; defence; and treason.

[114] Financial and economic matters; home affairs; trade and industry; energy; transport; social
security; regulation of the professions (though not the legal profession); employment; health and
medicines; media and culture; and miscellaneous matters including judicial remuneration and
equal opportunities. It should be noted that few of these headings are comprehensive, and many
of the reservations are subject to exceptions.

[115] SA 1998 s.29(4), provides that a provision which would not otherwise relate to reserved matters
but which modifies Scots private law or Scots criminal law as either applies to reserved matters
shall be treated as "relating to" reserved matters (and thus invalid) unless its purpose is to make
the law in question "apply consistently to reserved matters and otherwise".

[116] *Martin v Most* [2010] UKSC 10; 2010 S.C. (U.K.S.C.) 40 at [49]. That approach was endorsed
by Lord Hope in *Imperial Tobacco Ltd v Lord Advocate* [2012] UKSC 61; 2013 S.C. (U.K.S.C.)
153 at [16]. That approach has the benefit of expanding the scope of devolved competence given
the adoption of a "reserved powers model". What the court is talking about is more than a "loose
or consequential connection" to the reservation. But this line of reasoning was applied by the
Supreme Court in *Re Recovery of Medical Costs for Asbestos Disease (Wales) Bill* [2015] UKSC
3; [2015] 2 W.L.R. 481 at [25] to the equivalent provision of the Government of Wales Act 2006
(s.108(7)). Wales operates on a "transferred powers model" (although the government has
accepted a recommendation to change that: HM Government, *Powers for a Purpose: Towards a
Lasting Devolution Settlement for Wales* (The Stationery Office, 2015) Cm.9020) with the result
that this interpretation *narrows* the scope of devolution requiring as it does more than a "loose
and consequential connection" to the devolution. That was a 3:2 split decision and may well be
revisited by the Supreme Court in the future. It is a decision that appears to fall foul of Lord
Neuberger's warning that although the same language may be used in the different devolution
statutes, the court should be careful about interpreting each statute the same: *Attorney General v
National Assembly for Wales Commission* [2012] UKSC 53; [2013] 1 A.C. 792 at [50].

It is clear, however, that some ancillary impact on reserved matters is not to be taken as fatal to the validity of the provision. This emerges from para.3 of Sch.4, which provides that modifications of the law on reserved matters are permissible so long as they are

> "(a) incidental to, or consequential on, provision made (whether by virtue of the Act in question or another enactment) which does not relate to reserved matters; and (b) do not have a greater effect on reserved matters than is necessary to give effect to the purpose of the provision".

Moreover, s.101 provides that, where a provision of an Act of the Scottish Parliament[117] could be read in such a way as to be outside competence, that provision is to be read "as narrowly as is required for it to be within competence, if such a reading is possible, and is to have effect accordingly". As this implies, those acting under Acts of the Scottish Parliament will themselves need to consider whether its provisions require to be "read down" to avoid a conflict with reserved matters, for the legality of their own actings, if not the validity of the Act, may otherwise be vulnerable to challenge. The validity of the Act can be saved by a narrow reading; the actions taken under it, if outwith the scope of that reading, cannot.

6–21   There is a separate issue here, to which we shall have cause to return. Some incidental or consequential impact on reserved matters is permitted, provided it does not have a greater effect on reserved matters than is necessary to give effect to the purpose of the provision. The question is: who decides whether the effect on reserved matters is greater than necessary? Of course, the initial judgment is for the promoters of the legislation and the Scottish Parliament itself (and indeed for those who have a locus to initiate pre-Assent challenges to the competence of a Bill). But when the court comes to consider that judgment, what is the nature of its role? In the human rights context, a distinction has been drawn between primary and secondary judgments.[118] If the court's function is one of reviewing the reasonableness of the legislative choice, then it makes merely a secondary judgment. The court makes a primary judgment if it decides for itself whether the legislative choice is incompatible with human rights. It would appear that here, as in the human rights sphere, the court must make a primary judgment. It must determine at what point the effect of a provision on reserved matters becomes "greater than necessary" and then ask whether the Scottish Parliament went beyond that point. In the human rights sphere, the courts grant a certain latitude to the legislature, identifying the area within which, consistently with human rights, it has a free choice. But in relation to the reserved/devolved boundary the issue seems sharper. Intuitively, one would have thought a particular legislative choice has greater than necessary effect on reserved matters or it does not; a line must be drawn, not points on a spectrum, and it is to be drawn by the courts.

Enactments protected from modification

6–22   Schedule 4 to the Scotland Act complements the reservation of specified matters to Westminster by s.29 and Sch.5 and preserves certain existing legislation from

---

[117] Or of a Bill before the Scottish Parliament, or of subordinate legislation made by a member of the Scottish Government.
[118] R. Clayton and H. Tomlinson, *The Law of Human Rights* (Oxford: Oxford University Press, 2000) paras 5.122–5.124 and 5.133.

modification by the Scottish Parliament,[119] including the Scotland Act itself so far as it prescribes the principal features of the devolution settlement. Exempted from this general prohibition are modifications to a number of specified sections of the Scotland Act, most of which relate to the statutory versions of the privileges enjoyed by the Houses of Parliament at Westminster and thus have to do with the Scottish Parliament's internal procedures.

EU law

The Scottish Parliament cannot make laws which are inconsistent with EU law. **6–23** Section 126(9) of the Scotland Act defines "EU law" to mean, or include

> "(a) all those rights, powers, liabilities, obligations and restrictions from time to time created or arising by or under the EU Treaties, and (b) all those remedies and procedures from time to time provided for by or under the EU Treaties".

A Member State of the EU must take all necessary steps to ensure the fulfilment of its obligations arising from the EU treaties or resulting from action taken by the EU institutions. The UK is the entity recognised in international law as being bound by these obligations. But it is for the state to decide how to parcel out responsibility for securing observance of its international obligations as a matter of its internal domestic law. Thus, while Pt I of Sch.5 reserves "international relations, including relations with territories outside the United Kingdom, the European Union (and their institutions) and other international organisations", it expressly exempts from the scope of that reservation "observing and implementing international obligations, obligations under the Human Rights Convention and obligations under EU law".[120] So far as EU obligations fall within the scope of devolved competence, therefore, they are to be fulfilled by the devolved institutions, and by the same token the devolved institutions will be liable for any breach of EU law within that sphere.

Convention rights

The Convention rights are those fundamental human rights enshrined in the **6–24** European Convention on Human Rights that have been incorporated into the legal orders of the UK by the Human Rights Act 1998.[121] The Human Rights Act did not enter fully into force until 2 October 2000. Section 129(2) of the Scotland Act therefore provided for the Human Rights Act to be treated as if it were in force for the purpose of certain provisions of the Scotland Act, namely those relating to the devolved competence of the Scottish Parliament and Scottish Government, proceedings under the Act involving human rights questions and the definition of devolution issues.[122] The consequence of this was that the Scottish Parliament and Scottish Government were bound by the Convention rights for over a year before they became binding on other Scottish public

---

[119] The statutes or statutory provisions protected from modification include arts 4 and 6 of the Union with Scotland Act 1706 and of the Union with England Act 1707, so far as they relate to freedom of trade; Private Legislation Procedure (Scotland) Act 1936; European Communities Act 1972 s.1 and Sch.1; and Human Rights Act 1998.

[120] SA 1998 Sch.5 para.7(1) and (2).

[121] Human Rights Act 1998 s.1 and Sch.1.

[122] SA 1998 ss.29(2)(d), 57(2) and (3), 100, 126(1) and Sch.6.

authorities and on governmental bodies and public authorities south of the border.[123]

Common law

6–25 It is now established that there are, in addition to the limits imposed by s.29(2), common law limits on the competence of the Scottish Parliament.[124] However, it would only be in rare and exceptional circumstances that the Parliament would transgress these limits. Any such review is not on the traditional common law grounds of irrationality/unreasonableness but could only be justified where the Parliament had legislated so as to abrogate fundamental rights (in which case the Convention rights limit to its competence ought to be engaged) or otherwise to secure the rule of law.[125] It ought to be a rare occurrence that a common law challenge is stateable, let alone successful.

CONTROLLING LEGISLATIVE COMPETENCE

6–26 We have so far considered the statutory, and now also common law, limits on the Scottish Parliament's legislative power. We turn now to consider the enforcement of those limits. There are three parts to this: first, the measures in place to ensure that only Bills that are within the Parliament's competence are presented for Royal Assent; secondly, the procedures for challenging any measure, which despite those pre-Assent checks, reaches the statute book; and finally, the judicial approach to policing those limits which will include a discussion of the remedies available to the court.

Pre-assent checks

6–27 The Scotland Act provides for a number of devices designed to ensure, prior to the passage of a Bill into law, that it is within the Parliament's competence. In the case of government Bills, the member of the Scottish Government in charge of the Bill must, on or before its introduction in the Parliament, state that in their view the provisions of the Bill would be within the competence of the Parliament.[126] In the case of all Bills, the Presiding Officer must, on or before the introduction of a Bill, decide whether or not in her view its provisions would be within the competence of the Parliament and state her decision.[127] The form of these statements of competence and the manner in which they are to be made are provided for in rr.9.2 and 9.3 of the Standing Orders of the Scottish Parliament.

---

[123] The Convention rights became binding on the Lord Advocate on 22 May 1999, and on the Scottish Parliament and other members of the Scottish Government on 1 July 1999.

[124] *AXA General Insurance Co Ltd v Lord Advocate* [2011] UKSC 46; 2012 S.C. (U.K.S.C.) 122. See also: *Attorney General v National Assembly for Wales Commission* [2012] UKSC 53; [2013] 1 A.C. 792.

[125] *AXA General Insurance Co Ltd v Lord Advocate* [2011] UKSC 46; 2012 S.C. (U.K.S.C.) 122, per Lord Reed at [153].

[126] SA 1998 s.31(1).

[127] SA 1998 s.31(2). A negative statement by the Presiding Officer would not, however, block the Bill's further progress. It is, in practice, very persuasive. See, for example: the ill fated Civil Appeals (Scotland) Bill (which sought to abolish the right to appeal to what was then the House of Lords); the Presiding Officer stated that, in his view, the Bill was outside the Parliament's competence and its parliamentary process ended shortly thereafter (*Official Report*, 20 December 2006)

It is an anomaly of the present system that no similar statement need be made once any amendments have been made to the Bill. In *Salvesen v Riddle*, discussed below, amendments to the Agricultural Holdings (Scotland) Bill rendered certain of its provisions beyond the competence of the Parliament.[128] A requirement on the Presiding Officer and/or the responsible minister to restate his or her view on the competence of the Bill once it was in final form would not necessarily prevent a repeat of *Salvesen* but ought to reduce the risk of it happening.

Naturally, the views of the Scottish Ministers and/or Presiding Officer are not conclusive of the issue of competence,[179] and the Bill may yet have a variety of further hurdles to clear. If the Bill is passed by the Scottish Parliament, it is for the Presiding Officer to send it forward for Royal Assent.[130] But s.32(2) of the Scotland Act provides that she may not so submit it at any time during which the Advocate General, Lord Advocate or Attorney General is entitled to refer the Bill to the Supreme Court under s.33; where such a reference has been made but not disposed of; or where the Secretary of State has made an order under s.35 of the Act prohibiting the Presiding Officer from submitting the Bill for Royal Assent.[131]

A reference may be made under s.33 at any time during the four week period commencing with the passing of the Bill by the Parliament, although the Law Officers may notify the Presiding Officer that they do not intend to make a reference. In that event (subject to a s.35 order) the Presiding Officer may send the Bill for Royal Assent at once. If a reference is made in relation to a Bill, the Scottish Parliament may choose simply to wait until the reference is disposed of one way or the other. If the Supreme Court finds that the provisions of the Bill are within the powers of the Parliament, then the Presiding Officer may submit it for Royal Assent without further ado. If it does not so find, the Bill cannot be sent forward for Royal Assent in unamended form. The Parliament may in that event reconsider the Bill in a form designed to rectify the problems of the earlier version.[132] A reference to the Supreme Court may, of course, take some time to dispose of. This is particularly likely to be the case where the Bill raises some question of compatibility with EU law. Although the Supreme Court may competently deal with such a question itself, it may elect to refer the matter on to the Court of Justice for the European Union for a preliminary ruling under art.267 of the Treaty on the Functioning of the European Union.[133] In that event, the Scottish Parliament has the right under s.34 to resolve that it wishes to reconsider the Bill before the references (i.e. to the Supreme Court and to the Court of Justice of the European Union) are decided.[134] If it does so resolve, the Presiding Officer will notify the Law Officers accordingly and the person who made the reference must request its withdrawal. The Parliament may then

---

[128] See the discussion at para.6–33, below.

[129] See the speech of Lord Hope in *A v Scottish Ministers* [2001] UKPC D5; 2002 S.C. (P.C.) 63 at [7]: " . . . they are no more than statements of opinion, which do not bind the judiciary"; see also Lord Reed in *Imperial Tobacco Ltd v Lord Advocate* [2012] CSIH 9; 2012 S.C. 297 at [59]–[64].

[130] SA 1998 s.32(1).

[131] This latter is not a control over the competence of a Bill, but is considered here since it is grouped with the controls on competence within the scheme of the Scotland Act 1998.

[132] SA 1998 s.36(4).

[133] See para.10–20, below.

[134] The procedures for such reconsideration are contained in the Parliament's Standing Orders r.9.9

consider and vote on an altered version of the Bill which seeks to accommodate the concerns that gave rise to the original reference. Even if the Bill is passed in its amended form, however, it may still be the subject of a second reference by a Law Officer, should one of them remain unsatisfied as to its competence. No such reference has to date been made under the Scotland Act. However, the Attorney General has exercised his equivalent power under the Government of Wales Act 2006 and three such references have now been determined by the Supreme Court, including the very first legislative measure of the Welsh Assembly. Only one reference has resulted in a finding that the legislative provision was beyond the Assembly's legislative competence.[135]

6–28   The power of the Secretary of State to intervene under s.35 is quite different from the reference power conferred on the Law Officers by s.33. In making a reference, the Law Officers are raising questions of legislative competence in relation to a bill ("does the Parliament have the power to pass this law?"). An intervention by the Secretary of State has nothing to do with the legislative competence of the Scottish Parliament as such, despite the position of s.35 in the scheme of the Scotland Act. Thus even if a Bill is within the competence of the Scottish Parliament, the Secretary of State may make a s.35 order preventing its submission for Royal Assent in two situations: where it contains provisions which he has reasonable grounds to believe would be incompatible with any international obligations of the UK or with the interests of defence or national security; or where it contains provisions which modify the law as it applies to reserved matters and which he has reasonable grounds to believe would have an adverse effect on the operation of the law as it applies to reserved matters. As with the Law Officers, the Secretary of State may not exercise this power if he has notified the Presiding Officer that he does not intend to make an order under s.35. Subject to that, he may make such an order at any time during the four week period commencing with the passing of the Bill by the Parliament; within four weeks of any subsequent approval of the Bill in amended form; or within four weeks of a reference to the Supreme Court being decided or otherwise disposed of. The order must be laid before both Houses of the Westminster Parliament and is subject to annulment by resolution of either House.

Devolution and compatibility issues

6–29   It follows from the fact that a provision in an Act of the Scottish Parliament "is not law" if it is outwith the boundaries of legislative competence prescribed by s.29 of the Scotland Act that, even where a Bill has survived pre-Assent scrutiny, received Royal Assent and entered into force, its validity remains open to

---

[135] *Attorney General v National Assembly for Wales Commission* [2012] UKSC 53; [2013] 1 AC 792; *Re Agricultural Sector (Wales) Bill* [2014] UKSC 43; [2014] 1 W.L.R. 2622 both held the respective provisions were within competence. The third challenge saw the Supreme Court split 3:2, with the Recovery of Medical Costs for Asbestos Disease (Wales) Bill (which was designed to allow the NHS to recover the costs of treating the effects of asbestos related diseases for former employers and insurers) was outwith the legislative competence of the Welsh Assembly: *Re Recovery of Medical Costs for Asbestos Disease (Wales) Bill* [2015] UKSC 3; [2015] 2 W.L.R. 481. The reference was made not because the Counsel General doubted the competence of the measure (he argued for in the Supreme Court) but because a challenge by insurance companies was inevitable and he wanted to avoid years of litigation as the case made its way through the courts.

challenge.[136] Such a challenge normally constitutes a devolution issue in terms of para.1(a) of Sch.6:

"a question whether an Act of the Scottish Parliament or any provision of an Act of the Scottish Parliament is within the legislative competence of the Parliament".

It must be raised and resolved in accordance with the rules laid down by Sch.6. That position has been amended in relation to criminal proceedings. Where, in criminal proceedings, a challenge is raised based on an alleged incompatibility with EU law or Conventions rights, it is to be treated as a "compatibility issue" as opposed to a devolution issue.[137] A compatibility issue must be resolved in accordance with the rules laid down in ss.288ZB and 288AA of the Criminal Procedure (Scotland) Act 1995.

Under Pt II of Sch.6, proceedings for the determination of a devolution issue may be instituted by the Advocate General or the Lord Advocate, but devolution issues may equally be raised, either by way of claim or defence, by any person. So, for example, a person might seek judicial review of an Act of the Scottish Parliament in the Court of Session on the grounds that it is outside the competence of the Parliament; or, when charged with a criminal offence, plead the invalidity of the legislation under which he is charged or of the decision to prosecute him.

While only the Supreme Court has jurisdiction to pronounce on the competence of Scottish legislation prior to its receiving Royal Assent, a devolution issue or compatibility issue may be raised in any proceedings before a court or tribunal. However, a tribunal from which there is no right of appeal must refer a devolution issue which arises before it to the Inner House of the Court of Session. Other tribunals, and any court other than the Supreme Court or a court consisting of three or more judges of the Court of Session, may do so. In criminal matters, a court other than a court consisting of two or more judges of the High Court of Justiciary, may refer a compatibility issue arising in proceedings before it to the High Court. Where a devolution issue is raised before either the Court of Session or the High Court (that is, where it does not come before them on a reference from an inferior court) or a compatibility issue is raised before the High Court, the court may choose to refer the issue to the Supreme Court for resolution. In any event, an appeal against a determination by the Inner House of the Court of Session of a devolution issue lies to the Supreme Court. Similarly, there is a right of appeal to the Supreme Court in respect of a determination of both a devolution issue and a compatibility issue by a court consisting of two or more judges of the High Court of Justiciary, but only with the leave of the High Court or, failing that, with special leave from the Supreme Court itself.[138] Paragraph 37 of Sch.6 provides that any power to make provision for regulating the procedure before any court or tribunal shall include the power to make provision in relation to devolution issues.

---

[136] See *A v Scottish Ministers* [2001] UKPC D5; [2003] 2 A.C. 602 and *Adams v Scottish Ministers*, 2003 S.C. 171.
[137] SA 1998 Sch.6 para.1 (as amended by the Scotland Act 2012 s.36(4)). Where the vires of an Act of the Scottish Parliament is challenged on grounds other than incompatibility with EU law or Convention rights, it remains a "devolution issue" and determined in accordance with Sch.6,
[138] Prior to the entry into force of the Scotland Act 1998, there was no right of appeal in Scots criminal cases beyond the High Court of Justiciary.

Judicial review of competence

6–30 Where the competence of a provision of an Act of the Scottish Parliament is challenged, essentially three questions fall to be answered: (a) what, applying the ordinary rules of statutory interpretation, does the provision mean; (b) read in that way, does the provision fall within the legislative competence of the Parliament; and (c) if the answer to question (b) is "no", can the provision be read narrowly enough so as to bring it within the competence of the Parliament?[139] If the answer to that final question is "no" a declaration that the provision is "not law" should follow. The question of remedy then arises. Following a declaration that a provision is "not law", the legislature should normally be afforded an opportunity to correct the problem, especially where there may be follow on consequences for other parts of a legislative scheme. With that in mind, where the court decides that a provision of an Act of the Scottish Parliament is not within the legislative competence of the Parliament, the court is empowered to

"make an order—

    (a) removing or limiting any retrospective effect of the decision, or
    (b) suspending the effect of the decision for any period and on any conditions to allow the defect to be corrected".[140]

It is helpful to illustrate these issues with some examples.[141] First, we will consider the case of *Martin v Most*, where the Supreme Court had to consider the boundary of reserved matters and, in particular, when a provision "relates to" a reserved matter. Secondly, we will consider the first successful civil challenge to the competence of a legislative provision of the Scottish Parliament. But before that, the Supreme Court has set down a number of principles that apply when considering whether a provision of an Act of the Scottish Parliament is within legislative competence. It is there that we shall begin.

6–31 In *Imperial Tobacco Ltd v Lord Advocate* (which was an unsuccessful challenge to the ban on the display of tobacco or smoking related products and the ban on cigarette vending machines) Lord Hope set out three principles that should be followed when determining a challenge to the competence of a legislative provision of the Scottish Parliament.[142] They were:

    (1) Any question of competence must be determined by applying the particular rules that have been set out in s.29 of, and Schs 4 and 5 to, the Scotland Act 1998. It was not for the court to express a view on whether an issue was better legislated for by Holyrood or Westminster.

---

[139] SA 1998 s.101. Where the question is one of compatibility with Convention rights, the question should be answered under s.3 of the Human Rights Act 1998 (which requires that much the same exercise be undertaken): *DS v HM Advocate* [2007] UKPC D1; 2007 S.C. (P.C.) 1; *Salvesen v Riddell* [2013] UKSC 22; 2013 S.C. (U.K.S.C.) 236.

[140] SA 1998 s.102.

[141] For a review of the various legislative competence challenges, see C.M.G. Himsworth and C.M. O'Neill, *Scotland's Constitution: Law and Practice*, 3rd edn (Haywards Heath: Bloomsbury Professional, 2015) paras 14.24 to 14.26.

[142] *Imperial Tobacco Ltd v Lord Advocate* [2012] UKSC 61; 2013 S.C. (U.K.S.C.) 153.

The respective spheres of responsibility had been determined by the UK Parliament. Decisions based on federal systems were of limited assistance. It is important to remember that a provision may have a devolved purpose but nevertheless be outside competence.[143]

(2) The system of rules laid down by the Scotland Act 1998 "must, of course, be taken to have been intended to create a system for the exercise of legislative power by the Scottish Parliament that was coherent, stable and workable" but that is not a principle of construction. The rules in Scotland Act 1998 are to be interpreted in the same way as any other Act of Parliament.[144]

(3) Describing the Scotland Act 1998 as a "constitutional statute" offers no guide as to its proper interpretation. It is, within carefully prescribed limits, a generous settlement of legislative authority. There is no presumption that a provision of an Act of the Scottish Parliament is inside, as opposed to outside, competence.[145]

A few years later, in the first challenge to the legislative competence of a measure of the Welsh Assembly, Lord Hope restated those principles[146] and they have since been followed by the Supreme Court.[147]

Against that background we turn to *Martin v Most*. This case concerned the **6–32** maximum sentence that could be imposed for certain road traffic offences. Those sentences had been increased by s.45 of the Criminal Proceedings etc. (Reform) (Scotland) Act 2007, that being an Act of the Scottish Parliament. The competence of that provision was challenged on the basis it related to a reserved matter, namely the Road Traffic Offenders Act 1988. The question divided the Supreme Court 3:2 (with Lord Hope and Lord Rodger failing to agree on the outcome of a Scottish appeal for the first time in their period together on the highest court).[148] That division of opinion, and the final outcome of the appeal, is closely linked to the particular statutory provisions in dispute in that case and whether it was a rule that was special to a reserved matter. For present purposes, that disagreement can be set to one side. It is possible to identify some helpful guidance about how the reserved matters boundary is to be policed so far as s.29(2)(b) is concerned (a point on which the Justices all agreed). A provision is outside competence if it "relates to" (s.29(2)(b)) a reserved matter and a whether a provision "relates to" a reserved matter is to be "determined . . . by reference to the purpose of the provision, having regard (among other things) to its effect

---

[143] *Imperial Tobacco Ltd v Lord Advocate* [2012] UKSC 61; 2013 SC (U.K.S.C.) 153 at [13]. On the last point, Lord Rodger illustrated it in *Martin v Most* [2010] UKSC 10; 2010 S.C. (U.K.S.C.) 40 at [76]: the Scottish Parliament may have the devolved competence to alter the sentencing powers of the lower courts but if it does so in a manner than infringes Convention rights, the measure will be beyond competence.

[144] *Imperial Tobacco Ltd v Lord Advocate* [2012] UKSC 61; 2013 S.C. (U.K.S.C.) 153 at [14].

[145] *Imperial Tobacco Ltd v Lord Advocate* [2012] UKSC 61; 2013 S.C. (U.K.S.C.) 153 at [15].

[146] *Attorney General v National Assembly for Wales Commission* [2012] UKSC 53; [2013] 1 A.C. 792 at [78]–[81].

[147] *Re Agriculture Sector (Wales) Bill* [2014] UKSC 43; [2014] 1 W.L.R. 2622, per Lord Reed at [5]–[6].

[148] For a fuller analysis of this case, see C. Himsworth, "Nothing Special About That? Martin v HM Advocate in the Supreme Court" (2010) 14 Edin. L.R. 487.

in all the circumstances" (s.29(3)).[149] Lord Walker explained what he understood that phrase to mean:

> "Section 29(2)(b) prohibits legislation by the Scottish Parliament that 'relates to' reserved matters. That is an expression which is familiar in this sort of context, indicating more than a loose or consequential connection, and the language of sec 29(3), referring to a provision's purpose and effect, reinforces that."[150]

That guidance has since been endorsed by the Supreme Court on a number of occasions.[151] Lord Rodger explained that the clearest indication of the purpose of a provision will usually come from a report that gave rise to the legislation or of one of the committees of Parliament but very often the purpose will be clear from its context within the Act in question.[152] At the end of that paragraph, Lord Rodger doubted whether a clear example of an unlawful provision would come before the courts because of the pre-legislative measures that are in place. That observation conveniently brings us on to the case of *Salvesen v Riddell*.

6–33   *Salvesen v Riddell*[153] was the first successful civil challenge to an Act of the Scottish Parliament and was based on an incompatibility with art.1 of the First Protocol to the European Convention on Human Rights. It concerned s.72 of the Agriculture Holdings (Scotland) Act 2003. That provision related to the right to buy certain agricultural tenancies and sought to regulate any purported termination of such a tenancy. The background to the legislation is complicated and it is unnecessary to explain it in detail. For present purposes it is enough to note that on 3 February 2003 S had served a notice the effect of which was to terminate his lease to R on 28 November 2008. He expected to obtain vacant possession of the property on that date. However, the 2003 Act struck at any purported termination notice that was served on or after 22 September 2002. To that extent the legislation was retrospective. That provision was not set out in the White Paper that preceded the Bill nor the Bill as introduced into the Parliament (and thus certified by the responsible Minister and the Presiding Officer as within the Parliament's competence). It was the result of a government amendment and was said to be an "anti-avoidance" measure to prevent landlords avoiding the more favourable (to tenants) regime that the 2003 Act was going to introduce. Had the notice been served after 30 June 2003, the 2003 Act offered acceptable protections for landlords in the same position as S. The consequence for S, however, was that rather than receive vacant possession on 28 November 2008, on 12 December 2008 R served notice under the 2003 Act exercising his "right to buy". The Land Court upheld R's position. The provisions of the 2003 Act that allowed that turn of events were subsequently held to be beyond the competence of the Scottish Parliament. The declaration that the offending provision was not

---

[149] The court had to consider other questions as well, in particular the application of s.29(4) and para.2(3) of Sch.4 (was the rule of Scots criminal law that the Act sought to modify "special to a reserved matter"). They are complex issues (which have not been made any easier by the decision is *Most* accordingly Lord Rodger: [149]) which we are not going to explore for present purposes.

[150] *Martin v Most* [2010] UKSC 10; 2010 S.C. (U.K.S.C.) 40 at [49].

[151] *Imperial Tobacco Ltd v Lord Advocate* [2012] UKSC 61; 2013 S.C. (U.K.S.C.) 153, per Lord Hope at [16]; *Re Recovery of Medical Costs for Asbestos Disease (Wales) Bill* [2015] UKSC 3; [2015] 2 W.L.R. 481, per Lord Mance at [25].

[152] *Martin v Most* [2010] UKSC 10; 2010 S.C. (U.K.S.C.) 40 at [75].

[153] *Salvesen v Riddell* [2013] UKSC 22; 2013 S.C. (U.K.S.C.) 236.

law was originally made by the Inner House, on appeal from the Scottish Land Court (where the point had not arisen) and was upheld by the Supreme Court.[154] The case is significant as it highlights a complete failure of the pre-Assent safeguards that are designed to prevent legislation beyond the competence of the Scottish Parliament reaching the statute book: it was "hard not to see this provision as having been designed to penalise landlords in this group retrospectively" and was accordingly discriminatory[155]; the difference in treatment between landlords who served notice before and after 30 June 2003 had "no logical justification"[156]; s.72 did not pursue an aim that was reasonably related to the aim of the legislation as a whole[157]; and there was no way in which the clear and plain language of the 2003 Act could be read in such a way as to bring it within the legislative competence of the Parliament.[158] In those circumstances, it was surprising that none of the pre-Assent checks raised any concerns over the lawfulness of s.72 of the 2003 Act.

That brought the court to the question of remedy. In the Supreme Court Lord Hope observed that

> "the finding of incompatibility ought not to extend any further than is necessary to deal with the facts of this case, and it is important that accrued rights which are not affected by the incompatibility should not be interfered with".[159]

Such an approach demonstrates that some care will be required when forging the appropriate remedy. As we have already noted, s.102 of the Scotland Act allows the court to remove or vary the retrospective effect of its decision and/or suspend the effect for a period to allow the defect to be varied. Lord Hope declined to limit the retrospective effect of the decision, but went to hold that:

> "Decisions as to how the incompatibility is to be corrected, for the past as well as the future, must be left to the Parliament guided by the Scottish Ministers."[160]

In this particular case, that led the Supreme Court to suspend the effect of their decision for 12 months, whilst granting permission for the Lord Advocate to

---

[154] *Salvesen v Riddell* [2013] UKSC 22; 2013 S.C. (U.K.S.C.) 236. See the case note by D.J. Carr, "Not Law (but not yet effectively not law)" (2013) 17 Edin. L.R. 370. The Inner House decision is reported at *Salvesen v Riddell* [2012] CSIH 26; 2013 S.C. 69. On that decision, see: D.J. Carr, "Not Law" (2012) 16 Edin. L.R. 410; M.M. Combe, "Human Rights, Limited Competence and limited partnerships: *Salvesen v Riddell*", 2012 S.L.T. (News) 193.

[155] *Salvesen v Riddell* [2013] UKSC 22; 2013 S.C. (U.K.S.C.) 236, per Lord Hope of Craighead at [42].

[156] *Salvesen v Riddell* [2013] UKSC 22; 2013 S.C. (U.K.S.C.) 236, per Lord Hope of Craighead at [44].

[157] *Salvesen v Riddell* [2013] UKSC 22; 2013 S.C. (U.K.S.C.) 236, per Lord Hope of Craighead at [44]

[158] *Salvesen v Riddell* [2013] UKSC 22; 2013 S.C. (U.K.S.C.) 236, per Lord Hope of Craighead at [47].

[159] *Salvesen v Riddell* [2013] UKSC 22; 2013 S.C. (U.K.S.C.) 236, per Lord Hope of Craighead at [51].

[160] *Salvesen v Riddell* [2013] UKSC 22; 2013 S.C. (U.K.S.C.) 236, per Lord Hope of Craighead at [57].

return (to the Court of Session) to seek an extension of that period if necessary.[161] The question of remedy did not arise in *Martin* but Lord Hope considered it on an obiter basis. Again, he would have suspended the effect of a finding of incompatibility for two months to allow it to be corrected but also removed any retrospective effect of the decision (not surprising perhaps given it related to criminal sentences that may have been imposed and already served in full).[162] Any remedy will obviously have to be tailored to the specific circumstances but it appears the court will normally be prepared to suspend any declarator that a provision is "not law" for at least a limited period so as to allow the Parliament an opportunity to address the consequences of the court's decision.

PARLIAMENTARY COMMITTEES

6–34 In any institution, it is impracticable to expect all of its work to be done by the institution meeting in plenary session. Delegation to committees is therefore necessary; but it is also desirable, since committees charged with specific remits develop an expertise in their fields which enables the institution as a whole better to perform its functions. At Westminster, a distinction is drawn between general and select committees[163]; at Holyrood, the committees of the Scottish Parliament combine the functions of the two (and have other functions besides).

Westminster

6–35 General committees are appointed afresh by the House of Commons Committee of Selection as and when required and must reflect the party political balance in the Commons as a whole. They fall into four categories: public Bill committees, which are appointed to consider public Bills and which can now take evidence in relation to the provisions of the Bill from external witnesses and experts; those appointed to consider subordinate legislation; those appointed to consider EU documents; and the grand committees of Scotland, Wales and Northern Ireland.[164] The chair of a general committee is appointed by the Speaker. Select committees are appointed for the life of each Parliament, and fall into five categories:

(a) domestic committees;
(b) scrutiny committees;
(c) internal committees, which oversee aspects of the House's procedures and practices;
(d) the departmental select committees; and
(e) the committees charged with supervision of the work of the main officers of Parliament.

Although select committees have been a feature of parliamentary life for many years, the present structure of departmental select committees dates back only to 1979. They are charged with examining the expenditure, administration and

---

[161] *Salvesen v Riddell* [2013] UKSC 22; 2013 S.C. (U.K.S.C.) 236, per Lord Hope of Craighead at [57].
[162] *Martin v Most* [2010] UKSC 10; 2010 S.C. (U.K.S.C.) 40 at [43].
[163] General committees were known, until the 2006–2007 session, as standing committees.
[164] House of Commons Standing Orders r.84.

policy of "their" departments of state and associated public bodies. They have been criticised for failing to alter the nature of the relationship between Parliament and government. Such criticism is not altogether fair. Unlike the congressional committees in the United States, they are neither constituted nor staffed so as to allow them to be systematic in their scrutiny, and though they have the power to "send for persons, papers and records", they cannot compel the attendance of witnesses or the production of documents. Their investigations are therefore dependent upon ministerial co-operation to a significant extent. Even so, as the Select Committee on Procedure concluded in 1990, the new select committees provided "a far more vigorous, systematic and comprehensive scrutiny of ministers' actions and policies than anything that went before".[165] Since the committees are constituted to reflect political balance in the House as a whole, voting can split along party lines; but it is not an invariable practice. Some committees if not others have shown willing to challenge the government (possibly at some cost to any ministerial aspirations their members may harbour). Outwith the category of departmental select committees, furthermore, the Select Committees on Procedure, Public Accounts and Public Administration have done much valuable work on constitutional fundamentals in an effort to improve Parliament's capacity to hold the executive to account.[166] The role of select committees has been strengthened in recent years. The House as a whole now elects the chairs of most of the select committees, with members being elected by their respective parliamentary groups.[167] The Prime Minister now appears before the Liaison Committee of the House of Commons three times a year and a Backbench Business Committee has been established with the power to schedule business in the Commons chambers on days set aside for non-government business. Select committees have undertaken some well publicised and high profile investigations in recent years: the Culture, Media and Sport Committee's report on phone hacking[168], the Treasury Committee's reports into the banking crisis; and the Foreign Affairs Committee's report into the Iraq war decision[169] all spring to mind. These committees, however, remain under-resourced as compared to the government departments they are trying to monitor. These high profile reports aside, it open to doubt just effective the committees can be at holding the government to account.[170]

---

[165] House of Commons Select Committee on Procedure, *The Working of the Select Committee System: Second Report from the Select Committee on Procedure, Session 1989–90* (The Stationery Office, 1990) HC 19–I.

[166] See, e.g. House of Commons Procedure Committee, *Parliamentary Questions, Third Report of Session 2001–02* (The Stationery Office, 2002), HC 622; Select Committee on Public Administration, *Ombudsman Issues, Third Report of Session 2002–03* (The Stationery Office, 2003) HC 448, which excoriates the government for failing to make good its pledge to introduce legislation to reform the ombudsman system and for obstructing the work of the Parliamentary Commissioner; and the series of reports produced by the same committee in recent years on ministerial accountability.

[167] House of Commons Standing Orders r.122B. Chairs are now also subject to term limits, being the greater of two consecutive Parliament's (which will now ordinarily be 10 years) or 8 years (r.122A).

[168] House of Commons Culture, Media and Sport Committee, *News International and Phone-hacking, Eleventh Report of Session 2010–12* (The Stationery Office, 2012) HC 903.

[169] House of Commons Foreign Affairs Committee, *The Decision to go to War in Iraq, Ninth Report of Session 2002–03* (The Stationery Office, 2003) HC 813.

[170] See the discussion in Himsworth and O'Neill, *Scotland's Constitution: Law and Practice* (2015), para.10.9.

Holyrood

6–36 At Holyrood, the committees were expected to have a more important role to play, in large part due to the absence of a second chamber. The rules on the committees of the Scottish Parliament are contained in Ch.6 of the Parliament's standing orders. These require the Parliament to establish and maintain a number of mandatory committees. They are: the Standards, Procedures and Public Appointments Committee; the Finance Committee; the Public Audit Committee; the European and External Relations Committee; the Equal Opportunities Committee; the Public Petitions Committee; and the Delegated Powers and Law Reform Committee.[171] The remit of each of the mandatory committees is prescribed in the Parliament's standing orders.[172] These committees are established for the whole session of the Parliament.[173] The Parliament may also, on a motion of any member or from the Parliamentary Bureau, establish subject committees. These committees vary (their names at least) from one parliamentary session to the next. There are currently 10 subject committees: the Devolution (Further Powers) Committee; the Economy, Energy, and Tourism Committee; the Education and Culture Committee; the Health and Sport Committee; the Infrastructure and Capital Investment Committee; the Justice Committee; the Justice Sub-committee on Policing; the Local Government and Regeneration Committee; the Rural Affairs, Climate Change and Environment Committee; and the Welfare Reform Committee. The remit of each of these committees, and their duration, is determined by the Parliament.[174] Each committee, other than a private Bill committee, is required to have between 5 and 15 members. The Parliamentary Bureau is charged with drawing up a provisional list of members for each committee, having regard to party political balance and preferences expressed by MSPs, which must then be approved by the Parliament. The Parliament must also approve any changes to a committee's remit or membership.[175]

The functions of the parliamentary committees are extensive. Each is empowered to examine such matters within its remit as it may deem appropriate, or as may be referred to it by the Parliament or another committee, and report to Parliament thereon. Each is charged, within its remit, with considering the policy and administration of the Scottish Government (including financial proposals and administration), any proposal for legislation (whether before the Scottish Parliament or the Westminster Parliament), and any relevant European legislation or international convention. They may consider the need for reform of the law and to that end may initiate legislative proposals. In the latter respect, their impact has been slight. Only three committee Bills have been enacted by the Parliament.[176] But in general terms, it is fair to say that the greater part of the Parliament's work is done through its committees, and the verdict of civil society (if not of the often hostile Scottish media) on their performance to date has been

---

[171] Scottish Parliament Standing Orders r.6.1(5).
[172] Scottish Parliament Standing Orders rr.6.6–6.11.
[173] Scottish Parliament Standing Orders r.6.12(1).
[174] Scottish Parliament Standing Orders rr.6.1(3) and 6.12(2).
[175] Scottish Parliament Standing Orders r.6.3.
[176] The Interests of Members of the Scottish Parliament Bill (from the Standards and Public Appointments Committee), the Scottish Parliamentary Commissions and Commissioners etc. Bill (Review of the Scottish Parliamentary Corporate Body Supported Bodies Committee) and the Scottish Parliamentary Pensions Bill (Scottish Parliamentary Pension Scheme Committee).

broadly favourable.[177] The values identified by the Consultative Steering Group as underpinning the Parliament's work—public participation, accountability and power sharing—may have an aspirational flavour, but the committees have to a significant extent succeeded in capturing them. More recently, the Calman Commission was supportive of the Holyrood committees but raised some concern about their effectiveness at holding the government to account.[178]

PARLIAMENTARY PRIVILEGE

Westminster

The privileges of the Westminster Parliament are rooted in the law and custom **6–37** of Parliament. At the opening of each new Parliament, the Speaker formally claims from the Crown for the Commons "their ancient rights and privileges", namely freedom of speech; freedom from arrest; the exclusive right to regulate their composition; and exclusive jurisdiction over their internal affairs. The Houses of Parliament also assert an exclusive jurisdiction over the existence and extent of their privileges and over breaches of privilege and contempts of Parliament, which has in the past provoked confrontation with the courts.

Article 9 of the Bill of Rights 1689 provides that

> "the freedom of speech and debates or proceedings in Parliament ought not to be impeached or questioned in any court or place out of Parliament".

This confers on members of both Houses an immunity from civil and criminal liability in respect of words spoken during debates or in the course of parliamentary proceedings (although members may expose themselves to the disciplinary jurisdiction of the House itself). The precise scope of the privilege is unclear owing to the inexact nature of the term "proceedings in Parliament" but was recently considered by the Supreme Court in *R. v Chaytor*.[179] In that case, a number of MPs were charged with false accounting in relation to parliamentary expenses that they had claimed. Each pled that the Crown Court lacked jurisdiction to hear the case, it being excluded by art.9 of the Bill of Rights. Had that argument been upheld, it would have produced the unsatisfactory outcome that MPs accused of offences associated with their expenses claims were immune from prosecution in the ordinary courts and could only be dealt with by Parliament. That would be unlikely to inspire public confidence.[180]

---

[177] Procedures Committee of the Scottish Parliament, *Third Report 2003 (Session 1), The Founding Principles of the Scottish Parliament: the Application of Access and Participation, Equal Opportunities, Accountability and Power Sharing in the Work of the Parliament* (The Stationery Office, 2003) SPP 818. Perhaps the main source of disquiet about the committees stemmed from the tendency to go into private session rather more routinely than the public interest in transparency might warrant.

[178] Report of the Calman Commission, Commission on Scottish Devolution, *Serving Scotland Better: Scotland and the United Kingdom in the 21st Century* (The Stationery Office, 2009) Ch.6.

[179] *R. v Chaytor (David)* [2010] UKSC 52; [2011] 1 A.C. 684.

[180] Query whether the appellants, if dealt with by Parliament, could then have complained under art.6 of the European Convention on Human Rights? Parliament would hardly be a "fair and impartial tribunal", made up, as it would be, of political friends and political foes. The "fair minded and informed observer" may have a "reasonable apprehension" of bias. Indeed, there may be evidence of actual bias. For discussion of a similar argument in relation to the Scottish Parliament, see N.S. Ghaleigh, B. Kemp and P. Reid, "Politics as a Profession: Electoral Law, Parliamentary Standards and Regulating Politicians" [2012] P.L. 658.

The appellants' claim of privilege was unanimously rejected by the Supreme Court (sitting as a panel of nine Justices). The first point the court confirmed was that it was for the court, nor Parliament, to determine the limits of art.9.[181] The court then went on to explain why art.9 required to be read narrowly:

> "There are good reasons of policy for giving article 9 a narrow ambit that restricts it to the important purpose for which it was enacted—freedom for Parliament to conduct its legislative and deliberative business without interference from the Crown or the Crown's judges. The protection of Article 9 is absolute. It is capable of variation by primary legislation, but not capable of waiver, even by Parliamentary resolution. Its effect where it applies is to prevent those injured by civil wrongdoing from obtaining redress and to prevent the prosecution of members for conduct which is criminal."[182]

Given the breadth of the protection that art.9 affords, the court was persuaded that its ambit should be restricted to the core business of Parliament. Submitting claims for expenses was "an incident of the administration of Parliament; it is not part of the proceedings of Parliament".[183] Accordingly, art.9 did not prevent the trial proceeding. The appellants had a second argument. They also sought to rely on a second privilege: what was said to be the exclusive cognisance of Parliament. In short, they argued, that it was for Parliament to deal with the alleged (and subsequently proved) wrongdoing, not the courts. As Lord Rodger explained, not since 1667 had the House claimed exclusive cognisance in a case where a member was alleged to have committed an ordinary crime in the House or its precincts.[184] Furthermore, unlike the privilege that arises under art.9, the privilege of exclusive cognisance can be waived by the House.[185] The fact the House authorities had co-operated with the investigation that led to the charges and the failure by the Speaker to step in and assert privilege all suggested that the House did not consider the matter to fall within its exclusive cognisance.[186] The argument was disposed of by Lord Rodger thus:

> " . . . the mere fact that the House *could* treat the matter as one of contempt does not mean that the House *must* do so, On the contrary, if the conduct in question would also constitute an offence under the ordinary criminal law of England, then the individual can be prosecuted in the criminal courts in the usual way. The jurisdiction of the House to deal with the matter overlaps with the jurisdiction of the ordinary courts to deal with it as a criminal offence. In short, the matter does not fall within the exclusive cognisance of Parliament."[187]

Accordingly, the trials were allowed to proceed and in due course a number of MPs were convicted and sentenced to periods of imprisonment.

---

[181] *R. v Chaytor* [2010] UKSC 52; [2011] 1 A.C. 684, per Lord Phillips at [15].
[182] *R. v Chaytor* [2010] UKSC 52; [2011] 1 A.C. 684, per Lord Phillips at [61].
[183] *R. v Chaytor* [2010] UKSC 52; [2011] 1 A.C. 684, per Lord Phillips at [62].
[184] *R. v Chaytor* [2010] UKSC 52; [2011] 1 A.C. 684, per Lord Rodger at [117].
[185] *R. v Chaytor* [2010] UKSC 52; [2011] 1 A.C. 684, per Lord Phillips at [63].
[186] *R. v Chaytor* [2010] UKSC 52; [2011] 1 A.C. 684, per Lord Rodger at [123].
[187] *R. v Chaytor* [2010] UKSC 52; [2011] 1 A.C. 684, per Lord Rodger at [108] (emphasis in the original); see also Lord Phillips at [81].

As the Supreme Court explained, the most significant effect of the privilege of **6–38** freedom of speech is the absolute immunity enjoyed by MPs in the law of defamation, which rests on the notion that MPs should be able to speak freely in Parliament without any fear that what they say might later be used against them in court. This is not to say that a Member of Parliament cannot be sued in defamation at all; in respect of his utterances outwith the meaning of "proceedings in Parliament", he is as liable to be sued as anybody else.[188] Neither does it mean that no reference whatsoever may be made in court to parliamentary proceedings. Since 1980, the House of Commons has permitted reference to be made in court to *Hansard* and published reports of parliamentary committees. In *Pepper v Hart*,[189] the House of Lords (in its judicial capacity) held that, in interpreting ambiguous legislation, the courts might properly have regard to clear ministerial statements made during the passage of the legislation through Parliament. The courts have also established the practice of examining ministerial statements made in Parliament when considering applications for judicial review of the legality of ministerial decisions. Section 13 of the Defamation Act 1996 enables MPs to waive their privilege in order to pursue an action in defamation. Most recently in 2011, the privilege of freedom of speech attracted headlines when it was used to name two individuals who were said to have obtained "super-injunctions" to prevent publication of affairs they were said to have had. One individual was named in the House of Lords and shortly thereafter the injunction (which was not in fact a "super-injunction") was discharged. The other was named in the House of Commons but that did not lead to the injunction (which, again, was not "super") being discharged.[190] The constitutional propriety of freedom of speech being used in this way so as to substitute the view of an MP or a peer on whether an individual should be named for that of a High Court judge is dubious. In the case of the court, each party is protected by the right of appeal. The same is not true when a member of the legislature has taken matters into their own hands.[191]

It is not only parliamentary proceedings which attract the protection of the privilege, but also the publication of parliamentary proceedings. This was established by the Parliamentary Papers Act 1840, the enactment of which followed one of the great confrontations between Parliament and the courts over the existence and extent of parliamentary privilege. In *Stockdale v Hansard*,[192] it was held that privilege did not extend to the publication by *Hansard* of a report by the Inspectors of Prisons, which referred to an indecent book, published by Stockdale, found circulating in Newgate Prison. By resolution, the House of Commons responded by asserting its "sole and exclusive jurisdiction to determine upon the existence and extent of its privileges".[193] It added that the institution or prosecution of any action bringing the privileges of Parliament into discussion or decision by a court outwith Parliament itself constituted a breach of

---

[188] Although even here it is not possible to fortify one's case against an MP with reference to remarks he has made in Parliament, or rely on these to prove malice: see *Church of Scientology of California v Johnson-Smith* [1972] 1 Q.B. 522 QBD; *Prebble v Television New Zealand Ltd* [1995] 1 A.C. 321 PC (New Zealand).

[189] *Pepper (Inspector of Taxes) v Hart* [1993] A.C. 593.

[190] *CTB v News Group Newspapers Ltd* [2011] EWHC 1334 (QB).

[191] That, and other issues, arising from the episode are considered in P. Johnson, "What can the press really say? Contempt of court and the reporting of parliamentary proceedings" [2012] P.L. 491.

[192] *Stockdale v Hansard* (1837) 2 Mood & R. 9.

[193] H.C.J. 418 (1837).

privilege "and renders all parties concerned therein amenable . . . to the punishment consequent thereon".[194] The 1840 Act gave statutory force to the Commons' view of what the law was, making clear that the protection of absolute privilege from civil and criminal proceedings extended to papers published under the authority of Parliament as certified by an officer of either House. Qualified privilege applies to the publication of fair and accurate reports of parliamentary proceedings and papers, so that there will be no liability in defamation without proof of malice.[195]

6–39 The privilege of freedom from arrest protects members from civil arrest, but not from arrest in connection with criminal offences. Since the abolition of imprisonment for debt in the nineteenth century, it has had little practical significance.[196] The importance of the exclusive right to regulate its own composition has also been attenuated by the transfer of the right of the Commons to determine the result of disputed parliamentary elections to the ordinary courts.[197] The Houses of Parliament do retain the right to determine whether a person is disqualified from membership of either House, as when, in 1960, the House of Commons declared vacant the seat of Tony Benn MP after he succeeded to a viscountcy on the death of his father and barred him from the House. This jurisdiction is not, however, exclusive, as a person claiming that an individual disqualified from membership of the House of Commons by virtue of the House of Commons Disqualification Act 1975 has been elected to the Commons may apply under s.7 of the Act to the Judicial Committee of the Privy Council for a declaration to that effect.[198]

The privilege consisting of Parliament's exclusive right to control its own proceedings and to regulate its internal affairs without interference from the courts remains significant. It was on this basis that the ordinary courts declined to intervene in the celebrated case of *Bradlaugh v Gossett*.[199] Mr Bradlaugh, an atheist who had been refused the opportunity of taking the oath required before an MP may sit,[200] contested the legality of a resolution of the House of Commons to exclude him and sought an injunction to restrain the serjeant-at-arms from enforcing that resolution. The court held it had no jurisdiction to pronounce on

---

[194] Stockdale subsequently obtained judgment against *Hansard*, but the two holders of the office of the Sheriff of Middlesex were imprisoned by order of the Commons for attempting to enforce the judgment. The court dismissed their application for habeas corpus on the basis that it could not go behind the Speaker's warrant to the effect that the two men were guilty of a breach of privilege and contempt of Parliament: *Sheriff of Middlesex Case* (1840) 11 Ad. & El. 273. They were later released by the Commons upon undertaking not to execute any orders of the court against *Hansard*, which in turn led to their being imprisoned by the courts for contempt of court.

[195] But while the 1840 Act resolved the differences between Parliament and the courts over this aspect of freedom of speech, it did not resolve the basic jurisdictional conflict over who it is, Parliament or the courts, that has the last word over the existence and extent of privileges when claimed.

[196] However, collateral privileges flow from the basic principle underlying freedom from arrest, namely the right of Parliament to the uninterrupted attendance and services of its members, such as the exemption of MPs from jury service and from citation to attend court as witnesses.

[197] See now the Representation of the People Act 1983 Ch.2 Pt III and para.4–27, above.

[198] Curiously, this jurisdiction was not transferred to the Supreme Court. The Judicial Committee may direct that the issue be tried in the High Court of England and Wales, the Court of Session or the High Court of Northern Ireland, depending on the location of the constituency in question; if so, the decision of that court is final.

[199] *Bradlaugh v Gossett* (1884) 12 Q.B.D. 721 QBD.

[200] This in the days before provision was made allowing MPs to make a solemn affirmation: see now the Oaths Act 1978.

the matter. It is also on the grounds of this privilege that the courts decline to investigate alleged procedural defects in the legislative process when the validity of an Act of Parliament is challenged. As we have seen,[201] the effect of the "enrolled Bill rule" is that a court of law can do no more than look to the Parliamentary Roll:

" . . . if from that it should appear that a bill has passed both Houses and received the Royal Assent, no court can inquire into the mode in which it was introduced into Parliament, nor into what was done previous to its introduction, nor what passed in Parliament during its progress."[202]

If the enactment of legislation, whether public or private, has been obtained by fraud or other impropriety, or in contravention of the standing orders of Parliament, only Parliament can rectify matters by repealing the measure in question.

The Houses of Parliament retain a jurisdiction to deal with breaches of **6–40** privilege and contempts of Parliament. "Contempt of Parliament" is a generic term to cover any offences punishable by Parliament, namely conduct offensive to the authority and dignity of the Houses or, as Erskine May puts it[203]:

"Any act or omission which obstructs or impedes either House in the performance of its functions, or which obstructs or impedes any member or officer of such House in the discharge of his duty, or which has a tendency, directly or indirectly, to produce such results."[204]

The term "contempts" therefore includes breaches of privilege, that is, the infringement of any of the specific privileges noted above. The distinction between the two may be important, however, for while the Houses of Parliament cannot extend the scope of their own privileges and questions of the existence and extent of privilege may be addressed by the courts, the list of possible contempts remains open and the courts cannot question the causes of committal for contempt. Established examples of contempt include disorderly conduct within the precincts of Parliament; the obstruction of members going to or coming from the Houses; bribery, corruption and other species of dishonesty; and refusal to give evidence before parliamentary committees.

The fact that certain conduct is found to constitute contempt does not mean that Parliament will take any further action against the contemnor. The House of Commons resolved in 1978 only to use its powers of punishment when

---

[201] See para.3–02, above.
[202] *Edinburgh and Dalkeith Railway v Wauchope* (1842) 8 Cl. & F. 710 HL, per Lord Campbell. See also *British Railways Board v Pickin* [1974] A.C. 765, in which the House of Lords eschewed any jurisdiction to inquire into parliamentary procedures.
[203] *Erskine May Parliamentary Practice* (2011).
[204] For a discussion of the full range of powers that Parliament has, see: *Erskine May Parliamentary Practice* (2011) pp.197–201 ("Punishment of Members"); pp.254–258 ("Misconduct of Members or Officers"); and Ch.5 ("Rules governing the conduct of Members of both Houses and the disclosure of financial interests"), especially pp.85–88 ("Complaints and investigations (House of Commons)") and pp.95–98 ("Enforcement (House of Lords)").

"satisfied that to do so is essential to provide reasonable protection for the House, its members or its officers, from such improper obstruction or attempt or threat of obstruction as is causing or is liable to cause substantial interference with the performance of their respective functions".

Nevertheless, the range of penalties at the theoretical disposal of the House is considerable. A member may be expelled or suspended; members or "strangers" may be admonished or reprimanded at the Bar of the House. Persons may be committed for contempt by the High Court of Parliament, without recourse to the ordinary courts; and the House retains a power, last used in 1880, of imprisonment (although curiously it has no power to impose fines).[205] As we saw in relation to *R. v Chaytor*, where the conduct that constitutes the contempt also amounts to a crime, Parliament's jurisdiction to punish the contempt is co-existent with the court's jurisdiction to deal with the criminal conduct.

6–41   As to the House of Lords, Erskine May comments that "the Lords enjoy their privileges simply because of their immemorial role in Parliament as advisers of the Sovereign".[206] Just as much as the House of Commons, the House of Lords claims the exclusive right to be the judge of its own privileges and the power to punish breaches of privilege and contempts, although issues of privilege arise less frequently in the Upper House. The privilege of peerage confers immunity from civil arrest.[207] Article 9 of the Bill of Rights 1689 applies equally to the Lords as to the Commons in protecting freedom of speech. The House of Lords is master of its own affairs and decides, through the Committee for Privileges, the right of newly created peers to sit and vote and on claims to old peerages.[208] Lastly, the Lords have the power to commit a person for contempt and, unlike the Commons, also have a power to fine and to order security to be given for good conduct.[209]

6–42   Many of these privileges may appear archaic, but their underlying rationale remains broadly sound, as attested by the provision made in the Scotland Act to extend aspects of parliamentary privilege as developed at Westminster to the Scottish Parliament. Even so, as part of the general drive to modernise the workings of Parliament, a joint committee consisting of members of the House of Lords and of the House of Commons was established in July 1997 to review the law and practice of parliamentary privilege at Westminster and to make recommendations. The committee, chaired by Lord Nicholls of Birkenhead,

---

[205] It is questionable now whether it would be consistent with the international obligations of the UK under the Convention for either House of Parliament to resort to its penal jurisdiction. It is not merely that the procedures of the Houses may lack compatibility with art.6 (particularly the right to be tried before an independent and impartial tribunal) but also that, in so far as the categories of contempts are not closed, imposition of criminal liability could be regarded as contrary to art.7, which prohibits the retrospective creation of criminal offences. See, generally, *Demicoli v Malta* (1991) 14 E.H.R.R. 47.

[206] *Erskine May Parliamentary Practice* (2011) p.205.

[207] See *Stourton v Stourton* [1963] 1 All E.R. 606.

[208] In the *Wensleydale Peerage Case* (1856) 5 H.L. Cas. 958, the House of Lords decided that the life peerage created for the judge Sir James Parke did not entitle him to sit in Parliament. The Appellate Jurisdiction Act 1876 authorised the appointment of Lords of Appeal in Ordinary carrying with it a right to sit and vote in the Lords, while the Life Peerages Act 1958 provided for the conferment of life peerages on men and women with the right to sit and vote.

[209] Although here again, it seems unlikely that such power would ever now be used: see para. 6–40.

published its first report in April 1999.[210] The joint committee's approach to its task was informed by the following considerations:

> "The overall guiding principle is that the proper functioning of Parliament lies at the heart of a healthy parliamentary democracy. It is in the interests of the nation as a whole that the two Houses of Parliament should have the rights and immunities that they need in order to function properly. But the protection afforded by privilege should be no more than Parliament needs to carry out its functions effectively and safeguard its constitutional position. Appropriate procedures should exist to prevent abuse and ensure fairness. Thus the thread running through this report involves matching parliamentary privilege to the current requirements of Parliament and present-day standards of fairness and reasonableness."

In that light, the committee made a number of recommendations for change. It favoured abolition of existing privileges only in a few cases.[211] Otherwise, its proposals generally involved clothing existing privileges in statutory form or removing more glaring anachronisms. Thus, it recommended the enactment of legislation confirming the traditional view of art.9 of the Bill of Rights as a blanket prohibition on the examination of parliamentary proceedings in court, subject to specific and limited exceptions,[212] clarifying the meaning of the term "proceedings in Parliament", and replacing the provisions of the Parliamentary Papers Act 1840 with legislation in comprehensible form. It also called for the replacement of s.13 of the Defamation Act 1996 with new provision enabling the House, rather than an individual member, to waive privilege in court proceedings (and not merely those involving defamation). It favoured the introduction of new statutory offences of bribery and corruption, but noted that, since the prosecution of such offences would inevitably impact upon art.9, any prosecution should be subject to the consent of the Attorney General or Lord Advocate. The right of each House to administer its internal affairs within its precincts should be confined to activities directly and closely related to proceedings in Parliament and

> "Parliament should no longer be a statute-free zone in respect of Acts of Parliament relating to matters such as health and safety and data protection. In future, when Parliament is to be exempt, a reasoned case should be made out and debated as the legislation proceeds through Parliament".

While each House should retain its disciplinary and penal jurisdiction over its own members, the disciplinary procedures of both Houses should be revised to bring them into line with contemporary standards of fairness, including rights guaranteed by the European Convention on Human Rights. Parliament's jurisdiction over contempts committed by strangers should be transferred to the courts, although Parliament should retain a residual jurisdiction including a power to

---

[210] Joint Committee on Parliamentary Privilege, *First Report of the Joint Committee on Parliamentary Privilege* (The Stationery Office, 1999) HL 43–I, HC 214–I.

[211] The joint committee recommended abolition of freedom from arrest in civil cases and of the collateral privilege exempting members from citation to attend court as witnesses (although it considered that citations should not be issued against members without the prior approval of a judge).

[212] Such as that established by *Pepper v Hart* [1993] A.C. 593.

admonish in non-contentious cases. None of these proposals, however, have been enacted into law.

Holyrood

6–43   The Scottish Parliament and its members do not enjoy the same range of privileges as obtain at Westminster, and such "privileges" as they have are, like the Parliament itself, derived from the Scotland Act 1998. The Act extends two aspects of the privilege of free speech to the Scottish Parliament, its members and officers. First, by virtue of s.41, any statement made in proceedings of the Parliament and the publication under the authority of the Parliament of any such statement is absolutely privileged in the law of defamation. Even if an MSP makes a defamatory statement maliciously, or with the intention of injuring the reputation of the object of the statement, he cannot be held liable in respect of it (although, as at Westminster, he may fall foul of the disciplinary jurisdiction of the Parliament itself). Secondly, by virtue of s.42, certain proceedings of the Scottish Parliament—namely, parliamentary proceedings in relation to a Bill or subordinate legislation—are shielded from criminal liability for contempt of court. A fair and accurate report of such proceedings, provided it is made in good faith, is similarly protected. This immunity is narrower than that which obtains at Westminster: it would appear, for example, that contemptuous utterances made in the course of a general debate in the Scottish Parliament could result in the prosecution of the speaker. However, para.1 of Sch.3 requires standing orders to make provision for the prevention of conduct constituting contempt of court and to lay down a sub judice rule. This finds its expression in standing order r.7.3(2) which requires that members do not conduct themselves in a manner which would constitute a criminal offence or contempt of court and r.7.5 which prevents members from making reference to any matter in relation to which legal proceedings are active. It is therefore unlikely that many instances of contemptuous behaviour will arise from the proceedings of the Scottish Parliament. Like members of the Westminster Parliament, MSPs are exempt from jury service, but by virtue of s.85 of the Scotland Act, rather than freedom from arrest and its associated privileges. No immunity from arrest, either criminal or civil, is extended to MSPs by the Scotland Act.

The aspect of parliamentary privilege that finds the most echoes in the Scotland Act is that of exclusive cognisance of internal affairs. The underlying rationale for this privilege is not dissimilar to that found in art.9 of the Bill of Rights: namely, to prevent outside interference, and specifically interference by the courts, with the proceedings of the Parliament. Absent such privileges, the ordinary work of the Parliament could be obstructed by the commencement of legal challenges to its activities. The Scotland Act, therefore, provides that the validity of any proceedings of the Scottish Parliament is unaffected by any vacancy in its membership[213] or by the participation of a member who is subject to disqualification.[214] The validity of any act of the Presiding Officer or either of her deputies is unaffected by any defect in the officer's or their election,[215] and

---

[213] SA 1998 s.1(4).
[214] SA 1998 s.17(5).
[215] SA 1998 s.19(7).

the validity of an Act of the Scottish Parliament is unaffected by any invalidity in the proceedings of the Parliament leading to its enactment.[216]

The courts have largely acquiesced in Westminster's assertion of exclusive **6–44** jurisdiction over its internal affairs, and that there are still good reasons for this is reflected in these provisions of the Scotland Act. It is important to note, however, that the jurisdiction of the ordinary courts is not wholly excluded in relation to the internal workings of the Scottish Parliament. Certain aspects of its internal affairs are governed by the Scotland Act itself, or by subordinate legislation made under it, or by Scottish legislation required to be enacted by the Scotland Act. The rules on members' interests are an example. In *Whaley v Lord Watson of Invergowrie*,[217] the petitioners sought interim interdict to restrain Mike Watson MSP from proceeding further with the Protection of Wild Mammals (Scotland) Bill, on the grounds that he was in breach of the rules against paid advocacy. Lord Johnston refused the petitioners' motion, partly on the basis that the grant of the remedy would intrude upon the exclusive competence of the Parliament to regulate its own affairs. But, as the First Division subsequently made clear, that competence is not exclusive. The rules on members' interests were then contained in a statutory instrument made pursuant to the Scotland Act. Accordingly they were legal rules, enforceable as such by the ordinary courts.[218] The fact that the Standards Committee of the Scottish Parliament had a parallel jurisdiction to scrutinise alleged breaches of the rules on members' interests did not affect the point, nor was the court in any way bound by the fact that the Standards Committee had rejected a complaint that Mr Watson had breached the rule against advocacy.

A further issue raised by *Whaley* concerned the effect of s.40(3) and (4) of the Scotland Act. These provide that in any proceedings against the Scottish Parliament, the court shall not make an order for suspension, interdict, reduction or specific performance (or other like order) but may instead make a declarator. Similarly, in any proceedings against an MSP, the Presiding Officer or her deputies, any member of the staff of the Parliament or the parliamentary corporation, the court may make no coercive order, but must confine itself to declarator, if the effect of making a coercive order would be to give relief against the Parliament which is prohibited by s.40(3). In *Whaley*, it was argued that the court could not grant interdict against Mike Watson MSP because the effect of doing so would be to interdict the Parliament from proceeding with the Protection of Wild Mammals (Scotland) Bill. As the First Division held, however:

> "Section 40(4) of the 1998 Act is designed to prevent parties from obtaining in substance remedies affecting the Parliament which they could not obtain in proceedings against the Parliament. It follows that subsection (4) applies where proceedings for some legal wrong could lie against the Parliament. In

---

[216] SA 1998 s.28(5). See also s.50, which provides that the validity of any act of a member of the Scottish Government or of a junior Scottish Minister is unaffected by any defect in his nomination by the Parliament or, as the case may be, in the Parliament's agreement to his nomination; and s.69(3), which makes similar provision in respect of any procedural defects in the appointment of the Auditor General for Scotland.

[217] *Whaley v Lord Watson of Invergowrie*, 2000 S.C. 340.

[218] The position would have differed if the petition had raised a question of compliance with the standing orders, which do not require to be cast in legislative form and which are in fact contained in a resolution of the Parliament.

the present case . . . the petitioners seek to interdict the first respondent from breaching Article 6 of the members' interests order—a wrong which could be committed only by a member and which could never be committed by the Parliament itself . . . In other words, any interdict against the first respondent could not have the effect of interdicting a wrong by the Parliament."[219]

So, for example, even if there were a compelling argument that the Scottish Parliament was proposing to enact legislation trespassing upon reserved matters, the court could not restrain it from proceeding by way of interdict. Nor could it interdict the printing and publication of the Bill by the Clerk to the Parliament, because that would effectively amount to an interdict against the Parliament proper. But coercive remedies are competent against members and officers of the Scottish Parliament where s.40(3) is not implicated, even though their grant may involve some disruption to the Parliament's internal affairs.

6–45   Finally, there are certain parallels to be drawn between the inherent jurisdiction enjoyed by the Houses of Parliament at Westminster as the High Court of Parliament and the conferment of specific powers on the Scottish Parliament in relation to witnesses, evidence and discipline. Section 22 of the Scotland Act provides for the regulation of parliamentary proceedings by standing order, and gives effect to Sch.3 which specifies how certain matters are to be dealt with by standing orders. Among the matters that Sch.3 requires standing orders to cover are the withdrawal from a member of the Parliament of his rights and privileges.[220] But while, as such, the Scottish Parliament has an independent disciplinary jurisdiction over its members,[221] it does not, by contrast to Westminster, have an autonomous penal jurisdiction, either over members or strangers. Sections 22 and 23 provide for the power of the Parliament to compel the attendance of witnesses and the production of documents, the exceptions to and modalities surrounding that power, and for the creation of summary offences of refusing or failing without statutory justification or reasonable excuse to attend or co-operate as required. The Houses of Parliament at Westminster, as the High Court of Parliament, have powers in relation to compelling attendance and the production of evidence similar to those of the ordinary courts, and have jurisdiction to deal with any breaches of privilege or contempts involved in non-compliance with their requirements. These provisions of the Scotland Act provide a statutory statement of the extent to which the Scottish Parliament is to have an equivalent jurisdiction, and it should in particular be noted that criminal offences under these provisions will be triable in the ordinary courts, but not before the Parliament itself. Similarly, an MSP who takes part in any parliamentary proceedings in contravention of the rules on the registration of financial interests or the rules against paid advocacy will be guilty of a criminal offence punishable by a fine, but again triable by the ordinary courts rather than the Parliament. Lastly, s.43 provides that the Scottish Parliament is a "public body" for the purposes of the Prevention of Corruption Acts 1889 to 1916, with the

---

[219] *Whaley v Lord Watson of Invergowrie*, 2000 S.C. 340, per Lord President Rodger at 351.

[220] This is provided for by the Standing Orders r.1.7, in the following terms: "The Parliament may, on a motion of the Standards Committee, withdraw from a member his or her rights and privileges as a member to such extent and for such period as are specified in the motion".

[221] For a discussion of the Parliament's disciplinary jurisdiction, see: Ghaleigh, Kemp and Reid, "Politics as a Profession: Electoral Law, Parliamentary Standards and Regulating Politicians" [2012] P.L. 658.

consequence that the members (and staff) of the Scottish Parliament, unlike members of the Westminster Parliament, are subject to liability for offences involving the corrupt making or accepting of payments, in money or in kind, for activity or inactivity in connection with the public body's business.

STANDARDS

Westminster[222]

On several occasions in the past century, the House of Commons has had cause **6–46** to inquire into possible contempts of Parliament, breaches of privilege and other species of un-parliamentary conduct connected with links between a member's parliamentary role and outside financial (or equivalent) interests. A public register of members' interests was established in 1975. It proved insufficient to prevent the various misdemeanours which finally, in 1994, prompted the establishment of a Committee on Standards in Public Life

> "to examine current concerns about standards of conduct of all holders of public office, including arrangements relating to financial and commercial activities, and to make recommendations as to any changes in present arrangements which might be required to ensure the highest standards of probity in public life".

The committee published its first report, concerning the holding by MPs of paid outside interests, in May 1995. The report acknowledged the widespread loss of public confidence in the probity of MPs, but found no evidence of "a growth in actual corruption". What it did find was that almost 70 per cent of MPs, not including the Speaker and Ministers, had some form of financial relationship with outside bodies, ranging from company directorships and consultancies with lobbying firms and trade associations to sponsorship agreements with trade unions. The committee did not recommend the introduction of an outright ban on outside financial interests, taking the view that this would deter otherwise eligible and well qualified people from seeking election to the House of Commons: " . . . a Parliament composed entirely of full-time professional politicians would not serve the best interests of democracy." It did, however, recommend the establishment of a new Select Committee on Standards and Privileges and the appointment of a Parliamentary Commissioner for Standards, who would supervise compliance with a new Code of Conduct for MPs and report to the select committee on alleged breaches. It called for a specific prohibition on paid advocacy and the adoption of rules requiring members to deposit with the Commissioner for Standards, and thereby make available for public inspection, any agreements with bodies outside Parliament relating to the provision of services by them in their capacity as MPs, together with details of the remuneration received from any such employment. More generally, the committee set out seven general principles which were to be taken to govern all aspects of public life.[223] The House of Commons endorsed both the statement of principles and the specific recommendations of the committee in a free vote in

---

[222] See P. Leopold, "Standards of Conduct in Public Life" in J. Jowell and D. Oliver (eds), *The Changing Constitution*, 7th edn (Oxford: Oxford University Press, 2011) Ch.15.
[223] Namely selflessness, integrity, objectivity, accountability, openness, honesty and leadership.

November 1995, at the same time approving a resolution banning paid advocacy. The House subsequently approved a new Code of Conduct for MPs in July 1996.[224] It was enforced by the Select Committee on Standard and Privileges and after repeating the seven principles of conduct in public life, it set out eight rules dealing with matters such as general conduct, acceptance of gifts, lobbying and advocacy and registration of gifts. When in doubt, members were exhorted to seek the advice of the Parliamentary Commissioner for Standards. The Commissioner was also responsible for maintaining the Register of Members' Interests. Registrable interests include any pecuniary interest or other material benefit which a member receives and which might reasonably be thought by others to influence his actions, speeches or votes in Parliament, or actions taken in his capacity as an MP.[225] A proposal to make it an offence to fail to register a financial interest (as it is for MSPs) was dropped during the passage of the Parliamentary Standards Act 2009.[226]

Although the House of Lords did not come under the same sort of pressure as the House of Commons over standards of conduct, peers nevertheless adopted a code of conduct modelled on that applicable to MPs and containing the seven principles of public life, and a new Register of Lords' Interests requiring registration by peers of all relevant interests.[227]

6–47 None of that prevented the expenses scandal that hit Westminster in 2009. As we have already seen, some parliamentarians ended up in prison as a result of false expenses claims. Others simply appeared ludicrous: for example, the claim made for a duck pond! Using the freedom of information legislation, journalists sought, and were eventually given, details of the expenses claimed by parliamentarians.[228] The first report of the Committee on Standards in Public Life had noted a widespread loss of trust in parliamentarians in the late-1990s. In the aftermath of the expenses scandal, their standing fell even further. A number of reforms were introduced to try and arrest the decline and restore public trust and confidence in their representatives. First, the Parliamentary Standards Act 2009[229] was hurried through Parliament (and was promptly amended by the Constitutional Reform and Governance Act 2010). That Act concerned only the House of Commons[230] and established a new body corporate known as the

---

[224] The current version of the code was adopted on 14 April 2015, House of Commons, "Code of Conduct" (The Stationery Office, 2015), HC 1076, *http://www.publications.parliament.uk/pa/cm201516/cmcode/1076/1076.pdf* [Accessed 7 June 2015].

[225] The code of conduct divides registrable interests into the following 10 categories: directorships; remunerated employment, office, profession, etc.; the provision of services to clients where the services arise out of the member's position as an MP; sponsorships; gifts, benefits and hospitality in the UK exceeding a specified value; overseas visits; overseas benefits and gifts exceeding a specified value; land and property other than the member's personal residence(s) (or those of a spouse) which generate an income; shareholdings; and miscellaneous relevant interests not caught by any of the specific categories.

[226] See N. Parpworth, "The Parliamentary Standards Act 2009: A Constitutional Dangerous Dogs Measure?" (2010) 73 M.L.R. 262, 276

[227] The code of conduct took effect on 31 March 2002.

[228] Only after a complaint to the Information Commissioner, which was then upheld by the High Court: *Corporate Officer of the House of Commons v Information Commissioner* [2008] EWHC 1084 (Admin); [2009] 3 All E.R. 403.

[229] Parpworth, "The Parliamentary Standards Act 2009: A Constitutional Dangerous Dogs Measure?" (2010) 73 M.L.R. 262.

[230] Parliamentary Standards Act 2009 s.2.

Independent Parliamentary Standards Authority.[231] The Authority is now responsible for the salaries of MPs (both determining what they should be and their payment). Leaving the fixing of MPs salary to an independent body ought to have been an uncontroversial step. When the Authority determined that MPs should receive a 10 per cent pay rise following the 2015 general election, however, the political parties united to denounce the decision. Given public sector pay rises were capped at 1 per cent at the time the response was not surprising. If transferring MPs pay to an independent body was meant to take the sting out of it, the move failed spectacularly. The Authority's other key function is the administration of the MPs expenses scheme. The Authority also has a compliance officer who may conduct an investigation if he has reason to believe that any MP has been paid an amount under the expenses scheme that should not have been allowed.[232] Making a false or misleading claim under the expenses claim is also an offence punishable by a fine and/or a period of up to 12 months' imprisonment.[233]

The Independent Parliamentary Standards Authority works closely with the Parliamentary Commissioner for Standards.[234] The work of the Parliamentary Commissioner for Standards is overseen by the Standards Committee, who are also responsible for investigating specific complaints alleging a breach of the code of conduct.[235] Exceptionally, and without precedent, the Standards Committee has, since 2013, had at least two (and no more than three) lay members.[236] A separate committee, the Privileges Committee, now deals with any matters of privilege that are referred to it by the House of Commons.[237]

Holyrood

Certain provisions concerning the maintenance and enforcement of standards in **6–48** the Scottish Parliament are contained in the Scotland Act itself. Section 39 deals with members' interests.[238] Broadly, it reflects the rules laid down in the House of Commons following the first report of the Committee on Standards in Public Life. In addition, it requires provision to be made by or under an Act of the Scottish Parliament for a register of members' interests to be published and made available for public inspection. It specifies that contraventions of the provisions made pursuant to it shall constitute criminal offences punishable on summary conviction by a fine not exceeding level five on the standard scale. In addition, s.43 provides that the Scottish Parliament is a "public body" for the purposes of the Prevention of Corruption Acts 1889 and 1916. Thus members and staff of the Parliament may be subject to criminal liability for corruptly making or accepting payments, in money or in kind, for activity (or inactivity) in connection with the Parliament's business.

---

[231] Parliamentary Standards Act 2009 s.3; see *http://www.parliamentarystandards.org.uk* [Accessed 7 June 2015].

[232] Parliamentary Standards Act 2009 s.9.

[233] Parliamentary Standards Act 2009 s.10.

[234] See the Joint Statement of the Parliamentary Commissioner for Standards, the Chief Executive of the Independent Parliamentary Standards Authority and the Independent Parliamentary Standards Authority Compliance Officer (20 January 2015), *http://www.parliament.uk/documents/pcfs/ IPSA-Joint-Statement.pdf* [Accessed 7 June 2015].

[235] House of Commons Standing Orders r.149.

[236] House of Commons Standing Orders r.149A.

[237] House of Commons Standing Orders r.148A.

[238] "Member" includes the law officers, whether or not they are also MSPs.

The provisions required by s.39 was made on an interim basis by the Secretary of State under the Scotland Act 1998 (Transitory and Transitional Provisions) (Members' Interests) Order 1999.[239] The matter is now governed by the Interests of Members of the Scottish Parliament Act 2006. Section 1 of the 2006 Act provides for the establishment of a statutory Register of Interests of Members of the Scottish Parliament. The Act then makes provision in connection with "registrable interests", namely registrable financial interests falling within the eight categories set out in the Schedule.[240] The maintenance of the register is the responsibility of the Clerk to the Parliament, who shall arrange for its publication and shall make it available for public inspection. Within 30 days of taking the oath of allegiance or making a solemn affirmation, a member must lodge with the clerk a written statement giving details of his registrable interests or, as the case may be, declaring that he has none. In addition, he must give details of registrable interests which are no longer held if

"after taking account of all the circumstances, that interest is reasonably considered to prejudice, or to give the appearance of prejudicing, the ability of the member to participate in a disinterested manner in the proceedings of the Parliament".[241]

Further provision is made for late registration, voluntary registration, and for deletion of spent entries from the register. The 2006 Act then makes provision in connection with "declarable interests". A member has a declarable interest in any matter if he has or had a registrable financial interest in the matter which appears in his entry on the register. A member is required to declare, orally or in writing as the Parliament may determine, the existence of a declarable interest before taking part in any proceedings of the Parliament relating to the matter in question. The prohibition on paid advocacy is continued, as required by s.39(4) of the Scotland Act 1998. Finally, the 2006 Act provides for the sanctions which shall attach to breaches of its terms. As noted, s.39 of the Scotland Act requires that such breaches shall constitute criminal offences. In addition, the member concerned may be excluded from proceedings of the Parliament, or otherwise prevented or restricted from participating in such proceedings, for such period as the Parliament may determine.

6–49		Apart from the rules on the registration and declaration of financial and other interests and the prohibition on paid advocacy, MSPs are also constrained to abide by the terms of the Code of Conduct for Members of the Scottish Parliament. The code is drafted and reviewed by the Standards, Procedures and Public Appointments Committee. The current iteration (the fifth edition) was

---

[239] Scotland Act 1998 (Transitory and Transitional Provisions) (Members' Interests) Order 1999 (SI 1999/1350). See O. Gay, "The Regulation of Parliamentary Standards after Devolution" [2002] P.L. 422; D. Woodhouse, "Delivering Public Confidence: Codes of conduct, a step in the right direction" [2003] P.L. 511 (contrasting the regulatory regime adopted in Scotland favourably with that which obtains at Westminster).

[240] Namely, remuneration; related undertakings (essentially, unremunerated directorships or partnerships); election expenses; sponsorship; gifts; overseas visits; heritable property; and interests in shares.

[241] Interests of Members of the Scottish Parliament Act 2006 s.2(3). Where subsequent registrable interests are acquired, they must also be notified to the clerk within 30 days.

adopted in April 2011.[242] It makes provision in relation to the registration and declaration of interests and the rule against advocacy, general conduct and conduct in the Chamber, the regulation of cross-party groups and lobbying. Like the standing orders, but unlike the rules on members' interests, it represents a non-statutory form of self-regulation, alleged breaches of which will be investigated and dealt with primarily, if not exclusively, by the Parliament itself rather than by the courts. It has yet to be determined whether breaches of the standing orders or Code of Conduct are justiciable or not. While distinguishing their legal form from that of the Members' Interests Order in *Whaley*, the First Division was careful to avoid stating in terms that the court would have no jurisdiction over the Parliament's non-statutory regulatory devices. The standing orders, at least, are adopted under authority of s.22 of the Scotland Act, Sch.3 of which requires that specified provision be made therein.

The Code of Conduct is enforced by the Public Standards Commissioner for **6–50** Scotland. This office was created on 1 April 2011 when the Scottish Parliamentary Commissions and Commissioners etc. Act 2010 came into force.[243] It abolished the then existing office of Scottish Parliamentary Standards Commissioner but the new Commissioner simply assumed the same powers and responsibilities. The Commissioner is independent of the Parliament, the Scottish Government and the Parliamentary Corporation. That independence is secured in two ways: the Commissioner is appointed for a single non-renewable term of eight years and he can only be removed from office by the Scottish Parliament on a motion supported by two-thirds of all MSPs.[244] The functions of the Commissioner are essentially two-fold: he investigates any complaint that a member[245] has breached any of the "relevant provisions"; and he reports to the Parliament on the outcome of any such investigation. The "relevant provisions" are the Code of Conduct for MSPs, the Standing Orders of the Parliament and the 2006 Act.[246] The Commissioner makes no determination as to whether any provision has been breached: that is a matter for the Parliament to determine after he has reported.[247] In the first instance, his report is submitted to the Standards, Procedures and Public Appointments Committee[248] who are free to reach their own conclusion on the facts or direct the Commissioner to carry out any further investigations.[249] Having considered the matter, the committee then present their report to the Parliament who again are free to reach their own conclusion. The ultimate decision on whether a member has breached any of the relevant provisions therefore rests with the Parliament.

There is, however, a catch. The Commissioner is required to follow any directions given to him by the Parliament.[250] One of those directions requires him

---

[242] Scottish Parliament, "Code of Conduct for Members of the Scottish Parliament, Edition 5" (Scottish Parliament, 2011), *http://www.scottish.parliament.uk/msps/code-of-conduct-for-msps.aspx* [Accessed 6 June 2015].

[243] See P. Reid, "Public Standards in Scotland: A Rubik's Cube?" (2012) 16 Edin. L.R. 229.

[244] Scottish Parliamentary Commissions and Commissioners etc. Act 2010 s.9.

[245] Defined by Scottish Parliamentary Standards Commissioner Act 2002 s.20, to include the Scottish Law Officers, whether or not MSPs; and former MSPs and Law Officers (although the reach of this will be limited by the requirement in s.6(5)(c) that complaints be made within one year of the conduct in question).

[246] Scottish Parliamentary Standards Commissioner Act 2002 s.3.

[247] Scottish Parliamentary Standards Commissioner Act 2002 s.9.

[248] Scottish Parliament Standing Orders r.3A.4

[249] Scottish Parliamentary Standards Commissioner Act 2002 s.10.

[250] Scottish Parliamentary Standards Commissioner Act 2002 s.4(2).

to suspend his investigation and report the matter to the procurator fiscal where he is satisfied that the member under investigation has committed the conduct complained about and this conduct would amount to a criminal offence.[251] That direction, read together with s.17 of the 2006 Act and s.39(6) of the Scotland Act 1998, has the effect that whenever the Commissioner comes to the view that an MSP may have breached the rules on registration of an interest, he must refer the matter to the procurator fiscal *before* reporting to the Standards, Procedures and Public Appointments Committee. Thus, despite the statutory scheme leaving the final decision on whether or not a breach has occurred to the Parliament, where the Commissioner comes to the view that there has been a breach, the question will necessarily be referred for the procurator fiscal to consider whether criminal proceedings should be instigated. The consequences for an MSP's career of being so referred are likely to be fatal.

6–51   So it proved with Wendy Alexander. A brief account of her demise highlights a number of flaws in the current system.[252] In the autumn of 2007 Wendy Alexander was elected the leader of the Scottish Labour Party. She was elected unopposed. Nonetheless she ran a campaign and raised funds for that purpose. Those donations were subject to the Electoral Commission's then reporting requirements in terms of the Political Parties, Elections and Referendums Act 2000 and Alexander made a "voluntary" return at the end of the campaign.[253] In the course of writing "thank you" letters to contributors to her campaign Alexander noticed one of the donors, Mr Green, had a Jersey address. That was potentially significant: she was only allowed to receive donations from "permissible donors" and for an individual that meant they had to be on the electoral register.[254] It transpired Mr Green was not a permissible donor and the time to return the donation under the 2000 Act had expired. The Electoral Commission launched an investigation to determine what, if any action, should be taken against Alexander. For present purposes, we are interested in what the Scottish parliamentary authorities did. Alexander had not registered any of the donations to her campaign in the Register of Members' Interests. Under the 2006 Act Alexander was obliged to register any gift in excess of 1 per cent of her salary as an MSP (then £520).[255] That obligation was independent of the reporting requirements under the Political Parties, Elections and Referendums Act 2000. A complaint was lodged by an SNP researcher with the Commissioner about Alexander's failure. Having investigated the complaint the Commissioner concluded that Alexander should have registered the donations. This was contrary to the advice Alexander had received from the parliamentary clerks. Things got worse for Alexander. First, in response to the Commissioner's conclusion that the donations should have been registered she made a voluntary

---

[251] Scottish Parliamentary Standards Commissioner Act 2002 (Procedures, Reporting and Other Matters) Direction 2002 para.15. The full direction is contained in Vol.4 Annex 5 of the Code of Conduct for Members of the Scottish Parliament, *http://www.scottish.parliament.uk/Parliamentaryprocedureandguidance/Directions.pdf* [Accessed 7 June 2015].

[252] For a more detailed account of this episode and the issues it gave rise to, see Ghaleigh, Kemp and Reid, "Politics as a Profession: Electoral Law, Parliamentary Standards and Regulating Politicians" [2012] P.L. 658.

[253] It was voluntary because under the Political Parties, Elections and Referendums Act 2000 at that time, any donation under £1,000 did not need to be registered and all donations to the Alexander campaign fell below that level: s.62(11). The limit has since been raised to £1,500 (Political Parties and Elections Act 2009).

[254] Political Parties, Elections and Referendums Act 2000 s.54(2)

[255] Members of the Scottish Parliament Act 2006 s.5.

entry in the Register of Members' Interests. In doing so, she issued a press release advising that this had been done "in light of an opinion received from [the Commissioner]".[256] That trigger a fresh complaint: this time alleging that Alexander had breached the MSPs Code of Conduct by disclosing the existence of a complaint that was under investigation by the Commissioner.[257] Secondly, the Commissioner referred the matter to the procurator fiscal in terms of the direction.

Skipping to the conclusion of this sorry saga highlights the problems with the system. Having considered the Commissioner's report on the first complaint, the Standards, Procedures and Public Appointments Committee, by a majority, held that the donations should have been registered, presented their report to the Parliament and moved that it be approved and that Alexander be suspended for one sitting day.[258] After an acrimonious and fairly partisan debate, the Parliament refused to pass the motion.[259] Being an MSP, Alexander even had a vote: unsurprisingly, she voted against the motion! But the result was the Parliament, who under the Act is the only arbiter of whether there has been a breach of the relevant provisions, found that Alexander had not breached the rules. By this time she had already been referred to the procurator fiscal by the Commissioner and two months before the vote had resigned as leader of the Scottish Labour Party. As to the complaint about disclosing the existence of the Commissioner's investigation, that was rejected by the Standards, Procedures and Public Appointments Committee.[260]

This was not a particularly satisfactory episode for the Parliament. A political career had been ruined over a £950 donation that the politician had forfeited, which led to alleged failings that were ultimately not upheld. This was done in a fairly partisan atmosphere and just serves to underscore the point that self-regulation (now regarded as unacceptable for most other professions) is unlikely to secure public confidence in politics as a profession.

SCOTTISH AFFAIRS AT WESTMINSTER

It remains to consider the machinery provided at Westminster for the considera- **6–52** tion of Scottish affairs. For many years prior to devolution, special arrangements were made for the handling of Scottish business in the House of Commons, through time set aside for Scottish questions, the establishment of the Scottish Grand Committee, Scottish standing committees and the Select Committee on Scottish Affairs. Unsurprisingly, devolution entailed some reassessment of these arrangements.[261] The Select Committee on Procedure recommended, and the House by resolution accepted, that the range of questions that might properly be

---

[256] The full background facts to this issue are set out in Annex A to the Scottish Parliament Standards, Procedures and Public Appointments Committee, *7th Report, 2008 (Session 3), Complaint against Wendy Alexander MSP* (Scottish Parliament, 2008) SP Paper 150.

[257] The relevant provision of the code was para.9.1.4.

[258] Scottish Parliament Standards, Procedure and Public Appointments Committee, *6th Report, 2008 (Session 3), Complaint against Wendy Alexander MSP* (Scottish Parliament, 2008) SP Paper 142.

[259] Scottish Parliament, *Official Report*, cols 10577–10579 (4 September 2008).

[260] Scottish Parliament Standards, Procedures and Public Appointments Committee, *7th Report, 2008 (Session 3), Complaint against Wendy Alexander MSP.*

[261] House of Commons Select Committee on Procedure, *Procedural Consequences of Devolution, Fourth Report of Session 1998–99* (The Stationery Office, 1999) HC 185.

put to Ministers in the Scotland Office should be formally reduced to include only those matters for which they retained responsibility,[262] and that the time available for Scottish questions be reduced. The latter was given effect in November 1999, since when Scottish questions have taken place once every four weeks, lasting for 30 minutes.[263]

The Scottish Grand Committee, which consists of the full complement of Scottish MPs, was retained following devolution (despite a recommendation to the contrary from the Select Committee on Procedure) because, as the government pointed out

> "there will still be occasions after devolution where members representing constituencies in Scotland . . . will want to have debates on reserved matters for which time cannot be found on the floor of the House".

The Grand Committee has not met, however, since 2003.

The Scottish Affairs Select Committee is appointed by the House of Commons to examine the expenditure, administration and policy of the Scotland Office (including (i) relations with the Scottish Parliament and (ii) administration and expenditure of the offices of the Advocate General for Scotland (but excluding individual cases and advice given within government by the Advocate General)). Up to 11 MPs may be appointed to serve on it (not all of whom need represent Scottish constituencies).

---

[262] Corresponding provision is made in Scottish Parliament Standing Orders r.13.3.3.
[263] Naturally MPs remain free to table questions for written answers.

CHAPTER 7

GOVERNMENTS

As with parliaments, so too with governments: within the sphere of devolved **7–01** competence, the Scottish Government is the government of Scotland[1]; outwith that sphere, the UK Government continues to exercise executive authority north of the border. "Executive authority" is a concept of some complexity. Other than, perhaps, their width, there is no difficulty with the statutory powers of executive institutions—Ministers of the Crown, central government departments, the Scottish Administration and the penumbra of executive agencies, local and other public authorities operating to greater or lesser degree at arm's length from central or devolved government. Subtler questions arise, however, in relation to the non-statutory powers of governmental institutions, often (if not wholly accurately) referred to as "the prerogative". Explaining the nature of the prerogative requires something of a historical inquiry into the nature of that entity in which (if not whom) the prerogative is vested, namely the Crown. Broader questions arise about the extent to which prerogative powers are, or should be, subject to judicial control. The scheme of this chapter is therefore as follows. We begin with a consideration of the sources of executive power in a general sense. We then move on to an account of the institutional structure of executive government as that relates to Scotland. At one time, such an account would have been relatively straightforward, in so far as it involved a reasonably clear demarcation between the executive powers of central and local government.[2] Now, however (and leaving local government to a later chapter), executive authority is exercised at a variety of levels and in a variety of institutional settings. This is not simply a consequence of devolution, but also of what might be termed the "marketising" of the state. Particularly in the last 30 years, efforts have been made to improve the efficiency of government[3] by repackaging or reallocating aspects of executive authority to entities better able (in theory) to capture the efficient practices of the private sector. In some respects, as with privatisation and contracting out, the reallocation is clear, and the question which remains is whether and to what extent we should, nevertheless, continue to regard the powers and functions thus reallocated as public functions. In others, as with

---

[1] Although, as we shall see, the powers of the Scottish Ministers go beyond that sphere in various ways, particularly in that s.63 of the Scotland Act 1998 makes provision for the transfer of functions exercisable in or as regards Scotland by a Minister of the Crown to the Scottish Ministers. This goes beyond the provision made in s.53 for a general transfer to the Scottish Ministers of ministerial functions exercisable within devolved competence, which transfer occurred on 1 July 1999.

[2] Although there has always been a Scottish dimension to the government of the UK, which may be said to cut across this distinction.

[3] Some commentators detect ulterior motives in this process, and it is fair to say that marketisation, in its various guises, has tended to be at the expense of the powers of local authorities and at some cost too to accountability for the exercise of executive power.

executive agencies, the change is less obvious, being internal to the orthodox structure of government; but similar issues arise about the adequacy of political and legal controls over their powers.

THE CROWN AND PREROGATIVE

7–02 In one sense, the Crown is simply that "piece of jewelled headgear under guard at the Tower of London".[4] In another, the term serves as a synonym for the central executive government of the UK, for it is in the name of the Crown that executive acts of government are carried out.[5] The attribution to the Crown of acts of Ministers and officials might be "fictional" where they exercise statutory powers conferred on them in their official capacity. But the fiction is perhaps less obvious where prerogative powers are concerned. As Dicey explained:

> "The prerogative is the name for the remaining portion of the Crown's original authority, and is therefore . . . the name for the residue of discretionary power left at any moment in the hands of the Crown, whether exercised by the Queen herself or by her Ministers. Every act which the executive government can lawfully do without the authority of an Act of Parliament is done in virtue of this prerogative."[6]

Before the constitutional upheavals of the seventeenth century—provoked to no small extent by the claims of the Stuart kings to rule by prerogative right—the prerogative was clearly an autonomous source of governmental power. But civil war and the settlements of 1688–89 secured (although not without certain ambiguities) the subjection of the prerogative, both to Parliament and to the common law.[7] The power of Parliament to alter or abolish prerogative powers was conclusively established by the provisions of the Bill of Rights and Claim of Rights, which did exactly that; and by the Act of Settlement 1700,[8] which regulated the succession to the Crown. To the courts fell the task of determining

---

[4] *Town Investments Ltd v Department of the Environment* [1978] A.C. 359 HL, per Lord Simon at 397.

[5] *Town Investments Ltd v Department of the Environment* [1978] A.C. 359, per Lord Diplock at 380–382.

[6] A.V. Dicey, *The Law of the Constitution*, 8th edn (London: 1915) p.425. Dicey at p.424 also described the prerogative as "a term which has caused more perplexity to students than any other expression referring to the constitution"! See also, C.R. Munro, *Studies in Constitutional Law*, 2nd edn (London: Butterworths, 1999) Ch.8.

[7] Prior to that the position had not been clear, either in Scotland or England. In England, cases such as *Prohibitions del Roy* (1607) 12 Co. Rep. 63 (where the King was told that he must dispense justice only through his courts) and the *Case of Proclamations* (1611) 12 Co. Rep. 74 (where Coke CJ held that the King had not the power to alter the general law of the land by way of royal proclamation) must be set against those cases which conceded the autonomy of the prerogative, such as *Darnels Case* (1627) 3 State Trials 1 (where it was held sufficient answer to a writ of habeas corpus to state that the prisoner was detained by order of the King) and the *Case of Ship Money* (1637) 3 State Trials 826 (where a tax not authorised by Parliament was upheld as justifiable at a time of national emergency, of which the King alone was the judge). In Scotland, these questions figured less in case law and more in legal writings, but opinion was far from uniform. There is, however, evidence to suggest that Scots law treated the Crown and prerogative, both before and after the Revolution, with less deference than English law: see J.D.B. Mitchell, "The Royal Prerogative in Modern Scots Law" [1957] P.L. 304.

[8] As extended to Scotland pursuant to the Acts and Treaty of Union in 1707.

the existence and extent of prerogative powers when such were claimed, and, as has been held, it is now

> "350 years and a civil war too late for the Queen's courts to broaden the prerogative. The limits within which the executive government may impose obligations or restraints on citizens of the United Kingdom without any statutory authority are now well settled and incapable of extension".[9]

Now, therefore, the prerogative is a remnant (though far from an insignificant remnant) consisting of those legal attributes of the Crown in the sense of the Sovereign, exercisable by Her Majesty either as she sees fit or, more commonly, on the advice of her Ministers, or of the Crown in the sense of the central government.

It is sometimes said that it is on the basis of the prerogative that the government enters into contracts, employs its staff, holds and conveys property and so on. Certainly there is often no statutory authority for these functions. But in fact, these are less prerogative powers than the ordinary common law powers of any natural or legal person.[10] That is not to suggest that they are unimportant. In a manner even less visible than the prerogative, the common law powers of the Crown, exercisable by its agents in government (central and devolved) enable a wealth of governmental activity without any need for parliamentary authority. The constitutional legitimacy of this state of affairs is increasingly questionable.[11]

There are some prerogative powers that are said to be personal to the Queen. Ordinarily, it is said that the Queen has three rights: " . . . the right to counsel, the right to encourage and the right to warn."[12] That is true, and by and large that is where it stops: she reigns, but she does not rule. But it has been argued that the Queen has further rights, which she can exercise without reference to the advice of her Ministers.[13] These are said to be: the appointment of the Prime Minister and the Royal Assent to legislation. Prior to the Fixed-Term Parliaments Act 2011, that list would also have included the dissolution of Parliament. The suggestion that the Queen exercises any personal choice in these matters has been said to be both wrong and dangerous.[14] In relation to the first "personal prerogative" much of the academic speculation on the extent to which the Queen

---

[9] *British Broadcasting Corporation v Johns (Inspector of Taxes)* [1965] Ch. 32, per Diplock LJ at 79.

[10] It is generally said that the Crown is a corporation sole, and a legal person on that account.

[11] See B.V. Harris, "The 'Third Source' of Authority for Government Action" (1992) 108 L.Q.R. 626; A. Lester and M. Weait, "The Use of Ministerial Powers without Parliamentary Authority: the Ram Doctrine" [2003] P.L. 415. The issue has also been the subject of an inquiry by the House of Commons Select Committee on Public Administration: see its report *Taming the Prerogative: Strengthening Ministerial Accountability to Parliament, Fourth Report of Session 2003–04* (The Stationery Office, 2004) HC 422.

[12] W. Bagehot, *The English Constitution* (1867). For discussion of the significance of these three rights, see, e.g. Mitchell, "The Royal Prerogative in Modern Scots Law" [1957] P.L. 304; R. Brazier, *Constitutional Practice: The Foundations of British Government*, 3rd edn (Oxford: Oxford University Press, 1999).

[13] W.I. Jennings, *Cabinet Government*, 3rd edn (Cambridge: Cambridge University Press, 1959) p.394; V. Bogdanor, *The Monarchy and the Constitution* (Oxford: Clarendon Press, 1995) p.75.

[14] R. Blackburn, "Monarchy and the Personal Prerogatives" [2004] P.L. 546. See also, R. Blackburn, "The Royal Assent to Legislation and a Monarch's Fundamental Human Rights" [2003] P.L. 205.

could exercise a personal choice pre-dated the 2010 general election. Ordinarily
the result of an election makes the choice of Prime Minister clear and obvious.
Speculation surrounded how the Queen could (or should) act in the event of a
"hung" Parliament. As we saw in 2010, however, the politics of the result
resolved in such a way that again there was a clear and obvious choice of Prime
Minister.[15] It has also been argued that there is no "royal veto" based on the
personal views and beliefs of the monarch.[16] So far as it has been argued that
there are "constitutional grounds" on which the Queen could refuse Assent to a
Bill (for example, it subverted the democratic basis of the constitution)[17] that
must surely be a matter for the Supreme Court to resolve (and one that would test
the obiter statements about the limits on Parliament's legislative authority).[18] The
reality is there are so few examples of the Sovereign exercising her personal
prerogatives because as a matter of constitutional convention the Sovereign may
only act on the advice of her Ministers, who are in turn answerable to Parliament
for the advice they tender.[19] Any controls, then, are political and parliamentary,
and not "legal" in the sense they are reviewable by the courts.

The far greater portion of surviving prerogative power has in practice been
transferred to the Crown in the sense of the central government, and the
association of these prerogatives with the uniquely governmental functions of the
state is apparent when we note that they are mostly connected with foreign affairs
(e.g. the despatch and receipt of ambassadors, recognition of foreign states,
entering into international treaties),[20] defence (e.g. declaring a state of war or
national emergency, mobilising the armed forces) and the maintenance of the
peace and order of the realm. This is not to say that these areas are governed
solely by the prerogative. Since the precise extent of a given prerogative power
may be uncertain, or since its extent, though certain, is insufficient to meet the
ends of government, many "uniquely governmental" matters are in fact governed
wholly or partly by statute. Where this is the case, the powers provided by
Parliament override the prerogative, although the prerogative power only lapses
pro tanto and will revive on repeal of the legislation unless expressly abrogated
thereby.[21] Furthermore, the executive cannot exercise a prerogative power in a
manner that would derogate from the fulfilment of a statutory duty.[22]

7–03   The common law interlocks with these prerogative functions in two main
ways. First, as already noted, the courts have, at least since the Revolution of

---

[15] Which is exactly what Blackburn suggested would happen in responding to the "reams of
academic speculative theorising" on when and how the Queen would get involved in mediating
competing claims for the keys to Downing Street: Blackburn, "Monarchy and the Personal
Prerogatives" [2004] PL 546, 552. On the formation of the 2010 coalition, see: V. Bogdanor, *The
Coalition and the Constitution* (Oxford: Hart, 2011) Ch.2.

[16] See Blackburn's discussion of the constitutional crisis in Belgium in 1990 when King Baudouin,
a devote Catholic, refused to sign a Bill legalising abortion: Blackburn, "The Royal Assent to
Legislation and a Monarch's Fundamental Human Rights" [2003] P.L. 205.

[17] For a proponent of this argument, see: Brazier, *Constitutional Practice: The Foundations of
British Government* (1999).

[18] See the discussion at 3–13—3–14 above.

[19] For discussion of the operation of constitutional conventions, see paras 2–06—2–11, above.

[20] Ratification of international treaties is now subject to the Constitutional Reform and Governance
Act 2010 which requires that a treaty be laid before both Houses of Parliament for a period of 21
sitting days during which both Houses may resolve that the treaty should not be ratified.

[21] *Attorney General v De Keysers Royal Hotel Ltd* [1920] A.C. 508. *Burmah Oil Co (Burmah
Trading) Ltd v Lord Advocate* [1965] A.C. 75, per Lord Pearce at 143.

[22] *R. v Secretary of State for the Home Department Ex p. Fire Brigades Union* [1995] 2 A.C.
513.

1688–89, claimed jurisdiction to determine the existence and extent of prerogative power. But the courts did not, until relatively recently, inquire into the manner of exercise of an admitted prerogative. Their jurisdiction to do so was authoritatively established by the decision of the House of Lords in *Council of Civil Service Unions v Minister for the Civil Service.*[23] As Lord Scarman put it:

> " . . . if the subject matter in respect of which prerogative power is exercised is justiciable, that is to say if it is matter upon which the court can adjudicate, the exercise of the power is subject to review in accordance with the principles developed in respect of the review of the exercise of statutory power. . . . Today, therefore, the controlling factor in determining whether the exercise of prerogative power is subject to judicial review is not its source but its subject matter."[24]

Professor Craig sees *Council of Civil Service Unions v Minister for the Civil Service* as updating the heritage of the *Case of Proclamations*[25] and *Attorney General v De Keysers Royal Hotel Ltd.*[26]

The first denied the Sovereign any autonomous legislative power, independent of Parliament; the second affirmed the priority of statute over prerogative when they touched the same ground; and *Council of Civil Service Unions v Minister for the Civil Service* tells us that since the executive is subject to judicial control when acting pursuant to "the most legitimate discretionary power, that given by statute", it should in principle be subject to like control where its discretion is founded in the prerogative.[27] In practice, of course, the very subject matter of prerogative powers may render them immune from review as being non-justiciable: whether it is "right" to declare war, or purchase nuclear weapons, or enter into a particular international treaty are questions better left (at the present stage of the common law's development) to the political arena.[28] But non-justiciability has not been allowed to deprive *Council of Civil Service Unions v Minister for the Civil Service* of its effects. Thus in one case, the court held the Secretary of State's refusal to renew a passport to be reviewable, even though

---

[23] *Council of Civil Service Unions v Minister for the Civil Service* [1985] A.C. 374. A power of judicial review had been asserted by some judges in earlier cases, notably by Lord Denning MR in *Laker Airways Ltd v Department of Trade* [1977] Q.B. 643 CA (Civ Div). See also *R. v Criminal Injuries Compensation Board Ex p. Lain* [1967] 2 Q.B. 864 QBD, often regarded as the first instance of judicial review of the prerogative. Certainly the Court of Appeal treated the scheme for compensating victims of violent crime as established "under the prerogative" (it is now statutory), but "anyone may set up a trust or other organisation to distribute money, and for the government to do so involves no unique prerogative power": H.W.R. Wade and C.F. Forsyth, *Administrative Law*, 11th edn (Oxford: Oxford University Press, 2014) p.180.

[24] *Council of Civil Service Unions v Minister for the Civil Service* [1985] A.C. 374 at 407.

[25] *Case of Proclamations* (1611) 12 Co. Rep. 74.

[26] *Attorney General v De Keysers Royal Hotel Ltd* [1920] A.C. 508.

[27] P. Craig, "Prerogative, Precedent and Power" in C. Forsyth and I. Hare (eds), *The Golden Metwand and the Crooked Cord: Essays on Public law in honour of Sir William Wade QC* (Oxford: Oxford University Press, 1998) Ch.4.

[28] Although note that challenges were brought to the legality of government action in the sphere of treaty-making in *R. v HM Treasury Ex p. Smedley* [1985] Q.B. 657 and *R. v Secretary of State for Foreign and Commonwealth Affairs Ex p. Rees-Mogg* [1994] Q.B. 552, and although both were unsuccessful neither was dismissed as raising questions inherently unsuitable for judicial resolution. In matters of national defence, by contrast, see *Chandler (Terence Norman) v DPP* [1964] A.C. 763; *Lord Advocates Reference (No.1 of 2000)*, 2001 S.C.C.R. 296.

taken under the prerogative, as an "administrative decision affecting the rights of individuals and their freedom to travel" and of a wholly different order to decisions of high policy on matters of defence or foreign affairs.[29] In another, the court took the same view of the prerogative of mercy, an important feature of the criminal justice system the exercise of which was of critical importance to the individual.[30]

7–04   This continuum of gradual progress towards the proper subjection of governmental authority to the rule of law may now be updated further. The Crown Proceedings Act 1947, although principally concerned with defining the liability of the Crown in tort and delict in respect of acts committed by its servants or agents, also reserved the immunity from injunction and specific performance enjoyed by the Crown in England and extended its application to Scotland. The operative provision is s.21. This provides that in any civil proceedings against the Crown, the court cannot make an order for implement or grant interdict, but may "in lieu thereof make an order declaratory of the rights of the parties". It then provides that the court cannot in civil proceedings grant any interdict or make any order against an officer of the Crown if the effect of doing so would be to give relief against the Crown which could not have been obtained in proceedings against the Crown directly. North and south of the border, this was taken to mean (but for different reasons) that since neither interdict nor specific implement could be awarded against the Crown (qua Sovereign), neither remedy could be awarded against an officer of the Crown, which term is defined to include Ministers of the Crown and, now, members of the Scottish Government.

7–05   In *R. v Secretary of State for Transport Ex p. Factortame Ltd (No.2)*, the House of Lords were obliged as a matter of EU law to extend injunctive relief against the Crown where necessary to protect EU law rights.[31] Subsequently, in *M v Home Office*,[32] the House of Lords held the Home Secretary in contempt of court for disregarding an injunction requiring the Home Secretary to arrange for the immediate return to the jurisdiction of M, a Zairean asylum seeker. The injunction was granted as an emergency measure during the night, when it became apparent that, in breach of an undertaking to the court, the Home Secretary had countermanded arrangements to keep M in Britain. The following morning the judge discharged the injunction on the grounds that the authority of *Factortame* entitled him to grant injunctive relief against the Crown only where necessary to protect EU law rights, which were not here in issue. Nevertheless, during the currency of the injunction—a presumptively valid order of the court—the Home Secretary had ignored it. Giving the leading speech, Lord Woolf held that the reference in s.21 of the 1947 Act to "civil proceedings" was not apt to include proceedings for judicial review, so that the jurisdiction to grant injunctive relief in such proceedings, even where no question of EU law arose, was unimpaired.

7–06   Following *M v Home Office*, the question arose whether interdict was now to be regarded as available to restrain unlawful acts by the Secretary of State for

---

[29] *R. v Secretary of State for Foreign and Commonwealth Affairs Ex p. Everett* [1989] 1 All E.R. 655.

[30] *R. v Secretary of State for the Home Department Ex p. Bentley* [1993] 4 All E.R. 442.

[31] *R. v Secretary of State for Transport Ex p. Factortame Ltd (No.2)* [1991] 1 A.C. 603. Necessarily this involved recognition in Scotland that relief by way of interdict, interim or perpetual, would require to be granted against the Crown, despite s.21 of the 1947 Act, in like circumstances: see *Millar & Bryce Ltd v Keeper of the Registers of Scotland*, 1997 S.L.T. 1000.

[32] *M v Home Office* [1994] 1 A.C. 377.

Scotland or those acting on their behalf.[33] The Second Division held that it was not. The plain effect of s.21 had been to exclude interdict and implement in civil proceedings against the Crown. *M v Home Office*, having turned substantially on aspects of English procedure, was not authoritative as to the meaning of s.21 in Scotland. The question was revisited in *Davidson v Scottish Ministers*.[34] There it was argued that a coercive order might competently issue against the Scottish Ministers where, in light of the Human Rights Act 1998, the applicant's Convention rights were in issue. The Extra Division held that the right to an effective remedy for breaches of Convention rights did not entitle a litigant to a remedy of their choice and that appeals to the rule of law as requiring coercive orders to be granted against the Crown were to no purpose unless means were shown of construing the plain language of s.21 in that way. The applicant appealed to the House of Lords.[35] It was pointed out that, in light of *M v Home Office* and *McDonald v Secretary of State for Scotland*, s.21 of the 1947 Act applied with different effects north and south of the Border. There was nothing to indicate that the draftsman had intended such a distinction to obtain. In any event, it could not be justified. The House of Lords agreed, holding that references to "civil proceedings" in s.21 were to be read as excluding proceedings invoking the supervisory jurisdiction of the Court of Session in respect of acts or omissions of the Crown or its officers. Accordingly, in proceedings for judicial review, the remedies of interdict and implement may now competently be sought against the emanations of the Crown in Scotland. Similarly, where the Scottish Ministers breach an undertaking that has been given to the court in the context of such proceedings, it is open to the court to hold the Ministers in contempt.[36]

Gaps remain in the legal control of prerogative powers. That is not necessarily **7–07** objectionable, provided adequate and effective means of political and parliamentary control exist. Whether that is so, however, is questionable. Some observers have suggested that proper parliamentary control of the prerogative is inhibited by its invisibility. Up to a point, this seems correct. But certain exercises of the prerogative—the appointment of the Prime Minister not least amongst them—are highly visible, and it is rather difficult to see how Parliament could assert any more meaningful control over them. In other respects, as where decisions are taken about the deployment of armed forces and commencement of hostilities, the complaint may be less that these are prerogative decisions than that they require no a priori parliamentary authority. By convention, the House of Commons is now asked to vote in favour of military action, but, being a convention, it does not represent a legal limitation on the prerogative power. In any event, this relatively new convention is yet to be tested in urgent circumstances. Even if such powers were to be placed on a statutory footing, however, it is almost inconceivable that their exercise would be made subject to prior parliamentary approval. In some circumstances the government needs—and in no circumstances is it likely to surrender—the power to act of its own initiative. Any attempt to capture the prerogative in legislative form would have also to capture the flexibility necessary to enable the government to respond, with

---

[33] *McDonald v Secretary of State for Scotland*, 1994 S.C. 234.
[34] *Davidson v Scottish Ministers*, 2002 S.C. 205.
[35] *Davidson v Scottish Ministers* [2005] UKHL 74; 2006 S.C. (H.L.) 41.
[36] *Beggs v Scottish Ministers*, 2005 1 S.C. 342; *Smith v Scottish Ministers* [2015] CSOH 15; 2015 S.L.T. 131.

appropriate speed, to contingencies foreseen and unforeseen. Nor should it be thought that placing the prerogative on a statutory footing would render it more susceptible to judicial control. The justiciability of the subject matter of a power is not affected as such by its legal form. In sum, then, while there is force in the view that Parliament is insufficiently rigorous in its scrutiny of prerogative powers, it is not obvious that codification of the prerogative would improve the position.

UK GOVERNMENT

Prime Minister, Cabinet and Ministers of State

7–08 The appointment of the government is a prerogative act, and we have already noted many of the constitutional conventions surrounding this. The Queen is obliged by convention to appoint as Prime Minister the person who appears best able to command the confidence of the House of Commons and the Prime Minister then advises the Queen whom to appoint to ministerial office in their government, which advice she must follow. Identification of the Prime Minister is normally clear as the electoral system for the House of Commons is designed to produce a majority government. In 2010, however, it was several days after the election before it became apparent that David Cameron would be in a position to form a government. For as long as they retain the confidence both of the Commons and of their party (or, at least, their Cabinet), the powers of the Prime Minister are considerable indeed, not only by virtue of being in charge but also because, for practical purposes, the principal prerogatives of the Crown vest in them. Perhaps curiously, the office of Prime Minister receives little statutory recognition, and indeed received none at all prior to the enactment of the Chequers Act 1918. But they are very much a creature of constitutional convention, as also is the Cabinet. There are no legal rules in any Act of Parliament governing the composition, procedures and functions of the Cabinet.[37] As an institution, it emerged and developed in the late eighteenth century, and in the nineteenth century at least functioned very much as a collegiate body, likened by one former Prime Minister to a company's board of directors. Yet by 1963, according to one Cabinet Minister of the day, the Cabinet, like the Sovereign, had become a dignified rather than effective element of the constitution.[38] At first blush, that seems unsurprising. Government has grown immensely in volume, intensity and complexity, yet the Cabinet continues to meet weekly and is no larger now than it was a century ago. It is true that much of its work

---

[37] Apart from the fact that the Ministerial and Other Salaries Act 1975 restricts the number of salaried Cabinet posts to 20. See now, however, the Cabinet Manual that was prepared at the request of Prime Minister Brown to bring together in a single document the laws, conventions and rules that affect the operation of and procedures of government. The current iteration of the manual is HM Government, *The Cabinet Manual: A guide to laws, conventions and rules on the operation of government* (The Stationery Office, 2011) *https://www.gov.uk/government/uploads/system/uploads/attachment_data/file/60641/cabinet-manual.pdf* [Accessed 23 June 2015]. The manual is a valuable source of information on the functioning of government generally.
[38] R. Crossman, *British Government*. Crossman was not the only Cabinet Minister to hold this view.

is now delegated to cabinet committees, but this in itself may function to disperse power away from the Cabinet proper.[39] In Crossman's view, however, the consequence of the decline of cabinet government was an increase in the power of the Prime Minister, since the institutional mechanisms and constitutional conventions which once served a genuinely collegiate body, namely the conventions of confidentiality and collective responsibility, came to serve the Prime Minister instead.

The "presidential" style of leadership adopted by recent Prime Ministers may support Crossman's thesis, but it can be overstated. The extent of prime ministerial power seems very much a function of circumstances. If the premierships of Mr Blair and Mrs Thatcher might fairly be described as "presidential", the manner of Mrs Thatcher's fall from office, and the intervening premiership of Mr Major, indicate that there is more to central government than prime ministerial power alone. Moreover, as has been said, a focus on the Prime Minister obscures the point that

> "departments enjoy a greater degree of autonomy within the executive branch than is commonly acknowledged . . . by reason of the fact that their functions are vested directly in them".[40]

This autonomy is reinforced by the convention of individual ministerial responsibility to Parliament, whereby the Minister must answer for the actions of their department and associated public authorities.[41] The implication of this—and it may be to state the obvious—is that central government is a far more complex organism than it is sometimes depicted. One does not need to be an avid student of political economy to perceive that executive power is distributed far more widely than the inner circle of Prime Minister and Cabinet; in practice, much of it reposes with Ministers, officials and the web of agencies and public bodies beyond that.

Ministers are appointed by the Queen on the advice of the Prime Minister and **7–09** hold office at Her Majesty's pleasure. By convention, Ministers must be members either of the House of Commons or of the House of Lords. Section 2 of the House of Commons Disqualification Act 1975 provides that no more than 95 ministers may sit and vote in the House of Commons, and Sch.1 to the Ministerial and Other Salaries Act 1975 places limits on the total number of ministerial salaries that may be paid at any one time. These provisions are practical restrictions on the Prime Minister's powers of patronage, but there is no upper limit as such to the total number of Ministers that may be appointed

---

[39] The Ministerial Code states that matters which are solely the responsibility of an individual Minister, or which do not significantly engage the collective responsibility of Ministers, need not be taken either to Cabinet or even to committee. The job of committees is described in terms of settling issues brought before them at that level, or, if a decision of the full Cabinet is absolutely necessary, clarifying the issues and identifying the points of disagreement.

[40] T. Daintith and A. Page, *The Executive in the Constitution: Structure, Autonomy and Internal Control* (Oxford: Oxford University Press, 1999) pp.29 and 30.

[41] It may also be reflected in the conclusions reached by the Cabinet Secretary, having conducted a review at the Prime Minister's request in 1998, that cross-departmental issues were often not well handled.

provided the excess are peers and/or unpaid. Peers as Ministers are a necessary consequence of the statutory provisions and it is not at all uncommon for a political ally of the Prime Minister to be elevated to high ministerial office following the conferment of a life peerage.[42]

Some ministerial offices have a much longer historical pedigree than that of the Prime Minister. The office of the Lord Chancellor can be traced back to the thirteenth century; the office of Secretary of State emerged in England during the Tudor period, and from the eighteenth century two or more Secretaries of State were customarily appointed, dividing responsibility for home affairs and the colonies on the one hand and foreign affairs on the other. A Secretary of State for War was first appointed in 1794, and since then further Secretaryships of State have been created, merged and abolished as needs arise and lapse. The oldest government departments, such as the Treasury and the Home Office, are creatures of the prerogative; more modern manifestations of governmental activity may owe their origins to statute. Where new departments are created, the modern practice is to create by way of the prerogative a new Secretary of State, to whom functions are transferred by order made under the Ministers of the Crown Act 1975.[43] Once functions are vested in a Secretary of State, however, there is no need for further transfer orders when the distribution of functions between Secretaries is altered, for in law the office of Secretary of State is "in commission", one and indivisible, with the consequence that any one Secretary of State may act for or carry out the functions of any other.[44] In practice, however, each Secretary of State will normally confine themselves to the performance of functions related to the workings of their department.

Ministers are defined by s.8(1) of the Ministers of the Crown Act 1975 as the holders of "any office in Her Majesty's Government in the United Kingdom", a definition plainly apt to include the Secretaries of State, who head up government departments and sit in the Cabinet. Below Cabinet ministers in rank are Ministers of State, who share in the administration of departments and often have specific portfolios of their own. Their powers are largely statutory,[45] but as agents of the

---

[42] It is safe to say that by convention the Prime Minister requires to be a member of the House of Commons. The last peer to serve as Prime Minister was Lord Salisbury, who left office in 1902 (his nephew, Arthur Balfour, led the House of Commons and took the title of First Lord of the Treasury, which is normally held by the Prime Minister themselves). It appears that, following the resignation of Neville Chamberlain in May 1940, the King's preference for his replacement was Lord Halifax, but it became clear that Labour MPs would refuse to serve under Halifax in a wartime coalition Cabinet. Since the House of Commons controls supply, the Chancellor of the Exchequer and the Treasury Ministers also require to be Members of the House of Commons, but the position with regard to the other high offices of state may be more equivocal. Lord Carrington served as Foreign Secretary from 1979–82; and Lord Young as Secretary of State for Trade and Industry from 1987–89, so it probably cannot be said that there is any convention preventing the appointment of peers as senior non-Treasury Ministers if political realities permit.
[43] It is also common practice, when creating a new department, to incorporate it, usually as a corporation sole, so that it may hold property, enter into contracts, sue and be sued in its own name rather than in the name of the Crown: see Daintith and Page, *The Executive in the Constitution: Structure, Autonomy and Internal Control* (1999) pp.32 and 33.
[44] This is reflected in statutory drafting practice, which refers simply to "the Secretary of State", meaning "any one of Her Majesty's Principal Secretaries of State". See *Agee v Secretary of State for Scotland*, 1977 S.L.T. (Notes) 54.
[45] Again, drafting practice is to refer to "the Minister of the Crown" generically rather than specifically.

Crown they "can do anything an ordinary person can do provided that there is no statute to the contrary and Parliament has voted the money".[46]

Parliamentary secretaries assist with the parliamentary work of a department **7–10** and may have some limited administrative responsibilities. They are appointed by their ministerial chiefs with the written approval of the Prime Minister rather than by the Queen, and, as this implies, they are neither Ministers nor members of the government.

Scottish dimension to the UK Government

With the handover of powers from the UK Government to the Scottish **7–11** Government on 1 July 1999, the Scottish Office[47] was renamed the Scotland Office. The Ministers working within it at present are the Secretary of State for Scotland and a parliamentary under-secretary. Alongside the Scotland Office there is the Office of the Advocate General for Scotland (the UK Government's legal advisor on Scots law). It is important to note that, as well as ensuring the continuing representation of Scottish interests within the UK Government, the Secretary of State for Scotland has a number of powers under the Scotland Act 1998 in relation to such reserved matters as the conduct and funding of Scottish parliamentary elections,[48] the payment of grants into the Scottish consolidated fund and other financial transactions arising out of devolution,[49] and, perhaps most significantly, in relation to Scottish legislation and acts of the Scottish Government. As to the first, s.35 confers on the Secretary of State the power to make an order preventing the Presiding Officer from sending a Bill passed by the Scottish Parliament for Royal Assent if the Bill contains provisions which they have reasonable grounds to believe would be incompatible with any international obligations of the UK or with the interests of defence or national security, or which modify the law as it applies to reserved matters in a way which they have reasonable grounds to believe would have an adverse effect on the operation of the law in relation to reserved matters. Such an order may be made at any time within the four week period commencing with the passing of the Bill, and must be laid before both Houses of the Westminster Parliament. As to the second, the Secretary of State may by order made under s.58 direct the Scottish Government not to take action where they have reasonable grounds to believe that such action would be incompatible with any international obligations of the UK, or to act where they have reasonable grounds to believe such action to be necessary to give effect to any such obligations.[50] Section 58 also entitles the Secretary of State to revoke subordinate legislation made by the Scottish Government where one or more of the conditions for the exercise of the power under s.35 are met.

---

[46] Cabinet Office, *Agency Chief Executives Handbook* (The Stationery Office, 1996), para.16; and see Daintith and Page, *The Executive in the Constitution: Structure, Autonomy and Internal Control* (1999), pp.34 and 35. This is known as the "Ram doctrine": see HM Government, *The Cabinet Manual: A guide to laws, conventions and rules on the operation of government*, para.3.31

[47] As established in 1885; the original Secretary for Scotland assumed the full status of Secretary of State in 1926 (although the office did not attract a salary commensurate with those of other Secretaries of State until 1937).

[48] Scotland Act 1998 s.12, although, as we have seen, the Smith Commission has proposed that this function be devolved.

[49] Scotland Act 1998 Pt III.

[50] This may include a requirement that the Scottish Government introduce a Bill in the Scottish Parliament.

Since the Scotland Act 1998 devolved most of the issues falling within the responsibility of the Lord Advocate and Solicitor General for Scotland, it was considered appropriate that they should cease to be Ministers of the Crown in the UK Government and become members of the Scottish Government. But the UK Government continues to require advice from time to time on matters of Scots law and devolution issues arising under the Scotland Act, as it may also require to be represented in litigation arising out of the devolution settlement.[51] With that in mind, the Scotland Act established the new ministerial office of Advocate General for Scotland.[52] Apart from their role in relation to litigation and legal advice, the Advocate General has the power under s.33, in common with the Lord Advocate and Attorney General, to refer to the Supreme Court the question whether the provisions of a Bill passed by the Scottish Parliament are within its competence. They are also entitled, by virtue of s.98 and Sch.6, to institute proceedings for the determination of a devolution issue.

The Civil Service

7–12   In the background of the discussion so far has been the administrative machine that allows government to implement its policy: the Civil Service. The Civil Service is politically neutral with the result that when the government changes following a general election, the civil servants remain the same. Until recently, the Civil Service was established on a non-statutory basis although it was regulated to some extent by orders in council which are a form of legislation. Calls had long been made to place the Civil Service on a statutory footing, with the Blair Government of 1997 having made a joint commitment with the Liberal Democrats to introduce a Civil Service Bill.[53] Whilst a draft Bill was published in 2004, enacting it was never a sufficient priority to command the necessarily parliamentary time. The Constitutional Reform and Governance Act 2010 has, however, finally put the Civil Service on a statutory footing (but done little else to reform it). The 2010 Act applies to the Civil Service (except for the security services, Government Communications Headquarters ("GCHQ") and the Northern Ireland Civil Service) (s.1). A Civil Service Commission is established and it has responsibility for overseeing the recruitment of civil servants (ss.2 and 11–14). Management of the Civil Service is entrusted to the Minister for the Civil Service (who is invariably the Prime Minister) (s.3(1)), although management of the Diplomatic Service is entrusted to the Secretary of State (s.3(2)).[54] The management powers conferred on the Minister for the Civil Service and the Secretary of State include the power to make appointments (s.3(3)) and both are required to publish codes of conduct for the Civil Service and the Diplomatic Service respectively (ss.5 and 6).[55] Separate civil service codes may be published

---

[51] L. Clark, "Three Years On: The Role of the Advocate General for Scotland", 2002 S.L.T. (News) 139.

[52] Scotland Act 1998 s.87.

[53] Summarised by G. Drewry, "The Executive: Towards Accountable Government and Effective Governance?" in J. Jowell and D. Oliver, *The Changing Constitution*, 7th edn (Oxford: Oxford University Press, 2011) pp.207–209.

[54] As is drafting practice, the generic "the Secretary of State" is used in the Act but in practice, of course, it is the Foreign Secretary that is responsible for the Diplomatic Service.

[55] The Civil Service code is available at *https://www.gov.uk/government/publications/civil-service-code/the-civil-service-code* [Accessed 23 June 2015] and the Diplomatic Service code is available at *http://civilservicecommission.independent.gov.uk/wp-content/uploads/2014/06/Diplomatic-Code.pdf* [Accessed 26 August 2015].

for those civil servants that who serve the Scottish and Welsh Governments (s.5(2)).[56] Although some statutory basis for the Civil Service is welcomed, the 2010 Act represents fairly modest progress.

Under the 2010 Act the Minister for the Civil Service is also obliged to publish a "special advisors code" (s.8).[57] That requirement is part of the first statutory regulation of special advisors, a role which has grown in importance under recent governments.[58] Whilst career civil servants are apolitical, special advisors are appointed personally by a Minister (that appointment being approved by the Prime Minister) and whose appointment ends either when the Minister that appointed them ceases to hold office or the day following a general election (s.15). The Minister for the Civil Service is required to lay a report before Parliament annually about the special advisors (including the number of advisors and their cost) advising the government (s.16).[59] These measures were all introduced against a background of growing concern about the number and influence of such advisors. Although the existence of such advisors was nothing new, they doubled in number under the first Blair Government. In 2001 the Public Administration Select Committee recognised that the special advisors were an "established part of government" but that the role had to be put on a "firmer footing".[60] Arrangements were reviewed again in 2012 by the same committee and a number of further recommendations made.[61] In particular, the committee expressed concern that while the price of having a special advisor was that the Minister was *responsible* for the advisor's management and conduct (as opposed to being *accountable* for the actions of their civil servants) that responsibility remained "more theoretical than actual".[62] Ministerial responsibility is considered further in a moment.

Reinventing government

An account of departmental government is hardly a complete depiction of the organisation of the modern executive. Much, even most, of the work of government is in fact conducted at some distance from the ministerial core, as the result of what has been termed a "quiet revolution" in public administration.[63] It is a revolution often associated with the Thatcher Governments of the 1980s, and it is certainly true that much of its initial impetus stemmed from the Thatcherite

7–13

---

[56] The Scottish Code is available at *http://www.gov.scot/About/People/Directorates/Services-Groups/HR/HR/policies-guidance/conduct/Civil-Service-Code* [Accessed 23 June 2015].

[57] See Cabinet Office, Special advisers: code of conduct (The Stationery Office, 2010), *https://www.gov.uk/government/publications/special-advisers-code-of-conduct* [Accessed 23 June 2015], which includes a model contract for such advisors. The Scottish Government also has the power to appoint special advisors, details of which are available at: *http://www.gov.scot/About/People/14944/Special-Advisers* [Accessed 23 June 2015].

[58] For a comprehensive review of the role of the special advisor, see: B. Yong and R. Hazell, *Special Advisors: who they are, what they do and why they matter* (Oxford: Hart, 2014).

[59] An equivalent obligation is imposed on the First Ministers of Scotland and Wales: s.16(2) and (3).

[60] House of Commons Public Administration Select Committee, *Special Advisor: Boon or Bane? Fourth Report of Session 2000–01* (The Stationery Office, 2001) HC 293, para.81.

[61] House of Commons Public Administration Select Committee, *Special advisers in the thick of it, Sixth Report of Session 2012–13* (The Stationery Office, 2012) HC 134.

[62] House of Commons Public Administration Select Committee, *Special advisers in the thick of it, Sixth Report of Session 2012–13*, paras 90–91.

[63] M. Hunt, "Constitutionalism and the Contractualisation of Government in the United Kingdom" in M. Taggart (ed), *The Province of Administrative Law* (Oxford: Hart, 1997) Ch.4.

drive to roll back the frontiers of a state regarded as bloated and inefficient. But "new public management" in its various guises has become an international phenomenon, and in no sense is it (at least any longer) the preserve of the political right wing.

The commitment of the Conservative Governments of the 1980s and 1990s to rolling back the state manifested itself most prominently in the privatisation of state-owned industries. Within the government machine itself, freezes were imposed on civil service pay and recruitment and businessmen were brought in to advise on improving efficiency and effectiveness in the public sector. But, despite the government's best efforts at reinventing government and the transfer of over half of the state trading sector to private ownership, the level of public expenditure at the end of the 1980s was not noticeably different from its level in 1979: a near-doubling in real terms of welfare expenditure during the period kept the state's toll on annual gross domestic product at between 35 per cent and 40 per cent, where it remains yet. As the eighties gave way to the nineties, and the Thatcher administration was replaced by that of John Major, the reinvention of government began to focus less on the simple, if crude, objective of making government smaller and more on making what there was work better. This new approach was already in evidence by the close of the Thatcher years with the introduction of executive agencies and the emergence of private sector solutions to the perceived problems of government.

7–14 Executive agencies were spawned by the 1988 report *Improving Management in Government: The Next Steps*.[64] Having reviewed the organisation of the civil service and the way in which public services were provided, the authors of the report recommended that a complete separation be made between policy making functions and service delivery functions. The latter, covering an estimated 95 per cent of civil service activity, should be devolved to executive agencies instead of being (inefficiently) undertaken within the traditional structure of Whitehall departments. The government accepted the recommendations, and required all departments to review their activities in order to assess their suitability for hiving off to agencies. The rigour of the procedure intensified in 1991 with the introduction of "market testing".[65] This required departments to scrutinise particular functions and ask themselves, first, whether a particular function could be abolished; if not, whether it could be privatised; if not, whether its performance could be contracted out to a private company; and if not, whether it could be hived off to an executive agency. Only if the answer to all of these questions was "no" might things stay as they were.

As the *Next Steps* report had predicted, some 90 per cent of civil servants now work for agencies.[66] Each agency operates within the terms of a "framework document" which establishes the respective responsibilities of the relevant Minister and agency chief executive (who may be a civil servant but may equally be recruited from the private sector). The framework document also prescribes performance and financial targets, plus the operating arrangements for the

[64] K. Jenkins, K. Caines and A. Jackson, *Improving Management in Government: The Next Steps* (HMSO, 1988). See the discussion by Drewry in "The Executive: Towards Accountable Government and Effective Governance?" in *The Changing Constitution* (2011) pp.196–201.
[65] Cabinet Office, *Competing for Quality* (HMSO, 1991) Cm.1730.
[66] Cabinet Office, *List of Ministerial Responsibilities* (The Stationery Office, 2015) Pt IV lists 41 executive agencies for which UK Government Ministers are responsible. That is a significant reduction (from 90 in 2001). Executive agencies falling within the competence of the devolved administrations are now answerable to those administrations.

agency. Initially, and in theory at least, the chief executive answered to the Minister for their agency's operational efficiency and performance in implementing the policies settled by the Minister; the Minister, in turn, answered to Parliament for the agency's work and for the policies they had formulated. Now, the accountability of agencies to Parliament is more direct: written parliamentary questions are referred, where appropriate, to agency chief executives; agencies are subject to the jurisdiction of the Parliamentary Commissioner for Administration; and chief executives routinely appear before departmental select committees to answer for their operational effectiveness. Proposals to make chief executives directly responsible to select committees have, however, been rejected.[67]

The framework agreements between Minister and agency are not contracts, **7–15** nor could they be: agencies have no identity or legal personality separate from that of their parent departments. But they are intended to work like contracts and, as the *Next Steps* report envisaged, have brought about a fundamental shift in civil service thinking and working practices. The essence of that shift lies in the preference it represents for "marketised" solutions, modelled on the practices of the private sector, to public sector problems: " . . . contract has replaced command and control as the paradigm of regulation."[68] The ideas underpinning the reinvention of the state are now mainstream, and any notion that a Labour Government would halt or reverse these reforms was rapidly scotched after the 1997 election. On the contrary, Labour wholeheartedly endorsed the process and took it further, as part of its wider drive to modernise the machinery of government. As it sees the matter:

> "Most of the old dogmas that haunted governments in the past have been swept away . . . Better government is about much more than whether public spending should go up or down, or whether organisations should be nationalised or privatised. Now that we are not hidebound by the old ways of government, we can find new and better ones."[69]

In 2010, however, the coalition government took steps to arrest the seemingly endless expansion of non-governmental departments. The Public Bodies Act 2011 gave Ministers wide ranging powers to abolish, merge or otherwise modify the constitution of a large number of bodies. Under the coalition government's policy, a body should only exist at arm's length from government if it performs a technical function, its activities require political neutrality or it needs to act independently to establish facts. Where none of those tests are met, the activity should now be undertaken by a body that is democratically accountable at either national or local level. The result of this policy has been the review of the activities of over 900 bodies. As a result of the abolition of over 200 bodies and the merger of 170 more the total number should fall to approximately 600.

---

[67] See Treasury and Civil Service Select Committee, *The Role of the Civil Service, Fifth Report of 1993–94* (HMSO, 1994), HC 27, making the proposal and *The Civil Service: Taking Forward Continuity and Change* (HMSO, 1995) Cm.2748 rejecting it.
[68] Hunt, "Constitutionalism and the Contractualisation of Government in the United Kingdom" in *The Province of Administrative Law* (1997) p.12.
[69] White Paper, *Modernising Government* (HMSO, 1999) CM 4310.

GOVERNMENT OF SCOTLAND

7–16   It is well, when speaking of the government of Scotland post-devolution, to be careful with terminology. Just as at the UK level the functions of government are in no sense confined to the ministerial core, so too in Scotland executive authority does not repose in the Scottish Government alone. The "Scottish Government" refers to the nucleus of Scottish government, namely the First Minister, the Ministers appointed by her and the two Law Officers, collectively referred to as "the Scottish Ministers".[70] The Scottish Government in this sense is the central component of the wider "Scottish Administration", which also includes junior Scottish Ministers, non-ministerial office holders and civil servants appointed to the staff of the Scottish Administration.[71] But the UK Government as considered above, and indeed the supranational institutions of the European Union, remain relevant to the government of Scotland, whilst, at a lower level, there is the layer of Scottish public authorities exercising executive authority at arm's length from the ministerial core.

Scottish Government[72]

7–17   The UK model of parliamentary government is replicated in Scotland, although the 1998 Act casts the conventions that surround the formation of governments at the UK level in statutory form. Like the Prime Minister, then, the First Minister is appointed by the Queen from among the members of the Scottish Parliament; like the Prime Minister, they hold office at Her Majesty's pleasure.[73] They may resign their office at any time, and must do so if the Parliament resolves that the Scottish Government no longer enjoys the confidence of the Parliament.[74] Although the Queen carries out the formal task of appointment, she will act (the Scotland Act does not in terms require this, but it is plainly the intention) on the nomination of the Parliament as communicated to her by the Presiding Officer; and the Parliament must make its nomination within 28 days of a Scottish general election, the resignation of an incumbent First Minister, the office falling vacant for a reason other than resignation, or of the First Minister ceasing to be an MSP other than by virtue of a dissolution of the Parliament.[75] If the 28 day period expires without a nomination being made, s.3(1)(b) requires the Presiding Officer

---

[70] Scotland Act 1998 s.44. A person appointed to ministerial office in the UK Government may not be a member of the Scottish Government, or vice versa. The current crop of Scottish Ministers include those styled "Cabinet Secretaries" and the ministerial core has adopted the name "Scottish Cabinet", although there is no legal foundation for this.

[71] Scotland Act 1998 s.126(7). The non-ministerial office holders are defined by s.126(8) as the Registrar General for Births, Marriages and Deaths for Scotland, the Keeper of the Registers of Scotland and the Keeper of the Records of Scotland.

[72] Until the Scotland Act 2012 came into force, what is now called the "Scottish Government" was known (in legislation at least) as the "Scottish Executive". In fact, the Scottish Executive had "rebranded" itself at the Scottish Government in the autumn of 2007, *http://www.scotland.gov.uk/ News/Releases/2007/09/31160110* [Accessed 23 June 2015].

[73] Scotland Act 1998 s.45(1).

[74] Scotland Act 1998 s.45(2).

[75] Scotland Act 1998 s.46(2). Note that, whereas at Westminster an incumbent Prime Minister who wins a second general election simply continues in office without being reappointed, s.46(2)(a) seems clearly to envisage the re-nomination and reappointment of a victorious First Minister, even though they will in no sense have vacated the office. Provision is made in of the Standing Orders of the Scottish Parliament for the nomination and election of the First Minister (rr.4.1 and 11.10).

to propose to the Queen a date for the holding of an extraordinary general election, the result of which may produce a party balance in the Parliament more conducive to the nomination of one of its members to be First Minister.[76]

Once the First Minister has been appointed, it falls to them under s.47 of the Scotland Act to appoint the other members of the Scottish Government and the junior Scottish Ministers. The Scottish Ministers, like the First Minister, must be members of the Scottish Parliament and their appointment must meet with the formal approval of the Queen. The First Minister may not, however, seek Her Majesty's approval for any ministerial appointment "without the agreement of the Parliament".[77] Once appointed, the Scottish Ministers hold office at Her Majesty's pleasure (which is to say that they are, in theory, dismissible at will by the Queen). They may in any case be removed from office at any time by the First Minister, with no requirement of parliamentary agreement. A Minister who ceases to be an MSP (otherwise than by reason of a dissolution of the Parliament) ceases also to be a Minister. Otherwise, a Minister may resign at any time of their own choosing, and must do so if the Parliament resolves that the Scottish Government no longer enjoys the confidence of the Parliament. Junior Scottish Ministers are appointed by the First Minister under s.49, again with the approval of the Queen and the agreement of the Parliament as signified in accordance with standing orders, in order to assist the Scottish Ministers in the exercise of their functions. The conditions of tenure of office for junior Scottish Ministers are the same as those for the Scottish Ministers proper.

The position of the Law Officers differs in significant ways. The offices of **7–18** Lord Advocate and Solicitor General for Scotland are of some antiquity in Scottish government, the one dating back to the fourteenth century and the other to the sixteenth century. After the Anglo-Scottish union of 1707, the Lord Advocate became a member of the new government of Great Britain, and from 1746 (in which year the office of Scottish Secretary was abolished, not to be revived until the end of the nineteenth century) they assumed general ministerial responsibility for the government of Scotland in addition to their traditional legal duties. As members of the UK Government, the position of the Scottish Law Officers was somewhat anomalous. The normal constitutional convention requiring Her Majesty's Ministers to be members either of the House of Commons or of the House of Lords did not apply to them, although it did become customary to confer on the Lord Advocate a life peerage if they were not already a peer or an MP. Nonetheless, their ministerial responsibilities were extensive. They represented the Crown before the Scottish courts, advised the government on issues of Scots law, controlled the system of public prosecutions in Scotland and were in charge of the drafting of Bills applying to Scotland. Many of the functions relating to law reform and the machinery of justice which for England and Wales were performed by the Lord Chancellor were in Scotland vested in the Lord Advocate.

---

[76] There is no provision to prorogate this period, but see the decision of the House of Lords in *Robinson v Secretary of State for Northern Ireland* [2002] UKHL 32; [2002] N.I. 390 where the election of the First Minister and Deputy First Minister was upheld despite the time limit (in that case, six weeks: Northern Ireland Act 1998 s.16(8)) having been breached.

[77] As to the means by which the Parliament's approval is to be signified, see r.4.6 of the Standing Orders. Note that there is nothing in the Scotland Act 1998 to dictate to the First Minister how many Ministers they must appoint or what their portfolios should be (the only "named" members of the Scottish Government, the First Minister apart, being the Lord Advocate and the Solicitor General for Scotland).

Matters relating to Scots criminal law and procedure, the criminal justice system and the Scottish courts were prime candidates for devolution, and, as these encompassed most of the responsibilities of the Scottish Law Officers, it was deemed appropriate that they should cease to be Ministers in the UK Government and become instead members of the Scottish Government. This is provided for by the Scotland Act, although, as noted, the position of the Law Officers remains special and distinctive in a number of respects. Under s.48, it is now for the First Minister to recommend to the Queen the appointment of a person as Lord Advocate or Solicitor General (formerly, the Queen made the appointments on the advice of the Prime Minister). As with the Scottish Ministers and junior Scottish Ministers, the First Minister must secure the agreement of the Parliament before forwarding the names of their recommended candidates for appointment to Her Majesty. It is to be noted, however, that with the Law Officers it is the Queen who makes the appointments; she does not, as with the Scottish Ministers, simply approve the appointments made by the First Minister. Similarly, the First Minister cannot remove either of the Law Officers from office at their own discretion: only the Queen may do this when the First Minister so recommends with the agreement of the Parliament. This greater security of tenure than is enjoyed by other members of the Scottish Government is a reflection of the greater constitutional significance of the Law Officers' role in the administration of justice in Scotland, with a correspondingly greater need for a degree of independence on the Law Officers' part. The independence of the Lord Advocate is further secured by a number of provisions scattered throughout the Scotland Act. Section 48(5), for example, states in terms that

> "any decision of the Lord Advocate in his capacity as head of the systems of criminal prosecution and investigation of deaths in Scotland shall continue to be taken by him independently of any other person."

Section 29 limits the legislative competence of the Scottish Parliament so that it cannot remove the Lord Advocate from their position as head of the systems of criminal prosecution and investigation of deaths. Again, the general transfer of ministerial functions provided for by s.53 does not apply to the "retained functions" of the Lord Advocate (that is, those functions exercisable by them immediately before they ceased to be a Minister of the Crown and other statutory functions conferred on them alone after they ceased to be a Minister of the Crown). In all of these ways, then, the Scotland Act seeks to preserve the traditional autonomy enjoyed by the Law Officers in the discharge of their responsibilities.

Powers of the Scottish Government

7–19 Section 52(1) of the Scotland Act provides that "statutory functions may be conferred on the Scottish Ministers by that name". As devolution has taken root, the greater part of the Scottish Government's functions have begun to find their source in Acts of the Scottish Parliament and Scottish statutory instruments. Acts of the Westminster Parliament will in certain areas continue to confer functions on the Scottish Ministers. Otherwise, many of the Scottish Government's executive powers are founded on existing UK legislation, and to a lesser extent on executive powers rooted in the prerogative and the common law. The logic of devolution required not only that legislative competence over devolved matters be transferred from Westminster to the Scottish Parliament, but also that executive competence in these matters (and others) move from Ministers in the UK Government to the Scottish Ministers.

At one level, this was accomplished by a general transfer of ministerial functions (statutory or prerogative) exercisable within devolved competence, effected on 1 July 1999, by operation of s.53 of the Scotland Act.[78] To that extent, therefore, the devolved competence of the Scottish Ministers is co-extensive, in principle, with the legislative competence of the Scottish Parliament.[79] But s.63 then provides for the transfer of additional functions "exercisable by a Minister of the Crown in or as regards Scotland". These are functions the subject matter of which falls outside the legislative competence of the Scottish Parliament. The Parliament accordingly has no power to alter or abrogate such functions, although the Scottish Ministers are answerable to the Parliament for the manner of their exercise.

EU law and Convention rights

Compatibility with EU law is a condition of the validity of Acts of the Scottish **7–20** Parliament by virtue of s.29 of the Scotland Act; and by virtue of s.54, as reinforced by s.57(2), a condition of the legality of acts of members of the Scottish Government. But the relevance of EU law to Scottish legislation and executive decision making goes further than this. While Sch.5 of the Scotland Act reserves to Westminster competence over foreign affairs, including relations with the EU and European institutions, "observing and implementing . . . obligations under EU law" are expressly exempted from the scope of that reservation.[80] Thus the Scottish Parliament has a degree of positive competence in relation to the implementation in Scotland of EU law obligations. Similarly, s.2(2) of the European Communities Act 1972 together with Sch.2 to that Act empowers Ministers of the Crown to implement or give effect to the obligations of the UK arising under EU law. Now, by virtue of s.53 of the Scotland Act, so far as the s.2(2) power is exercisable within devolved competence, it is for Scottish purposes exercisable by the Scottish Ministers instead of by a Minister of the Crown. So, for example, if an EU directive were adopted requiring the Member States of the EU to take some specified action in the field of animal welfare, the Scottish Ministers could make the necessary subordinate legislation to give effect to the directive in Scotland and, to the extent that such latitude is allowed by the directive, could conceivably impose higher (or lower) standards than the rest of the UK. This reflects the tenor of the 1997 White Paper on devolution which emphasised that the new Scottish institutions should and would be involved in the processes of European policy formation and negotiation and in the scrutiny and implementation of EU obligations. By the same token, liability for breaches of EU law for which the Scottish Government was responsible would be laid at the Scottish Government's door.

---

[78] The concept of "devolved competence" for the purposes of s.53 is defined by reference to the definition of legislative competence contained in the Scotland Act 1998 s.29.

[79] Under the Scotland Act 1998 s.56, however, a number of statutory powers contained in pre-1998 enactments (mostly involving grant making and funding powers) continue, despite the terms of s.53, to be exercisable by a Minister of the Crown concurrently with the Scottish Ministers. The list of jointly exercisable powers may be extended by subordinate legislation. Provision is also made for the joint exercise of powers in relation to bodies, offices or office holders whose responsibilities touch on both reserved matters and devolved matters.

[80] A similar exception is made to the general reservation in respect of the UK's international obligations.

Yet the relatively straightforward division of labour in EU matters between London and Edinburgh as envisaged in the White Paper is complicated somewhat by the terms of s.57(1) of the Scotland Act. This provides that, despite the transfer to the Scottish Ministers by virtue of s.53 of functions in relation to observing and implementing obligations under EU law, any function of a Minister of the Crown in relation to any matter shall continue to be exercisable by them as regards Scotland for the purposes specified in s.2(2) of the European Communities Act 1972. A number of questions flow from this. First, what would happen if the Scottish Ministers adopted subordinate legislation to give effect to an EU obligation in Scotland, and then, pursuant to s.2(2), so too did a Minister of the Crown (and in a manner different from that of the Scottish Ministers)? The action of the Minister of the Crown could conceivably be raised before the courts as a "devolution issue" under s.98 and Sch.6 to the Scotland Act. But in view of the wording of s.57(1), there seems to be little doubt that in this context such trenching on the devolved competence of the Scottish Ministers is entirely lawful (and probably not accurately described as "trenching" at all). If this is correct, however, and if for this reason competence in relation to the observance and implementation in Scotland of EU obligations is properly to be regarded as shared, it is questionable how far the Scottish Government may properly be held liable for breaches of EU law. While the primary responsibility for the implementation of EU obligations falling within devolved competence may be that of the Scottish Ministers, there must on this reasoning always be a residual responsibility on the part of the UK Government because of s.57(1) and, as such, a residual liability founded on its failure to act to rectify breaches occasioned by the Scottish Ministers.[81]

7-21   As provided for by s.29 in relation to the legislative competence of the Scottish Parliament, by s.54 in relation to the devolved competence of the Scottish Government and as explicitly reinforced by s.57(2):

> " . . . a member of the Scottish Government has no power to make any subordinate legislation, or to do any other act, so far as the legislation or act is incompatible with any of the Convention rights."

Section 57(3) then provides that subs.(2) does not apply to an act of the Lord Advocate in prosecuting any offence, or in their capacity as head of the systems of criminal prosecution and investigation of deaths in Scotland, "which, because of subsection (2) of section 6 of the Human Rights Act 1998, is not unlawful under subsection (1) of that section". Section 6 of the Human Rights Act makes it unlawful for a "public authority" to act in a manner inconsistent with Convention rights unless, in terms of subs.(2), they are unable to act in any other way because of the terms of the primary or subordinate legislation pursuant to which they are acting.[82]

Intergovernmental relations

7-22   Only part of the story emerges from a consideration of the Scotland Act and the formal structures that are in place to regulate the government of Scotland. It is

---

[81] In practice, efforts would of course be made to avoid conflicts of this sort through the channels of co-operation and consultation established pursuant to the intergovernmental memorandums of understanding and supplementary concordats: as to which, see para.7–22, below.

[82] See, generally, I. Jamieson, "The Relationship between the Scotland Act and the Human Rights Act", 2001 S.L.T. (News) 43.

equally important to understand how the Scottish and UK Governments work together on a day to day basis. That relationship has evolved since the inception of devolution. It is inevitably tied to the prevailing political climate: between 1999 and 2007 there was a Labour led coalition in Edinburgh and a majority Labour Government in London. Since then, however, there is has been first a minority and now a majority nationalist Government in Edinburgh which has so far had to work with a Labour Government, then a Conservative led coalition and now a majority Conservative Government. The politics of the respective governments inevitably plays a significant part in their relationship. Despite those political difference, the need for good working relations between the Edinburgh and London governments remains.

Relations are governed by a memorandum of understanding and various "concordats". [83] The original memorandum of understanding, adopted in 2001,[84] set out the main principles on which inter-governmental relations would be conducted: communication and consultation, co-operation, exchange of information, statistics and research, and confidentiality.[85] The memorandum of understanding is a "statement of political intent" that was "binding in honour only". A number of further agreements supplement the memorandum of understanding. These include an agreement on the Joint Ministerial Committee and concordats on co-ordination of EU policy issues, financial assistance to industry, international relations and statistics. Although relations between Whitehall and the various devolved administrations would normally be done on a bilateral basis, the Joint Ministerial Committee was established consisting of the UK Government and the Scottish, Welsh and Northern Irish Ministers. Its terms of reference included: considering non-devolved matters which impinge on devolved responsibilities (and vice versa); to consider devolved matters if it is beneficial to discuss their respective treatment in different parts of the UK; to keep the arrangements for liaison between Whitehall and the devolved administrations under review; and to resolve disputes. The Joint Ministerial Committee was expected to meet once a year. In fact, there was no meeting of the committee between 2003 and 2008, when they resumed at the request of the Scottish First Minister.[86] The respective Secretaries of State were also given responsibility for "the promotion of good relations" between the UK Government and their respective devolved administration.

Assessing the impact of the memorandum of understanding and accompanying concordats in practice is difficult. The House of Lords Select Committee on the Constitution have doubted their usefulness.[87] At the Joint Ministerial Committee meeting in December 2014 it was agreed, having regard to the fundamental changes in the constitutional landscape since the memorandum of understanding

---

[83] For discussion, see: R. Rawlings, "Concordats and the Constitution" (2000) 116 L.Q.R. 257; A. Scott, "The Role of Concordats in the New Britain: Taking Subsidiarity Seriously" (2001) 5 Edin. L.R. 21.

[84] A new memorandum of understanding was published in October 2013 but the key provisions remain much the same.

[85] HM Government, *Memorandum of Understanding and Supplementary Agreements between the United Kingdom Government, Scottish Ministers, the Cabinet of the National Assembly for Wales and the Northern Ireland Executive Committee* (The Stationery Office, 2001) Cm.5240.

[86] House of Commons Justice Committee, *Devolution: A Decade On, Fifth Report of Session 2008–09* (The Stationery Office, 2009) HC 529, para.4.28.

[87] House of Lords Select Committee on the Constitution, *Devolution: Inter-Institutional Relations in the United Kingdom, Second Report of 2002–03* (The Stationery Office, 2002) HL Paper 28, para.38.

was originally prepared in 2000, that work would be commissioned on a revised memorandum of understanding.[88] That suggests that the various administrations found the memorandum of understanding to be of some continuing use.

GOVERNMENT ACCOUNTABILITY

7–23 Accountable government, like respect for the rule of law, is one of the hallmarks of a democratic society, and serves to distinguish it from a totalitarian state. It is often described as having two dimensions, explanatory and amendatory, the first implying an obligation to answer for and justify policies adopted and decisions taken, the second an obligation to acknowledge deficiency and error, where necessary, and to undertake to put things right (which may or may not involve a change in the responsible personnel).[89] The former is at least as important as the latter, although a tendency to focus on blame and sanction may obscure this. Plainly, in any democracy, the government will have the support of only a portion of the people to whom it is ultimately answerable via the ballot box. Not everyone will share its ideological persuasion, nor agree with its particular policies. But where a government accepts in good faith an obligation to explain itself and justify its actions (which implies at least that thought has been given to alternative means of pursuing its policy goals) it is easier to accept its choices; to that extent, accountable government is conducive to cohesion. In the same way, accountability reduces the risks of governmental fallibility. A government which feels obliged to account for its actions is the more likely to think things through properly in the first place, and although mistakes will inevitably be made—either because a policy is intrinsically flawed, or because it is poorly implemented—accountability in its amendatory form should ensure that they are rectified.

7–24 There is more than one way in which accountable government may be secured, and one may well obtain a better sense of the extent to which it is achieved in the UK by focusing less on the defects of particular mechanisms and more on the adequacy of all the mechanisms taken together. As noted, in the final analysis, a government is accountable to the people through periodic elections. If this control is sporadic and, often, blunted by the vagaries of the electoral process, it is nonetheless occasionally effective.[90] That apart, ongoing political accountability is traditionally held to be secured by parliamentary scrutiny of the executive, which rests on the constitutional doctrines of collective and individual ministerial responsibility to Parliament. We have touched on these doctrines already. Collective ministerial responsibility denotes the responsibility of all members of a government for all of its policies. However those policies are arrived at, it is the duty of each government Minister publicly to defend them, and if a particular

---

[88] Communiqué following meeting of the Joint Ministerial Committee on 15 December 2014, *https://www.gov.uk/government/news/joint-ministerial-committee-communique-december-2014* [Accessed 23 June 2015].

[89] C. Turpin, "Ministerial Responsibility" in J. Jowell and D. Oliver (eds), *The Changing Constitution*, 4th edn (Oxford: Oxford University Press, 2000) Ch.5.

[90] As in the 1997 general election, the result of which was as much a verdict on the outgoing Conservative administration as a mandate for its New Labour successor.

Minister cannot do so then, by convention, they should resign.[91] Individual ministerial responsibility, by contrast, denotes the responsibility of each Minister for everything that is done in their name by their department. In keeping with the traditional ideas of the anonymity and impartiality of the Civil Service, the Minister takes the credit for departmental successes; the corollary is that they should take the blame for departmental failures, even where they are not directly and personally implicated therein. Again, the sanction attaching to individual ministerial responsibility—that which gives the doctrine its teeth—is said to be resignation. In practice, of course, loss of office is not the automatic consequence either of a breach of collective ministerial responsibility or of departmental failure. In the former case, while the Minister who is unable to support a particular aspect of government policy may step down, and while the Prime Minister or First Minister may simply dismiss them, political considerations may militate against dismissal if the recalcitrant Minister is not otherwise minded to go. In the latter case, we have already seen that departmental wrongdoing is rarely attended by a ministerial resignation.[92] In neither case, in normal circumstances, is Parliament likely to be in a position to enforce the sanction by withdrawing its confidence, either from a particular Minister or the ministry as a whole.

But the ephemeral nature of the sanction does not deprive the doctrine of ministerial responsibility of all its force. There are numerous mechanisms, at Westminster and Holyrood alike, designed to facilitate parliamentary scrutiny of the executive. Questions are tabled by MPs and MSPs for oral or written answer. Motions and debates provide a means of requiring a Minister to appear and give an account. The parliamentary committees, moreover, furnish a specialised and systematic forum for control at various levels, through their pre-legislative and post-legislative scrutiny of executive measures and inquiries undertaken into matters falling within their respective remits. Considered in isolation, the adequacy of all of these devices is open to question. A key reason for this relates to the availability of information to Parliament. Political accountability cannot function unless information about the activities of governmental bodies is provided to Parliament and parliamentary committees. By and large, that information is in the hands of the government, which is therefore in a position to control its dissemination. Parliamentary questions, motions and debates may seek to elicit information, but are an inherently inefficient way of doing so. Ministers may and do refuse to answer questions on a variety of grounds. As for parliamentary committees, while they provide a sharper focus on governmental activity, their efficacy too is limited by their reliance on ministerial co-operation, deficiencies in the provision of information, their inherently party political make-up and the restrictions placed on the candour of officials appearing before them. Specific inquiries may be illuminating on occasion, but committees are not well suited to the ongoing audit of the departments they monitor. In all of these ways, the ability of parliamentary institutions to secure accountability is diminished.

---

[91] In terms of both the Ministerial Code and the Scottish Ministerial Code, upholding the principle of collective responsibility is one of the key duties of a Minister. Indeed in Scotland, where coalition governments were expected to be the norm, the principle of collective responsibility assumed on even greater importance than at Westminster: see B.K. Winetrobe, "Collective responsibility in devolved Scotland" [2003] P.L. 24.

[92] Both the Ministerial Code and Scottish Ministerial Code make clear, however, that an individual Minister may only remain in office for so long as they retain the confidence of the Prime Minister or First Minister as the case may be.

7–25   The reinvention of government has also heightened concern about the reach of parliamentary control. That reinvention involved drawing a distinction between the functions of policy making and policy execution, the latter of which is increasingly performed, whether by executive agencies, non-departmental public bodies or external contractors, at some distance from the ministerial core. It has been said, in light of these developments, that while the Minister remains accountable to Parliament for the delivery as well as the formation of government policy, they are only properly responsible for the latter.[93] On this reckoning, responsibility can only properly attach where a Minister is themselves culpable, either in the sense of being personally implicated in a serious departmental error or in the sense that they knew or should have known what was amiss. Beyond that, "pure vicarious headrolling is not required".[94] In principle, this seems unobjectionable: responsibility should be commensurate with the degree of power and control actually possessed. But in the reconfigured constitutional structure, it has led to the tactical employment by Ministers of a distinction between policy and operational matters, which implies that the Minister can be expected to know nothing about the latter.[95] What the distinction has allowed is the deflection of blame, away from the Minister and on to officials; and constitutional accountability to Parliament is diminished, not enhanced, if the extent of the Minister's duty to Parliament is to turn up and condemn the agency or quango charged with implementation.[96]

The parliamentary and academic criticism of this reworking of ministerial responsibility was amply justified by the instrumental way in which Ministers applied the policy/operational distinction. That distinction presupposes clarity and certainty in the division of roles where neither exists to any marked extent. It also led to major blind spots in parliamentary scrutiny, in so far as agency chief executives were no freer than other civil servants to attend select committees and give evidence unencumbered by ministerial directions. But it may be that what was (and is) needed is a conscious adjustment to the modern constitutional landscape. Professor Woodhouse[97] suggests that, within this environment, the political accountability of Ministers would be better captured by focusing on their role responsibility rather than causal responsibility in a simplistic sense. On that view, there is no reason why the Home Secretary should fall on their sword because a prison warder leaves a cell door open. But their general supervisory responsibility for ensuring, so far as possible, that such things do not occur should be acknowledged explicitly:

---

[93] This distinction between the general accountability of Ministers and their personal responsibility is not necessarily of recent provenance: something like it appears, for example, in the so called Maxwell-Fyfe guidelines, laid down by the Home Secretary in his response to the findings of the public inquiry into the disposal of land at Crichel Down in 1954: see *Hansard*, HC Vol.241, cols 1290 and 1291 (20 July 1954).

[94] G. Marshall (ed), *Ministerial Responsibility* (Oxford: Oxford University Press, 1989) p.11.

[95] D. Woodhouse, "The Reconstruction of Constitutional Accountability" [2002] P.L. 73, 75. In fact, the evidence suggests that Ministers concern themselves far more with operational matters than the distinction implies. Moreover, the flaws in a policy are likely to become apparent only when the policy is put into operation.

[96] For example, the fall out between the then Home Secretary Michael Howard and the Director General of the Prison Service, Derek Lewis, over responsibility for prison security. This episode is more full discussed by Drewry in "The Executive: Towards Accountable Government and Effective Governance?" in *The Changing Constitution* (2011) pp.203–205.

[97] Woodhouse, "The Reconstruction of Constitutional Accountability" [2002] P.L. 73, 75.

"Ministers are ... responsible for seeing that mechanisms are in place to provide them with the necessary and correct information so that they can respond to problems, if appropriate by taking direct control, and account to Parliament and the public. They are also responsible for ensuring that their departments have adequate human and financial resources to implement government policies, that those appointed as heads of executive agencies are suitably qualified, and that there are systems or procedures in place which minimise the dangers of errors being made. Such ... 'positive' responsibilities ... are supplemented by 'negative' responsibilities, so that the failure of ministers to intervene, when they should have done so, is not an appropriate excuse; neither is not knowing that something has happened when they should have known."[98]

Systemic operational failures should therefore be seen as engaging the responsibility (not merely the accountability) of the Minister, either because they have failed to ensure that an agency is staffed and funded sufficiently to perform its allotted task,[99] or because they have failed to step in to arrest and correct maladministration. According to Woodhouse, recent practice suggests that this lesson is being absorbed in governmental circles.[100] The duties of Ministers to account to Parliament and be held to account have been committed to paper, both at the Scottish and UK levels, in the latter case reflecting the terms of resolutions adopted by both Houses of Parliament.[101] But at least as important as recognising (if recognition it be) that ministerial responsibility does not stop with settling on a policy and charging others with its implementation is the insistence on the provision to Parliament of information.[102] The Scott Inquiry[103] into the sale of defence equipment to Iraq rightly identified this as the key to improved lines of political accountability. The entry into force of the Freedom of Information Act 2000 and the Freedom of Information (Scotland) Act 2002 has institutionalised the routine disclosure of official information and should make possible more effective scrutiny of government decision making than has been possible in the past. **7–26**

---

[98] Woodhouse, "The Reconstruction of Constitutional Accountability" [2002] P.L. 73, 78.

[99] As was the case with the establishment of the Child Support Agency, in the view both of the Parliamentary Commissioner for Administration and the House of Commons Select Committee on Social Services.

[100] Under reference to the inquiries into the sale of arms to Iraq (Inquiry into the Export of Defence Equipment and Dual-Use Goods to Iraq and Related Prosecutions, *Report of the Inquiry into the Export of Defence Equipment and Dual-Use Goods to Iraq and Related Prosecutions* (HMSO, 1996), HC 115), the failure to notify changes to the rules of entitlement to inherit a deceased spouse's state earnings related pension (Select Committee on Public Administration, *Administrative Failure: Inherited SERPS, Fifth Report of 1999–2000* (The Stationery Office, 2000), HC 433) and the supply of military equipment to Sierra Leone; and to the ministerial response to the Passport Agency crisis in the summer of 1999.

[101] The text of which is set out by Drewry in "The Executive: Towards Accountable Government and Effective Governance?" in *The Changing Constitution* (2011) p.205.

[102] Both ministerial codes stress that it is of "paramount importance that ministers give accurate and truthful information" to Parliament and require Ministers to be as open as possible with Parliament and the public, refusing to disclose information only when it would be in the public interest to do so.

[103] Inquiry into the Export of Defence Equipment and Dual-Use Goods in Iraq and Related Prosecutions, *Report of the Inquiry into the Export of Defence Equipment and Dual-Use Goods in Iraq and Related Prosecutions.*

Nor should the legal accountability of Ministers be neglected. The development of the law of judicial review may be seen in part as a response to the inadequacies of political channels of accountability. Even before the entry into force of the Human Rights Act 1998, the courts were able to insist that governmental powers were exercised lawfully, rationally and fairly, with appropriate regard to the fundamental rights of the citizen; now, all statutory powers fall to be read and given effect consistently with the Convention rights and may be the subject of declarations of incompatibility should this be impossible.[104] This growth in judicial review has been a source of considerable concern for the government and led to proposed reform of the procedure.[105] Between 1998 and 2012 the number of applications for judicial review (in England and Wales) rose from 4,500 to 12,400 (the bulk of the increase being accounted for by immigration claims). But the proposal to limit access to the courts for review of executive acts was widely criticised as an assault on the rule of law and the government pulled back from some of the more radical proposals. Finally, devolution itself has contributed in an important way to improving the accountability of government. By breaking government down into smaller parts and subjecting it to the control of separate parliaments or assemblies, devolution may well have made the attainment of political accountability more manageable and achievable.

---

[104] Acts of the Scottish Parliament which cannot be read and given effect consistently with the Convention rights are of course invalid and may be struck down.

[105] Ministry of Justice, *Judicial Review: Proposals for Further Reform* (The Stationery Office, 2013) Cm.8703.

CHAPTER 8

COURTS, JUDICIARY AND TRIBUNALS

Introduction

Put at its simplest, the function of the courts is to adjudicate on and determine **8–01** disputes of fact and law, meaning the law as laid down in and under statutes and the common law as expounded and applied by the courts themselves. The performance of this function is in no sense confined to professional judges sitting in the civil and criminal courts, but falls also to the many members (lay and legally qualified) of administrative tribunals.[1] Similarly, lay justices of the peace exercise significant judicial powers in relation to summary criminal justice and other matters in the district courts. Article 6 of the European Convention on Human Rights entitles every person, in the determination of their civil rights and obligations or of criminal charges against them, to a fair hearing, which is a matter of, among other things, the independence and impartiality of the tribunal in question. The one denotes freedom from constraint—and the appearance of constraint—by other institutions of the state; the other denotes absence of bias—and the appearance of bias—on the part of the individual decision maker.[2] With the incorporation of the Convention, as also with the devolution legislation, the courts have acquired a new and explicitly "constitutional" jurisdiction which has focused attention on the judicial role and on the relationship of the judiciary with other organs of the state.[3]

Scottish Judiciary

Though the legal system of Scotland is distinct from that of England and Wales **8–02** and that of Northern Ireland, the Scottish judiciary is not, at least in its upper echelons, exclusively Scottish. Since 1 October 2009, the UK Supreme Court has sat at the apex of the Scottish judicial system in civil matters. That court does not, however, sit at the head of the criminal justice system. The High Court of

---

[1] The system of tribunals in the United Kingdom was significantly reviewed, and streamlined, by the Tribunals, Courts and Enforcement Act 2007. The details of these changes are discussed where appropriate throughout this text. For a discussion of the system introduced by the 2007 Act, see: M. Elliott and R. Thomas, "Tribunal Justice, *Cart*, and Proportionate Dispute Resolution" (2012) 71(2) C.L.J. 297. Similar reforms have now been introduced to Scotland, see para. 8–11.

[2] *Findlay v United Kingdom* (1997) 24 E.H.R.R. 221 at [73]. The difference between independence and impartiality may be less pronounced than this implies: see Lord Irvine of Lairg, "Activism and Restraint: Human Rights and the Interpretative Process" [1999] E.H.R.L.R. 350, 356 and Lord Bingham in *Millar v Dickson* [2001] UKPC D4; 2002 S.C. (P.C.) 30 at [18].

[3] See S. Tierney, "Constitutionalising the Role of the Judge: Scotland and the new order" in A.E. Boyle et al (eds), *Human Rights and Scots Law* (Oxford: Hart, 2002) Ch.5.

Justiciary remains the court of final appeal for criminal matters in Scotland.[4] The UK Supreme Court has inherited the jurisdiction previous vested in the Judicial Committee of the Privy Council as the final court of appeal on devolution issues under s.98 and Sch.6 of the Scotland Act 1998, as well as the jurisdiction to determine "pre-Assent references" made in respect of Bills passed by the Scottish Parliament by one of the Law Officers.[5] That devolution jurisdiction, when exercised in the context of a criminal case, has proved politically controversial and prompted some ill-advised and intemperate remarks by members of the Scottish Government.[6] We will return to that shortly.

8–03   The UK Supreme Court was created by Pt 3 of the Constitutional Reform Act 2005.[7] The Supreme Court replaced the Appellate Committee of House of Lords thereby removing the final court of appeal from the Parliament and, it was said by the government of the day, completing the separation of powers. The jurisdiction of the Judicial Committee of the Privy Council, in matters of Scots, English and Welsh and Northern Irish law, and questions about the various devolution settlements, was also transferred to the new court.[8] Whether it was entirely necessary was a matter of debate but the removal of the judicial function of the House of Lords had probably become inevitable by the middle of the last decade. Whatever the strengths of the competing arguments, on 30 July 2009, the Appellate Committee of the House of Lords delivered their final judgments and come 1 October 2009, the judges that in July had been Lords of Appeal in Ordinary were sworn in as Justices of the Supreme Court.[9] Despite its name, the UK Supreme Court reigns supreme throughout the land in relation to only one type of case: a devolution matter. In those cases, the decision of the Supreme Court is binding in all legal proceedings and binds all courts, other than the Supreme Court itself.[10] In all other cases, a decision of the Supreme Court is to be regarded as a decision of a court of the part of the United Kingdom which gave rise to the appeal.[11] Thus a decision in an appeal from the Court of Appeal

---

[4] *McInnes (Paul) v HM Advocate* [2010] UKSC 7; 2010 S.C. (U.K.S.C.) 28, per Lord Hope of Craighead at [5]; *Fraser (Nat Gordon) v HM Advocate* [2011] UKSC 24; 2011 S.C. (U.K.S.C.) 113, per Lord Hope of Craighead at [11].

[5] Scotland Act 1998 s.33. No such references have yet been made.

[6] See the coverage of the then Justice Secretary's comments following the Supreme Court's decision in *Fraser*. For example, D. Leask, "MacAskill threat to end Supreme Court funding" (1 June 2011) *http://www.heraldscotland.com/news/crime-courts/macaskill-threat-to-end-supreme-court-funding-macaskill-threat-to-end-supreme-court-funding.13900094* [Accessed 9 June 2015].

[7] In language reminiscent of s.1(1) of the Scotland Act 1998, s.23(1) of the 2005 Act declares: "There is to be a Supreme Court of the United Kingdom"; see paras 6–02 and 6–03 of the second edition of this work for details of the Appellate Committee of the House of Lords and the Judicial Committee of the Privy Council.

[8] The territorial jurisdiction of the Judicial Committee is otherwise unaffected. It has physically moved location from Downing Street to the Supreme Court building in Parliament Square. See the rather curious proposal to breathe fresh life into the Judicial Committee so far as the United Kingdom was concerned in the (now discarded) House of Lords Reform Bill, which was introduced in Parliament on 11 July 2012. Clause 36 would have vested jurisdiction to resolve disputes about disqualification from the reformed House in the Privy Council and not the Supreme Court. The explanatory notes shed no light on why that choice was made.

[9] Constitutional Reform Act 2005 (2005 Act) s.24; all other than Lord Neuberger, who had been appointed as Master of the Rolls, assumed office as a Justice of the Supreme Court. Lord Neuberger did, however, return to the Supreme Court, as its President, in October 2012.

[10] 2005 Act s.41(3); "devolution matter" is defined in s.41(4) of the 2005 Act.

[11] 2005 Act s.41(2).

in London is binding only in England and Wales, but would ordinarily be very persuasive in both Scotland and Northern Ireland.

The continuing role of the Supreme Court in Scots law, in particular the extent to which it impacts on criminal law, has been something that the Scottish Government of Alex Salmond gave much thought. Both Professor Neil Walker and Lord McCluskey were commissioned to produce reports, the former being a more wide ranging consideration of the question of the final appellate jurisdiction in Scots law[12] and the latter focusing on the relationship between the High Court and the Supreme Court in criminal cases.[13] This led to an amendment to the Scotland Act 1998 to carve out certain criminal proceedings from the definition of "devolution matters". The Scotland Act 2012 introduced the following words to the end of para.1 of Sch.6 to the 1998 Act (which defines a devolution matter):

> "But a question arising in criminal proceedings in Scotland that would, apart from this paragraph, be a devolution issue is not a devolution issue if (however formulated) it relates to the compatibility with any of the Convention rights or with EU law of—
>
>> (a) an Act of the Scottish Parliament or any provision of an Act of the Scottish Parliament,
>> (b) a function,
>> (c) the purported or proposed exercise of a function, or
>> (d) a failure to act."[14]

Where such issues arise, they must now be dealt with as "compatibility issues" under the Criminal Procedure (Scotland) Act 1995. A "compatibility issue" is defined as

> "a question, arising in criminal proceedings, as to—
>
>> (a) whether a public authority has acted (or proposes to act)— (i) in a way which is made unlawful by section 6(1) of the Human Rights Act 1998, or (ii) in a way which is incompatible with EU law, or
>> (b) whether an Act of the Scottish Parliament or any provision of an Act of the Scottish Parliament is incompatible with any of the Convention rights or with EU law".[15]

Where such an issue arises, the procedures to be followed are set out in s.288ZB and s.288AA of the 1995 Act.[16] A compatibility issue can be referred to the Supreme Court by the High Court. Alternatively, an appeal lies to the Supreme

---

[12] Walker, *Final Appellate Jurisdiction in the Scottish Legal System* (The Stationery Office, 2010), *http://www.gov.scot/Resource/Doc/299388/0093334.pdf* [Accessed 9 June 2015].
[13] Lord McCluskey et al, *Final Report of Review Group: Examination of the Relationship Between the High Court of Justiciary and the Supreme Court in Criminal Cases* (Scottish Government, 2011), *http://www.gov.scot/resource/doc/254431/0120938.pdf* [Accessed 9 June 2015].
[14] Scotland Act 2012 s.36(4).
[15] Criminal Procedure (Scotland) Act 1995 s.288ZA(2), as inserted by the Scotland Act 2012 s.34(3).
[16] Inserted by ss.35 and 36(6) of the Scotland Act 2012, respectively.

Court, but only with the permission of either the High Court or the Supreme Court.[17] The Supreme Court only has jurisdiction to determine the compatibility issue. Once it has done so, the case must be returned to the High Court to proceed as appropriate.[18] That provision broadly reflects the procedure followed in *Fraser v HM Advocate* where the Supreme Court allowed the appeal but remitted the case to the High Court to determine whether permission should be granted to bring fresh proceedings and formally quash the conviction.[19] The "compatibility issues" provisions came into effect on 22 April 2013.[20]

8–04   The Court of Session and the High Court of Justiciary are the Supreme Courts of Scotland, with a network of sheriff and district courts operating below them. The Lord President is now the head of the Scottish Judiciary.[21] Prior to that change, each sheriff principal was responsible for his or her own sheriffdom whereas the Lord President was responsible for the Supreme Courts of Scotland. Scotland's supreme civil court is the Court of Session which can trace its roots back to the first half of the sixteenth century. Its jurisdiction is both original and appellate and extends over the whole of Scotland, in contrast to that of the sheriff courts. It is composed of the Lord President and Lord Justice Clerk, together with the Senators of the College of Justice or Lords of Session, as the Court of Session judges are collectively known[22] and has the power both at common law and under statute to regulate its own procedure by way of Act of Sederunt. Scotland's supreme criminal court is the High Court of Justiciary, and it is perhaps supreme in a truer sense than the Court of Session, for there is no right of appeal beyond the High Court sitting as an appellate body[23] except, as we have seen, in respect of what are now called compatibility issues, which carry a right of appeal to the UK Supreme Court. All judges of the High Court (the Lords Commissioners of Justiciary) have, since 1887, also been judges of the Court of Session. The head of the High Court is the Lord Justice General, an office which since 1836 has been held by the Lord President of the Court of Session. It has exclusive jurisdiction to try the most serious crimes, known as the pleas of the Crown, and concurrent jurisdiction with the sheriff court to try less serious crimes when a trial on indictment by solemn procedure (i.e. before a judge and jury of 15) is deemed appropriate by the prosecutor.[24] It was empowered to sit as an appellate court in 1926, the normal quorum being three,[25] and it too has power to regulate its own internal procedure by way of Acts of Adjournal.

The sheriff courts, which go back at least as far as the 12th century, are presently regulated by the Sheriff Courts (Scotland) Acts 1907 and 1971.

---

[17] Criminal Procedure (Scotland) Act 1995 s.288AA(5).

[18] Criminal Procedure (Scotland) Act 1995 s.288AA(2) and (3); s.288ZB(6) and (7).

[19] *Fraser v HM Advocate* [2011] UKSC 24; 2011 S.C. (U.K.S.C.) 113, per Lord Hope at [43].

[20] Scotland Act 2012 (Commencement No.3) Order 2013 (SI 2012/6).

[21] Judiciary and Courts (Scotland) Act 2008 s.2(1); in short, this places the Lord President at the head of all Scottish judges that sit in Scottish courts, other than those that are Justices of the UK Supreme Court

[22] The maximum number of Court of Session judges that may now be appointed, including the Lord President and Lord Justice Clerk, is 32: Court of Session Act 1988 s.1. Temporary judges may also be appointed to sit in the Court of Session in terms of the Law Reform (Miscellaneous Provisions) (Scotland) Act 1990 s.35.

[23] Criminal Procedure (Scotland) Act 1995 s.124.

[24] A prosecution will be brought in the High Court if a sentence of more than five years' imprisonment is sought, since the sheriff courts may only imprison convicted persons for up to five years. Where a sheriff considers that a sentence of five years is inadequate following conviction in the sheriff court, they may remit to the High Court for sentence.

[25] Criminal Procedure (Scotland) Act 1995 ss.103 and 104.

Scotland is divided into six sheriffdoms, each headed by a sheriff principal; each sheriffdom, bar one, is then subdivided into sheriff court districts based on the principal towns within the sheriffdom. For each district, there is at least one sheriff, the total number depending on the level of work involved. Their jurisdiction, although confined in the main to their particular districts, is extensive, encompassing both civil and criminal matters.[26] At the time of writing, an appeal lies for the decision of a sheriff to the sheriff principal of that sheriffdom. That right of appeal will be abolished when the operative part of the Courts Reform (Scotland) Act 2014 comes into force.[27] At present, the decision of a sheriff principal is only binding in his or her sheriffdom. Decisions of the new Sheriff Appeals Court (in which the sheriffs principal will sit along with appeal sheriffs)[28] shall have jurisdiction throughout Scotland. Unlike decisions of the sheriffs principal, which are binding only in their own sheriffdom, decisions of this new appeal court will be binding on all sheriffs. Other important changes being made to the sheriff courts by the Courts Reform (Scotland) Act 2014 include: the sheriff courts are to have *exclusive* competence in any action worth less than £100,000; the establishment of "summary sheriffs" to deal with low value case and many family law issues; and a central, all-Scotland jurisdiction personal injuries court[29] with the power to establish other all-Scotland specialised courts.[30] This package of reform was the subject of much debate as it made its way through Parliament. The principal components are due to come into force in the autumn of 2015.

More local still are the district courts, established of new by the District Courts (Scotland) Act 1975. A district court may consist of a stipendiary magistrate or of one of more lay justices of the peace.[31] The jurisdiction of justices of the peace is limited to minor offences and certain local administrative matters. They sit with a legally qualified clerk when hearing cases.

JUDICIAL INDEPENDENCE

Introduction

"Independence of a tribunal is required" explained Lord Carswell in *Kearney v* **8–05**
HM Advocate

> "in order that the public, seeing this, may feel confident in its ability to
> decide cases without any influence from the Executive being brought to bear

---

[26] Broadly, the civil jurisdiction of the sheriff courts covers small claims, summary causes and ordinary causes, the distinction between the three depending on the value of the claim involved. In criminal matters, the sheriff has jurisdiction to try all crimes other than the pleas of the Crown, and may conduct trials in accordance with summary or solemn procedure (i.e. in the latter case, with a jury).

[27] Courts Reform (Scotland) Act 2014 ("the 2014 Act") Pt 2 Ch.4.

[28] 2014 Act s.50.

[29] 2014 Act Pt 3 Ch.1.

[30] 2014 Act s.41.

[31] Only Glasgow has elected to appoint stipendiary magistrates (i.e. full time, salaried and legally qualified magistrates) in four of its district court areas. A stipendiary magistrate has powers in criminal matters approximating to those of the sheriff. This office is abolished by the 2014 Act s.128.

or any feeling that it needs to have regard to the views or wishes of the Executive in reaching its decisions."[32]

It is well established in the jurisprudence of the European Court of Human Rights that the way in which judges are appointed, their term of office and security of tenure, their mode of remuneration and the presence or absence of guarantees against outside pressure are all factors relevant to the question whether the tribunal presents a sufficient appearance of independence.[33] But it would be wrong to think that the importance of judicial independence only arrived with art.6 of the European Convention on Human Rights. It had long been recognised and protected by the common law. The structural independence of the Scottish judiciary has been reinforced in recent years by the Judiciary and Courts (Scotland) Act 2008 and the Courts Reform (Scotland) Act 2014. Both give the Lord President, and the sheriffs principal, responsibility for securing the efficient disposal of business within the courts for which they are responsible.[34]

The Judiciary and Courts (Scotland) Act 2008 placed an obligation upon a number of people, including the First Minister, the Lord Advocate, the Scottish Ministers and Members of the Scottish Parliament, to "uphold the continued independence of the judiciary".[35] This statutory obligation ought not to have been necessary as the importance of an independent judiciary in securing the rule of law in a democratic society should have been obvious to those that fall within the ambit of s.1 of the 2008 Act. Yet the constitutionalising of the courts role in modern society has increased the occasions where the courts are forced into a position where conflict with the executive appears inevitable. Respect for the importance of an independent judiciary normally prevents the executive from publically criticising judicial decisions that have gone against them. It is not always the case. To take one example: a series of decisions from the High Court in immigration cases in the early part of the last decade culminated in an unprecedented outburst by the then Home Secretary, David Blunkett. In response to a decision by the High Court that six asylum seekers were entitled to receive support from the National Asylum Support Service despite having failed, in the view of Home Office officials, to have claimed asylum as soon as was "reasonably practicable"[36] led the Home Secretary to declare he was "fed up" with a situation where "Parliament debates issues and the judges then overturn them".[37] He then stated his view that the judge, Collins J, had got it wrong. On the back of this Collins J found the unwelcome focus of the media's attention.[38]

As Lord Irvine LC put it, speaking extrajudicially:

---

[32] *Kearney (Arthur) v HM Advocate* [2005] UKPC D1; 2006 S.C. (P.C.) 1 at [62].

[33] *Findlay v United Kingdom* (1997) 24 E.H.R.R. 221 at [73].

[34] Judiciary and Courts (Scotland) Act 2008 ("the 2008 Act") s.2; 2014 Act ss.27–29.

[35] 2008 Act s.1(1).

[36] *R (on the application of Q) v Secretary of State for the Home Department* [2003] EWHC 195 (Admin).

[37] *The Times*, 20 February 2003.

[38] See the discussion in A. Bradley, "Judicial Independence Under Attack" [2003] P.L. 397; the Court of Appeal upheld the majority of Collins J decision (*R (on the application of Q) v Secretary of State for the Home Department* [2003] EWCA Civ 364; [2004] Q.B. 36) but were not subject to similar comment or coverage.

"But what about when the court disagrees with the executive? In a democracy under the rule of law, it is not mature to cheer the judges when a win is secured and boo them when a loss is suffered."[39]

It is not only the executive that can be perceived as threatening the independence of the judiciary. They are, however, in a privileged position. Not only do they have ready access to the media but they are involved in the appointment of the judiciary and are responsible for their remuneration. Accordingly, more formal mechanisms are in place to secure the independence of the judiciary from the executive in both of those regards. We will now discuss each of those in turn.

Judicial appointments

Judicial appointments in the United Kingdom were traditionally a matter for the **8–06** executive, although in Scotland steps were taken, within the limits imposed by the Scotland Act, to introduce a measure of independence and transparency into the process.[40] Judicial appointments are now regulated by statute and designed to ensure that the role of the executive in such appointments is minimised and the process is sufficiently transparent. The appointment of Justices of the Supreme Court is regulated by the Constitutional Reform Act 2005. There are to be no more than 12 Justices of the Supreme Court, each appointed by the Queen.[41] One of the Justices may be appointed to be the president of the court and another to be the deputy president.[42] A person is not qualified to be a Justice unless they have held high judicial office for a period of at least two years, have satisfied the judicial appointments eligibility condition on a 15 year basis or have been a qualifying practitioner for a period of at least 15 years.[43] "High judicial office", for the purposes of Scotland, means a judge of the Court of Session[44] and a "qualifying practitioner" is one who is an advocate or a solicitor with rights of audience before both the Court of Session and the High Court of Justiciary.[45] Selection is by a commission convened by the Lord Chancellor.[46] The commission reports to the Lord Chancellor, who has a limited right to veto a selection or require the commission to reconsider its selection.[47] Once the selection has been confirmed, the name is given to the Prime Minister who has no option but to

---

[39] Lord Irvine of Lairg, "The Impact of the Human Rights Act: Parliament, the Courts and the Executive" [2003] P.L. 308, 323.

[40] See "Judicial Appointments Reform", 2001 S.L.T. (News) 101. Put shortly, before the First Minister put forward any recommendation for appointment to judicial office, he took the advice of a Judicial Appointments Board established in 2002 with the functions of advertising posts, interviewing candidates and drawing up a shortlist of candidates considered suitable for particular appointments.

[41] 2005 Act s.23(2); the Crime and Courts Act 2013 (Sch.13) amended the 2005 Act so as to provide that the Supreme Court shall consist of not more than the full time equivalent of 12 judges and thereby allow for some form of part time working or job sharing by justices. The 2005 Act also makes provisions for appointment of acting judges (s.38) drawn from the supplementary panel (s.39) or from the ranks of Appeal Court judges in England and Wales and Northern Ireland or the Inner House of the Court of Session (s.38(8)).

[42] 2005 Act s.23(5).

[43] 2005 Act s.25(1).

[44] 2005 Act s.60(2).

[45] 2005 Act s.25(2); note the requirement to have rights of audience before both of the supreme courts of Scotland; rights of audience before only one of them is now sufficient to qualify a solicitor advocate for appointment to the Court of Session bench: 2008 Act s.21.

[46] 2005 Act ss.26–27 and Sch.8.

[47] 2005 Act ss.28–31.

recommend the appointment of that individual to the Queen.[48] The sole selection criterion is merit[49] although the commission making the selection must ensure that the Justices of the court, between them, have "knowledge of, and experience of practice in, the law of each part of the United Kingdom".[50] In the House of Lords this translated into a convention that there was ordinarily two Scottish Law Lords and one Northern Irish Law Lord. Thus far, that convention has continued in the Supreme Court.[51] Since 2013, it has been the practice of the Supreme Court to have a justice (an ad hoc member if necessary) with experience in Welsh law when considering devolution matters from Wales.[52]

8–07   Judicial appointments in Scotland are now regulated by a combination of the Scotland Act 1998 and the Judiciary and Courts (Scotland) Act 2008. The Lord President of the Court of Session and the Lord Justice Clerk are appointed by the Queen on the advice of the Prime Minister, although s.95(2) of the Scotland Act provides that the Prime Minister shall not recommend to the Queen the appointment of any person who has not been nominated by the First Minister; and before making any nomination, the First Minister must establish a selection panel in accordance with Sch.2 of the 2008 Act.[53] That panel is responsible for recommending to the First Minister individuals suitable for appointment to the vacant post.[54] The First Minister may not make a nomination under s.95(2) of the Scotland Act until that selection panel has made a recommendation.[55] The criteria for selection is "solely on merit" but the selection panel must also be satisfied that the candidate is "of good character".[56] All other judicial appointments in Scotland (both permanent and part time or temporary) now pass through the hands of the Judicial Appointments Board for Scotland, which was placed on a statutory footing by the 2008 Act.[57] The Board is independent of the Scottish Government and although judges of the Court of Session, sheriffs principal and sheriffs are still appointed by the Queen on the recommendation of the First Minister[58] an individual cannot be recommended by the First Minister to the Queen unless the Board has recommended his or her appointment to the office in question.[59] The Board consists of judicial (one Court of Session judge, one sheriff principal and one sheriff), legal (one advocate and one solicitor) and lay members. The number of lay members must be equal to the number of judicial

---

[48] 2005 Act s.26(3).
[49] 2005 Act s.27(5).
[50] 2005 Act s.27(8).
[51] The vacancy that arose following the untimely death of Lord Rodger of Earlsferry was filled by the Scottish judge Lord Reed and the vacancy created by the retirement of Lord Hope of Craighead was filled by another Scot, Lord Hodge. The Northern Irish Justice, Lord Kerr, has served on the court since is beginning.
[52] A policy announced by the President of the Supreme Court in a speech to the Institute of Government on 18 June 2013, *http://www.supremecourt.uk/docs/speech-130618.pdf* at para.20, and which has been adhered to when considered challenges to legislative acts of the Welsh Assembly: see, for example, *Re Agricultural Sector (Wales) Bill* [2014] UKSC 43; [2014] 1 W.L.R. 2622 where the Lord Chief Justice of England and Wales, Lord Thomas sat as an ad hoc justice.
[53] 2008 Act s.19(2).
[54] 2008 Act s.19(3).
[55] 2008 Act s.19(4).
[56] 2008 Act s.20.
[57] 2008 Act s.9 and Sch.1.
[58] Scotland Act 1998 s.95(4).
[59] 2008 Act s.11(1) and Scotland Act 1998 s.95(5).

and legal members and the chairman of the board must be a lay member.[60] The Board is charged with recommending to the Scottish Government suitable candidates for appointment to judicial office. The selection criterion is the same as that for the Lord President and Lord Justice Clerk: solely on merit, with the board being satisfied that the individual is of good character.[61] Subject to that criteria, the Board is to have regard to the need to encourage diversity amongst the judiciary.[62] Recommendations are made to the relevant Minister who can decide not to accept a recommendation. Where the Minister does so, they must give the Board reasons for that decision and the Board must reconsider its recommendation. It can, however, recommend the same individual again.[63]

The 2008 Act does not alter the statutory criteria of eligibility for appointment **8–08** to judicial office. To be appointed a sheriff principal or sheriff, one must have been legally qualified as a solicitor or advocate for at least 10 years.[64] By virtue of s.7 of the Bail, Judicial Appointments etc. (Scotland) Act 2000, which inserts a new s.11A into the Sheriff Courts (Scotland) Act 1971, the same condition of eligibility applies to the appointment of a person as a part time sheriff. This office is new, and was created in light of the abolition by the 2000 Act of the office of temporary sheriff following the decision of the High Court of Justiciary in *Starrs v Ruxton*.[65] Under art.19 of the Treaty of Union of 1707, appointments to the Court of Session bench are governed by a requirement of at least five years' standing as a member of the Faculty of Advocates. In 1990, eligibility was extended to sheriffs principal or sheriffs who have held office as such for a continuous period of at least five years, and also to solicitors who have enjoyed rights of audience in either the Court of Session or High Court of Justiciary for at least five years.[66]

It is hard to assess the extent to which the introduction of a statutory **8–09** appointments process has improved the standing of the judiciary. Whilst greater transparency in the process is to be welcomed, there is limited evidence to say one way or the other whether it has made a qualitative difference. Such research as there is has been done by the Judicial Appointments Board itself. The Board commissioned an external evaluation of itself in 2009 that surveyed the legal profession in Scotland for its views and perceptions of the judicial appointments process. The objective was two-fold: to understand the make up of the population that is eligible for appointment to judicial office and to understand the factors that encourage or deter eligible candidates from applying.[67] No firm conclusions were drawn from the survey but it did provide the Board with a better understanding of the composition of the pool of eligible candidates. In relation to diversity, however, there has been an increase in the number of women appointed to the Court of Session bench, with four of the last eight appointments being female.

---

[60] 2008 Act Sch.1 paras 3–4.
[61] 2008 Act s.12.
[62] 2008 Act s.14.
[63] 2008 Act s.11.
[64] Sheriff Court (Scotland) Act 1971 s.5.
[65] *Starrs v Ruxton*, 2000 J.C. 208.
[66] Law Reform (Miscellaneous Provisions) (Scotland) Act 1990 s.35(1), as amended by s.21 of the 2008 Act.
[67] MVA Consultancy for the Judicial Appointments Board for Scotland, *Continuous Improvement: An Analysis of Scotland's Judicial Appointments Process* (Edinburgh: MVA Consultancy, 2009) *http://www.judicialappointmentsscotland.org.uk/Publications/Research_Projects2/Continuous_ Improvement_An_Analysis_of_Scotland_s_Judicial_Appointments_Process_-_Volume_ 1_-_October_2009__final_.pdf* [Accessed 9 June 2015].

That may only represent 50 per cent of the appointments, but it represents an improvement in the bench where only nine of the 33 members are female.

Tenure and pay

8–10 At common law, it was presumed that a judicial office was held *ad vitam aut culpam* ("for life or until blame").[68] Statute now provides that judicial office holders shall retire at the age of 70, albeit there is provision for a judge to continue to sit on a part time basis, as a retired judge, until the age of 75.[69] Justices of the Supreme Court hold office "during good behaviour" and may be removed only on the address of both Houses of Parliament.[70] Judges of the Court of Session (and the Chairman of the Scottish Land Court) may be removed by the Queen, on the recommendation of the First Minister, if they have been found to be unfit for office on account of inability, neglect of duty or misbehaviour.[71] On the same grounds, a sheriff can be removed from office by the First Minister.[72] To secure the independence of the judiciary, strict procedures are prescribed before a judicial office holder can be removed from office.[73] These procedures are designed to insulate the judiciary, so far as possible, from political pressures and the threat of removal for political reasons. We have already seen how tempting it can be for politicians to launch attacks upon the judiciary. It is important that the judiciary should have nothing to fear. Chapter 5 of Pt 2 of the Judiciary and Courts (Scotland) Act 2008 now makes provision for the procedures to be followed before a judge of the Court of Session may be removed from office. This fulfilled the requirement of the Scotland Act, initially met by statutory instrument, to make such provision.[74] The 2008 Act also made provision for shrieval office holders that have since been replaced by fresh provisions in the Courts Reform (Scotland) Act 2014.[75]

8–11 The First Minister is required to constitute a tribunal to investigate and report on whether a judicial office holder is unfit to hold that office where the Lord President requests that they do so or in such other circumstances as the First Minister themselves thinks fit, having first consulted the Lord President.[76] Where a tribunal is constituted to investigate and report upon a judge of the Court of Session it shall consist of two members who have held high judicial office[77] (at

[68] *Mackay and Esslemont v Lord Advocate*, 1937 S.C. 860.
[69] Judicial Pensions and Retirement Act 1993 s.26; Law Reform (Miscellaneous Provisions) Act 1985 s.22; 2005 Act s.38; Sheriff Courts (Scotland) Act 1971 s.5A.
[70] 2005 Act s.33.
[71] Scotland Act 1998 s.95(6)–(8).
[72] Sheriff Courts (Scotland) Act 1971 s.12E.
[73] As the Supreme Court of Canada put it in *Valente v The Queen* [1985] 2 S.C.R. 673; (1985) 24 DLR (4th) 161 at [31]: "The essence of security of tenure ... is a tenure, whether until an age of retirement, for a fixed term, or for a specific adjudicative task, that is secure against interference by the Executive or other appointing authority in a discretionary or arbitrary manner."
[74] Scotland Act 1998 s.95(8); Scotland Act (Transitory and Transitional Provisions) (Removal of Judges) Order 1999 (SI 1999/1017).
[75] 2014 Act ss.21–25, replacing the provisions that were made by the s.40 of the 2008 Act. There is now a process for handling complaints against the judiciary which are now handled in accordance with the Complaints about the Judiciary (Scotland) Rules 2015.
[76] 2008 Act s.35(1); 2014 Act s.21(1) and (2); references to the 2008 Act relate to the provisions that concern judges of the Court of Session (including the Lord President and the Lord Justice Clerk) or the Chairman of the Scottish Land Court whereas references to the 2014 Act relate to the provisions that concern holders of shrieval office.
[77] As defined by s.60(2) of the 2005 Act.

least one of whom shall be, or have been, a judge of the Court of Session),[78] an advocate or a solicitor of at least 10 years standing and an individual who has never held high judicial office and has never been an advocate or a solicitor.[79] Where a tribunal is constituted to investigate and report on the holder of shrieval office, it shall consist of one member who is a qualifying member of the Judicial Committee of the Privy Council (who shall chair the tribunal and have a casting vote),[80] one member who holds the same shrieval office as the person under investigation, and an advocate or a solicitor of at least 10 years standing and an individual who has never been a qualifying member of the Judicial Committee of the Privy Council, nor held shrieval office nor ever been an advocate or a solicitor.[81] The selection of members of such a tribunal is to be made by the First Minister with the consent of the Lord President, unless it is the Lord President under investigation in which case the consent of the Lord Justice Clerk must be obtained.[82] Where the Lord President has requested that a tribunal be constituted, they may suspend the person who is to be subject to investigation from office until they order otherwise.[83] This power is in addition to the Lord President's power under s.34 of the 2008 Act to suspend a judicial officer holder where it is necessary for the purpose of maintaining public confidence in the judiciary. The tribunal may, prior to reporting to the First Minister, recommend that the person subject to their investigation be suspended.[84] Where the First Minister receives such a recommendation, they have a discretion as to whether to suspend the person under investigation.[85] The tribunal has the power to compel the attendance of any person to give evidence or to produce documents in their possession or under their control[86] and the procedure to be followed by such a tribunal may be prescribed by Act of Sederunt.[87] Having concluded their investigation the tribunal must submit a written report to the First Minister, which she must then lay before the Scottish Parliament, setting out the conclusions of the tribunal and their reasons for reaching those conclusions.[88] Where the tribunal has concluded that a holder of shrieval office is unfit to hold that office, the First Minister may then remove that person by order made by statutory instrument.[89] A similar conclusion in relation to a temporary judge of the Court of Session empowers the First Minister to remove that person from office.[90] Where a judge of the Court of Session has been found by the tribunal to be unfit to hold that office, the First Minister may recommend to the Queen that the individual be removed from office, but only after the Scottish Parliament, on the First Minister's motion, has resolved that she should make such a recommendation.[91]

---

[78] 2008 Act s.35(7).
[79] 2008 Act s.35(4).
[80] 2014 Act s.21(7).
[81] 2014 Act s.21(4).
[82] 2008 Act s.35(8); 2014 Act s.21(6).
[83] 2008 Act s.36(1); 2014 Act s.22(2).
[84] 2008 Act s.36(3); 2014 Act s.22(4).
[85] 2008 Act s.36(5); 2014 Act s.22(5).
[86] 2008 Act s.37(1); 2014 Act s.23(1).
[87] 2008 Act s.37(5); 2014 Act s.23(5). No such Act of Sederunt has yet been made.
[88] 2008 Act s.38; 2014 Act s.24.
[89] 2014 Act s.25.
[90] 2008 Act s.39.
[91] Scotland Act 1998 s.95(7).

8–12   What was not provided for, at least prior to the enactment of the Senior
Judiciary (Vacancies and Incapacity) (Scotland) Act 2006, was the maintenance
of the orderly conduct of judicial business in circumstances where either of
Scotland's two senior judges, the Lord President and the Lord Justice Clerk, was
incapacitated, or either office was vacant by reason of death, resignation or
removal. As the administrative functions of the Lord President increased, it
became more important to ensure continuity at the senior end of the judiciary.
The illness of the then Lord President, Lord Hamilton, in 2006 saw emergency
legislation, in the form of the Senior Judiciary (Vacancies and Incapacity)
(Scotland) Act 2006, introduced in the Scottish Parliament. The Bill completed
its parliamentary process in a single day. That Act has since been repealed and
its provisions broadly replicated in Ch.2 of Pt 2 of the 2008 Act. In the event of
incapacity, the 2008 Act makes provision for a written declaration to that effect
to be given to the First Minister by at least five of the eight judges (including the
Lord President or Lord Justice Clerk as appropriate) of the Inner House of the
Court of Session. That starts a procedure which is triggered automatically in the
event of a vacancy arising. Where the Lord President is unable to act, or their
office is vacant, their functions shall be carried out by the Lord Justice Clerk, and
those of the Lord Justice Clerk shall, in turn, be carried out by the senior Inner
House judge. Provision is also made in s.6 the 2008 Act for a situation in which
neither the Lord President nor the Lord Justice Clerk is able to act by reason of
incapacity or an event giving rise to a vacancy. The special procedures are
brought to an end either by a vacancy being filled in the ordinary way, or, in the
case of incapacity, by five Inner House judges giving a written declaration to the
First Minister to the effect that they are satisfied that the incapacity has been
overcome.

8–13   The tenure of those appointed to judicial office on a temporary basis initially
caused some problems after devolution. Tenure of judicial office is clearly a
necessary adjunct of judicial independence, and although Parliament may (and
does) override the presumption of the common law, any limitations on tenure
must not be such as to undermine the appearance of a tribunal's independence.[92]
Thus in *Starrs v Ruxton*,[93] the High Court of Justiciary held that, although the
initial appointment of temporary sheriffs by the executive was not inherently
objectionable, the brevity of their term of office (only one year), coupled with the
power (albeit unused) under s.11 of the Sheriff Courts (Scotland) Act 1971 to
recall a temporary sheriff's commission and the practice of appointing permanent
sheriffs from the pool of temporary sheriffs, was fatal to the compatibility of the
system with the right to a fair hearing before an independent and impartial
tribunal under art.6 of the Convention. This caused significant practical difficulties at the time. The Lord Advocate, in whose name all prosecutions are brought,
was required by s.57(2) of the Scotland Act 1998 to act in a manner that was

---

[92] For the approach of the European Court of Human Rights to this question, see *Campbell v United
Kingdom* (1984) 7 E.H.R.R. 165. The test is an objective one: whether there are grounds for
reasonable apprehension that the tribunal is not independent. On that basis, the court held a prison
board of visitors to constitute an independent and impartial tribunal, even though its members
were appointed for fixed terms of three years and were as a matter of law removable from office.
The court accepted, however, that as a matter of fact if not of law the government treated
members as irremovable during their terms of office.

[93] *Starrs v Ruxton*, 2000 J.C. 208.

compatible with Convention rights. Bringing, or continuing, a prosecution before a temporary sheriff was not so compatible. The Lord Advocate, or the local procurator fiscals on their behalf, therefore had no power to continuing criminal prosecutions before temporary sheriffs. A similar challenge to temporary judges in the High Court of Justiciary, who were appointed for a three year term, failed in *Kearney v HM Advocate*[94] as did a challenge to temporary judges in the Court of Session in *Clancy v Caird*.[95] As Lord Sutherland made clear in *Clancy* there is no inherent objection to a fixed term appointment:

> " . . . there can be no objection per se to the appointment of judges for a fixed term, provided that during that period there is security of tenure which guarantees against interference by the executive in a discretionary or arbitrary manner."[96]

Both as a matter of fact and law, temporary judges of the Court of Session do enjoy security of tenure during their term of office. Their independence and impartiality on that ground, at least, was therefore unimpeachable. The decision in *Starrs* led to the commissions of all temporary sheriffs being revoked and provision made in the Bail, Judicial Appointments etc. (Scotland) Act 2000 for their replacement by a new body of part time sheriffs.[97] Those provisions are now found in the Courts Reform (Scotland) Act 2014. Part time sheriffs, the number of which was previously capped at 80,[98] sit for between 20 and 100 days in any one year and they are appointed for a five year term, which is ordinarily renewable.[99]

It is not only the security of a judge's tenure which underpins their independence. The terms of their remuneration are also relevant to the question. The Act of Settlement of 1700, which was incorporated into Scots law by the Treaty of Union, provides that judicial salaries must be "ascertained and established"—in other words, not subject to executive discretion. The remuneration of Court of Session judges, sheriffs principal, sheriffs, members of the Lands Tribunal for Scotland and the Chairman of the Scottish Land Court is reserved to Westminster by para.L1 of Sch.5 to the Scotland Act; but payment of the salaries thus fixed is charged on the Scottish consolidated fund.[100] Parliamentary authority for the payment of judicial salaries is deemed to be permanent and does not require to be reviewed and renewed each year.[101] During their term of office, a judge's salary may be increased, but it may not be reduced.[102]

---

[94] *Kearney v HM Advocate* [2005] UKPC D1; 2006 S.C. (P.C.) 1.

[95] *Clancy v Caird*, 2000 S.C. 441.

[96] *Clancy v Caird*, 2000 S.C. 441 at [6].

[97] Sheriff Courts (Scotland) Act 1971 s.11A (as inserted by Bail, Judicial Appointments etc. (Scotland) Act 2000 s.7).

[98] Sheriff Courts (Scotland) Act 1971 s.11A(5). That provision, along with the rest of the 1971 Act, was repealed by the 2014 Act.

[99] 2014 Act ss.8 and 9.

[100] In relation to shrieval office holders, see 2014 Act s.16(13).

[101] Note, however, that in terms of the 2014 Act s.16, part time sheriffs are paid by the Scottish Ministers, at a rate determined by them, out of moneys earmarked for the Justice Department of the Scottish Government.

[102] 2005 Act s.34(4) (for Justices of the Supreme Court).

JUDICIAL IMPARTIALITY

8-14 Closely related to the idea of judicial independence is judicial impartiality.[103] Impartiality is fundamental to the integrity of the judicial role. If a judge has an interest of some kind in the outcome of proceedings before them, they must decline jurisdiction to decide the matter (or at least disclose their interest to the parties, so that they may decide whether they may properly sit). As Lord Hewart CJ famously put it: it is "of fundamental importance that justice should not only be done but should manifestly and undoubtedly be seen to be done". [104] The great difficulty in this area, as recent case law amply illustrates, is identifying at what point a judge's personal opinions, beliefs, relationships (personal or professional) cross the line into disqualifying bias. The devolution settlement and the incorporation of the Convention into national law have conferred on the judiciary a crucially important, and politically sensitive, jurisdiction that places a higher premium than ever on their impartiality.[105] The former Lord Chancellor, Lord Mackay of Clashfern, adverted to this when, looking ahead to the adoption of a human rights charter in the United Kingdom and the consequent involvement of judges in "political" decision making, he remarked:

> "The question which would then be asked, and to which an answer could not be postponed indefinitely, is whether the introduction of such a political element into the judicial function would require a change in the criteria for appointing judges, making the political stance of each candidate a matter of importance as much as his or her ability to decide cases on their individual facts and the law applicable to those facts. Following on from that is the question of how confidence in judicial independence and impartiality can be maintained, and whether their appointment should be subjected to political scrutiny of the sort seen in the United States."[106]

8-15 The very debate reveals the special value we place, and have always placed, on the impartiality of the judiciary. It is for this reason that judges are disqualified from membership of the House of Commons and Scottish Parliament.[107]

---

[103] They are separate and distinct concepts although not always readily differentiated. See, for example, the discussion in *Starrs v Ruxton*, 2000 J.C. 208, per Lord Prosser at 232 ("The two concepts appear to me to be inextricably interlinked, and I do not myself find it useful to try and separate the one from the other"); and per Lord Reed at 252–253 ("I do not regard it as necessary to attempt an exhaustive definition of the concepts of independence and impartiality or to define the distinction between them") and the judgement of Lord Carswell in *Kearney v HM Advocate* [2005] UKPC D1; 2006 S.C. (P.C.) 1 at [56]–[64].

[104] *R. v Sussex Justices Ex p. McCarthy* [1924] 1 K.B. 256 at 259.

[105] It has been argued that human rights protection, at least, does not draw the courts into matters of political controversy: the judicial role here is simply to define the sphere within which legislature and executive have a free hand. "[Rights] may not be submitted to the vote; they depend on the outcome of no elections", per Jackson J, *Virginia State Board of Education v Barnette* (1943) 319 U.S. 624. But it is difficult to reconcile this view with the very real controversy ignited by the Supreme Court's own pronouncements on issues such as abortion (*Roe v Wade* (1973) 410 U.S. 113), homosexuality (*Bowers v Hardwick* (1986) 478 U.S. 186; *Lawrence v Texas* (2003) 539 US 558), gay marriage (*Obergefell v Hodges* Unreported, 26 June 2015, US Supreme Court) and affirmative action (*Califano v Goldfarb* (1977) 430 U.S. 199; *Gratz v Bollinger* (2003) 539 US 244).

[106] Lord Mackay of Clashfern, quoted in R. Clayton and H. Tomlinson, *The Law of Human Rights* (Oxford: Oxford University Press, 2000) para.1.57.

[107] See House of Commons Disqualification Act 1975 s.1(1)(a) and the Scotland Act 1998 s.15(1)(a).

Similarly, convention requires a judge to dissociate themselves from party political matters.[108] A previous political career, whether as MP, MSP or Law Officer, is no bar to judicial appointment, although in certain situations, for example where a judge is called upon to rule judicially on the meaning and effect of legislation which they drafted or which, as Lord Advocate or Solicitor General, they promoted during its parliamentary passage, they will be unable to sit compatibly with art.6 of the Convention.[109]

It is well established that where a judge has a direct pecuniary or proprietary **8–16** interest in the outcome of a case before them, they are automatically disqualified from sitting.[110] Thus in *Dimes v Proprietors of the Grand Junction Canal*,[111] the Lord Chancellor was held to be disqualified from affirming a judgment of the Vice Chancellor in favour of the canal company by virtue of his substantial shareholding in the company. The categories of automatic disqualification were extended by the decision of the House of Lords in *R. v Bow Street Metropolitan Stipendiary Magistrate Ex p. Pinochet Ugarte (No.2)*,[112] overturning the earlier decision of the House of Lords in which it was held by a 3:2 majority that Senator Pinochet, as a past Head of State, enjoyed no immunity from arrest and extradition in respect of alleged crimes against humanity. Lord Hoffmann (who agreed with the speeches of Lord Nicholls and Lord Steyn, but who gave no separate reasons for holding that Pinochet was not entitled to immunity) turned out to be a director and chairman of Amnesty International Charity Ltd, while his wife had worked for Amnesty's International Secretariat since 1977. Amnesty International had sought, and been granted, leave to intervene in the first appeal to the House of Lords. In overturning that decision, Lord Browne-Wilkinson held:

> "[Although] the cases have all dealt with automatic disqualification on the grounds of pecuniary interest, there is no good reason in principle for so limiting automatic disqualification. The rationale of the whole rule is that a man cannot be judge in his own cause. In civil litigation the matters in issue will normally have an economic impact; therefore a judge is automatically disqualified if he stands to make a financial gain as a consequence of his own decision in the case. But if, as in the present case, the matter at issue does not relate to money or economic advantage but is concerned with the promotion of the cause, the rationale disqualifying a judge applies just as much if the judge's decision will lead to the promotion of a cause in which the judge is involved together with one of the parties."[113]

---

[108] On this basis, a Court of Session judge felt obliged to resign from a committee set up by the Leader of the Opposition in 1968 to formulate Conservative policy on the constitutional future of Scotland. Subsequently, in 1977, a sheriff was dismissed from office after using his judicial office as a platform for the promotion of his political beliefs.

[109] *Davidson v Scottish Ministers (No.2)*, 2005 1 S.C. (H.L.) 7.

[110] See, e.g. *R. v Rand* (1866) L.R. 1 Q.B. 230 QB; *R. v Camborne Justices Ex p. Pearce* [1955] 1 Q.B. 41 QBD.

[111] *Dimes v Proprietors of the Grand Junction Canal* (1852) 3 H.L. Cas. 759. There is a de minimis exception to this otherwise strict rule. For example, see the statement by the Supreme Court that justices with not ordinarily disclose small shareholdings: Supreme Court, "Disclosure of small shareholdings", *https://www.supremecourt.uk/procedures/disclosure-of-small-shareholdings.html* [Accessed 9 June 2015].

[112] *R. v Bow Street Metropolitan Stipendiary Magistrate Ex p. Pinochet Ugarte (No.2)* [2000] 1 A.C. 119.

[113] *R. v Bow Street Metropolitan Stipendiary Magistrate Ex p. Pinochet Ugarte (No.2)* [2000] 1 A.C. 119 at 135B.

In such cases there is no scope of fine distinctions and Lord Hewart CJ's famous dictum applies with its full force: disqualification is automatic and nothing more requires to be proved.[114] If the judge proceeds to decide nevertheless, their decision cannot stand.

This rule against bias also comes into play, even though the judge is not interested in the outcome or otherwise acting as a judge of their own cause, where for some other reason there are grounds for suspicion about their impartiality. The test is now settled. The task of the court is, first, to ascertain all the circumstances which have a bearing on the suggestion that a judge has an appearance of bias. The question is then whether a fair minded and informed observer, having considered the facts, would conclude that there was a real possibility that the judge was biased.[115] Yet while the test is simple to state, the subject of impartiality remains uncommonly resistant to classification and definition.[116] Those difficulties are considered further in Ch.14 where they are discussed in the context of grounds for judicial review.

TRIBUNALS

8-17 It is necessary to now consider the extensive tribunal system that has been introduced to support the work of the courts and to help relieve the burden that was placed upon them. As matters stand, the vast majority of tribunals fall under the remit of the UK Government. The Scottish Government has responsibility for those tribunals that fall wholly within devolved competence. The Smith Commission recommended that responsibility for the management and operation of all reserved tribunals (with two exceptions)[117] be devolved.[118] The UK Government included a draft clause to give effect to that proposal in their White Paper in response to the Smith Commission.[119] The current tribunal system has its origins in the report of Sir Andrew Leggatt, who was appointed by the UK

---

[114] *R. v Bow Street Metropolitan Stipendiary Magistrate Ex p. Pinochet Ugarte (No.2)* [2000] 1 A.C. 119, per Lord Browne-Wilkinson at 133B.

[115] *Porter v Magill* [2001] UKHL 67; [2002] 2 A.C. 357, per Lord Hope at [95]–[103].

[116] In *Locabail (UK) Ltd v Bayfield Properties Ltd* [2000] Q.B. 451 CA (Civ Div), while declining to list the factors which might give rise to an apprehension of bias, the Court of Appeal was at pains to stress that it could not "conceive of circumstances in which an objection could be soundly based on the religion, ethnic or national origin, gender, age, class, means or sexual orientation of the judge. Nor, at any rate ordinarily, could an objection be soundly based on the judge's social or educational or service or employment background or history, nor that of any member of the judge's family; or previous political associations; or membership of social or sporting or charitable bodies; or Masonic associations; or previous judicial decisions; or extra-curricular utterances (whether in textbooks, lectures, speeches, articles, interviews, reports or responses to consultation papers); or previous receipt of instructions to act for or against any party, solicitor or advocate engaged in a case before him, or membership of a [professional body]". Four joined appeals were considered by the Court of Appeal in *Locabail*; the outcome in one of those appeals, *Timmins v Gormley*, is not readily reconcilable with the tenor of the quoted passage. In Scotland, see *Hoekstra v HM Advocate (No.1)*, 2000 J.C. 387; 2000 S.L.T. 605.

[117] Those exceptions being the Special Immigration Appeals Commission and the Proscribed Organisations Appeals Commission.

[118] A step that was at least foreseen as a possibility in the Review of Tribunals, *Tribunals for Users: One System, One Service* (The Stationery Office, 2001) (the Leggatt Report) para.11.21, *http:/ /webarchive.nationalarchives.gov.uk/-/http://www.tribunals-review.org.uk/leggatthtm/leg-00.htm* [Accessed 9 June 2015].

[119] HM Government, *Scotland in the United Kingdom: An enduring settlement* (The Stationery Office, 2015) Cm.8990, *https://www.gov.uk/government/uploads/system/uploads/attachment_ data/file/397079/Scotland_EnduringSettlement_acc.pdf* [Accessed 9 June 2015].

Government in 2000 to review the "delivery of justice through tribunals other than ordinary courts of law". His remit was exceptionally wide and in August 2001 he produced his report that contained a significant number of recommendations for reform.[120]

The Tribunal, Courts and Enforcement Act 2007 gave effect to many of the Leggatt recommendations and drew together a diverse and wide ranging set of tribunals into a single, unified, structure.[121] It created a First-Tier Tribunal and an Upper Tribunal. Both are subdivided into chambers.[122] There are currently seven chambers of the First-Tier Tribunal: the General Regulatory Chamber; the Health, Education and Social Care Chamber; the Immigration and Asylum Chamber; the Property Chamber; the Social Entitlement Chamber; the Tax Chamber; and the War Pensions and Armed Forces Compensation Chamber. The functions of each chamber is set out in detail in the order.[123] The Upper Tribunal is currently divided into four chambers: the Administrative Appeals Chamber; the Immigration and Asylum Chamber of the Upper Tribunal; the Lands Chamber; and the Tax and Chancery Chamber. The Upper Tribunal ordinarily hears appeals from the First-Tier Tribunal but it is not exclusively an appellate body. The 2007 Act allows the Upper Tribunal (in particular, the Administrative Appeals Chamber) to assume responsibility for cases that would otherwise have to be raised by judicial review.[124] An appeal is allowed against a decision of the Upper Tribunal only in limited circumstances and lies to the Court of Session (or, in England, the Court of Appeal).[125] Leave must be granted and must first be sought from the Upper Tribunal. Leave can only be granted where the proposed appeal would raise some important point of principle or there is some other compelling reason for the court to hear the appeal.[126] It was proposed by the Leggatt review that express provision be made to exclude judicial review of un-appealable decisions of the Upper Tribunal.[127] That was not done and instead the Upper Tribunal was designated a "superior court of record".[128] An un-appealable decision of the Upper Tribunal may be judicially reviewed, but only where the same conditions are met for the granting of leave to appeal from the Upper Tribunal: there is some important point of principle or some other compelling reason.[129]

---

[120] Review of Tribunals, *Tribunals for Users: One System, One Service.*
[121] But not all tribunals have come under the new system. The most notable absentee is the Employment (and Employment Appeal) Tribunal.
[122] First-tier Tribunal and Upper Tribunal (Chambers) Order 2010 (SI 2010/2655).
[123] First-tier Tribunal and Upper Tribunal (Chambers) Order 2010 (SI 2010/2655) paras 3–8.
[124] Tribunal, Courts and Enforcement Act 2007 ss.20–21. No order transferring any such jurisdiction has yet been made.
[125] Tribunal, Courts and Enforcement Act 2007 s.13.
[126] Tribunal, Courts and Enforcement Act 2007 s.13(6) and (6A).
[127] Review of Tribunals, *Tribunals for Users: One System, One Service*, para.6.30–6.34.
[128] Tribunal, Courts and Enforcement Act 2007 s.3(5). This is a term that is unknown to the law of Scotland. For the reasons set out by Laws LJ in the Divisional Court in *R. (on the application of Cart) v Upper Tribunal* [2010] EWCA Civ 859; [2011] Q.B. 120 at [30]–[31] designation as a "superior court of record" did not exclude the Upper Tribunal from the court's judicial review jurisdiction.
[129] *Eba v Advocate General for Scotland* [2011] UKSC 29; 2012 S.C. (U.K.S.C.) 1, per Lord Hope at [48]; this decision should be read with the decision of the Supreme Court in *R. (on the application of Cart) v Upper Tribunal* [2011] UKSC 28; [2012] 1 A.C. 663 (both appeals were heard together and advised on the same day). See also: *SA v Secretary of State for the Home Department* [2013] CSIH 62; 2014 S.C. 1 and *EP v Secretary of State for the Home Department* [2014] CSIH 30; 2014 S.C. 706.

One of the concerns of the Leggatt review was the independence of the then system of tribunals.[130] In particular, representing as they do an alternative to court as opposed to an administrative process, it was important that the public have sufficient confidence that the tribunal they appealed to was sufficiently independent of the government it was reviewing.[131] That concern finds its expression in s.1 of the 2007 Act which extends the definition of the "judiciary" in s.3 of the Constitutional Reform Act 2005 (which requires various office holders to guarantee the continued independence of the judiciary) to cover members of a range of tribunals. The discussion about judicial independence applies mutatis mutandis to tribunal members.

8-18 The Leggatt Report, in Ch.11, considered some of the issues that devolution presented to the tribunal system proposed. So far as Scottish tribunals were concerned (that is, tribunals dealing with non-reserved matters), after reviewing the impact of the 2007 Act and a consultation on the introduction of Scottish tribunal service, the Scottish Parliament passed the Tribunals (Scotland) Act 2014. This Act largely replicates the system created by the 2007 Act. It came into force, in large part, on 1 April 2015. There will be a First-Tier Tribunal for Scotland and an Upper Tribunal for Scotland.[132] Both the First-Tier Tribunal for Scotland and Upper Tribunal for Scotland can be subdivided into chambers, although at the time of writing no order has been made doing so.[133] Provision is made for the appointment of chamber presidents and vice presidents, with a President of the Scottish Tribunals (who must be a Court of Session judge)[134] and a Head of the Tribunals (who is the Lord President).[135] All sheriffs are ex officio members of the First-Tier Tribunal for Scotland and all sheriffs (except part time sheriffs) and all judges of the Court of Session are ex officio members of the Upper Tribunal for Scotland.[136] Similar provision is made to allow certain judicial review cases to be transferred from the Court of Session to the Upper Tribunal for Scotland.[137] A duty equivalent to that imposed by s.1 of the Judiciary and Courts (Scotland) Act 2008 is imposed with respect to members of the tribunals.[138] Provision is made to appeal a decision of the Upper Tribunal for Scotland to the Court of Session. Such an appeal must be on a point of law and with the permission of the Upper Tribunal for Scotland or, where that has been refused, the Court of Session. Permission will only be granted where there are "arguable grounds for the appeal".[139] Nothing is said of judicial review in the Act but it is to be expected that it will remain available with respect to un-appealable decisions of the Upper Tribunal for Scotland but on similarly strict criteria.

---

[130] Review of Tribunals, *Tribunals for Users: One System, One Service*, s.2.

[131] Review of Tribunals, *Tribunals for Users: One System, One Service*, paras.218–2.22.

[132] Tribunals (Scotland) Act 2014 s.1; the Act provides that they will be known as the "First-Tier Tribunal" and the "Upper Tribunal" respectively. To avoid confusion with the UK equivalents, they will be referred to as the "First-Tier Tribunal for Scotland" and the "Upper Tribunal for Scotland" although it is recognised that "Scotland" is not formally part of their name.

[133] Tribunals (Scotland) Act 2014 s.20.

[134] Tribunals (Scotland) Act 2014 s.4.

[135] Tribunals (Scotland) Act 2014 s.2.

[136] Tribunals (Scotland) Act 2014 s.17.

[137] Tribunals (Scotland) Act 2014 s.57.

[138] Tribunals (Scotland) Act 2014 s.3.

[139] Tribunals (Scotland) Act 2014 s.48.

CHAPTER 9

LOCAL GOVERNMENT

Introduction

It is an unusual parliamentary session, at Westminster and Holyrood alike, that **9-01** does not see the enactment of at least one measure of greater or lesser significance relating to local government. This rash of legislation reflects a process aptly described by Professor Loughlin as a "politicisation and juridification" of relations between central and local government.[1] If that relationship is less characterised, now, by antagonism on the one hand and resistance on the other, it is nevertheless profoundly different from the traditional model, wherein the essential autonomy of local government was taken not only as given but as necessary to the health of the constitution.[2] Loughlin identifies four key features of that traditional model. The first was multifunctionality: local authorities were charged with the performance of a diverse range of functions, allocated to them not necessarily because, on an abstract economic analysis, they were the institutions best placed efficiently to perform them, but because their role was shored up by the features of local accountability, via the election of local councillors, and a degree of financial independence through their ability to raise local taxes. In keeping with these features of multifunctionality, representation and financial autonomy was the fourth: the conferment of broad discretionary powers on local authorities, which left them largely

> "free to decide on the precise pattern of the services which they delivered and even to redefine the nature of the services they provided".[3]

Local authorities were not, in this scenario, merely local agents for the implementation of central government policy. Within their accepted spheres of competence they enjoyed a substantial degree of freedom. Why then did this model break down?

At risk of oversimplification, the root cause was money. The share of national wealth consumed by local government increased five-fold in the period between

---

[1] M. Loughlin, "The Restructuring of Central-Local Government Relations" in J. Jowell and D. Oliver (eds), *The Changing Constitution*, 4th edn (Oxford: Oxford University Press, 2000) Ch.6 and I. Leigh "The Changing Nature of Local and Regional Democracy" in J. Jowell and D. Oliver (eds), *The Changing Constitution*, 7th edn (Oxford: Oxford University Press, 2011), Ch.9.

[2] This viewpoint was captured by the Royal Commission on Local Government in England, *Report of the Royal Commission on Local Government in England* (HMSO, 1969) Cmnd.4040 (the Redcliffe-Maud Report) in the following terms: "It is only by the combination of local representative institutions with the central institutions of Parliament, Ministers and departments, that a genuine national democracy can be sustained."

[3] Loughlin, "The Restructuring of Central-Local Government Relations" in *The Changing Constitution* (2000) p.140.

1890 and 1970. Over the same period, local authorities lost responsibility for income-generating trading activities, such as the local provision of utilities, whilst assuming responsibility for the delivery of welfare state services such as public housing and education. The costs associated with this, since they could not be met locally, required to be met by central government grants. As the financial dependency of the localities on the centre increased, so the latter could legitimately claim to take a closer interest in what local authorities were doing with the funds. For much of the post-war period, characterised by economic growth and a general political consensus on the virtues of the welfare state, the emerging tensions could be concealed. When, in the 1970s, economic growth faltered, the tensions became inescapably apparent. The Labour Governments of the time sought to address the public expenditure crisis through the well-established methods of consensus and dialogue, with little if any success. The election of the Conservative Government in 1979 marked the real watershed in central-local government relations, for this was a government committed not only to controlling public expenditure but also to a "rolling back" of the state in all its guises and a fundamental reappraisal of the assumptions which had underpinned the welfare state. The unwillingness of local government to co-operate with the centre in the pursuit of its objectives led central government to resort to what was, after all, always at its disposal: the sovereignty of Parliament. Disregarding the conventional restraints and understandings which had previously characterised central-local government relations, the Conservative administrations of the eighties and nineties progressively replaced with a prescriptive, regulatory framework the facilitative legislative framework within which local government was accustomed to working. Whole tiers of local government were simply swept away.[4] Short of that, local authorities were subjected to a battery of new duties in the interests of efficiency, some of which required the wholesale transfer of local authority functions to the private sector,[5] others of which imposed on local government a range of "market-mimicking" disciplines.[6] The central government vision for local government involved

> "a formal separation between service specification and service provision, requiring service provision to be achieved through market competition, and altering the governmental function to the residual one of planning only for services that the market cannot provide".[7]

It was an impoverished vision, and one understandably resented by local authorities of all political stripes.[8] As the House of Lords Select Committee on

---

[4] As with the abolition of the Greater London Council and the metropolitan borough councils in England in 1986, and, in Scotland, with the replacement of the regional and district councils by a single tier of unitary local authorities pursuant to the Local Government etc. (Scotland) Act 1994 ("the 1994 Act").

[5] As with the compulsory competitive tendering regime, introduced, initially, by the Local Government, Planning and Land Act 1980 and subsequently, in fortified form, by the Local Government Act 1988.

[6] See, e.g. Local Government Act 1988 s.35, which required district auditors in Scotland to undertake "value for money" audits to ensure that local authorities had made "proper arrangements for securing economy, efficiency and effectiveness in [their] use of resources".

[7] Loughlin, "The Restructuring of Central-Local Government Relations" in *The Changing Constitution* (2000) p.157.

[8] For an overview, see S. Jenkins, *Accountable to None: The Tory Nationalisation of Britain* (London: Hamish Hamilton, 1995).

Relations between Central and Local Government noted in 1996, its pursuit had damaged if not destroyed the older idea of mutually tolerant partnership between the centre and the localities:

> "This we believe will severely impair the ability of local government to respond to changing economic and social circumstances. [The Conservative legislation] will seriously dilute the legitimacy of local authorities, their institutional, administrative and political capacity and their ability to offer effective local services. They will also seriously diminish the accountability and responsiveness of government to the community at a time of growing social and economic stress.[9]

Many of the recommendations made by the select committee were picked up by **9–02** the Labour Party in advance of its election victory in 1997, and informed its first major White Paper on local government.[10] But Labour was in no sense bent on restoring the status quo ante. Explicitly or implicitly, its programme for local government accepted many of the elements of the Conservative reforms. It remained wedded to strict financial controls. Under the guide of "modernising" the management, performance and accountability of local authorities, it confined the discretion of local authorities in relation to their own internal organisation and introduced new, overarching codes on ethical standards. It insists on local authorities working in partnership with a variety of other agencies, whether public, private or voluntary in character. In the latest round of legislative initiatives, then, there remained a strong sense that central government still cannot bring itself to trust local authorities.

Whatever the ills bedevilling local government in Scotland, however, it lies within the competence of the Scottish Parliament, now, to address them. All matters relating to local government, and most of the functions of local authorities, fall within the devolved competence of the Parliament as defined by Sch.5 to the Scotland Act 1998, with the single exception of the franchise in local government elections.[11] In anticipation of devolution, the Secretary of State for Scotland established a Commission on Local Government and the Scottish Parliament, charged with considering how to build the most effective relations between local government and the Scottish Parliament and Executive, and how local authorities might best make themselves responsive and democratically accountable to the communities they serve. The commission, chaired by Sir Neil McIntosh, reported in June 1999.[12] Its recommendations ranged widely, including the establishment of formal working relationships between local authorities on the one hand and MSPs and the Scottish Executive on the other, the conferment on local authorities of a statutory power of general competence, the

---

[9] House of Lords Select Committee on Relations between Central and Local Government, *Rebuilding Trust* (HMSO, 1996) HL 97.
[10] HM Government, *Modern Local Government: In touch with the People* (The Stationery Office, 1998) Cm.4014.
[11] Although the Smith Commission recommended that this power be devolved (along with the power to determine the franchise for elections to the Scottish Parliament). See HM Government, *Scotland in the United Kingdom: An enduring settlement* (The Stationery Office, 2015) Cm.8990, para.1.4.5.
[12] Commission on Local Government and the Scottish Parliament, *Moving Forward: Local Government and the Scottish Parliament* (The Stationery Office, 1999) (the McIntosh Report).

Public Law

introduction of a four year term for local authorities and a system of proportional representation for local elections, the establishment of an independent inquiry into local government finance, and various changes to the way in which local authority business is conducted. Many of these proposals have been taken forward in some way, and are discussed further below. Perhaps inevitably, legislative initiatives to date have tended to have much in common with similar initiatives at Westminster (although there are significant differences of approach in some respects). It remains to be seen whether, in the future, central-local government relations in Scotland, and indeed models of local government, will develop along lines distinct from those which obtain south of the border.

STRUCTURE OF SCOTTISH LOCAL GOVERNMENT[13]

9–03 The present structure of local government in Scotland is the product of the Local Government etc. (Scotland) Act 1994, which took full effect on 1 April 1996. Prior to that, Scottish local government was organised on two basic levels, with nine regional councils and 53 district councils (together with three all purpose islands councils representing Orkney, Shetland and the Western Isles). The regional/district split was founded in the recommendations of the Royal Commission chaired by Lord Wheatley, which was appointed to inquire into the structure of local government in Scotland and which reported in 1969.[14] The touchstones of the Wheatley Report were that the structure of local government should be such as to enable local authorities to play "a more important, responsible and positive part in the running of the country", equipping them to deliver public services effectively, ensuring proper accountability for the exercise of their powers to the local electorate and securing, so far as possible, the participation of local people in decision making. With these objectives in mind, Wheatley rejected the idea of a single tier of all purpose local authorities in favour of a two tier system, wherein regional authorities would take responsibility for major strategic services and district councils would take charge of more "local" services. Little altered, the Wheatley recommendations were enacted into law by the Local Government (Scotland) Act 1973, much of which remains in force.

In 1991, however, the Secretary of State for Scotland announced the Government's intention to replace this structure with a single tier system of unitary authorities. Widespread opposition to the Government's plans counted for nought, and the proposals were duly enacted in the 1994 Act. The net result was the present, single layer of 32 unitary local authorities.[15] Certain functions

---

[13] See also C.M.G. Himsworth, *Local Government Law in Scotland* (Edinburgh T.&T. Clark, 1995); C.M.G. Himsworth, "Local Government in Scotland" in A. McHarg and T.J. Mullen (eds), *Public Law in Scotland* (Edinburgh: Avizandum, 2006); *Stair Memorial Encyclopedia, Reissue: Local Government* (London: LexisNexis).

[14] Royal Commission on Local Government in Scotland, *Report of the Royal Commission on Local Government in Scotland* (HMSO, 1969) Cm.4150 (the Wheatley Report).

[15] Which left Scotland "in terms of average population per elected council . . . about the most locally under-represented nation in Western Europe": see D. Wilson and C. Gane, *Local Government in the United Kingdom*, 3rd edn (Basingstoke: Macmillan, 1998).

were removed from local authority control altogether.[16] Arrangements were also put in place for the establishment of joint boards and other forms of joint arrangements between the new authorities. Such arrangements are not new—the 1973 Act makes provision for them, as amended by the 1994 Act—but the 1994 reorganisation brought about a significant expansion in their use, principally because many of the new authorities are too small in size to assume individual responsibility for particular functions in their areas. In some cases, joint arrangements are mandatory under the 1994 Act.[17] In others, it is for the local authorities to decide whether they wish to enter into joint arrangements, but it should be noted that where the Scottish Ministers consider that any functions should be discharged jointly by particular authorities, and that those authorities have failed to make any, or satisfactory, arrangements for the joint discharge of those functions, they may by order establish a joint board for those purposes after consulting the authorities in question.[18] The provisions in relation to joint arrangements are of interest, for they (or more accurately, the inevitable and acknowledged extension in their use) sit oddly with the rationale for abolishing the dual tiers of local government in the first place. The Government's case for shifting to a single tier of unitary authorities rested on the claims that the two tiers created confusion in the public mind about who was responsible for what, encouraged duplication of functions and hence waste, and were apt to generate friction between local authorities and hence delay and inefficiency. It is not obvious how the institution of a single tier of unitary authorities coupled with a proliferation of joint arrangements was supposed to address any of these problems, if problems they were.[19]

LOCAL AUTHORITIES—MEMBERSHIP AND ELECTIONS

Unless disqualified by virtue of the Local Government (Scotland) Act 1973 or any other enactment, a person is entitled to stand for election as a member of a local authority if they have attained the age of 18,[20] is a British subject, citizen of the Irish Republic or a citizen of the European Union, and is not subject to any **9–04**

[16] Water and sewerage functions were vested in three new water authorities pursuant to Pt II and Schs 7–11 of the Act (and see now the Water Industry (Scotland) Act 2002, which transferred the functions of the three water authorities to a single body, Scottish Water). Responsibility for the children's reporter system passed to the new Scottish Children's Reporter Administration pursuant to Pt III and Sch.12 of the Act; and responsibility for the promotion of tourism transferred to new area tourist boards established and appointed by the Secretary of State (or, now, the Scottish Ministers) (but see now the Tourist Boards (Scotland) Act 2006).
[17] The Scottish Ministers have the power under s.27 of the 1994 Act to establish joint boards to discharge the functions of two or more valuation authorities. Responsibility for structure planning under the Town and Country Planning (Scotland) Act 1997 is to be exercised in the context of "structure plan areas" designated by the Scottish Ministers, which may cover the area of more than one planning authority. In that event, the planning authorities concerned are to perform their function in accordance with such joint arrangements as they may adopt under ss.56–58 of the Local Government (Scotland) Act 1973 (1973 Act): see, generally, 1994 Act s.33.
[18] See s.20 of the 1994 Act, which inserts new ss.62A–62C into the 1973 Act for these purposes.
[19] Jean McFadden criticises joint arrangements on the further ground that, since they "tend to be officer-led rather than member-led, and since members [of joint boards] are appointed by their councils rather than directly elected, they lack democratic legitimacy and direct accountability to the electorate": *Stair Memorial Encyclopaedia, Reissue: Local Government*, para.447.
[20] The age restriction was reduced from 21 to 18 by s.8 of the Local Governance (Scotland) Act 2004, which amends s.29 of the 1973 Act.

legal incapacity, provided (this in contrast to parliamentary elections) they can show a relevant local connection. That is established where the person is a registered local government elector in the area of the authority, or the occupier (whether as owner or tenant) of any land or other premises in the area during the whole of the 12 month period preceding the election, or has their principal or only place of work in the area during that same period, or is resident in the area throughout that time.[21] This general entitlement to seek election is then subject to a number of grounds of disqualification. A person whose estate has been sequestrated by a court in Scotland or who has been adjudged bankrupt elsewhere than in Scotland is disqualified,[22] as is a person who has been convicted anywhere in the British Islands[23] of a criminal offence carrying a sentence of not less than three months' imprisonment at any time in the five years preceding their nomination or election,[24] and a person who is disqualified under Pt III of the Representation of the People Act 1983.[25] Section 31A of the 1973 Act, as inserted by s.7 of the Local Governance (Scotland) Act 2004, provides that a person elected as a member of a local authority who is also the holder of "any paid office or employment or other place of profit in the gift or disposal of the authority" is disqualified from remaining a member if they fail, prior to the "relevant day",[26] to resign from that office, employment or place of profit. The rule is intended to preserve the important distinction between members and officers of local authorities, but has the effect of excluding from membership of their own local authority not only senior managers and policy advisers but also staff in technical or manual occupations. More broadly still, a person who holds a "politically restricted post" in any local authority in Great Britain is disqualified from becoming a member of any other local authority.[27] Where it is claimed that a disqualified person is, or is seeking to become, a member of a local authority, proceedings may be brought before the sheriff principal under s.32 of the 1973 Act. The participation of a disqualified person in any proceedings of the council or its committees does not, however, affect the validity of any decisions taken therein.[28]

As to the timing of local government elections, in 2002, and in accordance with the recommendation of the McIntosh Report, four year terms were introduced for local government, with elections being synchronised with Scottish

---

[21] 1973 Act s.29.

[22] 1973 Act s.31(1)(b) and (2).

[23] That is, anywhere in the UK, the Republic of Ireland, the Channel Islands or the Isle of Man.

[24] 1973 Act s.31(1)(c).

[25] 1973 Act s.31(1)(d). This includes disqualification following conviction in respect of corrupt or illegal election practices.

[26] "Relevant date" is defined as "the day first occurring after that on which the person elected a member of the local authority was, under the local elections rules, declared to be so elected (no account being taken of a day which is a Saturday or Sunday or Christmas Eve, Easter Monday, or a bank holiday in Scotland . . . or a day appointed for public thanksgiving or mourning in Scotland".

[27] Local Government and Housing Act 1989 s.1. This provision is based on the recommendations of the Widdicombe Committee of Inquiry into Local Authority Business, *Report of the Committee of Inquiry into Local Authority Business* (HMSO, 1986) Cm.9797 and survived a challenge to its compatibility with art.10 of the European Convention on Human Rights, in *Ahmed v United Kingdom* (1995) 20 E.H.R.R. CD72 and (2000) 29 E.H.R.R. 1. See, generally, McFadden, *Stair Memorial Encyclopaedia, Reissue: Local Government*, paras 245 and 256; for criticism, see G.S. Morris, "Local Government Workers and Rights of Political Participation: Time for a change" [1998] P.L. 25.

[28] 1973 Act ss.33 and 43.

parliamentary elections.[29] Further change was to come, however. As we saw in Ch.4, above, from 2007 the single transferrable vote system was introduced for local government elections.[30] Then, in 2009, the link with the Scottish parliamentary elections was broken. The Scottish Local Government (Elections) Act 2009 required the next local government elections to be held in 2012, then in 2017 and thereafter every four years. The result is local government elections will now be held midway through the term of the Scottish Parliament.

LOCAL GOVERNMENT POWERS

Local authorities have no inherent powers to undertake functions of their own **9–05** choosing. They are creatures of statute, and everything that they do must find its source in law.[31] This is the ultra vires rule, and the restraint that it imposes on local authorities should not be lightly discounted. It is true that many local government powers and functions are cast in broad discretionary terms, but even where this is so the courts will insist that the powers are not exercised for purposes ulterior to those envisaged by the statute, or on the basis of irrelevant considerations, or in an unreasonable manner.

An important aspect of local authorities' functions, which may be seen as distinct from their role in providing, or facilitating the provision of, public services, relates to their powers to make subordinate legislation for their areas.[32] The nature of these measures varies. At one end of the spectrum, there are rules that are primarily administrative in character, such as orders made for the regulation of public processions under s.63 of the Civic Government (Scotland) Act 1982 (as amended by s.71 of the Police, Public Order and Criminal Justice (Scotland) Act 2006), structure and development plans drawn up under the Town and Country Planning (Scotland) Act 1997, and strategies as adopted, for example, under s.89 of the Housing (Scotland) Act 2001 and s.1 of the Antisocial Behaviour etc. (Scotland) Act 2004. The adoption of such rules, plans and strategies may be authorised or required by statute, and statute (or regulations made thereunder) may similarly prescribe or guide their content. Even non-statutory guidance or statements of policy published by a local authority may have a rule-like effect in certain circumstances, as where, for example, it provides the foundation for a legitimate expectation in judicial review proceedings, or for a finding of maladministration by the Scottish Public Services Ombudsman

---

[29] Scottish Local Government (Elections) Act 2002. This was perhaps not unwise, for the claims of local government to democratic legitimacy appear somewhat thin when local election turnouts habitually fail to rise above 25% of the local electorate.
[30] See para.4–11, above.
[31] And not merely in the words of a statute alone. The common law grounds for judicial review—illegality, procedural impropriety and irrationality—provide a further level of legal constraint, as do such other jurisprudential innovations as the extension to local authorities of a fiduciary duty to local taxpayers in the use and management of their funds: see *Bromley LBC v Greater London Council* [1983] 1 A.C. 768 HL, followed in Scotland by the Inner House in *Commission for Local Authority Accounts in Scotland v Stirling DC*, 1984 S.L.T. 442.
[32] This power is distinct again from the power of local authorities to promote or oppose private legislation. By virtue of s.82(1) of the Act 1973 a local authority may promote or oppose any private legislation where it is satisfied that it is expedient to do so, and may defray the expenses incurred in so doing. The decision to promote or oppose must be authorised by resolution of the council adopted in accordance with s.82(2) of the 1973 Act. For private legislative procedures, see paras 6–12—6–14, above.

where it is said that the local authority has failed to follow its own criteria. At the other end of the spectrum are the numerous statutory provisions authorising local authorities to make byelaws for their areas.[33] In addition to the more specific powers contained in such statutes as the Civic Government (Scotland) Act 1982 and the Local Government and Planning (Scotland) Act 1982, there is a general byelaw-making power in s.201 of the Local Government (Scotland) Act 1973, which provides that a local authority "may make byelaws for the good rule and government of the whole or any part of its area and for the prevention and suppression of nuisances therein". It should be noted, however, that quite apart from the limitations imposed on a local authority's byelaw-making power by the ultra vires rule, any byelaw adopted by the authority must first be confirmed by the Scottish Ministers (or such other confirming authority as the relevant legislation may specify). At least one month before the local authority applies to the Scottish Ministers for confirmation, it must give public notice of its intention to do so and advise members of the public of their right to object to the byelaw proposed.[34] The Scottish Ministers may, having considered any objections received, confirm the byelaw, with or without modifications, or refuse to confirm it.[35]

9–06   Where byelaws are duly adopted, the responsible local authority is obliged to review them at intervals not exceeding 10 years, to ensure that they are updated or revoked as necessary.[36] Where the authority proposes to revoke any byelaw, it must comply with the procedures as to advance publicity prescribed by s.202B of the 1973 Act. All local authorities are required to keep a register of byelaws containing a description of each byelaw and any offences or penalties attaching to it, its dates of confirmation and coming into force and the date on which it was last renewed. The register is open to public inspection free of charge, although a reasonable charge may be made for providing certified copies of byelaws.[37] The Civic Government (Scotland) Act 1982, as well as amending the rules and procedures relating to byelaws, also introduced a new form of subordinate legislation known as "management rules".[38] Unlike byelaws, management rules may be made by a local authority without the further approval of the Scottish Ministers, although the local authority must give public notice of its intention to adopt particular rules and accord to objectors the right to make representations before bringing the rule into effect (if this is what the authority decides to do). But management rules may only be made for the purpose of regulating the use of, and the conduct of persons on or in

> "land or premises which are owned, occupied or managed by the authority or are otherwise under its control and to which the public have access, whether on payment or not".[39]

---

[33] See, generally, McFadden, *Stair Memorial Encyclopaedia, Reissue: Local Government*, paras 276–301.
[34] Failure to follow these procedures would itself entitle the Court of Session to reduce the byelaw.
[35] 1973 Act s.202.
[36] 1973 Act s.202A.
[37] 1973 Act s.202C.
[38] Civic Government (Scotland) Act 1982 ss.112–118.
[39] Civic Government (Scotland) Act 1982 s.112(1).

Where an "authorised officer" of the local authority reasonably believes that a person is breaching or has breached the terms of a management rule, they may exclude or expel that person from the land or premises.[40] The local authority may make exclusion orders effective for up to one year in the case of persistent offenders.[41] Failure to comply with an exclusion order, or with an instruction to leave (or not to enter) land or premises, is a criminal offence.[42]

Over and above their functionally specific powers and duties, local authorities **9–07** have a variety of powers that may be described as ancillary or subsidiary.[43] Some of these are reasonably precise in their terms, such as the power conferred by s.83(3) of the 1973 Act to make contributions to charitable funds, appeals and the like. Others are (at least on their face) more permissive, although even the latest additions to the legislative corpus do not go so far as to confer on local authorities a power of general competence.[44] One such power is contained in s.69 of the 1973 Act.[45] This provides that

> "a local authority shall have the power to do anything (whether or not involving the expenditure, borrowing or lending of money or the acquisition or disposal of any property or rights) which is calculated to facilitate, or is conducive or incidental to, the discharge of any of their functions".

It is, in fact, nothing more than a statutory statement of the common law position in relation to the ultra vires rule,[46] and was for a long time widely understood as a generous enabling power. That belief was exploded by the decision of the House of Lords in *Hazell v Hammersmith and Fulham LBC*.[47] There, the local authority had entered into "interest rate swap" contracts with financial institutions.[48] It purported to do so on the basis of s.111 of the Local Government Act 1972, assuming that swaps could legitimately be entered into as being incidental to their borrowing powers. The House of Lords disagreed. It was for a local authority, acting prudently in accordance with its fiduciary duty to local taxpayers, to determine at the time of borrowing money whether it would be able to afford interest payments thereon. Speculating on the capital markets was neither conducive nor incidental to that function. Interest rate swap contracts

---

[40] Civic Government (Scotland) Act 1982 s.116.
[41] Civic Government (Scotland) Act 1982 s.117
[42] Civic Government (Scotland) Act 1982 s.118
[43] For a comprehensive survey, see McFadden, *Stair Memorial Encyclopaedia, Reissue: Local Government*, paras 315–356.
[44] Such as was recommended not only by the McIntosh Report but also by the Wheatley Report before that.
[45] The corresponding provision in England and Wales, the Local Government Act 1972 s.111, is in identical terms.
[46] As Lord Selborne LC put it in *Attorney General v Great Eastern Railway Co* (1880) 5 App. Cas. 473 at 478, the doctrine of ultra vires "ought to be reasonably, and not unreasonably, understood and applied, and whatever may fairly be regarded as incidental to, or consequential upon, those things which the legislature has authorised ought not (unless expressly prohibited) to be held by judicial construction to be ultra vires".
[47] *Hazell v Hammersmith and Fulham LBC* [1992] 2 A.C. 1 HL. In Scotland, see to similar effect *Morgan Guaranty Trust Co of New York v Lothian RC*, 1995 S.C. 151.
[48] It was far from being alone in this. Following the decision of the House of Lords in *Hazell*, over 200 actions were commenced, both by local authorities and banks, to recover sums paid under contracts held in *Hazell* to be ultra vires the local authorities.

were therefore ultra vires and void.[49] This is not to say that the ultra vires rule always operated against the interests of local authorities. In the *Credit Suisse* cases, the Court of Appeal held that agreements between the local authorities and the bank, whereby the authorities undertook to guarantee the borrowings of companies established by the authorities in purported performance of their functions, were ultra vires and unenforceable by the bank.[50]

The ramifications of these decisions went beyond the immediate financial consequences for local authorities and banks. Previously, local authorities had been regarded as low risk counterparties by financial and commercial institutions. That perception changed sharply for the worse, putting at risk the drive by central government to encourage (if not force) the contracting-out of service delivery and other forms of public/private partnership.

9–08   The government responded to this on a number of fronts. One of the first enactments of the Labour Government elected in 1997 was the Local Government (Contracts) Act 1997 which, while it does not abrogate the ultra vires rule in its application to local government contracts, significantly mitigates the risks associated with it. Its aim, in the words of the Minister responsible for piloting it through the House of Commons, was

> "to make explicit the power of a local authority to enter into contracts of the sort envisaged in public/private partnership schemes . . . and to provide a safe harbour, by protecting contractors and lenders, if an authority is later found to have entered into an arrangement which is invalid".

Section 1(1) makes clear the power of a local authority to enter into contracts with others for the provision of, or in order to make available, assets or services or both (whether or not together with goods) for the purposes of, or in connection with, the discharge of their functions. Where a local authority enters into such a contract, it has the power also to enter into a contract with a financial institution, where the latter makes a loan or provides any other form of finance to a party to the primary contract other than the local authority itself.[51] The Act then establishes a certification mechanism in respect of such contracts. Provided the certification requirements[52] are met by the local authority (and they are not especially rigorous), the validity of the certified contract cannot be questioned in any private law proceedings. It remains possible in public law proceedings for the court to hold the contract unlawful, but the court may order that the unlawful contract continue to have effect. Even if the contract is set aside, agreed contractual "discharge terms" will apply to determine compensation due, unless these too are ultra vires (or none have been agreed). In that event, statutory damages terms apply. In the context of certified contracts, therefore, the risks of invalidity are placed firmly on the shoulders of local authorities.

---

[49] See also *McCarthy & Stone (Developments) Ltd v Richmond upon Thames LBC* [1992] 2 A.C. 48 HL and, in Scotland, *SPH (Scotland) Ltd v City of Edinburgh Council* Unreported 25 June 2003 Outer House. For the consequences of *Hazell* on the law of unjust enrichment, see *Morgan Guaranty Trust Co. of New York v Lothian RC*, 1995 S.C. 151 and (in England) *Kleinwort Benson Ltd v Lincoln City Council* [1999] 2 A.C. 349 HL.

[50] *Crédit Suisse v Allerdale BC* [1997] Q.B. 306 CA (Civ Div) and *Credit Suisse v Waltham Forest LBC* [1997] Q.B. 362 CA (Civ Div).

[51] Local Government (Contracts) Act 1997 s.1(2).

[52] Local Government (Contracts) Act 1997 s.3(2)(a)–(g).

But contract is only one means through which local authorities may perform their functions. Broader enabling powers have also been enacted. The Local Government in Scotland Act 2003 proclaims itself in its long title as an Act "to provide anew about the way in which local authorities discharge their functions".[53] The three main parts of the Act make provision for the achievement by local authorities of "best value" in their delivery of public services, the introduction of a duty of "community planning" and for a power to advance community well being. The duty to secure best value is a duty to pursue "continuous improvement in the performance of [local authority] functions",[54] which in turn is defined in terms of maintaining an appropriate balance between the quality of performance and the costs of performance, both to the authority and to persons paying, fully or partly, for the services provided. In striking that balance, the authority must have regard to efficiency, economy, effectiveness and equal opportunities.[55] At the same time, Pt 1 relaxes certain of the restrictions imposed on local authorities' contracting powers[56] and on their powers to enter into trading arrangements for the provision of goods and services.[57] Moreover, with the formal introduction of best value, the compulsory competitive tendering regime contained in the Local Government Act 1988 is abolished.[58] It is to be noted, however, that whereas the compulsory competitive tendering regime only ever applied to around one-fifth of local authority functions, the duty to secure best value applies across the board. To that extent alone, its implications for local authorities are the more profound.

Monitoring compliance with s.1 falls to the Controller of Audit and the **9–09** Accounts Commission for Scotland.[59] On receipt of a report from the controller alleging failure by a local authority to comply with its duties, the commission may direct the controller to carry out further investigations or state its findings, with or without a preliminary hearing. On receipt of the commission's findings, the authority concerned is obliged to consider those findings at a meeting of the council and to notify the commission of any remedial action it proposes to take.[60]

Part 2 makes provision in relation to community planning. It is the duty of **9–10** each local authority to initiate, maintain and facilitate a "community planning

---

[53] The equivalent legislation south of the border is the Local Government Act 1999 and the Local Government Act 2000 Pt I. In many respects, the 1999 Act, 2000 Act and 2003 Act simply take forward, and give legislative force to, what was already taking place as a matter of local government or audit practice.

[54] Local Government in Scotland Act 2003 (2003 Act) s.1(1) and (2).

[55] 2003 Act s.1(3) and (4). Not only that, but the local authority must also perform its functions in relation to best value in such a way as to contribute to the achievement of sustainable development.

[56] Namely, the restrictions contained in the Local Government Act 1988 s.17(5)(a), (b) and (d), which prohibit local authorities from taking into account specified "non-commercial considerations" when deciding whether and on what terms to enter into contracts. It should be noted that these restrictions are not abrogated entirely, as was contended for in some quarters, but only in the circumstances defined in s.7(2)(a)–(c) of the 2003 Act. The restrictions in respect of non-commercial considerations elsewhere in s.17(5) of the 1988 Act are unaffected.

[57] 2003 Act ss.8 and 9. Note that in terms of the Local Authorities (Goods and Services) Act 1970, a local authority is obliged, before entering into any trading arrangement thereunder, to consider whether the arrangement will be likely to improve or promote the well being of either or both of its area and persons living in that area.

[58] 2003 Act s.60(1)(e) and (f).

[59] 2003 Act s.3.

[60] 2003 Act s.5. For the further enforcement powers vested in the Scottish Ministers, see below.

process".[61] The object of this process is to institutionalise consultation between the local authority, all public bodies responsible for providing public services in its area, and such community bodies and other bodies or persons as appropriate, in planning for the provision of, and providing, those public services.[62] Apart from local authorities themselves, health boards, the Police Service of Scotland, the Scottish Fire and Rescue Service, Scottish Enterprise, Highlands and Islands Enterprise and Strathclyde Passenger Transport Executive are required to participate in community planning.[63] Under s.19, local authorities and their community planning partners may request the Scottish Ministers to establish by order corporate bodies to "co-ordinate and further" community planning. Monitoring compliance with the duty of community planning is shared between the local authorities themselves,[64] the Scottish Ministers[65] and the Accounts Commission for Scotland.[66]

9–11   Part 3 concerns the power to advance well being, the nearest the legislation comes to conferring a power of general competence.[67] Under s.20(1), a local authority has the power

> "to do anything which it considers is likely to promote or improve the well-being of (a) its area and persons within that area; or (b) either of those".

The power includes power to incur expenditure; give financial assistance to any person; enter into agreements or arrangements with any person; co-operate with, facilitate or co-ordinate the activities of any person; exercise functions on behalf of any person; or to provide staff, goods, materials, facilities, services or property to any person.[68] On the face of this, there would seem to be few forms of innovation in service delivery that would now fall foul of the ultra vires rule. But it is not quite that generous. First, s.22(1) provides that nothing in s.20 is to be taken as enabling a local authority to do anything which, by virtue of a "limiting provision", it is unable to do.[69] Secondly, a local authority may not by virtue of s.20 do anything which would "unreasonably duplicate" something which a

---

[61] 2003 Act s.15(1).

[62] For definition of "public bodies" and "community bodies", see 2003 Act s.15(4).

[63] 2003 Act s.16(1). This list may be amended by the Scottish Ministers.

[64] Presumably the discharge of their duty to report from time to time under s.17(1) of the 2003 Act is intended to provide an opportunity for self-assessment.

[65] In addition to their power to issue guidance about community planning under s.18 of the 2003 Act and to adopt regulations governing the form, content and frequency of reports provided under s.17(1), the Scottish Ministers have the power under s.17(8) to call for reports and information from local authorities about the implementation by them of community planning, together with their wider enforcement powers under Pt IV of the Act.

[66] The Accounts Commission for Scotland has the power under s.1(1) of the Local Government Act 1992 to direct the publication of information about local authorities' standards of performance in such a way as to "facilitate the drawing of conclusions" about the discharge of their community planning functions.

[67] Pursuant to the enactment of the power to advance well being, essentially obsolete powers, including aspects of the power contained in s.83 of the Local Government (Scotland) Act 1973 (the general power of local authorities to incur expenditure) and ss.171A–171C of that Act (the power of local authorities to promote economic development in their areas) are repealed: see 2003 Act s.60(1).

[68] 2003 Act s.20(2).

[69] "Limiting provision" is defined as a provision in any enactment which expressly prohibits or prevents a local authority from doing something or which limits its powers in that respect. Mere absence of positive authority is not to be taken as a prohibition in this sense: 2003 Act s.22(2) and (3).

person other than the local authority is obliged or empowered to do pursuant to its statutory functions. In short, then, Pt 3 restates, albeit in relaxed form, the ultra vires doctrine. Perhaps for that reason, it is not attended by the usual raft of provision for ministerial monitoring and audit: whether a local authority has acted properly within the scope of its powers under s.20 will be, at least ultimately, a question for the courts.

However, Pt 4 makes overarching provision for enforcement of the duties **9–12** created by Pts 1–3. Among other things, it confers on the Scottish Ministers the power to issue "preliminary notices" and, thereafter, "enforcement directions" where it appears to the Scottish Ministers that a local authority has "significantly exceeded its power under section 20".[70] As with the enforcement powers conferred on the Scottish Ministers in relation to best value, accounting and community planning by ss.23 and 24, these are open to the objection that they allow the executive to dictate to an elected authority what it must do and how it must do it. But the objection to ss.26 and 27 goes further. They authorise the Scottish Ministers to determine questions of vires, which are questions of law; and an authority to which an enforcement direction is given is under a duty to comply with it.[71] Further, in issuing an enforcement direction, the Scottish Ministers may require the authority to take such action as is specified in the direction "being action calculated to remedy or prevent the recurrence of its significant excess of power".[72] It would, at least in principle, be open to an authority to resist such a direction on the basis that, if its action is intra vires, there is no legal basis for the direction; and if it is ultra vires, it is simply void ab initio (and unlikely to give rise to any liability to pay compensation to any person). Presumably if a local authority were to resist an enforcement notice in this way, it would fall to the Scottish Ministers to bring proceedings for an order requiring the authority to comply with its duty. But the right of the Scottish Ministers must depend on the validity of their own direction, and the court could not decide that without inquiring into the nature of the local authority's alleged breach of s.20. In that regard, moreover, a court is not confined to finding a given act or decision to be ultra vires only when the excess of competence is "significant".

It becomes apparent that, while there is much in the 2003 Act that is genuinely enabling, it falls a long way short of according autonomy to local authorities within the limits of the law. At all times, local authorities are required to have regard to guidance and regulations promulgated by the Scottish Ministers under the Act. The choices made by local authorities in the exercise of their functions in relation to best value, community planning and the promotion of well being may exceptionally be subject to judicial oversight, but they are routinely subject to ministerial oversight and audit control, both of which are reinforced by the rigorous reporting requirements laid on local authorities by the Act. In significant respects, the regime contained in the 2003 Act is more prescriptive and interventionist than the regime contained in the Local Government Acts 1999 and 2000 south of the border. Is this acceptable because the centre is now more local? No doubt, via the Scottish Government and Accounts Commission and thence the Scottish Parliament, all of this may be said to enhance the accountability of

---

[70] 2003 Act ss.26 and 27.
[71] 2003 Act s.27(7).
[72] 2003 Act s.27(1).

local authorities for the performance of their functions to the public. But there is a strong sense here that this accountability is but a by-product of, and secondary to, the consolidation of central control and supervision over the activities of local government in Scotland.

ORGANISATION OF LOCAL AUTHORITY BUSINESS

9–13 Within the UK and Scottish Government's, executive decisions are taken by Ministers, who answer for their decisions to Westminster or the Scottish Parliament. The organisation of local authority business is quite different: " . . . there is no source of executive authority other than the council itself."[73] But while the functions of local authorities are vested in the council for each local government area, it would obviously be impracticable for the full council to take every decision. Except where statute provides otherwise, therefore, the council may delegate its functions to committees, subcommittees, joint committees[74] or officers of the councils, though not to a single councillor.[75]

Local authorities are accorded a good deal of latitude as to how they carry out their business. They are required to hold a first meeting within 21 days of a local election, at which they must elect a convenor and, if they wish, a depute convenor.[76] Thereafter, it is largely up to individual authorities how often they hold meetings.[77] It is also, subject to the restrictions already noted, for each authority to decide whether and to what extent it wishes to delegate functions to committees and officers, and on the particular model of delegation it wishes to adopt. There is no longer any requirement that particular committees be

---

[73] Committee of Inquiry into Local Authority Business, *Report of the Committee of Inquiry into Local Authority* Business, para.5.2.

[74] Bearing in mind that committees must reflect the political balance of the full council.

[75] See, generally, 1973 Act s.56. Local authorities are not permitted to delegate major financial decisions, defined by s.56(6) as functions with respect to determining the level of council tax for their area and borrowing money. Note also s.82 of the 1973 Act, which requires the decision to promote or oppose private legislation to be taken by the full council. A number of statutory provisions also require certain reports to be considered by the full council, in the interests of publicity: see, e.g. Ethical Standards in Public Life etc. (Scotland) Act 2000, s.18, which requires the written findings of the Standards Commission to be considered at a meeting of the full council; and 2003 Act s.5, which requires a local authority, on receipt of a report by the Accounts Commission for Scotland on its compliance with the duty to secure best value, to consider the report at a meeting of the council and notify the commission of the remedial steps it proposes to take. Interestingly, like provision in the Local Government (Scotland) Act 1975 s.29, in relation to consideration of reports by the Commissioner for Local Administration in Scotland is repealed by the Scottish Public Services Ombudsman Act 2002.

[76] 1994 Act s.4. There is no statutory definition of the functions of a convenor or depute convenor, other than in para.3 of Sch.7 to the 1973 Act, which states that the convenor (or depute convenor) shall chair meetings of the council. At meetings where a vote is taken, the convenor or depute convenor has a casting vote in the event of a tie. In Aberdeen, Dundee, Edinburgh and Glasgow the convener of the council is known as the "Lord Provost".

[77] Apart from the requirement to hold a first meeting within 21 days of the election, the only other requirement is that a local authority should hold as many meetings as it thinks necessary. Schedule 7 to the 1973 Act makes provision in relation to the calling and conduct of meetings, but broadly it is for each council to regulate its own practice by way of standing orders. The usual pattern is for meetings of the full council to be held every four or six weeks, with a summer recess and Christmas break.

established. Again, it is for the council to provide for the conduct and procedures of committee meetings through standing orders of its own choosing.[78]

At various times, thought has been given to the adoption of different models **9–14** of organising local authority business. The Maud Committee recommended that each local authority should appoint a management board of five to nine councillors, to which all other committees would be answerable.[79] The Widdicombe Committee considered three different models—the management board, the ministerial model and the separation of powers model based on an elected or appointed executive—but found none of them to be sufficiently advantageous to justify a departure from prevailing practice. The Government revisited the issue in its 1998 White Paper.[80] In England and Wales, this was followed by a further round of consultation on new forms of governance for local authorities,[81] which led in turn to the provision contained in Pt II of the Local Government Act 2000.[82] This provides for the adoption by English and Welsh local authorities of "executive arrangements" under which certain functions of the local authority become the responsibility of the executive.[83]

Section 11 gives authorities a choice as to the form of their executive **9–15** arrangements between three options: an elected mayor, acting with two or more councillors appointed to the executive by them (the "mayor and cabinet" model); a councillor elected as executive leader by the council, acting with two or more councillors appointed by them or by the authority (the "leader and cabinet" model); or an elected mayor acting with an officer of the authority appointed by the council (the "mayor and council manager" model). Sections 13–17 then make provision for the denomination of executive functions. Consulting in Scotland, the McIntosh Commission found little support for any of these alternatives to the status quo.[84] As the commission noted, however, if Scottish local authorities do not have formal executives, majority groups constitute something very similar. In effect, many decisions of a local authority are in no sense taken in public meetings, but agreed in private meetings of the controlling group on the council. The McIntosh Committee, therefore, recommended that councils should review their procedures with a view to ensuring that policy proposals and matters for decision are subject to open debate, and that the council is able to scrutinise the majority group and hold it properly to account for its decisions. The Scottish Ministers chose to take this forward not by introducing legislation along the lines of Pt II of the Local Government Act 2000, but by requiring councils to review their organisational structures and appointing an

---

[78] 1973 Act s.62. The Local Government and Housing Act 1989 s.20, confers on the Scottish Ministers the power to prescribe standing orders to be adopted by local authorities, but the power has never been used. For the legal effect of standing orders, see *R. v Hereford Corp Ex p. Harrower* [1970] 1 W.L.R. 1424 DC.

[79] Committee of Inquiry into the Management of Local Government, *Report of the Committee of Inquiry into the Management of Local Government* (HMSO, 1969) Cm.4840 (the Maud Report).

[80] HM Government, *Modern Local Government: In touch with the People*.

[81] Department of the Environment, Transport and Regions, *Local Leadership, Local Choice* (The Stationery Office, 1999), Cm.4298 and Welsh Office, *A Stronger Voice for Local People: Consulting on the Draft Local Government Bill* (The Stationery Office, 1999).

[82] Separate provision was made in relation to London in the Greater London Authority Act 1999.

[83] Local Government Act 2000 s.10.

[84] Commission on Local Government and the Scottish Parliament, *Moving Forward: Local Government and the Scottish Parliament*.

advisory panel to assist them in that task. The panel reported in 2001.[85] All but three of Scotland's 32 local authorities undertook reviews of their internal structures, and all but three of those made some changes, involving either a streamlining of their existing committee systems, the introduction of formal executives, or the adoption of devolved structures of decision making.

So far as the organisation of local authority business in Scotland is concerned, then, statutory regulation is relatively light. Two areas into which statute does intrude, however, relate to public access to local authority meetings and to the policing of standards of conduct. As to the first, statutory rights of access to council meetings were accorded initially only to the press.[86] Substantially extended rights of access, for press and public, were provided for by the Public Bodies (Admission to Meetings) Act 1960, which applied to meetings of the full council and to education committees; this was extended again by the Local Government (Scotland) Act 1973 to all committee (but not subcommittee) meetings. The current law is contained in the Local Government (Access to Information) Act 1985, which inserted into the 1973 Act a new Pt IIIA and a new Sch.7A. It requires, first, that public notice of the time and place of all meetings, including meetings of committees and subcommittees, be posted at the offices of a local authority at least three clear days in advance or, that failing, at the time the meeting is called. Secondly, it provides that meetings of the council and any committee and subcommittee shall be open to the public. This general rule is then qualified in a number of ways. The council (or committee) has the power to exclude where necessary to prevent or suppress disorderly conduct.[87] It may also, acting by formal resolution, exclude the public from a meeting during consideration of an item of business that is likely to involve disclosure of "exempt information".[88] There is no provision for challenging a resolution to exclude, although it is in principle subject to judicial review and in one case the Court of Appeal apparently assumed that the exclusion of the public pursuant to an unlawful resolution would render invalid the subsequent proceedings and any decision taken therein.[89] Section 50A(2) of the 1973 Act further provides that the public must be excluded from a meeting during consideration of an item of business that is likely to involve disclosure of confidential information.[90] The right of access to meetings is then reinforced by provision for access to documents relating to meetings. Before a meeting, copies of the agenda, the report for the meeting and any background papers must be made available for

---

[85] Leadership Advisory Panel, *Scottish Local Government's Self-Review of its Political Management Structures: Report of the Leadership Advisory Panel* (Scottish Executive, 2001) (the MacNish Report).

[86] Local Authorities (Admission of the Press to Meetings) Act 1908.

[87] 1973 Act s.50A(8).

[88] 1973 Act s.50A(4). The categories of exempt information are defined in Sch.7A, and include information relating to individual employees, tenants, clients and other recipients of benefits from the authority; information concerning contracts of the authority; information relating to the prevention or investigation of crime; and legal advice given to the authority. "Information" is defined to include "an expression of opinion, any recommendations and any decision taken": s.50K(1).

[89] *R. v Liverpool City Council Ex p. Liverpool Taxi Fleet Operators' Association* [1975] 1 All E.R. 379 QBD, a case involving the Public Bodies (Admission to Meetings) Act 1960.

[90] "Confidential information" has a special meaning for these purposes, being confined by s.50A(3) of the 1973 Act to information provided by a government department on terms which forbid its disclosure to the public, and information the disclosure of which is prohibited by or under any enactment or by order of the court.

public inspection at the offices of the local authority.[91] A reasonable number of copies of the agenda and reports must be made available at the meeting itself for use by members of the public,[92] and after the meeting copies of the minutes, the agenda and any reports provided to members must be retained for six years and made available for public inspection.[93] All this accounted for, it should also be noted that the Freedom of Information (Scotland) Act 2002 now imposes on local authorities extensive statutory duties in relation to the disclosure of information held by them, both as a matter of routine publication and on request.

As to the probity of local councillors, the old patchwork of provision for controlling standards in public life has largely been replaced by the Ethical Standards in Public Life etc. (Scotland) Act 2000.[94] The Prevention of Corruption Act 1906 extended (and extends) to local councillors, and certain other species of unethical behaviour constitute criminal offences under the Local Government (Scotland) Act 1973.[95] Beyond that, the 1973 Act together with the Local Government and Housing Act 1989 made provision for a register of interests, and s.31 of the 1989 Act authorised the Secretary of State (or, post-devolution, the Scottish Ministers) to adopt a code of conduct by which all councillors undertake to be bound. The regulatory gap is obvious: on the one hand, a number of criminal offences dependent on the criminal standard of proof; on the other, a code, breach of which carries no formal sanction other than anything the member's party, the authority or the local electorate might happen to mete out. In its third report, the Committee on Standards in Public Life described the situation as wholly insufficient to secure public confidence in the probity of local government, and recommended the adoption of a national code of ethical standards to be enforced at local level.[96] **9–16**

The matter being devolved, the Scottish Government took over responsibility for consulting on these proposals, and came up with a framework for ethical standards differing from the committee's recommendations in two important ways. First, it extended the scope of the code beyond local government to include also "devolved public bodies". Secondly, it rejected the idea of local enforcement in favour of a national standards commission, charged with investigating complaints concerning breaches of the new codes of conduct. This framework is reflected in the 2000 Act.[97] The Scottish Ministers are charged with issuing a mandatory code of conduct for local councillors,[98] including provision about the registration and declaration of their interests and their ineligibility to participate

---

[91] 1973 Act s.50D.
[92] 1973 Act s.50B.
[93] 1973 Act s.50D. Where the minutes fail to provide a fair and coherent record of the proceedings, on account of removal of any references to "exempt information", the authority is required instead to make available a summary version of the record of the meeting. Background documents must also be retained and made available for inspection, but only for a period of four years following the meeting.
[94] In England and Wales, less onerous provision is made in the Local Government Act 2000 Pt III.
[95] See, e.g. 1973 Act s.38(2), which makes it a criminal offence to fail to declare an interest in a contract.
[96] Committee on Standards in Public Life, *Third Report—Standards of Conduct in Local Government in England, Scotland and Wales* (The Stationery Office, 1997) CM.3702–1.
[97] See, generally, D.W. Cobb, "Shutting the Door or Cleaning the Stable? The Ethical Standards in Public Life etc (Scotland) Act 2000", 2001 S.L.T. (News) 205.
[98] Standards Commission for Scotland, *The Councillors' Code of Conduct*, 3rd edn (Scottish Government, 2010) http://www.gov.scot/Publications/2010/12/10145144/0 [Accessed 9 June 2015].

in council business affecting those interests,[99] together with a model code of conduct for members of devolved public bodies containing a mixture of mandatory and optional provisions so that individual public bodies have some scope for tailoring the model code to suit their particular circumstances.[100] Every local authority and devolved public body is required by s.7 to set up, maintain and make available for public inspection a register of members' interests. Section 8 and Sch.1 then provide for the establishment of the Standards Commission for Scotland and the remainder of Pt 2 is devoted to the conduct of investigations where breaches of the codes of conduct are alleged to have taken place.

9–17 Section 9 and Sch.2 originally provide for the appointment of a chief investigating officer, who takes responsibility for the initial investigation of complaints made to the commission. Those functions have since been transferred to the Commissioner for Ethical Standards in Public Life in Scotland.[101] The commission may issue general directions to the commissioner relating to the performance of their functions, but may not direct them as to how they conduct particular investigations.[102] Investigations must be carried out in confidence, so far as possible, and should normally be completed within three months.[103] The commissioner has the same powers as the Court of Session to require the attendance and examination of witnesses and the production of documents,[104] although no one may be compelled to give evidence or produce documents that they could not be compelled to give or produce in civil proceedings in the Court of Session. Therefore it might be open for a witness to claim, say, confidentiality or privilege in relation to particular documents. Conceivably, the commissioner could treat such a claim as obstruction, which entitles them to certify the matter to the Court of Session. The Court of Session may in turn treat the matter as a contempt of court. On conclusion of an investigation, it is for the commissioner to decide whether or not to report to the Standards Commission.[105] If they are minded to report that the subject of the investigation has breached the applicable code of conduct, they must first give the subject a copy of their proposed report and accord them an opportunity to make representations thereon. But it should also be noted that the commissioner may or, if so directed by the commission, must submit an interim report on an investigation in progress, and that the commission may on receipt of such a report suspend the member concerned from office for a period not exceeding three months (which may, however, be renewed).[106] The commission may only exercise the power of suspension where

---

[99] Ethical Standards in Public Life etc. (Scotland) Act 2000 (2000 Act) s.1. "Interests" are defined by s.1(8) to include "pecuniary and non-pecuniary interests".

[100] 2000 Act s.2. Devolved public bodies are required to submit their individual codes of conduct for the approval of the Scottish Ministers within time limits stipulated by order made under s.3.

[101] Scottish Parliamentary Commissions and Commissioners etc. Act 2010. The functions were transferred via the Public Standards Commissioner for Scotland (Public Service Reform (Commissioner for Ethical Standards in Public Life in Scotland etc.) Order 2013 (SSI 2013/197)).

[102] 2000 Act s.10.

[103] Where it appears that the investigation will take longer to complete, the chief investigating officer must notify the commission, the individual subject to the investigation and the relevant authority or body of that fact: 2000 Act s.12(5).

[104] "Documents" includes information held by means of a computer or in any other electronic form: 2000 Act s.13(5).

[105] 2000 Act s.14.

[106] 2000 Act s.21.

satisfied that the further conduct of the investigation is likely otherwise to be prejudiced or (more broadly) that it would be in the public interest to do so. The commission is not required to hold a hearing before imposing a suspension, although the subject of the interim report must be given an opportunity to make representations on its contents.

Where the commissioner submits a final report under s.14 of the Act, the **9–18** commission may decide to take no further action, direct them to conduct further investigations or hold a hearing.[107] If a hearing is held, it must be conducted by at least three members of the commission, and the individual whose conduct is being considered is entitled to be heard, either in person or through a representative (legal or otherwise); but that apart, the procedure to be followed at the hearing is for the commission itself to determine.[108] The commission has the power to require the attendance of any person to give evidence and the production of documents, and is expressly authorised to examine witnesses on oath. Failure to attend a hearing, give evidence or produce documents, without reasonable excuse, is a criminal offence. At the conclusion of a hearing, the members of the commission must state their findings in writing and provide copies to the subject of the inquiry, the council or body concerned, any other person the commission considers should receive a copy, and any other person who pays a "reasonable charge" for a copy.[109] The findings, adverse or otherwise, must be considered at a full meeting of the council.

Where the commission's verdict is that the applicable code of conduct has **9–19** been breached, it has a number of possible sanctions at its disposal. It may censure the member concerned, but otherwise take no action; suspend that person, for a period not exceeding one year, from all or specified meetings of the council or body; or (in the case of a councillor) disqualify them from being, or being nominated for election as, or being elected as a councillor, for a period of up to five years.[110] A person who is found to have contravened a code of conduct and/or upon whom a sanction is imposed under s.19 may appeal to the sheriff principal within 21 days of the relevant decision.[111] The grounds for appeal, in the case of an appeal against a finding of breach of the code, are that the commission's finding was based on an error of law; that there was procedural impropriety in the conduct of the hearing; that the commission has acted unreasonably in the exercise of its discretion; or that the facts found to be proved by the commission do not support its decision. The grounds for appeal in the case of an appeal against the imposition of a sanction are narrower: that the sanction was excessive, or that the commission has acted unreasonably in the exercise of its discretion. In the first case, the sheriff principal may confirm or quash the

---

[107] For a list of hearings, and their outcomes, see Standards Commission for Scotland, "Concluded Investigations Referred from CES", *http://www.standardscommissionscotland.org.uk/full_list* [Accessed 9 June 2015].

[108] 2000 Act s.17.

[109] 2000 Act s.18. The section makes no provision for releasing the report in confidence or in redacted form, even though s.17 permits the commission to conduct hearings in private if it considers that this would be in the public interest.

[110] 2000 Act s.19. It is worth noting that both disqualification and suspension under s.21 could present problems for a local authority in terms of securing the necessary political balance on its committees, and could even deprive a majority group of its overall control of the council.

[111] 2000 Act s.22.

verdict of the commission, or quash the decision and remit the matter to the commission for reconsideration. In the second case, they may confirm or quash the sanction, or quash it and either substitute a different sanction or remit the matter to the commission. There is a further right of appeal from the decision of the sheriff principal to the Court of Session.

CHAPTER 10

THE EUROPEAN UNION

INTRODUCTION

To understand the Europe of today it is necessary understand the process of **10–01** evolution that has taken place. The current form of "Europe" came into being on 1 December 2009 with the entry into force of the Treaty of Lisbon. But the foundations for today's Union were laid in the early 1950s. We therefore begin by reviewing the evolution of what started as a six state coal and steel community and today exists as a 29 member social, economic and increasingly political Union. Against that background, we turn to consider the institutions of the EU, the form of legislation that it passes and the main ways in which EU law impacts on Member States. The substance of EU law is beyond the scope of this work.[1] Finally, we look at the key pieces of UK legislation that give effect to British membership of the European Union.

THE EVOLUTION OF THE EUROPEAN UNION

From the Coal and Steel Community to a draft constitution

The initial steps towards European integration were taken in 1952 when the **10–02** European Coal and Steel Community (the ECSC) was formed. Six nations (France, (the Federal Republic of) Germany,[2] Italy, Belgium, the Netherlands and Luxembourg) signed the Treaty of Paris. This was not an ordinary international treaty. It created a super-national body with independent institutions having the power to bind the Member States. In creating this "Community" the Member States transferred some of the powers normally exercised by sovereign states but for specific and defined purposes and for a limited period of time.[3] A number of institutions were created. A High Authority was the main executive institution with decision making power and responsibility for implementing the aims of the Treaty; an Assembly consisting of delegates from national parliaments and which

---

[1] Many texts are devoted to that subject, or more frequently one particular aspect of it. For general texts covering EU law see, for example D.A.O. Edward and R.C. Lane, *European Union Law* (Cheltenham: Edward Elgar, 2013); A. O'Neill, *EU Law for UK Lawyers* (Oxford: Hart, 2011), or P. Craig and G. De Burca, *EU Law: Text, Cases and Materials*, 5th edn (Oxford: Oxford University Press, 2011).

[2] Following German reunification in 1990, the Democratic Republic of Germany became part of the Communities without any amendment to the then existing treaties or a separate accession agreement. The consequence of the reunification of Germany was a significant increase in the Communities' territory and an additional 16 million people within its boundaries.

[3] European Coal and Steel Community Treaty art.97: the ECSC was formed for 50 years and therefore expired, naturally, on 24 July 2002.

exercised essentially supervisory powers; a Council, consisting of one representative from each Member State; and a court charged with the interpretation and application of the Treaty. As we shall see shortly, the European Union of today is structurally very similar to the model adopted by the six founding members of the ECSC.

After aborted attempts to form a European Defence Community and a European Political Community (foundering on French anxieties about German rearmament), discussions continued between the ECSC Member States about how to progress the project of European integration. Those discussions led to the foundation of two further communities in March 1957: the European Economic Community (the EEC) and the European Atomic Energy Community (the EAEC). These treaties entered into force on 1 January 1958 and were, unlike the time limited the ECSC, for an "unlimited duration".[4] The two new treaties followed the same scheme as the ECSC Treaty: there was an Assembly consisting of delegates from national parliaments, a Council and a court. The High Authority was, in the two new communities, known as the Commission. From the inception of the EEC and the EAEC, the three Communities shared a single Assembly and a single court. In 1967, the Councils of the respective Communities were merged and the ECSC High Authority and the EEC and EAEC Commissions came together to form the Commission of the European Communities. Although there remained three legally distinct Communities, they each now shared the same institutions and the distinctions began to blur.

In economic terms, the European Communities were a conspicuous success. In parallel to the European Communities, seven other countries formed the European Free Trade Association (the EFTA) in 1960.[5] Four of the EFTA members, however, sought membership of the Communities twice during the 1960s. A third attempt led to a Treaty of Accession being signed by Denmark, Ireland, Norway and the UK in January 1972. In the event, the Norwegian people declined membership in a referendum resulting in Norway failing to ratify the Treaty. The remaining countries did ratify the Accession Treaty and, as a result, became members of the three Communities on 1 January 1973. The 1970s ended with reform of the Assembly. Until that point, it comprised of delegates appointed by the respective parliaments of the Member States and it possessed limited powers.[6] Direct elections to what was now called the European Parliament took place for the first time in 1979. With direct election came at least some level of democratic legitimacy and thus a claim for greater powers. As we will see, over the coming years, the European Parliament would go on to acquire a number of additional powers. The 1980s started with the accession of Greece, who became the tenth Member State of the Communities, and the secession of Greenland. Although Greenland remained part of Denmark, in 1979 Greenland acquired the power to opt out of Danish treaty obligations and, following a referendum in 1982, did just that in relation to the Communities.[7] In 1985, five

---

[4] European Economic Community Treaty art.240; European Atomic Energy Community Treaty art.208.

[5] The seven were: Denmark, Norway, Austria, Portugal, Switzerland, Sweden and the UK.

[6] It had two main powers, both of them rightly regarded as "nuclear options": it could require the Commission, *en masse*, to resign and it could reject the budget prepared by the Commission. Otherwise, the Assembly was limited to trying to call the Commission to account where it considered that to be necessary.

[7] The result was the Communities lost over 50 per cent of its territory but less than 0.1 per cent of its population.

Member States entered into the Schengen agreement, the effect of which was the removal of border controls between their respective countries.[8] The work needed to implement the agreement was such that it was 10 years before the system came fully into force. On 1 January 1986 the Communities grew to 12 in number with the accession of Spain and Portugal.

1986 was, however, more noteworthy in the evolution of the Union for the adoption by the Member States of the Single European Act. Signed in February 1986, it came into force on 1 July 1987 and committed the Member States to an ambitious timetable to complete the "internal market" by the end of 1992. The Single European Act revived the integrationist momentum in the Communities. In addition to the commitment to the internal market, the Single European Act made important amendments to the legislative procedures of the Communities. These enhanced the role of the European Parliament and an amendment to the EEC Treaty allowed qualified majority voting (in place of unanimity) in an increased number of areas in the Council of Ministers. A new Court of First Instance was created to assist the Court of Justice, the Parliament was given a veto over the accession of new Member States and the Communities acquired an extended competence that now reached into economic and monetary union, social policy, social and economic cohesion and the environment.

The Single European Act produced significant momentum for further integra- **10–03** tion. Plans for economic and monetary union were developed alongside plans for deeper political integration. The result was another treaty: the Treaty on European Union, more commonly known as the Maastricht Treaty. The Maastricht Treaty was politically controversial. It was also subject to legal challenge in a number of Member States[9] and was initially rejected by the Danes in a referendum.[10] The Maastricht Treaty created the "European Union" and adopted the "three pillar" structure for the Union. The first of the three pillars was the existing Communities. The Communities were flanked by the other two pillars: a common foreign and security policy and co-operation on justice and home affairs. This unwieldy structure reflected the tension at the heart of the European Union between integration and intergovernmentalism. The Communities pillar was, as ever, a genuinely super-national structure which bound the Member States in ever-widening areas: a "new legal order of international law" as the Court of Justice put it.[11] The Maastricht Treaty also made a number of important changes to the treaties that founded the Communities, in particular the EEC Treaty. These included the renaming of the EEC as the European Community (the EC), the conferral of a number of new competences, the creation of citizenship of the EU and provision for achieving economic and monetary union and the adoption of a single currency. The other two pillars were, on the other hand, much more akin to traditional creations of international law. Neither of

---

[8] The original Schengen countries were Belgium, the Federal Republic of Germany, France, Luxembourg and the Netherlands.

[9] In the UK, those challenges came in the form of applications to the courts for interdict (in Scotland) and injunction (in England and Wales): *Monckton v Lord Advocate*, 1995 S.L.T. 1201 and *R. v Secretary of State for the Foreign and Commonwealth Office Ex p. Rees-Mogg* [1994] Q.B. 552 DC, respectively.

[10] The Treaty was initially rejected by Danes in a referendum by the narrowest of margins (there was less than 1% in it) but following a number of undertakings at the Edinburgh Summit in December 1992, the Treaty was approved by the Danish people the following year.

[11] *NV Algemene Transport- en Expeditie Onderneming van Gend en Loos v Nederlandse Administratie der Belastingen* (C-26/62) [1963] E.C.R. 1 at 12.

these pillars had supremacy over national laws nor direct effect.[12] The Maastricht Treaty also elevated the concepts of proportionality and subsidiarity to the status of general principles of Community law.[13] Their elevation ought to have provided some reassurance to those concerned about the pace and direction of European integration. Proportionality requires the Communities' institutions to go no further than is necessary to achieve the objectives of the treaties; subsidiarity requires that legislative and administrative action be taken at the most appropriate level, be it European, national or regional level. The other important aspect of the Maastricht Treaty was its endorsement of the concept of "variable geometry" or differential integration. This was intended to permit Member States to move towards integration at different speeds in difference contexts[14] and respond to the tension that existed, and continues to exist, amongst the Member States about their differing vision as to how far the project of European integration should go.[15] The difficulties with this multifaceted conception of the EU were reflected in the provision made in the Maastricht Treaty for a further intergovernmental conference in 1996 to consider "to what extent the policies and forms of co-operation introduced by this Treaty may need to be revised". The product of that further conference was a further treaty: the Treaty of Amsterdam.

10–04   The Treaty of Amsterdam was signed in October 1997. Before turning to consider that, in attempt to maintain some degree of chronology, three other developments should be noted. First, the European Economic Area (the EEA) came into being on 1 January 1994. The EEA consisted of the EU Member States on the one hand and six of the now seven Member States of the EFTA.[16] Secondly, in 1994 a further accession treaty was agreed, this time with Austria, Finland, Sweden and, for a second time, Norway. Each country held a referendum to ratify their accession to the EU and, for a second time, the Norwegian people rejected membership. There were no such difficulties in the other accession countries who duly joined the EU on 1 January 1995.[17] Finally, as noted above, the Schengen agreement (which removed border checks between the signatory countries) became fully operational on 26 March 1995 and by now

---

[12] Both supremacy and direct effect were key characteristics of the Communities and are discussed more fully below at paras 10–35—10–36. Supremacy has also been discussed in the context of its consequences for the sovereignty of the Westminster Parliament (at para.3–09).

[13] See para.10–25 below. Proportionality is discussed in Ch.11 (in relation to human rights) and Ch.14 (in relation to judicial review). So far as EU law is concerned, proportionality has significant differences. See *R. (on the application of Lumsdon) v Legal Services Board* [2015] UKSC 41; [2015] 3 W.L.R. 121 at [22]–[82].

[14] For general discussion, see D. Curtin, "The Constitutional Structure of the European Union: A Europe of bits and pieces" (1993) 30 C.M.L. Rev. 17; S. Weatherill, "The Provisions on Closer Co-operation" in D. O'Keeffe and P. Twomey (eds), *The Legal Issues of the Amsterdam Treaty* (Oxford: Hart, 1999) Ch.2.

[15] That lack of agreement on the vision for the future of Europe (closer integration along a federal model or an economic union that respects the sovereignty of the Member States) has rendered the EU an "essentially contested concept" (Z. Bankowski and E.A. Christodoulidis, "The European Union as an Essentially Contested Project" (1998) 4(4) E.L.J. 341).

[16] The EFTA Member States were by now Austria, Norway, Sweden and Switzerland (who remained from the time the United Kingdom was a member) along with Finland, Iceland and Liechtenstein. The Swiss people rejected the European Economic Area Treaty in a referendum and as a result it was only the other six EFTA members that joined the EEA.

[17] The consequence of their accession was the EFTA element of the recently created EEA was reduced to three: Iceland, Liechtenstein and Norway.

its signatories had expanded from five to nine.[18] Returning to the Treaty of Amsterdam, it modified the three pillar structure of the EU and made further changes to the Communities. The role of the European Parliament was further enhanced with an extension of the "co-decision" legislative procedure into new areas.[19] In the Council of Ministers, qualified majority voting was extended. The EC acquired further competences, many transferred from the third pillar, including visas, asylum, immigration and other policies related to free movement of persons. On a practical level, the biggest impact the Treaty of Amsterdam had was the renumbering of all the EC and Maastricht Treaty articles, which caused no end of confusion.[20] The Treaty of Amsterdam was met with a rather muted reception, perhaps because it failed to grapple with the pressing issue of constitutional and institutional reform that was necessary before further expansion of the Union. Those issues were again deferred to another intergovernmental conference and another treaty.

The Treaty of Nice was signed on 26 February 2001. It sought to ready the Union for expansion beyond its then membership of 15. The power of veto was removed for almost all matters and the weighting of votes in the Council and the allocation of seats in the European Parliament amongst the Member States were determined.[21] The structure and jurisdiction of the Court of Justice was also amended. After initially being rejected by the Irish people in a referendum, it was approved at the second attempt and entered into force on 1 February 2003.[22] Given, as we shall see, the Treaty of Nice has been superseded the most significant and lasting decision to come out of the intergovernmental conference that gave rise to the Treaty was the adoption, by way of a solemn proclamation, of the Charter of Fundamental Rights that had been drafted at the request of the European Council meeting in Cologne in July 1999.[23] The Charter contained many familiar rights, in language that was similar, and in places identical, to the rights set out in the European Convention on Human Rights. But it went further and set out a number of social and economic rights[24], which were afforded the same status as more traditional fundamental rights.[25] Having been "solemnly proclaimed", the Charter had no legal effect, it did not bind the Member States and it did not confer any rights on EU citizens. As such "soft law" has the habit of doing, it hardens over time and the Charter has now been adopted by the

---

[18] Spain, Portugal, Greece and Italy, although only the first two implemented the agreement when it became operational in 1995. The membership has grown further and now includes all EU Member States (with the exception of the UK and Ireland, who have not signed; Bulgaria, Croatia, Cyprus and Romania are obliged by the terms of their accession agreements to join but have not yet implemented the agreement), together with four non-Member States (Iceland, Liechtenstein, Norway and Switzerland).

[19] The co-decision procedure is discussed at para.12–32, above.

[20] The result being that both article numbers were invariably used, for example art.234 (ex art.177).

[21] The current rules on these matters are discussed above at paras 10–14 and 10–09, respectively.

[22] For the sake of completeness, it should be noted that between the signing of the Treaty of Nice and its coming into force, the very first Treaty, which founded the ECSC, expired on 24 July 2002 and brought that Community to an end. Much of its work was absorbed by the EC.

[23] The Charter is considered in more detail below at para 12–39. See also, Edward and Lane, *European Union Law* (2013) paras 6.114–6.118; O'Neill, *EU Law for UK Lawyers* (2011) paras 6.55–6.98.

[24] For example, rights to collective bargaining (art.28), social security (art.34) and healthcare (art.35).

[25] Articles 51 and 52 of the Charter.

Member States, giving it the same legal force as the treaties.[26] We will return to the Charter below.

The Treaty of Nice served its primary function and enabled the EU to expand and admit a further 10 members on 1 May 2004[27] taking the membership to 25. Accession treaties were agreed with Bulgaria and Romania the following year and they joined on 1 January 2007. Breaking the chronology slightly, the most recent country to join the EU was Croatia, who joined the Union on 1 July 2013, bringing the current membership to 28.[28]

A Constitution for Europe?

10–05 In February 2002, under the chairmanship of former French President Giscard d'Estaing, a "constitutional convention" was convened. In the summer of 2003, the convention agreed the text of a draft "Treaty establishing a Constitution for Europe". The draft constitution sought to bring together the various Treaties of the Communities and the Union in a single text. The proposed text was submitted to the President of the Council on 18 July 2003. After a series of inter-governmental conferences and several rounds of negotiation the final version of the Treaty Establishing a Constitution for Europe was signed in Rome on 29 October 2004. It would transpire that easy part had been done. To enter into force the Treaty, like all previous European treaties, required to be ratified by each of the Member States in accordance with their own constitutional procedures. As with Maastricht, judicial challenges followed in a number of Member States, none of which were successful.[29] Initially, ratification went smoothly. By the spring of 2005 nine Member States had ratified the constitution, including Spain where the electorate had supported ratification by an overwhelming majority in a referendum.[30] Referendums were due, however, in nine more Member Dtates.[31] First, in May 2005, the French people rejected the constitution by a margin of 55:45 (on a 70 per cent turnout). A few weeks later, the Dutch public also rejected the constitution, this time by a margin of 62:38 (on a 62 per cent turnout). Despite ratification by Estonia, Latvia, Luxembourg (after a positive

---

[26] See para.10–38 below and *Kucukdeveci v Sweden* (C-555/07) [2010] E.C.R. I-365.

[27] The new members were: the Czech Republic, Estonia, Cyprus, Latvia, Lithuania, Hungary, Malta, Poland, Slovakia and Slovenia.

[28] At the time of writing there are six "candidate countries" for membership of the EU. "Candidate countries" are those countries that are in the process of integrating EU laws into their domestic law. This is a change from the initial accessions, which provided a post-accession period of alignment. All admissions since (and including) the 2004 group of 10 have followed this pre-alignment model. The current "candidate countries" are: Albania, Iceland, Montenegro, Serbia, the former Yugoslav Republic of Macedonia and Turkey. Two more countries are "potential candidate countries" meaning they have sought membership but do not yet fulfill the membership criteria. Those counties are Bosnia and Herzegovina and Kosovo.

[29] In the United Kingdom, an attempt was made to prevent a Bill being introduced to Parliament to give effect to the Treaty: *R. (on the application of Southall) v Secretary of State for Foreign and Commonwealth Affairs* [2003] EWCA Civ 1002; [2003] 3 C.M.L.R. 18. For references to challenges in other Member States, see Edward and Lane, *European Union Law* (2013), para.1.50.

[30] The other countries that had ratified the constitution were Austria, Belgium, Cyprus, Greece, Hungary, Italy, Lithuania and Slovenia.

[31] It perhaps betrays the political sensitivity of the constitution in a number of countries that so many referendums were held when only Ireland was obliged by its constitution to hold one. The Dutch referendum was the first such plebiscite in its history.

referendum result) and Malta,[32] the French and Dutch electorate had effectively killed the constitution. The remaining referendums that had been promised by Member States (including the United Kingdom) were postponed and it was accepted that the anticipated date for the constitution to come into force (1 November 2006) was now unachievable.

The end of the constitution did not mark the end of the desire to reform the Union. In 2007 the Council agreed to hold another intergovernmental conference with a view to producing a fresh treaty that would draw heavily on the aborted constitution. The product of that conference was the Lisbon Treaty which was signed on 13 December 2007.

The Lisbon Treaty

The Lisbon Treaty entered into force on 1 December 2009. Much of the content **10–06** of the failed constitution was reflected in the Treaty but some of the more inflammatory provisions were excluded, such as provision on the flag and anthem of the EU and an express declaration of the supremacy of EU law.[33] The most significant difference between the constitution and the Lisbon Treaty was the structure adopted. Whereas the constitution would have resulted in a single document, the Lisbon Treaty reverts to the traditional formula of amending the existing treaties, albeit extensively. Articles 1 and 2 of the Lisbon Treaty list the changes to the EU and EC Treaties.[34] What was previously the EC Treaty was now to be known as the Treaty on the Functioning of the European Union (TFEU) and the heavily amended Maastricht Treaty was styled the Treaty establishing the European Union (TEU). The key points to note include: the Union "replace[d] and succeed[ed] the European Community"[35]; the Union acquired legal personality[36]; the pillar structure that was created by the Maastricht Treaty was largely removed with most of the third pillar (co-operation on justice and home affairs) absorbed by the Community form and common foreign and security policy brought within the Union; and there is no hierarchy between the TEU and TFEU and together they are known as "the Treaties".[37]

Before turning to consider the institutions that form the EU and the legislative powers of the Union, a word on the terminology employed may be helpful. For ease of reference, the discussion that follows refers to "the EU" and "the Union" and should be taken to include the collective structures of the European Union. Similarly, the phrase "EU law" will be employed which should be taken to include that which falls within the jurisdiction of the Court of Justice of the European Union. Finally, reference to treaty articles will invariably be to the TFEU or the TEU as amended by the Treaty of Lisbon. I have endeavoured to

---

[32] The parliaments of Germany, Finland and Slovakia had also approved the constitution and it was awaiting formal ratification by the president of each of those countries (in the case of Germany and Slovakia, after judicial challenges had been resolved).

[33] Of course, leaving these provisions out of the Treaty did nothing to change the fact that each of them existed and still exist.

[34] The list of amendments ran to well over 100 pages when the Lisbon Treaty was published in the *Official Journal*; [2007] OJ C306/1.

[35] Article 1 TEU; thus ended the European Community but the EAEC remains in place and continues to be governed by its own Treaty.

[36] Article 47 TEU; this was significant in that it allowed the EU to enter international treaties in its own right.

[37] Article 1 TEU; art.1(2) TFEU. The consolidated versions of the Treaties were published in the *Official Journal* in March 2010: [2010] OJ C83.

update, where appropriate, references in any quotes from the case law of the court to the current treaty provision to avoid the need to work back through the previous treaties.

THE INSTITUTIONS OF THE EU

Introduction

10–07 Article 13 TEU provides that the institutions of the EU shall be: (a) the European Parliament; (b) the European Council; (c) the Council; (d) the European Commission; (e) the Court of Justice of the European Union; (f) the European Central Bank; and (g) the Court of Auditors. The Parliament and the Council are vested with the legislative (and budgetary) functions of the EU.[38] The European Council has no legislative functions; it is there to provide "the Union with the necessary impetus for its development".[39] The executive functions of the EU belong to the Commission,[40] which is responsible to the European Parliament[41] and judicial functions rest with the Court of Justice.[42] It can be seen, therefore, that the EU possesses the same key organs as a conventional nation state. Each of those will now be considered in more detail.[43]

Two new, and at the time controversial, roles were introduced by the Treaty: a permanent president of the European Council and a High Representative of the Union for Foreign Affairs and Security Policy. The latter caused particular concern as, read with the provisions contained in Title V of the TEU, the spectre of the EU in its own right becoming a more prominent actor on the global stage appeared on the horizon. Before turning to consider the institutions created by the TEU, a few words about the new President of the European Council (the President) and the High Representative for Foreign Affairs and Security Policy (the High Representative) are necessary.

10–08 Prior to the entry into force of the Lisbon Treaty, the presidency of the European Council rotated around the Member States, each taking its turn to hold the six month presidency. The President of the European Council is now elected by the European Council, by qualified majority voting, for a term of two and a half years.[44] That term is renewable once.[45] The holder of that office cannot hold a national office.[46] The President is responsible for chairing the European Council and they shall "drive forward its work"; ensuring the preparation and continuity of the work of the European Council; they must "endeavour to facilitate cohesion and consensus" within the European Council; and report to the European Parliament after each meeting of the European Council.[47] The

---

[38] Articles 14(1) and 16(1) TEU.
[39] Article 15(1) TEU.
[40] Article 17(1) TEU.
[41] Article 17(8) TEU.
[42] Article 19(1) TEU.
[43] The European Central Bank and the Court of Auditors, along with other EU institutions such as the European Investment Banks and the Committee of the Regions, will not be discuss in this book. For a discussion of those institutions, see Edward and Lane, *European Union Law* (2013) Ch.4.
[44] Article 15(5) TEU; art.246 TFEU provides that should the office be vacated during its term, the Presidency shall be filled in accordance with the provisions of art.17(7) TEU.
[45] Article 15(5) TEU; art.246 TFEU
[46] Article 15(6) TEU.
[47] Article 15(6) TEU.

President also has an obligation to ensure external representation of the EU on issues concerning its common foreign and security policy.[48] The first President of the European Council was former Belgium Prime Minister Herman van Rompuy and took office on the entry into force of the Lisbon Treaty on 1 December 2009.[49] His term was renewed in June 2011[50] and he was replaced by the current President, Donald Tusk of Poland, on 1 December 2014.

There was no equivalent to the High Representative before the Lisbon Treaty. The High Representative is appointed by the European Council, again using qualified majority voting, and with the agreement of the President of the Commission.[51] Unlike the President, her term of office is not prescribed. The High Representative is responsible for the conduct of the EU's common foreign and security policy.[52] In addition, she presides over the Foreign Affairs Council[53] and serves as one of the Vice Presidents of the Commission, with a particular responsibility for ensuring the consistency of the EU's external actions.[54] The first High Commissioner was Baroness Ashton, from the UK. She also assumed office on 1 December 2009[55] and was replaced by the Italian Federica Mogherini on 1 November 2014.

Neither of the roles have proved as controversial as perhaps feared.[56] The High Representative has allowed the EU to have a more co-ordinated approach to foreign relations but rarely, if at all, at the expense of the Member States' autonomy on the diplomatic scene. Equally, the very idea of a "President of Europe", as it was styled by Euro-sceptics, was too much for some. The first incumbent, however, has not had, nor sought, the profile that some feared he would.

The European Parliament

The European Parliament, based in Strasbourg, currently has 751 members (MEPs) directly elected by the electorate of the 28 Member States. Seventy three of those MEPs were returned by the UK.[57] The number of MEP's is capped at 751 (750 directly elected representatives plus the President) and no Member State shall have fewer than six MEPs or more than 96.[58] The allocation of seats amongst the Member States is determined by the European Council, acting unanimously and on the initiative, and with the consent, of the European Parliament.[59] The current allocation was determined by the European Council in

10–09

---

[48] Article 15(6) TEU.

[49] Decision 2009/879 electing the President of the European Council [2009] OJ L315/48.

[50] Decision 2012/151 electing the President of the European Council [2012] OJ L77/17.

[51] Article 18(1) TEU; art.246 TFEU provides that should the office be vacated, the High Representative shall be replaced in accordance with the art.18(1) TEU.

[52] Article 18(2) TEU.

[53] Article 18(3) TEU.

[54] Article 18(4) TEU.

[55] Decision 2009/950 appointing the High Representative of the Union of Foreign Affairs and Security Policy [2009] OJ L328/69

[56] For a more amusing articulation of some of the concerns about creating the role, see the then Shadow Foreign Secretary, William Hague's, speech in Parliament on 21 January 2008, in particular at *Hansard*, HC Vol.470, cols 1261–1262 (21 January 2008).

[57] Six MEPs are drawn from Scotland, three from Northern Ireland and four from Wales. The remaining 60 represent England.

[58] Article 14(2) TEU. The number temporarily increased to 766 with the accession of Croatia in 2013 but was readjusted in advance of the European Parliamentary elections in May 2014.

[59] Article 14(2) TEU.

June 2013.[60] Pursuant to that decision, Germany has the maximum allocation of 96 MEPs (representing one MEP for every 838,739 citizens).[61] Malta, the smallest Member State, received the minimum allocation of six MEPs (representing one MEP for every 70,227 citizens).[62] The European Council are required to revise that allocation "sufficiently far in advance of" the 2019–2024 European parliamentary term.[63]

Members of the European Parliament are elected for a five year term.[64] They must be elected by direct universal suffrage in a free and secret ballot[65] using a system of proportional representation.[66] As we saw in Ch.4, the United Kingdom employs the closed list system in Scotland and England and Wales whereas the single transferrable vote is used in Northern Ireland.[67] The majority of Member States function as a single constituency for the purposes of European elections. The United Kingdom, along with Belgium, France, Italy and Ireland, are the exception in subdividing into constituencies. For the purposes of elections to the European Parliament, the United Kingdom is divided into 12 multi-member regions, with each region allocated between three and 10 MEPs depending upon its population.[68] Members of the European Parliament now receive a salary that is fixed at 38.5 per cent of the salary of a judge of the Court of Justice.[69] Prior to that system coming into force in 2009, an MEP was paid the equivalent of a member of their home parliament. That led to wide disparities between the salaries paid to MEPs of different Member States.

Although candidates usually stand under the banner of their national party, once in Strasbourg they generally organise themselves according to pan-European groups. There are currently seven political groups in the European Parliament together with a small group of non-attached members.[70] These European political parties are required to "contribute to forming European political awareness and to expressing the will of the citizens of the Union".[71]

---

[60] Decision 2013/312 establishing the composition of the European Parliament [2013] OJ L181/57.

[61] Based on the Eurostat population figures for 1 January 2013 (which were the most recent at the time of writing) *http://ec.europa.eu/eurostat/web/popultion-demography-migration-projections/population-data/main-tables* [Accessed 11 August 2015].

[62] Cyprus, Estonia and Luxembourg also received the minimum allocation, with their MEP-to-citizens ratio being 1 to 144,313, 220,802 and 89,507, respectively

[63] Decision 2013/312 establishing the composition of the European Parliament [2013] OJ L181/57 art.4.

[64] Article 14(3) TEU.

[65] Article 14(3) TEU.

[66] Decision 2002/772 amending the Act concerning the election of the representatives of the European Parliament by direct universal suffrage, annexed to Decision 76/787/ECSC, EEC, Euratom [2002] OJ L283/1; the decision further requires that either a list system is employed or the single transferrable vote system. In this context, see also art.223(1) TFEU.

[67] See para.4–10, above; the United Kingdom is one of nine Member States that employs the closed list system (along with Estonia, France, Germany, Greece, Hungary, Portugal, Romania and Spain). Malta and Ireland use the single transferrable vote system employed in Northern Ireland. The remaining Member States use a form of the open list system.

[68] Scotland, Northern Ireland and Wales each form a separate region. England is then divided into nine regions. The smallest regions are Northern Ireland and the North East (both with three MEPs). The South East is the largest region, returning 10 MEPs.

[69] Decision 2005/684 adopting the Statute for Members of the European Parliament [2005] OJ L262/1, art.10. At the time of writing this was approximately €7,950 per month.

[70] The current groupings, and their membership, can be found on the European Parliament's website, *http://www.elections2014.eu/en/european-political-parties* [Accessed 10 June 2015].

[71] Article 10(4) TEU.

European political parties are subject to regulations adopted by the European Parliament and the Council, acting in accordance with the ordinary legislative procedure.[72] To be recognised as a European political party, the party must meet the following conditions: it must have legal personality in the Member State in which its seat is located; it must be represented in one quarter of the Member States, either by MEPs or in the national or regional parliaments of the Member States; it must conform with the founding principles of the EU; and it must have either participated in elections to the European Parliament or expressed a desire to do so.[73]

The European Parliament exists to ensure that EU citizens are directly **10–10** represented at EU level.[74] As we have seen, its powers have expanded, in particular following the introduction of direct elections. The Parliament has the power to adopt its own rules and procedures[75] and, unless otherwise provided for in the treaties, acts by simple majority of the votes cast.[76] The European Parliament performs five main functions. First, as explained below, it plays a role in the appointment, and then holding to account, of the Commission.[77] So far as the appointment of the Commission is concerned, however, that role is limited to approval *en masse* of the nominees. The inability to reject individual candidates leaves the Parliament with a fairly blunt axe. Secondly, the European Parliament plays an important role in relation to the EU budget. Responsibility for the EU budget is shared between the Parliament, the Council and the Commission.[78] Preparation of the EU budget is a complex process and beyond the scope of this book. For present purposes, it is sufficient to note that the draft budget must be sent to the Parliament no later than 1 October in the year before it is to be implemented.[79] The Parliament then has 42 days to approve the budget or adopt amendments to the budget.[80] If the Parliament does neither, the budget is deemed to have been adopted.[81] Where amendments are proposed, a "Conciliation Committee", which has the task of reaching agreement on a joint text, is convened by the President of the Council and the President of the European Parliament.[82] The conciliation committee has 21 days in which to complete its task before returning the draft budget to both the Council and the Parliament.[83] The European Parliament then has the final say on the draft budget: if the Parliament, acting by a majority of its members, rejects the joint text of the draft budget, the Commission is required to submit a new draft budget.[84] If the budget is approved by the Parliament but rejected by the Council, the Parliament can, within 14 days of the Council's rejection of the joint text, approve the

---

[72] Article 224 TFEU.
[73] Regulation 2004/2003 on the regulations governing political parties at European level and the rules regarding their funding [2003] OJ L297/1 (as amended by Regulation 1524/2007 amending Regulation (EC) No 2004/2003 on the regulations governing political parties at European level and the rules regarding their funding [2007] OJ L343/5), art.3.
[74] Article 10(2) TEU.
[75] Article 232 TFEU.
[76] Article 231 TFEU.
[77] See para.10–16, above.
[78] Article 314 TFEU.
[79] Article 314(3) TFEU.
[80] Article 314(4) TFEU.
[81] Article 314(4)(b) TFEU.
[82] Article 314(4)(c) and (5) TFEU.
[83] Article 314(4)(c) and (5) TFEU.
[84] Article 314(7)(b) and (c) TFEU.

Parliament's amendments to the budget and adopt the budget. To do this, the Parliament must act by a majority of its component members and three-fifth of the votes cast.[85] As a result of those complex procedures, which have only been briefly outlined, the important role of the European Parliament in determining and approving the EU budget should be obvious.

The third important function of the European Parliament relates to its general supervisory powers. The Commission is responsible to the Parliament.[86] The Parliament may, at the request of a quarter of its component members, set up a temporary committee of inquiry to investigate alleged contraventions or malad-ministration in the implementation of EU law.[87] The European Parliament can also receive petitions, addressing any matter within the EU fields, from any citizen of the EU or any natural or legal person residing or having its registered office in a Member State.[88] An ombudsman, empowered to receive complaints from any citizen of the EU or any natural or legal person residing or having its registered office in a Member State, concerning allegations of maladministration in the activities of the EU institutions, bodies, offices or agencies (with the exception of the Court of Justice acting in its judicial capacity), shall also be elected by the European Parliament.[89] The ombudsman is elected following each European Parliamentary election and holds office for the duration of the Parliament's term.[90] They are eligible for re-election.[91]

Fourthly, the European Parliament is required to consent to a number of EU decisions in areas of constitutional or political importance. These areas include: composition of, and method of election to, the European Parliament[92]; the conclusion by the EU of specified categories of agreements with third countries or international organisations[93]; the accession of new Member States[94]; the secession of existing Member States[95]; and a number of specific policies in relation to judicial co-operation in criminal matters.[96] Fifth, and finally, the European Parliament now plays an important role in the passage of EU legislation. The legislative processes are discussed below.[97]

10–11   As will be apparent from that brief overview of the role and functions of the European Parliament, it has come a long way from its beginnings as an assembly of delegates sent by the Member States' respective parliaments. But a lot of work

---

[85] Article 314(d) TFEU.
[86] Article 17(8) TEU.
[87] Article 226 TFEU.
[88] Article 227 TFEU.
[89] Article 228(1) TFEU.
[90] Article 228(2) TFEU.
[91] Article 228(2) TFEU.
[92] Article 14(2) TEU and art.223 TFEU, respectively.
[93] Article 218(6) TFEU; in particular the European Parliament had to consent to the EU's accession to the European Convention on Human Rights (art.218(6)(a)(ii) TFEU) on which see para. 12–38.
[94] Article 49 TEU.
[95] Article 50 TEU; although quite what would happen if the rest of the secession process had been successfully navigated only for the European Parliament to refuse to consent is another matter given the right of Member States to withdraw from the EU "in accordance with its own constitutional requirements".
[96] For example, the formation of a European Public Prosecutors Office (art.86 TFEU) or the definition of certain criminal offences (art.83 TFEU).
[97] See paras 12–31—12–33.

still has to be done. The European Parliament exists to afford citizens of the EU democratic representation at EU level.[98] Average turnout across the EU at the most recent elections in 2014 was only 42.61 per cent.[99] That represents a continuation of the year-on-year decline in turnout at European elections since direct elections were first introduced (turnout had been 42.97 per cent in 2009).[100] Much still has to be done to connect the EU citizenry with their Parliament.

The European Council

The European Council has met regularly since the 1970s but with the entry into force of the Lisbon Treaty it was formally recognised by the treaties.[101] The European Council (which must be distinguished from "the Council", which is discussed below) consists of the Heads of State, or of Government, of the Member States,[102] together with the President of the European Council[103] and the President of the Commission.[104] Meetings of the European Council have more colloquially been referred as "summit meetings" or "European summits". The European Council has no legislative function (unlike "the Council") but exists to "provide the Union with the necessary impetus for development" and to set the general political direction and priorities.[105] The European Council is required to meet twice every six months, or when the President convenes a special meeting.[106] Decisions of the European Council should be taken by consensus, unless the treaties require otherwise.[107] The President is required to report to the European Parliament after each meeting of the European Council.[108] Despite having no legislative function, the European Council has proved to be a useful forum for bringing the leaders of the Member States together on a regular basis. Discussion is not necessarily restricted to areas of EU competence and the European Council provides a forum for the Member States to discuss areas of mutual concern and matters that are subject to intergovernmental co-operation. Decisions taken in the European Council are taken by the respective leaders in

10–12

---

[98] Article 10(2) TEU.
[99] The turnout figures are available on the European Parliament's website at *http://www. europarl.europa.eu/elections2014-results/en/election-results-2014/html* [Accessed 11 August 2015]. It is worth bearing in mind that in four Member States, voting is compulsory which results in higher turnout figures. The Member States are Belgium, Luxembourg, Greece and Cyprus.
[100] See *http://www.europarl.europa.eu/elections2014-results/en/turnout.html* [Accessed 11 August 2015]. Turnout in Slovakia was a mere 13% and was under 25% in another three Member States (Czech Republic, Poland and Slovenia).
[101] Article 13(1) TEU.
[102] For example, the UK would be represented by the Head of Government, the Prime Minister, as opposed to the Head of State, the Queen. France, however, would be represented by her President, the Head of State. Each Head of State/Government can be assisted by a Minister who may attend with them (art.15(3) TEU).
[103] See para.12–08 above.
[104] Article 15(2) TEU.
[105] Article 15(1) TEU.
[106] Article 15(3) TEU.
[107] Article 15(4) TEU. Accordingly, a vote in the European Council is rare. The UK Prime Minister (David Cameron) forced a vote over the appointment of the new Commission President in June 2014. He lost the vote 26:2. The Prime Minister's report to Parliament following the European Council meeting can be found at: *Hansard*, HC Vol.583, cols 559–601 (30 June 2014).
[108] Article 15(6)(d) TEU.

their capacity as representatives of the Member States. Any decision taken, therefore, is a decision of the Member States (and not of the Council). As a result, such decisions are immune from judicial review before the Court of Justice.[109]

The Council

10–13 The Council is a different creature and must be differentiated from the European Council. The Council, jointly with the European Parliament, is responsible for exercising the EU's legislative and budgetary functions.[110] The Council consists of representatives of each Member State, at ministerial level, who have the authority to commit the government of their Member State and to cast its vote.[111] The High Representative chairs the Council when it meets to discuss foreign affairs, otherwise the presidency of the Council is held by the Member States on the basis of equal rotation.[112] Decision 2009/881 provides that the presidency shall be held by groups of three Member States for 18 months.[113] Within the trio, each Member State shall hold the presidency for six months.[114] The grouping of Member States into trios for the purposes of the Presidency of the Council was developed to allow enhanced continuity and reflected an informal practice that had begun in early 2007. The order in which the Member States hold the presidency is determined by the European Council and by qualified majority.[115] The Council meets in different configurations depending upon the business to be discussed.[116] The configurations are determined by the European Council and by qualified majority.[117] There are currently 10 configurations of the Council: general affairs; foreign affairs; economic and financial affairs (including budget); justice and home affairs (including civil protection); employment, social policy, health and consumer affairs; competitiveness (internal market, industry, research and space); transport, telecommunications and energy; agriculture and fisheries; environment; and education, youth culture and sport (including audiovisual

---

[109] *European Parliament v Council of Ministers of the European Communities* (C181/91 and C248/91) [1993] E.C.R. I-3685; [1994] 3 C.M.L.R. 317 at [12].

[110] Article 16(1) TEU.

[111] Article 16(2) TEU. Not every Member State has to be represented at every meeting of the Council. A Member State can appoint another Member State as a proxy to vote on its behalf. However, a Member State cannot exercise more than one proxy (art.239 TFEU; Rules of Procedure of the Council arts 5 and 11).

[112] Article 16(9) TEU.

[113] Decision 2009/881 on the exercise of the Presidency of the Council [2009] OJ L315/50 art.1(1) and Annex 1, although the annex was misprinted originally and the correct version was subsequently published at [2009] OJ L344/56.

[114] Decision 2009/881 on the exercise of the Presidency of the Council art.1(2).

[115] Article 236 TFEU; the current order was determined by Decision 2007/5 determining the order in which the office of President of the Council shall be held [2007] OJ L1/11, which determines the order until 30 June 2020. The rotation of the presidency for the period from 1 July 2020 must be determined before 1 July 2017: Decision 2009/908 laying down measures for the implementation of the European Council Decision on the exercise of the Presidency of the Council, and on the chairmanship of preparatory bodies of the Council [2009] OJ L322/28, art.3. The UK will next hold the presidency between July and December 2017, along with Estonia and Bulgaria for the period July 2017 to December 2018. The current holder of the presidency (January to June 2015) is Latvia. The order of future presidencies can be found on the Council website, *http:// www.consilium.europa.eu/council/what-is-the-presidency?lang=en* [Accessed 10 June 2015].

[116] Article 16(6) TEU.

[117] Article 236 TFEU.

matters).[118] The Council is, however, a single entity despite the configurations structure. Accordingly, legislative measures adopted by the Council make no mention of the specific configuration that adopted the measure. The general affairs council deals with issues that cross a number of configurations and is responsible for ensuring consistency across the work of the other configurations.[119] The foreign affairs council is slightly different from the other configurations. It is responsible for elaborating, and ensuring consistency in, the EU's external action.[120] It is chaired not by the Member State holding the rotating presidency but by the High Commissioner.[121] The general affairs and foreign affairs, together with the economic and financial affairs council meet monthly. The remaining councils meet from time to time.

The Council is assisted in its work by a Committee of the Permanent Representatives of the Member States (more commonly referred to as "COREPER").[122] Permanent Representatives perform a function akin to an ambassador. The Committee of the Permanent Representatives of the Member States is responsible for preparing the work for all Council meetings and for ensuring the central rules and principles of the EU are observed.[123] Like the Council, the Committee of the Permanent Representatives of the Member States is chaired by the Permanent Representative (or their deputy) of the Member State that holds the presidency of the Council, save for the political and security committee, which is chaired be a representative of the High Representative.[124] The Committee of the Permanent Representatives of the Member States can set up, or approve, subcommittees or working parties to assist it with a view to carrying out certain preparatory work or studies as defined in advance.[125] In practice, these meetings, which are normally attended by civil servants from the appropriate field, are invaluable in assisting the Council in performing its core functions.

Voting in the Council is a complicated business. The Council can, in some **10–14** areas, act by simple majority and in some other areas it must act unanimously.[126] The default rule, however, is that the Council can act by qualified majority.[127] Qualified majority voting weights each Member States' vote by reference to their population. Determining the weightings is always a contentious matter. Since the accession of Croatia there have been 352 votes in the Council. France, Germany, Italy and the United Kingdom each have 29 votes. Malta has the fewest votes with three. A majority of Member States must be present to form a quorum.[128]

---

[118] That configuration was determined by Decision 2009/878 establishing the list of Council configurations in addition to those referred to in the second and third subparagraphs of Article 16(6) of the Treaty on European Union [2009] OJ L315/46, as amended by Decision 2010/594 amending the list of Council configurations [2010] OJ L263/12. Further details of the work of the different configurations can be found at *http://www.consilium.europa.eu/council/council-configurations?lang=en* [Accessed 10 June 2015].

[119] Article 16(6) TEU.

[120] Article 16(6) TEU.

[121] Article 18(3) TEU.

[122] Article 16(7) TEU; art.240(1) TFEU.

[123] Article 240(1) TFEU; Rules of Procedure of the Council art.19(1).

[124] Rules of Procedure of the Council art.19(4).

[125] Rules of Procedure of the Council art.19(3).

[126] An abstention, or an absence, does not prevent the Council acting unanimously: art.238(4) TFEU.

[127] Article 16(3) TEU. Unlike votes requiring unanimity, an abstention or absence can affect the outcome as it is effectively a "no" vote.

[128] Rules of Procedure of the Council art.11(4).

The operation of the qualified majority voting system was altered significantly by the Lisbon Treaty. At present, and until 1 April 2017, the Council operates under transitional arrangements.[129]

Until 31 October 2014, qualified majority voting required 260 votes, representing at least half of the Member States, to be cast in favour for the Council to adopt a measure that had been proposed by the Commission (as was normally the case).[130] The requirement for a "double majority" (votes cast and 50 per cent of the Member States) is to prevent the small Member States being overwhelmed by the larger members.[131] Where the Council acts otherwise then on the proposal of the Commission, in addition to reaching 260 votes two-thirds of the Member States must in favour.[132] Under either system, where an act is adopted by qualified majority voting, a Member State may request that a check is made to ensure that the qualified majority represents at least 62 per cent of the total population of the EU. If it does not, the measure is not adopted.[133] Where not all Member States participate in a vote (for example, where one or more of the Member States benefits from an opt-out), 55 per cent of the Member States participating in the vote, representing not less than 65 per cent of the population of the participating Member States, constitutes the necessary threshold to adopt a measure.[134]

Since 1 November 2014 a qualified majority has been defined as

> "at least 55% of the members of the Council, comprising at least fifteen of them and representing Member States comprising at least 65% of the population of the Union".[135]

A "blocking minority" must consist of at least four Member States otherwise a qualified majority shall be deemed to have been achieved.[136] Where not all Member States participate in a vote, the pre-November 1, 2014 rules for such situations continue to apply, other than where the Council does not act on a proposal from either the Commission or the High Representative, in which case the required majority is 72 per cent of the Member States participating in the vote, representing not less than 65 per cent of the population of the participating Member States.[137] Until 31 March 2017, a Member State can request that a decision be adopted in accordance with the pre-November 1, 2014 qualified majority voting system.[138] After 1 April 2017, there cannot be recourse to the previous regime.

---

[129] The transitional arrangements are prescribed in Protocol (No.36) on Transitional Provisions, which, for the rest of this section, is referred to as "the Protocol". Transitional arrangements are authorised by art.16(5) TEU.

[130] Article 3(3) of the Protocol, as amended by art.20 of the Croatian Accession Treaty. Prior to the accession of Croatia, 255 votes were required (out of a total of 345). The Croation Accession Treaty is availale at [2012] OJ L112/10.

[131] Two hundred and sixty votes could be achieved by only 13 Member States voting together (if the 12 with the largest allocation of votes all came together with the support of one other Member State).

[132] Article 3(3) of the Protocol, as amended by art.20 of the Croatian Accession Treaty.

[133] Article 3(3) of the Protocol, as amended by art.20 of the Croatian Accession Treaty.

[134] Article 3(4) of the Protocol.

[135] Article 16(4) TEU.

[136] Article 16(4) TEU.

[137] Article 238(3) TFEU.

[138] Article 3(2) of the Protocol.

The Commission

It is important to start by noting what the Commission is not. It is not the civil **10–15** service of the EU. The Commission has a civil service that supports it work. But so too does the Council and the Parliament. The Commission, based in Brussels, is more than simply the executive arm of the EU. The Commission is charged with promoting the general interest of the EU and taking appropriate initiatives to that end.[139] In particular, the Commission is responsible for: ensuring compliance with the treaties and measures adopted pursuant to them; overseeing the application of EU law under the control of the Court of Justice; executing the budget and managing programmes; and exercising co-ordinating, executive and management functions as laid down in the treaties.[140] In addition, the Commission has a significant legislative function. It alone has the power to initiate EU legislation under the ordinary legislative process.[141] Given the importance of this institution, and the vast power it possesses under the treaties, it is critical to an understanding of how the EU functions to understand how the Commission operates.

The Commission consists of a President and a number of Commissioners. **10–16** These are independent of the Member States.[142] The TEU provides that from 1 November 2014, the number of Commissioners (including the Commission President[143] and the High Representative) should correspond to two-thirds of the number of Member States, unless the European Council, acting unanimously, varies that number.[144] Prior to that, there was one Commissioner from each Member State.[145] The growth of the EU was believed to have rendered that model unworkable. Henceforth, Commissioners were to be chosen from among the nationals of Member States

"on the basis of a system of strictly equal rotation between Member States, reflecting the demographic and geographical range of all the member states".[146]

However, the European Council has departed from that rule. Following the Irish rejection of the Lisbon Treaty, and in response to concerns about departing from the one Commissioner per Member State approach, a commitment was given by the European Council to ensure that each Member State would continue to send a Commissioner.[147] Effect was given to that commitment in May 2013, the result

---

[139] Article 17(1) TEU.

[140] Article 17(1) TEU.

[141] Article 17(2) TEU; art.289(1) TFEU.

[142] Article 245 TFEU.

[143] This is the third "President" we have encountered. In an attempt to try to minimise confusion with the President of the European Council (Mr van Rompuy) and the President of the Council (currently Latvia), this President will be referred to as the "Commission President" throughout.

[144] Article 17(5) TEU.

[145] Article 17(4) TEU. Prior to 2004, the five largest Member States (France, Germany, Italy, Spain and the UK) each nominated two commissioners with one being nominated by each of the remaining Member States.

[146] Article 17(5) TEU.

[147] That commitment was given at a meeting of the European Council on 11–12 December 2009. See the note issued of the conclusions of that meeting, *http://consilium.europa.eu/uedocs/cms_data/docs/pressdata/en/ec/104692.pdf* [Accessed 10 June 2015].

of which is that the one Commissioner, one Member State approach continues to apply.[148]

The Commission President is responsible for laying down guidelines within which the Commission is to work, determining the internal organisation of the Commission and appointing the Vice Presidents of the Commission (other than the High Representative, who holds office as a Vice President of the Commission ex officio).[149] They can also require the resignation of a Commissioner.[150] The appointment of the Commission President previously required the unanimous agreement of the Member States. The Lisbon Treaty amended that procedure so as to remove the right of a Member State to veto a nominee for the position.[151] The European Council must now, acting by qualified majority, propose to the European Parliament a candidate for the position of Commission President. The European Parliament may then elect, by a majority of its component members, that nominee. If the nominee does not achieve sufficient votes in the Parliament, the European Council, again acting by qualified majority, shall propose a new candidate to the Parliament.[152] Commissioners are then nominated by the Council, "by common accord" with the President-elect.[153] Nominees are selected on the basis of suggestions made by the Member States. A nominee, whose independence shall be beyond doubt, should be chosen on the ground of their general competence and European commitment.[154] The proposed Commissioners, together with the (European Council) President and the High Representative, shall, as a collective, be subject to a vote of consent by the European Parliament.[155] If the Parliament consents, the Commissioners are then appointed by the European Council, acting by qualified majority.[156] Once appointed, the Commission's term of office is five years.[157] A Commissioner can be "compulsorily retired" by the Court of Justice, on application by either the Council or the Commission, where the Commissioner no longer fulfils the conditions required for the performance of their duties or has been guilty of serious misconduct.[158]

The Commission acts by a simple majority of its members.[159] It is collegiate and dissent is not formally recorded.[160] The President allocates each Commissioner with responsibility for one or more areas of EU activity. The Commission is divided into departments, known as directorates-general, and of which there are currently 33. Each directorate-general is responsible for a different area of EU

---

[148] Decision 2013/272 concerning the number of members of the European Commission [2013] OJ L165/98 art.1. In terms of art.3, the European Council must review the position either in advance of the appointment of the first Commission following the accession of the thirtieth member state or following the appointment of the current Commission.

[149] Article 17(6) TEU.

[150] Article 17(6) TEU. They cannot require the High Representative to resign but they can trigger the process by which she may be removed. The High Commissioner may only be removed by the European Council, acting by qualified majority.

[151] As the UK Prime Minister learned to his cost in June 2014 when he was unable to prevent the nomination of former Luxembourg Prime Minister Jean Claude Juncker, see fn.107, above

[152] Article 17(7) TEU.

[153] Article 17(7) TEU.

[154] Article 17(3) TEU.

[155] Article 17(7) TEU.

[156] Article 17(7) TEU.

[157] Article 17(3) TEU.

[158] Article 247 TFEU.

[159] Article 250 TFEU.

[160] Article 17(6)(b) TEU.

policy, for example climate change, energy, home affairs or trade. The portfolios of the directorates-general do not correspond exactly to the portfolios of the Commissioners and as will be obvious from the fact that there are 33 DGs and only 28 Commissioners, one Commissioner may have responsibility for more than one directorate-general. Each directorate-general is divided into directorates, which are in turn divided into units. A director-general (akin to a permanent secretary in Whitehall) is responsible for each directorate-general and they work closely with the Commissioner responsible for the directorate-general.

Evidently, the Commission has a very broad range of responsibilities. With **10–17** that comes significant power. The Commission plays a central role in the EU legislative process, which is considered in more detail below. In addition to its legislative role, the Commission exercises the executive functions of the EU. It has significant powers in relation to the adoption of subordinate legislation.[161] The Commission oversees the application of EU law and has the power to take enforcement action against Member States where they fail to comply with an EU obligation that is incumbent upon them.[162] The Commission also has the power to take enforcement action against legal or other persons, most notably in the sphere of competition law.[163] Finally, the Commission represents the EU at a number of different international organisations, in particular the World Trade Organisation.

The Commission is accountable to the European Parliament. We have already seen the role played by the Parliament in relation to the appointment of the Commission. The Parliament may also censure the Commission. A motion of censure requires a two-third majority of the votes cast, representing a majority of the component members of the European Parliament, to pass. Where such a motion is passed, the Commission, as a whole (including the High Representative), must resign.[164] Just as the Parliament's role in the appointment of the Commission is to support or reject the proposed Commissioners as a block, likewise the power to censure results in the removal of all of the Commissioners. It is therefore a fairly blunt instrument. The role of the European Parliament would be much enhanced if it had the option simply to censure an individual Commissioner.[165] Finally, the Commission is required to respond to questions put by the Parliament and its members.[166] The Commission has the right to attend all meetings of the Parliament and, at its request, to be heard.[167] This gives the Commission the opportunity to explain, or give an insight into, its thinking on legislative initiatives and timescales or other aspects of the EU law.

---

[161] These procedures are explained more fully in Edward and Lane, *European Union Law* (2013) paras 3.24–3.29.

[162] Article 258 TFEU. In the first instance, the Commission must deliver to the Member State concerned a "reasoned opinion" and give the state an opportunity to submit its observations. If the Member State does not comply with the opinion within the period prescribed by the Commission, the Commission is empowered to bring the matter before the Court of Justice.

[163] For an explanation of the Commission's enforcement powers in the sphere of competition law, see Edward and Lane, *European Union Law* (2013), paras 13.89–13.108.

[164] Article 234 TFEU. The censured Commission remain in office until their replacements have been appointed.

[165] That said, the Parliament did play a central role in bringing about the resignation of the Santer Commission in March 1999. See, generally, V. Mehde, "Responsibility and Accountability in the European Commission" (2003) 40 C.M.L. Rev. 423.

[166] Article 230 TFEU.

[167] Article 230 TFEU.

The Court of Justice of the European Union

10–18 Having formed the Commission with executive authority and rule making powers, it was necessary to have a judicial mechanism to review the exercise of those powers. The formation of the Court of Justice in the founding Treaties was therefore the necessary corollary of the Commission. What is now the Court of Justice of the European Union has evolved as the Communities developed and the Union was formed. Under the Lisbon Treaty, the Court of Justice of the European Union is charged with "ensur[ing] that in the interpretation and application of the Treaties the law is observed".[168] The court, in fact, comprises of three separate courts: the Court of Justice; the General Court; and the Civil Service Tribunal. We will consider each in turn.

The Court of Justice

10–19 The Court of Justice now comprises of 28 judges (one per Member State)[169] who are "assisted" by nine advocates general.[170] Judges and advocates general must be a person whose independence is beyond doubt, who possess the qualifications for appointment to the highest judicial offices in their respective countries or be jurisconsult of recognised competence.[171] Appointment is for a (renewable) six year term.[172] To avoid the mass replacement of the court and facilitate continuity in the membership of the court, the term of office of half of the judges and advocates general falls for renewal every three years.[173] Nominations for the court (which are usually made by the Member States) are now reviewed by a panel that produces a non-binding opinion on the suitability of the nominee for the office of judge or advocate general.[174] The panel was introduced by the Lisbon Treaty and consists of seven members, who are drawn from the Court of Justice, the General Court, Member States' supreme courts and lawyers of recognised competence. One of the members of the panel is proposed by the European Parliament. Members of the panel hold office for four years, a term that is renewable once.[175] Having received the opinion of the panel, judges and advocates general are appointed by "common accord" of the governments of the Member States.[176] A judge may only be removed from office if the unanimous opinion of the judges and the advocates general is that they no longer fulfil the

---

[168] Article 19(1) TEU.
[169] Article 19(2) TEU.
[170] Article 19(2) TEU. Article 252 TFEU prescribes that there be eight advocates general but the Council, acting unanimously, is given the power to increase that number. They did so by Decision 2013/336 increasing the number of Advocates-General of the Court of Justice of the European Union [2013] OJ L179/92 with the result that the number of advocates general increased to nine with effect from 1 July 2013 and shall increase to 11 from 7 October 2015.
[171] Article 19(2) TEU; art.253 TFEU.
[172] Article 19(2) TEU; art.253 TFEU.
[173] Article 253 TFEU; Statute of the Court of Justice art.9.
[174] Article 255 TFEU.
[175] Decision 2010/124 relating to the operating rules of the panel provided for in art.255 of the Treaty on the Functioning of the European Union [2010] OJ L50/18, which adopts the panel's rules of procedure. Decision 2010/125 appointing the members of the panel provided for in art.255 of the Treaty on the Functioning of the European Union [2010] OJ L50/20 appointed the initial panel, which include UK Supreme Court Justice Lord Mance. Lord Mance was one of three members of the original panel reappointed for a second term: Decision 2014/76 appointing the members of the panel provided for in art.255 of the Treaty on the Functioning of the European Union [2014] OJ L41/18.
[176] Article 19(2) TEU; art.253 TFEU.

requisite conditions or meet the obligations of their office.[177] The judges of the court elect one of their number to serve as the president of the court for a term of three years.[178] Since 2012, a vice president has also been elected and they also serve a three year term.[179]

The court sits in three different formations. First, the court divides itself into a number of chambers. Each chamber consists of either three or five judges and each chamber is chaired by a president. The chamber presidents are elected by the judges from within their number. Presidents of the five-judge chambers are elected for three years. Presidents of the three-judge chambers are elected annually.[180] Secondly, the court may convene as the "Grand Chamber". The Grand Chamber comprises of 15 judges and is presided over by the President of the Court. It also includes the Vice President of the Court and three presidents of chambers of five judges. The court must sit as the Grand Chamber where a Member State or an EU institution that is a party to the case so requests.[181] Finally, the court may sit as the full court, which requires not less than 17 judges to be present. The court shall convene as the full court when, having heard the advocate general, the case is considered to be of exceptional importance or when hearing specified case under the treaties.[182] Decisions of the court are only valid when an uneven number of judges sit in the deliberations on the case.[183] The quorum of a chamber (whether a three judge or a five judge chamber) is three; the quorum of the Grand Chamber is 11; and the quorum of the full court is 17.[184] Whatever the formation, the court only ever delivers a single judgment of the court; there are no dissenting or concurring opinions. Each case that is received by the court is assigned to a judge who is the "judge-rapporteur". They prepare a preliminary report and on the basis of that report the court, at a general meeting, determines which formation of the court should hear the case.

Each case is also assigned an advocate general. The advocates general are members of the court, who sit on the bench with the judges during oral hearings. The function of the advocate general is to "assist" the court.[185] After the oral hearing, the advocate general ordinarily prepares an "opinion" which is delivered in open court (and usually printed along with the report of the eventual judgment).[186] This is a "reasoned submission" on the case and is ordinarily more discursive than the judgment produced by the court (no doubt as a result of the necessary compromises made in drafting a single judgment of the court). Consequentially, although not an authoritative statement of EU law, an advocate

---

[177] Statute of the Court of Justice art.6; the same rule is applied to advocates general by art.8 of the Statute.

[178] Article 253 TFEU.

[179] Statute of the Court of Justice art.9a. The functions of the Vice President are set out in Decision 2012/671 concerning the judicial functions of the Vice-President of the Court [2012] OJ L300/47.

[180] Statute of the Court of Justice art.16.

[181] Statute of the Court of Justice art.16.

[182] Statute of the Court of Justice art.16. The Statute of the Court of Justice art.16 currently requires the court to sit as the full court for cases brought under arts 228(2) (removal of the ombudsman), 245(2) and 247 (removal of a commissioner) and 286(6) (removal of a member of the Court of Auditors).

[183] Statute of the Court of Justice art.17.

[184] Statute of the Court of Justice art.17.

[185] Article 19(2) TEU.

[186] It is no longer necessary for the court to receive an opinion from the Advocate General before giving judgment: art.252 TFEU

general's opinion can be helpful in understanding the judgment of the court and they can assist the development of EU law more generally.

10–20   In terms of art.19(3) TEU, the role of the Court of Justice is three-fold: to rule on actions brought by a Member State, an institution or a natural or legal person; to give preliminary rulings where requested to do so by the national courts of Member States; and to rule in other cases provided for in the treaties. Scratch below the surface and matters become more complicated than they first appear. The Court of Justice has made it clear that the EU is based on the rule of law and as such the court is entitled to review, when asked to do so, whether any EU measure conforms with the treaties and accordingly, where necessary, a natural or legal person may bring a direct action before the court.[187] There are essentially four categories of action that can be brought before the Court of Justice: direct actions, appeals,[188] preliminary references under art.267 TFEU and opinions. The details of these various forms of actions are beyond the scope of this work.[189] It is, however, appropriate to say a few words about the preliminary reference system, touching as it does on the relationship between the Court of Justice and national courts.

Article 267 TFEU provides:

> "The Court of Justice of the European Union shall have jurisdiction to give preliminary rulings concerning: (a) the interpretation of the Treaties; (b) the validity and interpretation of acts of the institutions, bodies, offices or agencies of the Union; Where such a question is raised before any court or tribunal of a Member State, that court or tribunal may, if it considers that a decision on the question is necessary to enable it to give judgment, request the Court to give a ruling thereon.
>
> Where any such question is raised in a case pending before a court or tribunal of a Member State against whose decision there is no judicial remedy under national law, that court or tribunal shall bring the matter before the Court."

The majority of cases that come before the Court of Justice (in 2013, 450 out of 699)[190] arrive by means of an art.267 reference. The reference procedure is not an appeal and while the parties to an action can request that the national court make a reference, it is ultimately a matter for the discretion of that court.[191] It is important to note the two functions that an art.267 reference can perform. First, the national court can request an opinion on the interpretation of EU law. This is an important mechanism by which the Court of Justice can ensure a uniform

---

[187] *Parti Ecologiste Les Verts v European Parliament* (294/83) [1986] E.C.R. 1339; [1987] 2 C.M.L.R. 343 at [23].

[188] That is to say appeals from the General Court. There is no right of appeal to the Court of Justice from any national court. This can be contrasted with the European Court of Human Rights which allows an individual to make an application provided they have exhausted their domestic remedies (European Convention on Human Rights art.35).

[189] See: Edward and Lane, *European Union Law* (2013) paras 5.30–5.154; O'Neill, *EU Law for UK Lawyers* (2011), Chs 3 (preliminary references) and 4 (direct actions).

[190] Court of Justice of the European Union, *2013 Annual Report of the Court of Justice of the European Union* (Court of Justice of the European Union, 2014) p.84; an increase from 302 references in 2009.

[191] *Willy Kempter KG v Hauptzollamt Hamburg-Jonas* (C-2/06) [2008] E.C.R. I-411 at [41].

interpretation of EU law throughout the Union.[192] Secondly, the national court can request an opinion from the Court of Justice on the validity of an act of an EU institution or body. Given the restrictive rules on standing which limit the ability of individuals to challenge the validity of acts of the EU institutions,[193] this limb of the art.267 reference procedure provides an important mechanism by which the validity of such acts can be judicially reviewed.

The point may be obvious but it bears mentioning: the Court of Justice can only rule on questions of EU law. It cannot interpret national law,[194] it cannot advise if national law is compatible with EU law[195] and it cannot annul, set aside or strike down national law.[196] The rules of the various national courts prescribe the procedure for that court referring a question to the Court of Justice.[197] But the question arises: when should a national court refer a question to the Court of Justice? Article 267 differentiates between national courts from which lies an appeal to a higher national court (these courts "*may*" refer a question) whereas a national court of last resort "*shall*" refer a question.[198] Practice obviously varies throughout the Member States: UK courts had, at the end of 2013, referred 561 cases since the UK joined what was then the EEC whereas Austria, who only joined in 1995, has referred 429 cases.[199] So far as Scotland is concerned, the Scottish courts have endorsed the approach outlined by Sir Thomas Bingham, MR (as he then was) in *R. v International Stock Exchange of the United Kingdom and Republic of Ireland Ltd Ex p. Else (1982) Ltd* where he said:

> " . . . if the facts have been found and the Community law issue is critical to the court's final decision, the appropriate course is ordinarily to refer the issue to the Court of Justice unless the national court can with complete confidence resolve the issue itself. In considering whether it can with complete confidence resolve the issue itself the national court must be fully mindful of the differences between national and Community legislation, of the pitfalls which face a national court venturing into what may be an unfamiliar field, of the need for uniform interpretation throughout the Community and of the great advantages enjoyed by the Court of Justice in

---

[192] *NV Algemene Transport- en Expeditie Onderneming van Gend en Loos v Nederlandse Administratie der Belastingen* (C-26/62) [1963] E.C.R. 1.

[193] Article 263 TFEU. The rules on standing in such applications are discussed in O'Neill, *EU Law for UK Lawyers* (2011) paras 4.21–4.36. See also *Inuit Tapiriit Kanatami v European Parliament* (C-583/11 P) [2014] Q.B. 648 Grand Chamber, noted by A. Kornezov, "Locus standi of private parties in actions for annulment: has the gap been closed" [2014] C.L.J. 25.

[194] For example, the request made of it in *Kleinwort Benson Ltd v Glasgow City Council* (C346/93) [1996] Q.B. 57; [1995] E.C.R. I-615.

[195] *Groupement National des Negociants en Pommes de Terre de Belgique v ITM Belgium SA* (C-63/94) [1995] E.C.R. I-2467; *Wilson v Ordre des Avocats du Barreau de Luxembourg* (C-506/04) [2006] E.C.R. I-8613; [2007] 1 C.M.L.R. 7.

[196] If asked to do so, the court will answer by explaining whether EU law precludes the national law in question but it is for the national court to disapply a provision of national law.

[197] For example, in the Court of Session, Rules of the Court of Session 1994 Ch.65.

[198] What exactly the national court of last resort is for Scotland is not as simple a question as might be expected. In civil matters, it is clearly the UK Supreme Court. But in criminal matters, it is probably the High Court of Justiciary, although a limited right of appeal, with leave, lies to the UK Supreme Court where a "compatibility issue" arises in terms of the Scotland Act 1998 (Sch.6 of that Act). A similar issue arises in England and Wales in cases where there is no right to apply to the UK Supreme Court for leave to appeal a decision of the Court of Appeal: *Chiron Corp v Murex Diagnostics Ltd (No.8)* [1995] All E.R. (E.C.) 88.

[199] Court of Justice of the European Union, *2013 Annual Report of the Court of Justice of the European Union*, pp.107–109.

construing Community instruments. If the national court has any real doubt, it should ordinarily refer."[200]

In reaching a decision on whether to refer a question to the Court of Justice, lower courts retain a discretion as to whether to make a reference. They may have regard to factors such as the importance of the issue or the likely expense and delay a reference would cause. It is open to a lower court to come to the view that it should give judgment itself and it would then become a matter for the appeal court to review. The lower courts are not prevented from making a reference by any national rules of precedence: it is open to the lower court to refer a question even where the higher court has ruled on the same point.[201]

Having taken a decision to refer a question to the Court of Justice, the framing of the question is, strictly speaking, a matter for the court. In practice, in Scotland at least, it is common for the parties to be asked to assist in that process.[202] The Court of Justice has issued guidance on the form and content for a preliminary reference that should, so far as possible, be adhered to.[203] Once the reference has been made, proceedings before the national court should be sisted (stayed). The delay in receiving an answer can be considerable.[204]

The General Court

10–21 The General Court (formerly known as the Court of First Instance) was founded in 1988 to assist the Court of Justice in discharging its functions. It consists of 28 judges (again, one from each Member State)[205] but it is not served by advocates general.[206] The conditions, term and method of appointment of the judges of the General Court, as well as the rules on the selection of, and the powers of, the president and vice president, are the same as that outlined above in relation to the Court of Justice.[207] There is provision for the General Court to sit as a Grand Chamber but the court ordinarily sits in chambers of three or five judges (five-judge chambers being referred to as "extended composition"). As with the Court of Justice, the judges of the General Court elect chamber presidents from amongst their number.[208] There is also provision for the General Court to sit in an appeal chamber (comprising of the President of the General Court and at least

---

[200] *R. v International Stock Exchange of the United Kingdom and Republic of Ireland Ltd Ex p. Else (1982) Ltd* [1993] Q.B. 534 CA (Civ Div) at 545; endorsed by the Lord President (Rodger) in *Booker Aquaculture Ltd v Secretary of State for Scotland*, 2000 S.C. 9 at 27.

[201] *Rheinmuhlen-Dusseldorf v Einfuhri und Vorratsstelle fur Getreide und Futtermittel* (C-166/73) [1974] E.C.R. 33.

[202] Although see, for example, *Scotch Whiskey Association v Lord Advocate* [2014] CSIH 38 where the court took on the task of drafting the reference itself and the parties were afforded an opportunity to correct any factual inaccuracies in the court's draft.

[203] Recommendations of the Court of Justice of the European Union to national courts and tribunals in relation to the initiation of preliminary ruling proceedings [2012] OJ C338/1.

[204] On the preliminary reference procedure generally see: A. Poole, "Arguing for and against references to the European Court of Justice", 2009 S.L.T. (News) 23; A. Arnull, "The Law Lords and the European Union: swimming with the incoming tide" (2010) 35 E.L. Rev. 57.

[205] Although art.19(2) TEU provides that the General Court shall include "at least one judge per Member State" thus allowing the membership of the court to be extended if necessary.

[206] Article 254 TFEU; Statute of the Court of Justice art.48. Provision is made in the Statute of the Court of Justice art.49 for one of the members of the court to discharge the functions of an advocate general but this rarely happens in practice.

[207] Article 19(2) TEU; art.254 TFEU.

[208] Statute of the Court of Justice art.50.

two chamber presidents).[209] An appeal chamber hears appeals from the specialised courts (of which there is, at present, only one: the Civil Service Tribunal).

The General Court's jurisdiction is now prescribed by art.256 TFEU. The **10–22** General Court has first instance jurisdiction in all actions raised directly by natural and legal persons. With the exception of those reserved to the Court of Justice or delegated to a specialist court, the General Court hears proceedings raised in terms of arts 263 (review of the legality of legislative acts and various acts of the institutions), 265 (action by a Member State against an institution for failure of that institution to act),[210] 268 (compensation for damage in accordance with art.340 (action for damages against an institution)), 270 (staff disputes) and 272 (arbitration) TFEU. The decision of the General Court in these cases is appealable to the Court of Justice, but only on a point of law.[211] As we have noted, the General Court also has jurisdiction to hear appeals from the specialist courts.[212] Finally, the treaties enable the General Court to assume jurisdiction to hear preliminary references in terms of art.267 TFEU.[213] At the time of writing no provision has been made to activate this jurisdiction.

The Civil Service Tribunal

The Civil Service Tribunal is, at the time of writing, the only specialist court to **10–23** have been established and was founded in 2004.[214] It comprises of seven judges who, unlike the other judges of the Court of Justice of the European Union, are appointed by the Council, acting unanimously.[215] They are appointed for a renewable six year term.[216] Similar provision is made for the election of a president by the members of the tribunal and the tribunal shall ordinarily sit in chambers of three.[217] Given the small number of judges, provision has been made for the appointment of temporary judges to cover in the event of the absence of one of the seven judges of the tribunal.[218] An appeal lies to the General Court on a point of law only (but the treaties envisage allowing appeals from the specialist courts on questions of fact too).[219]

EU LEGISLATION

Introduction

We have seen that legislative functions are vested in the European Parliament and **10–24** the Council. That the EU has legislative functions is a unique characteristic

---

[209] Decision 2013/C 313/09 Appeal Chamber [2013] OJ C313/5.
[210] The actual formulation of that article is not a model of clarity in terms of its drafting and should be referred to for its full terms.
[211] Article 256(1) TFEU.
[212] Article 256(2) TFEU.
[213] On which, see para.10–20, above.
[214] Decision 2004/752 establishing the European Union Civil Service Tribunal [2004] OJ L333/7. The power to establish further specialist courts is now found in art.257 TFEU.
[215] Article 257 TFEU.
[216] Statute of the Court of Justice Annex 1 art.2
[217] Statute of the Court of Justice Annex 1 art.4; this provision allows the tribunal, in certain determined cases, to sit with a single judge, five judges or as a full court.
[218] Statute of the Court of Justice art.62c.
[219] Article 257 TFEU; Statute of the Court of Justice Annex 1 art.11

amongst international bodies. The Member States have transferred to the EU the power to legislate in certain specified areas, which allows the EU institutions to take autonomous decisions within those spheres. How exactly legislation is enacted by the EU is a complicated process, with the appropriate route being dictated by the legal basis chosen for the measure in question. Before we turn to consider those processes, the types of EU legislation need to be examined for there are different forms that EU legislation can take (and each form of legislation has a different consequence for the Member States).

Forms of EU legislation

10–25 Article 288 TFEU provides: "To exercise the Union's competences, the institutions shall adopt regulations, directives, decisions, recommendations and opinions." Only regulations have general effect throughout the EU. Directives and decisions are binding (to differing degrees discussed below) on those to whom they have been addressed. Recommendations and opinions, however, have no binding force (but may have an indirect impact or influence on the interpretation of EU law). There is no hierarchy of legislative norm: a regulation does not rank ahead of a decision. However, regulations, directives and decisions can be either legislative, delegated or implementing acts. The nature of the act does not alter the character of the measure: an implementing directive is as much a directive as a legislative one. But it does affect their ranking in the overall hierarchy of norms.[220]

Before turning to consider the different forms of EU legislation, there are three points that are worthy of note. First, the EU is based on the principle of conferral.[221] That has the effect that the EU can

> "act only within the limits of the competences conferred upon it by the Member States in the Treaties to attain the objectives set out therein. Competences not conferred on the Union in the Treaties remain with the Member States".[222]

Those competences come in three parts. There are exclusive competences, such as the customs union and the necessary competition rules to ensure the functioning of the internal market.[223] In these areas of exclusive competence the Member States are forbidden from legislating or adopting legally binding acts, unless authorised to do so by the EU.[224] Next, there are shared competences. The default rule is that anything that falls within the ambit of the treaties is a shared competence unless otherwise stated.[225] Article 4(2) TFEU sets out a non-exhaustive list of shared competences. This includes matters such as the internal market, the environment and consumer protection. Member States' competence is, however, more restricted due to the doctrine of pre-emption. Article 2(2) goes on to provide: "The Member States shall exercise their competence to the extent that the Union has not exercised its competence." Thus, the Member State retains competence only until such time as the EU exercises its own competence. The

---

[220] See para.10–30 on the hierarchy of EU norms.
[221] Article 5(1) TEU.
[222] Article 5(2) TEU; a similar limit is imposed upon the institutions by art.13(2) TEU.
[223] Article 3(1) TFEU.
[224] Article 2(1) TFEU.
[225] Article 4(1) TFEU.

final part are areas in which the EU can carry out actions to "support, coordinate or supplement" the actions of the Member States.[226] Legal acts by the EU within these areas do not have a harmonising effect and do not fetter the competence of the Member State. In other words, the doctrine of pre-emption does not apply. Article 6 TFEU lists the areas in which the EU can play such a role and they include matters such as industry, culture and tourism. The second point of note is that the use of the powers and competences conferred on the EU is governed by the principles of proportionality and subsidiarity.[227] Subsidiarity requires that, other than areas which fall within the exclusive competence of the EU, the Union shall act

> "only if and in so far as the objectives of the proposed action cannot be achieved by the Member States . . . but can rather, by reason of the scale of effects of the proposed action, be better achieved at Union level".[228]

Proportionality requires that "the content and form of Union action shall not exceed what is necessary to achieve the objectives of the Treaty".[229] Each of these principles is considered further in a moment. Thirdly, the EU enjoys exclusive competence within certain prescribed areas. There is no list of exclusive competences of the Member States.[230] The treaties normally specify the form of act to be used. Where they are silent on the matter, the institutions may choose the form of legislative measure, in accordance with the principle of proportionality.[231]

Against that background, we now turn to consider each of the different types of EU legislative measure.

Regulations

"A regulation shall have general application. It shall be binding in its entirety and **10–26** directly applicable in all Member States."[232] The defining characteristic of a regulation is that their entry into force and application within the national legal orders of the Member States are wholly independent of any measure of reception into national law. In other words, they are directly applicable (not to be confused with direct effect, which is discussed below). Indeed, any purported implementation of a regulation into domestic law is not permitted:

> "The direct application of a Regulation means that its entry into force and its application in favour of or against those subject to it are independent of any measure of reception into national law. By virtue of the obligations arising from the Treaty and assumed on ratification, Members States are

---

[226] Article 2(5) TFEU.
[227] Article 5(1) TEU.
[228] Article 5(3) TEU.
[229] Article 5(4) TEU; proportionality now has a much greater prominence in domestic law in the United Kingdom. For a recent discussion of the concept in EU law, see the judgment of the UK Supreme Court in *R. (on the application of Lumsdon) v Legal Services Board* [2015] UKSC 41; [2015] 3 W.L.R. 121 at [22]–[82]. In relation to domestic law, see *Bank Mellat v HM Treasury* [2013] UKSC 39; [2014] A.C. 700 at [68]–[76] (Lord Reed).
[230] Other than, perhaps, national security: art.4(2) TEU.
[231] Article 296 TFEU.
[232] Article 288 TFEU.

under a duty not to obstruct the direct applicability inherent in Regulations and other rules of [EU] law. Strict compliance with this obligation is an indispensible condition of simultaneous and uniform application of [Regulations] throughout the [EU]."[233]

In short, a regulation becomes part of the Member States' legal system without any further action on their part.[234] A consequence of this is that regulations are capable of conferring rights on individuals that can be enforced directly by them before national courts. This is a characteristic of the concept of direct applicability that is shared with the concept of direct effect (and discussed further below). Once adopted, regulations must be published in the *Official Journal*. They enter into force on the date specified in the notice, failing which on the twentieth day following publication of the notice.[235]

Directives

10-27 "A directive shall be binding, as to the result to be achieved, upon each Member State to which it is addressed, but shall leave to the national authorities the choice of form and methods."[236] In many ways a directive is what a regulation is not: it does not have general application and it calls for implementation at Member State level. Directives therefore give the EU a greater flexibility and are appropriate where harmonisation is required rather than uniformity. First, they do not need to be addressed to all Member States therefore do not necessarily apply throughout the Union. Secondly, a directive leaves it to a Member State to decide how best to incorporate its requirements into domestic law whereas a regulation must be capable of being dropped into the legal system of all 28 Member States. With such an enlarged Union, that is an increasingly challenging task. Despite this, directives are often very prescriptive which leaves Member States little room in practice when it comes to implementation.

Directives applying to all Member States must be published in the *Official Journal* and take effect in the same way as regulations. Directives normally then allow the addressee Member States a specified period of time in which to transpose the measures into national law. The obligation rests on the Member States and any internal constitutional difficulties (for example, the failure by a devolved or sub-state executive to implement a directive) is of no interest to the EU.[237] Although a directive does not require to be implemented until a certain date, after its publication Member States must refrain from adopting any measure which would prevent the objective of the directive being achieved[238] and the courts of the Member States must interpret domestic law, as far as possible, in

---

[233] *Fratelli Variola SpA v Amministrazione Italiana delle Finanze* (C-34/73) [1973] E.C.R. 981.
[234] In the United Kingdom, a regulation is, of course, reliant upon the European Communities Act 1972 for its recognition in domestic law (*Thoburn v Sunderland City Council* [2002] EWHC 195 (Admin); [2003] Q.B. 151 at [59]).
[235] Article 297 TFEU.
[236] Article 288 TFEU.
[237] For an explanation of the obligation resting on the Member States see *Commission v Netherlands* (C-144/99) [2001] E.C.R. I-3541 at [15]–[17] of Advocate General Tizzano's opinion.
[238] *Inter-Environnement Wallonie ASBL v Region Wallonie* (C-129/96) [1997] E.C.R. I-7411; [1998] 1 C.M.L.R. 1057.

light of the wording and purpose of a directive.[239] Directives normally require Member States to notify the Commission of the measures taken to implement a directive. Failure on the part of the Member State to implement a directive, at all or correctly, within that period may expose the state to enforcement action by the Commission and liable in damages for that breach of EU law.[240] Furthermore, individuals may be able to rely directly on the provisions of the directive in proceedings before the national courts where the directive satisfies the conditions for direct effect.[241]

Decisions

"A decision shall be binding in its entirety. A decision which specifies those to **10–28** whom it is addressed shall be binding only on them."[242] Both regulations and decisions are binding in their entirety. What distinguishes the two measures is that decisions are only addressed to a limited number of persons.[243] Since the Lisbon Treaty a decision does not necessarily require an addressee but where it has one (and the addressee can be a Member State or a natural or legal person(s)) it is binding on them and only them. A decision without an addressee remains "binding in its entirety" but it is not clear on whom. Decisions are generally used to address specific issues or problems and where general measures, such as a regulation, would be inappropriate. In particular, Decisions are used to notify breaches of EU law or determinations that state aid is incompatible with the common market.

Recommendations and Opinions

"Recommendations and opinions shall have no binding force."[244] The Council, **10–29** and where specifically authorised by the treaties the Commission and the European Central Bank, may adopt recommendations.[245] Recommendations are adopted following the procedure that is applicable to the subject matter at issue.[246] Because recommendations and opinions have no binding force, they cannot create legal rights nor can they have direct effect. Nevertheless, national courts are required to take notice of them, in particular when they may inform the interpretation of other provisions of EU law.[247] In recent years, greater use has been made of these measures as vehicles for the development of EU policy as the

---

[239] *Marleasing SA v La Comercial Internacional de Alimentacion SA* (C-106/89) [1990] E.C.R. I-4135.

[240] *Francovich v Italy* (C-6/90) [1991] E.C.R. I-5357.

[241] On direct effect of directives, see para.10–36, above.

[242] Article 288 TFEU.

[243] See *Yusuf v Council of the European Union* (T-306/01) [2005] E.C.R. II-3533; [2005] 3 CMLR 49 at [185]. Although the Grand Chamber allowed an appeal against this decision, they endorsed the Court of First Instance's (as it then was) discussion of the difference between regulations and decisions: *Kadi v Council of the European Union* (C-402/05 P) [2009] 1 A.C. 1225; [2008] E.C.R. I-6351 at [237]–[247].

[244] Article 288 TFEU.

[245] Article 292 TFEU.

[246] Article 292 TFEU.

[247] *Grimaldi v Fonds des Maladies Professionnelles* (C-322/88) [1989] E.C.R. 4407; [1991] 2 C.M.L.R. 265 at [18].

old stress on uniformity has given way (as it inevitably had to in such an enlarged Union) to a new emphasis on flexibility.

Hierarchy of EU norms

10–30 The Lisbon Treaty introduced, for the first time, a hierarchy of EU norms.[248] The treaties sit at the top of that hierarchy. Below them, a distinction is now drawn between "legislative acts", "delegated acts" and "implementing acts".[249] A legislative act is a regulation, directive or decision adopted by the European Parliament and the Council, on the recommendation of the Commission.[250] A legislative act may delegate to the Commission to adopt non-legislative acts of general application "to supplement or amend non-essential elements of the legislative act".[251] The legislative act must explicitly define the objectives, content, scope and purpose of the delegation and the "essential elements" of the legislative act may not be delegated.[252] The legislative act may also impose conditions on the delegation.[253] Any non-legislative act adopted under a delegated power must include the word "delegated" in its title.[254] Both legislative and non-legislative acts are legally binding EU acts. Member States are required to adopt "all measures of national law necessary" to implement such acts.[255] Where uniformity is required in the implementation of a legislative act, that act shall confer implementing powers (ordinarily) on the Commission.[256] An implementing measure adopted by the Commission must use the word "implementing" in its title.[257]

EU legislative process

10–31 The EU legislative process, or rather processes, for there are several, is a complex business, primarily because there is not one institution identifiable as the legislature. As the EU has evolved so too has its legislative process, primarily by reference to the role played by the European Parliament. Initially, when it was known as the "Assembly", being consulted on a legislative proposal was about as much as it could expect. This did little to deter those concerned about the EU's "democratic deficit". The Lisbon Treaty sought to rationalise the previous approach to EU legislating, introducing the "ordinary legislative procedure" (which is the old process of "co-decision" by another name) and a new "special legislative process" (which to a large extent incorporates what were formerly

[248] The word "law" was used in the aborted EU Constitution and was replaced with "norm" come the Lisbon Treaty to avoid any federal connotations that may accompany the term "law"; on the hierarchy of EU norms generally, see P. Craig, "Delegated acts, implementing acts and the new Comitology Regulation" (2011) 36 E.L. Rev. 671.
[249] Articles 289, 290 and 291 TFEU, respectively.
[250] Article 289(1) TFEU. This is the "ordinary legislative" procedure and is discussed further at para.10–32, below.
[251] Article 290(1) TFEU.
[252] Article 290(1) TFEU.
[253] Article 290(2) TFEU.
[254] Article 290(3) TFEU.
[255] Article 291(1) TFEU.
[256] Article 291(2) TFEU.
[257] Article 291(4) TFEU.

known as the "consent" procedure and the "consultation" procedure).[258] We will start by considering the "ordinary legislative process".

Ordinary legislative process

Article 294 TFEU sets out the ordinary legislative process, which is now the **10–32** default method by which legislative measures are adopted by the EU.[259] The process has, essentially, six stages: proposal; first reading; second reading; conciliation; third reading; and signature and entry into force.[260] The process begins with the Commission (who have a near monopoly on initiating the ordinary legislative process)[261] submitting a proposal to the Council and the European Parliament. There then follows the "first reading" stage. The European Parliament goes first and adopts its position and communicates this to the Council. If the Council approves the Parliament's position, the proposal is adopted in the wording that corresponds to the position of the Parliament. The vast majority of legislative proposals are approved at this stage and then pass for signature and publication. If the Council does not approve the Parliament's position, it shall adopt its own position and communicate that to the Parliament, with full reasons as to why it adopted the position it has. The Commission is also required, at this stage, to inform the Parliament fully of its position. There then follows the "second reading".

At the second reading stage the Parliament has three months[262] to do one of three things. First, it can approve the Council's position at first reading in which case the act concerned shall be deemed to have been adopted. If the Parliament does nothing within three months of being informed of the Council's position at first reading the act is also deemed to have been adopted (in the wording that corresponds to the Council's position). Secondly, the Parliament can, acting by a majority of its component members, reject the Council's position with the result that the proposed act shall fail. Finally, the Parliament, again acting by a majority of its component members, may propose amendments to the Council's position at first reading. Where the Parliament proposes amendments, they are forwarded to the Council and the Commission, with the latter being required to deliver an opinion on the proposed amendments. Where the Parliament has proposed amendments, the measure then returns to the Council. The Council has

---

[258] Prior to the Lisbon Treaty there was process known as "co-operation". This was introduced by the Single European Act. In short, this required the Council to obtain the opinion of the Parliament on a legislative proposal of the Commission. The Parliament could not prevent a proposal being adopted but it could force the Commission to re-examine its proposal and require the Council to act unanimously, instead of by qualified majority, in certain circumstances. The "co-operation" procedure all but died out after the Treaty of Amsterdam and was finally done away with by the Lisbon Treaty.

[259] The narrative of the procedure that follows outlines the provisions of art.294 TFEU. Reference should be made to that article and individual footnotes have not been inserted to direct readers to the specific subparagraph of that article for every step of the process.

[260] Alas, words are the only tools at my disposal to explain the ordinary legislative procedure. But for those who prefer diagrams, the explanation on the European Parliament website will undoubtedly be of assistance, *http://www.europarl.europa.eu/external/appendix/legislativeprocedure/europarl_ordinarylegislativeprocedure_howitworks_en.pdf* [Accessed 10 June 2015].

[261] Article 294(15) TFEU makes provision for the very rare circumstances where a legislative proposal originates not from the Commission but from a group of Member States, the European Central Bank or the Court of Justice.

[262] This may be extended by a maximum of one month on the initiative of either the Parliament or the Council: art.294(14) TFEU.

three months to approve the amendments, in which case the act shall be deemed to have been adopted. The Council acts by qualified majority voting, unless the Commission has delivered a negative opinion on any amendments, in which case unanimity is required in the Council to approve those amendments. Where the Council does not approve any of the Parliament's amendments, the President of the Council, in agreement with the President of the European Parliament, shall, within six weeks, convene a meeting on the "conciliation committee".

The conciliation committee consists of members of the Council (or their representatives) and an equal number of MEPs. The purpose of the committee is to seek to agree a joint text based on the second reading opinions. The committee has six weeks[263] from when it is convened to reach such an agreement otherwise the proposed act shall be deemed not to have been adopted. The Commission takes part in the proceedings of the committee and "shall take all necessary initiative" with a view to reconciling the positions of the Parliament and the Council. If a joint text is agreed within the prescribed time, the proposal returns to the Parliament and the Council for the "third reading".

At the third reading stage, the Parliament and the Council can either pass or reject the agreed text; there is no scope for further amendment. The Parliament requires a simple majority to approve the text. The Council acts by qualified majority. Each body has six weeks in which to approve the proposed act.[264] If either body fails to approve the proposed act within that time, it shall be deemed not to have been adopted. If, however, both approve, the act is adopted subject to the final formalities. Those formalities require that the legislative act be signed by the President of the Parliament and the President of the Council and then be published in the *Official Journal*. It enters into force on the date specified by the act or, in the absence of any such date, on the twentieth day following publication in the *Official Journal*.[265]

Special legislative process

10–33 Article 289(2) TFEU provides for what is known as the special legislative process:

> "In the specific cases provided for by the Treaties, the adoption of a regulation, directive or decision by the European Parliament with the participation of the Council, or by the latter with the participation of the European Parliament, shall constitute a special legislative process."

Different provisions of the treaties specify what the special legislative process, in that instance, means. Usually it takes the form of requiring the Council to act unanimously and with the consent of, or at least having consulted with, the European Parliament. Consultation is the more common requirement. Where the European Parliament must be consulted the Council is not bound to follow the

---

[263] This may be extended by a maximum of two weeks on the initiative of either the Parliament or the Council: art.294(14) TFEU.
[264] This may be extended by a maximum of two weeks on the initiative of either the Parliament or the Council: art.294(14) TFEU.
[265] Article 297(1) TFEU.

Parliament's opinion but it must await it before proceeding.[266] The consent process is generally reserved for more sensitive areas of EU policy and issues concerning EU finance.[267] The margin required in the European Parliament to consent is prescribed by the relevant treaty article. Article 48(7) TEU allows the Council acting unanimously, and with the consent of the European Parliament, to dispense with the special legislative process and proceed by means of the ordinary legislative process (assuming no national parliament objects).

IMPACT OF EU LAW ON DOMESTIC LEGAL SYSTEMS

What we now turn to discuss are some of the main elements of EU law that have **10–34** a direct impact on the Member States. There are four aspects of EU law that are considered: primacy of EU law, direct effect, state liability for damages, and the protection of fundamental rights.

Primacy of EU law

As we saw earlier long before the United Kingdom negotiated membership of the **10–35** EU, the Court of Justice of the European Union had made it clear that EU law was a new and distinctive species of international law. Borne out of a modest dispute over an unpaid Italian electricity bill, the primacy of EU law was declared by the court in *Costa v ENEL*:

> "The transfer by the States from their domestic legal system to the Community legal system of the rights and obligations arising under the Treaty carries with it a permanent limitation of their sovereign rights, against which a subsequent unilateral act incompatible with the concept of the Community cannot prevail."[268]

Subsequently, the court went on to confirm that EU law in all its forms, not simply the treaties, prevails over national law, even where the conflicting national provision is constitutional in nature.[269] The court took the primacy of EU law to its logical conclusion in *Amministrazione delle Finanze dello Stato v Simmenthal SpA* where it held that a national court must

> "apply Community law in its entirety and protect rights which the latter confers on individuals, and must accordingly set aside any provision of

---

[266] If it fails to do so, any purported measure will be annulled: *Roquette Freres SA v Council of Ministers of the European Communities* (C-138/79) [1980] E.C.R. 3333. The Parliament must not, however, unreasonably delay its opinion: *European Parliament v Council of Ministers of the European Communities* (C-65/93) [1995] E.C.R. I-643.

[267] For example, arts 19(1) (action to combat non-discrimination), 25 (amending the rights enjoyed by citizens of the EU) or 311 (determining the EU's finances) TFEU.

[268] *Costa v Ente Nazionale per l'Energia Elettrica (ENEL)* (C-6/64) [1964] E.C.R. 585 at [14].

[269] *Internationale Handelsgesellschaft mbH v Einfuhr- und Vorratsstelle fur Getreide und Futtermittel* (C-11/70) [1970] E.C.R. 1125.

national law which may conflict with it, whether prior or subsequent to the Community rule".[270]

Thus national laws are not invalidated or struck down if inconsistent with EU law (unless national law prescribes that result)[271] but simply set aside and disapplied. Nonetheless, the rule as to the primacy of EU law has caused significant constitutional difficulties in a number of Member States. The difficulties so far as the UK is concerned are discussed in Ch.3, above and developed further below.[272] For now it is worth noting that the domestic constitutional implications for the UK of EU membership have not been exhaustively resolved. As the Supreme Court explained in *R. (on the application of Buckingham CC) v Secretary of State for Transport* were a provision of EU law to clash with a fundamental principal of the UK constitution, it would be for the British courts, applying domestic law, to resolve such a conflict: the answer is not to be found (exclusively at any rate) in the jurisprudence of the Court of Justice of the European Union.[273]

Direct effect of EU law

10–36 The treaties always contained a mechanism for their enforcement through the right of the Commission or another Member State to bring issues of non-adherence before the Court of Justice. In one of the earliest cases to come before the court, however, judicial enforcement was to go a step further. In *NV*

---

[270] *Amministrazione delle Finanze dello Stato v Simmenthal SpA* (C-106/77) [1978] E.C.R. 629.

[271] For example, an Act of the Scottish Parliament is *"not law"* to the extent it is inconsistent with EU law (Scotland Act 1998 s.29(2)). That results, however, from a provision of the Scotland Act, an Act of the UK Parliament, and not a rule of EU law.

[272] It is not only the courts of the UK that have had to struggle with the constitutional consequences of EU membership and the primacy of EU law. In France, the Conseil d'Etat at one time refused to question the validity of French legislation on the ground that it conflicted with Community law and declined to accept the doctrine of direct effect of directives (see, e.g. *Syndicat General de Fabricants de Semoules de France* [1970] C.M.L.R. 395; *Minister of the Interior v Cohn-Bendit* [1980] 1 C.M.L.R. 543) and has only relatively recently signalled its acceptance of the supremacy of Community law: P. Roseren, "The Application of Community Law by the French Courts from 1982 to 1993" (1994) 31 C.M.L. Rev. 315. The German constitution permits the transfer of sovereign powers to intergovernmental institutions, so to that extent the reception of the supremacy of EU law caused little difficulty. Less straightforward was the question whether EU law could take priority over the inalienable fundamental rights enshrined in the Basic law. Following the decision of the Court of Justice of the European Union in *Internationale Handelsgesellschaft*, the German Constitutional Court refused to renounce its right to uphold fundamental rights in German law even in the face of conflict with EU law (although it found on the facts of that case that no such conflict existed). Subsequently the German courts departed from this position, but in *Brunner v Treaty on European Union* [1994] 1 C.M.L.R. 57, the Constitutional Court, while confirming the legality of ratification of the Maastricht Treaty and acknowledging the primary responsibility of the European Court of Justice for the protection of fundamental rights, suggested that it retained the competence to perform this task if the European Court of Justice failed to do so adequately, and also asserted a right to review the legal instruments of the European institutions to ascertain whether they remained within the limits of the sovereign rights transferred to them.

[273] *R. (on the application of Buckingham CC) v Secretary of State for Transport* [2014] UKSC 3; [2014] 1 W.L.R. 324, per Lord Reed at [79] and per Lords Neuberger and Mance [203]–[205]. See also: P. Craig, "Constitutionalising constitutional law: HS2" [2014] P.L. 373. That of course differs from the scenario that presented itself to the House of Lords in *Factortame*, where the clash was between EU law and an "ordinary" Act of Parliament.

*Algemene Transport- en Expeditie Onderneming van Gend en Loos v Neder-
landse Administratie der Belastingen*,[274] a reference for a preliminary ruling from
a Dutch tax tribunal, the court addressed the question of the effect, as a matter of
Dutch domestic law, of what is now art.30 TFEU. The court held that, unlike
most international treaties, which only create mutual obligations between the
states party to them, EU law imposed obligations and conferred legal rights on
individuals as well. These rights would arise

> "not only when an explicit grant is made by the Treaty, but also through
> obligations imposed, in a clearly defined manner, by the Treaty on
> individuals as well as on member states and the Community institutions".

For a treaty article to have this direct effect of creating an enforceable individual
right, the court held that the provision in question required to be clear, negative,
unconditional, containing no reservation on the part of the Member State and
independent of any national implementing measure. Since what is now art.30
TFEU satisfied these criteria, the applicants in *Van Gend en Loos* were able to
invoke the protection of EU law in the proceedings before their national court.

Since then the doctrine of direct effect has expanded considerably, partly as a
consequence of the Court of Justice applying the criteria for direct effect in a
generous manner[275] and partly through the extension of the doctrine to other
measures of EU law besides articles of the treaties and regulations. Decisions
were held to be capable of having direct effect in 1970,[276] and in 1974 it was held
that directives too could have direct effect and create enforceable individual
rights.[277] There are however two important riders to note in relation to the direct
effect of directives. First, it is only after the expiry of the time period allowed for
implementation of the directive that its capacity for direct effect crystallises. The
reason for this is as follows. Directives leave some discretion to national
authorities in relation to implementation. That discretion would be meaningless
if individuals could, at any time, rely directly on the terms of a directive in
proceedings before national courts. However, it is equally important that, where
the directive requires enforceable rights to be conferred on individuals, Member
States should not be able to defeat that intention by implementing the directive
erroneously or not implementing it at all within the time allowed. In other words,
once the time limit for implementation has elapsed, the individual may rely
directly on the provisions of the directive in legal proceedings (provided that the
conditions for direct effect are satisfied, namely that it imposes upon the Member
State a clear, precise and unconditional obligation intended to create rights for

---

[274] *NV Algemene Transport-en Expeditie Onderneming van Gend en Loos v Nederlandse Administratie der Belastingen* (C-26/62) [1963] E.C.R. 1, more commonly referred to as *Van Genden
Loos*.

[275] For example *Defrenne v SA Belge de Navigation Aerienne* (SABENA) (C-43/75) [1976] E.C.R.
455 where the court held that the not particularly precise, nor negative, obligation in what is now
art.157 TFEU (that "[e]ach Member State shall ensure that the principle of equal pay for male and
female workers for equal work or work of equal value is applied") was capable of being directly
effective (a view that neither the Commission nor the Member States appeared to share at the
time).

[276] *Grad v Finanzamt Traunstein* (C-9/70) [1970] E.C.R. 825.

[277] *Van Duyn v Home Office* (C-41/74) [1974] E.C.R. 1337.

individuals).[278] National authorities cannot then plead their own mistake, tardiness or other shortcomings in their defence.[279]

Secondly, the Court of Justice of the European Union has consistently held that directives cannot produce horizontal direct effect, that is legal rights enforceable as between private parties.[280] Since the justification for according direct effect to directives at all is largely rooted in the desire to bind Member States to the proper discharge of their EU obligations, it stands to reason that the institutions of the state should be caught by the direct effect of a directive. So they are, because directives are capable of producing vertical direct effects, or effects binding on the state. But this does not provide convincing justification for horizontal direct effect: private persons are not responsible for the proper implementation of directives into national law, and accordingly it would be unfair to expect them to suffer the consequences of the government's failings. There is force in this reasoning. But another species of unfairness flows from distinguishing between the horizontal and vertical direct effect of directives in this way. By virtue of the vertical direct effect of directives, public employees obtain rights against their employer the benefit of which is denied to the employees of private sector organisations. The court has repeatedly made it clear that where an individual is entitled to rely upon a directive against a Member State, it does not matter in what capacity the latter is acting.[281] The court has acknowledged that this state of affairs is less than ideal, but points out that it is easily avoided provided the Member States properly implement directives into national law. As we noted above, national courts are required to interpret domestic law, as far as possible, in light of the wording and purpose of a directive.[282] That gives directives a limited "indirect" effect. However, it was the court's ruling in *Francovich v Italy* which further incentivised Member States to properly and timeously implement directives.

State liability for damages

10–37 In *Francovich*[283] individuals who had suffered loss due to the persistent non-implementation of a directive by the Italian authorities sued the Italian Government to make good the damage caused to them. The Italian court referred to the Court of Justice the question whether EU law recognised any principle of Member State liability in damages for failure to implement a directive. The court

---

[278] *Becker v Finanzamt Munster-Innenstadt* (C-8/81) [1982] E.C.R .53; *Foster v British Gas Plc* (C-188/89) [1991] 1 Q.B. 405 [1990] E.C.R. I-3313.
[279] At the risk of stating the obvious, where a Member State has properly and timeously implemented a directive, normally no issue of direct effect can then arise: *Johnston v Chief Constable of the Royal Ulster Constabulary* (C-222/84) [1986] E.C.R. 1651. But the matter is one of substance, not form. If an otherwise properly implemented directive is not being applied by a Member State correctly so that the rights that should be conferred have not, in fact, been conferred, the directive itself can be founded upon if it meets the relevant criteria: *Marks & Spencer Plc v Customs and Excise Commissioners* (C-62/00) [2003] Q.B. 866; [2002] E.C.R. I-6325.
[280] *Marshall v Southampton and South West Hampshire AHA* (C-152/84) [1986] E.C.R. 723; *Faccini Dori v Recreb Srl* (C-91/92) [1994] E.C.R. I–3325 at [20]; *Dominguez v Centre Informatique du Centre Ouest Atlantique* (C-282/10) [2012] 2 C.M.L.R. 14 at [37].
[281] *Marshall v Southampton and South West Hampshire AHA* (C-152/84) [1986] E.C.R. 723 at [49]; *Foster v British Gas Plc* (C-188/89) [1991] 1 Q.B. 405 [1990] E.C.R. I-3313 at [17]; *Dominguez v Centre Informatique du Centre Ouest Atlantique* (C-282/10) [2012] 2 C.M.L.R. 14 at [38].
[282] See para.10–27, above; *Marleasing SA v La Comercial Internacional de Alimentacion SA* (C-106/89) [1990] E.C.R. I-4135.
[283] *Francovich v Italy* (C-6/90) [1991] E.C.R. I-5357.

held that it did, provided that the directive was intended to confer rights on individuals (whether or not those rights also satisfy the criteria of direct effect); provided also that the content of the rights is capable of being identified from the provisions of the directive; and provided there was a causal link between the Member State's failure to fulfil its obligations and the loss sustained by the complainant. Subsequently, it was held that the *Francovich* doctrine was applicable to any breach by a Member State of EU law provided that the breach was "sufficiently serious".[284] The decisive criterion for proving a sufficiently serious breach of EU law is whether the Member State in question has "manifestly and gravely disregarded the limits on its discretion" imposed by EU law.[285] As EU law does not discriminate between the institutions of the Member States, in principle a liability in damages for breach of EU law can arise as a result of a judgment of the national court.[286] It will only be in truly exceptional circumstances that such a liability is likely to arise.[287]

In all of these ways—sometimes, admittedly, on slender textual foundations—the Court of Justice has built up a body of law designed to be effective in securing uniform judicial protection between the Member States in areas falling within EU competence. In this regard, the court has been as powerful, if not more powerful, an engine of European integration than the Commission.

Protection of fundamental rights

A fourth front is opening up in which the Court of Justice of the European Union **10–38** may further develop EU law. Fundamental (that is, human) rights are now a central tenet of EU law:

> "Fundamental rights, as guaranteed by the European Convention for the Protection of Human Rights and Fundamental Freedoms and as they result from the constitutional traditions common to the Member States, shall constitute general principles of the Union's law."[288]

It was not always so. The original Treaties of the Communities made no reference to fundamental rights. It was the court, after an initial reluctance,[289] that "discovered" implicit in the EU legal order rights that broadly reflected those of the Member States: international human rights treaties which the Member States

[284] *Brasserie du Pecheur SA v Germany* (C-46/93) [1996] Q.B. 404; [1996] E.C.R. I-1029; *R. v Secretary of State for Transport Ex p. Factortame Ltd (No.5)* [2000] 1 A.C. 524.
[285] See P. Craig, "Once More unto the Breach: the Community, the State and damages liability" (1997) 113 L.Q.R. 67; W. Van Gerven, "Bridging the Unbridgeable: Community and national tort Laws after *Francovich* and *Brasserie*" (1996) 45 I.C.L.Q. 507; T. Tridimas, "Liability for Breach of Community Law: Growing Up and Mellowing Down?" (2001) 38 C.M.L. Rev. 301. European Union institutions can also be found liable for damages for breach of EU law. See Edward and Lane, *European Union Law* (2013) para.5.96 and cases cited therein.
[286] *Kobler v Austria* (C-224/01) [2004] Q.B. 848; [2003] E.C.R. I-10239.
[287] *Kobler v Austria* (C-224/01) [2004] Q.B. 848; [2003] E.C.R. I-10239 at [51]–[59]. Examples would include a manifest disregard for the case law of the Court of Justice by the final court of appeal of a Member State or a blatant non-compliance with the obligation to make a preliminary reference.
[288] Article 6(3) TEU; art.2 TEU is to similar effect.
[289] For example, *Stork v High Authority of the European Coal and Steel Community* (C-1/58) [1959] E.C.R. 17.

were a party to supplied "*guidelines*" which should be followed[290] and the court drew "*inspiration*" from the constitutional traditions common to the Member States.[291] The most significant international treaty on human rights, common to all the Member States, is, of course, the European Convention on Human Rights. Prior to the Lisbon Treaty, the EU was not, and could not, be a party to the Convention.[292] Article 6(2) TEU now requires that the EU accede to the Convention.[293] A draft accession agreement was agreed between the EU and the Council of Europe in April 2013. That agreement was referred to the court for its opinion on whether it was compatible with EU law. An oral hearing took place in May 2014 and those Member States that participated, along with the EU institutions, supported the accession agreement. In June 2014, the advocate general gave his opinion that was, in effect, a qualified yes.[294] Against that background, it came as a surprise that the CJEU, in December 2014, issued its opinion and concluded that the accession agreement was *not* consistent with EU law.[295] That conclusion causes a number of problems: the EU cannot accede to the Convention until it has addressed the concerns raised by the court in its opinion[296]; the EU, however, remains bound by the terms of art.6(2) TEU and is thus under an obligation to accede to the Convention; that raises the prospect of enforcement proceedings being raised against the Commission for failing to comply with art.6(2) TEU; and the appetite on the part of the countries that are signatories to the European Convention but not members of the EU to embark on yet more (undoubtedly tortious) negotiations to revise the accession agreements must be doubted. Whether the EU will now accede to the Convention must be in serious doubt.

10–39   Failing to accede to the European Convention on Human Rights would not mean there is no human rights protection in EU law. On the contrary, the EU has its own document. The Charter of Fundamental Rights of the European Union was adopted by "solemn proclamation" in December 2000.[297] It was adopted not by the Member States but by the institutions of the EU. The Charter is wider in scope than most other fundamental rights treaties, covering socio-economic rights such as the right of collective bargaining and action (art.28), fair and just working conditions (art.31) and healthcare (art.35) in addition to the more

---

[290] *Nold Kohlen- und Baustoffgrosshandlung v Commission of the European Communities* (C-4/73) [1974] E.C.R. 491 at [13]

[291] *Kremzow v Austria* (C-299/95) [1997] E.C.R. I-2629.

[292] *Re Accession of the Community to the European Human Rights Convention* (Opinion 2/94) [1996] E.C.R. I-1759.

[293] The European Convention on Human Rights was previously open to signature by members of the Council of Europe. It was amended by Protocol No.14, art.17, which inserted a new art.59(2) to specifically allow the EU to accede to it.

[294] Opinion of the Court on the draft Accession Agreement of the European Union to the European Convention on Human Rights (Opinion 2/13), 13 June 2014, opinion of Advocate General Kokott, [2015] 2 C.M.L.R. 21.

[295] Opinion of the Court on the draft Accession Agreement of the European Union to the European Convention on Human Rights (Opinion 2/13), 18 December 2014, OJ C-62/2; [2015] 2 C.M.L.R. 21.

[296] It is perhaps worth noting that the court, as an EU institution, was part of the negotiation process for the accession agreement. During that process, a number of concerns raised by the court were addressed in the final agreement. The sheer number of objections now raised by the court to EU accession to the European Convention may therefore come as a surprise.

[297] The full text was published in the Official Journal (Charter of Fundamental Rights of the European Union [2000] OJ C364/1) and is available online at: *http://www.europarl.europa.eu/charter/pdf/text_en.pdf* [Accessed 10 June 2015].

traditional fundamental rights. Where a right protected by the Charter corresponds to an equivalent right in the European Convention, the Charter right has the same meaning and scope as the Convention right.[298] That breadth of rights was obviously not to everyone's taste with the UK and Poland negotiating a protocol to the Charter to clarify its application in their respective legal systems.[299] Initially, at least, the Charter was of limited practical effect: it did not have the same status as the treaties and it was binding on Member States only when implementing EU law.[300] That changed with the Lisbon Treaty. Article 6(1) TEU now provides:

> "The Union recognises the rights, freedoms and principles set out in the Charter of Fundamental Rights of the European Union of 7 December 2000, as adapted at Strasbourg, on 12 December 2007, which shall have the same legal value as the Treaties."[301]

Thus the Charter now has the same standing as the treaties. It features more regularly in judgments of the Court of Justice and has already been used on a number of occasions to strike down EU legislative measures for non-compliance.[302] The Supreme Court has confirmed that the Charter has direct effect in UK law and applies when the UK implements EU obligations.[303] The recent decision of the Employment Appeal Tribunal in *Janah v Libya*[304] gives an insight into the potential domestic consequences of the Charter. J claimed she had been unfairly dismissed from her post working at the Libyan embassy in London. Employment falls within the scope of EU law. Her claim was rejected by the Employment Tribunal on the basis it was barred by the State Immunity Act 1978.

---

[298] Article 52(3) of the Charter.
[299] Quite how much clarity it brought to matters is another question. The Charter did not extend the ability of British or Polish courts to any legislative or administrative acts inconsistent with fundamental rights and the socio-economic rights contained in Ch.IV of the Charter were declared not to create new justiciable rights. As a result of the decision of the Grand Chamber of the Court of Justice of the European Union in *R. (on the application of NS) v Secretary of State for the Home Department* (C-411/10) [2013] QB 102; [2012] 2 CMLR 9 at [119]–[122] and the High Court in *R. (on the application of AB) v Secretary of State for the Home Department* [2013] EWHC 3453 (Admin); [2014] 2 C.M.L.R. 22 at [11]–[14] any belief that the Protocol amounted to an opt-out was dispelled. On the Protocol generally see: O'Neill, *EU Law for UK Lawyers* (2011), paras 6.68–6.73.
[300] Article 51(1) of the Charter.
[301] The Charter as originally proclaimed was adapted in anticipation of its elevation to the status of primary law. The adapted version, which makes few substantive changes, was published in the *Official Journal*: [2007] OJ C303/1.
[302] For example, and perhaps most controversially, in *Digital Rights Ireland Ltd v Minister for Communications, Marine and Natural Resources* (C-293/12), [2015] Q.B. 127 where the Data Retention Directive was struck down for non-compliance with arts 7 (respect for private and family life) and 8 (protection of personal data). The UK response to this decision was to enact emergency legislation to effectively reinstate the provisions of the directive: Data Retention and Investigatory Powers Act 2014 (which received Royal Assent within three days of its first reading in the House of Commons). That too has been held to be incompatible with the EU law and the government afforded until March 2016 to remedy the problem: *R (on the application of Davis and others) v Secretary of State for the Home Department* [2015] EWHC 2092 (Admin).
[303] *Rugby Football Union v Consolidated Information Services* [2012] UKSC 55; [2012] 1 W.L.R. 3333.
[304] *Benkharbouche v Embassy of Sudan; Janah v Libya* [2014] 1 C.M.L.R. 40; [2014] I.C.R. 169. See A Sanger, "The State Immunity Act and the right of access to the court" (2014) 73(1) C.L.J. 1.

On appeal, the Employment Appeal Tribunal held that the relevant provisions of the 1978 Act were incompatible with J's right to a fair trial in terms of art.6 of the European Convention and art.47 of the Charter. So far as the European Convention issue was concerned, the 1978 Act could not be "read down" in terms of s.3 of the Human Rights Act 1998[305] but it could be disapplied as incompatible with the Charter.[306] This gives rise to an acute issue in the UK: as we shall see in the next chapter, it was a careful and deliberate choice not to confer on the courts a power to disapply an Act of Parliament where it conflicted with a Convention right; where, however, such a Convention right also finds expression in the Charter, and the case falls within the sphere of EU law, the courts have exactly that power in terms of the European Communities Act 1972. That conclusion was upheld by the Court of Appeal.[307] The exact interrelationship between the Charter, the European Convention on Human Rights, the Human Rights Act and the European Communities Act seems destined to occupy the minds of the higher courts in the coming years.

The scope of the Charter should not, however, be over-emphasised: as art.51(2) of the Charter makes clear, it does not establish any new power or task for the Union, or modify the powers or tasks defined by the treaties. It therefore only applies within the sphere of EU law.[308] It remains too early to tell just how extensive an impact it will have.

EU LAW IN THE UK

Introduction

10–40 We have already seen, in Ch.3, above, the impact of EU law on the doctrine of parliamentary sovereignty. Wrestling with issues like that is not unique to the UK and similar discussions can be found in the jurisprudence of supreme and constitutional courts throughout the EU.[309] We have also seen the special place that EU law has in the law of Scotland as one of the limitations imposed upon the competence of both the devolved Parliament and the Scottish Ministers. What we turn to consider now are the two primary legislative measures that give effect to, and regulate, EU law in the UK: the European Communities Act 1972 and the European Union Act 2011. It is then necessary to briefly consider the Scotland Act 1998, which gives EU law a special place in Scots law. Finally, given the promise of a referendum on continued membership, we briefly discuss some of the legal issues that would follow from a decision by the UK to leave the EU.

---

[305] On the operation of s.3 of the Human Rights Act 1998, see paras 11–07—11–10.

[306] *Benkharbouche v Embassy of Sudan; Janah v Libya* [2014] 1 C.M.L.R. 40; [2014] I.C.R. 169 at [69].

[307] *Benkharbouche v Embassy of Sudan; Janah v Libya* [2015] EWCA Civ 33; [2015] 2 CMLR 20. An appeal to the Supreme Court is currently pending.

[308] Although that may be expanding beyond its bounds as traditionally understood. See *Zambrano v Office National de l'Emploi (ONEm)* (C-34/09) [2012] Q.B. 265; [2011] E.C.R. I-1177; I. Solanke, "Using the citizen to bring the refugee in: *Gerardo Ruiz Zambrano v Office National de l'Emploi (ONEM)*" (2012) 75 M.L.R. 101; A. Hinarejos, "Extending Citizenship and the Scope of EU Law" [2011] C.L.J. 309.

[309] Edward and Lane, *European Union Law* (2013) para.6.19 and cases cited therein.

European Communities Act 1972

The 1972 Act was the mechanism by which the UK acceded to the EU on **10–41**
January 1, 1973.[310] When the UK joined what was then the European Economic
Community, effect had to be given to all existing EU law as well as ensuring the
future EU legislation could be effectively implemented in the UK. Section 2(1)
of the 1972 Act was designed to achieve those twin aims:

> "All such rights, powers, liabilities, obligations and restrictions from time to
> time created or arising by or under the Treaties, and all such remedies and
> procedures from time to time provided for by or under the Treaties, as in
> accordance with the Treaties are without further enactment to be given legal
> effect or used in the United Kingdom shall be recognised and available in
> law, and be enforced, allowed and followed accordingly; and the expression
> enforceable EU right and similar expressions shall be read as referring to
> one to which this subsection applies."[311]

Lord Denning described the effect of that provision in characteristically vivid
terms:

> "The Treaty does not touch any of the matters which concern solely
> England and the people in it. These are still governed by English law. They
> are not affected by the Treaty. But when we come to matters with a
> European element, the Treaty is like an incoming tide. It flows into the
> estuaries and up the rivers. It cannot be held back, Parliament has decreed
> that the Treaty is henceforward to be part of our law. It is equal in force to
> any statute."[312]

Lord Denning may have underestimated the impact of the accession to the EU.
Laws LJ, in *Thoburn v Sunderland City Council*, probably better captured the
impact of the 1972 Act: "It may be there has never been a statute having such
profound effects on so many dimensions of our daily lives."[313] In any event,
s.2(1) of the 1972 Act has the effect that all directly effective EU laws apply in
the UK without the need for further action. Section 2(2) confers power on Her
Majesty by Order in Council, or any designated Minister, to make regulations for
the purpose of implementing any EU obligation incumbent upon the UK (for
example, implementing a directive). Section 3 of the 1972 Act imposes an
obligation on the courts to determine any question of EU law "in accordance
with the principles laid down by and any relevant decision of the European
Court".[314]

As we saw in Ch.3, accession to the EU presented a formidable challenge to
the classic understanding of parliamentary supremacy. The 1972 Act contains no
plain declaration of the supremacy of EU law. Instead, the legislative effect of the

---

[310] The Treaty of Accession could not bring about that result because of the dualist nature of the UK:
international treaties can only change the law of the United Kingdom when Parliament gives
effect to them (*Attorney General for Canada v Attorney General for Ontario* [1937] A.C. 326 PC
(Canada)).

[311] European Communities Act 1972 s.2(1) (as amended).

[312] *HP Bulmer Ltd v J Bollinger SA* [1974] Ch. 401 CA at 418F.

[313] *Thoburn v Sunderland City Council* [2002] EWHC 195 (Admin); [2003] Q.B. 151 at [62].

[314] That can be contrasted with the obligation in the Human Rights Act to "take into account"
decisions of the Strasbourg court. See paras 11–05—11–06.

primacy of EU law is to be found tucked away in the middle of s.2(4): " . . . any enactment passed or to be passed . . . shall be construed and have effect subject to the foregoing provisions of this section." There it is: any enactment, which therefore includes an Act of Parliament, is to have effect subject to the provisions of EU law. There is no point in repeating the earlier discussion about how the British courts responded to the challenge this provision presented.

European Union Act 2011

10–42 The 2011 Act has been subject to significant confusion.[315] It appears to have two aims (perhaps out of concern that Lord Denning's "incoming tide" is closer to a tsunami?). First, it seeks to introduce various "locks", both legislative and in the form of a referendum requirement, before certain changes can be made to numerous aspects of EU law. As we will see, and leaving aside issues associated with the use of referendums in the United Kingdom (which are discussed in Ch.5, above), this has potentially profound constitutional implications. Secondly, it enacts what was originally billed by the then Foreign Secretary (William Hague) as a "sovereignty clause". Unlike the "locks", the "sovereignty clause" appears to lurk at the opposite end of the spectrum in terms of constitutional significance. We now turn to consider these two features of the 2011 Act.

The "locks"

10–43 Much of the 2011 Act is devoted to establishing a system that requires parliamentary and/or popular approval before the UK can assent to, or implement, numerous EU decisions. The "referendum locks" are contained in ss.2–6 of the 2011 Act. These complicated provisions are not readily amendable to a brief summary.[316] But they do provide a comprehensive code which is not to be construed expansively.[317] Section 2 provides that a treaty which amends either the TEU or the TFEU shall not be ratified unless it has been approved by Parliament and the "referendum condition" is met. The "referendum condition" requires: (a) the Act providing for the approval of the treaty shall provide that the provision approving the treaty is not to come into force until a referendum has been held as to whether or not the treaty should be ratified; (b) such a referendum is held; and (c) the majority of those voting in the referendum are in favour of ratifying the treaty. Similar provision is made in s.3 for an equivalent approval process where the TEU and/or TFEU are amendment in accordance with the simplified revision procedure in art.48(6) TEU. The referendum requirements of ss.2 and 3 are avoided where the treaty or decision does not fall within s.4 of the 2011 Act, or, in the case of s.3, where the "significance condition" is satisfied.[318] Section 4 is drafted in very broad terms and it will be rare that a treaty or

---

[315] See, for example, M. Gordon and M. Dougan, "The United Kingdom's European Union Act 2011; 'who won the bloody war anyway?' " (2012) 37 E.L. Rev. 3.

[316] The more detailed analysis of the European Union Act 2011 by Professor Craig is commended: P. Craig, "The European Union Act 2011: Locks, Limits and Legality" (2011) 48 C.M.L. Rev. 1915.

[317] *Wheeler v Office of the Prime Minister* [2014] EWHC 3815; [2015] 1 C.M.L.R. 46 at [28]. The case is a useful illustration of some of the apparent gaps in the convoluted provisions in ss.2–6.

[318] Section 3(4) of the 2011 Act provides: "The significance condition is that the Act providing for the approval of the decision states that— (a) the decision falls within section 4 only because of provision of the kind mentioned in subsection (1)(i) or (j) of that section, and (b) the effect of that provision in relation to the United Kingdom is not significant."

art.48(6) TEU decision does not fall within it.[319] Section 5 requires a Minister to lay a statement before Parliament confirming their view as to whether a treaty or decision falls within the scope of s.4 and their reasons for that conclusion. Section 6 then introduces another raft of decisions that require approval both by Parliament and in a referendum. A Minister "may not vote in favour of or otherwise support" a decision which falls within s.6. Such decisions range from a decision under art.48(7) TEU to move to qualified majority voting[320] or various decisions in relation to EU common defence or the European Public Prosecutor's Office to a decision to adopt the euro.[321] The case for a referendum on the latter is much more compelling than the former. Sections 7–10 then require statutory or parliamentary approval before a Minister may approve, vote in favour of or otherwise support a range of EU decisions.[322]

Leaving aside issues around the legality, as a matter of EU law, of a number **10–44** of the provisions of the 2011 Act[323] there are two main issues of domestic constitutional significance thrown up by the 2011 Act. The first is the requirement that an Act of Parliament shall not come into force until such time as a referendum has been held. It may be argued that the 2011 Act changes the "manner and form" of legislation.[324] Has Parliament redefined itself, for matters falling within the 2011 Act as a tricameral body consisting of Commons, Lords and the citizens?[325] On that argument, if Parliament were to pass an Act approving a treaty amendment or another decision that falls within the scope of the 2011 Act without holding a referendum and obtaining a positive result, the court should not recognise that Act as valid. There is some Commonwealth authority to support the "manner and form" argument.[326] As we saw in Ch.3, above however, on a classic understanding of the doctrine of parliamentary sovereignty, Parliament cannot bind its successors. Thus applying the orthodox view of sovereignty, it would be open to Parliament to dispense with the requirements of the 2011 Act in any particular case. It might be thought that the political cost of eliding the referendum requirement would be such that Parliament would never countenance such a thing. But the range of issues on which a referendum is now required is so vast. Take, for example, a proposed decision to adopt measures concerning unfair dismissal by the ordinary legislative process instead of the special legislative process in terms of art.153(2)

---

[319] Three specific carve-outs are made in s.4(4): "A treaty or Article 48(6) decision does not fall within this section merely because it involves one or more of the following— (a) the codification of practice under TEU or TFEU in relation to the previous exercise of an existing competence; (b) the making of any provision that applies only to member States other than the United Kingdom; (c) in the case of a treaty, the accession of a new member State." As Craig points out the language of this provision is complex and likely to be of limited practical significance. For example, accession treaties are often used to introduce other treaty amendments thus the exception is unlikely to apply: Craig, "The European Union Act 2011: Locks, Limits and Legality" (2011) 48(6) C.M.L. Rev. 1915, 1923–1924.

[320] See para.10–33, above.

[321] The full list is set out in s.6(5) of the 2011 Act.

[322] The matters covered by these sections are more fully explained by Craig, "The European Union Act 2011: Locks, Limits and Legality" (2011) 48 C.M.L. Rev. 1915, 1917–1920.

[323] See Craig, "The European Union Act 2011: Locks, Limits and Legality" (2011) 48 C.M.L. Rev. 1915, 1928–1936.

[324] See, for example, I. Jennings, *The Law of the Constitution*, 5th edn (London: University of London Press, 1959) Ch.4.

[325] V. Bogdanor, "Imprisoned by a Doctrine: The Modern Defence of Parliamentary Sovereignty" (2012) 32 O.J.L.S. 179.

[326] See para.3–05, above.

TFEU. Section 6 of the 2011 Act requires approval by Act of Parliament and by referendum before the Minister could vote in favour of such a measure. Pity the party activists that have to drum up enthusiasm amongst the electorate to traipse to a polling station on a damp Thursday evening to cast their vote on that issue. But pity more the Prime Minister who has to explain to Parliament that, after spending parliamentary time passing the necessary Act and tens of millions of pounds organising and winning a referendum, that the decision was not passed because, whilst the UK was organising its referendum, one or more Member States had changed their mind and the measure failed despite the British people giving it the thumbs up. So whilst the referendum "lock" may be politically binding on issues such as adopting the single currency or any substantial revision of the treaties, for many of the matters caught within the scope of the 2011 Act, it may be (and probably should be) a requirement more honoured in the breach than in the observance.

The second issue of note is the form of referendum. There are no turnout thresholds and a simple majority of the votes case is required for ratification.[327] As we discussed in Ch.5, above, issues of legitimacy arise when the turnout in a referendum falls significantly. Low turnout must be an issue of concern in relation to the 2011 Act. The "catch-all" manner in which it is drafted risks the British electorate being asked, at reasonably frequent intervals (at least for a country that has only ever had two nationwide referendums) to express a view on fairly technical points of EU law. There is no need to repeat the points made earlier about the democratic legitimacy of a referendum result in such circumstances.[328] But there threatens to be a substantial political price to pay for the UK as a result of these provisions. How often will the other Member States be prepared to put otherwise uncontroversial measures on hold for six months or so (and it is hard to envisage the necessary Act being passed and referendum held in less than six months)? And how will they react when, after such a pause, the UK returns to the Council to explain that on a 20 per cent turnout, 51 per cent of the electorate voted against the proposal to adopt the ordinary legislative process in relation to that regulation concerning unfair dismissal?

The "sovereignty clause"

10–45 Despite the constitutional implications of the "lock" provisions in the 2011 Act, it was what has now become s.18 of the Act that caused much of the debate as the Act made its way through Parliament. After various iterations, the form that was settled upon was this:

> "Directly applicable or directly effective EU law (that is, the rights, powers, liabilities, obligations, restrictions, remedies and procedures referred to in section 2(1) of the European Communities Act 1972) falls to be recognised and available in law in the United Kingdom only by virtue of that Act or where it is required to be recognised and available in law by virtue of any other Act."

As enacted, s.18 is simply a declaration of what the law is, and what it had always been understood to be:

---

[327] See ss.2(2)(c) and 3(2)(c) of the 2011 Act.
[328] See para.5–08, above.

"It is important now to declare—*and it must be made plain*—that the provisions of article 119 of the EEC Treaty take priority over anything in our English statute on equal pay which is inconsistent with article 119. *That priority is given by our own law. It is given by the European Communities Act 1972 itself*"[329] (emphasis added).

The counter-argument, that EU law contains the entrenchment of its own supremacy[330] and by importing EU law into domestic law Parliament thereby imported that entrenchment, was specifically rejected by the Divisional Court of the High Court in *Thoburn v Sunderland City Council*.[331] So quite why s.18 was required is unclear. It simply appears to declare exactly what the law has always been accepted by the courts to be. If, however, the "manner and form" argument in relation to the "locks" outlined above is correct Parliament has limited its sovereignty in relation to ratification of EU Treaty amendments and other decisions. If it can limit its sovereignty in that field, why not others? If that is correct, as Bogdanor points out, it is somewhat paradoxical, and ironic, that in seeking to defend parliamentary sovereignty against "the European's", Parliament in fact surrendered it.[332]

Scotland Act 1998

As we have seen, the Scottish Parliament has a limited legislative competence **10–46** and the Scottish Government has similar restraints imposed upon its powers.[333] One of those limits is EU law. That is unsurprising: the legislative competence of the UK Parliament is curtailed by EU law so it was inevitable that the same limitation would be placed on the Scottish Parliament.[334] International relations generally, and relations with the EU in particular, are reserved under the Scotland Act.[335] That reservation is qualified, however, so as to exclude from its scope the observance and implementation of obligations under EU law. It follows from this that in matters of EU law falling within the scope of devolved competence, it is for the Scottish Parliament and the Scottish Ministers, as appropriate, to take whatever action is necessary to comply with EU law. Even outwith the sphere of devolved competence, the impact of EU law on Scottish interests will often make it appropriate for the Scottish Parliament and/or Scottish Ministers to be

---

[329] *Macarthys Ltd v Smith* [1981] Q.B. 180 CA (Cid Div) at 200E–F; Lord Bridge made the same point in *R. v Secretary of State for Transport Ex p. Factortame Ltd (No.2)* [1991] 1 A.C. 603 at 659A: "Thus, whatever limitation of its sovereignty Parliament accepted when it enacted the European Communities Act 1972 was entirely voluntary. Under the terms of the Act of 1972 it has always been clear that it was the duty of a United Kingdom court, when delivering final judgement, to override any rule of national law found to be in conflict with any directly enforceable rule of [EU] law."

[330] *NV Algemene Transport- en Expeditie Onderneming van Gend en Loos v Nederlandse Administratie der Belastingen* (C-26/62) [1963] E.C.R. 1 and *Costa v ENEL* (C-6/64) [1964] E.C.R. 585.

[331] *Thoburn v Sunderland City Council* [2002] EWHC 195 (Admin); [2003] Q.B. 151 at [58]–[59].

[332] Bogdanor, "Imprisoned by a Doctrine: The Modern Defence of Parliamentary Sovereignty" (2012) 32 O.J.L.S. 179, 190.

[333] See paras 6–19 and 17–20.

[334] Although there are conceptual differences in the limitations: an Act of Parliament that is found to be incompatible with EU law is dis-applied, but not struck down whereas an Act of the Scottish Parliament is "not law" so far as it is incompatible with EU law. That distinction is as a result of the terms of the Scotland Act 1998 (s.29(2)) and has nothing to do with EU law itself.

[335] Scotland Act 1998 Sch.5 para.7(1).

consulted on legislative proposals, to assist in the formulation of the UK's policies in relation to the EU and even to represent the UK in meetings of the Council of Ministers.

Cessation of membership

10-47 Until the Lisbon Treaty was adopted there was no formal exit mechanism: the Union was "an ever-lasting Union".[336] It is true that Greenland left in 1985. That cessation was effected by a formal treaty amendment.[337] But it was the result of a change in internal Danish constitutional arrangements and a popular vote by the people of Greenland.[338] There is no example of an entire Member State having left. Given a mechanism now exists within the treaties to allow for cessation, unilateral and immediate cessation is probably prohibited.[339] In any event, that is an issue that may never arise and, at least, is much further down the road. In 2013, a private members' Bill was introduced which would require a referendum to be held before 31 December 2017 at which the electorate would be asked: "Do you think that the United Kingdom should be a member of the European Union?"[340] The Bill received the support of the government, or, at least, the Conservative part of the coalition government. Despite passing through the House of Commons, the Bill did not survive the House of Lords. However, the debate on continued membership of the EU goes on and a referendum by the end of 2017 has been promised. The European Union Reference Bill is, at the time of writing, before Parliament, and if passed will fulfil the pledge. In the event of a vote in favour of leaving the EU, and assuming Parliament then gave effect to that result,[341] the UK would have to invoke the procedure set out in art.50 TEU. That provides that a Member State may decide to withdraw in accordance with its own constitutional requirements.[342] A Member State must then notify the European Council of its intention to leave the Union, following which

> "the Union shall negotiate and conclude an agreement with that State, setting out the arrangements for its withdrawal, taking account of the framework for its future arrangement with the Union".[343]

Those negotiations shall be conducted in accordance with art.218 TFEU (the procedure for negotiating an agreement between the EU and a third country). The EU may conclude the cessation agreement by the Council acting by qualified majority having obtained the consent of the European Parliament. Withdrawal

---

[336] On the cessation provisions, see Edward and Lane, *European Union Law* (2013) paras 2.75–2.79.

[337] Treaty amending, with regard to Greenland, the Treaties establishing the European Communities [1985] OJ L29/1.

[338] In 1982, they voted in favour of withdrawing from the EU (which was then the EEC) by a narrow margin: 52:48 on approximately a 75% turnout.

[339] In which case, the European Union (Withdrawal) Bill, a private members' Bill introduced by Lord Pearson of Rannock in June 2014, would be inappropriate, providing as it did for the simple repeal of the European Communities Act 1972.

[340] European Union (Referendum) Bill cl.1.

[341] That may be stating the (at least politically) obvious but it was a point Lord Neuberger PSC reminded us of in relation to the Scottish independence referendum: a referendum result does not bring about change, only an Act of Parliament and Parliament is not, he said, bound by the result of any referendum: *Moohan, Petitioner* [2014] UKSC 67; 2015 S.L.T. 2 at [47].

[342] Article 50(1) TEU.

[343] Article 50(2) TEU.

takes effect on the date specified in the cessation agreement, failing which two years after the Member State notified the Council of its intention to leave the Union.[344] Should that state wish to rejoin the Union, it must apply for membership in accordance with the normal application procedure (art.49 TEU). These provisions have never yet been utilised.

For now, however, the UK remains a member of the EU and with that comes **10–48** the full suite of rights and obligations inherent in membership of the Union. If that is to change, it is likely to be at the specific behest of the UK electorate, expressed in a referendum. If that is so, both domestic and EU law will have to recalibrate to give effect to that decision of the people.

---

[344] Article 50(3) TEU.

CHAPTER 11

HUMAN RIGHTS

Introduction

11-01 It has been said that if the twentieth century had a "big idea" at all, it was the idea of human rights.[1] More accurately, the "big idea" was the codification, at national and international level, of these rights. The post-war period was characterised by the emergence of a new international order in which, in response to the atrocities perpetrated during the war and (in some cases) with a view to securing social and economic advancement, human rights featured prominently. The European Convention on Human Rights was a product of these times, adopted under the auspices of the Council of Europe and signed and ratified by the UK in 1951.[2] Unlike many other international treaties, the Convention provided a mechanism for its own enforcement in the European Court of Human Rights, which was established in 1958 following the acceptance by the requisite eight signatory states of its compulsory jurisdiction. The UK accepted the compulsory jurisdiction of the court in 1966, and granted its citizens the right of individual petition the same year.[3]

The consequences of this were two-fold. First, pressure grew for the adoption of a domestic bill of rights, whether by incorporation of the Convention into national law or otherwise.[4] At the same time, perhaps stung by the European Court's exposure of the deficiencies of the common law in defending individual freedom, the courts themselves began to develop, in various ways, a domestic human rights jurisprudence.[5] In order to understand the constitutional climate in which the Human Rights Act was eventually enacted in 1998, it is necessary to consider the nature and foundation of that jurisprudence, the development of which was part of a wider reappraisal of our constitutional traditions.

---

[1] R. Singh, *The Future of Human Rights in the United Kingdom: Essays on law and Practice* (Oxford: Hart Publishing, 1997) p.1.

[2] G. Marston, "The United Kingdom's Part in the Preparation of the European Convention on Human Rights" (1993) 43 I.C.L.Q. 819.

[3] Lord Lester, "UK Acceptance of the Strasbourg Jurisdiction: What really went on in Whitehall in 1965" [1998] P.L. 237.

[4] The argument for incorporation was never one of mere principle. In practical terms, it was difficult to see why, if British citizens were to have the benefit of the Convention rights at all, they should be obliged to resort to the European Court of Human Rights in Strasbourg to vindicate them.

[5] The initiative here was almost exclusively taken by the English courts. In Scotland, it was held in *Kaur v Lord Advocate*, 1980 S.C. 319, that the courts were not entitled to have regard to the Convention, whether as an aid to statutory construction or otherwise. This remained the position until the decision of the Inner House in *T, Petitioner*, 1997 S.L.T. 724.

PRE-INCORPORATION STATUS OF HUMAN RIGHTS

As we have seen, the UK adopts a "dualist" view of the relationship between **11–02** international treaties and domestic law.[6] On this view, a treaty does not form part of national law unless and until incorporated into the law by legislation. That failing, the treaty cannot create rights or duties enforceable before the national courts.[7] The rationale for this is that the making of a treaty is an executive, not a legislative, act, and the government should not be permitted to burden citizens with obligations unsanctioned by Parliament.[8] This is not to say that the Convention was without legal effect in the domestic laws of the UK. In England at least, the courts had regard to the Convention rights as an aid to the construction of ambiguous statutory provisions, on the presumption that Parliament would not have intended to legislate inconsistently with the UK's treaty obligations.[9] Further, where legislation was enacted specifically to comply with the UK's obligations under the Convention, the courts sought to read and give effect to it consistently with the Convention rights.[10] By the same token, the Convention provided a guide to the development of the common law.[11] More broadly, the courts began to recognise fundamental rights as factors material to the lawful and rational exercise of discretion by administrative officials. In so doing, they fashioned a domestic human rights jurisprudence offering, by the time of incorporation of the Convention, a level of protection comparable to, if by no means co-extensive with, that accorded under the Convention proper.[12] This manifested itself in different ways. One technique was to develop (or rediscover) a robust principle of statutory construction, whereby, in the absence of clear and express provision to the contrary, Parliament was taken to authorise no interference with fundamental rights.[13] In other cases, the human rights dimension influenced the rigour with which the court would test the reasonableness of the decision. Thus in *Bugdaycay v Secretary of State for the Home Department*,[14] where the applicant, an asylum seeker, sought judicial review of the Home Secretary's decision to deport him, Lord Bridge held:

> "The most fundamental of all human rights is the individual's right to life, and when an administrative decision under challenge is said to be one which

---

[6] And whether it should continue to do so in relation to issues of human rights has been disputed. See para.2–12, above.

[7] *JH Rayner (Mincing Lane) Ltd v Department of Trade and Industry* [1990] 2 A.C. 418 HL.

[8] For criticism of this doctrine in relation to human rights treaties, see Lord Steyn, "Democracy Through Law" [2002] E.H.R.L.R. 723. See above.

[9] *Waddington v Miah* [1974] 1 W.L.R. 683 HL.

[10] *Re Lonrho Plc* [1990] 2 A.C. 154 HL at 208 and 209.

[11] *Derbyshire CC v Times Newspapers Ltd* [1993] A.C. 534 HL.

[12] See J. Munro, "Judicial Review, Locus Standi and Remedies: The impact of the Human Rights Act 1998" in A.E. Boyle et al (eds), *Human Rights and Scots Law* (Oxford: Hart, 2002) Ch.6.

[13] Lord Browne-Wilkinson made the case for this approach in "The Infiltration of a Bill of Rights" [1992] P.L. 397. The technique was applied, by Lord Browne-Wilkinson and others, in a number of important decisions, including *R. v Secretary of State for the Home Department Ex p. Leech (No.2)* [1994] Q.B. 198 CA (Civ Div) (cf. in Scotland, *Leech v Secretary of State for Scotland*, 1993 S.L.T. 365); *R. v Secretary of State for Social Security Ex p. Joint Council for the Welfare of Immigrants* [1996] 4 All E.R. 385 CA (Civ Div); *R. v Lord Chancellor Ex p. Witham* [1997] 2 All E.R. 779 QBD; and *R. v Secretary of State for the Home Department Ex p. Pierson* [1998] A.C. 539 HL. For more venerable authority, see *Pyx Granite Co Ltd v Ministry of Housing and Local Government* [1960] A.C. 260 HL.

[14] *Bugdaycay v Secretary of State for the Home Department* [1987] A.C. 514 HL.

may put the applicant's life at risk, the basis of the decision must surely call
for the most anxious scrutiny."[15]

The effect of *Bugdaycay* was to prepare the way for the reception of something
resembling the principle of proportionality.[16] As early as 1996, in appropriate
cases, the courts were prepared to hold that

"the more substantial the interference with human rights, the more the court
will require by way of justification before it is satisfied that the decision is
reasonable".[17]

HUMAN RIGHTS ACT 1998

11-03 Against that background, the Human Rights Act 1998 was enacted, entering into
force on 2 October 2000, and bringing with it a significant change to the legal
landscape in the UK.[18] The avowed purpose of the Human Rights Act was to
"bring rights home" so as to allow UK citizens to rely upon the rights protected
by the Convention before the domestic courts.[19] The Human Rights Act is almost
unique, in that it cuts across almost all areas of law.[20] The Act did this not by
wholesale incorporation of the Convention but by creating a number of
"Convention rights" in exactly the same terms as those protected by the
Convention.[21] It is a very skilfully crafted statute. It required to balance the

[15] *Bugdaycay v Secretary of State for the Home Department* [1987] A.C. 514 at 531. The "anxious
scrutiny" doctrine, which essentially involves the substitution of orthodox *Wednesbury* review for
a level of control approaching review for proportionality, was subsequently adopted in cases
involving freedom of expression (see *R. v Secretary of State for the Home Department Ex p. Brind*
[1991] 1 A.C. 696 HL) and the right to respect for private life (see *R. v Ministry of Defence Ex
p. Smith* [1996] Q.B. 517 CA (Civ Div)), although in neither case to the advantage of the
applicant.
[16] The differences between *Wednesbury* review and proportionality review are discussed in the
speech of Lord Steyn in *R. (on the application of Daly) v Secretary of State for the Home
Department* [2001] 2 A.C. 532 HL.
[17] *R. v Ministry of Defence Ex p. Smith* [1996] Q.B. 517, per Lord Bingham MR at 554. See in
Scotland *Abdadou v Secretary of State for the Home Department*, 1998 S.C. 504. Conversely, the
orthodox *Wednesbury* standard continued to apply in areas not impinging upon fundamental
rights, particularly where the decision challenged involved questions of high economic or social
policy: see, e.g. *R. v Secretary of State for the Environment Ex p. Hammersmith and Fulham LBC*
[1991] 1 A.C. 521 HL; *East Kilbride DC v Secretary of State for Scotland*, 1995 S.L.T. 1238.
[18] As we have seen, the Scotland Act 1998 had ensured that the effects of Convention rights had
already been felt in Scotland.
[19] Home Office, *Rights Brought Home: The Human Rights Bill* (The Stationery Office, 1997),
Cm.3782, *https://www.gov.uk/government/uploads/system/uploads/attachment_data/file/263526/
rights.pdf* [Accessed 24 June 2015]; the UK was under no obligation to give domestic effect to
the Convention: *James v United Kingdom* (1986) 8 E.H.R.R. 123 at [84], *Observer v United
Kingdom* (1991) 14 E.H.R.R. 153 at [76], and *McCann v United Kingdom* (1995) 21 E.H.R.R. 97
at [153].
[20] For an eloquent description of the effects of the Human Rights Act 1998, see Lord Rodger's
comments at [179]–[185] in *Wilson v First County Trust Ltd (No.2)* [2003] UKHL 40; [2004] 1
A.C. 816 HL.
[21] The articles of the Convention which are prescribed as "Convention rights" are arts 2–12 and 14,
arts 1–3 of the First Protocol and art.1 of the Thirteenth Protocol, all read with arts 16–18 of the
Convention (Human Rights Act s.1(1)). They have effect subject to any derogation or reservation
by the UK (s.1(2)) and are set out in Sch.1. Section 1(4) provides that the Secretary of State may
amend the Human Rights Act as necessary to reflect any Protocol to the Convention signed and
ratified by the UK.

continuing sovereignty of Parliament, with the effective protection of the rights it contained whilst allowing those rights to reflect the domestic context within which they would be relied upon. Added to that is the fact that the Convention is a living, and evolving, instrument: the scope of any particular article today may not be what it was yesterday.[22] The Human Rights Act is, as we have seen, a "constitutional statute" which although not immune from express repel, it holds an elevated place in the constitution. Its status was best described by Lord Rodger of Earlsferry:

> "Although the Act is not entrenched, the Convention rights that it confers have a peculiar potency. Enforcing them may require a court to modify the common law. So far as possible, a court must read and give effect to statutory provisions in a way that is compatible with them. Rights that can produce such results are clearly of a higher order than the rights which people enjoy at common law or under most other statutes."[23]

In 2015, the Conservative Government was elected with a manifesto pledge to repeal the Human Rights Act and replace it with a "British Bill of Rights". What that would look like is unknown at the time of writing.

Before turning to consider the key provisions of the Human Rights Act[24] it is **11–04** appropriate to sound a note of caution. The Act, and the Convention rights it creates, despite Lord Rodger's elegant description, are secondary to the common law in relation to the protection of human rights. The Supreme Court recently took the opportunity to (again) remind the legal profession of that point:

> "What we now term human rights and public law has developed through our common law over a long period of time ... The growth of the state has presented the court with new challenges to which they have responded by a process of gradual adaption and development of the common law to meet current needs. This has always been the way of the common law and it has not ceased on the enactment of the Human Rights Act 1998, although since then there has sometimes been a baleful and unnecessary tendency to overlook the common law. It needs to be emphasised that it was not the purpose of the Human Rights Act that the common law should become an ossuary."[25]

---

[22] *Tyrer v United Kingdom* (1979–80) 2 E.H.R.R. 1 was the first time the Strasbourg court acknowledged the idea but it has since become firmly embedded in its case law. In the European Court on Human Rights, *Practical Guide to Admissibility Criteria* (Council of Europe/European Court of Human Rights, 2014) and reported at (2015) 60 E.H.R.R. SE8, the court states: "As a living instrument, the Convention must be interpreted in light of present-day conditions" (at para.7).

[23] *Wilson v First County Trust Ltd (No.2)* [2003] UKHL 40; [2004] 1 A.C. 816 at [180]. Lord Rodger's description of the Human Rights at [179]–[184] is worth reading in its entirely.

[24] It is not possible to discuss the substance of any, let alone all, of the Convention rights. They are considered in a number of specialist texts, including: Lord Lester, Lord Pannick and J. Herberg, *Human Rights Law and Practice*, 3rd edn (London: Lexis Nexis, 2009); Lord Reed and J.L. Murdoch, *Human Rights Law in Scotland*, 3rd edn (Haywards Heath: Bloomsbury Professional, 2011); Wadham et al, *Blackstone's Guide to the Human Rights Act 1998*, 7th edn (Oxford: Oxford University Press, 2015).

[25] *Kennedy v Charity Commission* [2014] UKSC 20; [2015] A.C. 455, per Lord Toulson at [133]; Lord Mance made similar comments at [46]. A similar point was made by Lord Reed in *R. (on the application of Sturnham) v Parole Board* [2013] UKSC 23; [2013] 2 A.C. 254 at [29] and *R. (on the application of Osborn) v Parole Board* [2013] UKSC 61; [2014] A.C. 1115 at [54]–[63].

With that note of caution ringing in our ears, we now turn to consider the specific provisions of the Human Right Act 1998.

Section 2: Status of European Court of Human Rights jurisprudence[26]

11–05 The Human Rights Act starts by explaining what regard domestic courts should have to decisions of the European Court of Human Rights in Strasbourg. Section 2(1) provides that domestic courts must "take into account" any decision of the European Court of Human Rights[27] "whenever made or given" so far as it is relevant to the question that is before the court. So decisions of the European Court of Human Rights are not binding on domestic courts.[28] However, domestic courts should: "In the absence of special some circumstances . . . follow any clear and constant jurisprudence of the European Court of Human Rights."[29] That dicta has evolved into what has now become known as the "*Ullah* principle":

> "It is of course open to member states to provide for rights more generous that those guaranteed by the Convention, but such provision should not be the product of interpretation of the Convention rights by national courts, since the meaning of the Convention should be uniform throughout the States party to it. The duty of national courts is to keep pace with the Strasbourg jurisprudence as it evolved over time: no more, but certainly no less."[30]

Lord Brown subsequently put his own twist on *R. (on the application of Ullah) v Special Adjudicator* when he explained the final sentence "could as well have ended: 'no less, but certainly no more'".[31] That approach to the Strasbourg jurisprudence has proved controversial[32] but it allowed Lord Rodger to produce his memorably succinct judgment in *Secretary of State for the Home Department v AF (No.3)*: "Strasbourg has spoken, the case is closed."[33] That statement is not absolute. In *R. v Horncastle* Lord Phillips explained the circumstances in which domestic courts can decline to follow Strasbourg jurisprudence:

---

[26] For an interesting discussion of this issue see, Lord Phillips, "Strasbourg Has Spoken" in A. Burrows, D. Johnston and R. Zimmermann, *Judge and Jurist: Essays in Memory of Lord Rodger of Earlsferry* (Oxford: Oxford University Press, 2013).

[27] Or an opinion or decision of the Commission or decision of the Committee of Ministers.

[28] This does nothing to the domestic rules of precedent: if a judge considers that a binding decision is inconsistent with European Court of Human Rights jurisprudence they must decide the case in accordance with the binding domestic authority. They can then, if appropriate, give leave to appeal. See: *Kay v Lambeth LBC* [2006] UKHL 10; [2006] 2 A.C. 465.

[29] *R. (on the application of Alconbury) v Secretary of State for the Environment, Transport and the Regions* [2001] UKHL 23; [2003] 2 A.C. 295, per Lord Steyn at [26].

[30] *R. (on the application of Ullah) v Special Adjudicator* [2004] UKHL 26; [2004] 2 A.C. 323, per Lord Bingham of Cornhill at [20].

[31] *R. (on the application of Al-Skeini) v Secretary of State for Defence* [2007] UKHL 26; [2008] 1 A.C. 153 at [106].

[32] See, for example R. Masterman, "Section 2(1) of the Human Rights Act 1998: Binding Domestic Courts to Strasbourg?" [2004] P.L. 725; J. Wright, "Interpreting Section 2 of the Human Rights Act: Towards an Indigenous Jurisprudence of Human Rights" [2009] P.L. 595; N. Bratza, "The Relationship between the UK Courts and Strasbourg" [2011] E.H.R.L.R. 505; Lord Irvine, "A British Interpretation of Convention Rights" [2012] P.L. 237.

[33] *Secretary of State for the Home Department v AF (No.3)* [2009] UKHL 28; [2010] 2 A.C. 269 at [98].

"The requirement to 'take into account' the Strasbourg jurisprudence will normally result in the domestic court applying principles that are clearly established by the Strasbourg court. There will, however, be rare occasions where the domestic court has concerns as to whether a decision of the Strasbourg court sufficiently appreciates or accommodates particular aspects of our domestic process. In such circumstances it is open to the domestic court to decline to follow the Strasbourg decision, giving reasons for this course. This is likely to give the Strasbourg court the opportunity to reconsider the particular aspect of the decision that is in issue, so that there takes place what may prove to be a valuable dialogue between the domestic court and the Strasbourg court."[34]

Horncastle was such a case (concerning the admissibility of hearsay evidence in criminal proceedings) where the Supreme Court refused to follow Strasbourg jurisprudence which did not stem from the Grand Chamber and which was not altogether clear.[35] That approach was explained further by Lord Neuberger in *Manchester City Council v Pinnock* where he said:

"This court is not bound to follow every decision of the European court . . . Where, however, there is a clear and constant line of decisions whose effect is not inconsistent with some fundamental substantive or procedural aspect of our law, and whose reasoning does not appear to overlook or misunderstand some argument or point of principle, we consider that it would be wrong for this court not to follow that line."[36]

The Supreme Court has since followed that approach, in particular in relation to prisoner voting rights.[37] Where there is a clear line of jurisprudence emanating from the Grand Chamber then giving domestic effect to it should not be controversial:

"A decision of the European Court of Human Rights is more than an opinion about the meaning of the Convention. It is an adjudication by the tribunal which the United Kingdom has by Treaty agreed should give definitive rulings on the subject."[38]

What of the situation where Strasbourg has yet to speak on the point? Is it for the Supreme Court to push the boundaries and expand the meaning and content of the Convention rights? Or should it await guidance from Strasbourg?

It has been held that it would be "highly undesirable" for the domestic courts **11–06** to get "out of step" with the Strasbourg interpretation[39] and that the "wiser

---

[34] *R. v Horncastle (Michael Christopher)* [2009] UKSC 14; [2010] 2 A.C. 373 at [11].

[35] *R. v Horncastle* [2009] UKSC 14; [2010] 2 A.C. 373, per Lord Brown of Eaton-under-Heywood at [120].

[36] *Manchester City Council v Pinnock* [2010] UKSC 45; [2011] 2 A.C. 104 at [48].

[37] *R. (on the application of Chester) v Secretary of State for Justice* [2013] UKSC 63; 2014 S.C. (U.K.S.C.) 25; [2014] A.C. 271, per Lord Mance at [27] and Lord Sumption at [121].

[38] *R. (on the application of Chester) v Secretary of State for Justice* [2013] UKSC 63; 2014 S.C. (U.K.S.C.) 25; [2014] A.C. 271, per Lord Sumption at [121].

[39] *M v Secretary of State for Work and Pensions* [2006] UKHL 11; [2006] 2 A.C. 91, per Lord Nicholls at [29].

course" is to wait until the Strasbourg court has spoken.⁴⁰ That would appear to
be the natural consequence of the *"Ullah* principle": no more, but certainly no
less; no less, but certainly no more. Lord Brown explained, in *R. (on the
application of Al-Skeini) v Secretary of State for Defence*, why it was important
that domestic courts did not get ahead of the Strasbourg court:

> "There seems to me, indeed, a greater danger in the national court
> construing the Convention too generously in favour of an applicant than in
> construing it too narrowly. In the former event the mistake will necessarily
> stand: the member state cannot itself go to Strasbourg to have it corrected;
> in the latter event, however, where Convention rights have been denied by
> too narrow a construction, the aggrieved individual *can* have the decision
> corrected in Strasbourg."⁴¹

If domestic decisions were to run ahead of the Strasbourg jurisprudence, short of
legislating to reverse any particular decision, the UK would be stuck with the
result. That, however, has given rise to what Lord Kerr described (in the course
of his dissent in *Ambrose v Harris*)⁴² as *Ullah*-type reticence.⁴³ *Ambrose*
concerned the content of art.6, the right to a fair trial and in particular the issue
of questioning of an accused person, before detention, without a solicitor present.
Was that compatible with art.6(3)(c) of the Convention? The task for the
Supreme Court, said Lord Hope, was to identify as best it can where the
Strasbourg court stands on the issue but not to expand the scope of art.6 further
than the Strasbourg jurisprudence justifies.⁴⁴ Lord Kerr disagreed:

> "I greatly doubt that Lord Bingham contemplated—much less intended
> —that his discussion of this issue [in *Ullah*] should have the effect of acting
> as an inhibitor on courts in this country giving full effect to Convention
> rights unless they have been pronounced upon by Strasbourg. I believe that,
> in the absence of a declaration by the European Court of Human Rights as
> to the validity of a claim to a Convention right, it is not open to courts of
> this country to adopt an attitude of agnosticism and refrain from recognising
> such a right simply because Strasbourg has not spoken."⁴⁵

⁴⁰ *Ambrose v Harris* [2011] UKSC 43; 2012 S.C. (U.K.S.C.) 53, per Lord Hope of Craighead at
[15], read with Lord Hope's comments in *Smith v Ministry of Defence* [2013] UKSC 41; [2013]
3 W.L.R. 69 at [42].
⁴¹ *R. (on the application of Al-Skeini) v Secretary of State for Defence* [2007] UKHL 26; [2008] 1
A.C. 153 at [106] (emphasis in the original). This was not a new statement and was consistent
with earlier comments by the House of Lords: *R. (on the application of Clift) v Secretary of State
for the Home Department* [2006] UKHL 54; [2007] 1 A.C. 484, per Lord Hope at [49] and *N v
Secretary of State for the Home Department* [2005] UKHL 31; [2005] 2 A.C. 296, per Lord Hope
at [25] and Lord Brown at [76].
⁴² *Ambrose v Harris* [2011] UKSC 43; 2012 S.C. (U.K.S.C.) 53.
⁴³ *Ambrose v Harris* [2011] UKSC 43; 2012 S.C. (U.K.S.C.) 53 at [126].
⁴⁴ *Ambrose v Harris* [2011] UKSC 43; 2012 S.C. (U.K.S.C.) 53 at [20].
⁴⁵ *Ambrose v Harris* [2011] UKSC 43; 2012 S.C. (U.K.S.C.) 53 at [128]; Lord Kerr has developed
these comments further when speaking extra-judicially, see *The UK Supreme Court: The Modest
Underworker of Strasbourg?*, Clifford Chance lecture, 25 January 2012, *http://www.supreme
court.uk/docs/speech_120125.pdf.*

Lord Kerr, joined by Lord Wilson, was again prepared to adopt a construction that would have developed the meaning of the Convention beyond the point reached by the Strasbourg Court in *Moohan, Petitioner*.[46] Again Lord Kerr was in a minority (this time because the majority held there was a "clear and consistent" line of authority that determined the question).[47] The unwillingness to develop Convention rights beyond the Strasbourg jurisprudence can appear difficult to reconcile with other features of the Convention rights system. First, the purpose of the Human Rights Act was to ensure domestic law provided a remedy for human rights violations.[48] It did this not by way wholesale incorporation of the Convention but by the creation of domestic law rights (called "Convention rights") that correspond to rights under the Convention. Being domestic rights, their interpretation is a matter for the domestic courts,[49] who should interpret them "like any other statute".[50] It also jars with the national authorities being viewed as the primary means of securing the rights protected by the Convention. The Convention is, as the Strasbourg Court has made clear, a living instrument, the interpretation of which evolves over time. That suggests that domestic courts ought to participate in that process of ensuring the Convention keeps pace with changes in society. That may, on occasion, require domestic courts to lead the Convention into new areas.[51] And in areas that the Strasbourg Court has left to fall within the "margin of appreciation", the domestic courts will have to reach their own view anyway (so uniformity through the contracting states is not inherent within the Convention).[52] Finally, it risks giving insufficient weight to the fact the Convention establishes minimum standards for rights protection: it represents the floor, not the ceiling.[53] But there are arguments the other way, not least the traditional rule of statutory construction whereby the court will try to interpret legislative provisions based on an international treaty in a way that does not put the UK in breach of those obligations.[54] Laws LJ, in a postscript to his judgment in *Children's Rights Alliance for England v Secretary of State for Justice*, called on the Supreme

---

[46] *Moohan, Petitioner* [2014] UKSC 67; 2015 S.L.T. 2 (prisoner voting case in relation to the Scottish independence referendum); see para.1–05, above.

[47] *Moohan, Petitioner* [2014] UKSC 67; 2015 S.L.T. 2, per Lord Hodge at [9]–[13].

[48] *Aston Cantlow and Wilmcote with Billesley Parochial Church Council v Wallbank* [2003] UKHL 37; [2004] 1 A.C. 546, per Lord Hope of Craighead at [44]; *R. (on the application of Quark Fishing Ltd) v Secretary of State for Foreign and Commonwealth Affairs* [2005] UKHL 57; [2006] 1 A.C. 529, per Lord Nicholls of Birkenhead at [34]; *R. (on the application of Al-Skeini) v Secretary of State for Defence* [2007] UKHL 26; [2008] 1 A.C. 153, per Lord Rodger of Earlsferry at [54].

[49] *Re McKerr* [2004] UKHL 12; [2004] 1 W.L.R. 807.

[50] *Re G (Adoption: Unmarried Couple)* [2008] UKHL 38; [2009] 1 A.C. 173, per Lord Hoffmann at [33]; cf. Lord Scott's comments in *R. (on the application of Animal Defenders International) v Secretary of State for Culture, Media and Sport* [2008] UKHL 15; [2008] 1 A.C. 1312 where at [44] he acknowledged that Convention right were domestic rights but they "are not merely part of domestic law".

[51] As appeared to be recognised by the majority in *Re G (Adoption: Unmarried Couple)* [2008] UKHL 38; [2009] 1 A.C. 173.

[52] *Re G (Adoption: Unmarried Couple)* [2008] UKHL 38; [2009] 1 A.C. 173, per Lord Hoffmann at [36].

[53] *Handyside v United Kingdom* (1976) 1 E.H.R.R. 737.

[54] For a critique of the case for domestic courts going beyond the Strasbourg jurisprudence, see A. Kavanagh, *Constitutional Review under the UK Human Rights Act* (Cambridge: Cambridge University Press, 2009) pp.155–164.

Court to revisit the *Ullah* principle in the hope that it may be reformed.[55] If they do, those that would advocate reform include the Lord Chancellor that was the architect of the Human Rights Act[56] and, to a lesser extent, the President of the Strasbourg Court itself.[57]

Section 3: The interpretive obligation

11–07   Section 3 of the Act provides:

> "(1) So far as it is possible to do so, primary legislation and subordinate legislation must be read and given effect in a way which is compatible with the Convention rights."[58]

This is the "interpretive obligation" laid on the courts by the Act, and it is one of the Act's key provisions.[59] The interpretative obligation contained in s.3 is a strong one (*"must* be read . . . "*)*[60] but one that is only engaged when a legislative provision, interpreted in accordance with the ordinary canons of statutory interpretation, produces a result that is incompatible with a Convention right. The first task is always to ascertain the "ordinary" interpretation of a provision (in other words, to understand the intention of Parliament when enacting the provision). Only then can it be determined if it is necessary to invoke s.3.[61]

---

[55] *Children's Rights Alliance for England v Secretary of State for Justice* [2013] EWCA Civ 34; [2013] H.R.L.R. 17 at [62]–[64]; see also Sir John Laws' third Hamlyn Lecture (J. Laws, *The Common Law Constitution* (Cambridge: Cambridge University Press, 2014)). On reform of the *Ullah* principle see M. Andenas and E. Bjorge, *"Ambrose*: is the *Ullah* principle wrong?" (2012) 128 L.Q.R. 319 and Masterman, "The Mirror Crack'd", UK Constitutional Law Association blog (February 13, 2013), *http://ukconstitutionallaw.org* [Accessed 24 June 2015]; and S. Ghandhi, *Al-Skeini* and the Extra-Territorial Application of the European Convention on Human Rights" in *Judge and Jurist: Essays in Memory of Lord Rodger of Earlsferry* (2013).

[56] Lord Irvine, "A British Interpretation of Convention Rights" [2012] P.L. 237.

[57] Bratza, "The Relationship between the UK Courts and Strasbourg" [2011] E.H.R.L.R. 505. Various judges have commented on the continuing debate in extra-judicial lectures, for example: Lady Hale, *"Argentoratum Locutum:* Is the Supreme Court Supreme?" (2012) 12 H.R.L.R. 65 and Lord Reed, "The Common Law and the ECHR" (Inner Temple, 11 November 2013, *http:// www.innertemple.org.uk/downloads/members/lectures_2013/lecture_reed_2013.pdf* [Accessed 1 September 2015]).

[58] As noted in *Ghaidan v Godin-Mendoza* [2004] UKHL 30; [2004] 2 A.C. 557 (see, in particular, the speeches of Lord Steyn at [45]–[48] and Lord Rodger at [118]), this wording is modelled on the approach prescribed by the European Court of Justice for the interpretation of domestic measures by reference to European directives: see *Marleasing SA v La Comercial Internacional de Alimentacion SA* (C-106/89) [1990] E.C.R. I-4135. Note also Lord Irvine, "The Development of Human Rights in Britain under an Incorporated Convention on Human Rights" [1998] P.L. 221, in which the then-Lord Chancellor identified the interpretive techniques employed in EU cases as providing useful guidance on the proper role of the courts under the Human Rights Act 1998 s.3(1).

[59] Section 3 in fact contains two obligations: to "read" legislation in a Convention compliant manner and to "give effect to" legislation in a Convention compliant manner. They are distinct obligations (*Ghaidan v Godin-Mendoza* [2004] UKHL 30; [2004] 2 A.C. 557, per Lord Rodger of Earlsferry at [107]). Although our primary focus here is how the court "reads" legislation, other public authorities (which are also required to apply s.3) will have to ensure not only their interpretation of legislation is in accordance with s.3 but they "give effect" to it in a Convention-compliant manner.

[60] The obligatory nature of s.3(1) should be stressed. Whereas the courts empowered to make them have a discretion in relation to declarations of incompatibility, s.3(1) is, as Lord Millett observed in *Ghaidan v Godin-Mendoza* [2004] UKHL 30; [2004] 2 A.C. 557 at [59], "a command".

[61] *S v L* [2012] UKSC 30; 2013 S.C. (U.K.S.C.) 20, per Lord Reed at [15]–[17].

The function of the courts under s.3(1) remains interpretive, not quasi-legislative. Plainly, s.3(1) does not permit the courts altogether to rewrite statutory provisions in order to achieve compatibility with the Convention rights[62]; if it did, s.4 (which, as we shall see in a moment, provides for declarations of incompatibility) would be redundant. Equally plainly, it goes beyond the established principles of statutory construction, such as that which permits the courts to interpret ambiguous statutory provisions consistently with the Convention rights. Even if the meaning of a provision, construed according to the ordinary principles of interpretation, admits of no doubt, s.3(1) may nonetheless require that the provision be given a different meaning.[63] In *R. v Lambert*,[64] for example, the House of Lords accepted that the language of s.28(3) of the Misuse of Drugs Act 1971, in imposing on an accused person a legal or persuasive burden of proof of their innocence, conflicted with the presumption of innocence enshrined in art.6(2) of the Convention. It was possible to "rescue" the provision, however, by resorting to the interpretive obligation in s.3(1) and taking the word "proves" to mean "gives sufficient evidence", so converting a legal burden into a merely evidential one.

In *Ghaidan v Godin-Mendoza*, Lord Nicholls observed that, in enacting s.3, Parliament intended the courts to be able to modify the meaning and effect of legislation "to an extent bounded only by what is 'possible'".[65] Parliament had specifically rejected a "reasonableness" test for s.3 during the passage of the Human Rights Act. What s.3 provides is, in effect, "a strong rebuttable presumption in favour of an interpretation consistent with the Convention rights".[66] What is less clear is where the limits of "possibility" lie. As Lord Nicholls noted in *Re S (Children) (Care Order: Implementation of Care Plan)*, the Act reserves the amendment of primary legislation to Parliament: "By this means, the Act seeks to preserve parliamentary sovereignty. The Act maintains the constitutional boundary." Accordingly

> "a meaning which departs substantially from a fundamental feature of an Act of Parliament is likely to have crossed the boundary between interpretation and amendment".[67]

This is not to say that interpretive devices such as "reading down" to narrow the scope of a provision, or "reading in" supplementary words or phrases if

---

[62] In this respect, s.3(1) may be contrasted with provisions in the constitutions of former British colonies in relation to laws incompatible with constitutional rights. Such provisions commonly authorise the courts to construe such laws "with such modifications, adaptations, qualifications and exceptions as may be necessary to bring them into conformity with the constitution", and clearly envisage the courts engaging in a quasi-legislative role: see *R. v Hughes (Peter)* [2002] UKPC 12; [2002] 2 A.C. 259.

[63] *R. v A (No.2)* [2001] UKHL 25; [2002] 1 A.C. 45, per Lord Steyn at [44]; *Ghaidan v Godin-Mendoza* [2004] UKHL 30; [2004] 2 A.C. 557, per Lord Nicholls at [30].

[64] *R. v Lambert (Steven)* [2001] UKHL 37; [2002] 2 A.C. 545.

[65] *Ghaidan v Godin-Mendoza* [2004] UKHL 30; [2004] 2 A.C. 557 at [32]. The same point had already been made by the House of Lords in *R. v A (No.2)* [2001] UKHL 25; [2002] 1 A.C. 45 at [44].

[66] *Ghaidan v Godin-Mendoza* [2004] UKHL 30; [2004] 2 A.C. 557, per Lord Steyn at [50].

[67] *Re S (Children) (Care Order: Implementation of Care Plan)* [2002] UKHL 10; [2002] 2 A.C. 291 at [37]–[40]. See also, e.g. *De Freitas v Permanent Secretary of Ministry of Agriculture, Fisheries, Land and Housing* [1999] 1 A.C. 69 PC (Antigua and Bermuda), per Lord Clyde at 79; *Ghaidan v Godin-Mendoza* [2004] UKHL 30; [2004] 2 A.C. 557, per Lord Nicholls at [33] and Lord Rodger of Earlsferry at [115].

necessary to secure compatibility, are excluded as impermissible amendments to the legislative language. The exercise is not purely linguistic, but purposive.[68] But s.3 does not go so far as to allow the courts to introduce into the operation of primary legislation rights and duties not sanctioned by Parliament. Neither does s.3 allow the courts to read and give effect to legislation in a way apt to have practical repercussions which the courts are ill equipped to evaluate. There may be several ways of reading and giving effect to a provision in order to achieve compatibility with the Convention rights. As the House of Lords repeatedly acknowledged,[69] the choice between them may well raise questions of social or economic policy or resource allocation requiring legislative, not judicial, resolution.

But while the limitations on the scope of the interpretive obligation are easily stated, their application is far from self-executing. *Ghaidan* provides a useful illustration. As amended, para.2 of Sch.1 to the Rent Act 1977 allowed the surviving spouse of a protected tenant of a dwelling house to succeed to the statutory tenancy on the tenant's death, if then living there. A person living with the original tenant as "his or her wife or husband" was treated as a spouse for these purposes. Mr Godin-Mendoza complained that the natural and ordinary meaning of this provision breached his rights under arts 8 and 14 of the Convention, since he was prevented from succeeding to the statutory tenancy of his late partner, with whom he had lived in a stable homosexual relationship for almost 20 years.

Applying s.3(1), the Court of Appeal read and gave effect to the provisions complained of so as allow the same sex partner of a deceased tenant to succeed to the statutory tenancy of the property in which both had lived.[70] The landlord appealed to the House of Lords. By a majority the House of Lords dismissed the appeal. There was no appreciable difference between their Lordships as to the scope of the interpretive function under s.3(1), and all were agreed that, as they stood, the relevant provisions of the Rent Act were incompatible with Mr Godin-Mendoza's Convention rights. The majority had no difficulty in interpreting para.2 of Sch.1 to the Rent Act as if it provided that a person, whether of the same or of the opposite sex, who was living with the original tenant in a long term relationship, was to be treated as the spouse of the original tenant. It mattered not (bearing in mind that s.3(1) involves a purposive approach to interpretation rather than semantic pedantry) that Parliament had started with the husbands and wives of deceased tenants and subsequently extended the protection of the legislation to those who had lived with the deceased as if married. Since it was not necessary to be married to qualify for that protection, the fact that homosexuals could not then marry was not to be regarded as the critical factor excluding them from its scope. So to hold involved no "judicial

---

[68] Lord Steyn, in particular, was at pains to emphasise this in a number of speeches: *R. v A (No.2)* [2001] UKHL 25; [2002] 1 A.C. 45 at [45]; *Ghaidan v Godin-Mendoza* [2004] UKHL 30; [2004] 2 A.C. 557 at [39]. See to like effect, e.g. *Somerville v Scottish Ministers* [2006] CSIH 52; 2007 S.C. 140 at [49] and [54].

[69] In addition to *De Freitas v Permanent Secretary of Ministry of Agriculture, Fisheries, Land and Housing* [1999] 1 A.C. 69 and *Re S (Children) (Care Order: Implementation of Care Plan)* [2002] UKHL 10; [2002] 2 A.C. 291, see also *R. (on the application of Anderson) v Secretary of State for the Home Department* [2002] UKHL 46; [2003] 1 A.C. 837; *Bellinger v Bellinger* [2003] UKHL 21; [2003] 2 A.C. 467.

[70] Thereby departing from the earlier decision of the House of Lords in *Fitzpatrick v Sterling Housing Association Ltd* [2001] 1 A.C. 27 HL, that a same sex partner could only succeed to the less secure assured tenancy.

vandalism"[71] or violence to the legislative text. Lord Rodger expressed the matter in the following terms:

"[The] key to what it is possible for the courts to imply into legislation without crossing the border from interpretation to amendment does not lie in the number of words that have to be read in. The key lies in a careful consideration of the essential principles and scope of the legislation being interpreted. If the insertion of one word contradicts those principles or goes beyond the scope of the legislation, it amounts to impermissible amendment. On the other hand, if the implication of a dozen words leaves the essential principles and scope of the legislation intact but allows it to be read in a way which is compatible with Convention rights, the implication is a legitimate exercise of the powers conferred by section 3(1)."

There is probably little in this passage with which Lord Millett, dissenting in *Ghaidan*, would disagree. Nonetheless, Lord Millett was unable to accept the interpretation favoured by his brethren as a proper exercise of the interpretive function under s.3(1). His Lordship accepted that s.3 required the court to

"take the language of the statute as it finds it and give it a meaning which, however unnatural or unreasonable, is intellectually defensible. It can read in and read down; it can supply missing words, so long as they are consistent with the fundamental features of the legislative scheme; it can do considerable violence to the language and stretch it almost (but not quite) to breaking point. The court must strive to find a possible interpretation compatible with the Convention rights. But it is not entitled to give it an impossible one, however much it would wish to do so. In my view, s.3 does not entitle the court to supply words which are inconsistent with a fundamental feature of the legislative scheme; nor to repeal, delete or contradict the language of the offending statute".[72]

The statutory provisions in question were concerned with spouses, or persons living together as husband and wife. A heterosexual couple could be married, or live together as husband and wife. A homosexual couple could not.[73] Lord Millett continued:

"By what is claimed to be a process of interpretation of an existing statute framed in gender specific terms, and enacted at a time when homosexual relationships were not recognised by law, it is proposed to treat persons of the same sex living together as if they were living together as husband and wife and then to treat such persons as if they were lawfully married. It is to be left unclear as from what date this change in the law has taken place . . .

---

[71] The expression is Lord Bingham's: see *R. (on the application of Anderson) v Secretary of State for the Home Department* [2002] UKHL 46; [2003] 1 A.C. 837 at [29].

[72] *Ghaidan v Godin-Mendoza* [2004] UKHL 30; [2004] 2 A.C. 557 at [67]–[68].

[73] The Bill which became the Civil Partnership Act 2004 was before Parliament during the hearing of the *Ghaidan* appeal. This creates a new legal relationship comparable to, but distinct from, marriage. Which statutes to amend by extending their reach to civil partners and persons living together as civil partners, and whether and to what extent the Act should be retrospective, were questions then being considered in the context of the legislative process, as Lord Millett pointed out.

Worse still, in support of their conclusion that the existing discrimination is incompatible with the Convention, there is a tendency in some of the speeches of the majority to refer to loving, stable and long-lasting homosexual relationships. It is left wholly unclear whether qualification for the successive tenancy is confined to couples enjoying such a relationship or, consistently with the legislative policy which Parliament has hitherto adopted, is dependent on status and not merit."[74]

11-08   What is "possible" as a matter of interpretation is context specific and cannot be resolved in the abstract. The scheme of the Human Rights Act, and statements made to Parliament by Ministers in the course of its enactment, make tolerably clear that declarations of incompatibility are (or were intended) to be a remedy of last resort, from which it follows that incompatibility with Convention rights, when it arises, is (or was intended) to be resolved by reliance on the interpretive obligation in most cases. But where the legislation has wide ranging implications, it will usually be appropriate to leave it to the legislature to determine these policy issues and enact fresh provision, rather than the court relying upon s.3 to "cure" the problem.[75] Where a curative interpretation is unachievable, the court will not suggest how the provision should be revised so as to achieve compatibility with Convention rights: that is a matter for Parliament.[76] But the proper limits of the interpretive function under s.3(1) are bound up with sensitivities as to the proper limits of the judicial role, for one thing, and with wider issues regarding the clarity and accessibility of the law, for another. Lord Abernethy alluded to these concerns in giving the opinion of the Registration Appeal Court in *Smith v Scott*.[77] In that case, the appellant submitted that s.3(1) of the Representation of the People Act 1983, which disenfranchises all persons serving a custodial sentence following conviction of a criminal offence (and which was held by the European Court of Human Rights to be incompatible with art.3 of the First Protocol to the Convention in *Hirst v United Kingdom (No.2)*)[78] could be rescued under s.3(1) of the Human Rights Act by reading in words to the effect that the disenfranchisement of a particular prisoner would depend on

---

[74] *Ghaidan v Godin-Mendoza* [2004] UKHL 30; [2004] 2 A.C. 557 at [99]–[100]. Lord Millett added that Parliament's consideration of the scope of the Civil Partnership Act was, to that extent, foreclosed by the decision of the majority. Lord Millett's approach echoes that of the New Zealand Court of Appeal in *Quilter v Attorney General of New Zealand* [1998] 1 N.Z.L.R. 523, in which the court rejected the argument that the prohibition of discrimination in the Bill of Rights Act 1990 required it to reinterpret the provisions of the Marriage Act in such a way as to extend its scope to same sex couples. It should, however, be said that the Bill of Rights Act 1990 requires that any interpretation adopted by the courts must be "reasonable". As Lord Steyn noted in *Ghaidan* at [44], this model was available to the draftsman of the Human Rights Act but was, clearly, rejected in favour of the stronger obligation now contained in s.3(1).

[75] *Re S (Children) (Care Order: Implementation of Care Plan)* [2002] UKHL 10; [2002] 2 A.C. 291; *R. (on the application of Wright) v Secretary of State for Health* [2009] UKHL 3; [2009] 1 A.C. 739, per Baroness Hale of Richmond at [39].

[76] *R. (on the application of Wright) v Secretary of State for Health* [2009] UKHL 3; [2009] 1 A.C. 739, per Baroness Hale of Richmond at [39]. Although Lord Neuberger has recently suggested that in some circumstances a declaration should not be made without the court having expressed some idea about how it could be remedied: *R. (on the application of Nicklinson) v Ministry of Justice* [2014] UKSC 38; [2014] 3 W.L.R. 200 at [127].

[77] *Smith v Scott* [2007] CSIH 9; 2007 S.C. 345.

[78] *Hirst v United Kingdom (No.2)* (2006) 42 E.H.R.R. 41. This is not an issue that has gone away and is considered at paras 4–13 above and 11–13 below.

the discretion of the sentencing judge. The Registration Appeal Court rejected this argument in explicit terms: such an interpretation would

> "depart substantially from a fundamental feature of the legislation. Without the benefit of consultation or advice, this Court would, in a real sense, be legislating on its own account, especially in view of the wide range of policy alternatives from which a 'possible' solution would require to be selected".[79]

The court further indicated that the approach to interpretation favoured by the majority in *Ghaidan* "appears to us to give rise to potentially significant difficulties in the consistent interpretation of legislation in the various courts which may have to apply it" and expressly reserved its opinion on the extent to which that approach might be followed and applied in the Scottish courts. Despite that note of caution having been sounded, *Ghaidan* remains the leading case on the application of s.3. And before parting with it, there is one final point to note. Whilst our discussion has focused on how the court grapples with the interpretation of a statute, s.3 is not limited to the court. It applies to everyone else (in particular public authorities) who has cause to interpret and give effect to legislation.[80] That flows from the obligation imposed on all public authorities (including the court) to act in manner that is compatible with Convention rights.[81] That produces a final consequence: a party need not be a "victim"[82] to plead s.3; it is sufficient that he or she has sufficient standing to raise the case.[83]

A Minister sponsoring a Bill in either House of Parliament must, prior to its **11–09** second reading, make a statement to the effect that the provisions of the Bill are compatible with the Convention rights or that, although they are unable to make a statement of compatibility, the government nevertheless wishes the Bill to proceed.[84] A statement of compatibility is clear evidence, appearing on the face of an enactment, that it was not the intention of the legislature to violate Convention rights, and it was thought it might provide a strong incentive to the courts (whatever the subject matter of the legislation) to find means of construing the legislation consistently with the Convention.[85] They have had no such effect:

---

[79] *Smith v Scott* [2007] CSIH 9; 2007 S.C. 345 at [27]
[80] *Ghaidan v Godin-Mendoza* [2004] UKHL 30; [2004] 2 A.C. 557, per Lord Rodger of Earlsferry at [106].
[81] Human Rights Act 1998 s.6; see para.11–14, below.
[82] See para.11–23, below.
[83] *R. (on the application of Rusbridger) v Attorney General* [2003] UKHL 38; [2004] 1 A.C. 357.
[84] Human Rights Act 1998 s.19. A statement to the effect that a Bill is outwith competence but the government wish to proceed in any event is rare (for example, ss.319 and 321 of the Communications Act 2003 which banned political adverts on TV—the European Court of Human Rights subsequently held the ban to be Convention compliant: *Animal Defenders International v United Kingdom* (2013) 57 E.H.R.R. 21). In the Scottish Parliament, the Presiding Officer must make a statement confirming whether or not in their view the provisions of any Bill introduced in the Parliament would be within the competence of the Parliament, which competence depends inter alia on compatibility with the Convention rights; and the Scottish Minister in charge of an Executive Bill must make a similar statement in respect of that Bill: Scottish Parliament Standing Orders rr.9.1 and 9.3(a).
[85] See Lord Irvine, "The Development of Human Rights in Britain under an Incorporated Convention" [1998] P.L. 221.

"These statements may serve a useful purpose in Parliament . . . But they are no more than expressions of opinion by the minister. They are not binding on the court, nor do they have any persuasive authority."[86]

Since 1 January 2002, the explanatory notes issued to accompany Westminster Bills have given an outline of the government's views on compatibility, although falling short of the disclosure of its legal advice sought by some.[87] Where a Bill is amended such that the Minister responsible for it forms the view that their statement of compatibility no longer holds true, it would be a breach of the Ministerial Code to present the Bill for Royal Assent without first informing Parliament of their revised view.[88] As to pre-incorporation enactments, there were indications of a tendency to examine parliamentary materials, on a rather broader basis than was countenanced by *Pepper v Hart*,[89] in order to ascertain the mischief against which the legislation was aimed and the legislature's reasons for adopting the enactment in the chosen form.[90] In *Wilson v First County Trust (No.2)*,[91] the Speaker of the House of Commons and the Clerk of the Parliament intervened to object to this use of *Hansard* as an encroachment upon art.9 of the Bill of Rights.[92] The House of Lords accepted that the Court of Appeal in that case had made inappropriate use of parliamentary material. Nevertheless, it was held that where the courts are assessing the compatibility of legislation with the Convention rights, it is necessary to identify the rationale for the legislation, an exercise that may involve reference to "additional background material". Such material may be found in published documents, such as government White Papers; or in statements made by Ministers or members in either House of Parliament during debate on a Bill. In either case, if relevant, the courts are entitled to take it into account without "questioning" proceedings in Parliament, intruding into the legislative process or ascribing to Parliament the views expressed by a Minister: "The court would merely be placing itself in a better position to understand the legislation."[93]

11–10   *Wilson v First County Trust Ltd (No.2)* also clarified one further matter relating to the reach of s.3(1) of the Human Rights Act. It is plain that the interpretive obligation applies to any enactment, whenever enacted. The courts cannot,

---

[86] *R v A (No.2)* [2001] UKHL 25; [2002] 1 A.C. 45, per Lord Hope of Craighead at [69].

[87] Lord Lester, "Parliamentary Scrutiny of Legislation" [2002] E.H.R.L.R. 432.

[88] Cabinet Office, *Guide to Making Legislation: ECHR* (The Stationery Office, 2009).

[89] *Pepper v Hart* [1993] A.C. 593.

[90] See, e.g. the Court of Appeal decision in *Wilson v First County Trust Ltd (No.2)* [2001] EWCA Civ 633; [2002] Q.B. 74. Having examined the legislative history of the Consumer Credit Act 1974, the Court of Appeal remarked that the parliamentary debates "tended to confuse rather than to illuminate" (at [36]), shedding no light on why Parliament thought it necessary to enact the provisions there in issue.

[91] *Wilson v First County Trust Ltd (No.2)* [2003] UKHL 40; [2004] 1 A.C. 816.

[92] This provides that the proceedings of Parliament shall not be impeached or questioned in any court or place outside Parliament.

[93] *Wilson v First County Trust Ltd (No.2)* [2003] UKHL 40; [2004] 1 A.C. 816, per Lord Nicholls at [64]. See also [140]–[144] per Lord Hobhouse. Lord Nicholls added that in most cases, reference to *Hansard* was unlikely to prove useful. The same was said of the doctrine established in *Pepper v Hart*, but lawyers nonetheless feel obliged to trawl through *Hansard* in search of ministerial statements or other material that may shed some favourable light on the meaning of statutory provisions (thereby increasing the costs of litigation). Lord Steyn has argued that the only defensible application of *Pepper v Hart* arises in situations where the government states in Parliament that a statutory provision means one thing and subsequently contends for a different meaning in litigation: *"Pepper v Hart*: A re-examination" (2001) 21 O.J.L.S. 59.

however, apply a Convention-proofed interpretation of an enactment to acts or events which occurred prior to the coming into force of the Act. In other words, events prior to 2 October 2000 are not measured against an interpretation of a provision founded upon s.3. To that extent, the Human Rights Act does not have retroactive effect. This distance from the commencement of the Human Rights Act, and having regard to the various limitation periods that operate, this issue will now rarely arise.

Section 4: Declarations of incompatibility

If it is not possible to read and give effect to a statutory provision consistently **11–11** with the Convention rights, then certain higher courts[94] may make a declaration of incompatibility in respect of the provision.[95] In relation to a provision of subordinate legislation, the same courts may make a declaration of incompatibility if satisfied that the provision is incompatible with a Convention right and that the parent statute (disregarding any possibility of revocation) prevents removal of the incompatibility.[96] For the purposes of the Human Rights Act, Acts of the Scottish Parliament constitute subordinate legislation.[97] However, a declaration of incompatibility under s.4 could never be appropriate in relation to a provision of an Act of the Scottish Parliament: as we saw in Ch.6, above, where such a provision is held to be incompatible with Convention rights it is ultra vires the Scottish Parliament and will held to be "not law". [98] It will be obvious that s.3 and s.4 work very closely together. The more than can be achieved through s.3, the less s.4 will have to be deployed. As we will see in a moment, s.4 can leave an applicant with a somewhat pyrrhic victory so limiting the use of s.4 is not necessarily a bad thing. But the other side of the coin is that the more cases that are resolved using s.3, the fewer that are returned to Parliament to resolve using the remedial mechanism that is provided for in the Human Rights Act (s.10). It calls for a careful balance to be struck.

Resort to s.4 "must always be an exceptional course"[99] and one that is **11–12** available only after the court has first tried to remedy the problem using s.3.[100] Where a court is considering whether to make a declaration of incompatibility, the Crown is entitled to notice of the proceedings and thereafter to be joined as a party to the proceedings.[101] The Crown in this sense is defined to include a

---

[94] For Scottish purposes, the Supreme Court, the Courts Martial Appeal Court, the Court of Session and the High Court of Justiciary sitting otherwise than as a trial court: Human Rights Act 1998 s.4(5)(a) and (d).

[95] Human Rights Act 1998 s.4(2); the remedy is a discretionary one and the court may refuse to make a declaration even where satisfied the impugned provision is incompatible with Convention rights. For example, where a declaration has already been made by another court, there is unlikely to be any merit in issuing a second declaration: *R. (on the application of Chester) v Secretary of State for Justice* [2009] EWHC 2923 (Admin); [2010] H.R.L.R. 6 at [32]–[44].

[96] Human Rights Act 1998 s.4(4).

[97] Human Rights Act 1998 s.21. So too does "any order, rules, regulations, scheme, warrant, byelaw or other instrument made by a member of the Scottish Government . . . in exercise of prerogative or other executive functions of Her Majesty which are exercisable by such a person on behalf of Her Majesty".

[98] Scotland Act 1998 s.29; see para.6–24 above, See also: I. Jamieson, "The Relationship between the Scotland Act and the Human Rights Act", 2001 S.L.T. (News) 43.

[99] *Ghaidan v Godin-Mendoza* [2004] UKHL 30; [2004] 2 A.C. 557, per Lord Steyn at [50].

[100] *Wilson v First County Trust Ltd (No.2)* [2003] UKHL 40; [2004] 1 A.C. 816, per Lord Nicholls at [14].

[101] Human Rights Act 1998 s.5(1) and (2).

Minister of the Crown (or any person nominated by them) and a member of the Scottish Government.[102] Granting of a declaration of incompatibility is a matter for the discretion of the court.[103] Where the offending provision has already been declared incompatible and the complaint is the failure to take remedial action, a further declaration is unlikely.[104] It is ordinarily not for the court to propose a solution to the incompatibility it is declaring,[105] but in exceptional circumstances that may be appropriate.[106] If a declaration of incompatibility is granted, however, it has no effect on

> "the validity, continuing operation or enforcement of the provision in respect of which it is given; and ... is not binding on the parties to the proceedings in which it is made".[107]

The sovereignty of Parliament is thus preserved. Rather, a declaration under s.4 triggers the power in s.10 to take remedial action. It is important to note that it is only a power. The Minister is not obliged to make a remedial order, nor need Parliament enact amending legislation, although any failure to do so in response to a declaration of incompatibility will provide the aggrieved individual with a strong case to take to Strasbourg.[108] Ultimately, however, redress is political:

> "But the court has no role to sanction government for such failures. Under the Human Rights Act 1998 the minister has no obligation to act on a declaration of incompatibility. If he does not, the complaint's remedy is to take proceedings in Strasbourg ... [and] failure by a member state of the Council of Europe to give effect to a decision of the European Court of

---

[102] Thus it might be appropriate for a member of the Scottish Government to be joined as a party to proceedings relating to a pre-commencement enactment (as defined in the Scotland Act 1998 s.53(3)) where that enactment confers functions exercisable post-devolution by the Scottish Ministers, either by way of the general transfer of functions provided for by s.53 or by way of a transfer of functions pursuant to s.63.

[103] "If the court is satisfied that the provision is incompatible with a Convention right, it *may* make a declaration of that incompatibility" (Human Rights Act 1998 s.4(2), emphasis added).

[104] *R. (on the application of Chester) v Secretary of State for Justice* [2013] UKSC 63; 2014 S.C. (U.K.S.C.) 25; [2014] A.C. 271, per Lord Mance at [39]. In that case, not only did the Supreme Court refuse to make a second declaration of incompatibility in relation to s.3 of the Representation of the People Act 1983, it also refused to make a declaration of incompatibility in relation to the near identically worded s.8 of the European Parliamentary Elections Act 2002.

[105] *R. (on the application of Wright) v Secretary of State for Health* [2009] UKHL 3; [2009] 1 A.C. 739, per Baroness Hale of Richmond at [39].

[106] *R. (on the application of Nicklinson) v Ministry of Justice* [2014] UKSC 38; [2014] 3 W.L.R. 200, per Lord Neuberger at [127]. Lord Wilson, in the same case (at [204]) said: "But a court will be of maximum assistance to Parliament in this regard if it not only identifies the factors which precipitate the infringement but articulates options for its elimination." *Nicklinson* was an exceptionally hard case concerning the proper interpretation of the Suicide Act 1961 and what, if any, right a person had to assisted suicide.

[107] Human Rights Act 1998 s.4(6)(a) and (b).

[108] This power is also exercisable where, following an adverse decision of the European Court of Human Rights in proceedings against the UK, it appears that a provision of legislation is incompatible with an obligation of the UK arising under the Convention: Human Rights Act 1998 s.10(1)(b). In neither case need the power in s.10 be used; it may be preferable to remedy the defect identified by the Convention or a declaration of incompatibility by way of primary legislation enacted in the normal way.

Human Rights sounds at the political level; it is as such not amendable to sanctions in national courts."[109]

This perhaps highlights an aspect of what Ewing called the "futility" of the Human Rights Act.[110]

Where there is a desire to respond positively to a s.4 declaration, a remedial order may be made by Her Majesty in Council[111] or in accordance with the procedures prescribed by Sch.2. The ordinary procedure[112] requires the relevant Minister of the Crown[113] to lay a draft of the remedial order before both Houses of Parliament after the expiry of a 60 day period commencing with the laying before both Houses of a document containing a draft of the proposed order and the "required information".[114] If during the 60 day period representations (including any parliamentary report or resolution) are made to the Minister in relation to the proposed order, the Minister must accompany the draft order laid under para.2(a) with a statement summarising the representations received and giving details of any changes made to the proposed order as a result thereof.[115] The draft order must then be approved by affirmative resolution of both Houses of Parliament within 60 days of its being laid in its final form.[116] Schedule 2 also provides for an urgent procedure, applicable in cases where the incompatible provision is contained in subordinate legislation which has been quashed, or declared invalid, by reason of its incompatibility with the Convention rights.[117] In such cases, the Minister may make a remedial order with immediate effect, but then lay the order before Parliament and declare that, because of the urgency of the matter, it was necessary to proceed without the order first being approved in draft by both Houses. Representations may be made to the Minister in relation to the order during the period of 60 days following its laying before Parliament, at the end of which period the Minister must lay before Parliament a statement summarising the representations and giving details of any changes they consider it appropriate to make to the original order in light thereof. If any changes are made, the Minister must make a further remedial order replacing the original order. The order (original or replacement) ceases to have effect at the end of a

---

[109] *R. (on the application of Chester) v Secretary of State for Justice* [2010] EWCA Civ 1439; [2011] 1 W.L.R. 1436, per Laws LJ at [27].

[110] K.D. Ewing, "The futility of the Human Rights Act" [2004] P.L. 829; K.D. Ewing, "The continuing futility of the Human Rights Act" [2008] P.L. 668; not that everybody agrees with Ewing: A. Lester, "The utility of the Human Rights Act: a reply to Keith Ewing" [2005] P.L. 249.

[111] By way of an Order in Council: Human Rights Act 1998 s.10(5).

[112] Human Rights Act 1998 Sch.2 para.2(a).

[113] That is, "the holder of an office in Her Majesty's Government in the United Kingdom": Ministers of the Crown Act 1975 s.8.

[114] Human Rights Act 1998 Sch.2 para.3(1). The "required information" is defined by para.5 as an explanation of the incompatibility which the proposed order seeks to remove, including particulars of the relevant declaration of incompatibility, funding or order; and a statement of the Minister's reasons for proceeding under s.10 and for making an order in the terms proposed. It should be noted that the Minister may only proceed under s.10 if they consider that there are "compelling reasons" for doing so (although it is inconceivable that their judgment in that matter could be challenged by way of judicial review).

[115] Human Rights Act 1998 Sch.2 para.3(2).

[116] In calculating the 60 day periods, no account is to be taken of any time during which Parliament is prorogued or dissolved, or both Houses are adjourned for more than four days: Human Rights Act 1998 Sch.2 para.6.

[117] Human Rights Act 1998 s.10(4) and Sch.2 para.2(b).

120 day period following the laying of the original order unless, during that time, both Houses of Parliament adopt resolutions approving it.[118]

11–13 The series of cases concerning the rights of convicted prisoners illustrates the limits of the Human Rights Act as a means by which to secure the protection of Convention rights. As we saw in Ch.4, above, s.3 of the Representation of the People Act 1983 bars any convicted prisoner who is, at the time of an election, serving a period of imprisonment from voting. Such a blanket ban on prisoners voting has long been held to infringe art.3 of the First Protocol[119] to the Convention.[120] As a result, a declaration of incompatibility was made by the (Scottish) Electoral Registration Court in relation to s.3 of the 1983 Act in 2007.[121] There has been, however, no political desire to amend the law so as to introduce a more proportionate ban. Indeed, when the matter surfaced again in 2011 the then Prime Minister told Parliament that the thought of enfranchising any serving prisoners made him feel physically ill and a proposed relaxation of the ban was overwhelmingly rejected by the House of Commons.[122] The matter returned to the Supreme Court in 2013 when a number of prisoners continued to complain about their inability to participate in elections.[123] There was nothing the Supreme Court was prepared to do: the ban could not be interpreted in a Convention-compliant manner under s.3[124]; it was for Parliament, using the remedial powers it has under s.10, to amend the legislation; and any further declarator would be pointless as Parliament had a draft Bill before it (although there was little prospect of it securing sufficient votes). This entire episode highlights the limits of the Human Rights Act, and thus the limits to the protection of fundamental human rights. However convicted prisoners may be regarded[125] the Grand Chamber of the European Court of Human Rights has held that their fundamental human rights have been infringed and that finding has

---

[118] But such lapse of the order will not affect the validity of anything previously done under it, or affect the power of the Minister to make a fresh remedial order: Human Rights Act 1998 Sch.2 para.4(4).

[119] For a summary of the general significance of art.3 of the First Protocol see Lord Collins' comments in *R. (on the application of Barclay) v Secretary of State for Justice* [2009] UKSC 9; [2010] 1 A.C. 464 at [52]–[59].

[120] *Hirst v United Kingdom (No.2)* (2005) 42 E.H.R.R. 41 Grand Chamber. It was not an unanimous decision and both the President, and the future President, of the court dissented. Despite that, the European Court of Human Rights has subsequently adhered to that line, despite repeated requests to depart from it: *Scoppola v Italy (No.3)* (2012) 56 E.H.R.R. 19 Grand Chamber; *Greens v United Kingdom* (2010) 53 E.H.R.R. 21; *McLean v United Kingdom* (2013) 57 E.H.R.R. SE8.

[121] *Smith v Scott* [2007] CSIH 9; 2007 S.C. 345. The matter was most recently considered by the Supreme Court in *Moohan, Petitioner* [2014] UKSC 67; 2015 S.L.T. 2 (a point on which the Supreme Court split 5:2).

[122] *Hansard*, HC col.493 (Vol.523) to 586 (10 February 2011) for a record of the debate.

[123] *R. (on the application of Chester) v Secretary of State for Justice* [2013] UKSC 63; 2014 S.C. (U.K.S.C.) 25; [2014] A.C. 271. Complaints were also founded upon alleged EU law rights and the identical ban under the European Parliamentary Elections Act 2002 (s.8) was also challenged.

[124] Given the range of possible options (discussed briefly in *R. (on the application of Chester) v Secretary of State for Justice* [2013] UKSC 63; 2014 S.C. (U.K.S.C.) 25; [2014] A.C. 271 by Lord Sumption at [114]) s.3 of the Human Rights Act was never likely to be suitable for an issue such as this

[125] And the applicants in *Chester* appear to be individuals who were particularly unlikely to encourage any sympathy or be likely to benefit from any modified ban (see *R. (on the application of Chester) v Secretary of State for Justice* [2013] UKSC 63; 2014 S.C. (U.K.S.C.) 25; [2014] A.C. 271, per Baroness Hale at [87] and [99]).

been accepted (however reluctantly) by the Supreme Court.[126] It is an infringement that has been allowed to persist. As Baroness Hale noted in *Chester*:

"Democracy is about more than respecting the views of the majority. It is also about safeguarding the rights of minorities, including unpopular minorities."[127]

It is unlikely that a s.4 declaration that affected a majority of the electorate would go uncorrected by the legislature. So it is always likely to be a minority group, and usually an unpopular minority, that will be the left with the pyrrhic victory that is a declaration that their fundamental human rights have been infringed which has no effect on the continuing validity, operation or enforcement of the offending provision. Whether they be serving prisoners or terrorist suspects[128] their rights ought to be treated equally:

" . . . it is the purposes of all human rights instruments to secure the protection of the essential rights of members of minority groups, even when they are unpopular with the majority. Democracy values everyone equally even if the majority does not."[129]

Public authorities

So far, the provisions we have considered have been principally aimed at the **11-14** court and how it secures the protection of Convention rights. Section 6 is, however, pivotal to the scheme of incorporation adopted by the Human Rights Act. It provides: "It is unlawful for a public authority to act in a way which is incompatible with a Convention right."[130] An "act" includes a failure to act but does not include a failure to introduce in, or lay before, Parliament a proposal for legislation or a failure to make any primary legislation or remedial order.[131] A public authority may only act in a manner which is incompatible with a Convention right when required to do so by primary legislation, or by secondary legislation made under it, and only then when the provision cannot be interpreted (pursuant to s.3) in manner that is compatible with the Convention right in issue.[132] But given the strength of the obligation under s.3 to strive for a

---

[126] Lord Sumption, in particular, sets out why the Grand Chamber's decision may not be sound: *R. (on the application of Chester) v Secretary of State for Justice* [2013] UKSC 63; 2014 S.C. (U.K.S.C.) 25; [2014] A.C. 271 at [113]–[137].

[127] *R. (on the application of Chester) v Secretary of State for Justice* [2013] UKSC 63; [2014] A.C. 271; 2014 S.C. (U.K.S.C.) 25 at [88]. Lord Sumption did not accept that serving prisoners constituted a minority in that sense: "But the present issue has nothing whatever to do with the protection of minorities. Prisoners belong to a minority only in the banal and legally irrelevant sense that most people do not do the things which warrant imprisonment by due process of law" (*R. (on the application of Chester) v Secretary of State for Justice* [2013] UKSC 63; 2014 S.C. (U.K.S.C.) 25; [2014] A.C. 271 at [112]).

[128] As was the case in perhaps the most celebrated s.4 declaration: *A v Secretary of State for the Home Department* [2004] UKHL 56; [2005] 2 A.C. 68. See para.13–09, below for a discussion of that case.

[129] *Ghaidan v Godin-Mendoza* [2004] UKHL 30; [2004] 2 A.C. 557, per Baroness Hale of Richmond at [132].

[130] Human Rights Act 1998 s.6(1).

[131] Human Rights Act 1998 s.6(6).

[132] Human Rights Act 1998 s.6(2).

Convention-compliant interpretation of legislation, recourse to s.6(2) is rare.[133] Three points are immediately apparent. First, it is critically important to identify who or what falls within the meaning of the term "public authority" because, secondly, the Act does not, at least directly, regulate relations between private parties. Finally, it is necessary to understand the territorial scope of the Human Rights Act: does the s.6 prohibition apply to public authorities that operate outside the UK?

Section 6 of the Human Rights Act defines "public authorities" as follows:

> "(3) In this section 'public authority' includes— (a) a court or tribunal, and (b) any person certain of whose functions are functions of a public nature but does not include either House of Parliament or a person exercising functions in connection with proceedings in Parliament. . . .
>
> (5) In relation to a particular act, a person is not a public authority by virtue only of subsection 3(b) if the nature of the act is private."[134]

This definition is not exhaustive: it was not thought necessary to define expressly bodies which are "obviously" public authorities, but only to make clear that the term included bodies which might otherwise be thought to fall outwith its scope.[135] It follows that "standard" public authorities, such as local authorities and government departments, are bound by the duty to act in conformity with the Convention rights in respect of all their activities, whereas "functional" public authorities—bodies some of whose functions are "functions of a public nature" —are bound only in the performance of those functions and not, by virtue of s.6(5), in respect of their private acts.[136] It is therefore key to understanding the breadth of the Human Rights Act that these two ideas ("functions of a public nature" and "nature of the act is private") are understood. Unsurprisingly, they have proved controversial.

During the passage of the Human Rights Bill through Parliament, the Home Secretary indicated that the means of distinguishing public from private functions should "relate to the nature and substance of the act, not to the form and legal personality".[137] It was also suggested that the way in which the courts —meaning, clearly, the English courts—have developed the concept of judicial review would offer valuable guidance.[138] Like s.6, the scope of judicial review in

---

[133] See para.11–07, above.

[134] Human Rights Act 1998 s.6(4) excluded the House of Lords acting in its judicial capacity from the definition of "Parliament". That provision was repealed by the Constitutional Reform Act 2005 as a consequence of the establishment of the Supreme Court.

[135] See R. Clayton and H. Tomlinson, *The Law of Human Rights* (Oxford: Oxford University Press, 2000) paras 5.05–5.08.

[136] This distinction between standard and functional public authorities was drawn by Clayton and Tomlinson, and was approved by the Court of Appeal in *Poplar Housing and Regeneration Community Association Ltd v Donoghue* [2001] EWCA Civ 595; [2002] Q.B. 48.

[137] *Hansard*, HC Vol.314, col.433 (17 June 1998).

[138] D. Pannick, "Who is Subject to Judicial Review and in Respect of What?" [1992] P.L. 1; *Aston Cantlow and Wilmcote with Billesley Parochial Church Council v Wallbank* [2003] UKHL 37; [2004] 1 A.C. 546, per Lord Hope of Craighead at [25]; *Poplar Housing and Regeneration Community Association Ltd v Donoghue* [2001] EWCA Civ 595; [2002] Q.B. 48, per Lord Woolf CJ at [65].

England turns on a distinction between public and private functions.[139] It has since been made clear by the House of Lords that the two are distinct.[140] The English jurisprudence could never be a complete guide, however, not least since s.2 of the Human Rights Act requires the courts to take account of the principles developed by the European Court of Human Rights, and that court has its own approach to what constitutes a public authority.[141] As has been said:

"It is only by ensuring that Convention rights are respected throughout our legal system and at all levels of society that the state can avoid liability in Strasbourg for permitting such violations [of the Convention rights]. This is the purpose of the Human Rights Act and it explains the non-incorporation of Article 13.[142] Unlike judicial review, the purpose is not limited to protecting individuals against abuses of power by the state and governmental bodies. While the presence of a governmental feature is probably conclusive of a body being a public authority within section 6, then, its absence should not be conclusive against it."[143]

In most cases, distinguishing public and private functions will present no **11–15** problem. But at the margins, it becomes more controversial. If the nature of a function and not its form is crucial, are private schools and hospitals to be treated as public authorities, at least to the extent that they provide education and health care.[144] Are charities, because of the nature of charitable objects and the state support they enjoy in terms of the tax advantages flowing from charitable status?[145] Are commercial organisations which contract to perform or provide

---

[139] Whether an function is "public" or "private" is not determinative of its susceptibility to review in Scotland; rather, the test is whether there is "a tripartite relationship between the person or body to whom the jurisdiction, power or authority has been delegated or entrusted, the person or body by whom it has been delegated or entrusted and the person or persons in respect of or for whose benefit that jurisdiction, power or authority is to be exercised": see *West v Secretary of State for Scotland*, 1992 S.C. 385, per Lord President Hope at 413. The distinction between "public" and "private" may now be relevant, however, in relation to the question of standing to bring judicial review proceedings in Scotland: *AXA General Insurance Co Ltd v Lord Advocate* [2011] UKSC 46; 2012 S.C. (U.K.S.C.) 122; see para.14–05 below.

[140] *YL v Birmingham City Council* [2007] UKHL 27; [2008] 1 A.C. 95, per Lord Bingham at [12]. See also W. Wade and C. Forsyth, *Administrative Law*, 11th edn (Oxford: Oxford University Press, 2014) p.149

[141] See, e.g. *Chassagnou v France* (1999) 29 E.H.R.R. 615 at [100].

[142] Article 13 enshrines the right to an effective remedy for breaches of the Convention rights. It is not a Convention right in terms of the Human Rights Act 1998 because (according to the government) it need not be: the fact of incorporation of the other Convention rights is sufficient to secure their effective protection in domestic law. But that is only true if the definition of public authorities under s.6 accurately reflects the scope of state responsibility in the Strasbourg Court for breaches by the state of its duty under art.1 of the Convention, to secure the Convention rights and freedoms to all within its jurisdiction, and in that regard "the state cannot absolve itself from responsibility by delegating its obligations to private bodies or individuals": *Costello-Roberts v United Kingdom* (1993) 19 E.H.R.R. 112 at [27]).

[143] K. Markus, *"Leonard Cheshire Foundation*: What is a Public Function?" [2003] E.H.R.L.R. 92, 96.

[144] The question assumes what is not necessarily the case, namely that the provision of education and health care involves, by definition, a public function. On this point, see, e.g. *Aston Cantlow and Wilmcote with Billesley Parochial Church Council v Wallbank* [2003] UKHL 37; [2004] 1 A.C. 546, per Lord Rodger of Earlsferry at [159]; *YL v Birmingham City Council* [2007] UKHL 27; [2008] 1 A.C. 95, per Lord Neuberger at [161]–[169]; and D. Oliver, "Functions of a public nature under the Human Rights Act" [2004] P.L. 329.

[145] See *RSPCA v Attorney General* [2001] 3 All E.R. 530 Ch Div.

services on behalf of a standard public authority? Are trade unions and professional bodies, because their functions relate to freedom of association (and may raise other significant questions, as in relation to the conformity of their procedures to due process guarantees)? Are religious organisations, because their functions relate to freedom of conscience and expression.[146] In some cases, such questions have been disposed of with relative ease. In *Marcic v Thames Water Utilities Ltd*, for example, no point was even taken about whether the defendant, as a privatised utility, was a public authority for the purposes of s.6.[147] Again, in *R. (on the application of A) v Partnerships in Care Ltd*,[148] it was held that a private psychiatric hospital, registered as a mental nursing home under the Registered Homes Act 1984 and licensed to receive patients detained under the Mental Health Act 1983, was a public authority for the purposes of s.6. A, an NHS patient, had been placed in the hospital for treatment of a personality disorder. The hospital managers decided to cease offering such treatment. Keith J held that the relevant statutory duties were laid directly upon the hospital as a registered facility and that the hospital managers were a body upon whom important statutory functions relating to the provision of appropriate care and treatment had been devolved. There was a strong public interest in securing the proper discharge of such functions. For those reasons, it was appropriate to place the hospital within the scope of s.6.

11–16		Both decisions accord with the government's stated intention that privatised or contracted-out methods of delivering public services should not exclude the provider from the coverage of the Human Rights Act.[149] The Court of Appeal considered the issue in *R. (on the application of Heather) v Leonard Cheshire Foundation*.[150] The foundation ran a nursing home for the disabled. Residents were placed in the home by social services and health authorities pursuant to their statutory duties to provide accommodation to those in need of care and attention by reason of age, illness or disability, and to their power to make arrangements for such accommodation to be provided by third parties. The foundation decided to close the home and the residents applied for judicial review, arguing that the foundation was a public authority and that its decision was in breach of art.8. The Court of Appeal held that "the role that [the foundation] was performing manifestly did not involve the performance of public functions".[151] Its reasons for so holding were that there was no material difference between the services provided by the foundation to privately funded and publicly funded residents, yet it was only in respect of the latter that it was said to be performing public functions; the degree of public funding, while relevant, was not conclusive; the foundation was not standing in the shoes of the local authorities or exercising any statutory powers; and, save for an element of regulation by the Care Commission,

[146] See *Aston Cantlow and Wilmcote with Billesley Parochial Church Council v Wallbank* [2003] UKHL 37; [2004] 1 A.C. 546.
[147] *Marcic v Thames Water Utilities Ltd* [2003] UKHL 66; [2004] 2 A.C. 42.
[148] *R. (on the application of A) v Partnerships in Care Ltd* [2002] EWHC 529 (Admin); [2002] 1 W.L.R. 2610.
[149] An intention no doubt born out of a desire to comply with the Strasbourg authority which did not allow liability under the Convention to be evaded by delegating public functions to private bodies. For example, *Costello-Roberts v United Kingdom* (1993) 19 E.H.R.R. 112
[150] *R. (on the application of Heather) v Leonard Cheshire Foundation* [2002] EWCA Civ 366; [2002] 2 All E.R. 936.
[151] *R. (on the application of Heather) v Leonard Cheshire Foundation* [2002] EWCA Civ 366; [2002] 2 All E.R. 936 at [35].

there was insufficient control exercised by the local authority over the foundation. The approach taken by the Court of Appeal was concerningly narrow given the prevalence of contracting-out and other forms of public/private partnership as a means of public service delivery. A reassuring note was sounded by the House of Lords in *Aston Cantlow and Wilmcote with Billesley Parochial Church Council v Wallbank*[152] where the House considered the approach to s.6(3). Without reference to *R. (on the application of Heather) v Leonard Cheshire Foundation*, let alone overruling it,[153] Lord Nicholls said:

> "Clearly there is no single test of universal application. There cannot be, given the diverse nature of governmental functions and the variety of means by which these functions are discharged today. Factors to be taken into account include the extent to which in carrying out the relevant function the body is publically funded, or is exercising statutory powers, or is taking the place of central government or local authorities, or is providing a public service."[154]

It appeared that the House of Lords was laying down a broad, functions-based, approach to "functions of a public nature".

The leading case on this matter is now *YL v Birmingham City Council*.[155] It **11–17** was a case that concerned the duty of the council to provide accommodation to YL, an 84 year old lady suffering from Alzheimer's. Under the National Assistance Act 1948, the council had a duty to make arrangements to provide YL with accommodation. Under s.26 of that Act, the council contracted an independent care home to accommodate YL. That home accommodated privately paying residents but the majority had at least part of their fees paid by the council. YL was one such resident who had the majority of her fees met by the council. Six months after YL moved into the home, the company running the home purported to terminate its contract with YL. Proceedings were commenced on behalf of YL in which, inter alia, a declarator was sought that the company running the home were exercising public functions for the purposes of s.6 of the Human Rights Act. When the case reached the House of Lords, it divided their Lordships 3:2, with the majority holding that the company was not exercising public functions. Lord Scott summarised his reasons for so holding in the following terms:

---

[152] *Aston Cantlow and Wilmcote with Billesley Parochial Church Council v Wallbank* [2003] UKHL 37; [2004] 1 A.C. 546.

[153] *R. (on the application of Heather) v Leonard Cheshire Foundation* [2002] EWCA Civ 366; [2002] 2 All E.R. 936 was cited in argument before the House of Lords (as was an earlier decision of the Court of Appeal in *Poplar Housing and Regeneration Community Association Ltd v Donoghue* [2001] EWCA Civ 595; [2002] Q.B. 48) but not referred to in the judgment.

[154] *Aston Cantlow and Wilmcote with Billesley Parochial Church Council v Wallbank* [2003] UKHL 37; [2004] 1 A.C. 546 at [12]. See also Lord Hope at [41]. Lord Rodger at [160], suggested that "the essential characteristic of a public authority is that it carries out a function of government which would engage the responsibility of the United Kingdom before the Strasbourg organs".

[155] *YL v Birmingham City Council* [2007] UKHL 27; [2008] 1 A.C. 95. For discussion of this case, see: S. Palmer, "Public, private and the Human Rights Act 1998: an ideological divide" [2007] C.L.J. 559; S. Choudhry, "Children in "care" after *YL*—the ineffectiveness of contract as a means of protecting the vulnerable" [2013] P.L. 519

"Southern Cross is a company carrying on a socially useful business for profit. It is neither a charity nor a philanthropist. It enters into private law contracts with the residents in its care homes and with the local authorities with whom it does business. It receives no public funding, enjoys no special statutory powers, and is at liberty to accept or reject residents as it chooses (subject, of course, to anti-discrimination legislation which affects everyone who offers a service to the public) and to charge whatever fees in its commercial judgment it thinks suitable. It is operating in a commercial market with commercial competitors."[156]

Lord Mance shared those concerns, and appeared to be troubled by the distinction that would fall to be drawn between self-funding residents (who would not engage the Convention) and (part-) publically funded residents (who would).[157] Likewise, Lord Neuberger recognised the force in the point that a person who would have a Convention rights claim if the service was provided by the council should not lose that simply because they have been contracted out. But that did not assist YL for a number of reasons. In particular, Lord Neuberger held that the council's duty was simply to *arrange* the provision of care, not to *provide* care so YL's was not a contracting out case.[158]

Lord Bingham and Baroness Hale dissented in forceful terms. Lord Bingham concluded his speech by saying:

"When the 1998 Act was passed, it was very well known that a number of functions formerly carried out by public authorities were now carried out by private bodies. Section 6(3)(b) of the 1998 Act was clearly drafted with this well-known fact in mind. The performance by private body A by arrangement with public body B, and perhaps at the expense of B, of what would undoubtedly be a public function if carried out by B is, in my opinion, precisely the case which section 6(3)(b) was intended to embrace. It is, in my opinion, this case."[159]

Lady Hale identified a number of important factors to be borne in mind when considering the reach of s.6(3)(b):

"While there cannot be a single litmus test of what is a function of a public nature, the underlying rationale must be that it is a task for which the public, in the shape of the state, have assumed responsibility, at public expense if need be, and in the public interest."[160]

The fact that YL made some contribution to the cost of the home did not prevent her care being a "function of a public nature". National Health Service dental care, as Lady Hale pointed out, is still a function of a public nature despite those

---

[156] *YL v Birmingham City Council* [2007] UKHL 27; [2008] 1 A.C. 95 at [26].
[157] *YL v Birmingham City Council* [2007] UKHL 27; [2008] 1 A.C. 95 at [116]–[117].
[158] *YL v Birmingham City Council* [2007] UKHL 27; [2008] 1 A.C. 95 at [146]–[153].
[159] *YL v Birmingham City Council* [2007] UKHL 27; [2008] 1 A.C. 95 at [20].
[160] *YL v Birmingham City Council* [2007] UKHL 27; [2008] 1 A.C. 95 at [65].

that can afford to do so paying for it.[161] Lady Hale concluded that applying the factors she had identified to YL, she had "no doubt" that Parliament intended her situation to fall within s.6(3)(b) and to the extent that the decision of the Court of Appeal in *R. (on the application of Heather) v Leonard Cheshire Foundation* suggested otherwise, it was wrong.[162]

Given the prevalence of contracting-out and other forms of public/private partnership as a means of public service delivery, the approach taken in *YL* matters. Whether the recipient of public services will be able to rely on their Convention rights should not turn on the happenstance of the identity and nature of the service provider. On the *YL* approach, there is a risk that it will. Whether a particular function is performed by a local authority directly or by a private company on a contracted-out basis, the function remains the same.[163] The fact that the identity of the body performing the function has changed is neither here nor there for the purposes of s.6 since, provided the function is of a public nature, the body is bound to act compatibly with the Convention rights, if only to that extent. *YL* has been subject to much criticism and attempts to amend the Human Rights Act to reverse its effects have failed.[164] As a result, the scope of this important provision of the Human Rights Act has been given a much narrower scope than was originally intended[165] and has left much uncertainty as to when the provider of a service will fall within the terms of the Act.

That brings us to the question of jurisdiction. This is an issue that will **11–18** normally present no problem whatsoever: a public authority based in the UK, that operates in the UK and whose acts have effect in the UK obviously falls within the scope of s.6. What of those public authorities that operate furth of the UK? Events in Iraq have been the main vehicle through which this question has been considered. Can a solider on deployment in the desert of Iraq rely on their Convention rights? Does an Iraqi citizen detained by the UK Army have Convention rights under the Human Rights Act? The answers to these questions have generated much litigation and have required the Supreme Court to consider the territorial scope of the Act.

Acts of Parliament do not, unless the contrary intention appears, have effect beyond the UK.[166] Accordingly, the starting position is that the obligations imposed on public authorities are only intended to apply within the UK. The territorial scope of the Convention is set out in art.1: "The high contracting parties shall secure to everyone within their jurisdiction the rights and freedoms defined in section 1 of this Convention." Article 1 is not a Convention right under the Human Rights Act but it does define the scope of the Act: the territorial scope of the Act was intended to be co-extensive with the territorial scope of the

---

[161] *YL v Birmingham City Council* [2007] UKHL 27; [2008] 1 A.C. 95 at [72].

[162] *YL v Birmingham City Council* [2007] UKHL 27; [2008] 1 A.C. 95 at [73].

[163] P. Craig, "Contracting Out, the Human Rights Act and the Scope of Judicial Review" (2002) 118 L.Q.R. 551, 556.

[164] Joint Committee on Human Rights, *Legislative Scrutiny: Health and Social Care Bill, Eighth Report of Session 2007–08* (The Stationery Office, 2008), HL 46; HC 303. Wade and Forsyth, *Administrative Law* (2014) p.148.

[165] The Secretary of State for Constitutional Affairs intervened in *YL* in support of her position.

[166] Francis A.R. Bennion, *Statutory Interpretation*, 6th edn (London: LexiNexis, 2013) pp.314–317 and 306. However, there is the curious practice of specifying that an Act applies to Northern Ireland with the consequences that Acts which are silent on the point are taken to apply only to Great Britain.

UK's obligations under the Convention.[167] Thus to understand the scope of the Human Rights Act it is necessary to understand the scope of the Convention. This was most recently considered by the Grand Chamber in *Al-Skeini v United Kingdom*.[168] At paras 131 and 132 of the judgment, the Grand Chamber explained:

> "131. A state's jurisdictional competence under article 1 is primarily territorial. Jurisdiction is presumed to be exercised normally throughout the state's territory. Conversely, acts of the contracting states performed, or producing effects, outside their territories can constitute an exercise of jurisdiction within the meaning of article 1 only in exceptional circumstances.
>
> 132. To date, the court in its case law has recognised a number of exceptional circumstances capable of giving rise to the exercise of jurisdiction by a contracting state outside its own territorial boundaries. In each case, the question whether exceptional circumstances exist which require and justify a finding by a court that the state was exercising jurisdiction extra-territorially must be determined with reference to the particular facts."

The Grand Chamber then discussed three distinct categories where extraterritorial jurisdiction could be found: state agent authority and control (for example, diplomatic staff working overseas)[169]; effective control over an area (for example, where a contracting state exercises some or all of the public powers ordinarily exercised by the government of that area)[170]; and the Convention legal space (for example, where the contracting state detains a foreign national overseas and holds them in a facility controlled by them).[171] In relation to that last category, the Grand Chamber went on to say:

> "It is clear that, whenever the state through its agents exercises control and authority over an individual, and thus jurisdiction, the state is under an

---

[167] *R. (on the application of Quark Fishing Ltd) v Secretary of State for Foreign and Commonwealth Affairs* [2005] UKHL 57; [2006] 1 A.C. 529, per Lord Nicholls of Birkenhead at [34]: "To this end the obligations of public authorities under sections 6 and 7 mirror in domestic law the treaty obligations of the United Kingdom in respect of corresponding articles of the Convention and its protocols. That was the object of these sections . . . Thus, and this is the important point for present purposes, the territorial scope of the obligations and rights created by sections 6 and 7 of the Act was intended to be co-extensive with the territorial scope of the obligations of the United Kingdom and the rights of victims under the Convention. The Act was intended to provide a domestic remedy where a remedy would have been available in Strasbourg. Conversely, the Act was not intended to provide a domestic remedy where a remedy would not have been available in Strasbourg."

[168] *Al-Skeini v United Kingdom* (2011) 53 E.H.R.R. 18; this was an appeal following the decision of the House of Lords in *R. (on the application of Al-Skeini) v Secretary of State for Defence* [2007] UKHL 26; [2008] 1 A.C. 153 in which the House had held that an Iraqi citizen that had died while in UK custody, and having been grossly mistreated by UK soldiers, was within the jurisdiction of the UK for the purposes of the Human Rights Act whereas five civilians who had been shot in a range of circumstances (some of which were hotly disputed) where not within the jurisdiction of the UK.

[169] *Al-Skeini v United Kingdom* (2011) 53 E.H.R.R. 18 at [134]; see also *Bankoviæ v Belgium* (2001) 11 B.H.R.C. 435; (2001) 44 E.H.R.R. SE5 at [71].

[170] *Al-Skeini v United Kingdom* (2011) 53 E.H.R.R. 18 at [135].

[171] *Al-Skeini v United Kingdom* (2011) 53 E.H.R.R. 18 at [136]; the example given is based on the circumstances of *Al-Saadoon v United Kingdom* (2009) 49 E.H.R.R. SE11.

obligation under article 1 to secure to that individual the rights and freedoms under section 1 of the Convention *that are relevant to the situation of that individual. In this sense, therefore, the Convention rights can be 'divided and tailored'."*[172]

The final part of that paragraph, in italics, is central to understanding jurisdiction in relation to persons detailed by a contracting state. In such circumstances (for example an insurgent detained in Iraq) the state would not be under an obligation to secure the detainees right to respect for family life or freedom of association. They would, however, as a minimum, require to secure the detainees art.2 (right to life) and art.3 (prohibition of torture) rights.

In relation to the Human Rights Act, the House of Lords and the Supreme **11–19** Court has had cause to consider jurisdictional scope on a number of occasions.[173] However, the first time the Supreme Court had the opportunity to consider the issue with the benefit of the Grand Chamber's decision in *Al-Skeini* was in *Smith v Ministry of Defence.*[174] One of the issues for the Supreme Court was: do soldiers on active service abroad fall within the UK's jurisdiction for the purposes of the Convention (and thereby within the scope of the Human Rights Act)?[175] While the court was divided on the other issues, they were unanimous in the answer to this question. As servicemen and women are under the control and authority of the state they are within its jurisdiction. Accordingly, they can rely upon their rights under the Human Rights Act.[176] Important in that extension of the territorial scope of the Act was the Strasbourg Court's decision that the package of rights contained with the Convention can, contrary what had previously been held,[177] be divided and tailored to fit the particular circumstances.[178] What is clear from the discussion in *Smith* is that the duty imposed on a public authority under s.6 of the Human Rights Act is capable of applying beyond the shores of the UK and for the benefit of people that are not citizens of this country. That presents a new and different dimension to the deployment of the armed forces overseas on missions such as that undertaken in Iraq.

---

[172] *Al-Skeini v United Kingdom* (2011) 53 E.H.R.R. 18 at [137] (emphasis added).
[173] *R. (on the application of Gentle) v Prime Minister* [2008] UKHL 20; [2008] 1 A.C. 1356, was the government under a duty, in terms of art.2, to obtain reliable legal advice before committing soldiers to war? The soldiers were not within the jurisdiction of the UK at the relevant time (Lord Bingham at [8](3)) and, in any event, art.2 did not prohibit the government from participating in an invasion that was unlawful in international law (Lord Rodger at [39]); *R. (on the application of Smith) v Oxfordshire Assistant Deputy Coroner* [2010] UKSC 29; [2011] 1 A.C. 1, did a soldier operating outside his base in Iraq fall within the jurisdiction of the UK for the purposes of the Convention? Private Smith collapsed while working off base. He was rushed back to base but died soon after due to heat stroke. The House of Lords held (6:3) that the soldiers operating abroad did not fall within the scope of the Convention.
[174] *Smith v Ministry of Defence* [2013] UKSC 41; [2014] A.C. 52.
[175] Two other issues were before the Supreme Court which were both important and interesting, but beyond the scope of this book: what duty did the state owe to soldiers when procuring equipment to be used in the battlefield and the scope of the doctrine of combat immunity. For a discussion of both of those issues, see: G. Junor, "A soldier's (human) rights when fighting abroad: the Supreme Court decides", 2013 S.L.T. (News) 251; R. Mullender, "Military Operations, fairness and the British state" (2014) 130 L.Q.R. 28.
[176] *Smith v Ministry of Defence* [2013] UKSC 41; [2014] A.C. 52, per Lord Hope of Craighead at [52].
[177] *Bankovic v Belgium* (2001) 45 E.H.R.R. SE5.
[178] *Smith v Ministry of Defence* [2013] UKSC 41; [2014] A.C. 52, per Lord Hope of Craighead at [48]–[49].

The horizontal effect of the Human Rights Act

11-20 The Human Rights Act is drafted to have vertical effect: it applies directly only to the organs of the state and other bodies falling within the definition of public authorities. But its potential horizontal effect—its application to purely private relationships—is considerable. This comes about in two ways. First, the interpretative obligation laid on the courts by s.3 applies, as we have seen, to all legislation in any proceedings, not merely in proceedings involving a public authority.[179] Through the medium of existing statutory provisions, read and given effect in a manner compatible with the Convention rights, those rights may become binding as between private parties; and if it is not possible to read and give effect to a provision consistently with the Convention rights, a declaration of incompatibility may be made. Secondly, the fact that courts and tribunals are themselves "public authorities" for the purposes of the Human Rights Act means that it is unlawful for them to act incompatibly with the Convention rights.

Different views have been expressed as to the effect of this. Sir William Wade argued that both the spirit of the Act and a literal construction of s.6 mean that, if a Convention right is relevant to proceedings before it, the court must decide in accordance with it, no less in a case between private parties than in a case against a public authority.[180] Sir Richard Buxton, on the other hand, insisted that the Convention creates rights only against the state (in its various manifestations) and that incorporation of the Convention rights did not change their content so as to render them enforceable against private parties.[181] Murray Hunt offers an intermediate position, in which the Convention rights will "pervade the law" but will fall short of creating wholly new private law causes of action.[182] In fact, the question of horizontal effect may be a subtler one than any of these accounts acknowledge.[183] Consider first the influence the Convention rights have on the development of the common law. Since that influence was making itself felt even prior to the enactment of the Human Rights Act, there is plainly no reason why the process should not continue. "Statutory horizontality"—bringing the Convention rights into play by means of the interpretative obligation—is plainly justified by the terms of s.3; to argue otherwise would be to deprive s.3 of a good deal of its meaning. In so far as public authorities may have powers to prevent breaches of the Convention rights, and may be liable under the Human Rights Act for failures to act as much as for their positive actions, a form of "intermediate horizontality" is created: if a private individual is not themselves bound to respect another's Convention rights, a public authority may be obliged

---

[179] Subject, however, to the presumption against retrospectivity, as explained by the House of Lords in *Wilson v First County Trust Ltd (No.2)* [2003] UKHL 40; [2004] 1 A.C. 816, see especially the speech of Lord Rodger at [186]–[214].

[180] H.W.R. Wade, "Horizons of Horizontality" (2000) 116 L.Q.R. 217. See also, e.g. Lester, Pannick and Herberg, *Human Rights: Law and Practice* (2009) pp.54–65.

[181] R. Buxton, "The Human Rights Act and Private Law" (2000) 116 L.Q.R. 48. Both Wade and Buxton cite statements made by the Lord Chancellor during the parliamentary passage of the Human Rights Bill in support of their views. Given the inherent conflict between these statements, one of which cheerfully countenances horizontal effect and the other of which plainly does not, this would not seem to be a question amenable to resolution under the *Pepper v Hart* doctrine: see A.J. Bowen, "Fundamental Rights in Private Law", 2000 S.L.T. (News) 157.

[182] M. Hunt, "The 'Horizontal Effect' of the Human Rights Act" [1998] P.L. 423.

[183] See I. Leigh, "Horizontal Rights, the Human Rights Act and Privacy: Lessons from the Commonwealth" (1999) 48 I.C.L.Q. 57.

to prevent them from actually violating them.[184] There is also authority for the proposition that a court must, in order to comply with s.6(1), conform its own procedures to the requirements of the Convention rights.[185] This would extend to what is termed "remedial horizontality", as seen where the court's decision to grant or withhold a remedy is determined by reference to the effect on the parties' Convention rights. Thus in *Karl Construction Ltd v Palisade Properties Plc*,[186] Lord Drummond Young recalled an inhibition granted on the dependence of the action between the parties on the grounds that its grant was incompatible with the defender's rights under art.1 of the First Protocol to the Convention. Previously the remedy was granted as of right in actions for payment of a sum or for damages, where the pursuer had included a warrant for inhibition in their summons. The Rules of the Court of Session required only that the summons be intimated to the defender. But the effect of an inhibition, once granted, is draconian: it freezes the whole of the defender's heritable assets, so that they are unable to use or dispose of them; the grounds for recall are (or were) limited; and the defender has no right to be compensated for wrongful use of the diligence. While Lord Drummond Young accepted that inhibition pursued a legitimate aim (namely, furthering the administration of justice by ensuring that assets are available to satisfy any decree granted in the pursuer's favour), he did not find that it struck the requisite "fair balance" between the general interests of the public and the rights of individuals to the use and enjoyment of their property. In other words, it was disproportionate.

In fact, the Human Rights Act appears to have horizontal effect in every **11–21** respect bar one: private individuals cannot sue one another for breaches of their Convention rights as such. Thus in *Douglas v Hello! Ltd*,[187] in which horizontality in the sense of "interpreting and developing the common law consistently with the Convention rights" was not taken to raise any difficulty, Keene LJ noted:

> "[Whether horizontality] extends to creating a new cause of action between private persons and bodies is more controversial, since to do so would appear to circumvent the restrictions on proceedings contained in section 7(1) of the Act and on remedies in section 8(1)."

---

[184] The analogy here is with the treatment of "positive obligations" arising under the Convention, i.e. those which require affirmative action by the state. Thus in *A v United Kingdom* (1998) 27 E.H.R.R. 611, the state was liable for failing to protect a child from punishment at the hands of his stepfather which was held to amount to inhuman and degrading treatment contrary to art.3 (the stepfather was acquitted by a jury, which accepted his defence of "reasonable chastisement" in his prosecution for assault). But see the likely limits to any such liability: *Mitchell v Glasgow City Council* [2009] UKHL 11; 2009 S.C. (H.L.) 21 and *Michael v Chief Constable of South Wales* [2015] UKSC 2; [2015] 2 W.L.R. 343.

[185] Thus, in *R. (on the application of A) v Lord Saville of Newdigate* [2001] EWCA Civ 2048; [2002] 1 W.L.R 1249, the Court of Appeal held that the Bloody Sunday Inquiry had breached the art.2 rights (right to life) of former soldiers called to give evidence by requiring them to attend the tribunal in Londonderry to do so. For an unequivocal acceptance of procedural and remedial horizontality in Scotland, see *Newman Shopfitters Ltd v MJ Gleeson Group Plc*, 2003 S.L.T. (Sh. Ct) 83 at [40].

[186] *Karl Construction Ltd v Palisade Properties Plc*, 2002 S.C. 270. See also, now, *Advocate General for Scotland v Taylor*, 2004 S.C. 339 at [34]; *Gillespie v Toondale Ltd*, 2006 S.C. 304.

[187] *Douglas v Hello! Ltd* [2001] Q.B. 967 CA (Civ Div).

Likewise in *Venables v News Group Newspapers Ltd*,[188] Dame Elizabeth Butler-Sloss P held that although the Convention rights could not found free-standing causes of action in private law proceedings, the court was obliged to act consistently with the Convention rights in adjudicating on common law causes of action. In *Douglas v Hello! Ltd (No.2)*,[189] Lindsay J drew on these cases and others[190] in holding the defendants liable to the claimants for breach of confidence but denying that there was any right of privacy under which Michael Douglas and Catherine Zeta-Jones were entitled independently to relief. In relation to breach of confidence, his Lordship held that the recent cases represented a fusion between older case law and the rights and duties arising under the Human Rights Act:

"Breach of confidence is an established cause of action but its scope now needs to be evaluated in the light of obligations falling upon the court under section 6(1) of the Human Rights Act. That can be achieved by regarding the often opposed rights conferred respectively by Arts 8 and 10 of the European Convention as absorbed into the action for breach of confidence and as thereby to some extent giving it new strength and breadth. The European Convention thus comes into play even in private law cases. It will be necessary for the courts to identify, on a case by case basis, the principles by which the law of confidentiality must accommodate Arts 8 and 10. The weaker the claim for privacy, the more likely it will be outweighed by a claim based on freedom of expression [but] a balance between the conflicting interests has to be struck."[191]

Lindsay J did not, however, rule out the possibility that the Human Rights Act might have to be accorded direct horizontal effect if such were necessary to secure compliance by a court with its duties under s.6(1). In *Douglas v Hello!*, denying the claimants a cause of action for invasion of privacy involved no conflict with the judge's s.6(1) duty because their privacy interests were sufficiently safeguarded by the cause of action for breach of confidence. But the law of confidence does not cover every possible invasion of privacy interests, as the decision of the European Court of Human Rights in *Peck v United Kingdom* made plain.[192] As Lindsay J put it:

"That inadequacy will have to be made good, and if Parliament does not step in then the courts will be obliged to. Further development by the courts may merely be awaiting the first post-Human Rights Act case where neither the law of confidence nor any other domestic law protects an individual who deserves protection."[193]

[188] *Venables v News Group Newspapers Ltd* [2001] Fam. 430.
[189] *Douglas v Hello! Ltd (No.2)* [2003] 3 All E.R. 996 Ch Div.
[190] Principally *Campbell v MGN Ltd* [2002] EWCA Civ 1373; [2003] Q.B. 633 (and see also the majority decision of the House of Lords at *Campbell v MGN Ltd* [2004] UKHL 22; [2004] A.C. 457) and *A v B Plc* [2002] EWCA Civ 337; [2003] Q.B. 195.
[191] *Douglas v Hello! Ltd (No.2)* [2003] 3 All E.R. 996 at [186].
[192] *Peck v United Kingdom* (2003) 36 E.H.R.R. 41. In that case, it was held that the applicant's right to privacy had been violated by the publication of images of him, captured on CCTV cameras in a public place, attempting to commit suicide.
[193] *Douglas v Hello! Ltd (No.2)* [2003] 3 All E.R. 996 at [229]. For discussion of these cases, and of the interaction between art.8 and art.10, in the context of an application for interim interdict, see *X v British Broadcasting Corp* [2005] CSOH 80; 2005 S.L.T. 796.

The section 6(2) "defence"

Section 6(2) of the Human Rights Act disapplies s.6(1) in two situations: first, **11–22** where a public authority could not, as the result of one or more provisions of primary legislation, have acted in any other way; or, secondly, where it was acting to give effect to or enforce statutory provisions which cannot be read and given effect in a manner compatible with the Convention rights. The first of these envisages a situation in which the public authority had no discretion at all, the second a situation in which such discretion as it had could not be exercised in conformity with the Convention. If that is the case then, assuming the act in question did breach a Convention right, the only remedy open to the litigant will be a declaration of incompatibility.[194]

Given the flexibilities of language, one would have thought that a public authority would be able to say that such discretion as it had could not be exercised compatibly with the Convention in very few cases. This in turn would seem to imply that public authorities have their own role to play in securing observance with the Convention rights, by considering whether, in any particular case, the Convention rights are engaged and how this might influence the decision it proposes to reach. But it is important to remember that the protection of Convention rights is a results business: what matters is that the decision a public authority takes is Convention compliant, the process by which it reaches that decision is irrelevant. The House of Lords made this point forcefully in two cases. First, in *R. (on the application of Begum) v Governors of Denbigh High School*, the House of Lords held that the Court of Appeal had fallen into error by holding that an individual's Convention rights had been breached by a public authority who had simply omitted to have regard to them.[195] That case concerned the uniform policy adopted by a non-denominational state school. Since a high proportion of the pupils were Muslim, the policy allowed girls to wear the shalwar kameeze and a headscarf, in the school colours, rather than the standard uniform. The claimant, a 14 year old pupil, wore the shalwar kameeze and headscarf without objection for her first two years at the school. She then claimed that she was obliged by her evolving religious beliefs to adopt the jilbab, a long, shapeless coat which more fully conceals the arms and legs. She appeared at the school thus attired and was sent home. She never returned to the school. She claimed that the school had violated her art.9 right to respect for her religious beliefs. The judge at first instance dismissed the claim. The Court of Appeal, without deciding whether as a matter of substance the uniform policy was incompatible with art.9, held that the school had breached her Convention rights by failing to reach its decision by a proper process of reasoning. The House of Lords disagreed. While domestic judicial review is normally concerned with the decision making process rather than the merits of the actual decision, challenges based on Convention rights are different. As Lord Hoffmann put it:

> "In domestic judicial review, the court is usually concerned with whether the decision-maker reached his decision in the right way rather than whether he got what the court might think to be the right answer. But Article 9 is

---

[194] The obvious drawback of this is that it has no effect on the validity, continuing operation or enforcement of the provision in respect of which it is made, and is not binding on the parties to the proceedings: see Human Rights Act 1998 s.4(6), and para.11–12, above.

[195] *R. (on the application of Begum) v Governors of Denbigh High School* [2006] UKHL 15; [2007] 1 A.C. 100.

concerned with substance, not procedure. It confers no right to have a decision made in a particular way. What matters is the result."[196]

Shortly afterwards, in another case, this time concerning the licencing of sex shops in Belfast, Lord Hoffmann made the point even clearer:

> "Either the refusal infringed the respondent's convention rights or it did not. If it did, no display of human rights learning by the Belfast City Council would have made the decision lawful. If it did not, it would not matter if the councillor's had never heard of article 10 or the First Protocol."[197]

The result is that even where a public authority has no regard to the possible infringement of a person's Convention rights, but happens upon a Convention-compliant decision, there is no ground for complaint. In that regard, challenges founded on an alleged infringement of a Convention right differ markedly from common law judicial review of a public authority's decision.

Section 7: Proceedings under the Human Rights Act

11–23 Section 7(1) of the Human Rights Act provides:

> "A person who claims that a public authority has acted (or proposes to act) in a way which is made unlawful by section 6(1) may— (a) bring proceedings against the authority under this Act in the appropriate court or tribunal, or (b) rely on the Convention right or rights concerned in any legal proceedings but only if he is (or would be) a victim of the unlawful act."

Judicial review is the normal vehicle by which to raise an issue under s.7(1)(a).[198] To that end, s.7(3) and (4) provide that the test of standing to apply for judicial review in such cases is status as a victim of the act complained of and not the ordinary common law requirements.[199] A person is a victim for the purposes of s.7(1) only if they would be a victim for the purposes of art.34 of the Convention.[200] To the extent that it is narrower than the common law test (and given the generous interpretation normally given to the "sufficient interest" test in England, it probably is), it is not acceptable to fall back on the common law test. To raise a challenge under the Human Rights Act, it is necessary to meet the test set in that Act.[201] It is therefore necessary to understand what is required to

---

[196] *R. (on the application of Begum) v Governors of Denbigh High School* [2006] UKHL 15; [2007] 1 A.C. 100 at [68]; see Lord Bingham at [29] to similar effect: "But the focus at Strasbourg is not and has never been on whether a challenged decision or action is the product of a defective decision-making process, but on whether, in the case under consideration, the applicant's Convention rights have been violated"; and Lord Nicholls at [68].

[197] *Belfast City Council v Miss Behavin' Ltd* [2007] UKHL 19; [2007] 1 W.L.R. 1420 at [13]; see also Lord Neuberger at [90].

[198] But not all claims under the Human Rights Act must be by means of judicial review. For example, where damages are sought for infringement of Convention rights, it is perfectly competent to proceed by means of an ordinary action in the sheriff court: *Ruddy v Chief Constable, Strathclyde Police* [2012] UKSC 57; 2013 S.C. (U.K.S.C.) 126.

[199] As to the common law requirements for standing, which have undergone substantial modification recently, see paras 14–04—14–07, below.

[200] Human Rights Act 1998 s.7(7).

[201] On the English rules on standing, see H. Woolf et al, *De Smith's Judicial Review*, 7th edn (London: Sweet & Maxwell, 2013), paras 2–006 to 2–009.

be a "victim" of an act for the purposes of the Convention. That requires consideration of art.34 of the Convention.[202]

Article 34 provides that the European Court of Human Rights may receive applications from any person, non-governmental organisation or group of individuals claiming to be a victim of a violation of one or more of the Convention rights. Local authorities and other organs of the state (what would be "core" public authorities in terms of s.6) cannot institute proceedings.[203] But legal persons and other bodies, including companies, newspapers, churches, trade unions and political parties, may be able to rely directly on at least some of the Convention rights. Pressure groups are not necessarily excluded, provided that, in common with individual applicants, they can demonstrate a reasonable likelihood that the measure complained of will be or was applied to them or their members, and provided they have authority to act on behalf of their members, who must be identified.[204] But recent experience in Scotland at least suggests that it remains difficult for pressure groups to persuade the court that they ought to be afforded standing.[205] The test applied by the Strasbourg Court in determining the scope of art.34 has been to ask whether the applicant was directly affected by the act or omission that is complained of. It is not necessary to show some financial loss or prejudice: that goes to the later question of just satisfaction and is irrelevant to the necessarily prior question of status as a victim.[206] So while the test of victimhood is narrower than the English test of "sufficient interest" it appears to be close to, although not absolutely coterminous with, the test introduced in Scotland by the Supreme Court in *AXA General Insurance Co Ltd v Lord Advocate*, which requires a petitioner to show that he or she is directly affected by a decision.[207]

But it should not be supposed that an active role for pressure groups in human rights litigation is excluded by the Human Rights Act. In Scotland and England alike it is open to them to fund, if not front, test cases in the human rights arena. More importantly, changes have been made to the rules of court north and south of the border to facilitate third party interventions in judicial review proceedings, whether or not involving human rights.[208] Rule 58.8A of the Rules of the Court of Session[209] provides that a person who is not directly affected by any issue raised in a petition for judicial review may nevertheless apply to the court for

---

[202] See generally: Woolf et al, *De Smith's Judicial Review* (2013), paras 2–044 to 2–058; Wadham et al., *Blackstone's Guide to the Human Rights Act 1998* (2015), paras 4.16–4.28.

[203] *Aston Cantlow and Wilmcote with Billesley Parochial Church Council v Wallbank* [2003] UKHL 37; [2004] 1 A.C. 546, per Lord Hope of Craighead at [46].

[204] See *Norris v Ireland* (1986) 8 E.H.R.R. CO75; and contrast *Open Door Counselling Ltd v Ireland* (1992) 15 E.H.R.R. 244.

[205] See, for example, *Christian Institute v Lord Advocate* [2015] CSOH 7; 2015 S.L.T. 72 where four charities (together with three individuals) sought to judicially review the competence of provisions of the Children and Young People (Scotland) Act 2014 (an Act of the Scottish Parliament) as, inter alia, incompatible with art.8 of the Convention. The Lord Ordinary held that none of the four charities qualified as a "victim" in terms of art.34 so as to enable them to challenge the Act on the basis it was incompatible with Convention rights (see [92]–[96]). At the time of writing, a reclaiming motion is pending before the Inner House.

[206] *Ilhan v Turkey* (2002) 34 E.H.R.R. 36; *JM v United Kingdom* (2011) 53 E.H.R.R. 6.

[207] *AXA General Insurance Co Ltd v Lord Advocate* [2011] UKSC 46; 2012 S.C. (U.K.S.C.) 122, per Lord Hope of Craighead at [63].

[208] The rules of the European Court of Human Rights make comparable provision for public interest interventions.

[209] Inserted by Act of Sederunt (Rules of the Court of Session Amendment No.5) (Public Interest Intervention in Judicial Review) 2000 (SSI 2000/317).

leave to intervene in the petition or in an appeal connected therewith. Where leave is granted, an intervention will normally take the form of a written submission, lodged with the court and copied to the parties, not exceeding 5,000 words in length, but the court may exceptionally allow longer written submissions to be made and may direct that it wishes to hear oral submissions from the intervener.[210] The Inner House has, however, recently adopted a very narrow reading of this rule that is unlikely to encourage applications (at appellate level at least).[211]

11–24	Proceedings under s.7(1) of the Human Rights Act must be commenced within one year of the date on which the act complained of took place.[212] That period is subject to any stricter time limit in relation to the procedures in question (for example, the soon to be implemented three month time limit for raising judicial review proceedings in Scotland) but subject to a discretion to extend the period where the court considers it equitable to do so in all the circumstances.[213] It is yet to be decided when time commences in relation to a continuing act but it has been suggested, obiter, that it would run from the date on which the breach ended.[214] Where, in proceedings under s.7(1)(a) or (b) of the Human Rights Act, the court finds that the public authority respondent is acting, or proposes to act, in a manner made unlawful by s.6(1), it may grant "such relief or remedy, or make such order, within its powers as it considers just and appropriate".[215] In the context of judicial review, the Court of Session may

> "make any order that could be made if sought in any action or petition, including an order for reduction, declarator, suspension, interdict, implement, restitution, payment (whether of damages or otherwise) and any interim order".[216]

It is now clear that s.21 of the Crown Proceedings Act 1947, which excludes the remedies of interdict and implement against the Crown (including, by virtue of Sch.8 to the Scotland Act 1998, the Scottish Ministers) in "civil proceedings", does not prevent the grant of either remedy in the exercise of the supervisory jurisdiction of the Court of Session on an application for judicial review.[217]

11–25	Section 8(2) of the Human Rights Act provides that damages may be awarded by a court having power to award damages or order the payment of compensation

[210] For the merits and demerits of "public interest" interventions, see S. Fredman, "Scepticism under Scrutiny" in T. Campbell, K.D. Ewing and A. Tomkins (eds), *Sceptical Essays on Human Rights* (Oxford: Oxford University Press, 2001), Ch.11; R. Charteris, "Intervention—in the Public Interest?", 2000 S.L.T. (News) 87.
[211] *Sustainable Shetland v The Scottish Ministers* [2013] CSIH 116
[212] Human Rights Act 1998 s.7(5).
[213] Human Rights Act 1998 s.7(5)(b). As to the new time limit for judicial review proceedings in Scotland, see: Courts Reform (Scotland) Act 2014 s.89, inserting a new s.27A into the Court of Session Act 1988.
[214] *A v Essex CC* [2010] UKSC 33; [2011] 1 A.C. 280, per Baroness Hale of Richmond at [113]. That would be consistent with what Lord Hope suggested in *Somerville v Scottish Ministers* [2007] UKHL 44; 2008 S.C. (H.L.) 45 at [51].
[215] Human Rights Act 1998 s.8(1).
[216] Rules of the Court of Session r.58.4.
[217] *Davidson v Scottish Ministers* [2005] UKHL 74; 2006 S.C. (H.L.) 41.

where a breach of the Convention rights is established.[218] But damages may only be awarded where such an award would be "just and appropriate": violation of one's Convention rights alone will not necessarily be sufficient.[219] Moreover, in deciding whether an award of damages is necessary to afford just satisfaction to the applicant, the court is required by s.8(3)(b) to consider the consequences of the award, which is likely to be regarded as calling attention to the risks of opening the floodgates to hundreds of other potential claims. Here as elsewhere, the court must take into account the principles applied by the European Court of Human Rights in deciding whether to award damages and, if so, in what amount. But the jurisprudence of the court in this respect has been justly criticised as inconsistent, opaque and premised upon unarticulated assumptions about the "value" of different types of application.[220] In their joint report on damages under the Human Rights Act, the Law Commission and Scottish Law Commission accepted that when the court awards damages, it seeks to restore the applicant to the position they would have been in but for the breach complained of.[221] But they were driven to remark upon the lack of principle in the case law of the court on the question of monetary redress. The report concluded that the entry into force of the Human Rights Act would involve little change to the law of damages in either jurisdiction, in that

> "where the courts ... have established appropriate levels of compensation for particular types of loss in relation to claims in tort or delict, it would seem appropriate for the same rules to be used in relation to a claim under the Human Rights Act".

In the event, the courts have proceeded in a different manner. In *R. (on the* **11–26** *application of Greenfield) v Secretary of State for the Home Department* Lord Bingham explained that the proper place to look for guidance on the appropriate level of damages was Strasbourg, not domestic authorities:

> "They are not inflexibly bound by Strasbourg awards in what may be different cases. But they should not aim to be significantly more or less generous than the court might be expected to be, in a case where it was willing to make an award at all."[222]

As Lord Bingham pointed out, the purposes of the Human Rights Act was not to provide a victim with a better remedy at home than they could get in Strasbourg; it was to provide them with the same remedy. Furthermore, a finding of violation will be an important part of any just satisfaction and damages will not ordinarily

---

[218] Where damages are sought, that can be done by means of an ordinary action in the sheriff court: *Ruddy v Chief Constable, Strathclyde Police* [2012] UKSC 57; 2013 S.C. (U.K.S.C.) 126. On damages under the Human Rights Act generally, see Wadham et al, *Blackstone's Guide to the Human Rights Act 1998* (2015) paras 4.54–4.71.

[219] M. Amos, "Damages for Breach of the Human Rights Act 1998" [1999] E.H.R.L.R. 178; R. Clayton, "Damage limitation: the Courts and Human Rights Act Damages" [2005] P.L. 429.

[220] A.R. Mowbray, "The European Court of Human Rights' Approach to Just Satisfaction" [1997] P.L. 647.

[221] Law Commission and the Scottish Law Commission, *Damages under the Human Rights Act 1998* (The Stationery Office, 2000), Law Com. No.266; Scot. Law Com. No.180, Cm.4853.

[222] *R. (on the application of Greenfield) v Secretary of State for the Home Department* [2005] UKHL 14; [2005] 1 W.L.R. 673 at [19].

be necessary to encourage high standards of compliance with the Convention.[223] More recently, the Supreme Court has offered guidance to lower courts when assessing damages in a Human Rights Act case:

> "First, at the present stage of the development of the remedy of damages under section 8 of the 1998 Act, courts should be guided, following *Greenfield*, primarily by any clear and consistent practice of the European court. Secondly, it should be borne in mind that awards by the European court reflect the real value of money in the country in question. The most reliable guidance as to the quantum of awards under section 8 will therefore be awards made by the European court in comparable cases brought by applicants from the UK or other countries with a similar cost of living. Thirdly, courts should resolve disputed issues of fact in the usual way even if the European court, in similar circumstances, would not do so."[224]

The consequence has been that rather than awards of damages under the Human Rights Act reflecting common law awards for similar complaints, damages are rarely awarded and when they are, tend to be significantly lower than would be expected at common law.

Sections 12 and 13: the press and religion

11–27 Sections 12 and 13 of the Human Rights Act have been described as the only blemishes on an otherwise beautifully drafted Act.[225] Nevertheless, they merit brief consideration. Section 12 applies if the court is considering granting any relief which, if granted, might affect the exercise of the Convention right to freedom of expression.[226] This was a matter of considerable public interest a few years ago following a spate of high profile "super injunctions" concerning, mainly, high profile footballers. It was also a matter of much misunderstanding: the real complaint was the granting of anonymised injunctions (where the applicants name was withheld).[227] If the person against whom such an order is to be granted is neither present nor represented such an order cannot be granted unless the court is satisfied that the applicant has taken all reasonably practicable steps to notify that person or there are compelling reasons why they should not

---

[223] *R. (on the application of Greenfield) v Secretary of State for the Home Department* [2005] UKHL 14; [2005] 1 W.L.R. 673 at [19].

[224] *R. (on the application of Sturnham) v Parole Board* [2013] UKSC 23; [2013] 2 A.C. 254, per Lord Reed at [39].

[225] *Wilson v First County Trust Ltd (No.2)* [2003] UKHL 40; [2004] 1 A.C. 816, per Lord Rodger of Earlsferry at [179].

[226] Human Rights Act 1998 s.12(1). "Relief" does not include a blanket order such as that available under s.11 of the Contempt of Court Act 1981. Where such a blanket order is made, s.12 is not engaged, as no "relief" is being granted. Common law fairness, however, requires that a person affected by such an order can apply promptly for its recall: *A v Secretary of State for the Home Department* [2014] UKSC 25; 2014 S.C. (U.K.S.C.) 151.

[227] For example, see *CTB v News Group Newspapers Ltd* [2011] EWHC 1232 (QB). It also highlighted the territorial scope of an injunction/interdict: it applies within the jurisdiction of the court. That was significant in *CTB* as whilst publication was restrained in England and Wales, the Glasgow-based *Sunday Herald* published the story anyway! More concerning was the Member of Parliament that, relying upon the privilege that attaches to statements made in Parliament, disclosed the identity of *CTB* in the House of Commons and thus thwarted the order that the court had been persuaded to grant having heard argument from both parties (see: P. Johnson, "What can the press really say? Contempt of court and the reporting of parliamentary proceedings" [2012] P.L. 491).

be notified.[228] It is only in exceptional circumstances that an interdict should be granted where advance notice has not been given.[229] In any case, s.12(3) requires the court to be satisfied that "the applicant is likely to establish that publication should not be allowed" before granting a pre-trial order. "Likely" does not mean "more likely than not"; it means the prospects of success are sufficiently favourable to justify making an order in all the circumstances of the case.[230] Finally, the court must have "particular regard" to the importance of the right to freedom of expression, taking into account the public interest in the material concerned and the extent to which it is already in the public domain. Regard should also be had to any relevant privacy code.[231] In reality, these provisions make little difference. The court must, in any event, strike a balance between art.8 (right to respect for private life) and art.10 (freedom of expression). If it were to prioritise one ahead of the other, that would likely result in the other right being infringed. The courts have therefore consistently downplayed the significance of s.12.[232]

Section 13 requires that "particular regard" be had to the Convention right of freedom of thought, conscience and religion (art.9) if a court's determination "might affect the exercise by a religious organisation (itself or its members collectively)" of that right.[233] Born out of a fear that the Human Rights Act may undermine the ability of the Church to refuse to marry same sex couples,[234] this provision appears to have even less significance than s.12. Under the Convention, where art.9 is engaged, any restriction on that right would have to be justified under the Convention. Consequently, s.13 does not give art.9 any greater weight than it already had.[235]

The role of the courts in human rights litigation

The Human Rights Act has given the courts, in particular the Supreme Court (and **11–28** the House of Lords before it), a much higher profile and has required it to intervene on matters that are at times the subject of considerable political controversy. These issues have ranged from the legality of the legislative and executive response to the threats presented in the post-9/11 world to the extent to which the government owe duties under the Human Rights Act to servicemen and women operating in a combat environment. The court's decisions have inevitably been controversial. Often cases require the court to balance competing interests and to assess the proportionality of any interference with a person or group's Convention rights. Proportionality as a concept was not introduced by the Human Rights Act but it is a prominent feature in many decisions under the

---

[228] Human Rights Act 1998 s.12(2).
[229] Committee on Super-Injunctions, *Report of the Committee on Super-Injunctions: Super-Injunctions, Anonymised Injunctions and Open Justice* (The Stationery Office, 2011), para.3.22.
[230] *Cream Holdings Ltd v Banerjee* [2004] UKHL 44; [2005] 1 A.C. 253. This approach was designed to give the court sufficient flexibility in cases where, for example, the consequences of disclosure may be particularly grave (per Lord Nicholls of Birkenhead at [22]).
[231] Human Rights Act 1998 s.12(4).
[232] The general approach to s.12 is best discussed by the Court of Appeal in *Ashdown v Telegraph Group Ltd* [2001] EWCA Civ 1142; [2002] Ch.149.
[233] Human Rights Act 1998 s.13(1).
[234] No person can be compelled to perform the marriage of a same sex couple: Marriage (Same Sex Couples) Act 2013 s.2.
[235] *R. (on the application of Amicus) v Secretary of State for Trade and Industry* [2004] EWHC 860 (Admin) at [41].

Act. Its application was recently explained by Lord Reed in *Bank Mellat v HM Treasury (No.2)*.[236] The passage merits repetition in full:

> "An assessment of proportionality inevitably involves a value judgment at the stage at which a balance has to be struck between the importance of the objective pursued and the value of the right intruded upon. The principle does not however entitle the courts simply to substitute their own assessment for that of the decision-maker. As I have noted, the intensity of review under EU law and the Convention varies according to the nature of the right at stake and the context in which the interference occurs. Those are not however the only relevant factors. One important factor in relation to the Convention is that the Strasbourg court recognises that it may be less well placed than a national court to decide whether an appropriate balance has been struck in the particular national context. For that reason, in the Convention case law the principle of proportionality is indissolubly linked to the concept of the margin of appreciation. That concept does not apply in the same way at the national level, where the degree of restraint practised by courts in applying the principle of proportionality, and the extent to which they will respect the judgment of the primary decision maker, will depend on the context, and will in part reflect national traditions and institutional culture. For these reasons, the approach adopted to proportionality at the national level cannot simply mirror that of the Strasbourg court."[237]

Lord Reed went on to set out the structured approach that should be adopted by the court when it is called upon to make an assessment of the proportionality of a particular measure:

> " ... it is necessary to determine (1) whether the objective of the measure is sufficiently important to justify the limitation of a protected right, (2) whether the measure is rationally connected to the objective, (3) whether a less intrusive measure could have been used without unacceptably compromising the achievement of the objective, and (4) whether, balancing the severity of the measure's effects on the rights of the person to whom it applies against the importance of the objective, to the extent that the measure will contribute to its achievement, the former outweighs the latter."[238]

The fourth question in particular appears apt to further politicise the court's role. Assessing whether the restriction on the individual's Convention rights is outweighed by the importance of the objective that is sought will often be a very political, and controversial, question.

---

[236] *Bank Mellat v HM Treasury (No.2)* [2013] UKSC 39; [2014] A.C. 700.
[237] *Bank Mellat v HM Treasury (No.2)* [2013] UKSC 39; [2014] A.C. 700 at [71]. Although Lord Reed was dissenting on the application of the test in that particular case, his analysis of the concept of proportionality was endorsed by the majority: per Lord Sumption at [20]. It has subsequently been followed by the Supreme Court: *Gaughran v Chief Constable of the Police Service of Northern Ireland* [2015] UKSC 29; [2015] 2 W.L.R. 1303.
[238] *Bank Mellat v HM Treasury (No.2)* [2013] UKSC 39; [2014] A.C. 700 at [74]; see also Lord Sumption at [20]. In that analysis Lord Reed drew on Lord Clyde's seminal discussion of proportionality in *de Freitas v Permanent Secretary of Ministry of Agriculture, Fisheries, Land and Housing* [1999] 1 A.C. 69 at 80 and Dickson CJ's discussion in the Canadian Supreme Court in *R. v Oakes* [1986] 1 S.C.R. 103.

Mention is made by Lord Reed of the related issue of the "margin of **11–29** appreciation" (or "degree of respect") to be afforded by the courts to the legislature and executive. That raises the question as to when the court should decline to decide a point and hold that another branch of government is better placed or better qualified to make the assessment. In *R. (on the application of Countryside Alliance) v Attorney General* (which was a challenge to the hunting bans), Lord Bingham made the point this way:

"The democratic process is liable to be subverted if, on a question of moral and political judgment opponents of the Act achieve through the courts what they could not achieve in Parliament."[239]

The balance is always a difficult one to strike, as Lord Brown's dissent in the same case demonstrates.[240] Questions of law, no matter how controversial, are always matters for the court. As Lord Hoffmann has explained:

"In a society based upon the rule of law and the separation of powers, it is necessary to decide which branch of government has in any particular instance the decision-making power and what the legal limits of that power are. That is a question of law and must therefore be decided by the courts.

This means that the courts themselves often have to decide the limits of their own decision-making power. That is inevitable. But it does not mean that their allocation of decision-making power to the other branches of government is a matter of courtesy or deference. The principles upon which decision-making powers are allocated are principles of law. The courts are the independent branch of government and the legislature and executive are, directly and indirectly respectively, the elected branches of government. Independence makes the courts more suited to deciding some kinds of questions and being elected makes the legislature or executive more suited to deciding others. The allocation of these decision-making responsibilities is based upon recognised principles. The principle that the independence of the courts is necessary for a proper decision of disputed legal rights or claims of violation of human rights is a legal principle. It is reflected in article 6 of the Convention. On the other hand, the principle that majority approval is necessary for a proper decision on policy or allocation of resources is also a legal principle. Likewise, when a court decides that a decision is within the proper competence of the legislature or executive, it is not showing deference. It is deciding the law."[241]

---

[239] *R. (on the application of Countryside Alliance) v Attorney General* [2007] UKHL 52; [2008] 1 A.C. 719 at [45]. See also *AXA General Insurance Co Ltd v Lord Advocate* [2011] UKSC 46; 2012 S.C. (U.K.S.C.) 122, per Lord Hope at [49] where speaking of the Scottish Parliament (but the point is more general) he said: "While the judges, who are not elected, are best placed to protect the rights of the individual, including those who are ignored or despised by the majority, the elected members of a legislature of this kind are best placed to judge what is in the country's best interests as a whole."

[240] *R. (on the application of Countryside Alliance) v Attorney General* [2007] UKHL 52; [2008] 1 A.C. 719 at [157]–[159].

[241] *R. (on the application of ProLife Alliance) v British Broadcasting Corp* [2003] UKHL 23; [2004] 1 A.C. 185 at [75]–[76].

Identification of questions of law, as distinct from questions of policy lying within the proper province of legislative or executive action, is not a value-neutral matter, and it might appear that, as the judges have gained confidence in the exercise of a human rights jurisdiction, there has been a greater readiness to identify as legal questions issues which would once have fallen without question into the "political" sphere. In *Secretary of State for the Home Department v Rehman*, a case concerning the Secretary of State's decision that it was "conducive to the public good" to deport a person because of their involvement with a group associated with terrorist activities in Kashmir, Lord Hoffmann added a postscript to his speech (that was delivered shortly after the 9/11 attacks), explaining that those attacks were:

> " . . . a reminder that in matters of national security, the cost of failure can be high. This seems to me to underline the need for the judicial arm of government to respect the decisions of ministers of the Crown on the question of whether support for terrorist activities in a foreign country constitutes a threat to national security. It is not only that the executive has access to special information and expertise in these matters. It is also that such decisions, with serious potential results for the community, require a legitimacy which can be conferred only by entrusting them to persons responsible to the community through the democratic process. If the people are to accept the consequences of such decisions, they must be made by persons whom the people have elected and whom they can remove."[242]

Lord Hoffmann's tone had changed by the time he delivered his speech in the *A v Secretary of State for the Home Department* case.[243] That case is discussed more fully in Ch.13, below. For now it is enough to note that it concerned the UK Government's decision to derogate from art.5 of the Convention (right to liberty) in the aftermath of 9/11, claiming there to be a "threat to the life of the nation" (no other signatory to the Convention took that view). Parliament then enacted provision for the detention of foreign terrorist suspects without trial and without limit of time.[244] Nine people detained under this provision challenged the lawfulness of their detention. The case came before a panel of nine Law Lords. The first question for the House of Lords was whether there was a "threat to the life of the nation". By a majority of 8:1, the House of Lords held that to be an assessment that was pre-eminently political and on which great weight should be accorded to the judgment of the executive and of Parliament and that the court should not interfere with it.[245] Lord Hoffmann, in a short speech that deserves to be read in full, dissented. "Nothing could be more antithetical to the instincts and traditions of the people of the United Kingdom" than the power that Parliament had conferred.[246] But he disagreed with his colleagues on the prior question of the threat faced by the UK:

---

[242] *Secretary of State for the Home Department v Rehman* [2001] UKHL 47; [2003] 1 A.C. 153 at [62].
[243] *A v Secretary of State for the Home Department* [2004] UKHL 56; [2005] 2 A.C. 68.
[244] Anti-Terrorism, Crime and Security Act 2001 s.23.
[245] See, for example, *A v Secretary of State for the Home Department* [2004] UKHL 56; [2005] 2 A.C. 68, per Lord Bingham at [27]–[29].
[246] *A v Secretary of State for the Home Department* [2004] UKHL 56; [2005] 2 A.C. 68 at [86].

"This is a nation which has been tested in adversity, which has survived physical destruction and catastrophic loss of life. I do not underestimate the ability of fanatical groups of terrorists to kill and destroy, but they do not threaten the life of the nation. Whether we would survive Hitler hung in the balance, but there is no doubt that we shall survive Al-Qaeda. The Spanish people have not said that what happened in Madrid, hideous crime as it was, threatened the life of their nation. Their legendary pride would not allow it. Terrorist violence, serious as it is, does not threaten our institutions of government or our existence as a civil community."[247]

The other members of the panel (Lord Walker dissenting; Lord Hoffmann offered no view on the point) went on to quash the derogation on the basis it breached art.14, discriminating as it did so as only to apply to foreign nationals. The offending provision was, as a result, declared incompatible with arts 5 and 14 of the Convention. As we have already seen, a declaration under s.4 of the Human Rights Act did not assist the appellants secure their release. But Lord Hoffmann's dissent show how attitudes to the issue of deference can change and how significant a role the courts can now play.[248]

THE FUTURE OF THE HUMAN RIGHTS ACT

In 2015 a Conservative Government was elected with a commitment to repeal the **11–30** Human Rights Act and to replace it with a "British Bill of Rights". This was not a new idea.[249] No firm proposals have been made at the time of writing but the manifesto pledged to

"... break the formal link between British courts and the European Court of Human Rights, and make our own Supreme Court the ultimate arbiter of human rights matters in the UK."[250]

As we have seen, however, the Human Rights Act requires only that domestic courts "take account of" Strasbourg jurisprudence. Decisions of that court are not binding and the Supreme Court can, if appropriate, decline to follow them.[251] Domestic jurisprudence prescribes the circumstances in which it is appropriate to take that course (the *Ullah* principle) and not the Convention or the Strasbourg Court. The courts have also repeatedly stressed that what the Human Rights Act

---

[247] *A v Secretary of State for the Home Department* [2004] UKHL 56; [2005] 2 A.C. 68 at [96].

[248] The Government did not welcome the decision with the then Home Secretary reasserting Parliament's right to be arbiter of what was necessary for the security of the country. See, for example, "Law lords 'simply wrong', says Straw", *The Guardian* (17 December 2014), http://www.theguardian.com/uk/2004/dec/17/terrorism.immigrationpolicy [Accessed 24 June 2015]. The recent decision in *R. (on the application of Nicklinson) v Ministry of Justice* [2014] UKSC 38; [2014] 3 W.L.R. 200 provides another illustration, this time not in the field of national security but assisted suicide, of the Justices having to wrestle with essentially moral issues.

[249] See, for example, Lord Bingham's defence of the Human Rights Act in 2010 when again the prospect of repeal appeared to be gathering political momentum: T. Bingham, "The Human Rights Act" [2010] E.H.R.L.R. 568.

[250] Conservative Party Manifesto (2015) p.60.

[251] *R. v Horncastle* [2009] UKSC 14; [2010] 2 A.C. 373. More recently, the Supreme Court declined to follow the Strasbourg jurisprudence in relation to prisoners' rights: *R. (on the application of Kaiyam) v Secretary of State for Justice* [2014] UKSC 66; [2015] 2 W.L.R. 76.

created were *domestic* rights and that, before resort was had to Convention rights, the ordinary protections of the common law should be considered for there the answer will often be found. As Lord Reed explained in *R. (on the application of Osborn) v Parole Board*:

> "The values underlying both the Convention *and our own constitution* require that Convention rights should be protected by a detailed body of domestic law . . . The Human Rights Act 1998 has however given domestic effect, for the purposes of that Act, to the guarantees described as Convention rights . . . The importance of the Act is unquestionable. It does not however supersede the protection of human rights under the common law or statute, or create a discrete body of law based on the judgments of the European court. *Human rights continue to be protected by domestic law, interpreted and developed in accordance with the Act when appropriate.*"[252]

The emphasis placed on the domestic (that is the common law) protection for fundamental rights suggests that repeal of the Human Rights Act may make little practical difference. It is also unclear whether repeal of the Act will be accompanied by withdrawal from the European Convention on Human Rights itself. The initial suggestion appears to be not. Whilst there is a commitment in the manifesto to repeal the Human Rights Act, there is no pledge to withdraw from the Council of Europe and with it the Convention. Thus if the Human Rights Act is repealed but the UK remains a party to the Convention then as a matter of international law, the UK would remain bounded by the obligations contained within it. There would, however, be no domestic remedy for any breach of those rights and recourse would inevitably be had to the Strasbourg Court.[253] Further, with the EU now committed to accede to the European Convention on Human Rights, withdrawal from the Convention whilst continuing membership of the EU appears unlikely.[254] Continued membership of the EU presents a further problem. As we saw in Ch.10, above, the Charter of Fundamental Rights (which replicates many of the rights contained in the Convention) now has force in domestic law,[255] the reach of which is yet to be determined but may be much more substantial than many expected.[256]

11–31   Repeal of the Human Rights Act will be far from straightforward. As we have seen when looking at the competences of the Scottish Parliament and Scottish Government, Convention rights (a term introduced by the Human Rights Act) are

---

[252] *R. (on the application of Osborn) v Parole Board* [2013] UKSC 61; [2014] A.C. 1115 at [56]–[57] (emphasis added).

[253] Although see Lord Kerr's dissent in *R. (on the application of SG) v Secretary of State for Work and Pensions* [2015] UKSC 16; [2015] 1 W.L.R. 1449 where he advocated that human rights enshrined in international treaties to which the UK is party should be directly enforceable in domestic law.

[254] Although the accession of the EU to the Convention, whilst required by the Treaties, has been blocked by the Court of Justice of the European Union: Opinion 2/13 of the Court on the draft Accession Agreement of the European Union to the European Convention on Human Rights [2014] OJ C-62/2 and see para.10–38, above.

[255] *Rugby Football Union v Consolidated Information Services Ltd* [2012] UKSC 55; [2012] 1 W.L.R. 3333.

[256] For example the decision in *Benkharbouche v Embassy of Sudan; Janah v Libya* [2014] 1 C.M.L.R. 40; [2014] I.C.R. 169 concerning the state immunity. See A. Sanger, "The State Immunity Act and the right of access to a court" (2014) 73 C.L.J. 1.

central to delimiting the competences of the devolved bodies. Repeal would also threaten to drive another wedge between the Scottish and UK Governments, with the former apparently content with the current Convention rights system (reflected, as it was, in the draft constitution for an independent Scotland that was published in advance of the 2014 referendum). The Scottish Government has stated its continuing support for the Act, which makes it unlikely that the Scottish Parliament would pass a legislative consent motion agreeing to the repeal of the Human Rights Act. By convention, such a motion is required where Westminster proposes to legislate on a devolved matter or alter the terms of the devolution statutes. Whilst the Human Rights Act is reserved (Sch.4 of the Scotland Act 1998) its repeal would require amendment of the Scotland Act 1998. Westminster may retain the legislative competence to enact such measures without the consent of the Scottish Parliament (s.28(7) of the Scotland Act 1998), so the refusal of the Scottish Parliament to pass a legislative consent motion would not present a legal bar to the repeal of the Human Rights Act. It would, however, present a significant political problem should the UK Government proceed to amend the terms of the devolution settlement against the wishes of the Scottish Parliament. Similar, if not more acute, problems arise in Northern Ireland where not only are Convention rights a feature of the devolved settlement but the Belfast Agreement (which underpins much of the peace process) appears to bind the UK (as a matter of international law) to

> "complete incorporation into Northern Ireland law of the European Convention on Human Rights (ECHR), with direct access to the courts, and remedies for breach of the Convention, including power for the courts to overrule Assembly legislation on grounds of inconsistency."[257]

If repeal of the Human Rights Act will require any part of that agreement to be revisited, it is certain to be a long and difficult process.

For now, however, the Human Rights Act remains in full force and we await the new government's proposals as to how their manifesto pledge will be implemented. While that is being considered, it is helpful to restate the two questions Lord Bingham asked some years ago of critics of the Human Rights Act: (a) which of the rights contained in the Act should be discarded? and (b) would you rather live in a country in which these rights were not protected by law?[258]

---

[257] Belfast Agreement, "Rights, Safeguards and Equality of Opportunity: Human Rights" (10 April 1998) para.2.
[258] T. Bingham, *The Rule of Law* (London: Allen Lane, 2010) p.84. Chapter 7 in its entirety should be read by anyone engaging in the debate on the future of the Human Rights Act.

CHAPTER 12

CITIZEN AND THE STATE

12–01 Most citizens will live their lives in blissful ignorance of many of the other topics covered in this book. That there is a parliament, a government and courts will be known to them but they will rarely, if ever, have caused to enquire into how they operate and how they relate to each other. Few, if any, voters will care about the detail of electoral law beyond knowing how to vote in the system that is then in use and having a general confidence that the system is "fair". The Scottish independence referendum perhaps was an exception to this and represented an unprecedented engagement in a host of constitutional issues. But, as we saw earlier, constitutional law is not just about institutions and how they operate. It is also about the interaction between the citizen and the state; the governed and the governors. This is the level of constitutional law that is likely to engage most citizens. Granted that most law abiding citizens may not take too close an interest in the police powers of arrest and detention but most will have a view on when the state can monitor their communications or access their personal information. Similarly, many citizens will never take part in a public march or protest but will value the fact that such demonstrations of public opinion are permitted and will have a view on how they are policed. So in this chapter we focus on the different ways in which the citizen interacts with the state and the manner in which state power can (or should) be exercised over its citizens. This involves a review of a number of different topics: state powers of surveillance, police powers of arrest, detention, search and questioning, maintenance of public order and the right to protest. But we will start with a brief comment on two issues that remain topical: immigration and access to information.[1]

CITIZENSHIP

12–02 Much of the continuing controversy around immigration centres on political questions: who should be allowed into the country; how many people should be allowed in; and on what terms should they be allowed in? In particular, the EU rules concerning free movement of people, which result in EU citizens[2] being exempt from the normal immigration rules, have proved especially controversial with the UK committed to seeking to negotiate their reform. The rules that regulate immigration and asylum are now vast and its capacity to generate

---

[1] From that list of issues, it will be obvious that a comprehensive review of any, let alone all, of those topics is beyond the scope of this book. Specialist texts will be referenced where appropriate.

[2] As well as members of the EEA States (Iceland, Liechtenstein, Norway and Switzerland).

jurisprudence appears boundless.[3] We are only going to touch upon one small area: given constitutional law concerns the relationship between the state and its citizens, how does one acquire citizenship of the UK?[4]

The need for rules on citizenship really arises as a consequence of international law governing states. As a matter of public international law, it is for each state to determine its own rules on who are its citizens and nationals.[5] Since the entry into force of the British Nationality Act 1981 on 1 January 1983, there have been five means by which British nationality can be acquired: birth or adoption; by descent; registration and naturalisation. A child born in the UK (which includes, for these purposes, the Channel Islands and the Isle of Man) or, since 2002, in a British Overseas Territory, qualifies for British citizenship if (a) the parents are married and at least one is a British citizen or settled in the UK; (b) the parents are unmarried, but the mother, at least, is a British citizen or settled in the UK; or (c) at the time of birth one or both of the parents is a member of the armed forces.[6] The common law rule that birth in the UK was in itself sufficient to acquire citizenship was abolished by the 1981 Act.[7] "Settled" means "ordinarily resident" and not subject to any restriction under the Immigration Act 1971 on the period for which one may remain in the UK.[8] A person aged under 18 who is not a British citizen and is adopted in the UK becomes a British citizen on adoption if one or both of the adoptive parents is a British citizen. A child born outside the UK acquires British citizenship by descent if at least one parent is a British citizen (otherwise than by descent) or is abroad in the service of the Crown. The rules for acquiring citizenship through registration or naturalisation are complex and not infrequently changed. Reference should be made to specialist texts.

Citizenship carries with it a number of significant consequences. In some countries (but not now in the UK) it can render you bound to a period of national service. Citizenship is often a prerequisite to owning land, gain employment, entering the civil service or obtaining certain political rights. "Aliens"[9] are subject to a number of restrictions (such as voting rights, membership of Parliament and appointment to civil or military office). In day to day life the most practical consequence of citizenship is the ability to obtain a British passport. It is a prerequisite to acquiring a British passport that the applicant has citizenship. A passport is not only important in allowing an individual to travel,[10] but also to obtain consular protection if necessary and to evidence their right of abode in the UK when re-entry is sought.[11] Issue, or refusal, of a passport is a prerogative

---

[3] For further details, see M. Phelan and M.J. Gillespie, *Immigration Law Handbook*, 9th edn (Oxford: Oxford University Press, 2015).

[4] For a detailed accounts, see L. Fransman, *British Nationality Law*, 3rd edn (Haywards Heath: Bloomsbury Professional, 2011); *Macdonald's Immigration Law and Practice*, edited by I.A. Macdonald and R. Toal, 9th edn (London: Lexis Nexis, 2014).

[5] I. Brownlie, *Principles of Public International Law*, 7th edn (Oxford: Oxford University Press, 2008) pp.383–385.

[6] Borders, Citizenship and Immigration Act 2009 s.42.

[7] British Nationality Act 1981 s.1.

[8] See generally s.50 of the 1981 Act, as amended by the Nationality, Immigration and Asylum Act 2002.

[9] That is people who are not citizens of the Commonwealth or the Republic of Ireland nor a British protected person (see British Nationality Act 1981 s.50).

[10] Entering and leaving the UK is now a statutory entitlement for those that have a right of abode in the UK: Immigration Act 1971 s.1.

[11] Immigration Act 1971 s.3(9).

power but is subject to judicial review.[12] If the Secretary of State refuses to issue a passport, cogent reasons must be provided in light of obvious consequences such a decision has for a person's ability to travel.[13]

ACCESS TO INFORMATION[14]

12–03 There are two sides to the access to information coin: freedom of information, which allows the public access to official information, and official secrets, which prevents the public access to official information. Governments have sought to protect "official" information for centuries, but a public right of access to such information is a relatively new, and important, development:

> "Modern democratic government means government of the people by the people for the people. But there can be no government by the people if they are ignorant of the issues to be resolved, the arguments for and against different solutions and the facts underlying those arguments. The business of government is not an activity about which only those professionally engaged are entitled to receive information and express opinions. It is, or should be, a participatory process. But there can be no assurance that government is carried out for the people unless the facts are made known, the issues publicly ventilated. Sometimes, inevitably, those involved in the conduct of government, as in any other walk of life, are guilty of error, incompetence, misbehaviour, dereliction of duty, even dishonesty and malpractice. Those concerned may very strongly wish that the facts relating to such matters are not made public. Publicity may reflect discredit on them or their predecessors. It may embarrass the authorities. It may impede the process of administration. Experience however shows, in this country and elsewhere, that publicity is a powerful disinfectant. Where abuses are exposed, they can be remedied. Even where abuses have already been remedied, the public may be entitled to know that they occurred. The role of the press in exposing abuses and miscarriages of justice has been a potent and honourable one. But the press cannot expose that of which it is denied knowledge."[15]

12–04 Freedom of Information legislation was introduced by the Blair Government, much to the regret of the Prime Minister.[16] The Freedom of Information Act 2000 and the Freedom of Information (Scotland) Act 2002 are the legislative instruments that secure a general right of access to information held by public bodies in Scotland with the general purpose of creating openness in government.[17] They make broadly similar provision, with the 2000 Act relating to

---

[12] *R. v Secretary of State for Foreign and Commonwealth Affairs Ex p. Everett* [1989] Q.B. 811 CA (Civ Div). On prerogative powers, see Ch.7, above.

[13] *R. (on the application of Ali) v Secretary of State for the Home Department* [2012] EWHC 3379 (Admin); *R. (on the application of Nazem) v Secretary of State for the Home Department* [2014] EWHC 2556 (Admin).

[14] See P. Birkinshaw, "Regulating Information" in J.L. Jowell and D. Oliver (eds), *The Changing Constitution*, 7th edn (Oxford: Oxford University Press, 2011) Ch.14.

[15] *R. v Shayler* [2002] UKHL 11; [2003] 1 A.C. 247, per Lord Bingham of Cornhill at [21].

[16] T. Blair, *A Journey* (London: Hutchinson, 2010) p.516

[17] *Beggs v Scottish Information Commissioner* [2015] CSIH 17; 2015 S.L.T. 251 at [26].

reserved functions and the 2002 Act relating to devolved functions. Both Acts came fully into effect on 1 January 2005. Since then, a number of stories owe their origins to this legislation: from the MPs expenses scandal in 2009, to how much it costs to police the Old Firm match, the public, and especially the press, have obtained hitherto unthinkable access to official documents.[18] As Lord Bingham explained knowledge of the facts is a necessary prerequisite to holding the government to account (and knowing when, and for what, to hold them to account). For a detailed discussion of the operation of this legislation, reference should be made to specialist texts,[19] but for present purposes it is worth noting some of the key provisions of the legislation[20]:

1) Section 1 of the 2002 Act provides for a broad right to information held by Scottish public authorities (s.1(1)). A broad range of bodies (from the Scottish Ministers and the Parliament to the various health boards to a range of quangos) fall within the meaning of "Scottish public authority" (s.3; Sch.1).

2) That general entitlement to information is promptly qualified by a range of exemptions that are set out in Pt 2 of the Act. The production of information that would compromise national security (s.31), law enforcement (s.35), relations between the governments of the United Kingdom (s.28) or undermine the convention of the collective responsibility of the Scottish Ministers (s.30), to take a few examples, can be resisted. The limits of these exemptions are both important and controversial, with the court having recognised a general public interest in disclosure of information.[21] Provision is also made to allow repeated or vexatious requests to be refused (s.14).

3) The Scottish Information Commissioner ("the Commissioner") is responsible for promoting good practice by public authorities and enforcing the regime (s.43; Sch.2). Where a public authority refuses a request for information, an appeal lies to the Commissioner (s.47). If satisfied that the public authority ought to have provided the information requested, the Commissioner may issue an enforcement notice requiring the authority to take steps to comply with the request within a specified period (s.51). The First Minister has a limited right to veto an enforcement notice (s.52). Following the Supreme Court's decision in *R. (on the application of Evans) v Attorney General*, which dealt with the equivalent provision in the 2000 Act, any such veto will have limited use.[22] Failure to comply with an enforcement notice may be reported to the court, with the court empowered to treat any failure in

---

[18] Not every story has lived up to expectations: after a 10 year legal battle to obtain access to letters sent by Prince Charles to senior members of the government, culminating in the Supreme Court quashing the Attorney General's veto of the disclosure order (*R. (on the application of Evans) v Attorney General* [2015] UKSC 21; [2015] 2 W.L.R. 813), when the letters were finally released the only real question that was raised was why the government fought for so long to prevent that happening.

[19] For example, K. Dunion, *Freedom of Information in Scotland in Practice* (Dundee: Dundee University Press, 2012).

[20] The discussion that follows takes place under reference to the 2002 (Scottish) Act but broadly equivalent provision is made under the 2000 Act.

[21] *Scottish Ministers v Scottish Information Commissioner* [2007] CSIH 8; 2007 S.C. 330 at [11].

[22] *R. (on the application of Evans) v Attorney General* [2015] UKSC 21; [2015] 2 W.L.R. 813.

the same way it would treat a contempt of court (s.53). An appeal, on a point of law, lies to the Court of Session against a determination by the Commissioner (s.56).[23]

12–05 On the other hand, there is the Official Secrets Act 1989. While the freedom of information legislation seeks to secure access to official documents, the Official Secrets Act has exactly the opposite objective. The 1989 Act is significantly narrower than its predecessor, s.2 of the Official Secrets Act 1911. That provision, however, had endured sustained and widespread criticism and it was increasingly difficult to enforce.[24] The 1989 Act replaced that provision and was intended to be more targeted. Its principal provisions are:

1) The disclosure, without lawful authority, of any information relating to security and intelligence (s.1), defence (s.2) or international relations (s.3) is prohibited. An offence is committed by a member of the security and intelligence services, or any person who is notified that they are subject to the provisions of s.1 of the Act, by the simple act of disclosure (s.1(1)). A disclosure by a Crown servant or government contractor (defined in s.12) is an offence if it is a "damaging disclosure" (ss.1(3), 2(1) and 3(1)).

2) It is generally a defence to show that the accused did not know, and had no reasonable cause to believe, that the information disclosed related to security and intelligence, defence or international relations or, where applicable, had no reasonable cause to believe the disclosure would be damaging (ss.1(5), 2(3) and 3(4)).

3) A disclosure is "damaging" if it, as relevant: (i) damages, or would be likely to damage, the work of any part of the security services (s.1(4)); (ii) damages, or would be likely to damage, the capabilities of the armed forces or results in the loss of life or injury to members of the armed forces or serious damage to their equipment and/or installations, or endangers British interests abroad, including the safety of British citizens (s.2(2)); (iii) endangers, or would be likely to endanger, the interests of the UK abroad, seriously obstructs the promotion or protection by the UK of those interests or endangers the safety of UK citizens abroad (s.3(2)).

4) There is no defence available that any disclosure was in the public interest. To the extent that represents an interference with the art.10 right of freedom of expression it is a justified interference (*R. v Shayler*).[25]

The 1989 Act, although narrower than its predecessor, still strikes at a wide range of material and covers a wide range of individuals. Prosecutions under the Act are, however, rare and hard to pursue successfully. Former members of the security services who wish to write and publish memoirs have to obtain

---

[23] And from there, if necessary, to the Supreme Court. For example: *Common Services Agency v Scottish Information Commissioner* [2008] UKHL 47; 2008 S.C. (H.L.) 184 and *South Lanarkshire Council v Scottish Information Commissioner* [2013] UKSC 55; 2014 S.C. (U.K.S.C.) 1.

[24] For example, the jury's acquittal in *R. v Ponting* [1985] Crim. L.R. 318 in the face of a direction from the trial judge that effectively excluded the line of defence.

[25] *R. v Shayler* [2002] UKHL 11; [2003] 1 A.C. 247.

permission to refer to information that would otherwise fall within the scope of the 1989 Act. The ordinary courts have no jurisdiction to judicially review (at least one founded on art.10 of the European Convention on Human Rights) a refusal to give such consent; jurisdiction belongs to the Investigatory Powers Tribunal.[26]

SURVEILLANCE[27]

The European Court of Human Rights has repeatedly made clear that an **12–06** interference with protected rights will never be justifiable if it lacks a legal base. The traditional premise of the common law, however, is that all is allowed except that which is specifically prohibited by law. The police as much as anybody else have had the benefit of this. What it meant in practice was that the police required no positive legal authority for their actions provided their actions did not amount to legal wrong. Hence in *Malone v United Kingdom*,[28] the claimant had no remedy before the domestic courts because the tapping of his telephone by the police was not unlawful; but he had a remedy before the European Court because there was no positive legal basis for what the police had done.[29] Again in *R. v Khan*,[30] the entirety of the evidence against the accused consisted in tape recorded conversations obtained via a listening device installed by the police in the house of a suspect. Since the installation of the device was not unlawful, the trial judge ruled the evidence admissible and the accused was obliged to plead guilty. Again, the European Court found that the individual's right to respect for his private life under art.8 had been breached.[31]

The European Court of Human Rights first accepted surveillance techniques as constituting an interference with the rights protected by art.8 in *Klass v Germany*.[32] As noted, any interference must be, among other things, prescribed by law, which is to say that the act in question must have some basis in domestic law (not necessarily statutory) and be "accompanied by adequate and effective safeguards . . . to protect against arbitrary interference".[33] In addition, the law must be sufficiently accessible and foreseeable, in the sense of being formulated with sufficient precision to enable one to foresee, with reasonable certainty, the

---

[26] *R. (on the application of A) v Director of Establishments of the Security Service* [2009] UKSC 12; [2010] 2 A.C. 1.
[27] See generally *Renton and Brown's Criminal Procedure*, 6th edn (Edinburgh: W. Green) paras. 5.21–5.29.
[28] *Malone v United Kingdom* (1984) 7 E.H.R.R. 14.
[29] Telephone tapping was placed on a statutory footing by the Interception of Communications Act 1985, which was repealed and replaced by the Regulation of Investigatory Powers Act 2000.
[30] *R. v Khan (Sultan)* [1997] A.C. 558.
[31] *Khan v United Kingdom* (2000) 8 B.H.R.C. 310. Covert entry upon and interference with property by the police, Her Majesty's Revenue and Customs, the National Crime Squad and the National Criminal Intelligence Service was placed on a statutory footing by Pt III of the Police Act 1997. See also *Hewitt v United Kingdom* (1989) 67 D.R. 88, which exposed the absence of legal basis for secret surveillance activities and prompted the enactment of the Security Services Act 1989 and the Intelligence Services Act 1994; and *Govell v United Kingdom* (1997) 23 E.H.R.R. CD101, which exposed the absence of legal basis for intrusive surveillance activities and led to the enactment of the Regulation of Investigatory Powers Act 2000. In a number of respects, these powers have been supplemented by the anti-terrorist legislation considered in Ch.13, below (which, as there discussed, is not as strictly tailored to anti-terrorism as it might be).
[32] *Klass v Germany* (1978) 2 E.H.R.R. 214.
[33] *Malone v United Kingdom* (1984) 7 E.H.R.R. 14 at [67] and [68].

consequences a given action may entail. This does not of course mean that potential subjects of surveillance require to be given advance warning of it, but the law must be sufficiently clear to give citizens

> "an adequate indication of the circumstances in which and the conditions on which public authorities are empowered to resort to this secret and potentially dangerous interference with the right to respect for private life and correspondence."[34]

A statutory code which confers discretion on police officers is not necessarily inconsistent with the requirement of foreseeability, provided that the scope of the discretion and the manner of its exercise are prescribed with adequate clarity and provided that some form of ex post facto control is available.[35]

If surveillance activities are shown to have a legal basis in this sense, they then fall to be justified by reference to the countervailing public interests specified in art.8(2). Justification premised on the protection of national security or public safety is readily established in the jurisprudence of the court.[36] When considering whether surveillance (and other aspects of police activity) are necessary for the prevention of disorder and crime, the court looks to the seriousness of the interference with the protected right, the nature of the crime involved, and the presence or absence of a judicial warrant for the activity in question. Thus an interference with privacy which could not be justified by reference to the public interest in preventing petty crime may well be justifiable where the relevant criminal activity is serious.[37] By the same token, where the extent of the interference is slight, the absence of prior judicial authorisation is unlikely to be fatal.

12–07   The Regulation of Investigatory Powers Act 2000[38] and its sister legislation in Scotland represented the most comprehensive attempt to date to place police intelligence on a proper statutory basis conform to the requirements of the Convention. The UK Act extends to Scotland, but in relation to the authorisation of surveillance activity, s.46 provides that no person may grant an authorisation if it appears that the proposed surveillance will take in place in Scotland.[39] In that

---

[34] *Malone v United Kingdom* (1984) 7 E.H.R.R. 14 at [67]. See also *Valenzuela Contreras v Spain* (1998) 28 E.H.R.R. 483 at [46], where the European Court of Human Rights sets out the minimum conditions to be met by a statutory code on telephone tapping.

[35] See *Silver v United Kingdom* (1983) 5 E.H.R.R. 347, where the court held that it was acceptable to limit the scope of discretionary powers, if not in the parent enactment itself, then in secondary legislation or guidance adopted under it.

[36] See, e.g. *Leander v Sweden* (1987) 9 E.H.R.R. 433, where the European Court of Human Rights found that internal terrorist activity amounted to a serious threat to national security, ample to justify the collection of information and maintenance of secret files on candidates for sensitive employment positions.

[37] Compare, for example, *McLeod v United Kingdom* (1998) 27 E.H.R.R. 493 and *Murray v United Kingdom* (1994) 19 E.H.R.R. 193.

[38] Regulation of Investigatory Powers Act 2000 ("RIPA 2000").

[39] Subject to RIPA 2000 s.46(2), which specifies the purposes for which an authorisation extending to Scotland may be granted under the UK Act. Such authorisations may be granted where necessary in the interests of national security or of the economic well being of the UK, or on the application of, or to authorise conduct by, a member of either of the intelligence services (MI5 and MI6), Her Majesty's forces, the Ministry of Defence, the Ministry of Defence Police, the Commissioners of Customs and Excise, and the British Transport Police.

case, the authorisation must be sought and granted under the Regulation of Investigatory Powers (Scotland) Act 2000 instead.[40]

The Regulation of Investigatory Powers (Scotland) Act 2000 is concerned only with covert surveillance,[41] of which there are three categories: directed surveillance, intrusive surveillance and the conduct and use of covert human intelligence sources.[42] Directed surveillance is non-intrusive covert surveillance undertaken for the purposes of a specific investigation or operation, in a manner likely to result in obtaining private information about any person, whether or not they are the subject of the operation.[43] The term "private information" includes any information relating to the person's private and family life.[44] Intrusive surveillance is covert surveillance carried out in relation to anything taking place on residential premises or in any private vehicle,[45] which involves the presence of someone in the premises or vehicle, or which is carried out by means of a surveillance device.[46] Covert human intelligence sources are defined as persons who establish or maintain a personal or other relationship with another person for the covert purpose of facilitating the covert use of that relationship to obtain information or to provide access to information to another person.[47]

Section 5 of the Regulation of Investigatory Powers (Scotland) Act 2000 **12–08** provides the legal basis for these activities. This provides that surveillance in any of the senses defined above shall be lawful for all purposes if it is conducted by a person in accordance with the terms of an authorisation granted under the Act. Authorisations should normally be in writing, but may be granted or renewed orally in any urgent case.[48] An authorisation will normally cease to have effect

---

[40] Regulation of Investigatory Powers (Scotland) Act 2000 ("RIP(S)A 2000").

[41] "Surveillance" includes monitoring, observing or listening to persons, their movements, conversations or other activities or communications; recording anything so monitored, observed or listened to; and surveillance by or with the aid of surveillance devices: RIP(S)A 2000 s.31(2). It does not include, among other things, any entry on or interference with property or wireless telegraphy, which would be unlawful unless authorised under Pt III of the Police Act 1997. Such surveillance is "covert" if it is carried out in a manner calculated to ensure that the subjects are unaware that it is or may be taking place: RIP(S)A 2000 s.1(8).

[42] RIP(S)A 2000 s.1(1).

[43] RIP(S)A 2000 s.1(2). Note the saving in s.1(2)(c), for unauthorised surveillance of the sort which occurs when a police officer, observing a person acting suspiciously, follows the person to find out whether they are engaged in some criminal activity.

[44] RIP(S)A 2000 s.1(9). Since this definition is expressly non-exhaustive, it would presumably extend to other species of private information, such as information about a person's business affairs.

[45] RIP(S)A 2000 s.31(1) defines "residential premises" as "so much of any premises as is for the time being occupied or used by any person, however temporarily, for residential purposes or otherwise as living accommodation (including hotel or prison accommodation that is so occupied or used)" (but excluding any common parts of a building). "Private vehicle" is defined as any vehicle "used primarily for the private purposes of the person who owns it or of a person otherwise having the right to use it" (but excluding vehicles rented for a particular journey). In his annotations to the Act, Dr Alastair Brown makes the point that the confinement of intrusive surveillance to residential premises and private vehicles must presumably be deliberate, since authorisations under Pt III of the Police Act 1997 may be sought in relation to business premises, and the zone of privacy under art.8 of the European Convention, has been held to extend to offices: *Niemietz v Germany* (1992) 16 E.H.R.R. 523.

[46] RIP(S)A 2000 s.1(3) and (4).

[47] RIP(S)A 2000 s.1(7). A purpose is covert if and only if the relationship is conducted in a manner calculated to ensure that one of the parties is unaware of the purpose; and a relationship is used covertly, and information disclosed covertly, if and only if it is used or disclosed in a manner calculated to ensure that one of the parties is unaware of the use or disclosure: RIP(S)A 2000 s.1(8).

[48] RIP(S)A 2000 s.19(1).

three months after its grant or latest renewal, unless it is an authorisation for the use of a covert human intelligence source, in which case the period is 12 months. Oral authorisations, or authorisations granted by a person entitled to grant them only in urgent cases, lapse after 72 hours.[49] An authorisation may be renewed by any person who would have been entitled to grant it as new at any time before it ceases to have effect, except where the application for renewal relates to the conduct and use of a covert human intelligence source.[50] An authorisation must be cancelled by the person who granted or last renewed it, if they are satisfied that the authorised conduct no longer satisfies the requirements of the Act.[51]

The controls applicable to directed surveillance and the use of covert human intelligence sources are broadly similar. Either may be authorised by an officer having the rank of superintendent or above, or, in cases of urgency, inspector or above.[52] A person designated by reference to their rank in any police force as having power to grant authorisations may exercise that power only on the application of an officer in the same force.[53] In either case, an authorisation may only be granted if the granter is satisfied that surveillance of the type specified in the application is both necessary for certain specific purposes and a proportionate method of achieving the applicant's objectives. The specified purposes are the prevention and detection of crime, the prevention of disorder, the protection of public safety and the protection of public health.[54] In relation to an authorisation of the use of a covert human intelligence source, the granter must also be satisfied that arrangements exist for ensuring that an appropriate police officer is charged with day to day responsibility for dealing with the source and for the source's security and welfare, and that there will at all times be another officer of the same force charged with general oversight of the use made of the source and the maintenance of proper records.[55] Only conduct of the description specified in the authorisation, which is carried on in the circumstances and for the purposes of the investigation or operation therein identified, is clothed with legality by the authorisation.[56]

12–09   Intrusive surveillance is subject to stricter controls, representing as it does a greater invasion of individual privacy. It may be authorised only by the chief constable of Police Scotland (or any other senior officer of Police Scotland

[49] RIP(S)A 2000 s.19(3).

[50] In that case, the authorisation may only be renewed by a person who is satisfied that a review has been carried out of the use made of the source and the tasks given to and information obtained from the source since the authorisation was granted or renewed, and who has considered that review: RIP(S)A 2000 s.19(6), (7).

[51] RIP(S)A 2000 s.20.

[52] RIP(S)A 2000 ss.6(1), 7(1) and 8(1); and see also the Regulation of Investigatory Powers (Prescription of Offices etc., and Specification of Public Authorities) (Scotland) Order 2010 (SSI 2010/350) (as amended).

[53] RIP(S)A 2000 s.11(1). The provision has limited significance following the establishment of Police Scotland (cf. Police and Fire Reform (Scotland) Act 2012) as its effect is that a designated officer in Police Scotland can only grant an application from a constable or other officer of Police Scotland.

[54] RIP(S)A 2000 ss.6(3), and7(3).

[55] RIP(S)A 2000 s.7(2)(c) and 7(6).

[56] RIP(S)A 2000 ss.6(4) and 7(4). It does not necessarily follow, however, that conduct falling outwith the scope of the authorisation is, by definition, unlawful (at least as a matter of domestic law), or that evidence thereby obtained would be inadmissible. While the European Court of Human Rights takes a dim view of interferences with individual rights which lack a positive legal base, it has also held that evidence gathered in breach of a protected Convention right may be admitted provided the overall fairness of the trial is not thereby impaired: see *Schenk v Switzerland* (1988) 13 E.H.R.R. 242.

designated by the chief constable for the purposes of the Regulation of Investigatory Powers (Scotland) Act 2000),[57] and only then if they are satisfied that it is both necessary for the purpose of preventing or detecting serious crime[58] and a proportionate method of achieving that end.[59] The grant or cancellation of an authorisation for intrusive surveillance must be notified to a Surveillance Commissioner[60] as soon as reasonably practicable, specifying such matters as may be prescribed by order of the Scottish Ministers.[61] A notice of the grant of an authorisation must state either that the approval of a commissioner is required before the authorisation can take effect, or that the case is one of urgency (giving reasons for this belief).[62] An urgent authorisation so notified takes effect from the time of its grant; in other cases, the authorisation takes effect only once the granter receives written notice of a commissioner's approval.[63] Where a commissioner is satisfied that, at the time an authorisation was granted, there were no reasonable grounds to believe that its grant was either necessary or proportionate, they may quash it with effect from the time of its grant or any renewal thereof; and if they are satisfied that there were no reasonable grounds for treating the case as urgent, they may likewise quash the authorisation as granted.[64] The chief constable may appeal to the Chief Surveillance Commissioner.[65] The incorporation of Surveillance Commissioners into this machinery reflects the jurisprudence of the European Court of Human Rights, and specifically its requirements that the powers of the state be subjected to a measure of judicial control.[66] In addition to this, s.23 confers on persons aggrieved by any form of surveillance activity falling within its scope a right to complain to the Investigatory Powers Tribunal (established by s.65 of the UK Act),[67] provided that the conduct in question is believed to have taken place in relation to that person or any of their property, and to have taken place in "challengeable

---

[57] Subject to RIP(S)A 2000 s.6(1A).

[58] "Serious crime" is defined as conduct constituting one or more offences for which an adult with no previous convictions could reasonably be expected to be sentenced to at least three years' imprisonment, conduct involving the use of violence, conduct resulting in substantial financial gain, or conduct by a large group of persons in pursuit of a common purpose: RIP(S)A 2000 s.31(6) and (7).

[59] RIP(S)A 2000 s.10(1) and (2). Section 10(3) expressly requires the chief constable to consider whether the information sought could reasonably be obtained by means other than intrusive surveillance.

[60] RIP(S)A 2000 s.13(1). Provision is made for the appointment of a Chief Surveillance Commissioner and other Surveillance Commissioners by RIP(S)A 2000 s.2. They require to be persons who hold or have held high judicial office in terms of the Constitutional Reform Act 2005, i.e. a judge of the Court of Session or High Court of Justiciary at least. Sheriffs, judges of the Crown or circuit courts of England and Wales, and judges of the county court of Northern Ireland, may be appointed Assistant Surveillance Commissioners under s.3.

[61] As to which, see the Regulation of Investigatory Powers (Notification of Authorisations) (Scotland) Order 2000 (SSI 2000/340).

[62] RIP(S)A 2000 s.13(3).

[63] RIP(S)A 2000 s.14.

[64] RIP(S)A 2000 s.15.

[65] RIP(S)A 2000 ss.16 and 17.

[66] See, e.g. *Klass v Germany* (1978) 2 E.H.R.R. 214; *Funke v France* (1993) 16 E.H.R.R. 297.

[67] The Investigatory Powers Tribunal is the only tribunal before whom proceedings can be raised against any of the intelligence services or various other complaints arising out of anything that has been (or may have been) done pursuant to RIPA 2000 or RIP(S)A 2000. For more information on this tribunal's role and function, as well as a list of its decisions, see *http://www.ipt-uk.com/default.aspx* [Accessed 7 July 2015].

circumstances"[68] or circumstances in which authorisation should have been sought.

12–10 The UK legislation applies in Scotland without qualification in relation to the interception of communications and the investigation of electronic data protected by encryption, and a little needs to be said about these. As to the first, it is an offence for a person to intercept, intentionally and without lawful authority, any communication in the course of its transmission by a public postal service, a public telecommunications system or a private telecommunications system (except that, in the latter case only, no offence is committed by a person who intercepts a communication where that person has the right to control the operation or use of the system, or who has the express or implied consent of such a person to the interception).[69] An interception has lawful authority if it is carried out under s.3 or 4 of the Regulation of Investigatory Powers Act 2000, or takes place in accordance with an "interception warrant" granted under s.5. Section 3 provides authority for interception of communications which are (or which are reasonably believed to be) sent by and to persons who have consented to the interception[70]; interceptions authorised under Pt II[71]; interceptions by the provider of a postal or telecommunications service; and interceptions carried out under s.49 of the Wireless Telegraphy Act 2006. Section 4 makes provision in relation to interceptions carried out in respect of a person outside, and using a public telecommunications service provided outside, the UK. The power to grant a warrant under s.5 is conferred on the Secretary of State, and they must exercise the power personally except in the limited circumstances in which s.7(2) permits a senior official to issue a warrant in the Secretary of State's stead. The power may be exercised only where the Secretary of State believes the interception to be necessary on grounds falling within s.5(3) and proportionate to what is sought to be achieved.[72] The grounds specified in s.5(3) are the protection of national security, the prevention or detection of serious crime[73] and the protection of the economic well being of the UK. Only a limited number of persons may apply for interception warrants, among them the Chief Constable of Police Scotland.[74]

The treatment of encrypted data is dealt with by Pt III. Where "protected information"[75] comes into the possession of a person, such as a police officer, by virtue of a statutory power to seize, detain, inspect, search or otherwise interfere

---

[68] RIP(S)A 2000 s.23(2). Surveillance takes place in challengeable circumstances if it is conducted, or purports to be conducted, pursuant to an authorisation issued under the RIP(S)A 2000 or under s.93 of the Police Act 1997 (authorisations to interfere with property or wireless telegraphy).

[69] RIPA 2000 s.1. The inclusion of private telecommunications systems extends the ambit of the original offence contained in s.1 of the Interception of Communications Act 1985, and fills the gap in the law identified by the House of Lords in *R. v Effik (Godwin Eno)* [1995] 1 A.C. 309 (to the effect that a conversation on a cordless phone, picked up by a radio receiver operated by police officers in the flat next door to that of the suspect, was not comprised in a public telecommunications system for the purposes of the 1985 Act) and *Halford v United Kingdom* (1997) 24 E.H.R.R. 523 (to the effect that the internal telephone network of Merseyside Police was not comprised in a public telecommunications system).

[70] RIPA 2000 s.3(2). Such consent might be inferred from, for example, the fact that a person sends an email on a system carrying a clear warning that messages might be intercepted.

[71] RIPA 2000 s.3(3). Pt II deals with surveillance, and is qualified in its application to Scotland: see below.

[72] RIPA 2000 s.5(2).

[73] Including where necessary to give effect to an international mutual assistance agreement.

[74] RIPA 2000 s.6(2)(g).

[75] Namely, electronic information which cannot, or cannot readily, be accessed or put into intelligible form without a "key" such as a password: RIPA 2000 s.56(1).

with documents or other property, or of a statutory power to intercept communications, or by other lawful means not involving the exercise of a statutory power,[76] that person may, subject to conditions, require a person whom they reasonably believe to possess the key to the information to disclose that key. A person wishing to impose such a disclosure requirement must first obtain written permission from a sheriff.[77] The sheriff must be satisfied that disclosure is necessary for the purposes, inter alia, of protecting national security, preventing or detecting crime or protecting the economic well being of the UK, and that it is proportionate to those ends.[78] The effect of a disclosure notice duly issued under s.49 is to oblige its subject, on pain of criminal penalty, to hand over the key to the information or otherwise to translate it into intelligible form.[79] A duty to make arrangements to ensure that keys disclosed pursuant to a s.49 notice, and information thereby obtained, are not used improperly, is laid on certain officials, including the chief constable of Police Scotland.[80]

In amongst the detail of the legislation, the significance of the powers **12–11** conferred by the Regulation of Investigatory Powers (Scotland) Act 2000 and its UK-wide sister Act can be lost. They are well illustrated by considering its interrelationship with the law of legal professional privilege. It is a cornerstone of the rule of law that communications between a client and their lawyer are privileged: it cannot be overridden "by some supposedly greater public interest".[81] It is central to the functioning of this privilege that it is absolute: unless a client can have complete confidence that what they disclose to their lawyer is protected there will be an inevitable chilling effect.[82] Yet there is an obvious risk that in monitoring communications of an individual, privileged material may also be intercepted. That risk is more significant where the subject of surveillance is in any sort of dispute with the government: the consequence being that their opponent in litigation potentially has access to their (thought to be) confidential discussions with their lawyers. In February 2015, in the course of proceedings before the Investigatory Powers Tribunal, the UK Government conceded that from January 2010 the regime for interception, analysis, use, disclosure and destruction of legally privileged material was not in accordance with law for the

---

[76] See, generally, RIPA 2000 s.49(1).

[77] RIPA 2000 s.49(2) and Sch.2.

[78] Specifically, the applicant for permission to issue a disclosure notice must show that it would not be reasonably practicable to access the encrypted information, or render it into an intelligible form, by means other than a disclosure notice: RIPA 2000 s.49(2)(d).

[79] The Government rejected suggestions that this provision might breach the right to a fair trial in art.6 of the European Convention, in so far as it might require a person to incriminate themselves, citing the decision of the European Court of Human Rights in *Saunders v United Kingdom* (1997) 23 E.H.R.R. 313 to the effect that "the right against self-incrimination does not extend to the use in criminal proceedings of material that may be obtained from the accused by the use of compulsory powers, but which has an existence independent of the will of the suspect, for example, documents recovered under a warrant".

[80] RIPA 2000 ss.55 and 56(1)(a).

[81] *Three Rivers District Council v Bank of England* [2004] UKHL 48; [2005] 1 A.C. 610, per Lord Scott of Foscote at [25]. *R. v Derby Magistrates' Court Ex p. B* [1996] A.C. 487: "It is a fundamental condition on which the administration of justice as a whole rests." W.G. Dickson, *A Treatise on the Law of Evidence in Scotland*, revised edition (Edinburgh: Clark, 1887) at para.1663 said: "By sacred and settled rule of law, communications between a party and his legal adviser regarding the subject of a suit depending or threatened are secure from disclosure." In support of that proposition, Dickson cited authority stretching back to the sixteenth century. It is a principle whose importance has not diminished with time.

[82] *Bolkiah v KPMG* [1999] 2 A.C. 222.

purposes of art.8(2) of the Convention and therefore unlawful.[83] That regime is currently based on codes of practice issued under s.71 of the Regulation of Investigatory Powers Act 2000. A consultation is, at the time of writing, under way to revise those codes and review the protections that are in place for privileged information.[84]

12–12   Of more general concern is the blanket retention of communications data. Pursuant to an EU directive[85] provision was made for the retention by telephone and internet service providers of "communications data".[86] This data includes the location, time and duration of any telephone call and similar data in relation to email traffic.[87] This data had to be retained by the service providers for 12 months.[88] In April 2014 the Court of Justice of the European Union ruled that the Data Retention Directive was a disproportionate interference with the right to respect for private life and to the protection of personal data (arts 7 and 8 of the EU Charter of Fundamental Rights).[89] Accordingly the directive was annulled with the consequence that the Data Retention (EC Directive) Regulations 2009 lacked any legal basis and were subsequently repealed. They were, however, replaced by the Data Retention and Investigatory Powers Act 2014 which essentially re-enacts the provisions of the 2009 Regulations. The 2014 Act completed its entirely parliamentary passage in just three days.[90] The significance of this communications data can be overlooked. It is often said, reassuringly, that the *content* of the communication is not retained just the date, time and place of, and the parties to, the phone call or email. That data can, however, be significant. Suppose person A is a high profile celebrity who is seeking treatment for a drug addiction. If person A sits on their smartphone replying to emails every week whilst waiting to be seen in the clinic, that communications data is sufficient to identify that person A regularly attends a particular location which can then be identified as a treatment clinic. From the communications data that the service providers are required to retain, much can be understood about a person's life, including very sensitive personal information. The collection, retention and use of this data must also be set in the context of the "Wikileaks" scandal and the public concern over the mass collection of surveillance data.

---

[83] See *Belhaj v Security Services* (Case No.IPT/13/132-9/H) Unreported 26 February 2015 Investigatory Powers Tribunal. The case went on for a hearing on remedies (a particularly difficult issue where confirming or denying a breach also discloses the fact that surveillance was underway and would breach the government's "neither confirm nor deny policy"). That determination (*Belhaj v Security Services* [2015] UKIPTrib 13_132-H) is available at *http://www.ipt-uk.com/ docs/ABDEL_HAKIM_BELHADJ_Final.pdf* [Accessed 7 July 2015].

[84] The Government's response to the consultation is currently awaited, *https://www.gov.uk/ government/consultations/interception-of-communications-and-equipment-interference-draft- codes-of-practice* [Accessed 7 July 2015].

[85] Directive 2006/24 on the retention of data generated or processed in connection with the provision of publicly available electronic communications services or of public communications networks and amending Directive 2002/58/EC [2006] OJ L105/54.

[86] Data Retention (EC Directive) Regulations 2009 (SI 2009/859).

[87] Data Retention (EC Directive) Regulations 2009 (SI 2009/859) Sch.1.

[88] Data Retention (EC Directive) Regulations 2009 (SI 2009/859) reg.5. The directive required that data be retained for not less than six and not more than 24 months (reg.6).

[89] *Digital Rights Ireland Ltd v Minister for Communications, Marine and Natural Resources* (C-293/12) [2015] Q.B. 127; [2014] 3 C.M.L.R. 44.

[90] The 2014 Act has been held by the High Court to be invalid (being inconsistent with EU law). The effect of the decision was suspended until 31 March 2016 to allow the Government to consider how to respond: *R (on the application of Davis and others) v Secretary of State for the Home Department* [2015] EWHC 2092 (Admin). Permission to appeal has been granted.

In May 2015, the government announced its intention to bring forward an Investigatory Powers Bill to "modernise the law on communications data". This will include "better equipping" law enforcement and intelligence agencies and filling gaps in the respective abilities to build the necessary intelligence and evidence. The existing law has been criticised by the Intelligence and Security Committee.[91] This followed on from criticism of the Regulation of Investigatory Powers Act 2000 ("RIPA is not fit for purpose") by the Home Affairs Select Committee[92] and in June 2015 the Independent Reviewer of Terrorism Legislation called for a complete overhaul of the legislative basis for surveillance and data retention.[93] Whatever form the government's proposed legislation takes, any attempt to extend the scope of the monitoring and data retention powers should be subject to the most close and anxious scrutiny.

ARREST AND DETENTION

Where surveillance is concerned, the individual may never be aware that their **12–13** privacy has been invaded, or may become aware only after the interference has ceased. But there is no ignoring the deprivation of liberty involved in arrest or detention,[94] which is why art.5 of the Convention provides as follows:

"No-one shall be deprived of his liberty save in the following cases and in accordance with a procedure prescribed by law: ... (c) the lawful arrest or detention of a person effected for the purpose of bringing him before the competent legal authority on reasonable suspicion of having committed an offence or when it is reasonably considered necessary to prevent his committing an offence or fleeing after having done so."

The right to liberty carries with it a number of ancillary rights, as set out in art.5(2)–(5): the right to be informed promptly and in a language one understands of the reasons for one's arrest and of any charge against one; the right to be brought promptly before a judge where arrested or detained in connection with a criminal matter; the right to be brought to trial within a reasonable time or to be released pending trial[95]; and the right to compensation where arrested or detained in a manner incompatible with art.5.[96] The Strasbourg Court has described the right to liberty as being at the heart of any political system that

---

[91] Intelligence and Security Committee of Parliament, *Privacy and Security: A modern and transparent legal framework* (The Stationery Office, 2015) HC 1075.
[92] House of Commons Home Affairs Committee, *Regulation of Investigatory Powers Act 2000, Eight Report of Session 2014–15* (The Stationery Office, 2014) HC 711.
[93] D Anderson, QC, *A Question of Trust: Report of the Investigatory Powers Review* (The Stationery Office, 2015).
[94] Except perhaps in situations where, through intoxication or other incapacity, the detainee is unaware of what is happening to them.
[95] Hence the Bail, Judicial Appointments etc. (Scotland) Act 2000, Pt 1 of which made provision for bail to be granted even in serious cases, where previously it had been unavailable.
[96] This right to compensation for continued detention has proved controversial in recent years, with a series of challenges by prisoners serving indeterminate sentences who complain that they are not in a position to satisfy the Parole Board that they are suitable for release because of a failure to provide them with access to the necessary treatments and/or courses during their detention. See, for example, *R. (on the application of Kaiyam) v Secretary of State for Justice* [2014] UKSC 66; [2015] 2 W.L.R. 76; *R. (on the application of Sturnham) v Parole Board for England and Wales* [2013] UKSC 23; [2013] 2 A.C. 254; *James v United Kingdom* (2013) 56 E.H.R.R. 12. In *Kaiyam*

purports to abide by the rule of law.[97] Whether a person has been deprived of their liberty in any particular case is treated by the court as a function not merely of the duration of the period in which the person was subject to restraint but also of the type, manner and effects of that restraint. It is the substance of the act and not its form that is crucial.[98]

12-14   We have already noted the approach of the Strasbourg Court to the question whether a given interference with fundamental rights is prescribed by, or in accordance with, the law. In addition, any arrest or detention must conform to the substantive standards prescribed by art.5(1)(c). So, for example, an arrest not founded on a reasonable suspicion would not constitute a lawful arrest. What is "reasonable" turns very much on what is known to the arresting officer at the material time, but the test is an objective one.[99] Scots law currently recognises two forms of apprehension by the police: "arrest" (whether at common law or under statute) and "detention" (under the Criminal Procedure (Scotland) Act 1995). The continuing need for these two methods of apprehension has been doubted[100] but, for now, they remain and we will consider each separately.

12-15   An arrest may be effected with or without a warrant, under statutory powers or at common law, but almost always arrests are made by police officers. The power of ordinary people to effect a "citizen's arrest" is strictly circumscribed in Scots law:

> "A private citizen is entitled to arrest without warrant for a serious crime he has witnessed, or where he has a moral certainty that the person he arrests has just committed a crime or perhaps where, being the victim of the crime, he has information equivalent to personal observation, as where the fleeing criminal is pointed out to him by an eyewitness. He has no power to arrest someone who has committed only a breach of the peace, although he may

---

the Supreme Court refused to follow the Strasbourg Court and hold that a breach of art.5 in these circumstances required the release of the prisoner (as that would require the release of someone the Parole Board were not yet satisfied was safe to release) and thus an award of damages was appropriate. Awards thus far have, where made, tended to be in the hundreds of pounds.

[97] *Winterwerp v Netherlands* (1979) 2 E.H.R.R. 387 at [37]. Note that art.5 of the European Convention, relates only to the fact of detention, not to the conditions thereof. The treatment of persons held in detention is covered by art.3, which prohibits torture and inhuman or degrading treatment or punishment: see in that regard, e.g. *Napier v Scottish Ministers* [2002] U.K.H.R.R. 308.

[98] Difficulties of definition can arise at the margins, as seen in *Goodson v Higson*, 2002 S.L.T. 202.

[99] Thus there was a breach of art.5 in *Fox v United Kingdom* (1990) 13 E.H.R.R. 157, where the applicants had been arrested under s.11(1) of the Northern Ireland (Emergency Provisions) Act 1978. Section 11(1) conferred a power of arrest on a constable in respect of "any person whom he suspects of being a terrorist". In *McKie v Chief Constable for Northern Ireland* [1985] 1 All E.R. 1, this was held by the House of Lords to involve a subjective test: whether the officer had such a suspicion, and whether it was honestly held. The issue before the European Court of Human Rights was not whether s.11(1) itself breached art.5 but whether there was, in the circumstances, sufficient evidence to give rise to a reasonable suspicion. The court found there was not, from which it follows that any power of arrest, common law or statutory, may only be exercised lawfully, in light of the Human Rights Act 1998, where there are "facts or information that would satisfy an objective observer that the person concerned may have committed the offence" (*Fox v United Kingdom* (1990) 13 E.H.R.R. 157 at [32]).

[100] The Carloway Review, *The Carloway Review, Report and Recommendations* (Scottish Government, 2011) para.5.0.4.

intervene to prevent the occurrence of such a breach . . . Arrests by private citizens are not encouraged, especially where they involve the use of any force, and the limitations on this right of arrest are strictly enforced by the court."[101]

Beyond this, in other words, the private citizen who purports to arrest a person may render themselves liable to conviction for assault.

An arresting officer must make it clear to the arrestee that they are under legal **12–16** compulsion and should tell them the (correct) reason for their arrest.[102] It is preferable to use the word "arrest" here, but

> "any form of words will suffice to inform the person that he is being arrested if they bring to his notice the fact that he is under compulsion and the person thereafter submits to that compulsion."[103]

Reasonable physical force may be used to effect an arrest, and it is an offence under ss.90–91 of the Police and Fire Reform (Scotland) Act 2012 to resist a lawful arrest or to escape from lawful custody.

A person who has been arrested and is in custody has the right under s.15(1) of the Criminal Procedure (Scotland) Act 1995 to have the fact of their custody and the place where they are being held intimated to a third party without delay, or with no more delay than is necessary in the interest of the investigation or prevention of crime or the apprehension of offenders. They must be informed of this entitlement on arrival at the police station. Under s.17(1) of the 1995 Act, they are also entitled to request the attendance of a solicitor at the place where they are being held; again, they must be informed of this right. These rights apply regardless of whether the individual was arrested with a warrant or without.

Arrest with a warrant is perhaps the ideal mode of arrest, being predicated upon prior judicial authorisation. When an arrest is deemed necessary (because there is sufficient evidence to bring charges), the procurator fiscal applies to the appropriate sheriff or district court for a warrant to arrest the suspect.[104] The warrant must be signed by the sheriff, stipendiary magistrate[105] or justice granting it, although execution may proceed, if not on the warrant itself, then on an extract copy signed by the clerk of court.[106] Arrest warrants normally also include warrant to search the arrestee and their property, including lockfast premises and places,[107] to remove any items likely to afford evidence of guilt, and to bring the accused before the court issuing the warrant or any other court

---

[101] *Renton and Brown's Criminal Procedure*, 6th edn, para.7–03 (R.7), cited with approval by the High Court of Justiciary in *Codona (Douglas) v Cardle*, 1989 J.C. 99; *Bryans (Peter Herd) v Guild*, 1990 J.C. 51; and *Wightman (David Alexander) v Lees*, 2000 S.L.T. 111.
[102] *Forbes (Robin Norman) v HM Advocate*, 1990 J.C. 215.
[103] *Alderson v Booth* [1969] 2 Q.B. 216 DC, per Lord Parker CJ.
[104] See Criminal Procedure (Scotland) Act 1995 s.34, in relation to warrants on petition (i.e. in the context of solemn proceedings) and s.135 in relation to summary warrants.
[105] This post is to be abolished by the Courts Reform (Scotland) Act 2014 s.128. When brought into force, any existing stipendiary magistrates will be appointed as summary sheriffs.
[106] Criminal Procedure (Scotland) Act 1995 s.296.
[107] See, e.g. Criminal Procedure (Scotland) Act 1995 s.135(1).

competent to deal with them,[108] and in the meantime to detain them as appropriate.[109]

A great many statutes confer powers of arrest without warrant on police officers (usually "in uniform") where certain specified conditions are satisfied. In keeping with the normal presumption whereby statutes authorising invasions of the liberty of the individual fall to be construed narrowly, the courts generally insist on strict compliance by the police with the terms of statutory powers of arrest. Failure so to comply renders the purported arrest an unlawful assault, which the individual is entitled to resist.[110]

12–17   The state of mind of an arresting officer is a matter which may require to be approached with greater rigour in light of the Human Rights Act. As we have seen, art.5 of the Convention only allows a person to be arrested on suspicion of having committed a criminal offence where there are reasonable grounds, objectively judged, for that suspicion. The domestic courts have not, in the past, tended to inquire too closely into the objective strength or weakness of the suspicion an arresting officer claims to have harboured at the relevant time; rather, provided it is shown that the suspicion was honestly held, it is for the accused to prove that the suspicion was unreasonable.[111] It is suggested that even where a statute confers a power of arrest which is worded in subjective terms, a court of review will require to satisfy itself that there was sufficient evidence to give rise to a reasonable suspicion (making such allowance as may be necessary for the urgency of the situation, and the need for the police officer to make a speedy decision) such as to justify the arrest. It has now been held that it is necessary for the arresting officer themselves to have a reasonable suspicion; it is not acceptable that they rely upon the instruction of a senior officer without some understanding of the basis on which the senior officer formed the view that arrest was justified.[112]

The same may be said of the common law power to arrest without a warrant. This power may be exercised where the arresting officer reasonably believes the arrestee to have committed an offence, but only so far as necessary "to prevent justice from being defeated".[113] Thus the power might properly fall to be exercised where there is a risk that a person will abscond unless arrested, or will commit further crimes, or interfere with the course of justice by, for example, disposing of stolen goods. Urgency may justify an arrest in the interests of justice; by the same token, the longer the lapse of time since the commission of an offence, the less obvious will be the necessity of arresting without warrant. Similarly, the more serious the offence the arrestee is suspected of having

---

[108] Note that justices of the peace may grant warrants to arrest persons in respect of offences the district courts are not competent to try.

[109] Criminal Procedure (Scotland) Act 1995 s.135(2). The power to detain the suspect pending trial must be read subject to s.22, which provides for liberation of a person arrested and charged with an offence that may be tried summarily upon that person's undertaking to appear in court; and to ss.22A–25, which make provision in relation to bail. The bail provisions of the 1995 Act as originally enacted were amended by the Bail, Judicial Appointments etc. (Scotland) Act 2000 to comply with the requirements of art.5 of the Convention.

[110] *Wither v Reid (Carol)*, 1980 J.C. 7; *Gillies v Ralph* [2008] HCJAC 55; 2009 J.C. 25.

[111] See, e.g. *McLeod v Shaw (William)*, 1981 S.L.T. (Notes) 93.

[112] *McKenzie v Murphy* [2014] HCJAC 132; 2015 S.C.L. 194.

[113] *Peggie v Clark* (1868) 7 M. 89, per Lord Deas.

committed, the easier it will be to justify arrest without warrant.[114] Generally, whether a given arrest is wrongful depends on whether it was reasonable for the arresting officer to believe it was justified. Here again, however, if it is shown that the belief was honestly held, it is for the arrestee to show that there were no reasonable grounds for it[115]; and again, it is questionable whether this approach is fully compatible with art.5.

Short of arrest, the police have powers to detain persons suspected of crime **12–18** and indeed potential witnesses to a crime. These are now contained in ss.13 and 14 of the Criminal Procedure (Scotland) Act 1995, as amended by Pt 3 of the Police, Public Order and Criminal Justice (Scotland) Act 2006. Section 13 is best regarded as a power of "quasi-detention". Where a constable has reasonable grounds for suspecting that a person has committed or is committing an offence at any place, s.13(1)(a) of the 1995 Act provides that they may require that person to give their name, address, date of birth, place of birth "in such detail as the constable considers necessary or expedient for the purpose of establishing the person's identity", and nationality; and may additionally ask them for an explanation of the circumstances which have given rise to the constable's suspicion.[116] Provisions that would allow the constable to take the person's fingerprints (only for the purposes of verifying the name and address of the person and whether they are suspected of having committed any other offence) have been passed by the Scottish Parliament but are not yet in force.[117] The constable may require that person to remain with them while they verify the name and address and/or notes the explanation offered, provided that this can be done quickly, and may use reasonable force to ensure that the person remains with them.[118] The constable must inform the person of their suspicion and of the general nature of the offence which they suspect the person has committed or is committing; and if necessary must inform the person why they are being required to remain with them. They must also inform the person that failure to comply with their requirements may constitute an offence for which they may be arrested without warrant.[119] Where the constable believes any other person to have information relating to the offence in question, s.13(1)(b) provides that they may require that person to give their name and address. They must inform that person of the general nature of the offence that they suspect has been or is being committed, and that the reason for the requirement is that they believe the person has relevant information. A person who fails to give their name and address without reasonable excuse is guilty of an offence.[120] Resort to the powers under s.13 is permissible only where the constable has reasonable grounds to suspect an

---

[114] Although note that a constable may arrest without warrant a person who is committing, or who leads the constable reasonably to apprehend, a breach of the peace: see, e.g. *Montgomery v McLeod*, 1977 S.L.T. (Notes) 77.
[115] See, e.g. *Cardle v Murray*, 1993 S.L.T. 525.
[116] The information that the person must provide is prescribed by s.13(1A) of the Criminal Procedure (Scotland) Act 1995.
[117] What will be s.13(1B) and (1C) of the 1995 Act, as introduced by the Police, Public Order and Criminal Justice (Scotland) Act 2006 s.82.
[118] Criminal Procedure (Scotland) Act 1995 s.13(2)–(4).
[119] Criminal Procedure (Scotland) Act 1995 s.13(5).
[120] Criminal Procedure (Scotland) Act 1995 s.13(6)(b). A police officer cannot, however, require a person detained under this provision to remain with them while they verify the particulars given.

offence has been or is being committed. As to what might constitute reasonable cause, the editors of *Renton and Brown's Criminal Procedure* note that it need not

> "rest upon personal ocular observation by the officer; [their suspicions] may stem from the observations of other persons, from 'information received' or from prior knowledge of the suspect's habits and background, as well as general knowledge of the area being policed."[121]

But it must, like the suspicion necessary to justify arrest, be founded on facts known, or imparted, to the constable and not the suspicion of someone else: a bald instruction to a constable to detain a suspect will not suffice.[122]

12–19 The status of a person required to "remain" under s.13 while a constable checks their name and address and/or notes their explanation is unclear. While the section must mean something less than detention (otherwise there would be no need for s.13 at all), a person can not only be required to remain but can be physically constrained to do so. Moreover, while the constable has the power to require an explanation of the circumstances which have given rise to their suspicion, they are not enjoined to administer a caution at this stage. Presumably if the circumstances were such that a constable felt a caution to be appropriate, the s.14 power to detain should be used instead (although this is not to say that anything volunteered by the person asked to remain would be inadmissible for want of a caution).

12–20 Section 14(1) provides that where a constable has reasonable grounds for suspecting that a person has committed or is committing an offence punishable by imprisonment,[123] they may, in order to facilitate the carrying out of investigations into the offence and as to whether criminal proceedings should be instigated against the person, detain that person. Reasonable force may be used. Where a person is detained, the constable may exercise the same powers of search as are available following arrest; again, reasonable force may be used. The detainee must be taken as quickly as is reasonably practicable to a police station or other premises, and may thereafter be taken elsewhere.[124] Detention must be terminated at the end of 12 hours,[125] and sooner if it appears that there are no longer grounds for detention or if the detainee is arrested or detained pursuant to another statutory provision. Provision is now made for a "custody review officer" (who must be of the rank of inspector or above who has not been

---

[121] *Renton and Brown's Criminal Procedure*, 6th edn, para.A4.27. In *Dryburgh v Galt*, 1981 J.C. 69, Lord Wheatley held that even an ill founded suspicion might constitute reasonable cause to suspect: " . . . the fact that the information on which the police officer formed his suspicion turns out to be ill-founded does not in itself necessarily establish that the police officer's suspicion was unfounded. The circumstances known to the police officer at the time he formed his suspicion constitute the criterion, not the facts as subsequently ascertained."

[122] *HM Advocate v B* [2013] HCJ 71; 2013 S.L.T. 810; *Renton and Brown's Criminal Procedure Legislation* (Edinburgh: W. Green) para.A4-27.

[123] *Houston (David) v Carnegie*, 2000 S.L.T. 333.

[124] *Menzies (Alastair Edward) v HM Advocate*, 1995 J.C. 166.

[125] That period was doubled from six hours by the Criminal Procedure (Legal Assistance, Detention and Appeals) (Scotland) Act 2010 in response to the Supreme Court's decision in *Cadder (Peter) v HM Advocate* [2010] UKSC 43; 2011 S.C. (U.K.S.C.) 13 (which we discuss shortly).

involved in the investigation) to authorise an extension of detention for a further 12 hours. Such an extension may only be authorised where the reviewing officer is satisfied that the continued detention is necessary to secure, obtain or preserve evidence related to the offence for which the person is being detained, the offence for which the person being detained is an indictable offence and the investigation is being conducted diligently and expeditiously. Before authorising an extension of detention, the detainee (or their solicitor) must be given the opportunity to make representations to the reviewing officer.[126] Where a person is released at the termination of a period of detention under s.14(1) they cannot be re-detained under the subsection on the same grounds or on any grounds arising out of the same circumstances.[127] Where a person has previously been detained pursuant to another statutory provision, and is then detained under s.14(1) on the same grounds or on any grounds arising from the same circumstances, the 12 hour detention period must be reduced by the length of their earlier detention.[128] A constable who detains a person under s.14 must inform the person at that time of their suspicion, of the general nature of the offence that they suspect has been or is being committed and of the reason for the detention.[129]

Detention is not to be used as a means of delaying arrest and charge. If sufficient evidence emerges to justify arrest of a detainee, detention must be terminated and must in any event be terminated after 12 (or 24) hours.[130] A statutory caution must be administered to the detainee, both at the time of detention and again on arrival at the place of detention. Section 14(7)(a) provides that the power to question a detainee is without prejudice to any relevant rule of law regarding the admissibility in evidence of any answer given. The common law applies a test of fairness to determine issues of admissibility, and a full common law caution should also be administered to a detainee prior to questioning to obviate the risk of evidence thereby obtained being held

---

[126] Criminal Procedure (Scotland) Act 1995 ss.14A and 14B (again, inserted by the 2010 Act in response to the *Cadder* decision).

[127] Criminal Procedure (Scotland) Act 1995 s.14(3); *HM Advocate v Mowat*, 2001 S.L.T. 738.

[128] Criminal Procedure (Scotland) Act 1995 s.14(2)–(4).

[129] Criminal Procedure (Scotland) Act 1995 s.14(6). The subsection also requires the following matters to be recorded: the place where detention begins and the police station or other premises to which the detainee is taken; the general nature of the suspected offence; the time when detention begins and the time of the detainee's arrival at the police station or other premises; the time of the detainee's release from detention or, as the case may be, the time of their arrest; the fact that the detainee has been informed of their right, both at the moment of detention and again on arrival at the police station, to refuse to answer any question other than to give their name and address (this is the statutory caution); the fact that the detainee has been informed of their rights under s.15(1)(b), namely the right to have intimation of their detention and of the place where they are being held sent to a person reasonably named by them (e.g. a friend or relative) without delay, or with no more delay than is necessary in the interests of the investigation or prevention of crime or the apprehension of offenders; (where the detainee exercises their rights under s.15(1)(b)) the time at which their request is made and the time at which it is complied with; and the identity of the constable who informs the detainee of these rights. Failure to record a particular detail will not necessarily render the detention unlawful, however: see, e.g. *Cummings v HM Advocate*, 1982 S.L.T. 487.

[130] In *Grant (Thomas) v HM Advocate*, 1990 S.L.T. 402, the accused was not arrested until some 20 minutes after the expiry of the six hour period, and objection was taken at his trial to the admissibility in evidence of statements he had made while detained. The High Court held that such lapses in compliance with the strict formalities did not of themselves vitiate what had taken place during the currency of the detention.

inadmissible.[131] Failure to administer the statutory caution is less likely to be fatal to a subsequent prosecution.[132]

Provision is made in relation to the rights of persons arrested or detained by ss.15 and 17. Section 15(1)(a) provides that a person[133] who has been arrested and is in custody is entitled to have the fact of their custody and the place where they are being held intimated to a person reasonably named by them without delay, or with no greater delay than is necessary in the interest of the investigation or the prevention of crime or the apprehension of offenders. Section 15(1)(b) provides that a person detained under s.14 is entitled to have the fact of their detention and the place where they are being detained intimated to a person reasonably named by them, again without delay or with no greater delay than necessary. A person arrested or detained must be informed of their rights under s.15(1), whichever applies, on their arrival at the police station (or other place of detention).[134]

12-21   Under s.15A of the 1995 Act a suspect that has been arrested (but not charged) or detained under s.14[135] has the right to have intimation sent to a solicitor of their arrest or detention, where they are being held and that the solicitor's professional assistance is required (s.15A(2)). The suspect also has the right to a private consultation with their solicitor before being questioned and at any time during such questioning (s.15A(3)). In exceptional circumstances, access to a solicitor may be delayed where to do so is necessary in the interests of the investigation, the prevention of crime or the apprehension of offenders. In those exceptional circumstances, questioning may begin (or continue) without the suspect having a private consultation with their solicitor (s.15A(7)). These provisions were introduced by the Criminal Procedure (Legal Assistance, Detention and Appeals) (Scotland) Act 2010 in response to the Supreme Court's decision in *Cadder v HM Advocate*.[136] Prior to *Cadder* a person detained under the 1995 Act had no right to consult a solicitor, only to have the fact of their detention intimated to a solicitor.[137] Detention, at that time, could last for no more than six hours and with no ability to defer the start of that time, obvious practical difficulties would have arisen (particularly in rural communities) in providing a right for a suspect to consult a solicitor before the police could

---

[131] *Tonge (David Albert) v HM Advocate*, 1982 S.L.T. 506.

[132] See, e.g. *Scott v Howie (Paul)*, 1993 S.C.C.R. 81. The statutory caution was not administered at the moment of detention, but at the commencement of questioning at the police station when both the statutory and common law cautions were given. The accused then made a statement, upon which the Crown founded at his trial. The High Court held that what had occurred was a procedural defect that did not vitiate the admissibility in evidence of the accused's statement (although it noted, obiter, that any statement made by the accused between the moment of his detention and the commencement of questioning would have been inadmissible).

[133] Other than a person falling within the Criminal Procedure (Scotland) Act 1995 s.15(4), namely a person who appears to be a child, i.e. a person under 16 years of age. In that case the police officer must without delay intimate the fact of the child's arrest or detention to the child's parent, if known. The parent must be allowed access to the child, unless there is reasonable cause to suspect that the parent has been involved in the alleged offence in respect of which the child was arrested or detained. In that event, the parent may be allowed access to the child. The nature and extent of any access under s.15(4) is subject to any restriction "essential for the furtherance of the investigation or the well-being of the [child]": s.15(5).

[134] Or on their arrest or detention, if they are arrested or detained at the police station itself.

[135] As well as a person that voluntarily attends a police station for the purpose of being questioned on suspicion of an offence or is detained under any other provision for the same purpose.

[136] *Cadder v HM Advocate* [2010] UKSC 43; 2011 S.C. (U.K.S.C.) 13.

[137] A person arrested on any criminal charge did have (and continues to have) the right to consult with a solicitor: s.17 of the Criminal Procedure (Scotland) Act 1995.

interview them. That was not the motive behind the absence of a right to consult a solicitor, as Lord Rodger explain in *Cadder*:

" . . . s.15 of the 1995 Act deliberately deprives the suspect of any right to take legal advice before being questioned by the police, in the hope that, without it, he will be more likely to incriminate himself during questioning." [138]

That gave Scots law a problem with art.6 of the European Convention for the Grand Chamber of the Strasbourg Court had, in *Salduz v Turkey*, held that

"in order for the right to a fair trial to remain sufficiently 'practical and effective' article 6(1) requires that, as a rule, access to a lawyer should be provided as from the first interrogation of a suspect by the police, unless it is demonstrated in light of the particular circumstances of each case that there are compelling reasons to restrict this right. Even where compelling reasons may exceptionally justify denial of access to a lawyer, such restriction—whatever its justification—must not unduly prejudice the rights of the accused under article 6. The rights of the defence will in principle be irretrievably prejudiced when incriminating statements made during police interrogation without access to a lawyer are used for a conviction." [139]

The High Court of Justiciary (sitting as a bench of seven) declined to follow *Salduz*, pointing to the range of other protections that Scots law afforded to accused persons so as to secure their right to a fair trial. [140] That approach was rejected by the Supreme Court. What *Salduz* did was to provide a right against "self-incrimination" and the other protections relied upon by the High Court (many of which went beyond what the European Convention on Human Rights would require) were not sufficient to protect that particular right. Indeed, as Lord Rodger explained, Scots law was "the very converse" of what Strasbourg required. [141] It was therefore a breach of art.6, and thus unlawful, for the prosecution to rely on evidence obtained during an interview where the suspect had not been afforded the opportunity to consult a solicitor. [142]

That gave rise to a number of problems. Leaving aside the political controversy it provoked, the practical issue for the prosecuting authorities was reassessing numerous cases to determine whether they had a sufficiency of evidence without such interviews. Eight hundred and sixty seven cases could not

---

[138] *Cadder v HM Advocate* [2010] UKSC 43; 2011 S.C. (U.K.S.C.) 13 at [90]–[91].
[139] *Salduz v Turkey* (2009) 49 E.H.R.R. 19 at [55]. Lord Rodger explains (at [67]) that this right could be traced back to the Strasbourg Court's decision in *Saunders v United Kingdom* (1997) 23 E.H.R.R. 313.
[140] *HM Advocate v McLean (Duncan)* [2009] HCJAC 97; 2010 S.L.T. 73.
[141] *Cadder v HM Advocate* [2010] UKSC 43; 2011 S.C. (U.K.S.C.) 13 at [93], but see Lord Rodger's discussion of the evolution of Scots law on this point at [73]–[93].
[142] Under the Terrorism Act 2000 "safety interviews" may be conducted without a solicitor being present where the urgency of the situation demands it. Such interviews have been held to be Convention-compliant: *Ibrahim v UK* (2015) 61 E.H.R.R. 9 (a decision of the Fourth Section which has been appealed to the Grand Chamber). See also: M. Seet, "Suspected Terrorists and the Privilege Against Self-Incrimination" [2015] CLJ 208.

proceed as a result.[143] Two other questions arose from the decision: how early in the process does a person have to be informed of their right to speak to a lawyer and can such a person waive their right to consult a lawyer (and if so, how)? The first question troubled the Supreme Court, particularly as a result of comments made by the President of the Strasbourg Court in his concurring opinion in *Salduz* where it was suggested that the obligation should begin from the moment a suspect was detained.[144] As Lord Hope pointed out in *Cadder*, having regard to the fact that a person could be detained under s.14 of the 1995 Act at any time of day or night anywhere in the country, urban or rural, the best that could ever be achieved was the presence of a solicitor within a short time after the person's arrival at a police station.[145] Even that may be difficult in particularly remote locations. In *Ambrose v Harris* the Supreme Court confirmed that the obligation to provide access to a solicitor began when a person has been effectively restrained to the point that they have no option but to remain with the police.[146] That will necessarily depend on the particular circumstances: questioning having been stopped at the side of the road was not enough but having been handcuffed and searched after a quantity of heroin was found was sufficient. In relation to waiver, that question returned to the Supreme Court in *HM Advocate v Jude* where the court confirmed that there was no absolute rule that an accused must receive legal advice before they can be held to have effectively waived their right of access to a solicitor.[147] Before any waiver can be effective, however, the accused must have been given an indication of the broad nature and the gravity of the offence they were suspected of[148] and their status as a suspect must be clear.[149] In response to the ruling, as we have seen, the Criminal Procedure (Legal Assistance, Detention and Appeals) (Scotland) Act 2010 was passed by the Scottish Parliament. This provided a statutory right of access to a solicitor but also saw the Parliament double (and make provision to allow the quadrupling of) the period of detention. Alongside that Act, Lord Carloway was asked to undertake a review of Scottish criminal law and practice. Lord Carloway's report was published in November 2011.[150]

12–22   The Carloway Review gave rise to the Criminal Justice (Scotland) Bill. Much of the headlines associated with that Bill concerned the proposed abolition of the requirement of corroboration (the need to have evidence from two independent sources to prove each essential fact in a criminal case).[151] That proposal has now been dropped. However, if enacted, the Bill will make significant changes to the powers of arrest, detention and search. In particular, the Bill would abolish the

---

[143] See Crown Office and Procurator Fiscal Service, "Crown review of cases after *Cadder v HMA*", *http://www.copfs.gov.uk/media-site/media-releases/247-crown-review-of-cases-after-cadder-v-hma* [Accessed 7 July 2015].

[144] *Salduz v Turkey* (2009) 49 E.H.R.R. 19, per Judge Bratza at para.O-I2.

[145] *Cadder v HM Advocate* [2010] UKSC 43; 2011 S.C. (U.K.S.C.) 13 at [37]. Lord Rodger made much the same point at [70].

[146] *Ambrose v Harris* [2011] UKSC 43; 2012 S.C. (U.K.S.C.) 53.

[147] *Jude (Raymond) v HM Advocate* [2011] UKSC 55; 2012 S.C. (U.K.S.C.) 222.

[148] *R v HM Advocate* [2012] HCJAC 165; 2013 S.C.C.R. 164. Detailed specification of the offences is not, however, required: *GM v HM Advocate* [2013] HCJAC 26; 2013 S.C.C.R. 176.

[149] *Renton and Brown's Criminal Procedure Legislation*, para.A4–33.

[150] The Carloway Review, *The Carloway Review, Report and Recommendations*, *http://www.scot-land.gov.uk/About/Review/CarlowayReview* [Accessed 7 July 2015].

[151] On corroboration generally, see Walker and Walker, *The Law of Evidence in Scotland*, edited by M.L. Ross and J. Chalmers, 4th edn (Haywards Heath: Bloomsbury Professional, 2015) para.5.14.

common law power of arrest (cl.50) and replace it with a new statutory power which would also replace detention under s.14 of the 1995 Act (cl.1).[152] The proposed power would allow a constable to arrest without a warrant where they had reasonable grounds to suspect the person has committed or is committing an offence. Where the offence is not punishable by imprisonment, the power of arrest may only be exercised if the constable is satisfied that it is not in the interests of justice to delay. A person may be arrested under the cl.1 power more than once for the same offence (cl.2). A 12 hour period of detention is retained (cl.11) but with provision for the need for continued detention to be reviewed after six hours (cl.9). After 12 hours, detention may only be continued if the person is charged with an offence (cl.11). Provision is made for "investigative liberation" (in other words, release on conditions) (cl.14). Such conditions may apply for no more than 28 days (cl.15). Detailed provisions are made for the interviewing of persons by the police, with many of the existing provisions restated (cll.23–29). At the time of writing the Bill is currently in stage 2 of its passage through the Scottish Parliament. It was put on hold whilst the Scottish Government commissioned a review of what further safeguards were necessary to implement the proposed abolition of the corroboration rule. In April 2015, the Justice Secretary confirmed that the Scottish Government would remove the corroboration provisions from the Bill to enable it to resume its parliamentary progress. Before that pause, the Justice Committee had published its stage 1 report, recommending a number of changes to the Bill.[153] It can be anticipated that the some of the provisions mentioned above will have been revised before they make it to the statute book.

SEARCH

At common law, the police are entitled to search without warrant the person of **12–23** anyone they have lawfully arrested or detained under s.14 of the Criminal Procedure (Scotland) Act 1995, and this right of search extends to fingerprinting and photographing the suspect.[154] Section 18(2) provides, more specifically, that a constable may take from a person arrested or detained fingerprints, palm prints and other such prints and impressions of an external part of the body as the constable reasonably considers it appropriate to take, having regard to the circumstances of the suspected offence in respect of which the person has been arrested or detained. Section 18(6) provides that the constable may also take, with the authority of an officer of a rank no lower than inspector, a sample of

---

[152] Lord Carloway explained that the two different means by which a suspect may be taken into custody no longer served any meaningful purpose and there should instead be a single period of custody that followed on from "arrest on suspicion" (The Carloway Review, *The Carloway Review, Report and Recommendations*, para.5.0.4)

[153] Justice Committee, *3rd report, 2014 (Session 4), Stage 1 Report on the Criminal Justice (Scotland) Bill* (Scottish Parliament, 2014), *http://www.scottish.parliament.uk/S4_JusticeCommittee/Reports/juR-14-03w.pdf* [Accessed 7 July 2015].

[154] *Adair v McGarry (James Lyon)*, 1933 J.C. 72; and see the Criminal Procedure (Scotland) Act 1995 s.14(7)(b). As amended by Pt 3 of the Police, Public Order and Criminal Justice (Scotland) Act 2006, ss.13 and s.14 of the 1995 Act now provide that, where a person has given their name and address pursuant to either of those sections, they may be required to provide their fingerprints (or a record of the skin of their fingers on an approved device) but only for the purposes of verifying their name and address and establishing whether they may be a person suspected of having committed another offence. That provision is not yet in force.

hair; a sample of fingernail or toenail (or of material under the nails); a sample
of blood or other body fluid, body tissue or other material from an external part
of the body by means of swabbing or rubbing; or a sample of saliva. Reasonable
force may be used. Before arrest, however, a person may not be searched at
common law.[155] Search before arrest must be justified by reference to some
statutory provision,[156] or must be founded on a warrant. It has been held that
warrants to search a person prior to arrest

> "will not be lightly granted, and will only be granted where the circum-
> stances are special and where the granting of the warrant will not disturb the
> delicate balance that must be maintained between the public interest on the
> one hand and the interest of the accused on the other."[157]

But the requirement of "special circumstances" seems to be met by any
intelligible explanation of the need for a warrant.[158] Provided the procurator
fiscal applying for the warrant is able to satisfy the court that it is likely to turn
up some useful evidence, it will normally be granted: the unusual cases will be
those in which the warrant is refused.

In relation to the search of premises, again the ideal form of search is that
which is authorised by a warrant. The need to obtain a warrant is removed where
a person consents to the search.[159] Arrest warrants normally include warrant to
search the arrestee's premises and vehicles for evidence,[160] but warrants to search
may be granted in the absence of arrest or charge, either under the numerous
statutory provisions which authorise this or at common law. Where the grant of
a warrant is conditional, on a constable giving information on oath that they have
reasonable cause to suspect, for example, the presence of drugs on particular
premises, the justice of the peace must inquire into the grounds for that suspicion
and satisfy themselves of its reasonableness,[161] and it would seem, in light of the
Human Rights Act 1998, that a justice should always so satisfy themselves
before granting any warrant to search.

A general warrant to search any premises for any article is incompetent.[162] A
search warrant must be specific in its terms and the police must keep within its
limits when conducting a search under it. As this implies, "law enforcement
officers cannot be treated as acting under and in terms of legal powers of which

---

[155] Unless they consent to what would otherwise be an assault: see, e.g. *Devlin v Normand*, 1992
S.C.C.R. 875. Searches carried out before arrest in situations of urgency may also be excused in
the interests of justice, and the evidence thereby obtained admitted at trial, subject to the
overarching test of fairness: see, e.g. *Bell (William Adamson) v Hogg*, 1967 J.C. 49.

[156] e.g. Misuse of Drugs Act 1971 s.23(2), which entitles a constable to detain and search a person
whom they have reasonable grounds to believe is in possession of a controlled drug; Civic
Government (Scotland) Act 1982 s.60(1)(a), which entitles a constable to search a person whom
they have reasonable grounds to suspect is in possession of any stolen property; and Criminal Law
(Consolidation) (Scotland) Act 1995 ss.48–50 conferring powers to search for offensive weapons
and knives a person is reasonably believed to have about them.

[157] *Morris v MacNeill*, 1991 S.L.T. 607, per Lord Justice Clerk Ross at 609. See, e.g. *Hay (Gordon)
v HM Advocate*, 1968 J.C. 40, where a warrant was granted for the taking of dental impressions.

[158] *Renton and Brown's Criminal Procedure*, 6th edn, para.5.08.

[159] *Davidson (Heather) v Brown*, 1990 J.C. 324.

[160] See, e.g. Criminal Procedure (Scotland) Act 1995 s.135.

[161] *Birse (Gordon Dickson) v HM Advocate*, 2000 J.C. 503.

[162] *Bell v Black and Morrison* (1865) 5 Irv. 57.

they are at the time in question ignorant and heedless".[163] Any search conducted in ignorance of the terms of the warrant will, therefore, be a random search and unlawful on that account. The manner of execution of a search warrant may also be relevant to its legality and hence to the admissibility in evidence of items recovered under it. Certainly where a search warrant restricts the class or number of persons who may execute it, any breach of those restrictions will render the search unlawful unless the irregularity is excusable.[164] It may also be the case that the unduly oppressive execution of a search warrant—for example, in the middle of the night, or by an unnecessarily large number of officers—may render the search unlawful as being a disproportionate invasion of the subject's privacy.[165] On the other hand, where police officers engaged on a lawful search of premises stumble across "plainly incriminatory" articles not covered by the warrant, such articles may be removed and will be admissible in evidence.[166]

There are a number of statutory provisions authorising the search without warrant of premises or vehicles, but at common law the power of the police to enter and search private premises is limited. As a starting point, it may be said that the right of a police officer to enter private premises for any purpose without a warrant and without the occupier's consent is no greater than that of any other member of the public; and if the police do so enter, they must be prepared to justify their conduct by reference to special circumstances before any evidence thus obtained may be held admissible:

> "Irregularities require to be excused, and infringements of the formalities of the law in relation to these matters are not lightly to be condoned. Whether any given irregularity ought to be excused depends upon the nature of the irregularity and the circumstances under which it was committed."[167]

An urgent need to obtain evidence, particularly in relation to serious offences, may justify a search without warrant of private property.[168] Other circumstances that may excuse an irregular search are the authority and good faith of those who obtained the evidence.[169] Even where evidence is illegally obtained, it does not necessarily follow, either as a matter of domestic law or under the Convention, that it is inadmissible in subsequent criminal proceedings.[170] Thus the Convention-proofing of police powers of entry, search and seizure may be less a matter for the police themselves, under reference to art.8 of the Convention, but rather a matter for the court in considering the admissibility of evidence under reference to art.6.

---

[163] *Hoekstra v HM Advocate*, 2002 S.L.T. 599, per Lord Justice General Cullen at [55]; see also *Leckie v Miln*, 1982 S.L.T. 177.
[164] *Singh (Manjit) v HM Advocate*, 2001 S.L.T. 812; but cf. *Hepburn (James) v Brown*, 1998 J.C. 63 and *Lord Advocates Reference (No.1 of 2002)*, 2002 S.L.T. 1017.
[165] *Chappell v United Kingdom* (1990) 12 E.H.R.R. 1.
[166] *Pringle v Bremner and Stirling* (1867) 5 M. (H.L.) 55; *HM Advocate v Hepper (Patrick)*, 1958 S.L.T. 160; *Drummond (Thomas) v HM Advocate*, 1992 J.C. 88.
[167] *Lawrie (Jeanie) v Muir*, 1950 S.L.T. 37 at 42.
[168] *HM Advocate v McGuigan (John)*, 1936 S.L.T. 161.
[169] In addition to *Lawrie v Muir*, see also, e.g. *Wilson (David James) v Brown*, 1996 S.L.T. 686; and *Webley v Ritchie*, 1997 S.L.T. 1241.
[170] *Schenk v Switzerland* (1988) 13 E.H.R.R. 242; *Khan v United Kingdom* (2000) 8 B.H.R.C. 310.

QUESTIONING

12-24 The rules on questioning are, in fact, rules on the admissibility of evidence: there being no point asking questions in a manner which, or in circumstances that, will result in the court refusing to admit the answers as evidence. There are forms of questioning which, whatever the worth of the information they elicit, must be regarded as so offensive to the values of the common law, as well as the Convention, as to render the information inadmissible (or its admission a breach of art.6) and the questioning itself unlawful and a breach of some other Convention right.[171] As a matter of constitutional principle, evidence obtain by torture is inadmissible and torture has, for centuries, been unlawful.[172] Beyond that, the Strasbourg Court has derived a right to silence from the presumption of innocence enshrined in art.6(2) of the Convention, such that a suspect cannot be obliged to answer questions[173] (although this is not to say that adverse inferences cannot be drawn from a suspect's silence).[174] Different issues are raised by compulsory powers of questioning, where the suspect is obliged to answer the questions put by a police officer or other investigative authority on pain of criminal penalty. In *Saunders v United Kingdom*,[175] it was held that the extensive use made by the prosecution at the applicant's trial of answers he had been compelled to give under ss.432 and 442 of the Companies Act 1985 violated the presumption of innocence and rendered his trial unfair. Even so, it does not follow that all compulsory questioning, and any evidence gleaned thereby, is contrary to art.6. As the Judicial Committee of the Privy Council held in *Brown v Stott*,[176] if the right in question is not absolute—and plainly the presumption of innocence is not—the question is whether the restriction or modification of the right pursued a legitimate aim, and whether there is a reasonable relationship of proportionality between the means employed and the aim sought to be realised.[177] The overarching question is always whether the trial viewed as a whole is fair.[178]

12-25 As a matter of Scots law, a person cannot be questioned further once they have been formally charged, about the offence with which they are charged.[179] But there is no general rule that the police cannot question a person after they have

---

[171] See, e.g. *Ireland v United Kingdom* (1978) 2 E.H.R.R. 25, where the European Court of Human Rights found the "five techniques" employed in the interrogation of terrorist suspects to constitute inhuman and degrading treatment contrary to art.3.

[172] See *A v Home Secretary* [2005] UKHL 71; [2006] 2 A.C. 221, especially per Lord Bingham at [51]. As Lord Rodger notes at [129], it has been unlawful in Scotland since the end of the seventeenth century (which was later than in England).

[173] *Funke v France* (1993) 16 E.H.R.R. 297 at [44].

[174] See *Murray v United Kingdom* (1996) 22 E.H.R.R. 313, although the court noted that it would be incompatible with art.6(2) of the Convention, to base a conviction wholly or mainly on an accused's silence or failure to answer questions or give evidence.

[175] *Saunders v United Kingdom* (1997) 23 E.H.R.R. 313.

[176] *Brown v Stott*, 2001 S.C. (P.C.) 43. That case concerned the obligation imposed by the Road Traffic Act 1988 to identify the driver of a car which, in this case, led to her conviction for drink driving.

[177] *Brown v Stott*, 2001 S.C. (P.C.) 43, per Lord Hope at 74–75.

[178] That is not, of course, merely a matter of the fairness of admitting particular items of evidence, but encompasses all the other incidents of a fair trial, such as the right to be tried within a reasonable time (*Dyer v Watson* [2002] UKPC D 1; 2002 S.C. (P.C.) 89), the right to an independent and impartial tribunal (*Starrs v Ruxton*, 2000 J.C. 208) and the right to equality of arms, one aspect of which may be the presence, absence or adequacy of the accused's legal representation (*Buchanan v McLean* [2001] UKPC D 3; 2002 S.C. (P.C.) 1).

[179] *Carmichael v Boyd (Ryan)*, 1993 J.C. 219.

been arrested, provided the questioning is not unfair,[180] and of course questioning is often the very point of detention under s.14 of the Criminal Procedure (Scotland) Act 1995. Whether the court will admit evidence obtained during questioning is ultimately one of fairness, and that is to be assessed in all of the circumstances.[181] Administration of a caution is a factor, but not a decisive factor, in determining fairness and thus admissibility. As Lord Justice General Hope explained in *Pennycuick v Lees*:

> "There is ... no rule of law which requires that a suspect must always be cautioned before any question can be put to him by the police or by anyone else by whom the inquiries are being conducted. The question in each case is whether what was done was unfair to the accused ...
>
> [It] is important to note that there is no suggestion in [this] case that any undue pressure, deception or other device was used to obtain the admissions."[182]

A person should ordinarily be cautioned prior to questioning and, to avoid any risk of rendering statements inadmissible, the common law caution should be re-administered as often as necessary during a long period of questioning, and administered afresh after any break in questioning. The "common law" caution requires the person to be told that they are not obliged to say anything, but that anything they do say will be taken down (and recorded) and may be used in evidence. The question of fairness is a question of fact and accordingly one that the Appeal Court will only rarely disturb. The fact part of a statement or interview is inadmissible does not necessarily mean that it falls to be excluded in its entirety.[183] Evidence obtained by threat or inducement, or where the questioning amounts to bullying, is inadmissible.[184] Placing two suspects in adjoining cells then stationing a police officer to overhear any conservation between the suspects is also unfair (indeed the court held it amounted to unauthorised intrusive surveillance in terms of the Regulation of Investigatory Powers (Scotland) Act 2000).[185] The court has come and gone on how strict a line it is prepared to take on what is "unfair" in terms of questioning. In *Codona v HM Advocate*, the Lord Justice General (Hope) held as follows:

> "In order that a statement made by an accused person to the police may be available as evidence against him, it must be truly spontaneous and voluntary. The police may question a suspect, but when they move into the field of cross-examination or interrogation, they move into an area of great difficulty. If the questioning is carried too far, by means of leading or repetitive questioning or by pressure in other ways in an effort to obtain from the suspect what they are seeking to obtain from him, the statement is likely to be excluded on the ground that it was extracted by unfair means. Lord Justice-General Emslie's definition of the words 'interrogation' and

---

[180] *Johnston (Derek) v HM Advocate*, 1993 J.C. 187.
[181] For a general discussion, see *Renton and Brown's Criminal Procedure*, 6th edn, paras 24.39–24.45
[182] *Pennycuick v Lees*, 1992 S.L.T. 763 at 765 and 766. See also, e.g. *Young v Friel*, 1992 S.C.C.R. 567; *HM Advocate v Graham (James)*, 1991 S.L.T. 416.
[183] *Lord Advocate's Reference (No.1 of 1983)*, 1984 J.C. 52.
[184] *Paul (Ross Duncan) v HM Advocate* [2013] HCJAC 13; 2014 S.C.C.R. 119.
[185] *HM Advocate v Higgins* Unreported 11 March 1993 High Court of Justiciary on appeal.

'cross-examination' in *Lord Advocates Reference (No. 1 of 1983)*, as referring only to improper forms of questioning tainted with an element of bullying or pressure designed to break the will of the suspect or to force from him a confession against his will, should not be understood as implying any weakening of these important principles."[186]

Plainly, the stricter the test of fairness then the easier it is for a trial judge to justify withholding evidence from the jury on the basis that no reasonable jury could conclude that it had been fairly obtained.

FREEDOM OF ASSEMBLY, PUBLIC ORDER AND PROCESSIONS

Introduction

12–26   "[One] of the features of a vigorous and healthy democracy [is] . . . that people are allowed to go out onto the streets and demonstrate"[187] and "demonstration and protest and civil disobedience have a long and indeed proud history" in the UK.[188] Despite that, the approach of the common law to freedom of assembly was "hesitant and negative, permitting that which was not prohibited".[189] For Dicey, freedom of assembly was no more than the consequence of the ordinary freedoms enjoyed by the individual:

> " . . . it can hardly be said that our constitution knows of such a thing as any specific right of public meeting . . . The right of assembly is nothing more than a result of the view taken by the Courts as to individual liberty of persons."[190]

Whatever view Dicey formed, it is now a matter that is heavily regulated by statute and in this part of the chapter, we are going to consider those regulations. However, this is an area that is heavily influenced by the European Convention on Human Rights and in particular art.10 (freedom of expression) but even more so art.11 (freedom of assembly and association). So it is with art.11 that we begin.

Article 11 of the European Convention on Human Rights

12–27   Article 11 of the Convention provides:

> "Everyone has the right to freedom of peaceful assembly and to freedom of association with others, including the right to form and to join trade unions for the protection of his interests."

---

[186] *Codona v HM Advocate*, 1996 S.L.T. 1100 at 1105.

[187] *Austin v Metropolitan Police Commissioner* [2009] UKHL 5; [2009] 1 A.C. 564 at [1]

[188] *Lord Advocates Reference (No.1 of 2000)*, 2001 J.C. 143 at [17]. See also *R. (on the application of Catt) v Association of Chief Police Officers* [2015] UKSC 9; [2015] 2 W.L.R. 664, per Lord Sumption at [19].

[189] *R. (on the application of Laporte) v Chief Constable of Gloucestershire* [2006] UKHL 55; [2007] 2 A.C. 105, per Lord Bingham at [34].

[190] Albert V. Dicey, *Introduction to the Study of the Law of the Constitution*, 8th edn (London: 1915) pp.169–170. Dicey also wrote (at p.169) that "the police have with us [in England] no special authority to control open-air assemblies". As we will now see, that is certainly no longer the case.

Article 11 is important as it provides a vehicle through which other rights, such as freedom of religion (art.9) and freedom of expression (art.10) can be secured.[191] "Assembly" is construed widely, including public and private meetings, marches, public processions and sit-ins. The right is confined to peaceful assemblies, but an assembly does not lose that character merely because it is marred by "incidental" violence or because it attracts a violent response from others:

> " . . . the possibility of violent counter-demonstrations, or the possibility of extremists with violent intentions, not members of the organising association, joining the demonstration cannot as such take away that right."[192]

As a consequence, art.11 carries with it a positive obligation on the state to provide assistance to those who wish to protest. Simply abstaining from interfering with a person's art.11 right is not sufficient for the state to fulfil its obligations. As the Strasbourg Court has explained:

> "A demonstration may annoy or give offence to persons opposed to the ideas or claims that it is seeking to promote. The participants must, however, be able to hold the demonstration without having to fear that they will be subjected to physical violence by their opponents; such a fear would be liable to deter associations or other groups supporting common ideas or interests from openly expressing their opinions on highly controversial issues affecting the community. In a democracy the right to counter-demonstrate cannot extend to inhibiting the exercise of the right to demonstrate."[193]

Organisers of an assembly, and not just the attendees, fall within the scope of art.11.[194]

Article 11 is, however, a qualified right: it may be restricted where to do so is necessary in a democratic society, pursuant to a legitimate aim and the restriction is prescribed by law. The legitimate aims are set out in art.11(2) and it is normally "public safety" or the "prevention of disorder or crime" that are relied upon to justify an interference with this right. The requirement that an interference is "prescribed by law" is not difficult to satisfy: the law must be sufficiently accessible and sufficiently foreseeable.[195] Whether a restriction is "necessary" is

---

[191] For example, *Metropolitan Church of Bessarabia v Moldova* (2002) 35 E.H.R.R. 13 at [118] where art.9 was required to be interpreted in accordance with art.11; and *Socialist Party v Turkey* (1998) 27 E.H.R.R. 51 at [41].
[192] *Christians Against Racism and Fascism v United Kingdom* (1980) 21 D.R. 138 at [4].
[193] *Plattform "Artze fur das Leben" v Austria* (1985) 13 E.H.R.R. 204 at [32]. See also B. Fitzpatrick and N. Taylor, "Trespassers *Might* Be Prosecuted: The European Convention and Restrictions on the Right to Assemble" [1998] E.H.R.L.R. 292; H. Fenwick, "The Right to Protest, the Human Rights Act and the Margin of Appreciation" (1999) 62(4) M.L.R. 491; D. Mead, "The Right to Peaceful Protest under the European Convention on Human Rights—A Content Study of Strasbourg Case Law" [2007] E.H.R.L.R. 345.
[194] *Christians Against Racism and Fascism v United Kingdom* (1980) D.R. 21 at 138. A requirement for prior approval does not, on its own, infringe art.11: *Rassemblement Jurassien v Switzerland* (1979) D.R. 17 at 93.
[195] *Sunday Times v United Kingdom* (1979–80) 2 E.H.R.R. 245 at [49].

normally the most challenging criteria to assess. "Necessary" is not synonymous with "indispensable" but nor does it have the flexibility of words such as "ordinary", "useful", "reasonable" or "desirable". What the use of the word necessary does imply is that there is a "pressing social need".[196] For a measure to be "necessary" it must also be proportionate. The requirements of proportionality have been discussed in Ch.11, above and Ch.14, below.[197] We will discuss some of the leading cases where the courts have had to assess the legitimacy of an interference with art.11. Before doing so, however, it is helpful to set out the statutory framework within which public processions and gatherings are now regulated.

Public processions and assemblies

12–28 As a general rule, public processions must be notified at least 28 days in advance to the relevant local authority and chief constable.[198] The local authority may, after consulting the chief constable, issue an order either prohibiting the procession or imposing upon it conditions as to its date, time, duration and route.[199] The considerations to which the authority must have regard in deciding whether to make such an order include the risk of damage to property or disruption of the life of the community, and whether the proposed procession would impose a disproportionate burden on the police. Section 64 of the 1982 Act provides a right of appeal to the sheriff against an order made under s.63. The sheriff may only uphold an appeal if they find that the local authority made an error of law or material error of fact, exercised its discretion unreasonably (in the *Wednesbury* sense) or otherwise acted beyond its powers.[200] It is an offence to hold a procession without giving notice as required by s.62 or in contravention of the terms of an order under s.63,[201] and to refuse to desist from taking part in such a procession when required to do so by a uniformed police officer.[202]

Section 12 of the Public Order Act 1986 confers supplementary powers on the police to impose additional (or different) conditions on a public procession should this prove necessary. The power is exercisable only where the senior

---

[196] *Sunday Times v United Kingdom* (1979–80) 2 E.H.R.R. 245 at [59]; *Handyside v United Kingdom* (1979–80) 1 E.H.R.R. 737 at [48]. In both cases, the court was considering art.10. The court has repeated this formulation in the context of art.8 in *Dudgeon v United Kingdom* (1982) 4 E.H.R.R. 149.

[197] For a recent discussion, in the context of whether an interference with art.8 was "necessary", see *Gaughran v Chief Constable of the Police Service of Northern Ireland* [2015] UKSC 29; [2015] 2 W.L.R. 1303.

[198] Civic Government (Scotland) Act 1982 s.62, as amended by s.70 of the Police, Public Order and Criminal Justice (Scotland) Act 2006. The Scottish Ministers may designate certain processions as being exempt from these notification requirements; and local authorities may waive the requirement of 28 days' notice in exceptional circumstances.

[199] Civic Government (Scotland) Act 1982 s.63, as amended by s.71 of the Police, Public Order and Criminal Justice (Scotland) Act 2006. These conditions may include a prohibition on the entry by the procession into any public place specified in the order.

[200] Civic Government (Scotland) Act 1982 s.64(4). Note that in *DPP v Jones* [2002] EWHC 110 (Admin), it was held that the imposition of ultra vires conditions (there, on a public assembly pursuant to the Public Order Act 1986 s.14) did not render the order as a whole invalid, since the unlawful conditions could simply be severed from the notice.

[201] Civic Government (Scotland) Act 1982 s.65(1).

[202] Civic Government (Scotland) Act 1982 s.65(2).

police officer present at the procession reasonably believes that it may lead to serious public disorder, serious damage to property or serious disruption of the life of the community; or that the purpose of the organisers is to intimidate others with a view to preventing them doing what they have a right to do or compelling them to do something that they have no right to do.[203] The conditions imposed must be those that the police officer believes to be necessary to prevent serious disorder, damage to property, disruption or intimidation. It is an offence to knowingly fail to comply with conditions imposed under s.12, although it is a defence to prove that the failure arose from circumstances beyond one's control.[204] It is also an offence to incite others to commit an offence contrary to s.12.[205]

Powers to regulate and control public assemblies are conferred directly upon the police by s.14 of the 1986 Act. If the senior police officer, having regard to the time, place and circumstances in which any public assembly is being or is intended to be held, reasonably believes that it may lead to serious public disorder, serious damage to property or serious disruption of the life of the community, or that the purpose of the organisers is intimidatory in the sense described above, they may give directions imposing on the organisers and participants such conditions as to the venue, duration and maximum number of persons who may take part as appear necessary to prevent such serious disorder, damage or disruption. These powers apply only to a public assembly, defined by s.16 as meaning "an assembly of twenty or more persons in a public place which is wholly or partly open to the air".[206] A person who organises or takes part in such an assembly, and who knowingly fails to comply with such directions, is guilty of an offence,[207] although it is a defence in either case to prove that failure to comply was due to circumstances beyond one's control. It is also an offence to incite others to commit an offence contrary to s.14.[208]

The powers of the police in relation to assemblies were augmented by the **12–29** Criminal Justice and Public Order Act 1994, which inserted new ss.14A–14C into the 1986 Act. Section 14A[209] prohibits "trespassory assemblies", meaning an assembly of 20 or more persons on land wholly in the open air to which the public has no or only limited right of access. If at any time the chief officer of police reasonably believes that a trespassory assembly is intended to be held and that it is likely to cause serious disruption to the life of the community or significant damage to the land or a building or monument on it (where the land, building or monument are of historical, architectural, archaeological or scientific importance), they may apply to the local authority for an order prohibiting for a specified period not exceeding four days all trespassory assemblies in an area not exceeding the area represented by a circle with a radius of five miles from a

---

[203] The power is exercisable in advance of the procession, but only where people are assembling with a view to taking part in it.
[204] Public Order Act 1986 s.12(4) and (5).
[205] Public Order Act 1986 s.12(6).
[206] "Public place" means "any road within the meaning of the Roads (Scotland) Act 1984" and "any place to which at the material time the public or any section of the public has access, on payment or otherwise, as of right or by virtue of express or implied permission".
[207] Public Order Act 1986 s.14(4) and (5).
[208] Public Order Act 1986 s.14(6).
[209] Criminal Justice and Public Order Act 1994 s.70.

specified centre. Section 14B prescribes the offences in connection with trespassory assemblies. Thus, a person who organises or takes part in an assembly which they know to be prohibited by an order made under s.14A is guilty of an offence, as is a person who incites others to take part in a prohibited assembly. Under s.14C, a uniformed police officer may stop a person whom they reasonably believe to be on their way to an assembly prohibited by an order made under s.14A and direct that person not to proceed in the direction of the assembly. This power is only exercisable within the area covered by the order. Failure to comply with the police officer's direction is an offence.

These provisions were considered by the House of Lords in *DPP v Jones*.[210] The defendants were arrested while participating in a peaceful, unobstructive assembly at a roadside near Stonehenge. At the material time, an order made under s.14A prohibiting trespassory assemblies in the vicinity of Stonehenge was in force. The defendants were convicted of offences under s.14B. By a bare majority, the House of Lords quashed the convictions. The critical element in the reasoning of the majority was the finding of fact by the justices of the peace that the defendants' presence at the scene involved no obstruction of the highway. That being so, it fell within the scope of what Lord Irvine LC at least was prepared to recognise as a common law right to use the highway for any reasonable purpose, provided that the activity in question did not amount to a public or private nuisance and did not unreasonably impede the public's primary right to pass and repass.[211] But this was the narrowest of victories for the claims of public protest. Only the Lord Chancellor's speech bore any relation to the analytical pattern established in other cases from the pre-Human Rights Act era involving fundamental rights, in that it identified the scope of the common law right and then insisted that this right was not to be whittled down in the absence of clear statutory words.[212] That apart, one could be forgiven for thinking that the House of Lords discerned no "constitutional issue" in *Jones* at all.

General police powers

12-30   Those specific statutory powers are in addition to the general duty imposed on the police by s.20 of the Police and Fire Reform (Scotland) Act 2012 to maintain order. For example, rallies and assemblies fall outside the scope of the 1986 Act if they are held indoors. In such circumstances, the duty imposed under s.20 of the 2012 Act, coupled with the common law power of the police to prevent or restrain breaches of the peace, provides potentially extensive scope for intruding

[210] *DPP v Jones (Margaret)* [1999] 2 A.C. 240.
[211] The other members of the majority were rather more equivocal on this point: Lord Hutton, for instance, went no further than saying that the common law right of assembly "is unduly restricted unless it can be exercised in some circumstances on the public highway". For Lord Slynn (dissenting), the common law recognised no common law right to use the highway other than for passage, and "reasonable incidental uses associated with passage".
[212] H. Fenwick and G. Phillipson "Public Protest, the Human Rights Act and Judicial Responses to Political Expression" [2000] P.L. 627, pertinently contrast the decision in *DPP v Jones* with those in the near-contemporaneous cases of *Reynolds v Times Newspapers Ltd* [2001] 2 A.C. 127 and *R. v Secretary of State for the Home Department Ex p. Simms* [2000] 2 A.C. 115. In both of these, freedom of expression, both as a common law "constitutional right" and as embodied in art.10 of the European Convention, and the values underpinning that freedom, were articulated and formed the starting point for their Lordships' reasoning.

upon freedom of assembly and expression.[213] The extent of the common law adjunct to statutory police powers was the subject of the decision of the House of Lords in *R. (on the application Laporte) v Chief Constable of Gloucestershire Constabulary.*[214]

The claimant was a passenger on one of three coaches travelling from London to join an anti-war demonstration at RAF Fairford in Gloucestershire. That airbase had become something of a focal point for the expression of opposition to the war in Iraq (it was the base for US B52 bombers that were involved in the conflict), and there had been previous incidents of violent disorder. There was evidence that particular groups were bent on violence at this particular demonstration. The police operation put in place to cover the demonstration was the largest of its kind ever undertaken by the Gloucestershire Constabulary. The day before the demonstration, a senior officer of the force issued a "stop and search" order under s.60 of the Criminal Justice and Public Order Act 1994. Pursuant to that order, the coaches coming from London were intercepted at a village some 5km from the airbase. The vehicles and their passengers were searched. The police found items including wire cutters and baseball bats that led them to conclude that some, but not all, of the people on the coach would commit a breach of the peace when they got to the airbase. Crucially, the chief constable accepted that no breach of the peace was imminent and there were no grounds on which to arrest any of the passengers. Nevertheless, the officer in charge of the operation ordered that the passengers be put back on the coaches and escorted back to London. The claimant subsequently applied for judicial review, contending that the chief constable had acted unlawfully by preventing her from participating in the demonstration and by forcibly returning her to London.

The House of Lords held unanimously that the actions of the chief constable were neither "prescribed by law" nor a proportionate interference with the claimant's rights. The starting point is that a police officer, indeed all citizens, are duty bound to take steps to prevent a breach of the peace occurring in their presence, whether by arrest or actions short of arrest.[215] Where, however, no breach of the peace had yet occurred a reasonable apprehension of an imminent breach was required before any form of preventative action was permissible.[216] To be imminent the officer concerned must "think that [the breach] is *likely* to happen".[217] Thus, as the chief constable had formed the view that a breach of the

---

[213] See, for example *Thomas v Sawkins* [1935] 2 K.B. 249, in which anticipation of a breach of the peace was held to justify uninvited entry on to private premises; and *McLeod v United Kingdom* (1999) 27 E.H.R.R. 493, in which the existence of this power (or its statutory equivalent under the Police and Criminal Evidence Act 1984) was held not to breach art.8 of the European Convention, but the manner of its exercise in the circumstances of that case (where there was no imminent and immediate threat of disorder) was held to be disproportionate. Equally, the preventive power has been held to permit the imposition of conditions on public meetings otherwise than on a statutory basis: see, for example, *Humphries v Connor* (1864) 17 I.C.L.R. 1; *Duncan v Jones* [1936] 1 K.B. 218; *Piddington v Bates* [1961] 1 W.L.R. 162.

[214] *R. (on the application Laporte) v Chief Constable of Gloucestershire Constabulary* [2006] UKHL 55; [2007] 2 A.C. 105.

[215] *R. (on the application Laporte) v Chief Constable of Gloucestershire Constabulary* [2006] UKHL 55; [2007] 2 A.C. 105, per Lord Bingham at [29], Lord Rodger at [61] and Lord Brown at [110].

[216] *R. (on the application Laporte) v Chief Constable of Gloucestershire Constabulary* [2006] UKHL 55; [2007] 2 A.C. 105, per Lord Bingham at [30]–[33], Lord Rodger at [62]–[68], per Lord Carswell at [101], Lord Brown at [113]–[114] and Lord Mance at [139]–[142].

[217] *R. (on the application Laporte) v Chief Constable of Gloucestershire Constabulary* [2006] UKHL 55; [2007] 2 A.C. 105, per Lord Rodger at [67] (emphasis in original).

peace was *not* imminent when he stopped the coaches he had no power to take preventative action and the decision to send the coaches back to London was unlawful.[218] In any event, four of the five Law Lords held that the police action was premature, was indiscriminate and therefore represented a disproportionate restriction upon the claimant's art.11 right.[219] In dealing with the indiscriminate nature of the chief constable's decision, the House of Lords referred to the Strasbourg decision in *Ziliberberg v Moldova* where the court held:

" . . . an individual does not cease to enjoy the right to peaceful assembly as a result of sporadic violence or other punishable acts committed by others in the course of the demonstration, if the individual in question remains peaceful in his or her own intentions or behaviour."[220]

In practice, a "one size fits all" approach to policing public demonstrations may be the only practical option. In *Laporte* the House of Lords were at pains to emphasise the respect that should be had for the decisions taken by officers who were on the ground.[221] In that case, however, they concluded that the decisions could not be justified and it is clear that the threshold for preventative intervention is a substantial one. It does not, however, follow from *Laporte* that in all circumstances the police are prohibited from taking general and untargeted preventative action.

12-31   *Austin v Commissioner of Police of the Metropolis* arose out of the 2001 May Day protests in London and concerned the controversial police tactic of "kettling".[222] "Kettling" involves the containment of a group of people by the police on public order grounds. On 1 May 2001, at about 14.00, a large group of protestors arrived in Oxford Circus and took the police by surprise. In 1999 and 2000 there had been a serious breakdown in public order during the May Day demonstrations and the organisers in 2001 had refused to co-operate with the police in relation to the planning of the event. When the group arrived in Oxford Circus, the police took the decision to contain them there and placed an absolute cordon around the group. That group included a number of people that had nothing to do with the demonstration, including at least two that were out on their

[218] *Moss v McLachlan* [1985] I.R.L.R. 76 DC, upon which the chief constable in *Laporte* placed much reliance, was held, somewhat reluctantly, to be consistent with this analysis. The earlier case arose against the backdrop of the miners' strike of 1984–1985, which was marked by outbreaks of violence between striking and working miners. The claimants in *Moss* were striking miners who were stopped some five minutes' journey time from a colliery on the Nottinghamshire coalfield. Apprehending violence, the police ordered the claimants to turn back. When they refused, they were arrested and charged with obstructing a police officer in the execution of his duty. Skinner J held that the preventive action taken by the police was justified, given the "close proximity in place and time" of the claimants to the colliery and the "imminent and immediate" threat of a breach of the peace occurring there.

[219] *R. (on the application Laporte) v Chief Constable of Gloucestershire Constabulary* [2006] UKHL 55; [2007] 2 A.C. 105, per Lord Bingham at [55], Lord Rodger at [85]–[91], Lord Carswell at [106] and Lord Mance at [152]–[155].

[220] *Ziliberberg v Moldova* (Application No.61821/00) Unreported 4 May 2004 European Court of Human Rights at [2]; see also *R. (on the application Laporte) v Chief Constable of Gloucestershire Constabulary* [2006] UKHL 55; [2007] 2 A.C. 105, per Lord Rodger at [83]: "In the eyes of the law therefore innocent bystanders caught up in a breach of the peace are to be regarded as potentially allies of the police officers who are trying to supress violence."

[221] *R. (on the application Laporte) v Chief Constable of Gloucestershire Constabulary* [2006] UKHL 55; [2007] 2 A.C. 105, per Lord Bingham at [55], Lord Rodger at [90] and Lord Carswell at [106].

[222] *Austin v Commissioner of Police of the Metropolis* [2009] UKHL 5; [2009] 1 A.C. 564.

lunch break. By 14.20 a complete cordon had been put in place by the police. A controlled release was planned but postponed with around 40 per cent of the group actively hostile towards the police. Officers were instructed to identify people that were obviously nothing to do with the protest and 400 such people were released. It was around seven hours before most of the people were released. During that time they had no access to food, water or toilet facilities. A number of those contained raised proceeding against the police alleging, inter alia, that their art.5 right to liberty had been infringed by the police tactics on 1 May 2001. Founding the claim on art.5 was significant as it is an unqualified right: if it was held that it had been infringed, that could not be justified in the public interest. In the event, the House of Lords held that the people detained within the cordon had not been deprived of their liberty. Lord Neuberger had no difficulty in finding that the police should, in certain circumstances, have the power to detain people to prevent serious public disorder:

> "Any sensible person living in a modern democracy would reasonably expect to be confined, or at least accept that it was proper that she could be confined, within a limited space by the police, in some circumstances." [223]

It was important that any such confinement was proportionate in all the circumstances. [224] That point was emphasised by the Strasbourg Court when it issued its judgment in the case. [225] That court also recognised the challenge facing the police, which made it important that the European Convention on Human Rights was not interpreted in a way that would make it impracticable to maintain public order. [226] This also serves to emphasis the difficult balance that has to be struck, not by lawyers in a courtroom but, in the first instance, by police officers on the ground, in securing both the Convention rights of individuals at the same time as preserving public order. [227]

Breach of the peace

Finally, a word about the common law offence of breach of the peace. The **12–32** breadth of the offence gave rise to doubts about its compatibility with the European Convention on Human Rights (being too inspecific so as to not be "prescribed by law"). In *Smith v Donnelly* the High Court reviewed the scope of this offence. S had been protesting at the Faslane Naval Base (home of the UK nuclear submarine fleet). She had lain down on the road to block the entrance to the base. When she refused to move, she was arrested and charged with having committed a breach of the peace. At her trial, S raised a devolution issue and argued that the definition of breach of the peace was too vague to be compatible with the European Convention. The definition, distilled from the existing authorities, of the offence adopted by the court was "conduct which does present

---

[223] *Austin v Commissioner of Police of the Metropolis* [2009] UKHL 5; [2009] 1 A.C. 564 at [58].

[224] *Austin v Commissioner of Police of the Metropolis* [2009] UKHL 5; [2009] 1 A.C. 564, per Lord Hope of Craighead at [34].

[225] *Austin v United Kingdom* (2012) 55 E.H.R.R. 14 at [60].

[226] *Austin v United Kingdom* (2012) 55 E.H.R.R. 14 at [56].

[227] In a similar vein, see *R. (on the application of Catt) v Association of Chief Police Officers* [2015] UKSC 9; [2015] 2 W.L.R. 664 where the blanket retention of information on attendees at political protests was upheld where only an element on the ground were a threat to public order.

as genuinely alarming and disturbing, in its context, to any reasonable person".[228] That formulation has been approved by the Strasbourg Court and an enlarged bench of the High Court.[229] As a consequence, any exercise of the Convention rights of expression, assembly or association must be done in a manner which would not, in that context, present as genuinely alarming or disturbing to a reasonable person. To so is to commit an offence and would justify interference with that person's Convention rights.

---

[228] *Smith v Donnelly*, 2002 J.C. 65 at [17].
[229] *Lucas v United Kingdom* (2003) 37 E.H.R.R. CD 86 and *Jones v Carnegie*, 2004 J.C. 136, respectively.

CHAPTER 13

TERRORISM AND THE CONSTITUTION

INTRODUCTION

The scourge of terrorism is not new. The UK has had to contend with the terrorist **13–01** consequences of the troubles in Northern Ireland (and, prior to that, with terrorist activities associated with the campaign for Irish home rule). Most other western European countries, albeit to lesser extents, have also required to confront domestic terrorism[1]; and Arab terrorism has long been a feature of European life. The nature of the UK's present response to terrorism, however, is relatively new—and is not, as might be thought, merely a reaction to the Al-Qaeda attacks on New York and Washington on 11 September 2001. At one level, it might be thought that the "globalisation" of terror demanded, and demands, unprecedented counter-terrorism measures.[2] At the same time, as the decision of the House of Lords in *A v Secretary of State for the Home Department*[3] makes abundantly clear, certain of those measures, when tested against the precepts of respect for fundamental rights, necessity and proportionality, raise unsettling questions. In refusing the Secretary of State's appeal in *J1 v Home Secretary*, the consequence of which was Abu Qatada's deportation was prevented, Jackson LJ succinctly captured the dilemma that terrorism presents the law:

> "I should add that this is a decision which I reach with little enthusiasm. The appellant has been closely associating with Islamist extremists who are involved in terrorism. Such people show scant regard for the rights to life of others. I have no doubt that the Secretary of State was entitled to conclude that the appellant's deportation was conducive to the public interest on national security grounds. The fact remains, however, that the UK is party to the ECHR and has incorporated its provisions into our domestic law. Everyone within our shores is entitled to protection under the ECHR, even those who are involved in or connected with terrorism. The courts are under a duty to uphold those rights and we do so in this case."[4]

It is in responding to terrorist threats where many, if not all, of the constitutional ideals discussed earlier come into sharp focus: closed trials, detention without

---

[1] Basque and Corsican separatists have waged terrorist campaigns against the governments of Spain and France; in Germany, Italy and Greece, extreme left wing terrorist organisations have engaged in campaigns of terrorist violence, usually involving the kidnapping and/or murder of prominent individuals.

[2] It might equally be thought that it is not merely the globalisation of terror that calls for a heightened response, but also—as witness the perpetrators of the suicide bombings in London on 7 July 2005—its "domestication".

[3] *A v Secretary of State for the Home Department* [2004] UKHL 56; [2005] 2 A.C. 68.

[4] *J1 v Secretary of State for the Home Department* [2013] EWCA Civ 279 at [94].

trial, "control orders", special advocates, reverse burdens of proof, the need to balance the rights of society with the rights of an individual determined to cause indiscriminate damage to that society. It is an area where there are rarely obviously right answers but selecting the wrong answer can be life threatening. With the stakes (and often emotions) so high it is perhaps unsurprising that it is the response to terrorism that has so often tested our commitment, as a society, to the rule of law and placed the separation of powers under almost unbearable strain. But as Lord Bingham reminded us, "It is, however, when human rights are under pressure that human rights guarantees are most important".[5]

This chapter is split in to two parts. First, we look briefly at some of the main anti-terrorism laws that are currently in place.[6] Secondly, we look at three different case studies to illustrate the tension that is placed on the constitutional principles discussed elsewhere in this text and to illustrate how difficult the balance is to strike but also how important it is that in seeking to protect and preserve the state we do not compromise the ideas that define it. But before that, it is helpful to remember that this is not a new problem. The UK has faced many of these questions before and has not always lived up to our modern day expectations. To illustrate that point, it is helpful to go back to May 1940 and tell the story of a successful Jewish businessman, Jack Perlzweig, who is now more commonly known as Robert Liversidge.[7]

13-02 On 29 May 1940 Mr Liversidge was arrested and taken to Brixton Prison. He was to remain there for nearly 20 months. He did not, however, know why he had been detained and was never charged with any offence. May 1940 was a time of great anxiety: the Second World War was in its second year and a German invasion appeared imminent. The previous year the Home Secretary had made the Defence (General) Regulations 1939. Regulation 18B provided:

> "The Secretary of State, if satisfied with respect to any particular person that with a view to prevent him from acting in any manner prejudicial to the public safety or the defence of the Realm it is necessary to do so, may make an order against that person directing that he be detained."

In May 1940 the Home Secretary signed an order authorising the detention of Mr Liversidge. In the spring of 1941 Mr Liversidge sought to challenge the lawfulness of his detention. At every stage his challenge failed and by September 1941 his appeal to the House of Lords was heard.[8] By then the issue had become a focused one: was it enough for the Home Secretary, acting in good faith, to believe he had reasonable cause to authorise Mr Liversidge's detention? Or did the Home Secretary actually have to have reasonable cause to found that belief? If it was the former, there was no role for the courts; if it was the latter, it was for the court to review whether the Home Secretary had reasonable cause for his belief.[9] The House of Lords preferred the former. Lord Macmillan, reflective of the majority view of the House, said:

[5] T. Bingham, "The Human Rights Act" [2010] E.H.R.L.R. 568, 575.
[6] As will become apparent in a moment, this is an area where the law changes often. So "current" means in force in early 2015.
[7] See also "Mr Perlzweig, Mr Liversidge, and Lord Atkin", in T. Bingham, *The Business of Judging* (Oxford: Oxford University Press, 2000) Ch.3.
[8] *Liversidge v Anderson* [1942] A.C. 206.
[9] *Liversidge v Anderson* [1942] A.C. 206, per Lord Macmillan at 248.

"In a matter at once so vital and so urgent in the interests of national safety, I am unable to accept a reading of the regulation which would prescribe that the Secretary of State may not act in accordance with what commends itself to him as a reasonable cause of belief without incurring the risk that a court of law would disagree with him ... ."[10]

The majority of the House of Lords was concerned that if the Home Secretary was required to demonstrate the reasonableness of his belief, he would be unable to do so due to the national security consequences of disclosing his sources.[11] In short, the highest court in the land had allowed the executive to claim, through delegated legislation, the power to detain any person without limit of time, without trial and without review by the courts.

Lord Atkin provided the sole dissent and it was a dissent that ensured Mr Liversidge his place in history:

"I view with apprehension the attitude of judges who on a mere question of construction when face to face with claims involving the liberty of the subject show themselves more executive minded than the executive ... In this country, amid the clash of arms, the laws are not silent. They may be changed, but they speak the same language in war as in peace. It has always been one of the pillars of freedom, one of the principles of liberty for which on recent authority we are now fighting, that the judges are no respecters of persons and stand between the subject and any attempted encroachment on his liberty by the executive, alert to see that any coercive action is justified in law. ...

I protest, even if I do it alone, against a strained construction put on words with the effect of giving an uncontrolled power of imprisonment to the Minister. ...

I know of only one authority which might justify the suggested method of construction: "'When I use a word", Humpty Dumpty said in a rather scornful tone, "it means just what I choose it to mean, neither more nor less." "The question is," said Alice, "whether you can make words mean so many different things." "The question is," said Humpty Dumpty, "which is to be master—that's all."' ... After all this long discussion the question is whether the words 'If a man has' can mean 'If a man thinks he has'. I am of opinion that they cannot, and that the case should be decided accordingly."[12]

That dissent, not least the reference to Humpty Dumpty, made Lord Atkin deeply unpopular with his colleagues and divided academic opinion at the time.[13] Although described as a "very peculiar decision"[14] it was not until 1979 that the House of Lords recognised that Lord Atkin had been correct all along:

---

[10] *Liversidge v Anderson* [1942] A.C. 206, per Lord Macmillan at 257.
[11] For example, *Liversidge v Anderson* [1942] A.C. 206, per Lord Macmillan at 254. As we will see below, this is a problem that the government of today still complains about.
[12] ???
[13] A. Paterson, *Final Judgment: The Last Law Lords and the Supreme Court* (Oxford: Hart Publishing, 2013) p.150
[14] *Ridge v Baldwin* [1964] A.C. 40, per Lord Reid at 73.

" ... the time has come to acknowledge openly that the majority of this House in *Liversidge v Anderson* were expediently and, at that time, perhaps, excusably, wrong and the dissenting speech of Lord Atkin was right."[15]

What is the relevance of the case to us today? It serves as a reminder that in times of crisis, it is easy to abridge the rights of those that are perceived to be a threat. In *Liversidge* the executive had claimed, Parliament approved, and the courts endorsed, a power to detain without limit of time on the say so of a government minister. Such an arbitrary power is clearly inconsistent with the rule of law. Yet in the 21st century, Parliament sought to vest similar powers in the executive, in response to what was said to be a threat to the life of the nation. As we will see, the courts were more vigilant on that occasion. Similarly, the House of Lords in *Liversidge* wrestled with the balance between the accused's right to know the case against him and the need for the security services to protect their sources and their methods. That is a debate that continues today and one that we will examine in the context of closed hearings. Before turning to consider how the courts have addressed those issues in more modern times, it is helpful first to look at the main features of the current anti-terrorism regime.

<h2 style="text-align:center">EMERGENCY POWERS AND TERRORISM[16]</h2>

"Civil contingencies"

13–03 Provision has been made for extensive emergency powers in the Civil Contingencies Act 2004. In the event of an "emergency", which includes "war, or terrorism, which threatens serious damage to the security of the United Kingdom",[17] an order conferring emergency powers on the executive may be made.[18] The scope of the emergency powers that can be conferred are listed in s.22 of the Act. No summary can adequately convey the breadth of the powers available. It is not clear what further powers the executive could require access to. However, extensive provision is now made to deal with terrorism in particular.

Terrorism legislation

13–04 The hallmark of the contemporary response to the "emergency" of terrorism is the abandonment of any pretence that the powers of the state should be temporary and exceptional in nature.[19] On the contrary, despite provision for regular review of the operation of anti-terrorist legislation and the inclusion of a quasi-judicial

[15] *R. v Inland Revenue Commissioners Ex p. Rossminster Ltd* [1980] A.C. 952, per Lord Diplock at 1011.
[16] L.K. Donohue, *Counter-Terrorist Law and Emergency Powers in the United Kingdom, 1922–2000* (Dublin: Irish Academic Press, 2001); C. Walker, *Terrorism and the Law* (Oxford: Oxford University Press, 2011).
[17] Civil Contingencies Act 2004 s.19(1)(c).
[18] Civil Contingencies Act 2004 s.20. Ordinarily this should be done by the Privy Council but in cases of particularly urgency may be made by the Prime Minister or another "senior Minister of the Crown" (s.20(3)).
[19] H. Fenwick, *Civil Rights: New Labour, Freedom and the Human Rights Act* (Harlow: Longman, 2000) Ch.3. As the author notes, counter-terrorism provision following the enactment of the Terrorism Act 2000 is more extensive than anything that obtained, at least on the British mainland, during the worst years of Irish terrorist violence.

layer within the relevant institutional machinery, anti-terrorist powers now have the stamp of something permanent and, indeed, given the frequency with which Parliament now legislates on the matter, routine. There is nothing accidental in this. In 1995, against the backdrop of a diminution of Irish terrorism and the emergence of a new species of radical Islamic terrorism, Lord Lloyd of Berwick was asked to lead an inquiry into whether, in the event of the achievement of permanent peace in Northern Ireland, any need would remain for specific anti-terrorism legislation in the UK. The report of Lord Lloyd's inquiry was published in October 1996.[20] It concluded that there was a need for permanent, UK-wide, legislation (a conclusion no doubt fortified by the bombing in Omagh in August 1998, in which 29 lives were lost). The recommendations of the Lloyd Report were largely implemented by the enactment of the Terrorism Act 2000.

That Act remains the basic foundation of counter-terrorism legislation in the UK. It has, however, been supplemented by a number of additional enactments, most of which have been passed by Parliament in remarkably short time scales. In the aftermath of the 9/11 attacks on the US, the Anti-Terrorism, Crime and Security Act 2001 ("surely the most draconian piece of legislation Parliament has passed in peacetime in over a century")[21] was rushed through Parliament, with only 16 hours of debate permitted on a Bill that ran to 129 clauses and eight Schedules, many of which contained powers that were a long way removed from what would be necessary to respond to the "emergency" situation. Significant additional powers were conferred on the executive, with resultant inroads made on civil liberties, without any proper scrutiny. This pattern of legislating in response to events has been repeated: the Prevention of Terrorism Act 2005 was passed and came into force within three months of the House of Lords' decision in *A v Secretary of State for the Home Department*,[22] introducing a system of "control orders" to replace the 2001 Act's provisions sanctioning detention of foreign nationals without limit of time; the Terrorism Act 2006 came in response to the 7/7 bombings in London; and the Terrorism Prevention and Investigation Measures Act 2011 abolished control orders (introduced by the 2005 Act) after a series of decisions criticising the system and a change in the political mood in relation to them.[23] In addition to those measures, Parliament has enacted the Counter-Terrorism Act 2008 (introducing, amongst other things, notification requirements for persons convicted of certain terrorism-related offences) and the Counter-Terrorism and Security Act 2015 (enacted, it asserts, to help reduce the UK national terrorist threat level). As the Terrorism Act 2000 was designed to be a permanent code responding to a permanent threat, it contains no provision for its periodic review. Subsequent Acts have generally included some provision for the review of their operation and continuing need.[24] The annual renewal of

---

[20] Lord Lloyd of Berwick, *Inquiry into Legislation against Terrorism* (The Stationery Office, 1996), Cm.3420. See also the government's consultation document, published in December 1998, Home Office and Northern Ireland Office, *Legislation against Terrorism: a consultation paper* (The Stationery Office, 1998) Cm.4178.

[21] A. Tomkins, "Legislating against terror: the Anti-terrorism, Crime and Security Act 2001" [2002] P.L. 205.

[22] *A v Secretary of State for the Home Department* [2004] UKHL 56; [2005] 2 A.C. 68.

[23] The Liberal Democrats went into the 2010 general election with a manifesto commitment to abolish control orders. The coalition agreement that then followed the election promised that control orders would be subject to an "urgent review" which led to their abolition in early 2011.

[24] See Walker, *Terrorism and the Law* (2011) paras 1.77–1.88. For example, ss.13–14 of the Prevention of Terrorism Act 2005.

counter-terrorism provisions, a feature of the legalisation throughout the 1970s and 1980s, is not now a feature of this type of legislation.

13–05   Just as we talked about in Ch.1 the ad hoc approach to constitutional reform, counter-terrorism legislation suffers from the same problem. In a field where the rights and liberties of individuals are inevitably involved, arguably the very worst time to legislate on the matter is in the aftermath of a terrorist attack when emotions are inevitable running high. The 2006 Act provides a good illustration of the concern. First, it created offences that are subject to no geographical limits.[25] That is a remarkable provision: a person of any nationality, who acts in a way which constitutes an offence under the 2006 Act, no matter where in the world, is liable to prosecution in the UK courts under the 2006 Act even if their acts have no connection whatsoever with this country and they were lawful where they were carried out. Secondly, it is a mark of just how complacent Parliament had become that it was seen as a triumph for civil liberty that the government's original proposal to permit the detention and interrogation of terrorist suspects for up to 90 days (a proposal that was based on little more than a request from the police) was reduced to a 28 day period.[26] At the time of enactment, the maximum period of detention under the Criminal Procedure (Scotland) Act 1995 was six hours. It is lamentable that against that background, legislating for a 28 day period of detention was regarded by many as a victory. These, and many other, provisions in the 2006 Act do little to alter the impression that the legislation (not only the 2006 Act, but other counter-terrorism legislation) is a recipe for abuse of civil liberty, mistreatment of innocent people and inevitable confrontation with the courts.

"Terrorism"

13–06 An exceptionally broad meaning is given to the word "terrorism" by s.1 of the Terrorism Act 2000:

> "(1) In this Act 'terrorism' means the use or threat of action where—
>
>> (a) the action falls within subsection (2);
>> (b) the use or threat is designed to influence the government or an international governmental organisation or to intimidate the public or a section of the public, and
>> (c) the use or threat is made for the purpose of advancing a political, religious, racial or ideological cause.
>
> (2) Action falls within subsection if it—
>
>> (a) involves serious violence against a person,
>> (b) involves serious damage to property,
>> (c) endangers a person's life, other than that of a person committing the action,
>> (d) creates a serious risk to the health and safety of the public or a section of the public, or
>> (e) is designed seriously to interfere with or seriously to disrupt an electronic system."

---

[25] Terrorism Act 2006 s.17.
[26] That period has since been reduced further to 14 days: Protection of Freedoms Act 2012.

Any "action" is not limited to one that takes place within the UK (s.1(4)) and an action that involves firearms or explosives is terrorism for the purposes of the 2000 Act even where s.1(1)(b) is not satisfied (s.1(3)). This definition of terrorism is significantly wider that the previous statutory definition of "terrorism".[27] Whilst the concept of "serious" violence and "serious" damage to property is now contained within the definition, the purposes and motivations that constitute "terrorism" are extended. Whether it is appropriate to use motivation in a definition that creates a criminal offences is controversial: motive is not normally a relevant consideration in the criminal law and requiring the prosecution to prove motive can act as an unnecessary additional hurdle in proving a case.[28] Furthermore, there are fundamental difficulties with any legal definition of terrorism. "One man's terrorist is another man's freedom fighter" is true (Nelson Mandela in South Africa to take probably the best known example) and thus what constitutes terrorism, and who is a terrorist, can change over time.[29] Before moving on, we should pause to note who is, according to the 2000 Act, a "terrorist".

A "terrorist" is defined as a person who has committed any one of a number of offences under the 2000 Act or who is, or has been, concerned in the commission, preparation or instigation of acts of terrorism.[30] Those offences include, for example, membership of proscribed organisations (s.11), assisting the funding of such organisations (ss.15–18) and various acts that are directed at the planning and carrying out of a terrorist attack (ss.56–63). Conviction for many of these offences now brings with it various notification requirements, which are imposed for a period of between 10 and 30 years, requiring an individual to notify the police on an annual basis of various pieces of prescribed information.[31] In addition, an individual subject to the notification requirements must inform the police of any intention to travel abroad.[32]

Terrorism prevention and investigation measures

One of the most challenging questions for the government is what to do with **13–07** people they believe (or possibly know) are terrorists but equally are unable to mount a prosecution against (normally due to a lack of admissible evidence). As already alluded to, and as discussed further below, the original solution (but only when the individual concerned was a foreign national) was to sanction his or her detention without trial and without limit of time. When that was (unsurprisingly) held to be unlawful, the concept of a "control order" was introduced. Under the Prevention of Terrorism Act 2005, the Secretary of State could make an order "against an individual that imposes obligations on him for purposes connected

---

[27] Contained in the Prevention of Terrorism (Temporary Provisions) Act 1989 s.20(1): " . . . 'terrorism' means the use of violence for political ends and includes any use of violence for the purpose of putting the public or any section of the public in fear."

[28] Walker, *Terrorism and the Law* (2011), para.1.122.

[29] C. Walker, "The legal definition of 'terrorism' in United Kingdom law and beyond" [2007] P.L. 331.

[30] Terrorism Act 2000 s.40(1).

[31] Counter-Terrorism Act 2008 Pt 4.

[32] Counter-Terrorism Act 2008 s.52. Counter-Terrorism Act 2008 (Foreign Travel Notification Requirements) Regulations 2009 (SI 2009/2493).

with protecting members of the public from a risk of terrorism".[33] These orders could be made for a (renewable) period of up to one year and allowed significant restrictions to be placed on the activities of an individual.[34] Any obligation imposed had to be one the Secretary of State (or the court) considered "necessary for the purposes connected with preventing or restricting involvement by that individual in terrorism-related activity".[35] Section 1(4) then set out a non-exhaustive list of 16 such obligations, which included restrictions in respect of the individual's work, business or other occupation, restrictions on their association or communications with specified persons or persons generally and restrictions on their residence and movement. They could also be required, among other things, to surrender their passport and to submit to electronic monitoring. Breach of the conditions of a control order was a criminal offence.[36] Where there was sufficient evidence to prosecute a suspect, that should be done rather than making a control order but it was not a precondition to making such an order that there be an absence of a realistic prospect of prosecution.[37] It will be obvious that the extent to which the liberty of a person subjected to a control could be restricted was significant. In principle, the conditions imposed could amount to a deprivation of liberty for purposes of art.5 of the Convention (and thus amount to a disproportionate and unlawful interference with the suspect's Convention rights).[38] It was a matter to be determined on the facts and circumstances of each case whether the conditions amounted to a deprivation of liberty.[39] The conditions had, however, to be significant: a 16 hour curfew could only cause a control order to be struck down if accompanied by other conditions that were "unusually destructive of the life the controlee might otherwise have been living".[40]

Politically, however, control orders came to be regarded as unacceptable and the coalition government elected in 2010 legislated to abolish them. In their place came "Terrorism Prevention and Investigation Measures" ("TPIMs"). Introduced by the Terrorism Prevention and Investigation Measures Act 2011, the Secretary of State may only make a TPIM where five conditions are met:

> 1) that the Secretary of State reasonably believes that the individual is, or
>   has been, involved in terrorism-related activity (defined as "the
>   relevant activity");

---

[33] Prevention of Terrorism Act 2005 s.1(1).

[34] There were in fact two forms of order: "non-derogating" orders (which could be made by the Secretary of State) and more restrictive "derogating" orders (which had to be made by the court). See para.12–12 of the previous edition of this work.

[35] Prevention of Terrorism Act 2005 s.1(3).

[36] Prevention of Terrorism Act 2005 s.9.

[37] *Secretary of State for the Home Department v E* [2007] UKHL 47; [2008] 1 A.C. 499, per Lord Bingham at [15]–[16] and Lord Carswell at [32].

[38] *Secretary of State for the Home Department v JJ* [2007] UKHL 45; [2008] 1 A.C. 385. Lord Hoffmann at [44] dissented, arguing that anything less than actual imprisonment or something that is for practical purposes little different was necessary before the absolute right contained in art.5 of the Convention was engaged: "Otherwise the law would place too great a restriction on the powers of the state to deal with serious terrorist threats to the lives of its citizens."

[39] *Secretary of State for the Home Department v AP* [2010] UKSC 24; [2011] 2 A.C. 1.

[40] *Secretary of State for the Home Department v AP* [2010] UKSC 24; [2011] 2 A.C. 1, per Lord Brown at [4].

2) some or all of the relevant activity is new terrorism-related activity;

3) that the measure is necessary for purposes connected with protecting members of the public from the risk of terrorism;

4) that the measure is necessary for purposes connected with preventing or restricting the individual's involvement in terrorism-related activity; and

5) either the court gives the Secretary of State permission to make the order or the urgency of the situation leads to the Secretary of State to reasonably conclude that the measure be imposed without obtaining such permission.[41]

The measures that can be imposed are set out in Sch.1 to the 2011 Act and relate to, amongst other things, residence, travel, the ability to transfer property, the use of electronic communication devices and the use of an electronic tag or other similar device.[42] Failure to comply with any measure imposed by a TPIM, without reasonable excuse, is an offence.[43]

When considering whether to grant permission, the court has to determine whether the Secretary of State's decision that conditions (1)–(4) are satisfied are "obviously flawed".[44] The court can reach its decision without the individual who will be subject to the TPIM being notified of the application, let alone being offered the opportunity to be heard.[45] Once made, a TPIM remains in force for one year and may only be renewed once (for a further year) if conditions (a), (3) and (4) are satisfied.[46] Within seven days of the TPIM being served on an individual, the court must hold a directions hearing at which the individual has the opportunity to attend.[47] A "review hearing", at which the court must review the Secretary of State's decision in relation to conditions (1)–(4) and whether they continue to be met, must be held as soon as reasonably practicable after the directions hearing.[48] The Secretary of State is required to keep under review whether conditions (3) and (4) continue to be met once a TPIM has been made[49] and the relevant police force must keep under review whether sufficient evidence is available to prosecute the individual.[50]

The Supreme Court has not yet had the opportunity to consider TPIMs but they are designed to be a much more tailored, and thus proportionate, means of dealing with terrorist suspects for whom there is insufficient admissible evidence to bring a prosecution. Terrorism prevention and investigation measures address the same problem that detention without trial or limit of time was designed to address. It is fairly remarkable that only a decade after Parliament authorised that unpalatable step, it considered the 2011 Act a sufficient response to the same perceived threat.

---

[41] Terrorism Prevention and Investigation Measures Act 2011 s.3.
[42] Terrorism Prevention and Investigation Measures Act 2011 Sch.1.
[43] Terrorism Prevention and Investigation Measures Act 2011 s.23.
[44] Terrorism Prevention and Investigation Measures Act 2011 s.6(3).
[45] Terrorism Prevention and Investigation Measures Act 2011 s.6(4).
[46] Terrorism Prevention and Investigation Measures Act 2011 s.5.
[47] Terrorism Prevention and Investigation Measures Act 2011 s.8.
[48] Terrorism Prevention and Investigation Measures Act 2011 ss.8(5) and 9.
[49] Terrorism Prevention and Investigation Measures Act 2011 s.11.
[50] Terrorism Prevention and Investigation Measures Act 2011 s.10.

TERRORISM AND THE RULE OF LAW

Introduction

13–08 Having outlined some of the central features of the legislative response to terrorism, it is now helpful to consider a few case studies where the application of these rules has tested our (or at least the courts') commitment to the rule of law. We start with the issue of detention without trial (a matter that you could have been forgiven for believing had been resolved by Lord Diplock's recognition that Lord Atken's dissent in *Anderson* had been correct all along). Next we consider the right to a fair hearing, in the sense of being entitled to know the case against you and to challenge it. Modern surveillance and intelligence gathering methods often rub up against the rules on admissibility of evidence and can present acute dilemmas for the prosecuting authorities. Finally, we consider the right to a fair hearing, in the sense of a public hearing. When can, and should, the court sit in private and on what basis can that be authorised?

Detention without trial

13–09 As we saw above, the precursor to TPIMs were "control orders" which were themselves a response to the court objecting to the detention of suspects without trial and without limit of time. That final proposition was established in *A v Secretary of State for the Home Department*: despite it now being more than a decade since it was handed down, it remains one of the most importance decisions to emerge from the UK's highest court this century.[51] In issue was s.23 of the Anti-terrorism, Crime and Security Act 2001 (which provided for the detention of non-nationals if the Home Secretary believed that their presence in the country was a risk to national security and it was not possible to deport them)[52] and the Human Rights Act 1998 (Designated Derogation) Order 2001 (which contained the UK's purported derogation under art.15 of the European Convention on Human Rights from the requirements of art.5(1), the right to liberty).[53] Three issues arose for the House of Lords (which sat as a then unprecedented panel of nine Law Lords) to determine: (a) was there a "threat to the life of the nation" which entitled the United Kingdom to derogate from its obligations under the Convention; (b) if so, was the 2001 Order lawfully made; and (c) if not, was s.23 of the 2001 Act nevertheless compatible with the Convention.

---

[51] *A v Secretary of State for the Home Department* [2004] UKHL 56; [2005] 2 A.C. 68.

[52] The bar on deportation arose from the Strasbourg jurisprudence that prohibits the signatories to the Convention returning a person to a country where there was a real risk that his or her rights would be violated in the receiving country (see *Chahal v United Kingdom* (1997) 23 E.H.R.R. 413).

[53] Human Rights Act 1998 (Designated Derogation) Order 2001 (SI 2001/3644). Any derogation pursuant to art.15 is permissible only "to the extent strictly required by the exigencies of the situation [and] provided that such measures are not inconsistent with [the state's] other obligations under international law". The UK remains the only signatory to the European Convention that has considered it necessary to derogate from its obligations under the Convention. That is telling. Not even in the aftermath of the Madrid bombings on 11 March 2003, in which more than 200 lives were lost, did the Spanish Government consider it necessary to adopt measures that would have required it to derogate from its Convention obligations. Against that background, it is perhaps surprising that the Grand Chamber took "as its starting point" in *A v United Kingdom* (2009) 49 E.H.R.R. 625 that "the activities and aims of the Al'Qaeda network had given rise to a 'public emergency threatening the life of the nation'" (at [216]).

In relation to the first issue, the majority held the question of whether there was a public emergency threatening the life of the nation such as to permit a derogation from the Convention was a pre-eminently political assessment to which the courts should afford great weight.[54] In the circumstances, there was no basis on which to displace the conclusion that such a public emergency justifying a derogation existed. Lord Hoffmann disagreed:

"This is a nation which has been tested in adversity, which has survived physical destruction and catastrophic loss of life. I do not underestimate the ability of fanatical groups of terrorists to kill and destroy, but they do not threaten the life of the nation. Whether we would survive Hitler hung in the balance, but there is no doubt that we shall survive Al-Qaeda. The Spanish people have not said that what happened in Madrid, hideous crime as it was, threatened the life of their nation. Their legendary pride would not allow it. Terrorist violence, serious as it is, does not threaten our institutions of government or our existence as a civil community."[55]

Those are comments that many would agree with but equally would be surprised that they emanated from a judge and not the Government itself. *A v Secretary of State for the Home Department*, perhaps more than any case that had preceded it, highlighted how the court can now be called upon to adjudicate on questions that a decade or so earlier would have been regarded as clealy non-justiciable.

The majority of the House may have supported the Government on the first question but they found against them on the remaining two. The 2001 Order was quashed, it being held that it was disproportionate to the aim pursued and was unjustifiably discriminatory. As a starting point, it is now generally accepted that internment without trial, more than anything else, plays directly into the hands of terrorists. As Lord Nicholls put it:

" ... indefinite imprisonment without charge or trial is anathema in any country which observes the rule of law ... Wholly exceptional circumstances must exist before this extreme step can be justified."[56]

But the Attorney General, on behalf of the UK Government, objected to the courts undertaking a detailed review of the choices made by the Government and by Parliament in response to the perceived terrorist threat. These were matters, argued the Attorney, which properly fell within the discretionary area of judgment that belonged to the "democratic organs of the state", namely Parliament and the Government.[57] That argument was firmly rejected by Lord Bingham:

"I do not in particular accept the distinction which [the Attorney General] drew between democratic institutions and the courts. It is of course true that the judges in this country are not elected and are not answerable to Parliament. It is also true ... that Parliament, the executive and the courts

---

[54] *A v Secretary of State for the Home Department* [2004] UKHL 56; [2005] 2 A.C. 68, per Lord Bingham at [27]–[29].
[55] *A v Secretary of State for the Home Department* [2004] UKHL 56; [2005] 2 A.C. 68 at [96].
[56] *A v Secretary of State for the Home Department* [2004] UKHL 56; [2005] 2 A.C. 68 at [74].
[57] *A v Secretary of State for the Home Department* [2004] UKHL 56; [2005] 2 A.C. 68, per Lord Bingham at [37].

have different functions. But the function of independent judges charged to interpret and apply the law is universally recognised as a cardinal feature of the modern democratic state, a cornerstone of the rule of law itself. The Attorney General is fully entitled to insist on the proper limits of judicial authority, but he is wrong to stigmatise judicial decision-making as in some way undemocratic."[58]

That was a particularly strong assertion of the legitimacy of the courts reviewing decisions of the executive (and of Parliament) even in areas concerned with national security. So far as the proportionality of the measure was concerned, the conclusion that it was disproportionate was "irresistible".[59] It was an immigration measure that had been adopted for a national security purpose, the result of which was an equally (or even more) dangerous British national could not be deprived of their liberty simply because they were British. That robbed the provisions of any rational connection between the aim pursued and the measure adopted. Furthermore, it was argued by the Government that the detention of the appellants was in a prison of three, not four, walls: they were free to leave at any time if they could find a safe country that will take them.[60] That, however, simply served to underscore the disproportionate nature of their detention: as Lord Bingham pointed out, if a detainee was to depart for a country as close as France, there free to pursue their criminal plans, it is hard to reconcile that with the UK Government's assertion that the only proportionate means by which to control the threat they present whilst in the UK was their internment without trial.[61]

In response to the decision, the Government were scathing: the decision was, said the then Foreign Secretary, "simply wrong".[62] But *A v Secretary of State for the Home Department* was a test of society's commitment to the rule of law and principles that are said to be fundamental to our way of life. Detention without trial on the whim of the executive has been objected to since the times of Magna Carta. What the decision in *A v Secretary of State for the Home Department* showed beyond doubt, however, was that the courts would be called upon to consider questions that would previously have been the preserve of the executive and that the response to terrorism would require the courts to review, and on occasion alter, the balance struck between the rights of society as a whole and those of a deeply unpopular (and dangerous) minority.

Right to a fair trial: knowing the case

13–10 Two other cases serve to illustrate how the court continues to engage with these extremely sensitive issues. Both concern the right to a fair trial, a concept that has long been regarded by the common law as a fundamental right and which is now

---

[58] *A v Secretary of State for the Home Department* [2004] UKHL 56; [2005] 2 A.C. 68 at [42].
[59] *A v Secretary of State for the Home Department* [2004] UKHL 56; [2005] 2 A.C. 68, per Lord Bingham at [43]. Only Lord Walker dissented on that point. Lord Hoffmann, having found there was no threat to the life of the nation that justified a derogation in the first place, expressed no view on the validity of the purported derogation or the compatibility of s.23 of the 2001 Act.
[60] *A v Secretary of State for the Home Department* [2004] UKHL 56; [2005] 2 A.C. 68, per Lord Hope at [123] and Baroness Hale at [230].
[61] *A v Secretary of State for the Home Department* [2004] UKHL 56; [2005] 2 A.C. 68 at [33]
[62] A comment made by Jack Straw, MP in the course of an interview on the Radio 4, *Today* programme on 17 December 2004. Reported in *The Guardian*, "Law Lords 'simply wrong', says Straw" (17 December 2004) *http://www.theguardian.com/uk/2004/dec/17/terrorism.immigrationpolicy* [Accessed 8 July 2015].

enshrined in art.6 of the Convention. It is ordinarily uncontroversial to suggest that the right to a fair trial carries with it the right that an accused person know the case against them, know what evidence is founded upon and to test and, if necessary, correct it.[63] So important was the right to a fair hearing, and with it the right of the accused to know the case against them, that "the importance of upholding it far transcends the significance of any particular case".[64] But again the response to terrorism tests our commitment to that seemingly uncontroversial principle. Often evidence against terrorist suspects will be gathered by the security and intelligence services using covert measures. Does the right to a fair trial necessitate the disclosure of evidence that would in turn expose the methods used by the security and intelligence services? To what extent does the right to a fair trial have to sit in a balance with the interests of national security? Those questions came before the House of Lords in a series of cases concerning the "control orders" regime that was introduced in the aftermath of the *A v Secretary of State for the Home Department* decision.

Under the (now repealed) Prevention of Terrorism Act 2005, the Secretary of State could make a "non-derogating control order" if they had reasonable grounds for suspecting that an individual was, or had been, involved in terrorism-related activity and they considered it necessary, for purposes connected with protecting members of the public from a risk of terrorism, to make a control order imposing obligations on the individual.[65] Before making such an order, however, the Secretary of State was required to apply to the court for permission to make the order.[66] Only if the grounds for the order were "obviously flawed" could the court refuse permission.[67] In making the application for permission, the question inevitably arose as to how much of the evidence could be provided to the individual concerned. Ordinarily "open" and "closed" evidence was made available to the court with only the former being made available to the individual concerned. The appointment of a "special advocate" ameliorated to some extent the consequences of withholding the "closed" evidence: a "special advocate" was appointed to represent the individual and would be given access to the "closed" material but they could not discuss that material with the individual and could not take instructions upon it.[68] The special advocate did not, however, remove the concern about withholding part (and often a significant part) of the evidence.[69] In *Secretary of State for the Home Department v MB* the House of Lords appeared divided on the issue.[70] Lord Bingham held that a person entitled to a fair hearing must have sufficient information, in whatever form, to allow them to challenge or rebut the case against them, with or without the assistance of a special advocate. Whether that had been done in any particular case would have to be determined by looking at the process as a whole.[71] At the other end

---

[63] *Kanda v Malaya* [1962] A.C. 322 PC (Federated Malay States), per Lord Denning at 337.

[64] *Ridge v Baldwin* [1964] A.C. 40, per Lord Morris at 113–114.

[65] Prevention of Terrorism Act 2005 s.2.

[66] Prevention of Terrorism Act 2005 s.3(1).

[67] Prevention of Terrorism Act 2005 s.3(2).

[68] See generally A. Kavanagh, "Special Advocates, Control Orders and the Right to a Fair Trial" (2010) 73 M.L.R. 836.

[69] See Lord Bingham in *Secretary of State for the Home Department v MB* [2007] UKHL 46; [2008] 1 A.C. 440 at [35] and Lord Woolf CJ in *R. (on the application of Roberts) v Parole Board* [2005] UKHL 21; [2005] 2 A.C. 738 at [83].

[70] *Secretary of State for the Home Department v MB* [2007] UKHL 46; [2008] 1 A.C. 440.

[71] *Secretary of State for the Home Department v MB* [2007] UKHL 46; [2008] 1 A.C. 440 at [34]–[35].

of the spectrum, Lord Hoffmann concluded that the presence of the special advocate provided a sufficient safeguard to secure a fair hearing and meet the requirements of art.6. The rest of the panel (Lady Hale and Lords Carswell and Brown) took a middle course: the presence of the special advocate would ordinarily provide a sufficient safeguard but in the rare cases where the material crucial to determining the reasonable basis of the Secretary of State's suspicions cannot be disclosed in any way, the presence of the special advocate may be insufficient to secure a fair hearing.[72] As Lord Brown concluded:

> "I cannot accept that a suspect's entitlement to an essentially fair hearing is merely a qualified right capable of being outweighed by the public interest in protecting the state against terrorism (vital though, of course, I recognise that public interest to be). On the contrary, it seems to me not merely an absolute right but one of altogether too great importance to be sacrificed on the altar of terrorism control."[73]

Unfortunately, the guidance provided by the House of Lords in *MB* was not easy to apply in practice, with the result that the question (how to balance the individual's right to a fair hearing against the public interest in maintaining the effectiveness of the intelligence and security services) again returned to the House of Lords.[74] In the meantime, the Grand Chamber in Strasbourg had issued its decision in *A v United Kingdom* where it held that a decision "based solely or to a decisive degree on closed material" was inconsistent with the Convention and could not be saved by the presence of a special advocate.[75] Despite Lord Hoffmann expressing serious concerns about the correctness of the decision,[76] the House of Lords held it had no choice but to follow the decision of the Grand Chamber.

This series of cases illustrates not only the strain that can be placed on hitherto accepted and uncontroversial principles but also the difficulty the court has in striking the balance between the individual interest and the wider public interest. The division of opinion amongst the House of Lords on both occasions shows that there is no clearly correct answer to these questions and again the courts are called upon to rule on matters that have inevitable consequences on the operation of the intelligence and security services.

---

[72] *Secretary of State for the Home Department v MB* [2007] UKHL 46; [2008] 1 A.C. 440, per Lady Hale at [68]–[74].

[73] *Secretary of State for the Home Department v MB* [2007] UKHL 46; [2008] 1 A.C. 440 at [91].

[74] *Secretary of State for the Home Department v AF (No.3)* [2009] UKHL 28; [2010] 2 A.C. 269.

[75] *A v United Kingdom* (2009) 49 E.H.R.R. 625 at [220].

[76] *Secretary of State for the Home Department v AF (No.3)* [2009] UKHL 28; [2010] 2 A.C. 269 at [70]–[74]: "There are practical limits to the extent to which one can devise a procedure which carries no risk of a wrong decision. It is sometimes said that it is better for ten guilty men to be acquitted than for one innocent man to be convicted. Sometimes it is a hundred guilty men. The figures matter. A system of justice which allowed a thousand guilty men to go free for fear of convicting one innocent man might not adequately protect the public. Likewise, the fact that in theory there is always some chance that the applicant might have been able to contradict closed evidence is not in my opinion a sufficient reason for saying, in effect, that control orders can never be made against dangerous people if the case against them is based 'to a decisive degree' upon material which cannot in the public interest be disclosed. This, however, is what we are now obliged to declare to be the law" (at [74]).

Right to a fair trial: open justice

The final, and most recent, example is another subset of the right to a fair trial: **13–11**
a public hearing:

> "Open justice. The words express a principle at the heart of our system of
> justice and vital to the rule of law. The rule of law is a fine concept but fine
> words butter no parsnips. How is the rule of law itself to be policed? It is
> an age old question. *Quis custodiet ipsos custodes*—who will guard the
> guards themselves? In a democracy, where power depends on the consent of
> the people governed, the answer must lie in the transparency of the legal
> process. Open justice lets in the light and allows the public to scrutinise the
> workings of the law, for better or for worse. Jeremy Bentham said in a well
> known passage quoted by Lord Shaw of Dunfermline in *Scott v Scott* [1913]
> AC 417, 477: 'Publicity is the very soul of justice. It is the keenest spur to
> exertion and the surest of all guards against improbity. It keeps the judge
> himself while trying under trial.'"[77]

But open justice too must admit of some qualification to accommodate the
concerns of national security. Again, however, how to balance this core principle
of the rule of law with the wider public interest has vexed the Supreme Court. In
Al Rawi v Security Service the Supreme Court had to consider whether the court,
in exercise of its inherent power to regulate its own procedures, could introduce
a closed material procedure.[78] A closed material procedure is different from
private hearings: in the latter the public are excluded but all parties attend (a
procedure frequently used in cases concerning children) whereas in the former
not only are the public excluded but so too is at least one of the parties. In *Al
Rawi*, the claimants alleged that they had been detained and mistreated at the
hands of various foreign authorities. They brought an action claiming damages
on various grounds, including false imprisonment, conspiracy to injure and
torture. The Security Service denied liability but indicated that they intended to
rely upon a substantial amount of material which could not be disclosed without
causing a real risk of harm to the public interest. They proposed that the material
be withheld from the claimants but made available to special advocates appointed
on their behalf. At first instance, the judge held that he could authorise such a
procedure under the court's inherent jurisdiction to regulate its own proceedings.
That conclusion was reversed by the Court of Appeal. A further appeal by the
Security Service to the Supreme Court failed. Although the court was the master
of its own procedure, it does not follow that it can do whatever it likes. It must
have regard to the fundamental principles of open justice and of fairness.[79] Those
principles are "extremely important and should not be eroded unless there is a
compelling case for doing so" and even then, if it is to be done at all, it should
be done by Parliament.[80] Lord Clarke was a sole dissenting voice: " . . . although
fundamental, the principles are not absolute and must yield where it is necessary

---

[77] *R. (on the application of Guardian News and Media Ltd) v City of Westminster Magistrates'
Court* [2012] EWCA Civ 420; [2013] Q.B. 618, per Toulson LJ at [1].
[78] *Al Rawi v Security Service* [2011] UKSC 34; [2012] 1 A.C. 531. See J. Ip, "Al Rawi, Tariq, and
the Future of Closed Material Procedures and Special Advocates" (2012) 75 M.L.R. 606.
[79] *Al Rawi v Security Service* [2011] UKSC 34; [2012] 1 A.C. 531, per Lord Hope of Craighead at
[72].
[80] *Al Rawi v Security Service* [2011] UKSC 34; [2012] 1 A.C. 531, per Lord Dyson at [48].

in the interests of justice that they do so."[81] The majority did not necessarily disagree that the principles were not absolute; the disagreement was caused by the majorities' insistence that the common law would, in no circumstances, permit a closed material procedure.[82] Following *Al Rawi* the law appeared clear:

> "The basic rule is that (subject to certain established and limited exceptions) the court cannot exercise its power to regulate its own procedures in such a way as will deny parties their fundamental common law right to participate in the proceedings in accordance with the common law principles of natural justice and open justice."[83]

In short, it was for Parliament to authorise such a procedure.

13–12   That stance was tested in *Bank Mellat v Her Majesty's Treasury (No.1)*.[84] In that case, the Treasury had imposed various financial restrictions upon Bank Mellat (a major Iranian commercial bank) under the Counter-Terrorism Act 2008. The bank sought to challenge the imposition of those restrictions. Both the judge that heard that application, and subsequently the Court of Appeal, received closed material from the Treasury and refused the bank's application. On appeal to the Supreme Court, the question arose as to whether that court could consider the closed material. The 2008 Act made specific provision authorising, indeed requiring, the High Court and the Court of Appeal (and the Court of Session in Scotland) to make rules to allow the Treasury to lay before the court material that could not be disclosed to the other party. No provision was made in the 2008 Act allowing (let alone requiring) the Supreme Court to make similar rules nor was any express power conferred by the Constitutional Reform Act 2005 (which established the Supreme Court) to allow a closed material procedure. A simple application of the majority view in *Al Rawi* would have resulted in the Supreme Court refusing to consider the closed material. Indeed, that was the view of Lords Hope, Kerr and Reed. "Two principles of absolute clarity govern the law in relation to the manner in which trials should be conducted", wrote Lord Kerr:

> "The first is that a party to proceedings should be informed of the case against him and should have full opportunity to answer that case in open court. The second principle is that the first principle may not be derogated from except by clear parliamentary authority."[85]

But the majority took a more nuanced view. As the Constitutional Reform Act 2005 provides for an appeal to the Supreme Court against *any* judgment that must necessarily include a judgment which is wholly or partly closed. If that is correct, for such an appeal to be effective, the hearing would normally have to include a

---

[81] *Al Rawi v Security Service* [2011] UKSC 34; [2012] 1 A.C. 531 at [177].
[82] *Al Rawi v Security Service* [2011] UKSC 34; [2012] 1 A.C. 531, per Lord Dyson at [27].
[83] *Al Rawi v Security Service* [2011] UKSC 34; [2012] 1 A.C. 531, per Lord Dyson at [22].
[84] *Bank Mellat v HM Treasury (No.1)* [2013] UKSC 38; [2014] A.C. 700. See H.J. Hooper, "Crossing the Rubicon: *Bank Mellat v Her Majesty's Treasury (No.1)*" [2014] P.L. 171; P. Scott, "Crossing the Rubicon: closed hearing in the Supreme Court" (2014) 18(1) Edin. L.R. 88.
[85] *Bank Mellat v HM Treasury (No.1)* [2013] UKSC 38; [2014] A.C. 700 at [101]. See also Lord Hope at [81] and Lord Reed at [133].

closed material procedure.[86] Accordingly, it was implicit that the Supreme Court had the authority to conduct a closed material procedure. Having split 6:3 on whether it was competent in principle to conduct such a procedure, the court then split 5:4 on whether, in that particular case, to conduct a closed material procedure.[87] The majority (who all confessed to having had real misgivings about the decision) held that they should examine the closed material.[88] Having crossed the Rubicon, it turned out there was nothing to see:

> " . . . there was no point in our seeing the closed judgment. There was nothing in it which could have affected our reasoning in relation to the substantive appeal, let alone which could have influenced the outcome of that appeal."[89]

That the Supreme Court was persuaded to embark upon a closed material procedure, in circumstances that had not been expressly authorised by Parliament, for no real benefit is regrettable. Lord Neuberger captures the dilemma for the majority that favoured viewing the material: despite having a strong suspicion that the closed material would have no impact upon the court's judgment, in the absence of the material and without submissions on it they could not be sure. The result of the Supreme Court being led to consider this material in closed session are a set of guidelines placing exacting demands on any party that again asks the Supreme Court to operate a closed material procedure[90] and a strong direction that the Supreme Court should never be placed in a position where it would have to issued a closed judgment.[91] But these steps represent an attempt to shut the stable door after the horse has bolted: almost all agree that the right at stake was a fundamental principle of the common law. It appears to have been compromised, however, for no material gain.

CONCLUSION

It is in responding to the threat posed by terrorism that our commitment, as a **13–13** society, to the rule of law is tested. Detention without trial, the restrictions imposed by "control orders" and compromising the common law ideal of a fair trial may be seen by some as an acceptable method by which to interrupt and then punish *actual* terrorists. But that proceeds on the assumption that *only* actual terrorists will be dealt with by these provisions. Once the possibility that an "ordinary" person, by which we mean a non-terrorist, may be unwittingly subjected to these procedures, their unacceptability should become plain. That is

---

[86] *Bank Mellat v HM Treasury (No.1)* [2013] UKSC 38; [2014] A.C. 700, per Lord Neuberger at [37] (with whom the majority agreed).
[87] Lord Dyson (the author of the leading judgment in *Al Rawi*) joined Lords Hope, Kerr and Reed in dissenting on this point.
[88] *Bank Mellat v HM Treasury (No.1)* [2013] UKSC 38; [2014] A.C. 700, per Lord Neuberger at [64].
[89] *Bank Mellat v HM Treasury (No.1)* [2013] UKSC 38; [2014] A.C. 700, per Lord Neuberger at [66]; see also Lord Dyson at [143].
[90] *Bank Mellat v HM Treasury (No.1)* [2013] UKSC 38; [2014] A.C. 700, per Lord Neuberger at [68]–[74]; see also Lord Hope at [96] and Lord Dyson at [145].
[91] *Bank Mellat v HM Treasury (No.1)* [2013] UKSC 38; [2014] A.C. 700, per Lord Hope at [98]–[100], endorsed by Lord Neuberger at [60].

not to suggest that striking the balance is easy. As we have seen, it can present the courts with some exceptionally difficult decisions.

Professor David Feldman cites a remark made by the then Home Secretary, Charles Clarke: "We cannot fight terrorism with one hand tied behind our back."[92] He responds by reference to Israel, a country with "more experience than any other of maintaining a functioning democracy under the rule of law in the face of a pervasive and long-running campaign of terrorist violence aimed at the destruction of the state."

In 1999, the Supreme Court of Israel ruled that the use of torture to combat terrorism was unlawful. It was contended that this disabled the government and security services from effectively combating terrorist threats. The President of the Court answered thus:

> "This is the destiny of a democracy—it does not see all means as acceptable, and the ways of its enemies are not always open before it. A democracy must sometimes fight with one hand tied behind its back. Even so, a democracy has the upper hand. The rule of law and the liberty of an individual constitute important components in its understanding of security. At the end of the day they strengthen its spirit and this strength allows it to overcome its difficulties."[93]

What the Home Secretary failed to appreciate when complaining about having one hand tied behind his back is that is exactly the destiny of a democracy; a point that has been made repeatedly over the years. In his seminal work on the rule of law, Lord Bingham cites the words of Christopher Dawson, penned during the darkest days of the Second World War:

> "As soon as men decide that all means are permitted to fight an evil then their good becomes indistinguishable from the evil that they set out to destroy."[94]

A similar sentiment was expressed by Lord Hoffmann in *A v Secretary of State for the Home Department* when he reminded us that:

> "the threat to the life of the nation ... comes not from terrorism but from laws such as these. That is the true measure of what terrorism may achieve."[95]

Despite those warnings from history, the extensive powers, enacted in the name of combatting terrorism, often in the aftermath of a traumatic event, now appear to be a permanent feature of our laws and of our constitution. Every time the

---

[92] D. Feldman, "Human rights, terrorism and risk: the roles of politicians and judges" [2006] P.L. 364, 370.

[93] *Public Committee against Torture v Israel* (1999) 7 B.H.R.C. 31 at [39]. Lord Hoffmann's remarks in *A v Secretary of State for the Home Department* are a clear echo of the sentiments expressed here.

[94] H.C. Dawson, *The Judgement of the Nations* (London: Sheed and Ward, 1943) p.8, cited by T. Bingham, *The Rule of Law* (London: Allen Lane, 2010) p.159.

[95] *A v Secretary of State for the Home Department* [2004] UKHL 56; [2005] 2 A.C. 68 at [97].

response to terrorism comes to be debated in Parliament, it becomes apparent that neither the government nor, to a material extent, Parliament, have grasped the essential truth of these statements that the greatest threat presented by terrorism is the wilful sacrifice of hitherto fundamental civil liberties in the so called defence of those self same liberties.

CHAPTER 14

JUDICIAL REVIEW

Introduction

14–01 An application for judicial review invokes the supervisory jurisdiction of the Court of Session, meaning that "super-eminent" power of a supreme court to ensure that all those vested with a legal authority exercise that authority in accordance with the law.[1] As Clyde and Edwards note, while the supervisory jurisdiction has a long history, it is only relatively recently that the term "judicial review" has fallen into normal usage as a way of referring to it. Judicial review is sought by way of petition brought in accordance with Ch.58 of the Rules of the Court of Session.[2] After a brief discussion of the constitutional context of judicial review and its history in Scotland, we turn to consider this topic in three parts. First, we discuss the procedural issues associated with a petition for judicial review such as standing, time limits and requirements for leave. Secondly, we discuss the substantive grounds of judicial review. Finally, the remedies the court may grant a successful petitioner are briefly considered.

CONSTITUTIONAL CONTEXT AF JUDICIAL REVIEW[3]

14–02 Judicial review is fundamental to, and lies at the very heart of, the rule of law. It is: "The process by which the courts enforce compliance by public authorities with the law."[4] But it is also important to be clear about what judicial review is not. It does not involve the substitution of a judge's decision for an administrative decision they find to be wrong. It is not an appellate process, and the substantive grounds on which it may be sought are limited (if elastic). The issue is not whether the "right" or "wrong" decision was made, or whether a better

---

[1] Lord Clyde and D.J. Edwards, *Judicial Review* (Edinburgh: W. Green, 2000) para.1.01; also A. O'Neill, *Judicial Review in Scotland: A Practitioner's Guide* (Edinburgh: Butterworths, 1999) paras 1.03–1.05; A.W. Bradley and C.M.G. Himsworth, "Administrative Law", *Stair Memorial Encyclopaedia* (Edinburgh: Butterworths, 1995).

[2] Act of Sederunt (Rules of the Court of Session 1994) (SI 1994/1443) Ch.58, which replaced r.260B as introduced by the Act of Sederunt (Rules of Court Amendment No.2) (Judicial Review) 1985 (SI 1985/500). Rule 260B implemented the recommendations of the Dunpark Working Party on Procedure for Judicial Review of Administrative Action, which was appointed by the Lord President in light of remarks made by Lord Fraser of Tullybelton in *Brown v Hamilton DC*, 1983 S.C. (H.L.) 1 and *Stevenson v Midlothian DC*, 1983 S.C. (H.L.) 50, regretting the lack, in Scotland, of an expedited procedure for judicial review comparable to that established in England by reform of the rules of the court in 1977; see, now, for England, Supreme Court Act 1981 s.31 and CPR r.54.

[3] For a fuller discussion, see *De Smith's Judicial Review*, 7th edn, Woolf et al (eds) (London: Sweet & Maxwell, 2013) para.1–012 to 1–031; P.P. Craig, *Administrative Law*, 7th edn (London: Sweet & Maxwell, 2012) Ch.1.

[4] T. Bingham, *The Rule of Law* (London: Allen Lane: 2010) p.60.

decision could have been taken, but whether the decision was taken in accordance with the law.[5] That includes not only the law as enacted by Parliament, but also the fundamental characteristics of the rule of law.[6] That implies, at least in cases involving the review of statutory powers, that the decision maker acted within the four corners of the power conferred upon them, and this basic principle of legality, otherwise known as the ultra vires doctrine, provides a compelling constitutional justification for what the courts do in the context of review. Some, however, go further, and insist that the common law provides its own justification for what the courts do on review. This is not to contradict the sovereignty of Parliament, because the "higher order" rights endorsed by the courts in their recent jurisprudence are woven into the very structure of constitutional democracy within which Parliament operates. As Sir John Laws puts it, such rights "are not a consequence of the democratic process, but logically prior to it".[7] As will be seen in the discussion concerning standing, the constitutional justification for judicial review is better understood as being grounded in the rule of law.[8] As Lord Reed explained in *AXA General Insurance Co Ltd v Lord Advocate*:

> "Judicial review under the common law is based upon an understanding of the respective constitutional responsibilities of public authorities and the courts. The constitutional function of the courts in the field of public law is to ensure, so far as they can, that public authorities respect the rule of law. The courts therefore have the responsibility of ensuring that the public authority in question does not misuse its powers or exceed their limits."[9]

In a modern constitutional democracy the legislature ought to adhere to the rule of law and the courts ought to presume the legislature has so acted.[10] As we have seen in Ch.3, above, whether Parliament retains the power to legislate in a manner which does not respect a fundamental feature of the rule of law is now unclear: are there some common law rights that are so fundamental to our constitution that not even Parliament can override them?[11] The answer to that question is awaited.

DEVELOPMENT OF JUDICIAL REVIEW IN SCOTLAND

As traditionally understood, there was nothing inherently "public" about the **14–03** supervisory jurisdiction of the Court of Session. Naturally the nature of that

---

[5] *Reid v Secretary of State for Scotland*, 1999 S.C. (H.L.) 17 at 41: "Judicial review involves a challenge to the legal validity of the decision. It does not allow the court of review to examine the evidence with a view to forming its own view about the substantial merits of the case."

[6] On those fundamental characteristics, see Bingham, *The Rule of Law* (2010).

[7] J. Laws, "Law and Democracy" [1995] P.L. 72.

[8] *Eba v Advocate General for Scotland* [2011] UKSC 29; 2012 S.C. (U.K.S.C.) 1, per Lord Hope at [8]: "The rule of law ... is the basis on which the entire system of judicial review rests."

[9] *AXA General Insurance Co Ltd v Lord Advocate* [2011] UKSC 46; 2012 S.C. (U.K.S.C.) 122 at [142].

[10] *De Smith's Judicial Review* (2013) para.1–021.

[11] *Taylor v New Zealand Poultry Board* [1984] 1 N.Z.L.R. 394, per Sir Robin Cooke at 398.

jurisdiction is apt to include many actings by public authorities. As Lord Kinnear held in *Moss Empires Ltd v Assessor for Glasgow* [12]:

> "Wherever any inferior tribunal or administrative body has exceeded the powers conferred on it by statute to the prejudice of the subject, the jurisdiction of the Court to set aside such excess of power as incompetent and illegal is not in doubt."

But the supervisory jurisdiction is invoked in many other cases where the decision making power in question is derived not from statute but from some other instrument such as a contract and thus not "public" in an intuitive sense.[13]

The procedural changes introduced in 1985 did not (and could not) affect the jurisdiction of the Court of Session. But the advantages of the new application for judicial review in terms of expedition and, consequently, economy, were such as to prompt consideration of its proper scope. That exercise was greatly influenced, for a time, by developments in England as to the scope of judicial review there.[14] The principle of "procedural exclusivity" meant that in England, a person wishing to complain of an infringement of "public law rights" was obliged to proceed by way of judicial review. This made it imperative to identify correctly the nature of one's claim, for a public law claim brought by way of ordinary action risked being struck out, without any inquiry into the merits, as an abuse of the process of the courts. Reliance on this approach in Scotland was criticised as introducing unnecessary technicality at variance with the historical foundations of the supervisory jurisdiction in Scots law.[15] An authoritative statement of the scope of judicial review was finally provided in *West v Secretary of State for Scotland*, in which Lord President Hope held as follows[16]:

> "The Court of Session has power, in the exercise of its supervisory jurisdiction, to regulate the process by which decisions are taken by any person or body to whom a jurisdiction, power or authority has been delegated or entrusted by statute, agreement or any other instrument . . . The cases in which the supervisory jurisdiction is appropriate involve a tripartite relationship between the person or body to whom the jurisdiction, power or authority has been delegated or entrusted, the person or body by whom it has been delegated or entrusted and the person or persons in respect of or for whose benefit that jurisdiction, power or authority is to be exercised."

Plainly, therefore, judicial review is not confined to the statutory or prerogative powers of public authorities alone. Provided a reviewable jurisdiction exists, the supervisory jurisdiction may also extend to the acts and decisions of bodies

---

[12] *Moss Empires Ltd v Assessor for Glasgow*, 1917 S.C. (H.L.) 1 at 6.
[13] Hence, e.g. the susceptibility of arbiters to judicial review: see *Forbes v Underwood* (1886) 13 R. 465 and, more recently, *Shanks & McEwan (Contractors) Ltd v Mifflin Construction Ltd*, 1993 S.L.T. 1124.
[14] See, e.g. *Connor v Strathclyde RC*, 1986 S.L.T. 530; *Tehrani v Argyll and Clyde Health Board*, 1989 S.C. 342; *Safeway Food Stores Ltd v Scottish Provident Institution*, 1989 S.L.T. 131.
[15] Lord Clyde, "The nature of the supervisory jurisdiction and the public/private distinction in Scots administrative law" in W. Finnie, C.M.G. Himsworth and N. Walker, *Edinburgh Essays in Public Law* (Edinburgh: Edinburgh University Press, 1991) p.281.
[16] *West v Secretary of State for Scotland*, 1992 S.C. 385 at 413.

which are not obviously "public" at all.[17] By the same token, however, just because a body is a public authority does not mean that all its acts and decisions will be subject to judicial review. In *West* itself, review was incompetent because the dispute between Mr West and the Secretary of State was essentially contractual, relating to the terms and conditions of Mr West's employment as a prison officer.[18] But while there is certainty at the core, uncertainty at the margins remains, and it may be that the Inner House will require at some point to revisit the test prescribed in *West*.[19] As it is, it is possible that, where the court finds difficulty in applying the tripartite relationship criterion to the facts before it,[20] the test collapses into something akin to the public/private divide used to determine the scope of review in England.

PROCEDURAL ISSUES

Standing to bring judicial review proceedings

If judicial review is grounded in the rule of law, then access to judicial review is **14–04** of fundamental importance. For over a century, standing to bring judicial review proceedings was regulated by the two part private law test requiring both "title" and "interest".[21] That required a party to judicial review proceedings be "a party (using the word in its widest sense) to some legal relationship which gives him some right which the person against whom he raises the action either infringes or denies" (the requirement for "title")[22] and to establish that they have some real interest to enforce or protect, involving their "pecuniary rights and status", rather than seeking to resolve some academic point on a hypothetical set of circumstances (the requirement for "interest").[23] Although strictly speaking these were two distinct requirements, situations where there was title but no interest (or vice versa) were rare and in practice the distinction was meaningless. Nevertheless, the formal requirement to show "title and interest" led to increasingly unsatisfactory results. In *Rape Crisis Centre v Secretary of State for the Home*

---

[17] In addition to the cases on arbiters cited at fn.13, above see also *St Johnstone Football Club v Scottish Football Association Ltd*, 1965 S.L.T. 171 and *Gunstone v Scottish Womens Amateur Athletic Association*, 1987 S.L.T. 611 (sporting bodies); *McDonald v Burns*, 1940 S.C. 376 (religious bodies); *Crocket v Tantallon Golf Club*, 2005 S.L.T. 663 and *Smith v Nairn Golf Club* [2007] CSOH 136; 2007 S.L.T. 909 (disciplinary disputes arising in golf clubs). For a recent example of a football club successfully judicially reviewing a decision of the Scottish Football Association, see *Rangers Football Club Plc, Petitioner* [2012] CSOH 95; 2012 S.L.T. 1156.

[18] But employment matters may in certain circumstances be reviewable, see e.g. *Malloch v Aberdeen Corp*, 1971 S.C. (H.L.) 85; *Rooney v Chief Constable, Strathclyde Police*, 1997 S.L.T. 1261; *Maclean v Glasgow City Council*, 1997 S.C.L.R. 1049.

[19] For discussion of *West*, see W.J. Wolffe, "The Scope of Judicial Review in Scots Law" [1992] P.L. 625 and C.M.G. Himsworth, "Public employment, the supervisory jurisdiction and points West", 1992 S.L.T. (News) 257.

[20] As witness the differing outcomes in *Naik v University of Stirling*, 1994 S.L.T. 449 and *Joobeen v University of Stirling*, 1995 S.L.T. 120.

[21] Clyde and Edwards, *Judicial Review* (2000), Ch.10; O'Neill, *Judicial Review in Scotland: A Practitioner's Guide* (1999) paras 6.04–6.11 and A. O'Neill, *Judicial Review in Scotland: A Practitioner's Guide*, 2nd edn (London: LexisNexis, 2007) paras.14.03 and 14.04.

[22] *D & J Nicol v Dundee Harbour Trustees*, 1915 S.C. (H.L.) 7.

[23] *Swanson v Manson*, 1907 S.C. 426; although that phrase should not be regarded as exhaustive: *Scottish Old People's Welfare Council, Petitioners*, 1987 S.L.T. 179.

Department,[24] the petitioners (a limited company which provided advice and assistance to rape victims) was held to have no title to challenge the decision of the Home Secretary to allow Mike Tyson, a high profile boxer but convicted rapist, to enter the UK in order to compete in a fight in Glasgow. The Home Secretary's decision was taken under the Immigration Act 1971, and the Immigration Rules promulgated thereunder. Those provisions created no legal nexus between the petitioners and the Home Secretary. In other words, there was no relationship between the Rape Crisis Centre and the Home Secretary and as a consequence the centre had no "title". That conclusion appeared even more unacceptable in light of a similar challenge in England. Permission had been sought from the High Court in London to challenge a decision to allow Tyson to enter the UK to fight in Manchester. Permission was refused, not because the applicant lacked the necessary standing, but because the court was not satisfied that there were arguable substantive grounds for interfering with the Home Secretary's decision.[25] The Lord Ordinary in the *Rape Crisis Centre v Secretary of State for the Home Department* had reached the same conclusion as the English court with respect to the substantive grounds. But arguably this element of the decision merely papers over the cracks which are apparent in the test for showing title: had the petitioner's complaint on the merits been well founded, Scots law would have offered it no form of redress as it then stood. Given the core function of judicial review is securing the rule of law, that result could be regarded as problematic.

Much was said about the unsatisfactory state of the law following *Rape Crisis Centre v Secretary of State for the Home Department*. Criticism of the rules on standing, grounded as they were in private law, had long been made and calls made for a systematic review of the issue.[26] Those calls were echoed after *Rape Crisis Centre v Secretary of State for the Home Department*, most notably by Lord Hope in a lecture to the Administrative Law Bar Association.[27] Scots law was also becoming increasingly out of step with other common law jurisdictions, most noticeably England and Wales, and set in the context of the purpose of rules on standing (in a public law context) "title and interest" were increasingly seen as unsuitable.[28] The review of the civil justice system in Scotland, chaired by Lord Gill, concluded[29]:

> " . . . we are persuaded that the current law on standing is too restrictive and that the separate tests of title and interest should be replaced by a single test: whether the petitioner has demonstrated a sufficient interest in the subject matter of the proceedings."

As discussed below, that was one of a number of recommendations made in relation to judicial review. But before the Scottish Parliament could legislate to

---

[24] *Rape Crisis Centre v Secretary of State for the Home Department*, 2000 S.C. 527; *Scottish Old People's Welfare Council, Petitioners*, 1987 S.L.T. 179 provides a similar example.

[25] *R. v Secretary of State for the Home Department Ex p. Bindel* [2001] Imm. A.R. 1.

[26] C.R. Munro, "Standing in Judicial Review", 1995 S.L.T. (News) 279.

[27] Lord Hope of Criaghead, "Mike Tyson comes to Glasgow—a question of standing" [2001] P.L. 294.

[28] On the latter point, see T. Mullen, "Standing to Seek Judicial Review" in A. McHarg and T. Mullen, *Public Law in Scotland* (Edinburgh: Avizandum: 2006) pp.255–261.

[29] Scottish Civil Courts Review, *Report of the Scottish Civil Courts Review* (The Stationery Office, 2009) Ch.12 at para.25.

give effect to Lord Gill's recommendations, the Supreme Court intervened to modernise the rules of standing for judicial review.

We have already considered the case of *AXA General Insurance Co Ltd v Lord* **14–05** *Advocate* in relation to the continuing discussion of the sovereignty of Parliament and in relation to the review of the legislative competence of the Scottish Parliament. For present purposes, however, it is the influence of the case on the rules on standing in judicial review which are important. The case was a challenge to provisions of the Damages (Asbestos-related Conditions) (Scotland) Act 2009 which were said to be beyond the competence of the Scottish Parliament. AXA was an insurance company challenging the competence of legislation which imposed upon it liability to meet claims for damages. Both the Lord Advocate and the Attorney General entered appearance to defend the legislation. The third to tenth respondents were individuals whose pending actions for damages hinged on the competence of the 2009 Act. The Inner House held that these individuals had no title and interest to enter the action to defend its validity, despite being amongst the class of potential beneficiaries of the 2009 Act.[30] As Lord Reed explained in the Supreme Court, that produced a perplexing result: AXA had standing to challenge the validity of the 2009 Act, but the third to tenth respondents—whom AXA might have been required to pay compensation to, as the potential beneficiaries of the Act—had no right to be heard in response.[31] That absurdity sounded the death knell for "title and interest" as the test for standing in the public law sphere:

" . . . the time has come when it should be recognised by the courts that Lord Dunedin's dictum [in *D&J Nicol v Dundee Harbour Trustees*] pre-dates the modern development of public law, that it is rooted in private law concepts which are not relevant in the context of applications to the supervisory jurisdiction, and that its continuing influence in that context has had a damaging effect on the development of public law in Scotland. This unsatisfactory situation should not be allowed to persist. The time has come when the courts should cease to use the inappropriate terminology of title and interest in relation to such applications, and should refer instead to standing, based upon a sufficient interest."[32]

Moving to a test based on sufficient interest better allows the court to perform its core function in public law matters of preserving the rule of law, a task that was being inhibited in Scotland by a rights-based approach to standing.[33] What constitutes "sufficient interest" will vary according to the circumstances of a given case, as the rule of law does not require the court to hear and adjudicate

---

[30] *AXA General Insurance Co Ltd v Lord Advocate* [2011] CSIH 31; 2011 S.C. 662 at [56]–[58].
[31] *AXA General Insurance Co Ltd v Lord Advocate* [2011] UKSC 46; 2012 S.C. (U.K.S.C.) 122 at [156].
[32] *AXA General Insurance Co Ltd v Lord Advocate* [2011] UKSC 46; 2012 S.C. (U.K.S.C.) 122, per Lord Reed at [171]; Lord Hope reached the same conclusion (at [62]): "As for the substantive law, I think that the time has come to recognize that the private law rule that title and interest has to be shown has no place in applications to the court's supervisory jurisdiction that lie in the field of public law. The word 'standing' provides a more appropriate indication of the approach that should be adopted." That suggests that the rules of title and interest remain in what could be called "private law" judicial reviews (for example, those involving golf clubs and their members: see fn.17).
[33] *AXA General Insurance Co Ltd v Lord Advocate* [2011] UKSC 46; 2012 S.C. (U.K.S.C.) 122, per Lord Reed at [169].

upon every allegation of illegality levelled at a public body.[34] It will often require a person to demonstrate a particular interest in the matter, otherwise they may well be regarded as a mere busybody and denied standing.[35] But equally there will be cases where any individual, by mere virtue of the fact that they are a citizen, will have a sufficient interest to draw an alleged unlawful act of a public body to the attention of the court:

> "The rule of law would not be maintained if, because everyone was equally affected by an unlawful act, no one was able to bring proceedings to challenge it."[36]

14–06 Two points arise from the Supreme Court's rewriting of the rules on standing. The first is the constitutional justification for doing so. The court, in both *AXA General Insurance Co Ltd v Lord Advocate* and *Walton v Scottish Ministers*, repeatedly made the point that the purpose of judicial review was to secure the rule of law and changes to the rules on standing were necessary to ensure that objective was achieved. Lord Reed went so far as to describe the preservation of the rule of law as the "essential function of the courts".[37] That pronouncement appears to signal the end of the ultra vires doctrine as *the* constitutional underpinning of judicial review. Furthermore, the decision in *AXA* ought to be understood as marking a liberalisation of Scots public law. Following *AXA*, Scotland adopted the same liberal approach to standing as England and Wales but not the concomitant limitations or conditions such as strict time limits for initiating a judicial review and the requirement to obtain leave to commence proceedings. Those limiting conditions will be introduced in Scotland when the relevant provisions of the Courts Reform (Scotland) Act 2014 are brought into force in September 2015. But, one may observe that, despite the lack of such limitations following *AXA*, there was no flood of public law litigation hitting the Scottish courts.

Since *AXA* the Court of Session has continued to take a cautious approach to standing in judicial review matters.[38] Lord Reed reiterated the liberalisation of standing in *Walton*: the Supreme Court had

> "intended to put an end to an unduly restrictive approach which had too often obstructed the proper administration of justice: an approach which presupposed that the only function of the court's supervisory jurisdiction was to redress individual grievances, and ignored its constitutional function of maintaining the rule of law."[39]

That was necessary to respond to the narrow view taken by the Inner House of Mr Walton's interest in the construction of the new Aberdeen bypass. The

---

[34] *AXA General Insurance Co Ltd v Lord Advocate* [2011] UKSC 46; 2012 S.C. (U.K.S.C.) 122, per Lord Reed at [170].

[35] *Walton v Scottish Ministers* [2012] UKSC 44; 2013 S.C. (U.K.S.C.) 67, per Lord Reed at [94].

[36] *AXA General Insurance Co Ltd v Lord Advocate* [2011] UKSC 46; 2012 S.C. (U.K.S.C.) 122, per Lord Reed at [170].

[37] *AXA General Insurance Co Ltd v Lord Advocate* [2011] UKSC 46; 2012 S.C. (U.K.S.C.) 122 at [169].

[38] See C. McCorkindale, "Public Interest Litigants in the Court of Session" (2015) 19 Edin. L.R. 248.

[39] *Walton v Scottish Ministers* [2012] UKSC 44; 2013 S.C. (U.K.S.C.) 67 at [90].

distance between Mr Walton's house and the proposed route denied him "sufficient interest", so far as the Inner House was concerned, despite his active role in the campaign against the proposed development. It was that conclusion that Lord Reed was addressing when the case reached the Supreme Court and it was held that Mr Walton did have "sufficient interest" to raise proceedings. In *Christian Institute v Lord Advocate*,[40] a case concerning the provisions of the Children and Young People (Scotland) Act 2014 requiring every child have a "named individual" appointed to look out for their interests, a narrow view was again taken to the question of standing. A number of the petitioners (the Christian Institute, the Family Education Trust and the Young ME Sufferers Trust) were held to have insufficient interest. In reaching that view, the Lord Ordinary had regard to their failure to participate in the pre-legislative consultation and the call for evidence by the relevant parliamentary committee. That, said the Lord Ordinary, left him unconvinced that the petitioners had shown a genuine concern about the legislation before raising proceedings.[41] Furthermore, the rule of law was secured by the other petitioners who each had children that would be affected by the proposed legislation and accordingly had been found to have standing.[42] Expecting a petitioner to have actively participated in the legislative process as a means of demonstrating "genuine concern" about the legislation, so as to then grant standing would result in a substantial barrier being placed in the way of those that sought to raise public interest proceedings and it has the potential to undermine what the Supreme Court sought to achieve in *AXA*. Experience thus suggests that whilst the test for standing in Scotland may now be the same as England and Wales, it nevertheless remains harder for an applicant to clear the hurdle north of the border.

Before turning to consider the other procedural issues in relation to judicial review, it should be noted that a different test for standing applies to claims alleging a breach of a Convention right. Under the Human Rights Act 1998 a petitioner is required to demonstrate not that they have "sufficient interest", but rather that they are a "victim" within meaning of art.34 of the Convention.[43] A "victim" ordinarily requires that a person be directly affected by a specific act or omission. It is not necessary to show that they suffered damage (though that is relevant for the question of "just satisfaction" under art.41) nor that they suffered no damage under national law. **14-07**

Standing to intervene in judicial review proceedings

Since 2000, the Rules of the Court of Session (RCS r.58.8A) have allowed for public interest interventions. This allows the court to grant leave to a person or organisation to intervene in judicial review proceedings where the case raises, and the applicant seeks to address, a matter of public interest, that the propositions to be advanced by the applicant are relevant to the case and likely to assist the court and allowing the intervention will not unduly delay proceedings or prejudice the rights of the other parties (RCS r.58.8A(6)). Where **14-08**

---

[40] *Christian Institute v Lord Advocate* [2015] CSOH 7; 2015 S.L.T. 72. A reclaiming motion against this decision was heard in June 2015.

[41] *Christian Institute v Lord Advocate* [2015] CSOH 7; 2015 S.L.T. 72 at [93].

[42] *Christian Institute v Lord Advocate* [2015] CSOH 7; 2015 S.L.T. 72 at [94].

[43] Human Rights Act 1998 s.7; see Craig, *Administrative Law* (2012) para.25–024; *De Smith's Judicial Review* (2013) paras 2–044 to 2–058.

permission is granted, the intervention will, save in exceptional circumstances, be in the form of a written submission not exceeding 5,000 words (RCS r.58.8A(8) and (9)). Such applicants are rare and only once has one been granted.[44] That application was granted in favour of Alcohol Focus Scotland in the challenge to the Alcohol (Minimum Unit Pricing) (Scotland) Act 2012. That application was granted at first instance. When the case was reclaimed, a fresh application to intervene in the Inner House was refused, perhaps surprisingly given the decision at first instance.[45] An even more restrictive approach was taken in *Sustainable Scotland v Scottish Ministers*[46] where the Inner House refused an application by the Royal Society for the Protection of Birds to intervene in an appeal concerning the granting of consent for a wind farm on Shetland that was said to have harmful consequences for rare bird species. Having been consulted at an early stage, making its position clear to the Ministers during that consultation, and then having failed to either judicially review the decision or seek to intervene in the Outer House, it was, said the Lord Justice Clerk (Carloway), "inappropriate" to allow the Royal Society for the Protection of Birds to enter proceedings at the appeal stage.[47] By taking such a restrictive approach to such interventions, the Scottish courts seem to remain out of step with many other jurisdictions' more permissive rules.[48]

Time

14–09 There is at present no general time period within which a petition for judicial review must be presented. Certain statutes impose a time limit, for example the one year limit under the Human Rights Act 1998.[49] But where there is no specific time limit imposed by statute, the matter is regulated by the common law principles of *mora* (delay), taciturnity and acquiescence. That will change in September 2015 when s.89 of the Courts Reform (Scotland) Act 2014 is brought into force and s.27A of the Court of Session Act 1988 is introduced. At common law, all three elements—i.e. *mora* (delay), taciturnity, and acquiescence—had to be present for the plea to be sustained.[50] Delay alone was not sufficient, although the court has observed that:

> "In the field of administrative law, where a challenge is made against some decision or action the effects of which may be limited in time, the court will be more quick to infer from silence and inactivity that a person is acquiescing in a changed state of affairs ... Judicial review is a process designed to give speedy consideration to problems which arise, and when time is of materiality. In such a situation, potential litigants should lose no time in raising proceedings."[51]

[44] *Scotch Whiskey Association, Petitioner* [2012] CSOH 156.
[45] *Alcohol Focus Scotland, Applicants* [2014] CSIH 64.
[46] *Sustainable Scotland v Scottish Ministers* [2013] CSIH 116.
[47] *Sustainable Scotland v Scottish Ministers* [2013] CSIH 116 at [11].
[48] R. Charteris, "Intervention—in the public interest?", 2000 S.L.T. (News) 87; McCorkindale, "Public Interest Litigants in the Court of Session" (2015) 19 Edin. L.R. 248.
[49] Human Rights Act 1998 s.7(5).
[50] *Somerville v Scottish Ministers*, 2007 S.C. 140.
[51] *Watt v Secretary of State for Scotland* [1991] 3 C.M.L.R. 429, per Lord Weir at 440.

There is acquiescence where inaction on the part of the petitioner amounts to implied consent to the changed state of affairs.[52] It is an aspect of personal bar, which Clyde and Edwards describe in terms of a representation by the petitioner:

> "Where A has by his words or conduct justified B in believing that a certain state of facts exists, and B has acted on such belief to his prejudice, A is not permitted to affirm against B that a different state of facts existed at the same time."[53]

It is for the party pleading *mora*, taciturnity and acquiescence to establish the plea by reference to all the surrounding circumstances as well as the simple fact of the passage of time. It is not a matter simply for the discretion of the court.[54] So, for instance, in *Uprichard v Fife Council*,[55] Lord Bonomy sustained the plea where the petitioner had allowed 19 weeks to elapse after the granting of planning permission for a golf-related development in St Andrews before lodging her petition. This was because the petitioner had apparently acquiesced in the grant; the developers, who had incurred expenditure in the order of £1 million since the grant, would suffer undue prejudice; and the lateness of the challenge would have "a disruptive effect on good administration".[56]

Section 27A of the Court of Session Act 1988 will, however, provide for a **14–10** strict three month time limit:

> "(1) An application to the supervisory jurisdiction of the Court must be made before the end of—
>
> > (a) the period of 3 months beginning with the date on which the grounds giving rise to the application first arise, or
> > (b) such longer period as the Court considers equitable having regard to all the circumstances."

That provision is the result of the recommendation of the Gill Review which recommended the introduction of a time limit in Scotland and proposed a test in identical terms to the current English rules.[57] The Scottish courts can be expected to turn to the English courts for guidance when the new rules come into force.

---

[52] In *Hanlon v Traffic Commissioner*, 1988 S.L.T. 802, Lord Prosser at 805 noted that "the length of any delay before implications of acquiescence arise will be almost infinitely variable depending on the circumstances". See also, e.g. *Atherton v Strathclyde RC*, 1995 S.L.T. 557; *McIntosh v Aberdeenshire Council*, 1998 S.L.T. 93.

[53] Clyde and Edwards, *Judicial Review* (2000) para.13.20.

[54] *Pickering v Kyle and Carrick DC* Unreported, 20 December 1990 Outer House; *Edgar Road Property Co LLP v Moray Council* [2007] CSOH 88.

[55] *Uprichard v Fife Council*, 2000 S.C.L.R. 949.

[56] See also, e.g. *Swan v Secretary of State for Scotland*, 1998 S.C. 479, per Lord President Rodger at 487: "It is, of course, the case that judicial review proceedings ought normally to be raised promptly and it is also undeniable that the petitioners let some months pass without starting these proceedings. None the less, in considering whether the delay was such that the petitioners should not be allowed to proceed, we take into account the situation in which time was allowed to pass.' See also the remarks of Lord Diplock in *O'Reilly v Mackman* [1983] 2 A.C. 237 HL at 280–281 to a similar effect: "The public interest in good administration requires that public authorities and third parties should not be kept in suspense as to the legal validity of a decision the authority has reached in purported exercise of decision-making powers for any longer period than is absolutely necessary in fairness to the person affected by the decision."

[57] Scottish Civil Courts Review, *Report of the Scottish Civil Courts Review*, Ch.12, paras 38–39.

The English Civil Procedure Rules require that a claim must be filed "promptly" and, in any event, within three months of the ground of claim arising (subject to the court retaining a discretion to extend the time limit where appropriate).[58] The overriding obligation is one of "promptness" which can see an application for judicial review refused even where it is made within three months.[59] Doubts have been expressed about the compatibility of the "promptness" requirement with both EU law and the Convention,[60] with the "promptness" requirement having been held to lack sufficient certainty to comply with both EU procurement and environmental regulations.[61] Whether those same concerns read across to "pure" common law, domestic, grounds of challenge is a question that has divided the Court of Appeal.[62] With those doubts in mind, the English court should hesitate before striking out a claim on the ground it was not brought "promptly" despite the fact it was brought within three months.[63] Those concerns resulted in the requirement for "promptness" not being included in what is now s.27A of the Court of Session Act 1988. An application that is made within three months of the decision complained of will therefore not be refused as out of time.

14–11   Petitions may be brought too soon as well as too late. There may be a complaint of prematurity where the applicant has failed to resort to an available statutory or other alternative remedy.[64] The rule reflects the underlying character of the supervisory jurisdiction, which exists to correct those wrongs for which no other remedy is provided; but it is not absolute, and in "exceptional circumstances" a failure to exhaust alternative remedies will not bar a petition for review.[65] Where the petitioner has failed to resort to their statutory remedy because of some mistake or procedural irregularity on the part of the respondent[66] recourse to judicial review will be permitted.[67] Other material factors include the adequacy of the alternative remedy[68]; the nature of the petitioner's complaint[69]; and, sometimes, considerations of pure practicality.[70] Also, where

---

[58] CPR r.54.5; see generally *De Smith's Judicial Review* (2013), paras 16–053 to 16–061.

[59] For example, *R. v Secretary of State for Health Ex p. Alcohol Recovery Project* [1993] C.O.D. 344; see generally, *De Smith's Judicial Review* (2013), para.16–055 and Craig, *Administrative Law* (2012) para.27–036.

[60] *R. (on the application of Burkett) v Hammersmith and Fulham LBC* [2002] UKHL 23; [2002] 1 W.L.R. 1593.

[61] *Uniplex (UK) Ltd v NHS Business Services Authority* (C-406/08) [2010] 2 C.M.L.R. 47; *R. (on the application of Buglife: The Invertebrate Conservation Trust) v Medway Council* [2011] EWHC 746 (Admin); [2011] 3 C.M.L.R. 39.

[62] *R. (on the application of Berky) v Newport City Council* [2012] EWCA Civ 378; [2012] 2 C.M.L.R. 44.

[63] Craig, *Administrative Law* (2012) para.27–036.

[64] Clyde and Edwards, *Judicial Review* (2000), Ch.12; O'Neill, *Judicial Review in Scotland: A Practitioner's Guide* (1999) paras 6.12–6.22; and see also RCS r.58.3(2).

[65] *British Railways Board v Glasgow Corp*, 1976 S.C. 224.

[66] As in *Moss Empires Ltd v Assessor for Glasgow*, 1917 S.C. (H.L.) 1 where the assessor omitted to inform the petitioner of its right of appeal.

[67] Where it is the petitioner's agent who fails to advise of a right of appeal, a like leniency is not shown: see, e.g. *R. v Secretary of State for the Home Department Ex p. Al-Mehdawi* [1990] 1 A.C. 876 HL; *Ouafi v Secretary of State for Home Department*, 1997 S.L.T. 544.

[68] See, e.g. *Accountant in Bankruptcy v Allans of Gillock Ltd*, 1991 S.L.T. 765.

[69] In *British Railways Board v Glasgow Corp*, 1976 S.C. 224, Lord Wheatley held that averments of ultra vires or fraud would constitute "exceptional circumstances" justifying recourse to the supervisory jurisdiction.

[70] As in, e.g. *City Cabs (Edinburgh) Ltd v City of Edinburgh DC*, 1988 S.L.T. 184, where the decision challenged was of general application and one application for judicial review was thought to be a more expeditious way of dealing with the matter than via a large number of statutory appeals.

there is real uncertainty whether the alleged unlawfulness is going to occur, an application may be dismissed as premature. Thus in *Scottish National Party v Scottish Television Plc*,[71] Lord Eassie remarked that the subject matter of the application (allocation by the companies of broadcasting time for the Scottish National Party's party political broadcasts prior to the 1997 general election) was premature since neither company had at that point actually taken a decision on the question.[72]

Permission to raise proceedings

Section 89 of the Courts Reform (Scotland) Act 2014 will also introduce a **14–12** requirement that permission be sought to raise judicial review proceedings. What will be s.27B of the Court of Session Act 1988 will provide:

"(1) No proceedings may be taken in respect of an application to the supervisory jurisdiction of the Court unless the Court has granted permission for the application to proceed.

(2) Subject to subsection (3), the Court may grant permission under subsection (1) for an application to proceed only if it is satisfied that—

(a) the applicant can demonstrate a sufficient interest in the subject matter of the application, and

(b) the application has a real prospect of success."

Subsection (3) requires an application that seeks review of a decision of the Upper Tribunal for Scotland pass the "second appeals test".[73] That test requires, in addition to showing sufficient interest and a real prospect of success, that the applicant must also demonstrate that the application would raise a point of principle or practice or there is some other compelling reason to allow it to proceed. That test is a stringent one, designed to permit review in only rare and exceptional cases so as to ensure a compelling injustice cannot occur.[74] An error of law, even a compelling one, is not in itself enough to satisfy the second appeals test.[75] Although currently confined to attempts to review decisions of the Upper Tribunal, the introduction of a requirement to seek leave to appeal from the Inner House to the Supreme Court (and from the sheriff appeal court (when it comes into being) to the Inner House) is likely to see the "second appeals test" become more widely applied in civil litigation in Scotland.

The court may determine whether to grant permission without holding an oral hearing (s.27B(5)). Where permission is refused without an oral hearing, the applicant may, within seven days, request a review of that refusal at an oral hearing. That request must be considered by a different Lord Ordinary (s.27C). Where permission is refused after an oral hearing (or it is granted on conditions or only on particular grounds) a further appeal, again within seven days, may be made to the Inner House (s.28D). The policy memorandum accompanying the Bill (at para.186) envisages rules of court being introduced that will require the

[71] *Scottish National Party v Scottish Television Plc*, Unreported 15 May 1997 Outer House.
[72] J. Beatson, "The need to develop principles of prematurity and ripeness for review" in C. Forsyth and I. Hare (eds), *The Golden Metwand and the Crooked Cord: Essays in Honour of Sir William Wade QC* (Oxford: Clarendon, 1998) Ch.4.
[73] See *Eba v Advocate General for Scotland* [2011] UKSC 29; 2012 S.C. (U.K.S.C.) 1.
[74] *SA v Secretary of State for the Home Department* [2013] CSIH 62; 2014 S.C. 1.
[75] *EP v Secretary of State for the Home Department* [2014] CSIH 30; 2014 S.C. 706 at [31].

applicant to serve on the respondent(s) and any interest parties, within seven days of lodging the petition: (a) the petition; (b) a time estimate for the permission hearing; (c) any written evidence in support of the petition; (d) copies of any documents the petitioner intends to rely upon; and (e) a list of essential documents for advance reading by the court. The respondent(s) and/or interested parties would have 21 days to answer the petition and could oppose the granting of permission. Coupled with the introduction of a three month time limit to raise proceedings, the burden on the would be applicant is significantly increased.

Introducing a requirement to obtain permission will mark a significant change in judicial review proceedings in Scotland. At present, a petitioner requires to obtain first orders from the court to allow service of the petition.[76] Any suggestion that the requirement to obtain first orders could be used as a filter device akin to a leave requirement was rejected by the Inner House in *EY v Secretary of State for the Home Department*[77]: first orders should only be refused in exceptional circumstances, for example where the court clearly lacks jurisdiction or the averments are incomprehensible of gibberish.[78] On any view, the test a petitioner has to satisfy is a very low one. That fell to be contrasted with the position in England and Wales. Permission must be obtained from the High Court to commence judicial review proceedings.[79] Permission may be granted in whole or in part[80] and will be granted where the application is "arguable".[81] If the applicant seeks to introduce new grounds after permission has been granted, permission must be sought for those new grounds before they can be added.[82] Since 2000, the would be respondent can make representations as to why permission should be refused.[83] Permission is invariably determined in the first instance without a hearing,[84] with brief written reasons being provided explaining why permission has been granted or refused.[85] Where permission is refused, or granted in part only or subject to conditions, the applicant can request that the decision be reconsidered at a hearing.[86] There are no set criteria to be applied when considering whether to grant permission. The most common ground on which permission is refused is that the claim is unarguable and in reaching that conclusion it has been said that the court should apply a similar test to that governing applications for summary judgment.[87] Whatever the test that is applied, there has been a marked reduction in the number of applications for permission that have been granted over the last three decades.[88] It can be seen

---

[76] RCS r.58.7.

[77] *EY v Secretary of State for the Home Department* [2011] CSIH 3; 2011 S.C. 388.

[78] *EY v Secretary of State for the Home Department* [2011] CSIH 3; 2011 S.C. 388 at [16]; see also *Eba v Advocate General for Scotland* [2011] UKSC 29; 2012 S.C. (U.K.S.C.) 1, per Lord Hope of Craighead at [28].

[79] See generally, *De Smith's Judicial Review* (2013), paras 16–044 to 16–052 and Craig, *Administrative Law* (2012), paras 27–032 to 27–035.

[80] CPR r.54.12(1)(ii).

[81] *De Smith's Judicial Review* (2013) para.16–049. That is a lower test that has been adopted in Scotland ("real prospect of success").

[82] CPR r.54.15.

[83] CPR r.54.8.

[84] CPR PD 54A para.8.4.

[85] CPR r.54.12(2).

[86] CPR r.54.12(3).

[87] *De Smith's Judicial Review* (2013) para.16–050; see also *Sharma v Brown-Antoine* [2006] UKPC 57; [2007] 1 W.L.R. 780.

[88] V. Bondy and M. Sunkin, "Accessing Judicial Review" [2008] P.L. 647.

that the requirement for leave introduced by the Courts Reform (Scotland) Act 2014 is largely based on the English rules.

The new rules are based on the recommendations of the Gill Review. That **14-13** review concluded that a requirement to obtain leave[89] should be introduced in Scotland, broadly along the lines of Pt 54 of the Civil Procedure Rules.[90] The test they recommended was whether the petition had a real prospect of success, in the sense that it is not fanciful.[91] That should not require the court to be satisfied that, on the balance of probabilities, the petition will succeed.[92] Decisions on whether or not to grant leave would, the Gill Review anticipated, be reached without the need for an oral hearing.[93] The Gill Review anticipated that the introduction of a leave requirement would work well to filter out unmeritorious claims at an early stage and forcing respondents to make early concessions where a challenge was obviously well founded.[94] Introducing such a requirement would create a marked difference between a public law challenge instigated by means of a petition for judicial review and a private law challenge instigated by means of a summons. The former could only be brought with the leave of the court whereas the latter could be brought as of right, with the onus resting on the defender(s) to show why the action should not proceed and without the ability to have a case struck out or summarily dismissed.[95] The court would also have to guard against being over-zealous in its application of any leave requirement: a case (albeit rarely) that appears wholly unarguable may go on to succeed on the merits. If leave is too readily refused, the court's "essential function", namely securing the rule of law, will be compromised.

It is too early to know what effect these new rules will have on judicial review **14-14** in Scotland. Considering how the equivalent requirements have worked in England may, however, give some indication. Research carried out by Bondy and Sunkin[96] indicated that many solicitors that worked for applicants did not object to the requirement to seek permission. It had a two-fold benefit for many: it disposed of unmeritorious claims at an early stage (and without significant expense) and where permission was granted, it gave the respondent good reason to consider settlement. That latter point is likely to be especially true in Scotland where the test for permission has been set at "real prospect of success" as opposed to the English requirement that the application be "arguable". A note of caution is, however, appropriate. Every well founded application that is turned away at the permission stage is an unlawful decision that is allowed to stand. Thus taking too hard a line at the permission stage risks undermining the court's fundamental purpose in exercising its supervisory jurisdiction, namely, enforcing the rule of law. Bondy and Sunkin's research also highlighted the importance of

---

[89] "Leave" and "permission" are synonymous in this context, with "leave" being the preferred language in England and Wales until 2000.

[90] Scottish Civil Courts Review, *Report of the Scottish Civil Courts Review*, Ch.12, para.51.

[91] Scottish Civil Courts Review, *Report of the Scottish Civil Courts Review*, Ch.12, para.52.

[92] Scottish Civil Courts Review, *Report of the Scottish Civil Courts Review*, Ch.12, para.54.

[93] Scottish Civil Courts Review, *Report of the Scottish Civil Courts Review*, Ch.12, para.52.

[94] Scottish Civil Courts Review, *Report of the Scottish Civil Courts Review*, Ch.12, para.50; how effective or necessary a leave (or permission) requirement is has been questioned: Craig, *Administrative Law* (2012) para.27–035; Bondy and Sunkin, "Accessing Judicial Review" [2008] P.L. 647.

[95] Other than in the sheriff court where summary dismissal is competent (if rarely used): OCR r.17.2.

[96] Reported in Bondy and Sunkin, "Accessing Judicial Review" [2008] P.L. 647.

the judiciary being consistent in their application of the test: success rates at the permission stage ranged from 11 per cent with one judge to 46 per cent with another. If the choice of judge plays a significant role in the prospect of success, and where an oral hearing is likely to become the exception rather than the rule, there is a real risk that the potential for inconsistency could produce a sense of dissatisfaction with the system. Should the permission hurdle not only filter out unmeritorious claims but also encourage the resolution of well founded claims, the number of judicial decisions is likely to reduce. In itself that is not a bad thing but in a jurisdiction the size of Scotland, sufficient cases have to come before the court to ensure the common law can continue to develop and evolve.

Expenses

14–15 Any litigation is expensive. Where litigation is commenced in the public interest, cost becomes a particularly acute issue. Expenses rules in Scotland ordinarily see the successful party recover only a proportion of their expenses from the other side. In cases concerning the vindication of private rights, that general rule is acceptable. Where there is a risk that a party will be deterred from bringing public interest litigation (which, as Lord Reed explained in *AXA General Insurance Co Ltd v Lord Advocate*, enables the court to discharge its core function in securing the rule of law) there is cause for concern. For that reason, the court can, in appropriate circumstances, make an order to restrict a party's liability in expenses (a "protective expenses order"). The effect of a protective expenses order is to limit the applicant's exposure in expenses and thus offer a measure of protection against any adverse award that may be made in the event their claim is unsuccessful. The power to make a protective expenses order exists at common law[97] and is now, in relation to environmental cases at least, regulated by the Rules of Court.[98] So far as the common law power is concerned, it arises from the court's general and wide discretion to regulate all matters of expenses. A consequence of that is any award (being discretionary) will rarely be interfered with on appeal.[99] In exercising that discretion, the Court of Session has had regard to the approach taken by the English courts to similar applications and, in particular, what have become known as the *Corner House* principles.[100] In that case, the Court of Appeal set out the following principles that govern applications for a protective expenses order:

1) the issues raised must be of general public importance;
2) the public interest requires that the issues be resolved;
3) the party seeking the protective expenses order has no private interest in the outcome of the case;
4) having regard to the financial resources of the party seeking the protective expenses order and the likely costs involved, it is fair and just to make the order; and

---

[97] *McArthur v Lord Advocate*, 2006 S.L.T. 170.
[98] RCS r.58A.
[99] *McGinty v Scottish Ministers* [2013] CSIH 78; 2014 S.C. 81 at [62].
[100] *R. (on the application of Corner House Research) v Secretary of State for Trade and Industry* [2005] EWCA Civ 192; [2005] 1 W.L.R. 2600.

5) if the protective expenses order is not made the applicant is likely to discontinue proceedings (and would be acting reasonably to do so).[101]

Applications to the Court of Session under the common law power have had limited success and even when granted the cap on expenses has been fixed at what appeared to be a high level.[102]

Rule of Court 58A, made to fulfil the UK's obligations under the Aarhus Convention, now regulates the award of protective expenses orders in environmental cases. The overall aim of a protective expenses order is to ensure that proceedings are not prohibitively expensive for the applicant (RCS r.58A.2(3)) and can be sought by a party that is either an individual or a non-governmental organisation promoting environmental protection (RCS r.58A.2(2)). Where a protective expenses order is granted it must limit the applicant's liability in expenses to the respondent to the sum of £5,000 and must also limit the respondent's liability in expenses to the applicant to the sum of £30,000 (RCS r.58A.4). In other words, the price an applicant pays for limiting their potential exposure in expenses is a cap on the amount they can recover from the respondent if they are successful. Applications under this rule, as opposed to at common law, have fared little better.[103] Just as the rules on standing have, in form, been brought into line with the current rules in England and Wales but continue to be applied in a more restrictive manner, the same is true of protective expenses orders. A protective expenses order remains a rare occurrence in public law proceedings in Scotland and that has an inevitable chilling effect.

Territorial scope of judicial review

The Court of Session's jurisdiction extends throughout Scotland thus the **14–16** territorial scope of its supervisory jurisdiction ought to be, and invariably is, uncontroversial. What, however, of a petition from an asylum seeker who entered the UK in London but was required by the Secretary of State to move to Glasgow while their application was determined. The decision to refuse their application for asylum was then taken by tribunals sitting in England. Does the Court of Session have jurisdiction to review the decision? Those are broadly the circumstances the House of Lords had to consider in *Tehrani v Secretary of State for the Home Department*.[104] It was held that the Court of Session had jurisdiction where there was "a sufficient connection with Scotland".[105] In assessing whether such a connection exists, the court should have regard to whether the petitioner is resident in Scotland, whether the "harmful effects" of the decision will be felt in Scotland and whether the decision under challenge

---

[101] *R. (on the application of Corner House Research) v Secretary of State for Trade and Industry* [2005] EWCA Civ 192; [2005] 1 W.L.R. 2600 at [74].

[102] For example, *McGinty v Scottish Ministers* Unreported 28 January 2010 Outer House, where the cap was set at £30,000.

[103] For example, *Carroll v Scottish Borders Council* [2014] CSOH 30; 2014 S.L.T. 659; *Friends of Loch Etive, Petitioner* [2014] CSOH 116; *John Muir Trust, Petitioner* [2014] CSOH 172A; *Gibson, Petitioner* [2015] CSOH 41 where applications were refused.

[104] *Tehrani v Secretary of State for the Home Department* [2006] UKHL 47; 2007 S.C. (H.L.) 1.

[105] *Tehrani v Secretary of State for the Home Department* [2006] UKHL 47; 2007 S.C. (H.L.) 1, per Lord Nicholls of Birkenhead at [23] and Lord Rodger of Earlsferry at [99]–[101].

was taken in exercise of a UK-wide jurisdiction.[106] That gives rise to the possibility that both the Court of Session and the High Court could have jurisdiction to hear a challenge to the same decision. In the event that both courts were seized of jurisdiction, the rules of forum non conveniens would determine which court decided the issue.[107] Until such time as tighter rules on leave and time limits come into effect in Scotland, dual jurisdiction offers a person who has been refused permission by the High Court in England a second chance to have their case heard, without leave, by the Court of Session. Once the Courts Reform (Scotland) Act 2014 has come into force, this issue is likely to rendered largely academic.

Ouster of judicial review

14–17 While factors such as prematurity, delay and exhaustion of alternative remedies may have the effect of excluding or limiting the availability of judicial review, preclusive or ouster clauses have that explicit objective. The courts have effectively declined to give effect to certain forms of ouster clause,[108] holding that, at most, all they are capable of doing is excluding the possibility of appeal as distinct from review, or that an ouster is effective only to protect intra vires determinations.[109] In principle, any such clause now falls to be tested against the common law canon of statutory interpretation to the effect that the subject's right of access to the court is not to be eroded other than by clear statutory language[110] and the parallel right of access to the courts under art.6 of the Convention.

A distinction must however be drawn between attempts to oust the jurisdiction of the courts outright, and those that limit it in some way. One example of this is to provide that a certificate or statement by the responsible authority stating the existence of a fact shall be "conclusive evidence" thereof, so that it is not open to the aggrieved individual to adduce evidence tending to show that the facts are not as so stated.[111] Another commonplace technique is for statutes conferring a right of appeal on a point of law to provide that the appeal must be taken within a specified, and usually short, period of time. The object of the statutory scheme is to oust the supervisory jurisdiction in favour of an exclusive, and time limited, statutory remedy. In *Smith v East Elloe Rural DC*,[112] the House of Lords held that the applicant was indeed confined to her statutory remedy, and although the speeches in *Anisminic Ltd v Foreign Compensation Commission*[113] appeared to

---

[106] *Tehrani v Secretary of State for the Home Department* [2006] UKHL 47; 2007 S.C. (H.L.) 1, per Lord Hope of Craighead at [60] and Lord Rodger of Earlsferry at [103].

[107] *Tehrani v Secretary of State for the Home Department* [2006] UKHL 47; 2007 S.C. (H.L.) 1, per Lord Rodger of Earlsferry at [106].

[108] Such as "finality clauses", which provide that the decision of a body shall be final; or "shall not be questioned" clauses, which provide that the decision shall not be questioned in any court of law whatever.

[109] *Anisminic Ltd v Foreign Compensation Commission* [1969] 2 A.C. 147.

[110] *Raymond v Honey* [1983] 1 A.C. 1; *R. v Lord Chancellor Ex p. Witham* [1998] Q.B. 575.

[111] In *R. v Registrar of Companies Ex p. Central Bank of India* [1986] Q.B. 1114 CA (Civ Div), Dillon LJ noted that a computer search had unearthed over 300 instances of "conclusive evidence" clauses. For a home grown example, see the Freedom of Information (Scotland) Act 2002 s.31(2), which provides that a certificate signed by a member of the Scottish Executive stating that information is exempt from the freedom of information regime on national security grounds shall be conclusive of that fact.

[112] *Smith v East Elloe Rural District Council* [1956] A.C. 736.

[113] *Anisminic Ltd v Foreign Compensation Commission* [1969] 2 A.C. 147.

cast doubt on *East Elloe*, its authority has been confirmed on a number of occasions since.[114]

<h2 style="text-align:center">GROUNDS FOR JUDICIAL REVIEW</h2>

In *Council of Civil Service Unions v Minister for the Civil Service*,[115] Lord **14–18** Diplock summarised the grounds on which judicial review may be sought as follows:

> "Judicial review has I think developed to a stage today when one can conveniently classify under three heads the grounds on which administrative action is subject to control by judicial review. The first ground I would call 'illegality', the second 'irrationality' and the third 'procedural impropriety'."

These three headings, illegality, irrationality and procedural impropriety, each comprise a number of more specific principles of review, many of which interact or overlap. They are also elastic, in that the courts have progressively extended their scope and meaning, and do not necessarily exhaust the field. Lord Diplock himself anticipated the future reception into domestic administrative law of review on grounds of proportionality, a principle akin to which was being applied by the courts even in advance of the enactment of the Human Rights Act.

Illegality

In one sense, a decision could be said to be illegal whatever the reason for the **14–19** court's intervention. But as a discrete head of review, illegality means something narrower than this. In *Council of Civil Service Unions v Minister for the Civil Service* Lord Diplock explained what he meant by illegality:

> "By 'illegality' as a ground of judicial review I mean that the decision-maker must understand correctly the law that regulates his decision-making power and must give effect to it."[116]

Judicial review involves the control of powers, and at the most basic level this means ensuring that a given power is only exercised in the circumstances envisaged and on the conditions imposed by the donor, whether Parliament or some other body. Where the decision maker misinterprets or fails to apply the conditions of the grant of their power, or jurisdiction, they confer on themselves

---

[114] See, e.g. *R. v Secretary of State for the Environment Ex p. Ostler* [1977] Q.B. 122 CA (Civ Div); *R. v Cornwall CC Ex p. Huntington* [1994] 1 All E.R. 694 CA (Civ Div). As Simon Brown LJ put it in the latter case: " . . . the intention of Parliament when it uses an *Anisminic* clause is that questions as to validity are not excluded. When paragraphs such as those in *Ex p. Ostler* are used, then the legislative intention is that questions as to invalidity may be raised on the specified grounds in the prescribed time and in the prescribed manner, but that otherwise the jurisdiction of the court is excluded in the interests of certainty."
[115] *Council of Civil Service Unions v Minister for the Civil Service* [1985] A.C. 374 at 410. Lord Diplock's classification was adopted in Scotland in *Edinburgh DC v Secretary of State for Scotland*, 1985 S.C. 261.
[116] *Council of Civil Service Unions v Minister for the Civil Service* [1985] A.C. 374 at 410.

an authority it was never intended that they should have.[117] Thus the court on review will as a matter of principle ascertain whether the conditions for an exercise of jurisdiction were met, and if it finds that they were not will[118] reduce the decision as being ultra vires. Review on this ground is often discussed in terms of error, whether of law or of fact, on the part of the decision maker. But review for illegality goes further than this. A grant of power may be more or less prescriptive in the conditions it imposes on the power's exercise. But even where it apparently imposes no conditions, the courts presume that powers are granted subject to certain implied limitations. Although this is explained in terms of assumed legislative intent, these limitations are very much the product of judicial innovation, and have greatly extended the scope of review for illegality.

Jurisdiction and error

14–20 We have seen that the supervisory jurisdiction is to be distinguished from appellate procedures. One of the consequences of this distinction was that, since the supervisory jurisdiction is concerned only with the legal validity of decisions and not with their rightness or wrongness, errors were not reviewable and the only possibility of correcting these depended on the availability of a right of appeal.[119] This was never an absolute rule. An error, whether of law or of fact, which vitiated the power of a body to act or decide might be reviewed because in making such an error the decision maker stepped outside the four corners of their jurisdiction, conferring on themselves an authority they did not have. Such errors were (and are) described as "jurisdictional" errors, and the scope of review on this basis depended upon where the courts drew the line between such errors and non-jurisdictional errors that the body was at liberty (subject to any appeal) to make.

In this area, the decision of the House of Lords in *Anisminic* remains a landmark.[120] That case arose out of the fallout from the Suez crisis in 1956. Anisminic claimed compensation for property lost in Egypt during the crisis. It complained that the Foreign Compensation Commission had erred in determining that the successor in title to its property was required by the relevant Order in Council to be a British national. Anisminic argued that there was no such requirement in the order. Section 4(4) of the Foreign Compensation Act 1950, however, purported to exclude the court's jurisdiction to review any determination by the Foreign Compensation Commission. The core question (was Anisminic entitled to compensation?) was one that fell squarely within the Foreign Compensation Commission's jurisdiction. The question for the House of Lords was whether the court could review the alleged error concerning the subsidiary question (does the successor in title require to be a British national?). By a majority, the House held that it had jurisdiction to review that decision. By

---

[117] Thus in *McColl v Strathclyde RC*, 1983 S.L.T. 616, it was held that the local authority's statutory duty to provide "wholesome water" did not entitle it to fluoridate the water in the interests of dental health.

[118] On when the court might decline to reduce a decision which has been held to be flawed, see *King v East Ayrshire Council*, 1998 S.C. 182; *Anderson v Secretary of State for Work and Pensions*, 2002 S.L.T. 68.

[119] As Lord Reid explained in *Armah v Governor of Ghana* [1968] A.C. 192 at 234: "If a magistrate or any other tribunal has jurisdiction to enter on the inquiry and to decide a particular issue, and there is no irregularity in the procedure, he does not destroy his jurisdiction by reaching the wrong decision. If he has jurisdiction to go right he has jurisdiction to go wrong."

[120] *Anisminic Ltd v Foreign Compensation Commission* [1969] 2 A.C. 147.

asking itself the wrong question, and imposing an erroneous requirement, the Foreign Compensation Commission had, said the House of Lords, exceed its jurisdiction and the decision was a nullity.[121] The significance of the decision in *Anisminic* was explained by Lord Diplock in *Re Racal Communications Ltd*:

> "The break-through made by *Anisminic* … was that, as respects administrative tribunals and authorities, the old distinction between errors of law that went to jurisdiction and errors of law that did not, was for practical purposes abolished. Any error of law that could be shown to have been made by them in the course of reaching their decision on matters of fact or of administrative policy would result in their having asked themselves the wrong question with the result that the decision they reached would be a nullity."[122]

That interpretation of *Anisminic* was slow to take hold and it was not until the decision of the House of Lords in *R. v Lord President of the Privy Council Ex p. Page*[123] that the Lord Diplock view that the distinction between errors of law going to jurisdiction and errors of law within jurisdiction had been abolished was accepted.[124]

It appeared for some time that the law of Scotland was determined to follow a different course from that south of the border. That difference arose from the comments of the Lord President (Emslie) in *Watt v Lord Advocate*.[125] Although strictly speaking his remarks were obiter, the Lord President expressed the view that

> "however much this is to be regretted, the Court of Session has never had the power to correct an intra vires error of law made by a statutory tribunal or authority exercising statutory jurisdiction".[126]

That can be seen to be at odds with what the House of Lords held in *Anisminic* as interpreted and applied later by Lord Diplock and then Lord Browne-Wilkinson. That was unfortunate as the Scottish courts have, on numerous occasions, stressed that there was no difference between Scotland and England so far as the substantive grounds of judicial review were concerned.[127] As time went on, the application of the Lord President's comments in *Watt* became increasingly patchy, with some judges simply ignoring it.[128] In *Gillies Ramsay Diamond v PJW Enterprises Ltd* the argument that *Anisminic* rendered the distinction drawn in *Watt* unnecessary was mentioned but the court found it unnecessary to

---

[121] *Anisminic Ltd v Foreign Compensation Commission* [1969] 2 A.C. 147, per Lord Reid at 171.
[122] *Re Racal Communications Ltd* [1981] A.C. 374 at 383. See also *O'Reilly v Mackman* [1983] 2 A.C. 237, per Lord Diplock at 278.
[123] *R. v Lord President of the Privy Council Ex p. Page* [1993] A.C. 682.
[124] *R. v Lord President of the Privy Council Ex p. Page* [1993] A.C. 682, in particular Lord Browne-Wilkinson at 701–702.
[125] *Watt v Lord Advocate*, 1979 S.C. 120.
[126] *Watt v Lord Advocate*, 1979 S.C. 120 at 131.
[127] *Brown v Hamilton DC*, 1983 S.C. (H.L.) 1, per Lord Fraser at 42; *West v Secretary of State for Scotland*, 1992 S.C. 385, per Lord President Hope at 402 and 405; *Somerville v Scottish Ministers* [2006] CSIH 52; 2007 S.C. 140 at [123].
[128] For example, *Mooney v Secretary of State for Work and Pensions*, 2004 S.L.T. 1141 and *Donnelly v Secretary of State for Work and Pensions* [2007] CSOH 1; 2007 S.C.L.R. 746.

decide the point.[129] In *Eba v Advocate General for Scotland*, the Supreme Court
accepted the time had finally come to recognise that what was said by the Lord
President in *Watt* was irreconcilable with what had been decided in *Anisminic* and
it should no longer be followed. Thus by a somewhat circuitous route the law of
Scotland is now consistent with that of England and Wales: the Court of Session
has the power to correct any error of law by an inferior tribunal.

14–21   That general statement is, however, subject to qualification. The error must
affect the decision that was taken and not simply be a subsidiary or incidental
matter that was of no consequence to the final decision.[130] Furthermore, the court
will decline to intervene where errors of fact or law could be recognised as being
within the functions of the body concerned.[131] In *Wordie Property Ltd v Secretary
of State for Scotland*,[132] Lord President Emslie held that a decision of the
Secretary of State acting within their statutory remit would be ultra vires if they
improperly exercised a discretion confided to them, in particular "if [their
decision] is based upon a material error of law going to the root of the question
for determination".[133] More broadly, the language of "error" suggests that legal
questions are susceptible only of one, objectively verifiable, answer. That is not
(or not always) the case, as is apparent in the decision of the House of Lords in
*R. v Monopolies and Mergers Commission Ex p. South Yorkshire Transport
Ltd*.[134] There, the commission had power to take action where it was satisfied that
a monopoly situation existed in "a substantial part of the United Kingdom". The
commission purported to exercise this power on the basis of a monopoly situation
found to exist in an area amounting to only 1.65 per cent of the total area of the
UK. The company argued that in treating so small an area as "substantial", the
commission had erred in law and its decision was accordingly ultra vires. The
House of Lords disagreed:

> "The courts have repeatedly warned against the dangers of taking an
> inherently imprecise word and by redefining it thrusting on it a spurious
> degree of precision . . . The question is whether the Commission has placed
> the phrase broadly in the right part of the spectrum of possible meanings
> [and] within the permissible field of judgment . . . The statutory criterion of
> jurisdiction might itself be so imprecise that different decision makers, each
> acting rationally, might reach differing conclusions when applying it to the
> facts of a given case. In such a case, the court is entitled to substitute its own
> opinion for that of the person to whom the decision has been entrusted only
> if the decision is so aberrant that it cannot be classed as rational."[135]

---

[129] *Gillies Ramsay Diamond v PJW Enterprises Ltd*, 2004 S.C. 430 at [37]–[38].
[130] Clyde and Edwards, *Judicial Review* (2000) para.22.24.
[131] *R. v Lord President of the Privy Council Ex p. Page* [1993] A.C. 682.
[132] *Wordie Property Ltd v Secretary of State for Scotland*, 1984 S.L.T. 345.
[133] *Wordie Property Ltd v Secretary of State for Scotland*, 1984 S.L.T. 345 at 347. See also *R. v Lord
President of the Privy Council Ex p. Page* [1993] A.C. 682 at 701, where Lord Browne-Wilkinson
held that in order to justify intervention the error complained of required to be "relevant and
material".
[134] *R. v Monopolies and Mergers Commission Ex p. South Yorkshire Transport Ltd* [1993] 1 W.L.R.
23, followed in Scotland in *Stagecoach Holdings Ltd v Secretary of State for Trade and Industry*,
1997 S.L.T. 940. See also, e.g. *R. v Broadcasting Complaints Commission Ex p. Granada
Television Ltd* [1995] E.M.L.R. 163 CA (Civ Div); *R. v Radio Authority Ex p. Bull* [1998] Q.B.
294 CA (Civ Div); *R. v Broadcasting Standards Commission Ex p. BBC* [2000] 3 W.L.R. 1327
CA (Civ Div).
[135] *R. v Monopolies and Mergers Commission Ex p. South Yorkshire Transport Ltd* [1993] 1 W.L.R.
23, per Lord Mustill.

This is not to say that the courts will always accord a generous margin of interpretation to the primary decision maker. In appropriate cases, particularly those involving fundamental rights, they may confine the "spectrum of possible meanings" so closely as to leave only one answer to a given question of statutory interpretation, such that the decision maker falls into error if they fail to answer that question correctly.[136] Of course, it is *Eba* that highlights the most obvious limit on the court's willingness to correct errors of law. As we have seen, the result of the "second appeals test" that must be satisfied before a challenge to an otherwise unreviewable decision of the Upper Tribunal will be entertained is that an error of law on the part of the tribunal is not sufficient, in and of itself, to justify the court exercising its supervisory jurisdiction.[137] As Wade and Forsyth explain, where, for example, a tribunal has found X liable to pay a certain sum of money to Y but that decision is marred by an error of law, it is an error that will go uncorrected if the second appeals test cannot be satisfied but the same error could be pled in defence should Y raise an action for payment against X. At that point, the validity of the decision requires to be determined (in private law proceedings) irrespective of the second appeals test.[138] That sort of anomaly suggests the last word has yet to be written about intra vires errors of law.

What then of errors of fact? As with errors of law, "jurisdictional" errors of **14–22** fact have always been reviewable.[139] Where material findings of fact are reached on the basis of no evidence, again the courts will intervene.[140] But "outside those categories, we do not accept that a decision can be flawed in this court, which is not an appellate tribunal, upon the ground of mistake of fact".[141] Such an approach is not without justification. While a court on review may fairly regard itself as best placed to provide an authoritative interpretation on questions of law (subject to the qualifications noted above), it does not follow that it is best placed to determine questions of fact. The primary decision maker may have arrived at their findings of fact after a lengthy process of evaluation, possibly hearing witnesses or considering representations, and their function may involve the application of specialist expertise or experience. For a court on review to denominate such findings as erroneous, other than where the error is manifest, involves a substitution of judgment that is less easy to justify or explain. It seems clear, however, that the courts are increasingly willing to intervene on the basis of errors of fact, even where the finding of fact is not a condition precedent to the exercise of jurisdiction. In *R. v Parliamentary Commissioner for Administration*

---

[136] See, e.g. *R. (on the application of Adan) v Secretary of State for the Home Department* [2001] 2 A.C. 477.

[137] See para.14–12, above.

[138] H.W.R. Wade and C. Forsyth, *Administrative Law*, 11th edn (Oxford: Oxford University Press, 2014) p.224.

[139] *R. v Secretary of State for the Home Department Ex p. Khawaja* [1984] A.C. 74; *Tan Te Lam v Superintendent of Tai A Chau Detention Centre* [1997] A.C. 97 PC (Hong Kong).

[140] *Colleen Properties Ltd v Minister of Housing and Local Government* [1971] 1 W.L.R. 433 CA (Civ Div); *R. v Hillingdon LBC Ex p. Islam* [1983] 1 A.C. 688.

[141] *R. v London Residuary Body Ex p. Inner London Education Authority, The Times*, 24 July 1987 DC, per Watkins LJ. After consideration of the "difficult and elusive issue" of whether error of fact qualified as an independent ground of review, the Court of Appeal in *Wandsworth LBC v A* [2000] 1 W.L.R. 1246 CA (Civ Div), adopted this analysis, citing also the observation of Lord Brightman in *R. v Hillingdon LBC Ex p. Puhlhofer* [1986] A.C. 484 HL at 518 that "it is the duty of the court to leave the decision [as to the existence of a fact] to the public body to whom Parliament has entrusted the decision-making power, save in a case where it is obvious that the public body, consciously or unconsciously, was acting perversely".

Ex p. Balchin,[142] where the question was whether the Parliamentary Ombudsman had asked himself the wrong question in deciding whether or not there was maladministration, Sedley J held that "if there is such an error, it does not have to be defined as one of law or of fact (the latter too being reviewable if crucial to the decision)".[143] Further, the courts may now require to be more rigorous in their review of the factual basis of decisions because judicial review might otherwise fail to satisfy the requirements of art.6 of the European Convention on Human Rights. European and domestic case law recognises that breaches of art.6 by a primary decision maker may be "cured" where there is recourse to a higher court or tribunal having "full jurisdiction" and which does meet the guarantees of art.6.[144] This need not in all circumstances involve a full right of appeal,[145] but in certain contexts the restriction of the supervisory jurisdiction to questions of legal validity may deprive it of the fullness of jurisdiction necessary to secure compliance with the fair hearing guarantees.[146] Baroness Hale explained in *R. (on the application of Wright) v Secretary of State for Health*, what was necessary to allow judicial review to amount to full jurisdiction:

> "What amounts to 'full jurisdiction' varies according to the nature of the decision being made. It does not always require access to a court or tribunal even for the determination of disputed issues of fact. Much depends upon the subject matter of the decision and the quality of the initial decision-making process. If there is a 'classic exercise of administrative discretion', even though determinative of civil rights and obligations, and there are a number of safeguards to ensure that the procedure is in fact both fair and impartial, then judicial review may be adequate to supply the necessary access to a court, even if there is no jurisdiction to examine the factual merits of the case."[147]

Wrongful delegation[148]

14–23   "Wrongful delegation" is one of a number of heads of review that arise out of a proper construction of the power that confers a discretion upon a decision maker. Who is to take the ultimate decision? What factors can the decision maker have regard to in reaching a decision? For what purposes may the discretion be exercised? Each of these questions is answered by understanding the true scope of the power that has been conferred on the decision maker. Where the wrong person takes the decision, or irrelevant considerations are taken into account or the power exercised for an illegitimate purpose, review on the ground of illegality is available.

---

[142] *R. v Parliamentary Commissioner for Administration Ex p. Balchin* [1998] 1 P.L.R. 1 QBD.

[143] *R. v Parliamentary Commissioner for Administration Ex p. Balchin* [1998] 1 P.L.R. 1 at 5. See also *Anderson v Secretary of State for Work and Pensions*, 2002 S.L.T. 68.

[144] *R. (on the application of G) v X School Governors* [2011] UKSC 30; [2012] 1 A.C. 167. See also: Wade and Forsyth, *Administrative Law* (2014) pp.381–383.

[145] *Bryan v United Kingdom* (1995) 21 E.H.R.R. 342.

[146] *Kingsley v United Kingdom* (2001) 33 E.H.R.R. 13.

[147] *R. (on the application of Wright) v Secretary of State for Health* [2009] UKHL 3; [2009] A.C. 739 at [23]; see also the concurring opinion of Mr Bratza of the European Commission of Human Rights in *Bryan v United Kingdom* (1995) 21 E.H.R.R. 342 at [354].

[148] In relation to both unlawful delegation and the rule against fettering, see generally Wade and Forsyth, *Administrative Law* (2014) Ch.10; Craig, *Administrative Law* (2012) Ch.18.

Wrongful delegation arises where it is argued that the decision maker lacked competence to arrive at the decision complained of as the power to take such decisions was conferred on another. In *Vine v National Dock Labour Board*,[149] for example, the House of Lords granted a declaration that the dismissal of a registered dock worker was invalid because the board, instead of deciding the matter itself, had improperly entrusted the decision to its disciplinary committee. But, although the maxim *delegatus non potest delegare* has been applied at the cost of official convenience,[150] it is not to be regarded as an absolute rule. Rather, it reflects a special canon of statutory construction, which may be displaced by indications of a contrary legislative intent. In any particular case, the question for the court is: does the provision that empowers A to take the decision allow A to delegate that task to B? In general, a statute that authorises one level of delegation does not authorise a further delegation.[151]

The principle applies to powers of all kinds, but is likely to apply with greater rigour to powers classified as "legislative" or "judicial" (bearing in mind that such classifications should be approached with caution). While administrative processes are subject to the rule against wrongful delegation, greater tolerance tends to be shown to large or busy or multi-functional organisations.[152] On occasion, the application of the rule shades explicitly into procedural impropriety, as where decisions have been struck down because of delegation to an outside body or because of participation by non-members in the taking of decisions.[153] Similarly, arrangements characterised as "acting under dictation" have been held to fall foul of the rule,[154] although this might be better described as a species of wrongful fettering of discretion.

A special rule, the *Carltona* principle, applies to central government, whereby officials are treated as the Minister's alter ego.[155] Originally conceived in relation to the UK Government, the same principle also applies to the Scottish Ministers.[156] Exceptionally, statutes may exclude the *Carltona* principle and require a particular Minister take a decision,[157] but it was held in *R. v Secretary of State for the Home Department Ex p. Oladehinde*[158] that the implication of

---

[149] *Vine v National Dock Labour Board* [1957] A.C. 488 HL.

[150] *R. v Gateshead Justices Ex p. Tesco Stores Ltd* [1981] 1 All E.R. 1027 QBD.

[151] *Barnard v National Dock Labour Board* [1953] 2 Q.B. 18 CA.

[152] *R. v Race Relations Board Ex p. Selvarajan* [1976] 1 All E.R. 12 CA (Civ Div); *R. v Independent Broadcasting Authority Ex p. Whitehouse, The Times*, 4 April 1985 CA (Civ Div).

[153] As in *Leary v National Union of Vehicle Builders* [1971] Ch. 34 ChD.

[154] As in *H Lavender and Son Ltd v Minister of Housing and Local Government* [1970] 1 W.L.R. 1231; [1970] 3 All E.R. 871 QBD.

[155] *Carltona Ltd v Commissioner of Works* [1943] 2 All E.R. 560 CA; most recently explained by Lord Reed in *R (on the application of Bourgass and others) v Secretary of State for Justice* [2015] UKSC 54 at [48]–[52]. For a practical application of the policy, see *R. v Skinner (Edward George)* [1968] 2 Q.B. 700 where S challenged his conviction for drink driving on the grounds that the breathalyser used to take the incriminating sample had not been approved (under s.7(1) of the Road Safety Act 1967) by the Minister personally. The appeal was unceremoniously dismissed.

[156] *SHBA Ltd v Scottish Ministers*, 2002 S.L.T. 1321; *Beggs v Scottish Ministers* [2007] UKHL 3; 2007 S.L.T. 235. For a discussion of the limits of the principle, see *Somerville v Scottish Ministers* [2007] UKHL 44; 2008 S.C. (H.L.) 45 (where the actions of a prison governor did not fall to be attributed to the Scottish Ministers).

[157] For example *H Lavender and Son Ltd v Minister of Housing and Local Government* [1970] 1 W.L.R. 1231; [1970] 3 All E.R. 871.

[158] *R. v Secretary of State for the Home Department Ex p. Oladehinde* [1991] 1 A.C. 254 HL.

exclusion is not easily to be drawn. Local authorities in Scotland benefit from a general authority to delegate their functions to subcommittees and officers.[159]

The rule against fettering

14–24 The whole point of discretionary powers is to allow the latitude for reaching decisions in accordance with the public interest and with the circumstances and merits of particular cases. It follows that a public authority entrusted with discretionary powers cannot validly disable its decision making freedom, whether by entering into contracts, making representations or adhering to over-rigid rules or policies, such that it disposes of a case or application without considering its particular merits. Again, the rule against fettering is not absolute. It should also be noted that the promises, representations and assurances given by a public authority may generate legitimate expectations on the part of citizens, which may be protected by a court on review.[160]

Public authorities enter into contracts as a matter of routine, but as most contracts fetter freedom of action in some way there may be difficult questions of degree in determining exactly how far the authority may validly bind itself as to the future. In a number of cases, the courts have held that contracts entered into by public authorities were ultra vires and void because they were incompatible with the authority's wider statutory functions.[161] This is not to say that a public authority should in all circumstances be freed from its private law obligations, or that an authority is never competent to limit its discretion by entering into contracts. As Lord Blackburn held in *Attorney General v Great Eastern Railway Co*[162]:

> "The doctrine of ultra vires ought to be reasonably, and not unreasonably, understood and applied, and whatever may fairly be regarded as incidental to, or consequential upon, those things which the legislature has authorised ought not (unless expressly prohibited) be held by judicial construction to be ultra vires."

As Viscount Simonds later explained in *British Transport Commission v Westmorland CC*,[163] a public authority cannot by contract sterilise or renounce "part of its statutory birthright". There will require to be a fairly manifest incompatibility between the contract and the authority's statutory functions in order to satisfy this test.[164]

14–25 Short of contract, a public authority may make representations or give assurances to members of the public, from which it seeks subsequently to resile. May it do so? Unquestionably, where there has been reliance on a representation or assurance, substantial injustice may be done where the public authority goes

---

[159] Local Government (Scotland) Act 1973 s.56.
[160] On which, see para.14–39, below.
[161] *Ayr Harbour Trustees v Oswald* (1883) 10 R. (H.L.) 85; (1883) 8 App. Cas. 623; *Birkdale District Electric Supply Co Ltd v Southport Corp* [1926] A.C. 355 HL.
[162] *Attorney General v Great Eastern Railway Co* (1880) 5 App. Cas. 473 HL.
[163] *British Transport Commission v Westmorland CC* [1958] A.C. 126 HL.
[164] See, e.g. *R. v Hammersmith and Fulham LBC Ex p. Beddowes* [1987] Q.B. 1050 CA (Civ Div).

back on its word. Equally, however, an ultra vires representation or assurance, if enforced, could have the effect of enlarging the scope of a public authority's powers beyond the limits prescribed by the legislature. In some cases, the courts drew an analogy between the representations of public authorities and common law doctrines of estoppel or personal bar in order to hold that an authority could not, adversely to the interests of the citizen, resile from a representation relied on by them.[165] The House of Lords has conceded the similarity between the private law concepts of estoppel/personal bar and the public law concept of legitimate expectations, but added that

> "public law has already absorbed whatever is useful from the moral values which underlie the private law concept of estoppel and the time has come for it to stand upon its own two feet."[166]

The key moral value underpinning the doctrine of estoppel is that it would be unconscionable for a person to deny what they have represented or agreed. But in the field of public law, this principle cannot be given its full force because there may be wider public interests at stake which justify departing from the representation or assurance in question.[167]

A complaint of unlawful fettering may also arise in circumstances where the over-rigid application of a rule or policy is said to have precluded proper consideration of an individual's claim or case.[168] In one sense, there is much to be said for the adoption of rules and policies. They may speed up decision making processes, and conduce to greater consistency and certainty. But responsiveness is an equally important virtue of administrative decision making—indeed, it is in the interests of responsiveness that discretionary powers are conferred—and the task of the court in this regard is to reconcile the competing objectives. It is clear that an authority charged with a discretionary power may develop and apply a policy as to the approach they will adopt in the generality of cases; they may not, however, adopt a rule that certain applications will always be refused.[169] As Lord Browne-Wilkinson held in *R. v Secretary of State for the Home Department Ex p. Venables*:

---

[165] This approach is especially associated with Lord Denning: see *Robertson v Minister of Pensions* [1949] 1 K.B. 227 KBD; *Wells v Minister of Housing and Local Government* [1967] 1 W.L.R. 1000 CA (Civ Div); *Lever Finance Ltd v Westminster (City) LBC* [1971] 1 Q.B. 222 CA (Civ Div). Lord Denning's reasoning in *Robertson* was disapproved by the House of Lords in *Howell v Falmouth Boat Construction Co Ltd* [1951] A.C. 837 HL. Nor did arguments of personal bar avail the applicant in *Western Fish Products Ltd v Penwith DC* [1981] 2 All E.R. 204 CA (Civ Div).

[166] *R. (on the application of Reprotech (Pebsham) Ltd) v East Sussex CC* [2002] UKHL 8; [2003] 1 W.L.R. 348, per Lord Hoffmann at [35].

[167] Note, however, that in circumstances where an individual has suffered loss through reliance on a representation or assurance by a public authority, a remedy in damages might lie on the basis of negligent misstatement, as in *Ministry of Housing and Local Government v Sharp* [1970] 2 Q.B. 223 CA (Civ Div).

[168] As with representations and assurances, the adoption of rules and policies may also generate legitimate expectations which the courts will protect as a matter of procedural fairness.

[169] *R. v Port of London Authority Ex p. Kynoch Ltd* [1919] 1 K.B. 176 CA; *R. v Torquay Licensing Justices Ex p. Brockman* [1951] 2 K.B. 784 KBD; *British Oxygen Co Ltd v Minister of Technology* [1971] A.C. 610 HL.

" . . . the position is different if the policy adopted is such as to preclude the person on whom the power is conferred from departing from the policy or from taking into account circumstances which are relevant to the particular case in relation to which the discretion is being exercised. If such an inflexible and invariable policy is adopted both the policy and the decisions taken pursuant to it will be unlawful."[170]

Where a policy is adopted, it must be one that is based on relevant considerations and does not pursue an improper purpose.

Relevant considerations

14–26 In exercising a discretion, the decision maker must have regard only to relevant considerations. This requires that irrelevant considerations are disregarded and account is taken of any considerations that are necessarily relevant to the decision. For example, in *Ex p. Venables*,[171] the Home Secretary acted unlawfully in having regard to public petitions and other publically expressed opinions when he fixed the minimum tariff to be served by two children who had been sentenced to detention at Her Majesty's pleasure for their murder of a small boy. Those public views were irrelevant to the question to be determined by the Home Secretary, namely, the minimum period of imprisonment necessary to satisfy the twin objectives of punishment and deterrence.[172] Whilst having regard to an irrelevant consideration will likely render the decision unlawful, failure to have regard to a relevant consideration does not necessarily have the same result. There are some considerations that *are* relevant to the decision that is being taken, and *may*, but not *must*, be taken into account.[173] The failure to have regard to a relevant consideration that *may* be taken into account can only be reviewed on the ground that it was unreasonable (in the *Wednesbury* sense) not to have regard to it.[174] Irrelevant considerations as a ground of review shade into the pursuit of improper or extraneous purposes, simply because both issues have to be addressed by reference to the policy and purposes of the statute read as a whole when interpreting the exercise of statutory authority. The difficulty is that most statutes do not make explicit which considerations are "relevant" and which purposes "proper". That ultimately becomes a matter for the court. Given

---

[170] *R. v Secretary of State for the Home Department Ex p. Venables* [1998] A.C. 407 HL at 433. Although compare with *Belfast City Council v Miss Behavin' Ltd* [2007] UKHL 19; [2007] 1 W.L.R. 1420 where what was effectively a blanket ban on licenced sex shops was upheld by the House of Lords.

[171] *R. v Secretary of State for the Home Department Ex p. Venables* [1998] A.C. 407.

[172] *R. v Secretary of State for the Home Department Ex p. Venables* [1998] A.C. 407, per Lord Goff of Chieveley at 490–491; per Lord Steyn at 526: "It would be an abdication of the rule of law for a judge to take into account such matters. The same reasoning must apply to the Home Secretary when he is exercising a sentencing function. He ought to concentrate on the facts of the case and balance considerations of public interest against the dictates of justice. Like a judge the Home Secretary ought not to be guided by a disposition to consult how popular a particular decision night be . . . The power given to him requires, above all, a detached approach"; per Lord Hope of Craighead at 537.

[173] *R. v Somerset CC Ex p. Fewings* [1995] 3 All E.R. 20 CA (Civ Div).

[174] *R. (on the application of Hurst) v London Northern District Coroner* [2007] UKHL 13; [2007] 2 A.C. 189, per Lord Brown at [57], citing with approval the words of Cooke J in the New Zealand case of *CREEDNZ Inc v Governor General* [1981] 1 N.Z.L.R. 172.

the open-textured nature of the exercise, majority decisions are commonplace and the distinctions between the cases often appear rather fine.[175]

Improper purpose

A wide discretion is often conferred on public bodies and it is important that it **14–27** is exercised for the purpose it was given. Where a discretion is exercised for a purpose other than that for which it was conferred, the resultant decision is liable to be reduced. Ascertaining the purpose of the discretion is ordinarily the result of the court construing the underlying statute. The borderline can, at times, be a fine one. This category of review is best illustrated with some examples.[176] *Congreve v Home Office* concerned TV licences for colour televisions.[177] The Home Secretary announced that, from 1 April the TV licence fee would increase from £12 to £18. C had a licence that was to expire on 31 March and on 26 March he renewed it, paid the existing £12 fee and was issued with a licence until 29 February the following year. Twenty four thousand, five hundred other people renewed licences after the increase was announced but before it was effective in an attempt to save £6.[178] The Home Office wrote to these individuals demanding the extra £6 or their licence would be revoked (the Home Secretary had a general statutory power to revoke a TV licence).[179] Many paid (the "timid ones" according to Lord Denning)[180] but not C. In November of that year, the Home Office issued a final demand failing which the licence would be revoked and if a new, £18, licence was not purchased, he would be prosecuted should he use his colour TV. C raised an action for a declaration that revocation of his licence would be unlawful. The Court of Appeal accepted that the Home Secretary had a discretion to revoke a TV licence. That discretion was not, however, unlimited and could not be exercised improperly or in a manner that would be considered arbitrary. C had obtained what was then a valid licence. It was not appropriate for the Home Secretary to use the threat of revocation as a means to demand a further payment.

Highland RC v British Railways Board, the "Glasgow ghost trains" case, provides another suitable example.[181] The case concerned the Fort William to London sleeper train, a nightly service that ran in each direction. After privatisation of the railways in the 1990s[182] British Railways Board retained this service. The board had a statutory obligation to ensure that its revenues met its

---

[175] Consider, in this regard, cases raising the question of whether and to what extent a public authority may properly rely on financial or resource considerations in taking discretionary decisions: e.g. *R. v Cambridge DHA Ex p. B* [1995] 2 All E.R. 129 CA (Civ Div); *R. v Gloucestershire CC Ex p. Barry* [1997] A.C. 584 HL; *R. v Sefton MBC Ex p. Help the Aged* [1997] 4 All E.R. 532 CA (Civ Div); *R. v East Sussex CC Ex p. Tandy* [1998] A.C. 714 HL; in Scotland, *MacGregor v South Lanarkshire Council*, 2001 S.C. 502.
[176] As Craig notes, the law reports "abound with examples" of decisions being struck down on this basis and a number of further examples are given in Craig, *Administrative Law* (2012), para.19–009.
[177] *Congreve v Home Office* [1976] Q.B. 629 CA (Civ Div).
[178] A "bright idea" according to Lord Denning and one that had received considerable promotion in the press in the run up to the increase, with the Minister seemingly happy for that to happen (*Congreve v Home Office* [1976] Q.B. 629 at 652).
[179] At that point, under the Wireless Telegraphy Act 1949 s.1(4).
[180] *Congreve v Home Office* [1976] Q.B. 629 at 648.
[181] *Highland RC v British Railways Board*, 1996 S.L.T. 274.
[182] Railways Act 1993.

expenditure, i.e. that it did not run at a loss.[183] The board came under pressure from central government to make cuts in its budget and resolved to cancel the Fort William to London service. Ordinarily that would not be a problem as the board enjoyed a wide discretion to decide what services to run on the rail network. However, the Fort William to London service was the only timetabled passenger service than ran over three small areas of track in and around the Glasgow area. Discontinuing the service would therefore have the effect of triggering the statutory closure procedures.[184] That would have involved a public consultation and would have delayed the withdrawal of the service by at least three months. In attempt to avoid engaging that process, the board introduced three new services that would run across the affected parts of track once a day, all late in the evening. These were not in fact new services but were existing services re-routed. There was, by the board's own admission, little or no passenger benefit as a result of the changes.[185] Indeed, one service travelled down the affected part of track to a station, simply to reverse it back up and into Glasgow Queen Street station. The question, therefore, was whether the board had the power to exercise their discretion in such a way as to frustrate the closure provisions contained in the Railways Act 1993. The Inner House of the Court of Session was not impressed:

> "We agree with the Lord Ordinary that it is difficult to believe that Parliament could have intended that these procedures could be defeated by the provision of a service for the carriage of passengers on that line which is admitted to be of no benefit to the travelling public."[186]

The board's decision was thus unlawful.

Breach of Convention rights

14–28 In Ch.11, above we considered the provisions of the Human Rights Act 1998 in detail and, in particular, saw that as a result of s.6 of the Act it is now unlawful for a public authority to act in a manner which is incompatible with Convention rights. Any claim founded upon s.6 may be brought by way of judicial review. To the extent that such claims form another ground of "illegality" there are two points that are worthy of note. First, in relation to each of the grounds considered above the court was asking itself whether the decision maker had reached their decision in the correct manner. It was not concerned with the substance of the decision. A Convention rights challenge is often different. Whilst some rights, such as art.6, are primarily concerned with procedural guarantees, others, for example arts 8–10, are designed to afford a substantive protection. Accordingly, the court has to concern itself with the merits of the decision and not simply the procedure by which it was made. As Lord Hoffmann explained:

---

[183] Transport Act 1968 s.41(2).
[184] Railways Act 1993 ss.37–50, in particular s.37 for present purposes.
[185] *Highland RC v British Railways Board*, 1996 S.L.T. 274 at 280.
[186] *Highland RC v British Railways Board*, 1996 S.L.T. 274 at 279; see also 280 where the Lord President (Hope) also justified the conclusion on the basis of error of law: "The decision was outwith the board's powers because it was based on an error of law which lay at the root of the question which the board had to decide."

"In domestic judicial review, the court is usually concerned with whether the decision-maker reached his decision in the right way rather than whether he got what the court might think to be the right answer. But Article 9 is concerned with substance, not procedure. It confers no right to have a decision made in a particular way. What matters is the result."[187]

It follows that the converse is true: just as defective procedure is not fatal if nevertheless a Convention-compliant decision is reached, an impeccably reasoned decision is of no avail if the decision maker still reaches the wrong decision.[188] The second point to note is a related one and concerns an issue that was raised in *Belfast City Council v Miss Behavin' Ltd.*[189] There the council were criticised for not having even considered whether the decision in question was compatible with art.10 of the Convention. That ground of criticism was rejected by the House of Lords, it again being made clear that in the realm of Convention rights, what matters is the result:

"Either the refusal infringed the respondent's convention rights or it did not. If it did, no display of human rights learning by the Belfast City Council would have made the decision lawful. If it did not, it would not matter if the councillor's had never heard of art.10 or the First Protocol."[190]

PROCEDURAL IMPROPRIETY

As with review for illegality, procedural impropriety covers a variety of more **14–29** specific grounds of attack. Lord Diplock described this category thus:

"I have described the third head as 'procedural impropriety' rather than failure to observe basic rules of natural justice or failure to act with procedural fairness towards the person who will be affected by the decision. This is because susceptibility to judicial review under this head covers also failure by an administrative tribunal to observe procedural rules that are expressly laid down in the legislative instrument by which its jurisdiction is conferred, even where such failure does not involve any denial of natural justice."[191]

At one level, it may involve nothing more than ensuring that prescribed procedural standards have been observed; but the application of common law

---

[187] *R. (on the application of Begum) v Denbigh High School Governors* [2006] UKHL 15; [2007] 1 A.C. 100 at [68]; see Lord Bingham (at [29]) to similar effect: "But the focus at Strasbourg is not and has never been on whether a challenged decision or action is the product of a defective decision-making process, but on whether, in the case under consideration, the applicant's Convention rights have been violated." See also: *R. (on the application of Nasseri) v Secretary of State for the Home Department* [2009] UKHL 23; [2010] 1 A.C. 1, per Lord Hoffmann at [12]–[15].

[188] *R. (on the application of Nasseri) v Secretary of State for the Home Department* [2009] UKHL 23; [2010] 1 A.C. 1, per Lord Hoffmann at [14]; *Huang v Secretary of State for the Home Department* [2007] UKHL 11; [2007] 2 A.C. 167 at [11].

[189] *Belfast City Council v Miss Behavin' Ltd* [2007] UKHL 19; [2007] 1 W.L.R. 1420.

[190] *Belfast City Council v Miss Behavin' Ltd* [2007] UKHL 19; [2007] 1 W.L.R. 1420, per Lord Hoffmann at [13]; see also Lord Neuberger at [90].

[191] *Council of Civil Service Unions v Minister for the Civil Service* [1985] A.C. 374 at 411.

standards of natural justice and fairness goes much further than this, even to the extent of "supplying the omission of the legislature"[192] where necessary to ensure that decision makers act fairly in their dealings with the citizen.

Compliance with prescribed procedural requirements

14–30 Statutes conferring power on public authorities commonly impose procedural conditions, such as the serving of notice, a duty to consult, or a requirement to give reasons for a decision once taken. A distinction is sometimes made in this regard between mandatory and directory procedural requirements: non-compliance with the former, but not the latter, is said to be fatal to the validity of a decision. The utility of the distinction, other than as a very general guide, may be questioned. It has been held, for example, that a condition may be both mandatory and directory: mandatory as to substantial compliance, but directory as to precise compliance.[193] Equally, like many of the distinctions drawn in administrative law, it is far from self-executing. Statutes rarely make clear what the effect of non-compliance with a prescribed procedural requirement is to be, so that it falls to the courts to determine the issue. This is a question of construction to be decided by reference to the whole scheme and purpose of the measure, weighing the importance of the condition, the prejudice to private rights and interests flowing from non-compliance and the claims of the wider public interest.[194] Seen in that light, as Lord Hailsham LC remarked in *London and Clydeside Estates Ltd v Aberdeen DC*,[195] the mandatory/directory distinction presents "not so much a stark choice of alternatives as a spectrum of possibilities in which one compartment or description fades gradually into another". Again in *R. v Secretary of State for the Home Department Ex p. Jeyeanthan*,[196] Lord Woolf MR held that "it is much more important to focus on the consequences of the non-compliance" than to seek to force procedural requirements into rigid categories.

Even where a statutory procedural code is comprehensive in its coverage, the courts may be called upon to decide whether it has been properly fulfilled. A statutory duty to consult is unlikely to stipulate that the consultation be "genuine" and conducted in a manner which allows interested parties a reasonable opportunity to respond. A duty to give reasons will not insist in terms that the reasons are adequate, intelligible and properly connected to the facts. But the courts will add these glosses to the statutory language as a matter of necessary implication, to ensure that the express requirements operate effectively. A wider question is whether a statutory procedural code is exhaustive or whether the courts may supplement it with further procedural conditions. In the past, the

---

[192] *Cooper v Wandsworth Board of Works* (1863) 14 C.B. N.S. 180.

[193] *R. v Chief Constable of Merseyside Police Ex p. Calveley* [1986] Q.B. 424 CA (Civ Div).

[194] Instances where non-compliance with a prescribed requirement has been held to render a decision ultra vires include *Moss Empires Ltd v Assessor for Glasgow*, 1917 S.C. (H.L.) 1 and *London and Clydeside Estates Ltd v Aberdeen DC*, 1980 S.C. (H.L.) 1 (failure to notify a party of a right of appeal); *Perfect Swivel Ltd v City of Dundee District Licensing Board (No.1)*, 1993 S.L.T. 109 (failure to notify right of appeal to a sheriff); *Stakis Plc v Boyd*, 1989 S.L.T. 333 (commencement without sworn information of proceedings to condemn unfit food).

[195] *London and Clydeside Estates Ltd v Aberdeen DC*, 1980 S.C. (H.L.) 1.

[196] *R. v Secretary of State for the Home Department Ex p. Jeyeanthan* [2000] 1 W.L.R. 354 CA (Civ Div).

tendency was restrictive.[197] Now, as Lord Bridge held in *Lloyd v McMahon*,[198] it is clear that the courts will "not only require the procedure prescribed by the statute to be followed, but will readily imply so much and no more to be introduced by way of additional procedural safeguards as will ensure the attainment of fairness".

A striking instance of this occurred in *R. v Secretary of State for the Home Department Ex p. Fayed*.[199] The Fayed brothers had applied for naturalisation as British citizens under s.6(1) and 6(2) respectively of the British Nationality Act 1981. Without reasons, their applications were refused. Prior to giving his decision, however, the Home Secretary had indicated in a press release that the applications were regarded as especially difficult and sensitive. The brothers were not told why this was so. The Court of Appeal therefore held that, even though s.44(2) provides that the Home Secretary is "not required to assign any reason for the grant or refusal of any application", the Home Secretary was nonetheless obliged to act fairly in arriving at his decision. He was therefore required to give the applicants sufficient information as to the nature of his concern so that they would be able to make representations. The refusal was quashed.

NATURAL JUSTICE

Introduction

The twin principles of natural justice—*nemo iudex in sua causa* and *audi alteram* **14–31** *partem*—state, first, that no one may be a judge of their own cause (the rule against bias) and, secondly, that everyone has the right to be fairly heard. Both principles are derived from and rooted in judicial decision making processes, but have been extended by the courts in the exercise of their supervisory jurisdiction to the proceedings of inferior tribunals, whether statutory or domestic, and to more strictly administrative decision making procedures.[200] Judicial and administrative decision making processes do, however, differ considerably. To that extent, subjecting administrative officials to standards of procedural fairness crafted for a judicial context may not always be appropriate, for if the right to a fair hearing in an administrative setting meant what it means in a judicial setting, the administrative process would grind to a halt. On the other hand, it is recognised that administrative decisions may affect individuals' rights and interests as much as, if not more than, judicial decisions in the modern administrative state. For that reason, and also because intervention on procedural grounds is perceived as less likely to intrude upon the substance and merits of administrative decisions, the most vigorous development of administrative law has occurred in the context of natural justice.

---

[197] See, e.g. *Wiseman v Borneman* [1971] A.C. 297 HL, in which Lord Reid held that the courts could only properly extend statutory procedures where "it is clear that the statutory procedure is insufficient to achieve justice and to require additional steps would not frustrate the apparent purpose of the legislation".

[198] *Lloyd v McMahon* [1987] A.C. 625 HL at 703.

[199] *R. v Secretary of State for the Home Department Ex p. Fayed* [1998] 1 W.L.R. 763 CA (Civ Div).

[200] The scope for their application to legislative decision making processes appears, however, to be limited: see, e.g. *Bates v Lord Hailsham of St Marylebone* [1972] 1 W.L.R. 1373 ChD.

Rule against bias

14-32 We have already examined the application of this rule to judges and judicial decision makers in the context of judicial independence and impartiality in Ch.8, above, to which reference is made. There it was seen that where a decision maker has a direct pecuniary or proprietary interest in the outcome of proceedings before them, the consequence is automatic disqualification.[201] The categories of automatic disqualification were extended by the House of Lords in *R. v Bow Street Metropolitan Stipendiary Magistrate Ex p. Pinochet Ugarte (No.2)*, to include interest in the sense of the promotion of a cause in which the judge is involved together with one of the parties.[202] In either case, the maxim that justice must not only be done but must manifestly and undoubtedly be seen to be done[203] applies with its full force: disqualification is automatic and nothing more than the fact of the interest requires to be proved. If the disqualified judge proceeds nonetheless to decide, their decision cannot stand.[204] The rule against bias also comes into play, even though the judge is not financially interested in the outcome or otherwise acting as a judge of their own cause, where in some other sense their conduct or behaviour gives rise to a doubt about their impartiality. Here the test is whether the circumstances were such as to give a fair-minded and informed observer a reasonable apprehension of partiality or bias on the judge's part.[205]

14-33   As ever, the test can be stated quite easily but its application in practice is another thing. A fixed list of circumstances in which apparent bias will be found is probably impossible to prescribe as the question will always turn on the facts of the particular case. In *Locabail (UK) Ltd v Bayfield Properties Ltd* the Court of Appeal (which comprised Lord Bingham CJ, Lord Woolf MR and Sir Richard Scott VC) set out circumstances which they could not conceive of founding a valid objection. These included: religion, ethnic or national origin, gender, age, class, means or sexual orientation.[206] The court also set out circumstances which would ordinarily not found a valid objection: the social, educational, service or employment background of the judge (or their family), previous political associations, extra-curricular utterances or previous instructions to act for or against any party, solicitor or advocate instructed in the case now before the judge.[207] The case law offers some examples of how the rule has been applied, for example the sheriff who criticised striking miners could not then preside over the summary trial of one such miner[208] or the sheriff who invited one of the parties, who was the local Member of Parliament, into chambers so they could be formally introduced failed the test of apparent bias[209] and when a judge described the European Convention on Human Rights as "a field day for crackpots, a pain

---

[201] *Dimes v Proprietors of the Grand Junction Canal* (1852) 3 H.L. Cas. 759; *Wildridge v Anderson* (1897) 25 R. (J.) 27, per Lord Moncreiff at 34.

[202] *R. v Bow Street Metropolitan Stipendiary Magistrate Ex p. Pinochet Ugarte (No.2)* [2000] 1 A.C. 119.

[203] *R. v Sussex Justices Ex p. McCarthy* [1924] 1 K.B. 256 KBD, per Lord Hewart CJ at 262.

[204] Even where the disqualified judge sits as a member of a panel, their participation will suffice to vitiate the decision of the panel as a whole: see *Hoekstra (Lieuwe) v HM Advocate (No.2)*, 2000 J.C. 391 and *Davidson v Scottish Ministers (No.2)* [2004] UKHL 34; 2005 1 S.C. (H.L.) 7.

[205] *Porter v Magill* [2001] UKHL 67; [2002] 2 A.C. 357, per Lord Hope at [103].

[206] *Locabail (UK) Ltd v Bayfield Properties Ltd* [2000] Q.B. 451 CA (Civ Div) at [25].

[207] *Locabail (UK) Ltd v Bayfield Properties Ltd* [2000] Q.B. 451 at [25].

[208] *Bradford v MacLeod*, 1986 S.L.T. 244.

[209] *Doherty v McGlennan*, 1997 S.L.T. 444.

in the neck of judges and legislators and a goldmine for lawyers" in a national newspaper an appeal that he had heard and which turned on Convention law arguments had to be reheard by a fresh bench.[210] But in any given case, the question comes down to whether or not the "fair-minded and informed observer" would have a "reasonable apprehension" of bias on the part of the decision maker. *Locabail* gives us guidance on what does, and does not, found a "reasonable apprehension" but what are the characteristics of the "fair-minded and informed" observer?

The "fair-minded and informed" observer is not the same as the judge who is considering the question: there would have been no need to create this fictitious character if they were. They have been said to be one that pays attention to the woods, not the trees and who is not to be attributed with a mastery of the minutiae[211] but is someone who is "neither complacent nor unduly sensitive or suspicious".[212] In *Helow v Secretary of State for the Home Department*,[213] Lord Hope explained that the characteristic that they be "fair-minded" required that they be the sort of person that

> "always reserves judgment on every point until she has seen and fully understood both sides of the argument. She is not unduly sensitive or suspicious ... But she is not complacent either. She knows that fairness requires that a judge must be, and must be seen to be, unbiased. She knows that judges, like anybody else, have their weaknesses. She will not shrink from the conclusion, if it can be justified objectively, that things that they have said or done or associations that they have formed may make it difficult for them to judge the case before them impartially".[214]

That they be "informed" requires

> "that before she takes a balanced approach to any information she is given, she will take the trouble to inform herself on all matters that are relevant. She is the sort of person who takes the trouble to read the text of an article as well as the headlines. She is able to put whatever she has read or seen into its overall social, political or geographical context. She is fair minded, so she will appreciate that the context forms an important part of the material which she must consider before passing judgment".[215]

Yet even with that guidance, difficulties arise. Is there a single, universal fair-minded and informed observer so that the fair-minded and informed observer on the London Underground will be of the same mind as the fair-minded and informed observer on the Edinburgh tram or, as the case may be, the Queen Market Square in Belize? That question divided the Privy Council in *Belize Bank*

[210] *Hoeskstra v HM Advocate (No.2)*, 2000 J.C. 391; this case is also an example of an extra-judicial utterance founding recusal.
[211] *Davidson v Scottish Ministers (No.2)* [2004] UKHL 34; 2005 1 S.C. (H.L.) 7, per Lord Bingham at [8].
[212] *Johnson v Johnson* (2000) 201 C.L.R. 488, per Kirby J at [53], cited with approval in *Lawal v Northern Spirit Ltd* [2003] UKHL 35; [2004] 1 All E.R. 187, per Lord Steyn at [14].
[213] *Helow v Secretary of State for the Home Department* [2008] UKHL 62; 2009 S.C. (H.L.) 1.
[214] *Helow v Secretary of State for the Home Department* [2008] UKHL 62; 2009 S.C. (H.L.) 1 at [2].
[215] *Helow v Secretary of State for the Home Department* [2008] UKHL 62; 2009 S.C. (H.L.) 1 at [3].

Ltd v Attorney General of Belize.[216] That case illustrates another difficulty in
applying the test: how much knowledge is to be attributed to this "informed"
observer? We know from Lord Hope in *Helow* that they will inform themselves
of what is relevant. This will include all facts that are capable of being known by
members of the public[217] but not the same amount of information as another
member of the tribunal under attack.[218] In *Belize Bank* the majority attributed to
the reasonably informed observer a fairly detailed knowledge of how a senior
civil servant would have gone about recommending members of a commission to
the responsible Minister[219] and they ended up being endowed with much more
knowledge than the ordinary Belizean would have had yet the purpose of the
exercise was to ensure the ordinary Belizean would have faith in the tribunal. So
the risks are clear and the court has to take care to ensure that the "fair-minded
and informed observer" is not carved too much in the image of the court
itself.

These rules have been applied readily to the decisions of disciplinary
bodies,[220] administrative tribunals[221] and other bodies performing judicial and
quasi-judicial functions,[222] but at one time it appeared that different criteria
applied in relation to administrative authorities. In some cases, for example, it
was held that the test for bias could not apply to policy-based decisions, such as
those of planning authorities, since these were "radically different" from the
decisions of tribunals, which arrive at objective decisions according to rules.[223]
However, as Sedley J pointed out in *R. v Secretary of State for the Environment
Ex p. Kirkstall Valley Campaign Ltd,*[224] this kind of pigeonholing—distinguishing between administrative and judicial functions for the purposes of determining
the application of the rules of natural justice—was supposedly done to death by
the House of Lords in *Ridge v Baldwin.*[225] In *Kirkstall Valley,* an urban
development corporation as local planning authority had granted outline planning
permission for a retail development on part of a rugby club's property. The
applicant complained that this decision was vitiated by the participation of three
members and an officer of the corporation, each of whom had disqualifying

---

[216] *Belize Bank Ltd v Attorney General of Belize* [2011] UKPC 36, comparing Lord Dyson at
[75]–[76] and Lord Brown at [113].
[217] *Gillies v Secretary of State for Work and Pensions* [2006] UKHL 2; 2006 S.C. (H.L.) 71, per Lord
Hope at [17].
[218] *Gillies v Secretary of State for Work and Pensions* [2006] UKHL 2; 2006 S.C. (H.L.) 71, per Lady
Hale at [39].
[219] *Belize Bank Ltd v Attorney General of Belize* [2011] UKPC 36, per Lord Kerr at [42]; Lord Brown
dissented.
[220] *Palmer v Inverness Hospitals Board of Management,* 1963 S.C. 311.
[221] *Barrs v British Wool Marketing Board,* 1957 S.C. 72.
[222] *Brown v Executive Committee of the Edinburgh District Labour Party,* 1995 S.L.T. 985.
[223] *R. v Amber Valley DC Ex p. Jackson* [1985] 1 W.L.R. 298 QBD; *R. v St Edmundsbury BC Ex p.
Investors in Industry Commercial Properties Ltd* [1985] 1 W.L.R. 1168 DC. In both of these
cases, local planning authorities had entered into contracts with developers for the exploitation of
land owned by the authorities, and had undertaken to do their best to procure planning permission
(to be granted by themselves). In *Investors in Industry,* Stocker LJ considered that the
disapplication of the rule against bias in such circumstances was justified because, were it
otherwise, "an administrative impasse would occur in any case where a planning authority had,
quite properly, become involved in some development within its area". See to similar effect the
licensing decisions in *R. v Reading BC Ex p. Quietlynn Ltd* (1987) 85 L.G.R. 387 and *R. v
Chesterfield BC Ex p. Darker Enterprises Ltd* [1992] C.O.D. 465.
[224] *R. v Secretary of State for the Environment Ex p. Kirkstall Valley Campaign Ltd* [1996] 3 All E.R.
304 QBD.
[225] *Ridge v Baldwin* [1964] A.C. 40.

pecuniary or personal interests in the development such as to constitute a real danger of bias. Although the application failed on the merits, Sedley J accepted the applicant's argument that the test for bias was a uniform test applicable to all bodies, judicial or administrative, which are subject to control by judicial review. His Lordship explained the *Investors in Industry* line of cases[226] as being concerned not with bias but with a different principle:

> "[The] decision of a body, albeit composed of disinterested individuals, will be struck down if its outcome has been predetermined whether by the adoption of an inflexible policy or by the effective surrender of the body's independent judgment."[227]

It may therefore be said that the distinction between judicial and administrative functions no longer determines the application of the rule against bias, although it may continue to influence the rigour with which the rule is applied in any particular case. As Sedley J observed[228]:

> "[What] will differ from case to case is the significance of the interest and its degree of proximity or remoteness to the issue to be decided and whether, if it is not so insignificant or remote as to be discounted, the disqualified member has violated his disqualification by participating in the decision."

Planning and licensing cases illustrate a particular problem with the application **14–34** of the rule against bias to administrative decisions. What might be described as "structural bias" is often built into particular statutory schemes, as where a Minister or local authority is charged with responsibility both for promoting development or adopting policies and for determining appeals.[229] Viewed from the perspective of the right to a fair hearing in the determination of civil rights and obligations under art.6 of the Convention, none of this is necessarily objectionable, provided the decision maker is subject to subsequent judicial control by a court or tribunal having sufficiently full jurisdiction to secure compliance with art.6.[230] In practice, such decisions are generally subject, if not to judicial review, then to a statutory right of appeal on a point of law to the Court of Session.[231] Following the entry into force of the Human Rights Act 1998, it was held north and south of the border that neither judicial review nor a statutory appeal on a point of law was sufficient to "cure" the structural bias there complained of.[232] *R. (on the application of Alconbury Developments Ltd) v Secretary of State for the Environment, Transport and the Regions* was appealed to the House of Lords, where it was held that the availability of judicial review and/or statutory appeal on a point of law was sufficient to ensure compliance with

---

[226] Which were described as "plainly correct".

[227] *R. v Secretary of State for the Environment Ex p. Kirkstall Valley Campaign Ltd* [1996] 3 All E.R. 304 at 321.

[228] *R. v Secretary of State for the Environment Ex p. Kirkstall Valley Campaign Ltd* [1996] 3 All E.R. 304 at 325.

[229] See, e.g. *Franklin v Minister of Town and Country Planning* [1948] A.C. 87; *City of Glasgow DC v Secretary of State for Scotland (No.1)*, 1993 S.L.T. 198.

[230] *Bryan v United Kingdom* (1995) 21 E.H.R.R. 342. See para.14–22.

[231] See, e.g. Town and Country Planning (Scotland) Act 1997 s.58.

[232] *County Properties Ltd v The Scottish Ministers*, 2000 S.L.T. 965; *R. (on the application of Alconbury Developments Ltd) v Secretary of State for the Environment, Transport and the Regions* [2001] UKHL 23; [2002] 2 AC 295.

Public Law

art.6, with the consequence that the relevant statutory provisions were compatible with the Convention.[233] It should, however, be noted that this will not invariably be the case. Thus in *Kingsley v United Kingdom*,[234] the European Court held that judicial review proceedings were insufficient to cure the possibility of bias on the part of the Gaming Board of Great Britain in deciding to revoke the applicant's certificate of approval, because all that the court on review could do was quash the revocation and order the decision to be taken afresh by a differently constituted panel. In some circumstances, therefore, only a full rehearing by an appellate body will satisfy the requirements of art.6.

Right to a fair hearing

14–35 In *Board of Education v Rice*,[235] Lord Loreburn remarked that the duty to afford a fair hearing is "a duty lying upon anyone who decides anything". This was in keeping with older authorities,[236] which insisted on the observance of fair procedures by public authorities and private or domestic bodies alike.[237] But in the first half of the twentieth century, during what has been termed the "long sleep" of public law,[238] there was a tendency, perhaps most marked in the English courts,[239] to restrict the application of principles of natural justice to circumstances in which the decision maker acted judicially or the decision affected actual legal rights or privileges.[240] It is for this reason that the decision of the House of Lords in *Ridge v Baldwin*[241] is so often credited with reawakening public law and establishing the foundations of modern administrative jurisprudence. There, a chief constable who had lately been acquitted of criminal charges was dismissed from office by the local watch committee. He was not invited to attend the committee's meeting but later learned of the resolutions adopted at the meeting, upon which the committee had based their decision. He sought a declaration that the purported termination of his appointment was illegal, ultra vires and void as being in breach of natural justice. By a majority, the House of Lords held that an official such as the chief constable, who was dismissible only for cause, was entitled to notice of the charge against him and to an opportunity to be heard before being dismissed, and quashed the decision of the committee. In doing so, the majority based themselves firmly on the nineteenth century case law and disapproved the impediments to the application of natural justice that had been imported by the more recent decisions.

---

[233] *R. (on the application of Alconbury Developments Ltd) v Secretary of State for the Environment, Transport and the Regions* [2001] UKHL 23; [2003] 2 A.C. 295. Following this decision, the Inner House reversed the first instance decision of Lord Macfadyen in *County Properties*: see *County Properties Ltd v Scottish Ministers*, 2002 S.C. 79.

[234] *Kingsley v United Kingdom* (2001) 33 E.H.R.R. 13.

[235] *Board of Education v Rice* [1911] A.C. 179 HL at 182.

[236] Perhaps most notably *Cooper v Wandsworth Board of Works* (1863) 14 C.B. N.S. 180.

[237] In the latter case, often on the basis of implied terms: see, e.g. *Enderby Town Football Club v Football Association* [1971] Ch. 591.

[238] Stephen Sedley, "The Sound of Silence: Constitutional Law without a Constitution" (1994) 110 L.Q.R. 270.

[239] cf. Bradley and Himsworth, "Administrative Law" in *Stair Memorial Encyclopaedia* (1995), para.10.

[240] See, e.g. *Local Government Board v Arlidge* [1915] A.C. 120; *Franklin v Minister of Town and Country Planning* [1948] A.C. 87; *Nakkuda Ali v Jayaratne* [1951] A.C. 66 PC (Ceylon).

[241] *Ridge v Baldwin* [1964] A.C. 40.

There are good reasons to insist on a fair hearing. Not only is a fair hearing liable to produce better results but it is likely to produce an outcome that is more readily accepted by those it affects. "Justice is", Lord Reed explained in *R. (on the application of Osborn) v Parole Board* "intuitively understood to require a procedure which pays due respect to persons whose rights are significantly affected by decisions taken in the exercise of administrative or judicial functions".[242] That requires that a person so affected, provided they have something relevant to contribute, be entitled to participate in the decision making process.

However, the right to a fair hearing cannot mean the same thing in all contexts **14–36** and it is impossible to lay down rules of universal application. In some situations, as was implicitly acknowledged in *Re HK (An Infant)*[243] by the adoption of the terminology of "fairness" or "a duty to act fairly", it may not involve a hearing as such at all. At its fullest, as seen in the proceedings of the ordinary courts, the right to a fair hearing requires notice of the case one has to answer, an oral hearing in public, conducted in accordance with the rules of evidence, legal representation, the right to cross-examine, a reasoned decision, and a right of appeal.[244] It is with a fair and open hearing that justice and the rule of law are best secured.[245] But the right to a fair hearing does not equate to the right to an oral hearing. An oral hearing is required where it is necessary to secure a fair procedure and that will be determined by all the circumstances of the case.[246] Plainly, an oral hearing is not appropriate in the context of much administrative decision making. Thus while the application of the duty to act fairly does not turn

---

[242] *R. (on the application of Osborn) v Parole Board* [2013] UKSC 61; [2014] A.C. 1115 at [68]. See also *Secretary of State for the Home Department v AF (No.3)* [2009] UKHL 28; [2010] 2 A.C. 269, per Lord Phillips at [63]: " . . . feelings of resentment that will be aroused if a party to legal proceedings is placed in a position where it is impossible for him to influence the result".

[243] *Re HK (An Infant)* [1967] 2 Q.B. 617 QBD.

[244] See *Al-Rawi v Security Service* [2011] UKSC 34; [2012] 1 A.C. 531, in particular Lord Dyson at [10]–[15] where the Supreme Court held that only Parliament could abrogate the principles of open and natural justice so the court had no inherent power to authorise a closed material procedure (i.e. where evidence was presented to the court but withheld from one of the parties): "The open justice principle is not a mere procedural rule. It is a fundamental common law principle" (at [11]). That strong position must now be read subject to what was said (and done) by the Supreme Court in *Bank Mellat v HM Treasury (No.2)* [2013] UKSC 38; [2014] A.C. 700 where it was held that the Supreme Court had the implicit authority to hold a closed hearing where the tribunal against whom the appeal was taken had express statutory authority to hold closed hearings. On that question, the dissents of Lords Hope, Kerr and Reed are powerful (and compelling). See H.J. Hooper, "Crossing the Rubicon: *Bank Mellat v Her Majesty's Treasury (No.1)*" [2014] P.L. 171.

[245] "Open justice. The words express a principle at the heart of our system of justice and vital to the rule of law. The rule of law is a fine concept but fine words butter no parsnips. How is the rule of law itself to be policed? It is an age old question. *Quis custodiet ipsos custodes*—who will guard the guards themselves? In a democracy, where power depends on the consent of the people governed, the answer must lie in the transparency of the legal process. Open justice lets in the light and allows the public to scrutinise the workings of the law, for better or for worse. Jeremy Bentham said in a well known passage quoted by Lord Shaw of Dunfermline in *Scott v Scott* [1913] AC 417, 477: 'Publicity is the very soul of justice. It is the keenest spur to exertion and the surest of all guards against improbity. It keeps the judge himself while trying under trial' ": *R. (on the application of Guardian News and Media Ltd) v City of Westminster Magistrates' Court* [2012] EWCA Civ 420; [2013] Q.B. 618, per Toulson LJ at [1].

[246] Where a decision is challenged on the basis there ought to have been an oral hearing, it is for the court to determine whether, in the circumstances, a fair procedure was followed and not whether the decision to hold an oral hearing was "reasonable" (in the *Wednesbury* sense): *R. (on the application of Osborn) v Parole Board* [2013] UKSC 61; [2014] A.C. 1115, per Lord Reed at [65].

on whether the decision maker acted judicially or otherwise, the content of the duty will depend on "the character of the decision making body, the kind of decision it has to make and the statutory or other framework in which it operates".[247]

It follows, then, that functional distinctions are not deprived of all vitality: the more nearly "judicial" a decision making process, then, all other things being equal, the stricter will be the demands for fairness.[248] Clearly, however, this is not the only factor material to determining the scope of the duty to act fairly. In so far as it pertained to the threatened destruction of the pursuer's property, *Errington v Wilson*[249] may be said to illustrate also the relevance of the nature of the right or interest affected by the decision under attack.[250] Another factor relates to the stage that a given decision making process has reached. Often, a decision is arrived at only on completion of a number of procedural steps, such as a preliminary investigation or a public inquiry or consultation. In some cases, statutory procedural codes applicable to the preliminary stages of a process have been held to be exhaustive of the duty to act fairly.[251] On the other hand, it was held in *Re Pergamon Press Ltd*[252] that a Department of Trade and Industry inspector conducting an inquiry into a company's affairs under the Companies Acts was obliged, before publishing a highly critical report, to communicate the gist of their findings to the persons concerned and accord them an opportunity to respond. But that was the extent of the super-added duty to act fairly.[253] The extent to which the duty to act fairly applies to preliminary or interim stages of a decision making process will therefore depend on a combination of factors: the terms of the statutory procedural code itself, the impact of the preliminary inquiry upon the individual, the proximity of the challenged decision to the final outcome, and, perhaps also, the nature of the inquiry undertaken. The more "investigative" an inquiry, the less likely are the courts to impose additional procedural safeguards over and above those prescribed by Parliament, in order to avoid hindering what may already be a difficult and delicate task.

Lastly, the duty to act fairly may be limited, even excluded, in situations where it would normally otherwise apply by reference to overriding public interests. A clear instance of this is *Council of Civil Service Unions v Minister for the Civil Service*,[254] where the House of Lords held that the applicants' legitimate expectation of consultation prior to changes being made to the terms and conditions of staff at Government Communications Headquarters was defeated by the interests of national security. Again in *R. v Gaming Board for Great Britain Ex p. Benaim*,[255] the Court of Appeal held that the board was "under a

---

[247] *Lloyd v McMahon* [1987] A.C. 625, per Lord Bridge at 702.
[248] See, e.g. *Errington v Wilson*, 1995 S.L.T. 1193.
[249] *Errington v Wilson*, 1995 S.L.T. 1193.
[250] See also *McInnes v Onslow-Fane* [1978] 1 W.L.R. 1520 ChD, where Sir Robert Megarry VC distinguished between the levels of procedural protection to which an initial applicant for a benefit, an applicant for renewal of a benefit and the holder of a subsisting benefit, which benefit is revoked, would be entitled.
[251] *Wiseman v Borneman* [1971] A.C. 297; *Pearlberg v Varty* [1972] 1 W.L.R. 534 HL; *Bushell v Secretary of State for the Environment* [1981] A.C. 75 HL.
[252] *Re Pergamon Press Ltd* [1971] Ch. 388 CA (Civ Div).
[253] In *Maxwell v Department of Trade and Industry* [1974] Q.B. 523 CA (Civ Div), it was held that fairness did not oblige the inspector to allow cross-examination of witnesses by the subject of a report.
[254] *Council of Civil Service Unions v Minister for the Civil Service* [1985] A.C. 374.
[255] *R. v Gaming Board for Great Britain Ex p. Benaim* [1970] 2 All E.R. 528 CA (Civ Div).

duty to act fairly, but not very fairly" in rejecting applications for gaming licences on the basis of undisclosed information passed to them by the police. The public interest in maintaining the confidentiality of information leading to the detection of crime or wrongdoing outweighed the applicants' claim to be entitled to know the charges against them and to make representations in their own defence.[256] That decision must now be regarded as wrong, or at least unacceptable under art.6 of the European Convention (which applies to the determination of civil rights and obligations as well as criminal proceedings). The Strasbourg Court has held, and the Supreme Court has (reluctantly) accepted, that where a decision is based "solely or to a decisive degree" on material that is withheld from one party, the requirements of a fair hearing can *never* be satisfied.[257]

Duty to give reasons[258]

Statutes often require that decisions made under them should be supported by reasons. But it has been long asserted that, statute apart, there is no general common law duty to provide reasoned decisions.[259] However, developments in this area have been such that the sum of the exceptions to the general principle probably outweighs the principle itself.[260]

14–37

There are a number of rationales for requiring that reasons be provided. Reasons may be required where the effect of their absence is to frustrate a right of appeal or review.[261] Alternatively, where all the facts and evidence before the court point in favour of a decision other than that which was actually taken, the court may be entitled to infer, in the absence of reasons to the contrary, that the decision lacks a rational basis.[262] As Lord Keith observed in *R. v Secretary of State for Trade and Industry Ex p. Lonrho Plc*:

> " ... if all other known facts and circumstances appear to point over-whelmingly in favour off a different decision, the decision-maker who has given no reasons cannot complain if the court draws the inference that he had no rational reasons for his decision."[263]

---

[256] This should be taken as illustrative only. It may be, now, that in such circumstances the courts would hold the applicants entitled at least to know the gist of what had been said against them, bearing in mind the possibility that the information might be false or malicious: *R. v Secretary of State for the Home Department Ex p. Fayed* [1998] 1 W.L.R. 763 and *Kingsley v United Kingdom* (2002) 33 E.H.R.R. 13.

[257] *A v United Kingdom* (2009) 49 E.H.R.R. 79 Grand Chamber; *Secretary of State for the Home Department v AF (No.3)* [2009] UKHL 28; [2010] 2 A.C. 269. The problem is most acute in relation to counter-terrorism and national security where (it is said) disclosing some evidence to the accused will compromise the work of the security services. This problem is considered in Ch.13, above in more detail. See also J. Jackson, "Justice, security and the right to a fair trial: is the use of secret evidence ever fair?" [2013] P.L. 720; A. Kavanagh, "Special Advocates, Control Orders and the Right to a Fair Trial" (2010) 73(5) M.L.R. 836.

[258] See *De Smith's Judicial Review* (2013) paras 7–085 to 7–116; Craig, *Administrative Law* (2012) paras 12–028 to 12–037.

[259] *Stefan v General Medical Council* [1999] 1 W.L.R. 1293 PC, per Lord Clyde at 1300.

[260] M. Elliott, "Has the Common Law Duty to Give Reasons Come of Age Yet?" [2011] P.L. 56.

[261] *Minister of National Revenue v Wrights Canadian Ropes Ltd* [1947] A.C. 109 PC (Canada) (appeal); *R. v Secretary of State for the Home Department Ex p. Dannenberg* [1984] Q.B. 766 CA (Civ Div) (review); *Stefan v General Medical Council* [1999] 1 W.L.R. 1293.

[262] *Padfield v Minister of Agriculture, Fisheries and Food* [1968] A.C. 997.

[263] *R. v Secretary of State for Trade and Industry Ex p. Lonrho Plc* [1989] 1 W.L.R. 525 at 539–540.

In *R. v Civil Service Appeal Board Ex p. Cunningham*,[264] the Court of Appeal relied in part on this reasoning. There, the applicant sought judicial review of the board's decision to award him, by way of compensation for unfair dismissal, a sum some two-thirds less than an industrial tribunal would have awarded. But Lord Donaldson MR went further, stating that a "judicialised" tribunal is bound to provide outline reasons for its decisions, sufficient to disclose the matters to which it directed its mind, and that failure to do so is a breach of natural justice. In *R. v Secretary of State for the Home Department Ex p. Doody*,[265] the House of Lords indicated that the very importance of a decision to the individual affected by it may be such that, in fairness and without more, reasons should be provided for the decision. This serves not some instrumental end (although instrumental ends, such as ensuring that the decision maker properly and conscientiously addresses their mind to the issues to be decided, are important) but the more abstract, non-instrumental goal of ensuring that administrators treat those subject to their decisions with the appropriate degree of respect. Thus the more important or fundamental the nature of the individual's right or interest in question, the more likely it is that the discipline of fairness will require reasons to be given. Because, ultimately, if it is not clear why one person has lost or has had their right interfered with or restricted, justice will not have been done.[266]

It is not always appropriate, however, that the courts should impose this obligation on public authorities. In *R. v Higher Education Funding Council Ex p. Institute of Dental Surgery*,[267] the institute challenged the council's assessment of its research (upon which the level of government funding depended) because it was unsupported by reasons. Sedley J held that the council was not required to recite the reasons for its decision as it depended on an unquantifiable exercise of "pure academic judgment". The courts are also conscious of the resource implications of duties to give reasons, and concede that the interests of the complainant must be balanced against administrative efficiency and convenience.[268] It is generally said that, where reasons are required, they must be "proper, adequate and intelligible"[269] in the circumstances of the particular case. If reasons are provided which disclose a failing on the part of the decision maker (for example, having had regard to an irrelevant consideration) it is no defence to say that there was no duty to give reasons.[270]

---

[264] *R. v Civil Service Appeal Board Ex p. Cunningham* [1992] I.C.R. 817 CA (Civ Div).
[265] *R. v Secretary of State for the Home Department Ex p. Doody* [1994] 1 A.C. 531 HL.
[266] *English v Emery Reimbold & Strick Ltd* [2002] 1 W.L.R. 2409, Lord Phillips MR at [16].
[267] *R. v Higher Education Funding Council Ex p. Institute of Dental Surgery* [1994] 1 W.L.R. 242 DC.
[268] A like balance is recognised in the jurisprudence of the European Court of Human Rights. In *Helle v Finland* (1997) 26 E.H.R.R. 159, the court held that "while Article 6(1) obliges the courts to give reasons for their judgments, it cannot be understood as requiring a detailed answer to every argument adduced by a litigant. The extent to which the duty to give reasons applies may vary according to the nature of the decision at issue. It is moreover necessary to take into account, inter alia, the diversity of the submissions that a litigant may bring before the courts and the differences existing in the Contracting States with regard to statutory provisions, customary rules, legal opinion and the presentation and drafting of judgments. That is why the question whether a court has failed to fulfil the obligation to state reasons, deriving from Article 6 of the Convention, can only be determined in the light of the circumstances of the case".
[269] *Re Poyser and Mills Arbitration* [1964] 2 Q.B. 467 QBD.
[270] *Rooney v Strathclyde Joint Police Board* [2008] CSIH 54; 2009 S.C. 73, per Lord Reed at [32].

Unfairness as an abuse of power

It is not always possible to categorise unfairness on the part of a public authority **14–38**
as bias, or a failure to give a hearing, or a breach of a legitimate expectation, or
any other specific head of procedural impropriety. Nevertheless, the unfairness
complained of may be of such a degree as to call for redress. In *R. v Inland
Revenue Commissioners Ex p. Preston*, the House of Lords held that such would
be appropriate where unfairness in the exercise of statutory powers amounted to
an excess or abuse of power.[271] The principle recognised in *Preston* was applied
by the Court of Appeal in *R. v Inland Revenue Commissioners Ex p. Unilever
Plc*.[272] There, departing from a well-established practice, the Revenue relied on
a statutory time limit as defeating claims for loss relief. The Court of Appeal
accepted that there had been no such "clear, unambiguous and unqualified
representation"[273] as to generate a legitimate expectation on Unilever's part that
the former practice would continue to be followed. Even so, Sir Thomas
Bingham MR noted that the categories of unfairness were not closed and that, in
all the circumstances "to reject Unilever's claims in reliance on the time limit,
without clear and general advance notice, [was] so unfair as to amount to an
abuse of power by the Revenue". Again in *R. v National Lottery Commission Ex
p. Camelot Group Plc*,[274] Richards J quashed the decision of the commission to
reject two rival bids to run the national lottery but to reopen the bidding process
to one of the bidders. It was accepted that the enabling legislation accorded a
wide discretion to the commission as to how it would perform its functions,
but,

> "such a marked lack of even-handedness between the rival bidders calls for
> the most compelling justification, which I cannot find in the reasons
> advanced by the Commission in support of its decision . . . The Commis-
> sion's decision to negotiate exclusively with The People's Lottery was, in
> all the circumstances, so unfair as to amount to an abuse of power."

Legitimate expectations[275]

The principle of legitimate expectation has developed to "protect persons from **14–39**
gross unfairness or abuse of power by a public authority".[276] It first appeared in
relation to issues of procedural fairness: where a person had a legitimate
expectation that a public body would take a decision in a particular way.[277] For
example, in *Attorney General of Hong Kong v Ng Yuen Shiu* where the Hong
Kong authorities had announced that illegal immigrants would be interviewed
and each case determined on its merits. Thus, where the authorities purported to
expel the applicant, who had entered Hong Kong illegally from Macau some
years previously, the assurance given that all illegal immigrants would be

---

[271] *R. v Inland Revenue Commissioners Ex p. Preston* [1985] A.C. 835, per Lord Scarman at 851; per
Lord Templeman at 866–867.
[272] *R. v Inland Revenue Commissioners Ex p. Unilever Plc* [1996] S.T.C. 681 CA (Civ Div).
[273] As required by the decision of the Court of Appeal in *R. v Inland Revenue Commissioners Ex p.
MFK Underwriting Agents Ltd* [1990] 1 W.L.R. 1545 QBD.
[274] *R. v National Lottery Commission Ex p. Camelot Group Plc* [2001] E.M.L.R. 3 QBD.
[275] See *De Smith's Judicial Review* (2013) Ch.12; Craig, *Administrative Law* (2012), Ch.22.
[276] *Rainbow Insurance Co Ltd v Financial Services Commission* [2015] UKPC 15, per Lord Hodge
at [51].
[277] The judgment of Lord Denning in *Schmidt v Secretary of State for Home Affairs* [1969] 2 Ch. 149
CA (Civ Div) is believed to be the first reference to the idea of legitimate expectations.

interviewed had given rise to a legitimate expectation that should be enforced.[278] The Board described the principle thus: " . . . that a public authority is bound by its undertakings as to the procedure it will follow, provided they do not conflict with its duty."[279] In that case it was an express statement by the public body that had given rise to the legitimate expectation. Such an expectation can also be implied from a public body's past practice or conduct. For example, where the Inland Revenue consistently accepted claims for a tax refund, despite the claim being submitted after the time limit, the taxpayer had a legitimate expectation that its claim would not be rejected, without good reason, as out of time.[280] That case illustrates another aspect of what can be called procedural legitimate expectations. The consistent practice of accepting such claims late gave rise to a legitimate expectation that the Inland Revenue would not change that policy abruptly and without warning.[281] In such cases it is not the change in policy itself that frustrates a legitimate expectation but the process by which that change was made.

Implicit in what we have said is that the expectation is legitimate, " . . . nobody can have a legitimate expectation that he will be entitled to an ultra vires relaxation of a statutory requirement".[282] That rule is long established.[283] Where the expectation is said to be based upon an express promise or statement, the representation must be "clear, unambiguous and devoid of relevant qualification".[284] Whether a representation meets that test is assessed by asking how, on a fair reading of the promise, it would have been reasonably understood by those to whom it was made.[285] Other factors are relevant in determining whether a *legitimate* expectation has arisen. For example, the source of the representation is important. The more specific the representation, the easier it will be to establish a legitimate expectation.[286] A representation contained in a letter specifically addressed to the applicant will found a stronger case than one based on a representation in a general circular addressed to a large group. The knowledge of the applicant is also relevant: could they have foreseen that the public body would be likely to change its policy or decision? If so, a legitimate expectation

---

[278] *Attorney General of Hong Kong v Ng Yuen Shiu* [1983] 2 A.C. 629.

[279] *Attorney General of Hong Kong v Ng Yuen Shiu* [1983] 2 A.C. 629 at 638G.

[280] *R. v Inland Revenue Commissioners Ex p. Unilever Plc* [1996] S.T.C. 681. See also *Council of Civil Service Unions v Minister for the Civil Service* [1985] A.C. 374, per Lord Fraser at 401.

[281] *R. (on the application of Niazi) v Secretary of State for the Home Department* [2008] EWCA Civ 755, per Sedley LJ at [70].

[282] *Rainbow Insurance Co Ltd v Financial Services Commission* [2015] UKPC 15, per Lord Hodge at [52]. See also *De Smith's Judicial Review* (2013), paras 12–072 to 12–080.

[283] *R. v Attorney General Ex p. ICI Plc* (1986) 60 TC 1 CA (Civ Div), per Lord Oliver at 64G; *R. v Inland Revenue Commissioners Ex p. MFK Underwriting Agents Ltd* [1990] 1 W.L.R. 1545, per Bingham LJ at 1569; *Ali Fayed v Advocate General for Scotland*, 2004 S.L.T. 798, per Lord President Cullen at [115]–[119].

[284] *R. v Inland Revenue Commissioners Ex p. MFK Underwriting Agents Ltd* [1990] 1 W.L.R. 1545, per Bingham LJ at 1569; *R. (on the application of Bancoult) v Secretary of State for Foreign and Commonwealth Affairs (No.2)* [2008] UKHL 61; [2009] 1 A.C. 453, per Lord Hoffmann at [60].

[285] *R. (on the application of Association of British Civilian Internees (Far East Region)) v Secretary of State for Defence* [2003] EWCA Civ 473; [2003] Q.B. 1397, per Dyson LJ at [56].

[286] *R. v Ministry of Agriculture, Fisheries and Food Ex p. Hamble (Offshore) Fisheries Ltd* [1995] 2 All E.R. 714 QBD; *R. v Secretary of State for Health Ex p. United States Tobacco International Inc* [1992] Q.B. 353 DC.

is unlikely to arise.[287] These factors, not one of which is in itself decisive, are pointers not rules and each case must be judged in the round.[288]

Even where the expectation is legitimate, and is strong, it can still be overridden by a sufficient public interest.[289] It is, however, for the public body to justify its frustration of an otherwise legitimate expectation. As Laws LJ explained in *R. (on the application of Nadarajah) v Secretary of State for the Home Department*:

> "The principle that good administration requires public authorities to be held to their promises would be undermined if the law did not insist that any failure or refusal to comply is objectively justified as a proportionate measure in the circumstances."[290]

Whether the applicant relied upon the representation to their detriment is a relevant consideration at this stage.[291] The ultimate question is whether the frustration of a legitimate expectation is proportionate to the legitimate aim that is pursued.

Our discussion so far has been of legitimate procedural expectations (the way **14–40** in which decisions are taken). It is now well established that where a representation by a public body is sufficiently clear, unambiguous and lacking any relevant qualification, it can also produce a legitimate expectation of a *substantive* benefit. The classic example remains the case of *R. v North and East Devon HA Ex p. Coughlan*.[292] Miss Coughlan had been rendered tetraplegic in a road accident in 1971. She was a resident at the local authority nursing home called Mardon House. When she moved in she had been assured by the local authority that this would be her "home for life". This assurance, albeit the phrase "home for life" had never been used, had been repeated to Miss Coughlan and other residents several times.[293] Time passed and the local authority came to the view that Mardon House was uneconomic and it should be closed with Miss Coughlan, and the other residents, being housed elsewhere. Miss Coughlan sought judicial review of the decision to close Mardon House on the ground she had a legitimate expectation that it would be her "home for life" and to close it would be an abuse of power. The Court of Appeal held the "clear promise" that had been given to Miss Coughlan produced a legitimate expectation that it would be honoured unless there was an overreaching justification for doing otherwise. The representation was such that "strong reasons" were required to resile from the promise that had been given and where to keep the promise would not be inconsistent with any other statutory or common law duties that were incumbent upon the local authority, a decision not to honour the promise would be the

---

[287] *R. v Gaming Board of Great Britain Ex p. Kingsley (No.2)* [1996] C.O.D. 241.

[288] *R. (on the application of Nadarajah) v Secretary of State for the Home Department* [2005] EWCA Civ 1363, per Laws LJ at [69].

[289] *Council of Civil Service Unions v Minister for the Civil Service* [1985] A.C. 374; *Rainbow Insurance Co Ltd v Financial Services Commission* [2015] UKPC 15, per Lord Hodge at [51].

[290] *R. (on the application of Nadarajah) v Secretary of State for the Home Department* [2005] EWCA Civ 1363 at [68]. That passage has been endorsed by the Privy Council: *Paponette v Attorney General of Trinidad and Tobago* [2010] UKPC 32; [2012] 1 A.C. 1 at [38].

[291] *R. (on the application of Bancoult) v Secretary of State for Foreign and Commonwealth Affairs (No.2)* [2008] UKHL 61; [2009] 1 A.C. 453, per Lord Hoffmann at [60].

[292] *R. v North and East Devon HA Ex p. Coughlan* [2001] Q.B. 213 CA (Civ Div).

[293] *R. v North and East Devon HA Ex p. Coughlan* [2001] Q.B. 213 at [84].

equivalent of breach of contract in private law.[294] Having examined the local authorities reasons for breaking their word to Miss Coughlan, the Court of Appeal had "no hesitation" in concluding that the decision was unlawful.[295]

14-41   The last word has yet to be written about the doctrine of legitimate expectations (whether procedural or substantive). It is, however, a concept that is "rooted in fairness".[296] Having reviewed the authorities as they then stood, Laws LJ summarised where the law currently stands:

> "The power of public authorities to change policy is constrained by the legal duty to be fair (and other constraints which the law imposes). A change of policy which would otherwise be legally unexceptionable may be held unfair by reason of prior action, or inaction, by the authority. If it has distinctly promised to consult those affected or potentially affected, then ordinarily it must consult (the paradigm case of procedural expectation). If it has distinctly promised to preserve existing policy for a specific person or group who would be substantially affected by the change, then ordinarily it must keep its promise (substantive expectation). If, without any promise, it has established a policy distinctly and substantially affecting a specific person or group who in the circumstances was in reason entitled to rely on its continuance and did so, then ordinarily it must consult before effecting any change (the secondary case of procedural expectation). To do otherwise, in any of these instances, would be to act so unfairly as to perpetrate an abuse of power."[297]

Thus where a legitimate expectation has arisen, a public body which wishes to frustrate that expectation will have to demonstrate that to do so is proportionate in all the circumstances. That invariably calls upon the court to undertake a substantive review of the underlying decision.

SUBSTANTIVE REVIEW

Introduction

14-42 So far, judicial review has been seen as a procedure by which the court can review the decision making process. Did the decision maker act within the limits of their powers? Did they only have regard to relevant considerations? Has the decision maker provided appropriate reasons for this decision? Did the person affected by the decision have an adequate opportunity to participate in the

---

[294] *R. v North and East Devon HA Ex p. Coughlan* [2001] Q.B. 213 at [86].

[295] *R. v North and East Devon HA Ex p. Coughlan* [2001] Q.B. 213 at [89].

[296] *R. v Inland Revenue Commissioners Ex p. MFK Underwriting Agents Ltd* [1990] 1 W.L.R. 1545, per Bingham LJ at 1569; *R. v Inland Revenue Commissioners Ex p. Preston* [1985] A.C. 835, per Lord Scarman at 851: "I must make clear my view that the principle of fairness has an important place in the law of judicial review, and that in an appropriate case is a ground on which the court can intervene to quash a decision made by a public officer or authority in purported exercise of a power conferred by law"; *R. v North and East Devon HA Ex p. Coughlan* [2001] Q.B. 213 at [71]; *R. (on the application of Nadarajah) v Secretary of State for the Home Department* [2005] EWCA Civ 1363 at [68], where Laws LJ described the principle as "a requirement of good administration by which public bodies ought to deal straightforwardly and consistently with the public".

[297] *R. (on the application of Niazi) v Secretary of State for the Home Department* [2008] EWCA Civ 755, per Laws LJ at [51].

decision making process? All of this is consistent with what Lord Hope said in *West* about the function of judicial review, " . . . there is no jurisdiction to review the judgement of the inferior tribunal or jurisdiction on the merits of the action, which has been entrusted to them alone."[298] But what if the individual still insists that the decision is in some sense legally flawed? Where the decision is "unreasonable" or, increasingly, "disproportionate" the court retains the right to intervene. We will discuss what is meant by "unreasonable" or "disproportionate" in a moment. Before that, however, it is worth pausing to consider the constitutional implications of the court undertaking substantive review of decisions.

First, there is a similar objection to that which is made when a party complains of an unlawful delegation: the discretion or decision making power has been vested not in the court but in the chosen decision maker. It is for that chosen decision maker to exercise the discretion within the limits of their authority. But the answer to that complaint is the answer that underlies the entire system of judicial review: an unreasonable decision is unlawful because the court assumes that Parliament (or the other source of the decision maker's power) cannot have intended to permit the decision maker to act unreasonably.[299] But that is not to suggest there are no limitations on the courts' ability to undertake substantive review of decisions. There are decisions which the courts, whether on constitutional grounds (namely, respect for the doctrine of the separation of powers) or having regard to the limitations on its institutional competence, should be very slow to interfere in. As to the constitutional grounds, as Lord Bingham explained in *R. (on the application of Countryside Alliance) v Attorney General*:

> "The democratic process is likely to be subverted if, on a question of moral or political judgment, opponents of the Act achieve through the courts what they could not achieve in Parliament."[300]

Those comments were made in the context of a Convention rights challenge but they apply equally to a case seeking review at common law. The institutional limitations of the court were explained by Lord Carswell in *R. (on the application of Bancoult) v Secretary of State for Foreign and Commonwealth Affairs (No.2)*:

> "Decisions about how far to accommodate such concerns are very much a matter for ministers, who have access to a range of information not available to the courts and are accountable to Parliament for their actions."[301]

Where a decision involves the allocation of finite resources or deciding between competing claims on public finances, the court will rarely be in as good as position as the decision maker to assess those competing demands.[302]

---

[298] *West v Secretary of State for Scotland*, 1992 S.C. 385 at 397.

[299] Wade and Forsyth, *Administrative Law* (2014) p.287.

[300] *R. (on the application of Countryside Alliance) v Attorney General* [2007] UKHL52; [2008] 1 A.C. 719 at [45]. See also, *AXA General Insurance Co Ltd v Lord Advocate* [2011] UKSC 46; 2012 S.C. (U.K.S.C.) 122, per Lord Hope at [49].

[301] *R. (on the application of Bancoult) v Secretary of State for Foreign and Commonwealth Affairs (No.2)* [2008] UKHL 61; [2009] 1 A.C. 453 at [132].

[302] See, for example, L.H. Hoffmann, "The COMBAR Lecture 2001: Separation of Powers" (2002) 7 J.R. 137.

14-43 The classic formulation of the test of reasonableness remains that of Lord Greene MR in *Associated Provincial Picture Houses Ltd v Wednesbury Corp*: the court may interfere if a decision is "so unreasonable that no reasonable authority could ever have come to it".[303] That is clearly a very difficult test to satisfy. In *Council of Civil Service Unions v Minister for the Civil Service*, Lord Diplock preferred to talk of irrationality rather than unreasonableness:

> "By 'irrationality' I mean what can by now be succinctly referred to as '*Wednesbury* unreasonableness'. It applies to a decision which is so outrageous in its defiance of logic or of accepted moral standards that no sensible person who had applied his mind to the question to be decided could have arrived at it."[304]

That language is perhaps unfortunate in that it suggests some sort of extreme behaviour on the part of the decision maker. Accordingly, the circumstances in which the test is satisfied ought to be rare.

Wednesbury unreasonableness can take a variety of forms.[305] It may strike at decisions tainted by an element of fraud, dishonesty or bad faith.[306] It may also apply where it is said that a public authority has attributed excessive weight to one factor over others in arriving at a decision.[307] Decisions that are unduly oppressive or onerous in their effect on the citizen may also be struck down as unreasonable. Thus in *Mixnam's Properties Ltd v Chertsey Urban DC*,[308] the House of Lords quashed conditions attached to caravan site licences as unreasonable, being "a gratuitous interference with the rights of the occupiers". The quasi-penalty cases of *Congreve v Home Office*[309] (where the Home Secretary revoked television licences which had been purchased just in advance of a substantial increase in their cost) and *Wheeler v Leicester City Council*[310] (where the council revoked the licence of a local rugby club to use council-owned recreation grounds because of the club's failure to stop four of its members from joining a tour to South Africa) are other illustrations of judicial

---

[303] *Associated Provincial Picture Houses Ltd v Wednesbury Corp* [1948] 1 K.B. 223 at 230.
[304] *Council of Civil Service Unions v Minister for the Civil Service* [1985] A.C. 374 at 410.
[305] J. Jowell and A. Lester, "Beyond *Wednesbury*: substantive principles of administrative law" [1987] P.L. 368.
[306] See, e.g. *Roncarelli v Duplessis* (1959) 16 D.L.R. (2d) 689. The "boycott" cases may also fall into this category: see *R. v Ealing LBC Ex p. Times Newspapers Ltd* (1987) 85 L.G.R. 316 (where the council's ban on Murdoch newspapers, adopted to express councillors' disapproval of a "tyrannical employer", was quashed on *Wednesbury* grounds) and *R. v Derbyshire CC Ex p. The Times Supplements Ltd* [1991] C.O.D. 129 (where a similar ban based on the publication by *The Times* of articles critical of councillors was struck down). In *R. v Lewisham LBC Ex p. Shell UK Ltd* [1988] 1 All E.R. 938 DC, however, the council's boycott of Shell's products—motivated by a desire to pressurise the company to sever its links with South Africa—was held illegal but not unreasonable, although "very near the line".
[307] See, e.g. *R. v Director of Passenger Rail Franchising Ex p. Save our Railways*, *The Times*, 18 December 1995 CA.
[308] *Mixnam's Properties Ltd v Chertsey Urban DC* [1965] A.C. 735. Such a case would now fall to be dealt with in terms of art.1 of the First Protocol to the European Convention, and accordingly the principle of proportionality would apply.
[309] *Congreve v Home Office* [1976] Q.B. 629.
[310] *Wheeler v Leicester City Council* [1985] 1 A.C. 1054.

intervention to control oppressiveness. Although the respondents had in both cases acted to achieve a legitimate aim, the manner of their actions was excessive in that they punished those who had done no wrong. Arbitrariness, perversity or absurdity is liable to be condemned as unreasonable, not only where it is manifest but also where

> "there is an absence of logical connection between the evidence and the ostensible reasons for the decision, where the reasons display no adequate justification for the decision, or where there is an absence of evidence in support of the decision."[311]

The demise of *Wednesbury* reasonableness (in favour of a test of proportionality) has been on the horizon for a long time now.[312] Some attempts have been made to soften the language and ask only whether the decision is one that a reasonable decision maker could reach.[313] *Wednesbury* reasonableness remains, for the time being at least, as a ground of review.[314] There is an undoubted overlap between the two and often the same result will be reached whether by "reasonableness" or "proportionality".

Proportionality

In *Council for Civil Service Unions v Minister for the Civil Service*,[315] Lord **14–44** Diplock alluded to the possible future reception of a free standing doctrine of proportionality going beyond the traditional grounds of judicial review. In *R. v Secretary of State for the Home Department Ex p. Brind*,[316] the House of Lords declined to adopt a test of proportionality going beyond that of irrationality or unreasonableness as traditionally understood. But *Brind* did not rule out the reception of proportionality review altogether.[317] It would have been passing strange if it had, since the House of Lords had already accepted that

> "the court . . . must be entitled to subject an administrative decision to the most rigorous examination, to ensure that it is in no way flawed, according to the gravity of the issue which the decision determines".[318]

---

[311] S.A. De Smith et al, *De Smith, Woolf and Jowell's Principles of Judicial Review* (London: Sweet & Maxwell, 1999) para.12–018.
[312] *R. (on the application of Association of British Civilian Internees (Far East Region)) v Secretary of State for Defence* [2003] EWCA Civ 473; [2003] Q.B. 1397, per Dyson LJ at [34]: "Although we did not hear argument on the point, we have difficulty in seeing what justification there now is for retaining the *Wednesbury* test."
[313] *Boddington v British Transport Police* [1999] 2 A.C. 143; see also *De Smith's Judicial Review* (2013), para.11–024.
[314] And it is not without its defenders: J. Goodwin, "The last defence of *Wednesbury*" [2012] P.L. 445.
[315] *Council for Civil Service Unions v Minister for the Civil Service* [1985] A.C. 374.
[316] *R. v Secretary of State for the Home Department Ex p. Brind* [1991] 1 A.C. 696.
[317] Lord Ackner and Lord Lowry were concerned that to adopt such a test would "inevitably involve inquiry into and a decision upon the merits", but the view of the majority was that *Brind* was not an appropriate occasion for applying a stricter standard of scrutiny than *Wednesbury*.
[318] *Bugdaycay v Secretary of State for the Home Department* [1987] A.C. 514, per Lord Bridge at 531.

Proportionality, in this sense, is now a prominent feature of public law, not only in relation to legitimate expectations but, as we saw in Ch.11, above, human rights as well. As Lord Drummond Young recently explained, overall, what proportionality in this sense requires "is consideration of the balance between the public interest in the measure under challenge and the private interest of the person affected by it".[319] That necessarily requires the court to make a value judgment, but, as we have seen, judicial review is not a mechanism by which the court can substitute its own assessment for that of the decision maker. That has seen the court take a structured and analytical approach to the question. That structured approach of the common law is most often attributed to Lord Clyde's judgment in the Privy Council case of *De Freitas v Permanent Secretary of Ministry of Agriculture, Fisheries, Lands and Housing* where he explained that three questions required to be asked by the court:

> " . . . whether: (i) the legislative objective is sufficiently important to justify limiting a fundamental right; (ii) the measures designed to meet the legislative objective are rationally connected to it; and (iii) the means used to impair the right or freedom are no more than is necessary to accomplish the objective".[320]

That discussion took place in the context of the constitution of Antigua and Barbuda but was regularly applied by the UK courts when called upon to determine a question of proportionality.[321] That tripartite approach did undergo some modification[322] and in *Bank Mellat v HM Treasury (No.2)*, the Supreme Court explained how the courts should now address the question of proportionality. In a passage that merits repetition in full, Lord Reed explained:

> "As assessment of proportionality inevitably involves a value judgment at the stage at which a balance has to be struck between the importance of the objective pursued and the value of the right intruded upon. The principle does not however entitle the courts simply to substitute their own assessment for that of the decision-maker. As I have noted, the intensity of review under EU law and the Convention varies according to the nature of the right at stake and the context in which the interference occurs. Those are not however the only relevant factors. One important factor in relation to the Convention is that the Strasbourg court recognises that it may be less well placed than a national court to decide whether an appropriate balance has been struck in the particular national context. For that reason, in the Convention case law the principle of proportionality is indissolubly linked

---

[319] *Main v Scottish Ministers* [2015] CSIH 41; 2015 S.L.T. 349, Lord Drummond Young at [49].
[320] *De Freitas v Permanent Secretary of Ministry of Agriculture, Fisheries, Lands and Housing* [1999] A.C. 69 PC (Antigua and Barbuda) at 80.
[321] For example, *R. (on the application of Daly) v Secretary of State for the Home Department* [2001] UKHL 26; [2001] 2 A.C. 532.
[322] See, for example, *R. (on the application of Razgar) v Secretary of State for the Home Department* [2004] UKHL 27; [2004] 2 A.C. 368; *Huang v Secretary of State for the Home Department* [2007] UKHL 11; [2007] 2 A.C. 167; *R. (on the application of Aguilar Quila) v Secretary of State for the Home Department* [2011] UKSC 45; [2012] 1 A.C. 621.

to the concept of the margin of appreciation. That concept does not apply in the same way at the national level, where the degree of restraint practised by courts in applying the principle of proportionality, and the extent to which they will respect the judgment of the primary decision maker, will depend on the context, and will in part reflect national traditions and institutional culture. For these reasons, the approach adopted to proportionality at the national level cannot simply mirror that of the Strasbourg court."[323]

Lord Reed went on to set out the structured approach that should be adopted by the court when it is called upon to make an assessment of the proportionality of a particular measure:

" ... it is necessary to determine (1) whether the objective of the measure is sufficiently important to justify the limitation of a protected right, (2) whether the measure is rationally connected to the objective, (3) whether a less intrusive measure could have been used without unacceptably compromising the achievement of the objective, and (4) whether, balancing the severity of the measure's effects on the rights of the person to whom it applies against the importance of the objective, to the extent that the measure will contribute to its achievement, the former outweighs the latter."[324]

This structured approach to proportionality, requiring the court to address four questions, has been subsequently endorsed by the Supreme Court.[325] In relation to the third question, the courts must not apply that requirement too literally. To do so would permit only a single response and would deny the decision maker any margin of appreciation.[326] Properly understood, therefore, the third question requires the court to be satisfied that the measure selected by the public body is within the range of measures that can reasonably be considered as required to fulfil the policy objective.[327] In practice, it will normally be the fourth question that proves the most challenging. This question did not feature in Lord Clyde's initial explanation of proportionality in *De Freitas* but the need to balance the interests of society with those of individuals or groups within society had been recognised by the House of Lords as a part of the proportionality exercise that

---

[323] *Bank Mellat v HM Treasury (No.2)* [2013] UKSC 39; [2014] A.C. 700 at [71]. Although Lord Reed was dissenting on the application of the test in that particular case, his analysis of the concept of proportionality was endorsed by the majority: Lord Sumption at [20].
[324] *Bank Mellat v HM Treasury (No.2)* [2013] UKSC 39; [2014] A.C. 700 at [74]; see also Lord Sumption at [20]. In that analysis Lord Reed drew on Lord Clyde's seminal discussion of proportionality in *De Freitas v Permanent Secretary of Ministry of Agriculture, Fisheries, Lands and Housing* [1999] A.C. 69 at 80 and Dickson CJ's discussion in the Canadian Supreme Court in *R. v Oakes* [1986] 1 S.C.R. 103.
[325] *Gaughran v Chief Constable of the Police Service of Northern Ireland* [2015] UKSC 29; [2015] 2 W.L.R. 1303.
[326] *Bank Mellat v HM Treasury (No.2)* [2013] UKSC 39; [2014] A.C. 700, per Lord Reed at [75]. For a practical application of that approach, see *Main v Scottish Ministers* [2015] CSIH 41; 2015 S.L.T. 349, in particular Lord Justice-Clerk Carloway at [35]–[36].
[327] *Main v Scottish Ministers* [2015] CSIH 41; 2015 S.L.T. 349, per Lord Drummond Young at [48]. For a practical application of that approach, see Lord Justice-Clerk Carloway at [35]–[36].

"should never be overlooked or discounted".[328] By the time this question is reached, the court will already have found that there was no less intrusive measure that could have obtained the desired objective. What is left is a value judgment for the court.

14–45   What will now be apparent is that there is a significant overlap between unreasonableness/irrationality and proportionality. Whether a decision maker has acted reasonably in balancing the competing relevant factors in reaching their decision or whether there is a rational connection between means and ends are two issues that arise in an "unreasonableness" challenge but which have a strong affinity with the concept of proportionality.[329] But whilst the courts have long been willing to assess the reasonableness of a decision taken by a public body, they continue to deny that proportionality can be relied upon as a self-standing ground of review in the same way.

REMEDIES

14–46   In exercising its supervisory jurisdiction on an application for judicial review, the court may grant or refuse the petition or any part of it, with or without conditions.[330] In particular, the court may

> "make such order in relation to the decision in question as it thinks fit, whether or not such order was sought in the petition, being an order that could be made if sought in any action or petition, including an order for reduction, declarator, suspension, interdict, implement, restitution, payment (whether of damages or otherwise) and any interim order."[331]

Generous as this is (and plainly the remedies listed are not exhaustive), there are certain limitations on the court's remedial jurisdiction. In deciding whether to grant a particular remedy, it has been said that the court should have regard to the wider interest in good administration.[332] Remedies in the context of judicial review are a discretionary matter.[333] As Lord Carnwath explained in *Walton*, the court's discretion in relation to granting a remedy is effectively a counter-balance to the widening of the rules of standing.[334] Damages may be awarded only where

---

[328] *Huang v Secretary of State for the Home Department* [2007] UKHL 11; [2007] 2 A.C. 167, per Lord Bingham at [19]. Lord Bingham cited *R. (on the application of Razgar) v Secretary of State for the Home Department* [2004] UKHL 27; [2004] 2 A.C. 368 in support. In that case, Lord Bingham explained that striking a fair balance between the rights of the individual and the interests of the community as a whole was inherent in the entire proportionality exercise (see [17]–[20]).

[329] *De Smith's Judicial Review* (2013) para.11–084.

[330] RCS r.58.4(a).

[331] RCS r.58.4(b).

[332] *King v East Ayrshire Council*, 1998 S.C. 182, per Lord President Rodger at 196.

[333] To the extent there was any doubt about that in Scots law (cf. *Anderson v Secretary of State for Work and Pensions*, 2002 S.L.T. 68) that was removed by the Supreme Court in *Walton v Scottish Ministers* [2012] UKSC 44; 2013 S.C. (U.K.S.C.) 67.

[334] *Walton v Scottish Ministers* [2012] UKSC 44; 2013 S.C. (U.K.S.C.) 67 at [103].

their award would otherwise be competent.[335] It is now clear, however, that the court is not prevented by s.21 of the Crown Proceedings Act 1947 from granting the remedies of interdict or implement, ad interim or otherwise, against the Crown (including the Scottish Ministers) in the context of an application for judicial review.[336]

---

[335] The reference to "payment (whether of damages or otherwise)" in r.58.4(b) appears to countenance the award of monetary redress even absent a cause of action, but if such power exists it appears only to have been exercised twice: *Kelly v Monklands DC*, 1986 S.L.T. 169 and *Mallon v Monklands DC*, 1986 S.L.T. 347.

[336] It was established in *R. v Secretary of State for Transport Ex p. Factortame Ltd (No.2)* [1991] 1 A.C. 603 HL that s.21 did not prevent the grant of injunction or interdict where the Crown was said to have infringed the applicant's rights under Community law (see also, in Scotland, *Millar & Bryce Ltd v Keeper of the Registers of Scotland*, 1997 S.L.T. 1000). In *M v Home Office* [1994] 1 A.C. 377, the House of Lords had held that "civil proceedings" did not include proceedings for judicial review in England, so that the equivalent remedies of injunction and specific performance might competently be granted against the Crown in such proceedings even where no Community law element existed. In *McDonald v Secretary of State for Scotland*, 1994 S.C. 234, the Second Division held that the plain effect of s.21 had been to exclude interdict and implement in civil proceedings against the Crown and that *M v Home Office*, having turned substantially on aspects of English procedure, was not authoritative as to the meaning of s.21 in Scotland. However, in *Davidson v Scottish Ministers* [2005] UKHL 74; 2006 S.C. (H.L.) 41, the House of Lords held that there was no basis for interpreting the words "civil proceedings" as they appear in s.21 differently north and south of the border.

Index